P9-DBN-385
Butte Coypeau
place Maubert
LA RIVIERE DE SEINE

Cities and People

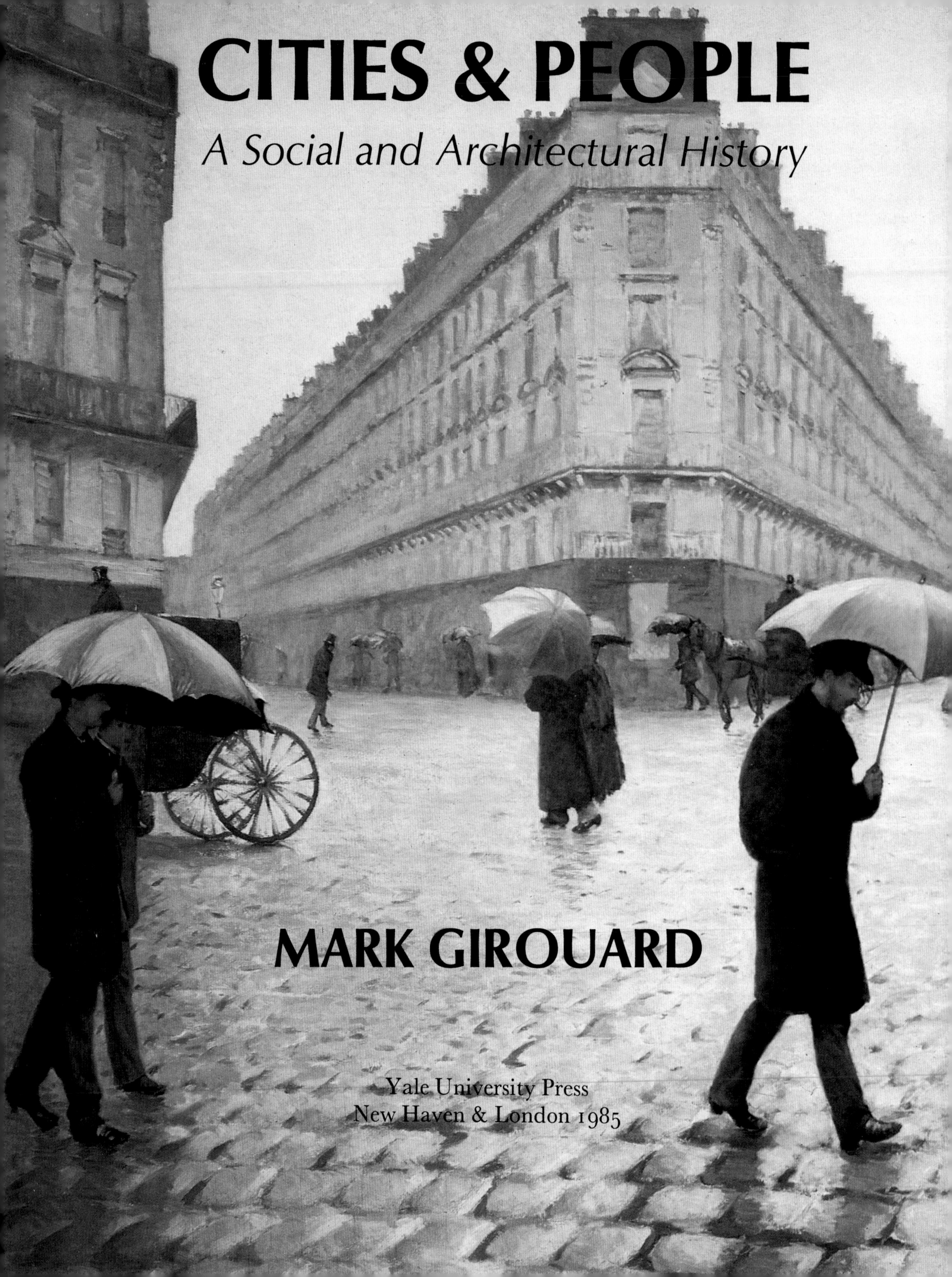

CITIES & PEOPLE

A Social and Architectural History

MARK GIROUARD

Yale University Press
New Haven & London 1985

To My Father For His Birthday

Designed by Dorothy Girouard

Filmset in Monophoto Baskerville in Great Britain by BAS Printers Limited, Over Wallop, Hampshire
Printed in Italy by Amilcare Pizzi s.p.a., Milan
Library of Congress card number 85-40461
ISBN 0-300-03502-0

(Front end paper) Aerial view of Paris in 1615 by Mathieu Merian

(previous page) Gustave Caillebotte. Detail from *Paris, a Rainy Day* (intersection of the Rue de Turin and the Rue de Moscou) (Art Institute of Chicago).

PREFACE

All big cities are romantic places in the sense in which William Morris used the word: 'by romantic I mean looking as if something was going on'. Henry James, in an article on London, wrote about 'the rumble of the tremendous human mill' and how it is 'supremely dear to the consistent London lover'. Lovers of cities of all kinds will know what he means, and how there is a roar, a throb or a sensation of life in any great city that lifts their heart or stirs their blood whenever they leave the station or walk out from the hotel, and savour a city for the first time. It is an exciting sensation for some, but can be a frightening one for others, especially for those who are working in a strange city rather than just passing through it. The rumble seems to become the inhuman sound of a mill which is remorselessly chewing up human beings. Even Henry James felt something like this about London in certain moods. 'I have been crushed', he wrote, 'under a sense of the mere magnitude of London—its inconceivable immensity . . . The place sits on you, broods on you, stamps on you . . .'

But the more anyone living in a city gets to know it, the more this impersonality vanishes, so that although he can still savour the throb of a city as a whole, he begins to distinguish the endless different elements of which it is made up, different societies, different groups, different races, different religions, different family nexuses, to some of which he gains access himself, if he did not start with it, and all of which are constantly overlapping and interacting. Over the centuries these interactions have produced much suffering and wastage, but also most of what makes human life endurable or enjoyable, in the country as well as the town.

This book is concerned with western cities from the Middle Ages up to the twentieth century, in terms of who did what, why, where and when. It aims to start with the functions which have drawn people to cities, and to work outwards from them to the spaces and buildings which grew up to cater for them. It has grown out of many years walking many miles in cities round the world, at all times of the day and night. At a certain stage I find that savouring cities in ignorance or drinking them in visually is not enough; I want to find out, not just who designed the buildings and when they were built, but why they were built. Conventional guidebooks, and even many standard histories of cities, often answer the first two questions without throwing much light on the third one.

The subject is so huge that I have had to be very selective. I have concentrated on the cities which were recognized at the time as having star quality, and were visited or imitated accordingly. I have tried to deal with these in sufficient detail to give some idea of what it was like to live in, for example, Bruges in the fifteenth century or Manchester in the nineteenth. Inevitably, many beautiful or interesting cities are dealt with summarily, if at all. I have used the term 'city' according to instinct rather than any cut-and-dried definition. There is a certain stage of cosmopolitanism and complexity at which a town becomes a city; everyone is aware of it, although the border between the two is inevitably imprecise. It is arguable that Washington, for instance, has only become a city in the last five or ten years. Clearly, the possession of a cathedral or a Lord Mayor does not necessarily make a town into a city in this sense. Size is important, but only relative size: the cities of the Middle Ages were no bigger than minor provincial towns of today, but they seemed huge places to their contemporaries. In fact, the more one gets to know medieval cities, the more resemblances to modern

New York skyline, Roger Mann.

cities appear, on the debit side as well as the credit. The biggest medieval cities were not as complex as modern ones, but they were not nearly as simple as the impression of unity suggested by the first dramatic view of a girdle of walls with towers rising behind it might suggest; nor were they the happy ideal communities projected by some enthusiasts. There was just as much exploitation and misery in them as in any modern city.

Any book concerned with the history of cities is bound to treat of individual buildings and questions of town planning, but there are many excellent books on these subjects already, and I do not pretend to deal exhaustively with either. I am not conscious

of having any particular message or theory; there is no shortage of books which have, many of them written by people who intensely dislike big cities and all that they stand for. Inevitably, however, I have my own predilections. I was brought up to believe that one lived in the town or the country (or if one was rich enough, in both) and to despise the suburbs; the suburbs are still a strange land to me, although one which I hope I now regard with interest rather than contempt. My sympathies and admiration go out to those who have loved cities but fought to remedy their defects without destroying them: to the often forgotten heroes who supplied them with drainage, services, transport, hospitals, schools and open spaces.

ACKNOWLEDGEMENTS

A great many people have assisted me with this book, and its inevitable inaccuracies are due to me rather than to them. My first thanks must go to Kenneth Ponting, most delightful and helpful of men, who was unstinting with information and material to do with the textile trade, before his sadly premature death. In Bruges Andries Van den Abeele has dealt patiently and with unfailing success with too many requests for help and information, and Henk Zantkuyl has been equally helpful and generous in Amsterdam, out of the store of his unequalled knowledge. I must thank Fred and Simone Warner, Charles Jencks and Denys Lasdun for suggestions and introductions in Tokyo, and Eric Klestadt for showing me round it and for his endless kindness there; Martin Foley and Indalessio Martinez for showing me around Mexico City, Alfonso Govela for help there, and Martin Foley and Marita Martinez del Rio de Redo for assistance with illustrations; Stephen Fox for two days intensive touring in Houston; Robert Winter for guiding me round Pasadena; my sister-in-law Roberta Frank for taking me to Riverside and Westwood Mall in Chicago; Jerzy Limon, for showing me Gdansk, and Professor Edward Cieslak for information; Lori Cornidis for interpreting and hospitality in Vienna; Maurice Shellim for much kindness and for showing me his achievements in the Park Street Cemetery in Calcutta, Colin Amery for sending me to the Fairlawn Hotel there, Baskar Chandra for guiding me, and the British Council for help and introductions; the French Embassy in London for introductions at the Bibliothèque Nationale; Eve Borsook for help in Florence and Professor Hidetoshi Hoshimo for talking to me about the Florentine textile trade; J. G. Links for help, suggestions and loans of books on Venice; Chung Wah Nan for raising my spirits in Hong Kong; Minette Broderick, Robert Grey, Anne Hawker and Victoria Newhouse for help in New York, Marilyn Perry for the loan of her apartment there; Erkinger and Claudia Schwarzenberg, Alain Camu, Charles and Maggie Jencks, John and Dagmar Searle, my parents-in-law Frank and Margaret Dorf, my brother-in-law Michael Dorf and my sister and brother-in-law Teresa and Kenneth James, for help and hospitality in Tuscany, Belgium, Los Angeles, Berkeley, Chicago, Washington, Warsaw and Mexico City; Christopher Lowry, of Thomas Cook's, for organizing me round the world; Erik Aerts, Walter Krause, Rosemary Mulcahy, Rosalys Coope, J. M. Richards, Dr Vermaut, Donald Insall, Hugh Honour, John Fleming, Andrew Saint, John Munro, John Archer, Juergen Schulz, Marc Ryckaert, Mireille Attar, Amanda Trafford, Pearl Ofoego, Harriet Waugh, William Curtis, Malcolm Campbell and Minoru Takeyama for help, information or suggestions at different times and places; and Edward Piper and Richard Coward for their photographs. I thank Primrose Newman, Miranda Davies, John Nicoll, Faith Hart, Celia Jones and Mary Carruthers for constant help at home and at my publishers; Ann Walker for her patience in accepting typing at short notice; and my father for checking the galleys. The book would never have made its deadline without Greta Soggot, and would never have been written without the London Library.

(right) Amsterdam. The main avenue of the Plantage in 1725 (Amsterdam Historical Museum).

CONTENTS

1. (right) Merchants arrive at a fifteenth-century city. Detail from MS 9231, f. 118r (Bibliothèque Royale, Brussels).

2. (following page) Looking up into the apse, Sancta Sophia, Constantinople.

Part I THE CITY REBORN

'Town air brings freedom'

Medieval legal maxim

1 The Revival of the West

In the ninth and tenth centuries, when the Roman settlements of the west had shrunk to populations of a few thousand people making do with patched-up corners of their sacked and gutted cities, while the colonnades crumbled, and weeds sprouted from amphitheatres and temples, Constantinople floated like a vision above the waters of the Bosphorus, still inviolate, still powerful, the biggest, richest and most sophisticated city in the world. Visitors from the west brought home wonderful stories, in which truth and fantasy were curiously mixed, for a big city was completely outside their experience. When the first view of Constantinople exploded on their vision, it must have filled them with the same kind of awe and amazement as filled immigrants from Europe when they approached Manhattan from the sea, in the years before inferior copies had spread round the world. But at least photographs and illustrations had given the latter some idea of what to expect; visitors to Constantinople would have been taken completely by surprise. No adequate techniques of depicting cities had been developed, and the first reasonably reliable illustrations of Constantinople date from after the Turkish conquest in 1453.

Walls and churches were the features of the city most

3. (previous page) The early fifth-century Theodosian walls, Constantinople.

4. (above) Sketch plan of Byzantine Constantinople.

5. (right) Detail from a view of Constantinople by Melchior Lorichs, 1599 (Royal Netherlands University, Leiden).

described by contemporary visitors, and almost the only ones of which substantial remains survive today.[1] The peninsula on which the city was built was surrounded by about twelve miles of walls; they were double on the landward side and single along the water, and were punctuated by 37 gates and 486 towers. Inside were several hundred churches and chapels and about eight hundred thousand inhabitants; around were the waters of the Bosphorus to the south, and the harbour of the Golden Horn to the east, crowded with sailing ships and galleys of all shapes and sizes from all over the Mediterranean and the Black Sea; above water and walls a confusion of roofs and domes rose up to the presiding dome of Sancta Sophia. When Sancta Sophia was lit at night, from over a thousand lamps hanging on brass chains from its dome and arches, the whole building glowed through the thin marble panels that took the place of glazing. It was used as a lighthouse by ships at sea twenty miles and more away.

The main entrance to the city was through the Golden Gate, so called because its iron gates were sheathed in plates of gold. Its parapet was crowned with statues of elephants; its central gate was only opened for an emperor when he made a state entry or returned from victory in war. From here the main street of the city ran for about three and a half miles to the great open square of the Augustaeum, between Sancta Sophia and the imperial palace. The street was lined most of the way with one- or two-storeyed colonnades, and there were other colonnades along other main streets, so that it was possible to walk under cover all over the city; and under the streets, subterranean waterways and vast cisterns supported on forests of columns were linked with aqueducts from the surrounding countryside to bring running water to every quarter. There were further colonnade-lined squares; there was the great open space of the Hippodrome, where the emperor and empress and a frantic audience of sixty thousand people watched chariot races between the two factions of the Greens and the Blues. There were obelisks and columns in a row down the centre of the Hippodrome, four gilded horses proudly prancing above the emperor's box, statues and monuments everywhere in the city, a huge statue of the Emperor Justinian riding a bronze horse on top of a column sheathed with brass; and in the palace itself, or rather in one of the many palaces, the emperor, God's viceroy on earth, lived out a ritual as elaborate and splendid as anything that took place in the churches. In 949 Liudprand, Bishop

S. Sophia

of Cremona, described his reception by the Emperor Constantine Porphyrogenitus in one of the halls of the main palace on the edge of the promontory below Sancta Sophia. Before the emperor's throne was a man-made tree 'of bronze gilded over, the branches of which were filled with birds, also made of gilded bronze, which uttered cries, each according to its varying species'. The throne itself 'was of immense size and was guarded by lions, made either of bronze or of wood covered over with gold, who beat the ground with their tails and gave a dreadful roar with open mouth and quivering tongue'. The bishop approached; the lions roared, the birds sang; the bishop sank to his knees and lowered his head three times to the ground, in the prescribed fashion; by the time he had lifted his eyes the throne had secretly and silently risen by invisible machinery, and the emperor was a god-like golden figure, high and remote up above him.[2]

Marvels such as these; the wealth everywhere; the jewels over the throne in the Blachernes palaces, which were said to light the room by their own radiance, the statues in the city that were said to move and speak, the other statues from the mouths of which wine and honey flowed on feast days; the relics in the churches, 'as many as in all the rest of the world', according to one account, ranging from the veil of the Virgin to the head of St John the Baptist, and the pillar at which Christ was scourged to the adze with which Noah built the Ark; the holy men living as hermits on the tops of columns down by the harbour; the pillars in Sancta Sophia each of which, if rubbed against, was said to cure a particular disease; the pagan magic of the Palladium, a sacred image of the goddess Pallas said to have been brought by Aeneas from Troy to Rome, and transferred by Constantine to the base of a great porphyry column in the forum of his new city; all these and much else made Constantinople a place of wonder and of pilgrimage. But for the west it was more than that. It had a practical function. Constantinople, and in many cases Constantinople only, could provide goods which the west wanted. More than any other factor, it was the means adopted to obtain these goods which stimulated the gradual revival of trade in western Europe; and out of this revival emerged the western city as we know it today.

The upper level of the arcades on the main street of Constantinople were only for the use of pedestrians; but the lower arcades, and arcades and halls elsewhere in the city and in Pera across the waters of the Golden Horn, were crowded to bursting with shops both retail and wholesale. These shops feature much less prominently in the descriptions of visitors than churches, relics, palaces, walls, monuments and marvels, but they were at least as important. Byzantine Constantinople at its prime was the biggest luxury shopping centre in the world, and most of its luxury goods were produced in its own workshops. Gold came in from the Caucasus and the Urals, ivory from Africa, pearls from the Persian Gulf and Ceylon, precious stones from Egypt, Persia and India, raw silk from China and different areas of Byzantium, linen from the Peloponnese and cotton from Asia Minor, and were transformed in specialist workshops confined to different quarters of the city and carefully regulated by the central government. Constantinople produced jewellery of every description; crowns and royal regalia; jewel-studded crosses, reliquaries, croziers and book-covers of gold and enamel; boxes, cups, horns, figures and figured triptychs of ivory; goblets and chalices of crystal and onyx bound in silver; bronze-plated doors, illuminated manuscripts and icons; and all kinds of fabrics, for dresses, robes, vestments and hangings, ranging from figured linens and cottons to cloth of gold and the silks for which Constantinople was especially famous, above all the purple silks made in the royal workshops and confined by law to royal use or royal gifts.

But Constantinople was also a major market for raw materials, imported both from its own empire and from outside. All the metals, ivory, precious stones and other materials used in its workshops could be bought there in their unworked state. So could the spices essential for medieval cooking, ginger from India and China, cloves from the Moluccas, pepper from Malabar, saffron from Cilicia, sugar from Cyprus, and exportable delicacies such as honey, nuts and raisins, and ingredients used to fix or colour dyes, such as indigo, kermes, saffron, brazilwood and alum. Last but not least were the drugs used in contemporary medicine, mostly for purges: galingale, cassia, aloes, senna, wormwood and China rhubarb. Cooking spices, dyeing ingredients, medical drugs and even raw cotton and sugar all tended to be lumped together by medieval merchants under the general title of spices.

It was the city's function as a huge and complex market that generated most of the ships crowding the harbour, and filled the arcades and bazaars with a confusion of nations. As a Spanish rabbi, Benjamin of Tudela, put it in 1161: 'Great stir and bustle prevails at Constantinople in consequence of the conflux of many merchants who resort thither both by land and by sea, from all parts of the world for purposes of trade, including merchants from Babylon and Mesopotamia, from Media and Persia, from Egypt and Palestine, as well as from Russia and Hungary . . .'—and also from the west.[3]

The darkness of the Dark Ages in western Europe can be exaggerated. Trade never died completely, and by the tenth century was reviving; Rome, though as a city only a shadow of its imperial self, was still a powerful religious centre where church fittings and ecclesiastical goods were in continuous demand; and the courts of the Frank, Lombard and German invaders, and the monasteries and cathedrals which they founded, were eager for the products of Constantinople. Their success in getting them is witnessed by the superb Byzantine artefacts, and the decaying remains of equally superb Byzantine textiles, which can be found in cathedrals and museums all over western Europe. In order to obtain these and more everyday goods the west had to solve two problems, however; how best to get access to eastern markets, and how best to pay for the goods which could be bought there.

The access of outsiders to Constantinople and other Byzantine towns was jealously controlled, and customs duties were high. Traders, if admitted at all, were hedged about with restrictions and limited to short visits. In the tenth century the Italian towns which remained part of the Byzantine empire—Naples, Amalfi, Gaeta, Ravenna, Salerno and Venice—received preferential treatment. But the mainland cities among these were under continual pressure from the invaders from the north, and gradually succumbed to them; alternatively, they fraternized with them, were regarded with suspicion in Constantinople, and finally lost their privileges there. Only Venice, securely isolated on its islands, could maintain itself as an increasingly independent, but to begin with loyal, subject of Byzantium. It was in a bargaining position of great strength, able to do deals with western rulers in return for getting them eastern goods, and with Constantinople in return for its loyalty and support. By the end of the eleventh century it had acquired the privilege of trading free of customs over almost all the Byzantine Empire, together with its own permanent district or colony within the walls of Constantinople. By the mid-twelfth century there were 10,000 Venetians living in the city, and the population of Venice itself was probably in excess of 100,000. What had started in the fifth century as a settlement of refugees from the mainland, and had grown to modest prosperity on the basis of trading in salt from its sea-marshes, had become one of the great success stories of the world.

Constantinople, by virtue of its location and its access to both sea and land routes, was ideally situated to transmit the products of the east to the west. But to begin with the west had no important manufactures to offer in return and few raw materials which Constantinople wanted. It traded with a little iron and timber, with any gold specie it could get hold of, and above all with eunuchs and slaves, mostly Slavs kidnapped in central Europe (hence the word 'slave'). Bishop Liudprand's presents to the emperor included four young eunuchs bought in Verdun-sur-Meuse, which specialised in this particular trade.[4] But when the Slavs were converted to Christianity the business ceased to be respectable.

There was, however, one industry which began to develop in the west, and the products of which merchants could sell readily in the east. The rainy districts in north-western Europe, England above all, produced better quality wool than was available anywhere in the east. By the twelfth century cloth woven from this wool, mainly in Flanders, was coming to Constantinople by way of Italy, with Venice as the main intermediary. What for centuries was to remain the main, though certainly not the only, generator of trade and urban life in western Europe, had been established; silks and spices moved from east to west, woollen textiles moved from west to east; and the western textile industry grew and flourished accordingly.

The situation, however, was both complex and changing. It was complicated by the existence of the Mohammedan world, and by the tensions between Mohammedans and Christians, between eastern and western Christians, between different groups of Mohammedans, and between different factions among the western merchants. The attitude of the west to Byzantium was far from being one of uncritical admiration; wonder was mixed with distrust, envy and even contempt. Relations were not improved by religious differences, which came to a crisis in 1054; the Church split in two, and in western eyes Constantinople, the greatest repository of Christian relics in the world, was now in the hands of heretics. Moreover, in spite of its amazing secular wealth it contained the contrasts and complexities of all great cities. The unsophisticated country soldiers or inhabitants of small towns who came there from the west could find these very upsetting. 'The town', wrote Odon de Deuil in the 1140s, 'is dirty and smelly, and given over in many places to perpetual gloom. The rich, in effect, build in the main streets, and abandon the lanes and backlands to strangers and the poor, and to murder, theft and all the other crimes which flourish in the dark . . . Everything is in excess of this city; it is richer than anywhere else, but also wickeder.'[5]

The rich were upsetting too. The women painted themselves; they ate over-elaborate food; worst of all, the men hired others to fight for them: 'they have no martial spirit, and, like women, are unfit for warlike enterprises'.[6] In 968, five pieces of purple silk which Bishop Liudprand of Cremona had bought in Constantinople for the Frankish Emperor Otto were confiscated on the ground that they were not for export. 'How improper and insulting it is', the bishop wrote in a fury to his emperor, 'that these soft, effeminate creatures, with their long sleeves and hoods and bonnets, idle liars of neither gender, should go about in purple, while heroes like yourself, men of courage,

6. A Byzantine in a litter. Miniature from the MS of the Byzantine History of Skyllitzes (National Library, Madrid).

skilled in war, full of faith and love, submissive to God, full of virtues, may not.'[7] He revenged himself by pointing out to the Byzantine bureaucrats that their precious purple silks were in fact being smuggled abroad by merchants from Amalfi and Venice, and sold in Italy to prostitutes and conjurors.

The Byzantine Greeks, on their side, dismissed the westerners as barbarians. They despised them, but increasingly they needed them. They needed help in their struggle against the Mohammedans whose power gradually but inexorably increased at their expense. Pisa and Genoa had built up navies to fight against Moorish pirates in the western Mediterranean; Constantinople made alliances with both cities for the sake of their navies and, to the fury of Venice, rewarded them with customs concessions and with their own districts and trading rights in Constantinople, Pisa in the late eleventh century and Genoa in 1155. But Venice, Genoa and Pisa were all prepared to trade with the Mohammedans in the intervals of fighting with them, in spite of occasional fulminations from the pope. The Mohammedan caliphs had conquered Egypt and Syria from Arabia in the seventh century and established a Mediterranean presence; they had as much access to the east as the Byzantines, more, indeed, as their power increased, and they were equally interested in buying western textiles. Alexandria had always been an alternative to Constantinople as a market in which to buy eastern spices, as well as Egyptian cottons, papyrus and luxury goods. Merchants came to it from all over Europe and the near east. It was from Alexandria that two Venetian merchants (possibly in collusion with local Christians) purloined the body of St Mark and smuggled it back to their home town in or around 828; there were said to be ten ships from Venice in the harbour at Alexandria at the time.

By the last decades of the twelfth century the power of Venice, Pisa and Genoa in the Byzantine Empire was very great, but also much resented. It was estimated that 60,000 Italians were living in Constantinople. There were constant incidents, massacres, arrests, expulsions, reconciliations and playing off of one city against the other. In 1200 a Crusade was organized in Europe, to attack the Mohammedans in Egypt. The bulk of the troops came from France, Flanders and Germany, but the transporting ships were hired from Venice, and the Crusaders could only afford to pay two-thirds of the bill. With the enthusiastic connivance of Venice, the Crusade was diverted to Constantinople. Its objective was to instal Alexius, an exiled claimant to the Byzantine throne, as the eastern emperor; Alexius promised to bring the eastern Church back to Rome, assist the Crusade and pay the remaining money due to Venice out of the Byzantine treasury.

On 26 June 1203 the western fleet sailed into the Bosphorus before the walls of Constantinople. The Venetians, of course, knew all about the city, but most of the Crusaders were seeing it for the first time. Much had changed in the previous three hundred years, but Constantinople was still an immeasurably larger and richer city than any in the west. Its inhabitants swarmed onto its roofs and battlements and gazed at the western fleet; the Crusaders crowded the decks and gazed back at the huge and resplendent city, appalled at their own effrontery. But they persisted. The city walls were stormed and breached; the reigning emperor fled; to prevent further fighting the city government agreed to Alexius being set up as co-emperor with his ancient and blind father. Alexius was murdered in a palace revolution, and another emperor installed, in defiance of the Crusaders, who had settled across the Golden Horn at Galata. The Crusaders stormed the walls again and occupied the city. Three days of rape, massacre and looting followed. Geoffrey of Villehardouin, one of the Crusaders, described the booty: 'gold and silver, and vessels and precious stones, and samite, and cloth of silk, and robes vair and grey, and ermine, and every choicest thing found upon the earth. And well does Geoffrey of Villehardouin, the Marshal of Champagne, bear witness that never, since the world was created, had so much booty been won in any city.'[8]

Venice's share included the four gilded horses which (according to one theory) had crowned the royal box in the Hippodrome. These were triumphantly installed over the portals of St Mark's, and with a brief interval in Paris under Napoleon have remained there ever since. Their move symbolised a shift in the balance of power. Western Europe could no longer be seen as a cultural satellite of Byzantium, and Venice was securely installed as its commercial capital. But its Byzantine connection was still much in evidence; in effect it was a smaller Constantinople in the west. St Mark's was a Byzantine church, its altars and treasury resplendent with all the artefacts from the east. The two columns on the piazzetta, surmounted by St Theodore and the Lion of St Mark, echoed the similar, if grander, columns of Constantinople, just as the arcaded piazza and the arcaded market buildings on the Rialto had been inspired by its streets and forums; the two-storey arcades around the Doge's Palace were an echo of similar arcades in Constantinople. The people who walked in the arcades wore Byzantine clothes, ate Byzantine food and painted their faces in the Byzantine way. It seems likely that the houses in which the richer merchants lived also derived from Constantinople, although the almost complete destruction of Byzantine houses in the latter city makes it impossible to be certain.[9]

But, although the balance had shifted, the pattern remained basically the same. It was still dominated by the west–east movement of textiles, and the east–west movement of silks and spices; and this movement was controlled more than ever by Venice and Genoa. As a result of a series of wars Genoa managed to push Pisa out of a leading role in the Mediterranean by the end of the thirteenth century. Genoa and Venice continued to compete for supremacy until Venice moved securely into the lead as a result of its resounding victory over Genoa at Chioggia in 1380. Venice had supported the Latin kingdom which had been installed in Constantinople after the conquest and sack in 1204; Genoa almost inevitably supported the Greeks, and helped to bring back a Byzantine emperor to Constantinople in 1261. Its rewards included access to the Black Sea, leading to a series of colonies there, its own Genoese town at Pera, across the Golden Horn from Constantinople, and one of the richest alum mines in the known world, at Phocaea, in Asia Minor. Alum was of the greatest importance for the textile industry, because it was used as a fixative for dyes. Venice, meanwhile, acquired trading stations and islands all round the eastern Mediterranean, including the islands of Crete and (much later and more briefly) Cyprus. In the far east Venetians and Genoese penetrated to India and China, and established friendly relations with the Tartar khans in Trebizond, Tabriz and Astrakhan. In the west both cities pioneered the sea route through the Straits of Gibraltar, and from the late thirteenth century were sending merchant fleets bi-annually to Flanders and England.

Flanders was the first great centre of the textile industry in western Europe, exporting north to Russia and the Baltic, west to England and south to Spain, in addition to its eastern trade, which supplied Italy as well as Byzantium and the Levant. But inevitably other areas began to develop their own industries and to produce cloth for export as well as for local use, to the discomfiture of Flemish trade. In the fourteenth century northern Italy, in particular Florence and Milan, became major exporters of high-quality cloth to the east, as well as suppliers of the Italian market. English cloth had acquired a high reputation by the mid-thirteenth century, at which date cloth from Stamford and other English towns was on sale in Venice, but England had produced only small quantities and sold most of its wool for export; in the 1330s it put very high export duties on wool and began to develop its own textiles, and in the course of the fifteenth century these grew to dominate the European market.

The European textile trade and industry, and its satellites, the trade in wool, silk, flax and the ingredients used in dyes, became extraordinarily complex, owing to the endless varieties of textiles which were produced, the great demand for them, the numbers of towns and districts competing to supply both finished articles and raw materials, and the changing fortunes of the suppliers. New markets were constantly being exploited, and new lines developed. In the fourteenth century, for instance, Flanders compensated for loss of sales in Italy and England by expanding its sales in Germany and the Baltic; the diminishing exports of English wool led to an enormous expansion of sheep-farming in Spain; and western Europe began to produce its own silk textiles, notably at Lucca.

But the whole of medieval trade was complex, not just the textile trade. Important though textiles and spices were, they were not the only goods being traded. Apart from anything else, the areas which wanted to buy imported textiles and spices had to have something to offer in return. All round the Baltic new German trading towns came into existence on the basis of importing textiles and spices and exporting Russian furs, wax and honey, and corn and timber from Poland and eastern Germany; in the fourteenth century they and a number of inland north German towns joined together to form the Hanseatic League. Throughout Europe trade in corn, timber, iron, salt and wine flourished. The corn trade was especially important because, as cities and populations grew, they ceased to be able to feed themselves from their own hinterlands. Apulia, Calabria and Sicily supplied Florence, Venice and Genoa, Sardinia and North Africa supplied Barcelona, Valencia and Majorca. Prussia and Poland became the granary of northern Europe and despatched many thousands of tons of corn annually to London and other English towns, and to Flanders. The settlement and development of Prussia was part of a great German colonization of former Slav lands which absorbed the overspill of German populations, and supplied the needs of the populations that

7. Detail from *Il Leone di San Marco* by Vittore Carpaccio (Palazzo Ducale, Venice).

8. (right) Detail from *The Martyrdom of the Franciscans at Centa* by Pietro Lorenzetti (Church of S. Francesco, Siena).

remained. In famine years, countries would go anywhere for corn: Baltic corn could land up in the Mediterranean, and in 1317 a Genoese convoy is recorded as carrying corn from Morocco to Sandwich in England.

The great Genoese and Venetian galleys, loaded with pepper or alum, bales of cloth or sacks of sugar or corn, dominated the Mediterranean but were far from having a monopoly of the carrying trade there. Medieval shipping was as complex and competitive as medieval trade in general. In the Mediterranean ships from Ragusa (now Dubrovnik) in Dalmatia, from Barcelona, Valencia and other ports in Catalonia, and from Marseilles and Narbonne in Provence, jockeyed for cargoes; and swarms of little boats, pedlars of the sea, sailed along the coasts from harbour to harbour, buying and selling as they went. In the Baltic the monopoly of the Hanseatic towns was being disputed in the fifteenth century by Dutch and English ships. All over Europe the navigable rivers formed great internal highways, crowded with every kind of craft.

The variety of medieval trade is endlessly fascinating. In the fourteenth century Genoa was importing slaves from the Russian steppes and selling them in Florence and Siena; the Sienese painter Pietro Lorenzetti had models on his doorstep when he

wanted to depict a martyrdom which had taken place on the Black Sea.[10] In the fifteenth century English merchants from Bristol were swapping alabaster reredoses from Nottinghamshire for dried fish in Iceland, and Augsburg merchants were importing raw cotton from Syria by way of Venice for their textile industry, and exporting copper and silver from the Tyrol mines in return. Papal bulls were written in Rome on Mohammedan papyrus imported from Alexandria, the cosmopolitan nature of which in 1168 can be gathered from the description written by Benjamin of Tudela: 'People from all Christian kingdoms resort to Alexandria, from Valentia, Tuscany, Lombardy, Apulia, Amalfi, Sicilia, Rakuvia, Catalonia, Spain, Roussillon, Germany, Saxony, Denmark, England, Flanders, Hainault, Normandy, France, Poitou, Anjou, Burgundy, Mediana, Provence, Genoa, Pisa, Gascony, Aragon and Navarre. From the west you meet Mohammedans from Andalusia, Algarve, Africa and Arabia, as well as from the countries towards India, Savila, Abyssinia, Nubia, Yemen, Mesopotamia and Syria, besides Greeks and Turks. From India they import all sorts of spices, which are bought by Christian merchants. The city is full of bustle and every nation has its own *fondaco* [combined business and living quarters] there.'[11]

A vivid idea of the range of goods bought and sold by medieval merchants is given by the 'Book of Descriptions of Countries and of Measures of Merchandise' compiled between about 1310 and 1340 by Francesco Balducci Pegolotti, a Florentine who worked for the merchant and banking firm of the Bardi in London, Antwerp and Cyprus.[12] The book deals with products, prices, weights and measures in all the areas with which Italian merchants had dealings. It mentions over six hundred different commodities, and over seven hundred places, ranging from Aberconway to Astrakhan, from Damascus to Dunfermline, and from Mecca to Majorca. It lists the English monasteries with wool for sale, and the different staging posts from Armenia to China, and describes what commodities were for sale in the markets of, for instance, Rhodes, Naples, Bruges and Constantinople, and very often where they came from.

It was not till the end of the eighteenth century, however, that the west developed a city as large as Constantinople. However impressive the ramifications of medieval commerce, by modern standards the quantities involved were minute, and the cities which developed out of it were little second-rate towns. Bruges, the great marketing and distributing centre of medieval Flanders, had a population of perhaps 35,000. The populations of Milan and Venice, the two biggest cities in western Europe, are unlikely to have been much more than 150,000 before the Black Death struck them, and may well have been less. At the peak of its production of cloth in the mid-fourteenth century Florence was producing 80,000 pieces of cloth a year; in the 1850s one warehouse alone in Manchester had a yearly turnover of 100,000 bales of cotton cloth.[13] The Florentine firm of the Bardi, which was one of the three biggest banking firms in Europe in the fourteenth century, had a managerial and clerical staff of about one hundred, at branches spread out all over Europe; the Medici, in the next century, never had more than sixty, dispersed over eight cities. All the forges of Styria, which by the fifteenth century was the leading iron-making centre in Europe, produced perhaps 2,000 tons a year; one steel mill today produces as much in a day. The biggest Venetian or Genoese galley would look like a cockle shell, if put next to a modern cargo ship. Medieval commerce involved small numbers of people moving many different types of merchandise in small quantities across great distances and against great odds.

9. (right) Francesco Sassetti and his son Teodoro. Attributed to Domenico Ghirlandaio (Metropolitan Museum of Art, New York).

2

Manufacture, Trade and Money

There was a great deal of variation in the scale of operation of merchants. At one end was someone like Benedetto Zaccaria of Genoa (*c.* 1240–1307) who owned dye-works in Genoa, alum mines in Asia minor, plantations in Chios and a trading-station in the Crimea, controlled, at intervals, a seaport near Seville and another in Syria, traded in spices, cutlery, cloth, furs, linen, salt and grain, lent money in Florence and advised kings in France, sold alum in Flanders, acted on occasion as admiral, pirate and spy as well as merchant, could make jokes in French, and pioneered the first recorded sea-voyage from Italy to England.[1] The smaller fish included English wool merchants like the Celys of London and the Brownes of Stamford, whose sphere of operations was confined to the Cotswolds, the Norfolk marshes, the Welsh borders or the Yorkshire and Lincolnshire wolds, where they bought their wool, and the wool staple at Calais or the Flemish fairs, where they sold it.[2]

The Italians became the big fish, because they were

10. The Medici palace in Milan. From Filarete's *Treatise on Architecture* (Biblioteca Nazionale Centrale, Florence).

more effective. One can get some idea of the sophistication and complexity which Italian commerce had reached by the mid-fifteenth century if one takes a look at Francesco Sassetti, partner in the firms of Amerigo Benci and Francesco Sassetti of Geneva and Lyons, and Francesco Sassetti and Giovanni Zampiri of Avignon.[3] One can literally take a look, for his portrait was painted in the 1460s. He stands with downcast eyes, wearing the rich but sober dress of a prosperous merchant; his son Teodoro, rather more gaily dressed, looks up to him. Behind is the lake and city of Geneva.

Sassetti's companies were in fact part of the great Medici empire, and the Medici family were the partners and the biggest shareholders in both of them, although their name did not feature in their titles. In the mid-fifteenth century there were Medici companies in Florence, Avignon, Bruges, Geneva (moved to Lyons in 1466), London, Milan, Pisa, Rome and Venice. There were also Medici agents in Bologna, Genoa, Lübeck, Naples and Valencia. Sassetti had worked in the Avignon company in the 1440s, had risen to become junior partner and manager, and had moved to Geneva by 1453. In 1458 he returned to Florence, but retained his Avignon and Geneva partnerships. In Florence he became what amounted to managing director of the central company, which co-ordinated all the others.

The whole conglomerate rested on the basis of Florence's position as one of the biggest textile-manufacturing cities in Europe, and much of its business consisted of exporting Florentine woollens and silks. But basically it dealt in anything which it thought would make a profit, or oblige an important customer, from slaves to olives. The conglomerate also included two companies manufacturing woollen textiles and one manufacturing silk textiles, both in Florence, and a money-changing and deposit-banking business in a shop by the Mercato Nuovo, also in Florence. The various companies were prepared to supply castrati-singers for S. Giovanni in Laterano in Rome, keep the Duke of Burgundy and Edward IV of England afloat with loans, and run the papal alum mines at Tolfa. Like all merchants of the time, the Medicis believed in diversification.

In 1470 there was a staff of five in the Geneva branch, and eight in Lyons. The staff normally lived and worked in one building. A description of the very grand Medici building in Milan gives some idea of how it was arranged. On the ground floor there were a series of 'fondaci', rooms in which merchandise was stored and sold, including one specifically reserved for cloth; there was also a room 'where they write and oversee the books of the bank'. The rooms on the first floor included a magnificent suite in which the managing partner, Pigallo Portinari, lived and entertained.[4]

The conglomerate had long got past the stage when individual merchants travelled from place to place with their own goods. The managing partners in the different branches stayed put in their cities, and used carriers to move goods to and fro in between. Each branch was run as an independent business, and kept its own separate accounts at the other branches. If, for instance, Sassetti when in Geneva thought that the Geneva account in Venice needed to be increased, there was no need for him to go to the trouble and risk of sending coins to Venice. Instead, he bought what was called a bill of exchange.[5] He would make a short term loan of the required sum of money to another merchant in Geneva, who would agree that his (the borrower's) agent in Venice would repay the debt to the Medici branch there in six weeks' time. The borrower's brief note of instruction to his agent constituted the bill. He would normally use the loan to buy goods in Geneva in order to dispatch them to Venice, where their sale enabled it to be repayed. The rate of exchange quoted in the bill would be calculated to give Sassetti as lender a profit, in effect to give him interest. But if the rate of exchange in Venice turned out to be different from what Sassetti in Geneva had calculated, his profit was affected accordingly.

This introduced an element of risk, and as a result making a profit on bills of exchange was not condemned by the church as usury, as a straightforward interest-bearing loan would have been. The different branches also increased their capital by accepting deposits, but they dealt with the problem of usury by calling the annual payment made in return a 'discretionary one', and in bad years did not pay it. In all commercial dealings usury presented a permanent obstacle to be got round if possible, like the tax laws today. In addition to accepting and making loans, the various Medici companies did a big business in buying and selling bills of exchange, for the convenience of others as well as themselves. This was the banking, as opposed to the merchant, side of their business.

In later life Sassetti grew careless. Lorenzo de' Medici, the head of the firm, lost interest in it except as a source of money for his political ambitions and patronage of the arts. Sassetti (who had himself sculpted as a Roman, in a toga) followed his example. At the end of the fifteenth century most of the companies were in trouble, and closed down one by one. The whole firm finally folded up in 1494; but in its prime it had been formidable.

Such a complex and relatively sophisticated organization was at the end of a long road, which led back to clusters of traders and buyers congregating in open market-places all round Europe. Virtually all medieval cities grew up round a market or a fair, or both. Some markets started up on new sites, most commonly outside a castle or abbey, which gave them protection, and by a river or a harbour, which supplied a means of transport, or a river ford, which attracted traffic. Nuremberg, for instance, started up in the eleventh century under the shade of an imperial castle on a hill, by a ford over the River Pegnitz. Other markets developed on an earlier nucleus. Florence started as a Roman settlement, fell into decay during the barbarian invasions, and revived in the ninth and tenth centuries, when the Roman forum became the medieval market-place.

Many of these market settlements never became larger than a small village or small town, crouched in the shadow of the castle. Others developed into powerful independent or semi-independent cities. They did so because they contributed to a more than local system of distribution, on the basis of either trade or manufacture or both. Success in trade called for the ability to exploit markets, combined with a key position in a

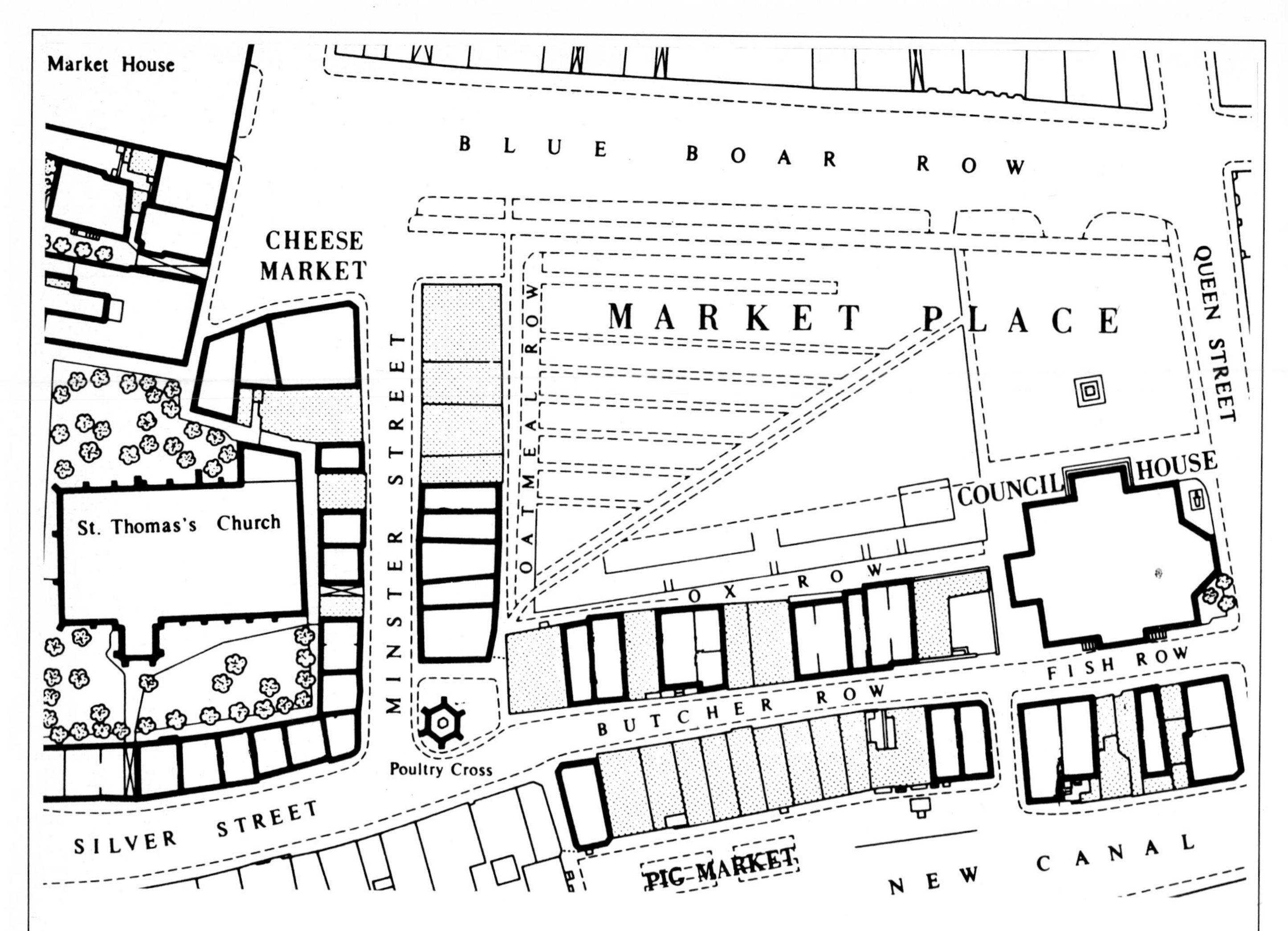

11. The market-place, Salisbury. It was originally open from Blue Boar Row to New Canal and St Thomas's to Queen Street (Royal Commission on Historical Monuments, England).

communication network, often where goods were shifted from one form of transport to another. At Gdansk, for instance, corn and timber coming down the Vistula on its way to the Low Countries or England was transferred from barges to sea-going ships, at Lübeck back to land for transport across the neck of the Danish peninsula to Hamburg; once the superiority of the sea-route through the Jutland Straits had been established by the end of the fifteenth century, Lübeck's position as a city of the first importance was gone for ever.

Florence revived under the protection of its bishop, who was the local representative of the Holy Roman Emperor beyond the Alps; as in many Italian cities in the early Middle Ages he became a semi-independent territorial ruler as well as a spiritual one. Local rulers not only provided protection to markets and fairs, they often actively promoted them, because they were both a useful convenience to them and a source of revenue, derived from renting the stalls, taxing the sales, and (in the case of markets) letting land on which the stall-holders could build houses. An enterprising ruler could achieve a great deal. In the late twelfth and thirteenth centuries the fairs of Champagne (held at Troyes and neighbouring towns) became the main European marts for the exchange of all kinds of merchandise, and especially for the meeting of Flemish and Italian merchants to buy and sell Flemish textiles and eastern spices. The fairs flourished because the counts of Champagne made roads, built halls, arranged for adjacent rulers to grant safe-conducts to merchants travelling through their territory to the fairs, and set up special courts which enforced contracts made there. The great northern market at Bruges flourished, as did the whole textile industry in Flanders, partly because of

12. The Palazzo del Broletto (1215), Como.

13. The Lonja (1483), Valencia.

the privileges and good government provided by a series of enterprising counts of Flanders.

In the early stage of a city's growth one open market-place accommodated commerce of all kinds, partly because the local ruler, who rented out the space, did his best to prevent it taking place anywhere else. When the bishop of Sarum (who was the local landowner as well as the local bishop) abandoned his inconvenient hill top cathedral and the settlement round it and laid out the new town of Salisbury in the early thirteenth century, country peasants, town craftsmen, dealers in food and prosperous merchants were put to buy and sell together in one large market-place; meat, poultry, eggs, fish and bread for daily use, kitchen pots and sacks of grain, and the wool, yarn and cloth on which the growth and success of the town depended was each given its own area.[6]

A similar arrangement existed in the market-place of Lübeck when it was founded in 1158.[7] And in both cities the market-place developed in a similar way, as did the market-places in countless other towns all over Europe. The more prosperous stall-holders gradually turned their stalls into more and more permanent structures, until they finally became houses, with shops on the ground floor. At Salisbury Butcher, Fish and Pot Rows cut into the space of the original market; at Lübeck the different trades were less segregated, but a mixture of chandlers, shoemakers, goldsmiths, apothecaries, haberdashers and others built even more houses, and reduced the market-place to its present size, which is unimpressively small for so important a medieval town. In both places cloth was bought and sold on the ground floor of a civic building put up on another portion of the market-place, in the form of the Rathaus at Lübeck, and the

14. (above) The Cloth Hall (1200–1304), Ypres.

15. (right) Antwerp. Looking across to the Butchers' Hall (1501–3) from the cathedral tower.

Bishop's Guildhall at Salisbury. But country people continued to come in to sell their eggs, chickens and other goods in the open space that remained.

Covered markets, as in the Bishop's Guildhall, were an early development. They were often obtained by building on or over the existing market square, rather than in another part of the town. A combination which remained common for several centuries was a building of two or more storeys with an open arcade at ground level for market activities, and a room or rooms above for the town council. One of the earliest examples is the Palazzo del Broletto at Como, inscribed with the date 1215, but the type soon spread all over Europe. A variation was to build an open arcaded building of one storey only. Pleasing examples of this are provided by Gothic market 'crosses' in England, such as the still surviving Poultry Cross in Salisbury market-place, an elegant (but much restored) little hexagonal building vaulted round a central column and surmounted by a cross.

More elaborate still were the enclosed halls devoted entirely or mainly to marketing. Since a commodious and impressive hall helped attract trade, these could be prestigious and expensive buildings. They tended to be confined to the most prosperous section of the cities' business. The Flemish cloth halls are an obvious and splendid example.

The grandest of them was the cloth hall at Ypres. Before it was blown to pieces in the 1914–18 war, it was impressive evidence of the early prosperity of the Flemish cloth trade and the enlightenment of Count Baldwin IX of Flanders, who started to build it in 1200. By the time it was completed in 1304, it consisted of a building 433 feet long, bigger in fact than most cathedrals, with gigantic halls on two floors to either side of a central tower. Although in use all the year round, its primary function was to contain and advertise the annual cloth fair which was opened in state by the mayor and council in one of the upper halls.[8]

The buildings known as *lonjas* in Spain are sometimes referred to as exchanges, but were market halls rather than exchanges, and contained stalls selling a variety of goods, including the raw silk which later gave its name to the superb Lonje de Seta in Valencia and Palma. Halls were also built for or by butchers and fishmongers, who were always among the richest of the tradesmen catering for local consumption; the butchers had a way of establishing a monopoly position in which trade was confined to a specifically limited number of families, an arrangement which could bring them great prosperity in an expanding city. The grandest surviving example of these is the huge butchers' hall built in Antwerp in 1501–3. It has a large vaulted hall on the ground floor, originally for sales, and rooms on the floors above for the meetings and festivities of the butchers' guild.[9]

In Paris the French kings moved the main market inland from its earlier site on the Place de Grève, by the Seine, and built a series of much less ambitious single-storey halls from the late twelfth century onwards, on sites later to be occupied by the great cast-iron market halls of the Third Empire. The 'selds' built in considerable numbers in and around Cheapside in London in the thirteenth and fourteenth centuries were even more modest; they were covered private bazaars, mostly not at all large, which were let out to tenants who sold their goods from boxes, chests, cupboards or benches.[10] Local rulers were always eager to build market halls, partly to stimulate trade in cities in their dominions, partly because of the income which they derived from renting stalls in them. They (or in some cases the town council, or any other person or body who had acquired the market rights from the overlord) always endeavoured to establish such halls in a monopoly position, and even if the town's citizens obtained freedom to buy and sell elsewhere, visiting merchants were usually compelled to use them. In London, for instance, it was decreed in 1388–9 'that no foreigner or stranger should sell any woollen cloth but in the Bakewell hall, upon pain of forfeiture thereof'; Bakewell or Blackwell Hall was the house and hall which the city corporation had acquired from a rich citizen, Thomas Bakewell, and turned into a cloth hall; the hall was rebuilt in 1588. Its greatest days came in the sixteenth and seventeenth centuries, when much of the cloth trade of England passed through it.[11]

From at least the fourteenth century shops became increasingly common, however, either as the result of converting market stalls, as already described, or on sufferance or by concession in other parts of the town. The smaller shops had a common form all over Europe, a form similar to that surviving in fishmongers' and butchers' shops in England today. Goods were sold from an open counter letting on to the street; the opening was not glazed, but was shuttered up when the shop was empty. The shop could vary from the minimum of one room, having shelves for storage and often a workshop at the back; or contain two rooms, with a room at the back for storage, or for working or living in; or be expanded to two or more floors, with living accommodation above and perhaps a cellar below for storage. It was preferable to live over or next to the shop, both for security and for convenience, but it was not always possible for a shopkeeper to find, or perhaps afford, accommodation attached to a shop in a desirable location, which could be no more than a permanent booth in the market, or one of a row of single rooms let on the ground floor of a larger building; it was common for merchants or prosperous citizens to let out the cellars or street frontage of property belonging to them in the centre in this way. In larger shops, a ledge beneath open window space could be used for display only, and sales took place inside.

Shopkeepers in medieval cities often made substantial fortunes and figured with some prominence in city life and politics. Grocers, fishmongers, butchers and goldsmiths tended to be especially prosperous. The richer shopkeepers often in fact traded in goods other than their particular speciality, and were to some degree merchants. The line between wholesaling and retailing was seldom sharply drawn; almost all wholesalers were prepared to sell retail as well.

But in the commercial world it was the merchants, the men who concentrated on wholesale buying and selling on a more than local scale, who had the most prestige, made the most money, built churches, endowed almshouses, hospitals and monasteries and by the later Middle Ages were running most medieval towns, including those the wealth of which was based on manufacture. The shops and workshops depended on the merchants to supply them with goods and raw materials, and to discover and exploit markets for their

16. (top left) A street of shops in the late fifteenth century. Detail from the *Gouvernement des Princes* (Bibliothèque de l'Arsenal, Paris).

17. (bottom left) A shop in Vlamingstraat, Bruges. Detail from a portrait by P. Pourbus, 1551 (Groeningemuseum, Bruges).

18. (above) A money-changer. From the Codex De Spheare by Marco dell'Avogaro (Biblioteca Estense, Modena).

products. The merchants put up the most capital, took the biggest risks and, if they were successful, made the biggest profits. As a group they were able, ambitious and thrusting. They had to be, for they worked against great odds. The early generations of merchants in any rising city often started with little or no capital, and usually travelled themselves with their goods, in danger of storm, shipwreck or pirates at sea, of bandits and robber barons by land, forced to pay an interminable succession of tolls to endless different jurisdictions on their routes, constantly changing their sacks and bundles of merchandise from one form of transport to another, bearing the weight of many months' and sometimes years' gap between buying goods and selling them, and not always certain whether, when they got their goods to the end of their long and painful journey, there would be any demand for them.

They also had to work unbuttressed by any kind of esteem. Unlike Victorian merchants, they had no lobby to tell them how wonderful they were. They were put firmly in their place, down in the Third Estate below the nobility and the clergy. Money might give them power, but as merchants they had no status, and they could only acquire it by somehow achieving nobility or knighthood, or membership of a city council or governing body. According to the teaching of the Church, although money-making did not destroy a man's hope of salvation, it did not improve it. Moreover, they were always skating close to activities which could be condemned as usury. Many merchants made at least occasional straightforward interest-bearing loans, and compensated by charging extra high interest as danger money. Almost all merchants had a bad conscience.

The central location of the Italian merchants on the Mediterranean put them in a strong position to dominate the movement of goods from east to west and north to south, and they built on to their geographical advantages by their business methods, which were far in advance of those used by other nations. Then, as now, a successful merchant not only had to make the right judgment as to what and where to buy and sell, he also had to have sufficient funds available in the right place at the right time. Much of the growth of cities over the centuries has been the result of improving techniques of raising capital and of moving it. The Italians were pioneers of both, owing to their resourcefulness in forming different kinds of partnership and opening up branches, and to their invention of the bill of exchange early in the fourteenth century. In addition they pioneered shipping-insurance and invented double-entry book-keeping: the latter enabled them to keep track of the value of what they had in stock as well as of their cash in hand, and to know where they stood financially.

The firms which specialized in making and accepting loans and dealing in bills of exchange, all on an international scale, were known as *banchi grossi*. They were the great and famous Italian banking firms of the Middle Ages and early Renaissance, such as the Bardi, Peruzzi and Alberti in the fourteenth century, and the Medici, Pitti, and Strozzi in the fifteenth. There were thirty-three *banchi grossi* in Florence in 1472. Genoa, Siena and Lucca were also important banking centres. Sienese banking flourished in the thirteenth century because Siena acquired a special relationship with the papacy; branches of Sienese companies were the main transmitters of papal revenues to Rome from all over Europe. For much of the fifteenth century the Medici took over as the main papal bankers, before they ultimately moved on from supplying papal finance to supplying popes; there were four Medici popes between 1513 and 1605.

Banchi grossi were based on partnerships, which were usually dominated by one family. They opened branches round Europe. In the fourteenth century the Florentine Alberti had branches, at various times, in Florence, Avignon, Seville, Rhodes and Naples. In the late fourteenth and early fifteenth centuries Francesco de Marco Datini, who came from the Tuscan textile town of Prato, but whose business headquarters were in Florence, had other branches in Avignon, Pisa, Genoa, Barcelona, Valencia, Majorca and Ibiza. The progress of these great Italian companies was not uniformly successful; in the 1340s, for instance, all the big Florentine companies went bankrupt, as the result of a panic caused by Edward III's failure to repay his loans to the Bardi and Peruzzi, the biggest of the Florentine firms. It was in an effort to avoid this kind of disaster that the Medici and other fifteenth-century merchants replaced single monolithic companies by separate companies for each branch, controlled by what amounted to a holding company in the home city.

All *banchi grossi* started as merchant companies or partnerships, and combined the two activities; they were merchant bankers in a far more precise sense than the firms which are so called today. Their banking activities grew out of their commercial activities, and helped to facilitate them. The wealth of Florence was based on cloth, not banking; banking was a service which grew out of its textile industry. The articles of association of the various Medici companies invariably state that their partnerships are formed 'for the purpose of dealing in exchange and in merchandise, with the help of God and good fortune'.[12]

Banchi grossi formed the top tier of three levels referred to in medieval Italy as *banchi*. Below them came the *banchi in mercato* and the *banchi di pegni*.[13] The latter was another term for pawnshop. No ingenious quibble was ever found to make pawnbroking acceptable to the Church; it was unequivocally condemned as usury, and no serious Christian could be a pawnbroker, although state and city governments had no qualms about licensing Jews to run their local pawnshops. All medieval cities of any size had these, and they dealt in anything from crown jewels to a weaver's loom or a housewife's set of pots and pans. Jewish pawnbrokers had one curious set of rivals. The inhabitants of Asti and Chieri in Piedmont risked the Church's law and specialized in pawnbroking. They formed lonely little communities all over Europe, condemned by the Church and ostracized by the other Italian merchants. They were known as Cahorsins, or Lombards, the latter a confusing description, because in some countries (such as England) any Italian merchant was called a Lombard.

Money-changers were a grade above the pawnbrokers in status and respectability though not necessarily in degree of profit. They were known as *banchieri in mercato*, because the counters or *banchi* from which they derived their name were usually set up in shops or little covered stalls on or near one of the city markets. Their basic occupation of changing money was a complex and important one, owing to the great variety of local coinage current in medieval Europe. They sat behind their stalls with their scales and piles or pouch of coins, as money-changers did all over the world, and had done for centuries. In Italy by the fifteenth century they were also beginning to act as transfer and deposit banks in the modern sense, always, however, on a local level.

Other nations tagged a long way behind the Italians in their financial methods. The Flemish money-changers in Bruges began to engage in deposit and transfer banking in the mid-fourteenth century, about a hundred years after the Italians, but they were little if at all imitated elsewhere in Flanders, and not at all in the rest of northern Europe. Bills of exchange only appeared in English merchant practice in the late fifteenth century, and in 1518 an employee of the great Fugger company of Augsburg wrote of double-entry bookkeeping: 'This rich-making art is little liked by the Germans'.[14] The most financially enterprising nation in medieval Europe after the Italians were the Catalans. Catalan merchants (who from 1137 formed part of the Kingdom of Aragon) flourished on the increasing export of Spanish wool to Italy, and also traded with north-west Africa and all round the Mediterranean; in 1311 they even captured Athens, and established a dukedom there. They used similar contracts to the Italian merchants and pioneered the first public deposit banks, which were set up in Barcelona in 1402, and Valencia in 1407.

Money-changers only needed a stall in the market-place, or a small shop near it. Pawnbrokers needed space to store their pledges, and usually lived and worked out of the centre in less prosperous areas, where they did most of their business. But involved as they were in constant buying and selling and in constant and essential picking up of information most medieval merchants and merchant bankers had no doubt as to where they wanted to live and to keep their merchandise. They lived close to the market, market hall or shops with which they were most concerned, and stored their merchandise below, next to or above their place of residence, both for convenience and for security; medieval towns had little in the way of effective police, and were constantly devastated by fire. Since the most profitable form of buying and selling tended to remain in the neighbourhood of the original market-place, the most prosperous merchants usually lived in the centre, on or a few blocks away from the market square. Retailers and craftsmen who sold their own products were often legally compelled to sell in a market or market hall, and, even if they were not, wanted their shops or stalls to be close to where the main buying and selling were going on and the richest potential customers lived; so they also gravitated to the centre, lived above or next to their work-place if they could (again, for convenience and security) or, if not, as close to it as possible. The merchants, having the most money, were likely to get the best and the largest plots; the richer shopkeepers, however, could compete with them and, as has been pointed out, the dividing line between merchant and rich shopkeeper was never a firm one.

A merchant needed space for storage, displaying wares, and keeping records on the one hand, and for living in on the other. The first three requirements could, at the simplest level, be supplied in one big room, with a table or ledge for display, a desk for writing on and shelves for storage. But operatives on a large scale needed more space, which might be obtained by storehouses at the rear, cellars below, attics up in the roof, or a mezzanine immediately above the shop. A vaulted cellar or vaulted ground floor room with small windows had the advantage that it could be made more-or-less

19. (left) A Florentine street-scene. Detail from *The Resurrection of Tabitha* by Massaccio and Masolino (Sta Maria del Carmine, Florence).

20–1. (above) Two merchants' houses. The fifteenth-century house in Nuremberg, later lived in by Albrecht Dürer, and the late fifteenth-century Palazzo Corner-Spinelli, Venice.

fireproof and burglar proof—such cellars often had direct access to the street by a ramp or steps. Goods liable to suffer from the damp, like grain or dried fish, were better stored up beneath the roof. Many documents relative to Florentine shops refer to *purghi*; these may have been the mezzanine floors which are prominently shown in contemporary depictions of Florentine streets, and were usable either for storage, or for residence in the case of a smaller shopkeeper renting the lower half of a building.[15] Warehouses in the sense of sizeable and separate buildings entirely occupied for storage scarcely existed in the Middle Ages, except for grain; the quantity of goods being dealt with was not enough to produce them. The 'warehouses' which feature in medieval English documents were usually no more than a room or rooms in a larger building.

A combination of forces all over Europe produced that most typical feature of medieval towns, the row of high merchants' houses, usually from four to six storeys high, with a lower portion for business, a middle for residence, and sometimes further space for storage in the attics. There are numerous stylistic variations and variations in plan and material, high stepped or pointed gables to throw off rain and snow in the north, flatter-pitched roofs, parapets and roof terraces in the south. There are contrasts in size, and in opulence of carved or moulded detail depending on the prosperity of the town and the richness of the individual merchant. But the basic pattern remains remarkably the same.

In some cases the individual sites were large enough to allow space for an internal courtyard; but the long narrow plots running back from the street frontage, which were more typical of medieval towns, usually produced a solid rectangular main building, although there was often stabling or more storage on the open ground at the back, reached by a covered way running through the house. The amount of available space varied, and with it the potential for open space within a plot; on the whole, then as now, the more prosperous the city and the more commercially desirable the area, the greater the congestion and the height of the buildings.

The division of workplace, storage and living-space in one building can be seen in different forms, in, for instance, the twelfth-century house on the Rheingasse in Cologne, the fourteenth-century Palazzo Davanzati in Florence and the fifteenth-century Palazzo Corner-Spinelli in Venice, all belonging to rich merchants. Merchant bankers were likely to live in much the same way. The splendid building occupied by the Milan branch of the Medicis in the mid-fifteenth century, although low for a building in the centre of a big town of that date, was a variation on the type. The arrangement could also serve equally well for a prosperous shopkeeper. Either merchant or shopkeeper, for instance, could have rented the shop which the dean and chapter of St Paul's built as a speculation in Bucklersbury in the City of London in 1405. It was built of timber on a plot about eighty feet by twenty, and contained cellars and four storeys, including garrets in the attic. On the ground floor above the cellars were a 'great shop' and a 'sotelhouse' in front, and a warehouse, approached through a covered alleyway and a small internal courtyard, at the back; the living-floors were above the shop, sotelhouse and warehouse.[16]

Italian merchants and merchant bankers did not confine their business to each others' premises. An information network was essential to their success, and for the convenience of collecting information they began to congregate in one particular place at one time of the day. This was probably the origin of the merchants' or bankers' loggias of which the Gothic Loggia or Foro dei Mercanti at Bologna, which dates from 1382–4, is perhaps the earliest recorded example; it may also have been one of the functions of the early Renaissance Loggia della Mercanzia in Siena (1417). In Bruges in the fifteenth century the Italian merchants congregated on a little square known as the Buerseplaats, from a family of Bruges innkeepers who owned two houses on the square; the Florentines built a small wooden loggia in front of their consulate, which was also on the square. In London the Italians met in Lombard Street in the open, 'walking in the rain when it raineth, more like pedlars than merchants',[17] for London was still a relatively unsophisticated provincial city. All such meeting places inevitably developed into places where at any rate the first stages of buying and selling goods or bills of exchange were negotiated; they were the embryos of the full-scale bourses or exchanges of later centuries, and of the discovery that commerce in goods could go on without the actual goods being on show, except perhaps in sample. It was an important discovery because it ultimately led to a complete separation of the business parts of a city from the warehousing and marketing parts.

Some of the goods being dealt with in medieval cities, at all levels from market stalls to the counting houses of merchant bankers, were inevitably made in the actual city, or its immediate environs, rather than being imported from a distance.

Although there were many medieval towns which grew and prospered on the basis

22. The Loggia dei Mercanti (1382–4), Bologna.

of importing and exporting, and the manufactures of which were limited to supplying a purely local network, there were others which were known largely or entirely for the products which they made or processed for export over Europe and beyond. Cordova became famous for its leather, Toledo for its swords, Limoges for its enamel, Nottingham for its carved alabaster, Fabriano for its paper. Milan and later Nuremberg were the Birminghams of the later Middle Ages, producing a wide variety of exquisitely finished metal objects, from locks to suits of armour; both were conveniently close to iron mines, in the Alps and the Harz Mountains. Lüneburg, a Hanseatic town not far from Hamburg, owed its prosperity to adjacent salt-pans, and quarries for building plaster. Most of these industries were carried on in small workshops, where the products made in the back were often offered for sale in the front. Some, like brewing, tanning and paper-making needed water. Some used water power: by the end of the Middle Ages water was being used to work hammers in forges, draw wire, throw silk in order to make silk thread, and pound wood or rags as part of the paper-making process, as well as for fulling and for grinding corn. All these industries congregated along a river, stream or canal. Tanning was so malodorous and fulling so noisy that they were often kept out of the centre by specific city regulations. But, other things being equal, any workshop which sold the products from its own premises graduated as close as it could to the centre, along with shops of all kinds.

23–4. Two views of the Fonte d'Ovile (1262), outside the Porta Ovile, Siena.

But textiles, especially woollen textiles, dominated medieval manufacture, even more than they dominated medieval trade. Textiles could be used for clothing, bedding, towelling or hangings, the demand for them was widespread and almost insatiable, they were easy to package, travelled well, and did not easily decay, the wool with which to make them was available in abundance, and by the later Middle Ages raw silk and flax for linen was being produced in Europe too. The textile industry and trade were far and away the biggest source of employment in Europe after agriculture, and much of the resources of agriculture went into supplying their needs. Textiles made monarchs and merchants rich, stimulated trade of all sorts, but also caused wars and revolutions, tore cities in half and sometimes all but destroyed them.

One reason why the woollen textile industry employed so many people was that it was easily the most complex type of manufacture in medieval Europe. There could be twenty or more different processes between cutting the wool off the sheep's back and delivering the final bale of cloth.

As a result, a special class of entrepreneurs emerged. They were known in England as clothiers, in Italy as *lanaiuoli*, in France as *drapiers*, and in Flanders as *lakenkopers*. They bought wool from the merchants, and sold cloth back to them. In between they organized and financed all the many stages of the production process. Some of the work was done on their own premises, but in the main they worked on the putting-out system, sending wool out to country-women for spinning, yarn to weavers for weaving

25. The cloth market, Bologna, in 1411. From the *Matricula Societatis Draperiorum* (Museo Civico, Bologna).

in their own houses, and cloth to independent dyers for dyeing in their own workshops. They could operate on a comparatively large scale, organizing a complex and widespread work-force adding up to a hundred or more people, or, on a small scale, involving only a dozen or fewer; in the latter case they were likely to be working themselves in one of the processes, perhaps as a weaver, fuller or dyer. They were in an intermediate position between merchants and artisans, and in different cities could become supporters of the former, or champions of the rights of the latter; it depended, usually, on the attitude of the merchants and the scale of their own operations.

At least three of the wool-textile processes needed water: fresh, clean water, the more abundant and faster-flowing the better. Water was needed for washing wool, dyeing yarn or cloth, and fulling cloth. Fulling was the process by which cloth was steeped in water and pounded, in order to clean it of the oil used in the weaving process, and to firm and thicken it. The pounding was originally done manually, or by stamping with the feet, but from the thirteenth century fulling-mills powered by water-wheels became increasingly common: Don Quixote mistook the thumping of the great hammers in a fulling-mill for the tread of a party of giants, and set off to do battle accordingly.[18] A fulling-mill needed a stream or river with a sufficient fall to turn the water-wheel; textile workers in flat countries had to continue fulling in the traditional way.

A good supply of fresh water was essential as the basis for a textile town. Seaports or ports up tidal waterways seldom had enough fresh water available with which to establish a big textile industry, for salt water was no use in the wool processes; they often developed a small one, as Genoa did on the basis of two small streams which tumbled down the precipitous slopes on which the city was built, to north and south of its centre. Venice, however, used its wealth of waterways and shipping to overcome its lack of any but rainwater supply: it brought in fresh water by boat, and also sent cloth out by boat to be fulled at its subject-city Treviso. As a result, in the sixteenth century it was able to build up a flourishing wool-textile industry.

The problem of water was especially great in the drier countries of the Mediterranean. Siena, for instance, used the greatest ingenuity to tunnel and conduit water from any available local springs to covered cisterns on the skirts of its hilltop site. On the basis of these it built up a sizeable textile industry, out of which grew an extremely important banking industry. For a time it could compete with Florence as an equal, and even soundly defeat it at the Battle of Montaperti in 1260. But the amount of water that it could get hold of was inevitably limited, whereas Florence had the Arno. As a means of transport the Arno was limited, though by no means useless. Only small boats could get up to the weir just below the town; bulky goods had to be disembarked at Signa,

26. A *tiratoia* or drying-shed by the Arno, seen through the Ponte alle Grazie. Detail from a drawing by Giuseppe Moricci.

and carried the last seven or eight miles by road. Upstream the only function of the river as a means of transport was to float logs down from the mountain forests. But it was as a source of industrial water that the Arno effectively created Florence as a major medieval textile centre. Swirling down from the Appenines, brown and muddy and liable to flood the town in winter, sometimes drying to a trickle in summer, it none the less supplied fast-flowing water in far more abundant quantities than Siena could ever hope for. Moreover, there were streams in the hills to north and south of Florence which could power fulling-mills within convenient reach of the city. So Florence prospered, rose to a population of around 100,000 and grew powerful, while Siena stuck at a population-level of about 30,000, and dwindled to a sleepy satellite of Florence.

There were hundreds of textile towns, large and small, all over Europe, but Florence and Ghent became the biggest. Ghent was the first to develop, and by the mid-thirteenth century already had a population estimated to have been in the region of 60,000.

Although Florence, and Tuscany in general, had had a long-established textile industry, it was a minor one, based on local wool of poor quality. For good-quality cloth Florence, like the rest of Italy, went to Flanders or England, especially the former. Then, during the thirteenth century, it developed a new industry, importing unfinished Flemish cloth and finishing it. Its merchants went up to the Champagne fairs to buy the cloth and brought it down to Florence for dyeing, fulling and the other finishing processes, followed by sale either for use in Italy or for export via Venice to the Levant. The city flourished, the population grew, and in the 1170s the walls were enlarged accordingly. The next step was to buy wool rather than cloth from the north, and to carry out the whole manufacturing process in Florence. Florentine merchants first came to England to buy wool in the second half of the thirteenth century; during the fourteenth century cloth-making became far more important in Florence than finishing Flemish cloth, the population rose to its peak and between 1284 and 1333 the walls of the city were enlarged again, to their maximum extent.

By 1350, just before the Black Death approximately halved Florence's population, its textile industry was producing 85,000 pieces of cloth a year, and may have employed as many as 30,000 people.[19] In 1427 the textile workers amounted to about 45.5 percent of the work-force.[20] Their number was made up of artisans, *lanaiuoli* and those retail shopkeepers who specialized in textiles. At the apex were the merchants; they were essential to the industry, although they dealt in many other goods besides, and were often engaged in banking activities as well. It was they who imported wool from England (and later from Spain, Provence and the Balearics), sold it in Florence to the *lanaiuoli*, bought back the bulk of the finished cloth, and sold it for export round Europe and the Levant. Moreover, the *lanaiuoli* needed capital, to buy wool (and often dyeing materials, which they sold on credit to the dyers), buy or rent premises, and pay the artisans. They frequently went into partnership with a merchant or merchant banker, who supplied most of the capital, while they provided the management and the expertise. In any labour dispute they and the merchants invariably sided together.[21]

The artisans were numerically much the biggest section of the industry, and on the average much the poorest. There was a good deal of variation, however. Their various branches, especially the dyers, wool-washers and carders (who separated the wool fibres in preparation for spinning), tended to include small firms of a few workers. An artisan who ran his own business could be moderately prosperous, and in the case of the dyers rather more than that. But many of the actual wage-earners worked for a pittance, were laid off in slack times and were reduced to borrowing from their immediate employers, or the *lanaiuoli*, who would mercilessly impound looms, tools, furniture or bedding if they did not repay the debt.

The industry was controlled by two guilds or *arti*, the older Arte de Mercanti di Calimala, which was originally concerned with buying and finishing Flemish cloth, but increasingly concentrated on finishing and dyeing cloth of all kinds, and the Arte della Lana, which dealt with all processes of the industry. The latter became much the most important. Its headquarters were in the centre of Florence, next to the Or San Michele. It had its own court, prison and police, and the penalties which it imposed included flogging, mutilation, fines, exclusion from work, and on occasion even death. It gradually acquired possession of most of the fulling-mills around Florence, and of the *tiratoi* in the city, the great open sheds in which wet cloth was 'tentered' by being fixed on hooks to dry and be stretched into shape. Merchants and *lanaiuoli* could both belong to the guild, and ran it together, with the power of the merchants predominating.

The artificers, although they had to belong and contribute to the guilds, were not allowed to become officers in them, vote in elections, or play any part in running them. Nor were they allowed to form guilds of their own. They were called *sottoposti*, official underdogs. There was nothing unusual about this. All over Europe the merchants did their best to keep artisans in their places; if formed into guilds of their own, the guilds were, to begin with, organized, legislated for and supervised by the merchants or the city establishment and were designed to impose standards of work and behaviour rather than to be a self-regulating and self-protecting union. Artisans often lived in separate suburbs outside the city walls, and it could be a matter of debate in a city council whether to extend the walls to protect them, with the risk of admitting a potentially powerful and disaffected element inside the city.

It is not surprising that they often were disaffected and, forming as they did large groups living together and nursing similar grievances, were able to make trouble. In the late thirteenth and fourteenth centuries appalling contests involving textile workers took place all over Europe. As early as 1225 the weavers and fullers of Valenciennes in north France deposed the town government, looted the rich, and declared a commune. In the late thirteenth century the textile workers of Ypres, Ghent and Bruges seized power, and when the merchants who ran the cities called in the help of the King of France routed his army at the Battle of Courtrai in 1302. In 1328 the French in return massacred an army of peasants and artisans at the Battle of Cassel. Meanwhile, in the adjoining dukedom of Brabant, the weavers, fullers and other textile workers had briefly seized power and abolished the merchant guilds, only to be ruthlessly suppressed in 1306 by the Duke of Brabant; for a time artisans in the workers' suburb outside the walls of Brussels were liable to the death penalty if found inside the gates after curfew.

In Florence in 1345 a wool-carder, who had been organizing protest meetings among his fellow workers, was arrested during the night along with his two sons and hastily hanged. In Siena in 1371 a rising of the wool-carders in the quarter of Ovile ended in their wholesale massacre; in 1385 the artisan-dominated rule of the Riformatori ended in the expulsion of four thousand artisans, an event from which the Siena textile industry never recovered. Political troubles in Florence in 1378 developed into the famous revolt of the Ciompi, during which the cloth workers and the lesser guilds took over the city for four years. In Flanders there were further textile worker revolts in 1379, led by Ghent, always the most radical of the Flemish textile cities.

The troubles were usually started less by wage-earning workers than by small entrepreneurs, who were disgruntled by being kept out of any share in running the city by the merchants or the big employers. The mainspring of the Ciompi revolt was the dyers, and the masters running small firms of carders, combers and wool workers, who wanted to have their own independent guilds. The results varied a good deal. The textile workers were most successful in Ghent, where from 1302 their guilds had a dominant role in the city. They were partially successful in Bruges and, except for brief intervals, failed completely in Brabant and Italy.

Textile towns inevitably generated specialized areas and buildings. In Florence the industry was approximately divided into three concentric zones, although it did not

27–8. Two details from paintings by I. N. van Swanenburgh, showing wool-combing and wool-washing by the canals of Leiden (Stedelijk Museum de Lakenhal, Leiden).

always work out as neatly as that. The warehouses of the merchants were in the centre, the artisans were on the periphery, and the *lanaiuoli* were in between. Their premises were known as *botteghe di lana*, and there were two hundred and seventy nine of them in 1380, in four separate areas.[22] *Botteghe* varied a good deal in size, but none was very large; around five to fifteen people could be employed in them, exclusive of outworkers. The less prosperous *lanaiuoli*, or the managers employed by the richer ones, probably lived over the *botteghe*. There were no cloth halls in the centre, as there were in Flemish towns, because in Italy there was no legal compulsion to use halls, and most buying and selling was carried out on individual premises.

In all textile towns artisans lived where they could afford to live, and where the nature of their work suggested. This meant that in general they lived, and often worked, on the outskirts of the city, where lodging was cheaper, and that those whose work involved water lived near it. In Florence the dyers lived and worked upstream (where the water was cleanest) along the north bank of the Arno beyond the church of Sta Croce. The wool-washers worked downstream, on flights of steps leading down to the river, and lived in very poor neighbourhoods adjoining. The fullers increasingly lived and worked out of the city, along the hill streams to north and south. The weavers kept their looms at home, were poorly paid, and lived in poor areas away from the water and on the edge of the city. It took a weaver about a month to weave a piece of cloth; he would walk into the centre to collect his yarn and back again to deliver the finished cloth. The carders normally worked under supervision in the premises of the *lanaiuoli*.

29. The amphitheatre at Arles, as converted into a fortified enclave in the Middle Ages and later. From an engraving after J. B. Guibert (British Museum).

The houses of the poorer artisans were mainly of one, or at the most two storeys, and many must have been little more than shacks.[23] Late medieval almshouses in Flemish towns were mainly built for indigent cloth-workers, and probably give some idea of what poor artisan houses were like, but translated from timber into brick by the money of the benefactors who built them. The dyers lived more substantially, and had their vats in cellars under their living-quarters or in yards at the back. But in the artisan areas the *tiratoi* were much the most distinctive buildings connected with the industry. They were a specifically Italian feature, roofed over to prevent the sun from harming the colours of dyed cloth, but open at the sides to promote through draughts for drying the cloth. In northern Europe, where protection from the sun was less important, the cloths were stretched on tenter racks arranged in serried rows in open fields and yards around the edge of the town.

The textile industry produced a type of medieval town as distinctive as the mill towns of the nineteenth century, and to be found, with variations, all over Europe. The type survived through the sixteenth and seventeenth centuries, for there were few changes in the techniques and organization of the industry in that period, so that pictures of late sixteenth-century cloth towns probably give much of the feel of medieval ones. Wool, yarn and cloth in all their various stages were on the streets everywhere. Wagons, sleds or mules trundled or carried bales of cloth or huge sacks of wool, to or from the wharves or the city gates, or out to the fulling mills and the country cottages of the spinning women. Other loads glided by in barges along rivers or canals, the banks of which were crowded with wool-washers washing fleeces. House fronts were festooned with yarn or wool hung out to dry, the great drying sheds were crammed with cloths which burst out from them like washing out of a hamper, and the northern cities were surrounded with fields of cloth instead of corn. In the artisan quarters drying-sheds, hospitals built by merchants with a conscience and the great churches of the preaching friars rose out of the little cottages, and there were pawn shops on the street corners. The weavers' areas must have been quiet places, with little traffic except for solitary weavers coming home crouched under a load of yarn, and the click of the looms set up close to the windows or in the street in front of their doors.

It is hard to get the feel of all this in the towns today, for the whole way of life and most of the buildings have gone. On the whole it was the grandest and most prestigious buildings connected with the industry, such as cloth halls and guild houses, which were most recorded and survived best. The houses and premises of clothiers, retail shopkeepers and dyers must survive in some numbers, although little work has been done in identifying or recording them. But virtually all the cheaply built houses of the poorer artisans have long ago crumbled to dust or been cleared away, the last *tiratoi* went in the nineteenth century, and all the tenter fields have been built over.

The artisans' quarters tend to have remained working-class areas, however, even if the buildings have mostly been renewed and the occupation of the inhabitants has changed. Wandering through them one can still sometimes get a flavour of their original character. Perhaps the best place in which to do so is in the poorer quarters of Siena, hot and quiet in the sun down the steep slopes next to the city walls, a world away from the high narrow streets of fortified palazzi along the hill crests or the great sweep of the Campo. The cool clear water is still splashing in the great caves of the medieval fountains; and the bigger houses in the dyers' area near the Fonte della Branda, where St Catherine of Siena's birthplace is today a shrine embellished in the Renaissance, remind one that the dyers enjoyed a modest prosperity and that Catherine of Siena's father was a dyer.

What one cannot get in Siena today is any feeling of its original skyline in the thirteenth and fourteenth centuries. Like other Italian cities, it was a miniature Manhattan of towers. Most of them were family towers, and they dominated the skyline far more effectively than the towers of the churches, or of the city walls and civic buildings. They were the towers of the city nobility.

Many cities round Europe had what can conveniently be called a nobility, although its members did not always call themselves noble. They were distinct from the great landowners or church magnates who came to cities like London or Paris to attend the court or sit in council or parliament, and acquired a house in the town to live in while they were there. The houses could be very grand (the Hôtel de Cluny in Paris, which was the town house of the abbots of Cluny, is a good example), the arrival or departure of their owners, attended by a mounted household of a hundred or more attendants, could be a sensational sight, but they were likely to stand empty for much of the year, and their owners were little concerned with the day to day life of the city.

The city nobility lived mainly in the cities, and owned land both in the city and outside it. Some of them had been granted nobility by kings or emperors as a reward for service in war, or owned what were called in the Middle Ages fiefs, properties held in return for military service (which was not always exacted), ownership of which could confer nobility. Others seem to have been called noble merely on the strength of ownership of land and ancient lineage. Many were descended from the senior household officers of the local rulers under the protection of whose castles or abbeys their city had originally

30. Family towers at Lucca. From a fourteenth-century manuscript (Archivo Capitolare, Lucca).

taken shape, and had owned property in the city from its very beginning. In many cities they did not take part in trade. Metz, for instance, was dominated from the thirteenth century by five groups known as *paraiges*, the kernel of which was made up of descendants of the household officials of the bishop of Metz.[24] They owned most of the town, and did not take part in commerce or banking, although after a while they intermarried, very selectively, with the families of Metz merchants and bankers as these grew in wealth and power.

In Italy the city nobles took freely to commerce and finance without any stigma attaching to their nobility as a result. The reason was perhaps that in early medieval Italy the country was, on the whole, poor, and the towns rich, whereas in northern Europe, with the exception of Flanders, the opposite tended to be the case; the Italian nobles could not support their style of life on their country rents, and came into the towns to increase their income. But in some cases, as in Siena, expanding cities which acquired territorial possessions compelled the local nobility to take up residence, in order to keep them under control.

It was a policy of dubious value, for city nobles formed one of the most troublesome elements in the medieval towns where they settled. Unlike self-made merchants, who tended to be hard-working, sober, thrifty and cautious, they were violent, flamboyant and quarrelsome; they looked down on everyone else, had an absurdly touchy sense of honour, and their feuds ravaged the towns. Moreover, they invariably congregated together in family groups or clans, the power of which was increased by their amalgamating with each other or absorbing outsiders.

It was these groups which built the family towers. Each tower (or sometimes group of towers) provided the fortified element in a complex of buildings occupied by an individual family or group of families, usually legally bound together by articles of association which specified how the complex was to be shared. The complex often contained a central square, a chapel or church, and a loggia, along with a cluster of dwellings

31. Genoa in 1481. From a sixteenth-century copy by C. Grassi of a late fifteenth-century picture. In the foreground is the city's war fleet, the ships of which were paid for by individual *alberghi* and carry their arms (Museo Navale, Genoa).

which could include shops, tenements and workshops occupied by retainers and dependants running right the way down the social scale, all of whom would turn out to fight for the clan if needs be.

Considerable rivalry existed between clans as to who could build the highest tower. At Florence the tower of the Tosinghi is said to have been 250 feet high.[25] It has long since been demolished, along with all but the bottom stumps of a handful of family towers; according to one reckoning these may have numbered as many as four hundred at their peak. At Bologna, where the first known articles of clan association date from 1177, there is documentary evidence for one hundred and ninety-four family towers; only two survive, both out of the perpendicular, one docked of its upper stages, but one still of amazing height. In all cities the towers were steadily reduced in number, as one faction won over another, or the merchants took control from the nobles. The biggest remaining collection is at S. Gimignano, where there are thirteen, including the tower of the town hall, and even this relatively modest assembly is extraordinary enough.

In some cases a clan or family moved into the remains of a Roman theatre or amphitheatre and adapted it as a warren of family houses. In Rome the Theatre of Marcellus was occupied in turn by the Pierleoni, the Savelli and the Orsini, and the Fiancigani and the Annibaldi fought for possession of the Colosseum. An eighteenth-century view of the amphitheatre in Arles, made before it was cleared out in the early nineteenth century, gives a vivid impression of one of these curious little towns within a town.[26] When Anselmo Adornes visited Genoa in the fifteenth century he described how 'generally all the members of a parentage or lineage live together in a single quarter or around a single square. There they sometimes own in common a church and a house with a loggia where every day the members of the family meet to discuss trivial or family matters.'[27] In Genoa the clans were called *alberghi*; they were represented on the city council, and dominated Genoese political, social and economic life. They were

32. Two family towers in Bologna.

33. (right) The Virgin Mary protecting Siena. From a sixteenth-century engraving.

based on noble landowning families who had moved into Genoa in its early days. But in course of time the family clans amalgamated with others and admitted new members, including non-noble merchants, in order to increase their power, and a number of completely artificial new clans were created, some of which lacked any noble element. Nevertheless it was the family loyalties, life-style and violent feuds of the original nobility which set the Genoese pattern.[28]

In Florence a very different situation existed. In 1292 the equivalents of the nobles in the Genoese *alberghi* were officially declared *magnati*, only in order to penalize them. They were not allowed to become Priors, as the members of the Signoria, which formed the executive government of Florence, were called; they were excluded from a number of other offices and not allowed to serve as the consul or rector of a guild. They had been pushed out of power by the newer merchant families. Even so, many of them retained great wealth and prestige and exerted a considerable influence on Florentine politics from behind the scenes, not least because the richer merchant families continued to intermarry with them.

The noble families had always owned property, and the new merchants put their profits into buying it, inside the city and out. In the course of time, the grander merchant families acquired substantial city holdings. For reasons of prestige a rich merchant was likely to live in a house with a sizeable garden, mainly occupied by his business and his family; but elsewhere in the city both nobles and new merchants owned buildings or shares in buildings which were subdivided and let out for a wide variety of uses, and the gardens or yards of which had been developed and covered with more buildings. As property was often divided up, as a result of providing marriage portions or dividing an inheritance among children, by the later Middle Ages both the plan of medieval cities and their ownership pattern had usually grown extraordinarily complex. But by then much of the property belonged to different branches of the Church.

3 Church and State

Nobles, merchants, shopkeepers, entrepreneurs and artisans all lived under the authority of the Church. Its importance in the medieval city can scarcely be exaggerated; in terms of buildings it is made abundantly clear by any visit to a historic medieval city, and even more by bird's-eye views or prospects made before the alteration and destruction of later centuries. However grand the town halls or market halls, however formidable the walls or the ruler's castle, however cumulatively impressive the private towers, in every medieval town nothing could equal ecclesiastical buildings for combined splendour of architecture and richness of furniture and fittings.

Cities, groups and individuals were often violently critical of the clergy, and prepared to manipulate the Church remorselessly to their own advantage. Nevertheless, the Church, and the scriptures as interpreted by it, were accepted as providing the only channel through which God spoke to man, and the only route to heaven. Its influence was all pervasive. It laid down the standards of both private and public morality, and by its law on usury conditioned the conduct of business. Almost all holidays were church holidays, almost all education was church education. Collectively, every town endeavoured to obtain protection against war,

34. Lüneburg in the mid-fifteenth century. Detail from a picture by Hans Bornemann (Church of St Nicholas, Lüneburg).

fire, plague and famine by acquiring as many religious relics as possible, and by enlisting one particular saint as its patron. Surviving pictures of the Virgin Mary stretching her robe to shield the city of Siena vividly conjure up the sense which a medieval city had of being under special protection. But this protection came through the Church and was epitomized in building: at Siena by the cathedral church of the Assumption of the Virgin, presiding over the skyline of Siena at the highest point of the city.

One practical result of the Church's position was that in every medieval city it invariably became the biggest property owner. Genuine piety and fear of hell-fire combined to see to this. There were many individuals in the Middle Ages who relentlessly pursued their own self-interest through their lives, but in old age trembled under the shadow of death and the fear of what might come after it. They did their best to escape the possibility of an eternity in hell by gifts or legacies to the Church, and by organizing and paying others to pray or say masses for their souls after death. Merchants were especially liable to feelings of guilt because most of them were conscious of having practised usury in their time, or of having steered dangerously close to it.

The ecclesiastical framework in a medieval town of any size was almost always a complex one. To begin with, there was the basic structure of spiritual rule, ultimately deriving from the pope, and usually wielded in a town of any size by a bishop or abbot-bishop in his cathedral (where authority invariably extended beyond the city), and by the priests in their parishes under him. But overlaid on this were all the varieties of religious houses founded or endowed by rulers, merchants and other benefactors. A town which was in any way connected with a king or a powerful duke or count was likely to be ringed with an especially superb collection of religious foundations, built, endowed and enlarged by successive generations of rulers. But commoners were equally active, if on a smaller scale, either in making new foundations, rebuilding old ones, or enlarging them with chapels dedicated to the use of guilds, fellowships and other organizations, or to the saying of masses for individuals who were usually buried in them. Their bequests went to endow a variety of functions, for it was accepted that education, health and everything else that today would be lumped under the heading of social services were the province of the Church.

35. Cologne from the river. Detail of a woodcut by Anton Woensam, 1523.

New religious foundations were usually set up on the outskirts of the town, where land was abundantly available. They tended to be endowed with orchards, gardens and fields as well as land for building. As time went on they were inevitably left property elsewhere in the town, and as it grew they frequently increased their income by developing what had previously been open ground with shops or housing. In addition to acquiring property, the Church almost always acquired privileges, and often sovereignty over a greater or lesser area. The most common privilege was that of holding a market or a fair; sovereignty could derive from a lay ruler handing over some of his own rights to a religious institution, or from the fact that the ruler was a bishop or an abbot in the first place, and kept himself and his establishment apart, for reasons of security and prestige. The cathedral, and the bishop's palace by it, took the place of the castle. Sometimes, when the city was prosperous and the cathedral revenues relatively small, the cathedral became more closely identified with the city. This happened in many Italian cities. In Florence the Arte della Lana took over responsibility for the fabric of the cathedral, and organized the building of Giotto's campanile and Brunelleschi's dome; the Arte di Calimala had even earlier made itself responsible for the Baptistery. The city government contributed lavishly, by imposing special taxes or earmarking existing funds. The cathedral had become a symbol of civic pride. Any physical sense of separation between it and the rest of the city has long since vanished, and one has to look at a street plan to see how it once occupied its own patch in the north-east corner of the original walled town. At Siena, on the other hand, one still gets the feeling of the Duomo being apart from the city; the division became even stronger in some English cathedral cities, above all at Lincoln, where the cathedral still floats on its hilltop above the main part of the city, in another and more ethereal world.

Parish churches were, by their nature, spread all over the town. Religious houses tend to show the date of their foundation by their position; the earlier ones are closer to the centre. The foundation of the Franciscan and Dominican Orders in the early thirteenth century, swiftly followed by the Carmelites and a number of others, brought to cities a new kind of religious Order, which concentrated on preaching, teaching and missionary work. New churches, designed like huge magnificent barns in order to be effective vehicles for preaching, rose up in cities all over Europe. They were usually built just outside the walls; but in most cities these were soon extended to include them, during the boom years of the late thirteenth and early fourteenth centuries.

The Church had always accepted the Christian duty of looking after the sick, the poor and those in trouble, and specific buildings were built for this purpose from the very early Middle Ages. The principle behind them was that nobody who was in genuine need and asked to be taken in was turned away. To begin with, a single institution would impartially accept ill people, lunatics, pilgrims, pregnant mothers, foundling children, orphans and the decrepit aged. Specialized institutions appeared in the course of the Middle Ages, but all types continued to be called hostels or hospitals, and some foundations (such as the Hôtel Dieu in Paris) continued their policy of accepting everyone, although a degree of specialization was likely to appear within their complex of buildings.[1]

Some hospitals were run by fraternities of laymen, notably the Order of the Holy Spirit, which was founded by a Frenchman, Guy de Montpellier, in the late twelfth century and taken up shortly after its foundation by Pope Innocent III, who gave it what became the hospital of Sto Spirito in Sassia in Rome as its headquarters. But most were under religious control, and many were built and run by religious Orders specifically founded for the purpose. Money came freely from all kinds of sources, for to endow or enrich a hospital was considered as praiseworthy a deed as building a church or founding a monastery. Hospitals were built and endowed by monarchs, bishops, individual pious laymen, or by guilds and fraternities; the latter usually confined their hospitals to their own sick or impoverished members, but sometimes opened them to everyone.

The earlier hospitals contained a single great room, sometimes divided up by pillars, with a chapel opening into the room. The kitchen was normally in an adjoining but free-standing building. As hospitals expanded, or the need for some form of subdivision was accepted, multi-ward hospitals began to appear. Ward was often added to ward in a very *ad hoc* manner. Largely by accident the great hospital of Sta Maria Nuova in Florence developed an approximately cross-shaped plan in the fourteenth century, and this was taken up and formalized in other Italian hospitals in the fifteenth century. The most influential example was the huge Ospedale Maggiore in Milan, which was begun in 1456. Its fame spread cross-shaped hospitals all over Europe and ultimately across the Atlantic to Spanish America.

The cross-shaped plan enabled four wards to have a view of a common altar at the crossing. At the Ospedale Maggiore there were two crosses, one for men and one for women, separated by a very large court containing a chapel. At the Hospital de la Santa Cruz (1504–14) in Toledo and the Hospital Real de Dementes (begun 1504) in Granada, the male and female wards were one above the other. The two Spanish hospitals were both for lunatics, and in the former a splinter of the True Cross was embedded in a huge cross of wood encrusted with silver, and hung in the open centre, which rose up through both floors.

Hospitals were among the earliest and the largest public buildings, other than churches, in medieval towns. They vied in size with market halls and the great halls built for justice or council by rulers or cities. The Hôtel Dieu in Paris was started in

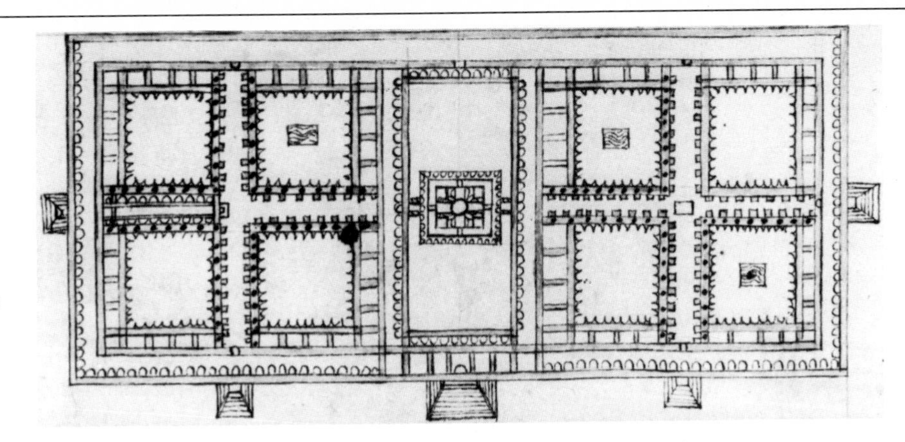

36. Plan of the Ospedale Maggiore, Milan. From Filarete's *Treatise on Architecture* (Biblioteca Nazionale Centrale, Florence).

37. The Hospital de la Santa Cruz (1504–14), Toledo.

38. Almshouses of 1480 in Boeveriestraat, Bruges.

the 1190s, to replace an earlier hospital which had been demolished for the rebuilding of Notre Dame. By 1260 a series of additions had produced 375 feet of wards, built along the water like a disjointed snake. At Tonnerre in Burgundy the Hôpital Notre Dame-de-Fontenille, of *c.* 1200, consisted of a hall 288 feet by 61, with a chapel at the end. The reason for so formidable a building in a small town was that the hospital was founded by the widowed queen, Margaret de Bourgogne, to atone for her sins during her married life and 'with a desire to merit the reward which the Evangelist has promised us'.[2] She lived next to the hospital, ran it herself, and personally nursed the patients.

But biggest of all was the Ospedale Maggiore in Milan. It was planned from the start to be a rectangular block measuring about 920 by 350 feet, and ended up much as it was planned, although it took several centuries to build. Ancillary accommodation for staff and services was grouped round and under the two great cross-shaped wards. Narrow subdivided corridors ran all round the wards and contained latrines, one to each bed; a drain, fed with water from the canal at the back of the hospital, ran under the latrines and was washed out regularly by means of sluice gates.

The actual water supply at the Ospedale Maggiore seems to have been much less sophisticated. But other medieval hospitals were even less adequately serviced, and the problems of keeping them and the patients in them clean must have been insuperable, especially during epidemics when the wards became appallingly crowded. As medieval medicine was anyway rudimentary it is not surprising that one of the portals of the Hôtel Dieu in Paris carried the inscription 'Here is the House of God and the Door to Heaven'. Hospitals gave shelter, food, and minimal medical attention to the sick and old, but essentially they were places for them to die in, fortified by the rites of the Church. The view of altar or chapel from the wards epitomized this function, and many hospital entries were indistinguishable from cathedral portals. The chapels, glowing with stained glass, gilding and painting, must have seemed like a glimpse of paradise to the inmates, lying in the stink of disease and death in the wards.

The Ospedale Maggiore contained single rooms for gentlemen 'who will be kept separate from the commoners, through respect'.[3] Cubicles, curtaining and bunk beds first appeared in the wards perhaps in the fifteenth century, and later became a standard arrangement. The inmates of hospitals for old people began to be put, more humanely, into rooms or even separate houses rather than wards. The result was the almshouse, which appears in Venice by the fourteenth century, if not earlier, and in the fifteenth century was common all over Europe. Almshouses could be built with a chapel and a common hall, with a priest or warden to oversee the inmates, but often they consisted of no more than a row of little houses. A similar arrangement appeared for both leper villages and plague-houses. Unlike ordinary hospitals, these were invariably isolated outside the town. They could be very large. The biggest was once again in Milan, where the Lazaretto, built for plague victims in 1488, consisted of an enormous hollow square with the walls lined internally with 288 little cells, all with a view of the altar under an open canopy in the centre of the square.[4]

Medieval education was entirely run by the clergy in northern Europe, and clergy predominated in it in Italy. But, in terms of buildings, the results were much less noticeable than the hospitals. Many schools were held within a religious complex or actually in a church, and the numbers involved were seldom large. The universities, of which nearly eighty were founded between the mid-twelfth century and 1500, produced much greater congregations of teachers and students: the University of Paris, one of the first and in medieval times the most famous of universities, developed as a by-product of the cathedral school at Notre Dame, and by the thirteenth century had several thousand teachers and students, and dominated the Left Bank of Paris. But in Paris and elsewhere both the students and teachers housed themselves to begin with in existing buildings, and when new buildings came to be built, they were of a very modest nature.[5] Teachers, and even more students, were normally poor, often desperately poor. It was not until the late fourteenth century that universities, and the colleges which formed part of them, began to acquire the kind of benefactor and endowments which had been flooding into hospitals for centuries, and even then there were relatively few of them. English universities, for some reason, attracted more money than continental ones, as was nobly exemplified in William of Wykeham's New College in Oxford, founded in 1379, and Henry VI's King's College in Cambridge, founded in 1440.

All university teachers and students were clerics. All clerics, including those not ordained as priests but in minor Orders, were automatically exempt from the civil law, and could only be tried in an ecclesiastical court. In any large town this meant that several thousand people were outside the civil law. This exemption, combined with the frequent existence of territories within the city in which clerics exerted civil power as well, contributed to the complex and often chaotic power structure which was to be found in every medieval city. The impression of unity suggested by their compact massing and clusters of wall-encircled towers rising out of the open countryside was almost always deceptive.

To begin with, admittedly, the structure of power was usually straightfoward enough. In the early Middle Ages almost all medieval towns were dominated by a lay or ecclesiastical ruler, who in many cases had created them and in any case protected them. Although the ruler often admitted the authority of an overlord, he was the immediate source of authority and law, and had the armed force with which to enforce them; the land in the town all belonged to him, and its occupants paid rent to him. The inhabitants were, to a large extent, at his mercy.

Inevitably, as a town grew in wealth, richer members began to chafe against the control of king, bishop or count, to resent being at the mercy of their courts and seeing them cream off the profits of tolls and markets, and to fight for increasing degrees of independence. The struggle for power was as likely to be led by members of the ruler's household and administrative staff, or families descended from them, as by merchants, especially if the ruler was often away and his servants grew independent in his absence. In time the two groups usually coalesced to form what in the sixteenth century tended to call itself the patriciate.

A prosperous town had the great bargaining power of being able to lend money to, or buy privileges from, rulers chronically in need of the former, and therefore ready to sell the latter. Friction between lord and overlord could often be exploited by a town to its own advantage. Privileges were seldom gained without a struggle; but rulers were unwilling to take too drastic action against communities from whom much of their wealth and prestige was derived. Endless varieties of a basically similar process went on all over Europe, with endlessly different results.

The town councils which emerged were selected according to a great variety of different systems. Some were effectively appointed by the ruler, some were self-perpetuating bodies drawn from the original property owners or the merchant guild, that is from the richest element of the city. Councils could be elected or selected to represent town wards, or different social groups, or guilds, or combinations of the three. Most cities developed at least two councils, the larger of which was often selected on a wider franchise. But in the end it was usually the richer citizens who ran their cities, even those which appeared to have a more broadly based constitution. In Florence, for instance, the government of the Priors, which lasted, with gaps, for two hundred years from 1283, put executive power into the hands of a Signoria of six Priors elected by the *arti*, the guilds, according to a complex system by which the seven most important *arti* had the most power. But the system was dominated by the merchants, who could belong to any number of guilds with the operation of which they had a connection; members of the Medici family, for instance, often belonged simultaneously to the three most powerful *arti*, the Lana, the Calimala and the Cambio. Even in the Flemish town councils, which were more truly guild-based, the weavers', fullers' and other guilds were run by entrepreneurs and employers, rather than by wage-earning craftsmen.

The inner council that ran Nuremberg was typical of the out-and-out oligarchies. It was made up of forty-five patricians and eight commoners. Its senior members were the seven Elders and the three Hauptmänner, one of whom, called the Losunger, was the first man of the city. The government had always been based on an elite, and by 1516 could be described as follows: 'The government of our city and of the common weal rests in the hands of ancient families, people whose ancestors, even back in the earliest days, were also members of the government and ruled the city. Foreigners who have settled here, and common people, have nothing to say, nor ought they to, for all power is of God, and only those may exercise it whom the Creator has endowed with special wisdom . . . The families whose members may be Elders are few in number, and even fewer those who may become Hauptmänner. A mere handful only become Losunger.'[6]

What the merchants or leading families endeavoured to acquire for their cities was, to begin with, the greatest possible degree of independence within the city boundaries: the right to make their own laws, have their own courts, appoint their own council, fix their own taxes, run their own markets and enjoy the market revenues, collect their own customs, recruit their own army, even if only a part-time citizen one, and build their own walls; and, as the reverse image of this, to be as free as possible from the laws, courts, council, taxes, market, customs and army of the ruler. If they were sufficiently successful in this to gain independence, or something approaching it, the next step was to extend their own laws and rule over the surrounding countryside. Their success, both internally and externally, was very variable; city councils could be formidably powerful bodies or subservient lackeys of the monarch, and surrounding territories could vary from a few square miles of land and a couple of villages to the far-extended empires of Genoa and Venice.

Even though medieval kings never obtained power as absolute as that belonging to some of their seventeenth-century successors, a city which was also the main seat of a powerful ruler was always going to be dominated by him. Paris was an important trading centre but there was never any doubt about the Paris merchants' submission to the French kings, securely and splendidly based in the centre of the city and the

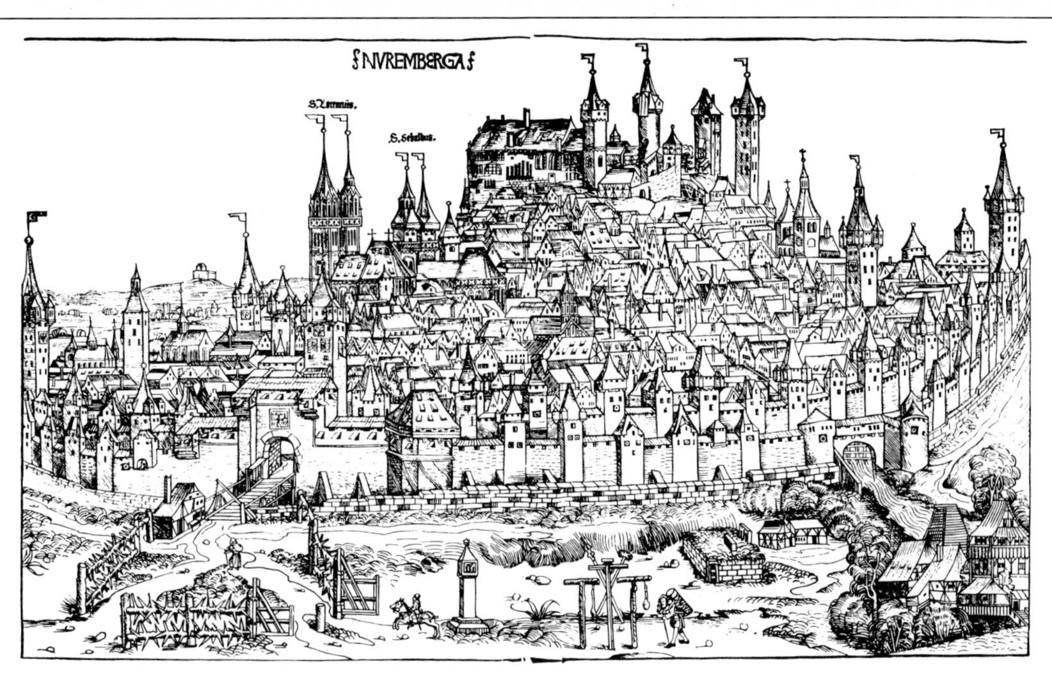

39. View of Nuremberg. From the woodcut by Hartmann Schedel in *Liber Cronicarum*, 1493.

greatest monarchs in Europe. London, where the king's base was well outside the City, at Westminster, achieved a greater degree of independence, but could never ignore his power and authority.

At Nuremberg, on the other hand, the castle which so formidably crowned the skyline gave a misleading picture of the balance of authority in the city. It was in fact two castles, one originally built by the emperor, the other the seat of his representative, the Burggraf, under whose protection the town had come into existence in the eleventh century. But by Nuremberg's great days in the fifteenth and sixteenth centuries, the Burggraf had lost most of his power (the city bought his castle from him in 1427) and the emperor was only an occasional visitor; although the city acknowledged his overlordship it was to a large extent independent. An even greater degree of freedom was to be found in cities like Florence and Siena, where the overlordship of the emperor, safely across the Alps, became negligible except on his long-spaced-out southern excursions, and that of the bishops, who in the early days had virtually ruled the cities, had vanished except for its spiritual element.

It was a big 'except', however. And in all medieval cities, in addition to freedom from secular law, different elements of the Church were likely to have acquired some kind of temporal jurisdiction in different portions of the city, as already described. Since secular individuals and secular groups were also constantly acquiring rights of all kinds from a grateful, impoverished or feeble ruler, the power map of an individual medieval city was likely to be almost as complex and confusingly full of overlapping jurisdictions, large and small, as the power map of medieval Europe.

A bird's-eye view of medieval Paris suggests a pleasingly simple arrangement of territories: the residence, courts, chapel and seat of government of the king on the Île de la Cité; the town hall, markets, and houses of merchants and artisans on the Right Bank; the university and the living quarters of its teachers and students in the smaller settlement on the Left Bank. But in fact neither land-use nor areas of jurisdiction were as simple as that.[7] The king soon moved over from the Cité and acquired additional residences on the Right Bank; here also was the Châtelet, the seat of the Prévôt de Paris, who represented the king in the city. The merchants had a secondary area and secondary markets on the Left Bank. The boundaries of jurisdiction between the king, represented by the Prévôt, the king's court of the Parlement, and the town council

40. The Palais on the Île de la Cité, Paris. From *Les Très Riches Heures du Duc de Berry* (Musée Condé, Chantilly).

were hopelessly confused. The members of the university were all clerics and technically independent of civil jurisdiction. The king owned and ran the main markets, but the butchers had a semi-independent settlement of their own by the Châtelet. And scattered over the whole city were the great religious houses, founded or endowed by kings and queens from the sixth century onwards: St Germain-des-Prés, Ste Geneviève, St Victor, St Germain-l'Auxerrois, St Martin-des-Champs and the Temple, all of which had their own little patches of land with their own jurisdiction, into which groups which wanted to be free of the city laws tended to retreat. Prostitutes clustered in the Rue Bourg l'Abbé, the territory of the Abbey of St Martin. Artisans anxious to be free of the guilds crowded into the territories of the Temple (belonging to the Knights Templar and later the Knights of St John of Jerusalem) on the edge of the Marais to the north-west, and of the Commanders of St John of the Lateran, which had acquired another independent territory on the Left Bank. Several of the religious houses had been granted the right to hold fairs by the king, the most famous and longest lasting of them being the six-week Foire de St Germain, held by the Abbey of St Germain-des-Prés. This acquired its own permanent buildings, and, like most fairs, had its own court and jurisdiction while the fair lasted.

In York the city held its court in the Guildhall and had its council chamber on the river bridge; to the west was the cathedral close, from which the diocese and archdiocese were administered, to the east the castle, which was the administrative centre of the county. Both had their own law courts, houses and communities, both were completely independent of the city, and it of them. The three together made up three little separate worlds, as to some extent they still do today. The cathedral precinct or close at York

41. Interior of the Town Hall, Lübeck, with a court in process. From the painting by Hans Heemsen (St Annen Museum, Lübeck).

was never walled, however; the cathedral close at Salisbury, also originally independent of the city, had its own walls and gatehouses, unlike the city, which could not afford them. It still gives a vivid feeling of the nature of these little independent territories.

In Bruges the separate but overlapping territories of the court and city were honeycombed by no fewer than twelve independent patches of property belonging to the provost and canons of the great collegiate church of St Donatien; they were ruled by their own judges, bailiff, clerk and courts, and partly occupied by prostitutes and unlicensed pawnbrokers. In Florence the powerful Arte della Lana had its own court, prison and powers of life and death, besides contributing with the other guilds to the general government of the city. In London, Novgorod and Bergen the Hanseatic League acquired privileged enclaves, which were in effect slices of foreign territory free of local laws and having their own courts, government and trade rights.

A number of medieval cities were made up of two or more independent towns, each with its own set of magistrates. The diffusion could reflect the development of the castle enclave as a separate organization, but also be caused by separate but adjacent foundations, sometimes having different racial origins. Multiple towns were especially common in Hanseatic cities. Gdansk consisted of Aldstadt and Rechtstadt, Berlin of Berlin itself and Kölln; three more municipalities were added in the seventeenth century, and they were only united to form the single city of Berlin in 1710.

The tower societies and tower complexes in Italian towns were examples of private territories preserved by force rather than legal right. Sometimes, however, a feudal seigneury with its own recognized jurisdiction was enveloped by the growth of a city, but retained its independence. This happened to the Vaernewicj family in Ghent when

42. The great hall of the Palais, Île de la Cité, Paris. From an engraving by J. A. du Cerceau.

the city walls were extended in the late fourteenth century; the family continued to dispense justice in its own little court, lived off its income from landed property, but also intermarried with the Ghent burghers and sat on the city council.[8]

However, in spite of these complexities, most medieval cities contained two major sources of power, a ruler, whose power extended outside the city, and a city government, the power of which was confined to the city's boundaries. Sometimes, of course, as in Italian cities which gained control of enough territory to form city-states, the two were combined.

The buildings which grew up round the seat of a ruler were conditioned by his needs. Apart from the residential element, at the very least he needed a place in which to make laws, a place in which to take counsel and a place in which to sit in judgment. At the simplest level, all three functions could be accommodated at different times in one large hall. But specialization soon set in and tended to produce the combination of a great hall, for events involving large numbers of people (from banquets to parliaments), and smaller, though never small, rooms for courts and inner councils. Westminster Hall in London and the great hall of the Palais in Paris were originally used for both banquets and courts; the courts left the hall of the Palais comparatively early on, but stayed in Westminster Hall until 1820.

Once a city had acquired a sufficient degree of independence it required the same type of accommodation as the ruler, if not necessarily on the same scale. In a small city, court, council and lawmaking could all go on in the same big room, literally a town hall; from early on rooms of this type were built in the market-place, and were usually placed above an open loggia which was used as a covered market.

As cities grew richer it became common for them to acquire the same kind of accommodation as was to be found in the ruler's castle or palace: a big room for the main council, a smaller one for the executive magistrates, a strong-room for money and records, and one or two rooms for clerks. The provision of these usually entailed the rebuilding of the town hall, the more splendidly the better, as a matter of prestige. The commercial element normally dropped out, but not always; the town hall at Torun in Poland, which was built in and after 1393, contained shops on the ground floor

43. The Vladislav Hall (*c.* 1490–1502) in Prague Castle.

and a market hall, a hall for the town council and courtrooms on the floor above.

The Rathaus in the Hanseatic city of Lüneburg still retains almost all its medieval decorations and fittings, a miraculous survival due to the city's poverty and stagnation in the seventeenth and eighteenth centuries. There is nothing as complete in Italy. A basic difference between northern town halls and Italian ones was that in Italy the town hall was usually residential. Moreover, in many Italian towns, again unlike the north, the executive and judicial functions were separated, instead of being combined in the city magistrates. Justice was the province of the official known as the Podesta, who was invariably the citizen of another place, since Italian cities were so torn with feuds that they could not rely on a local citizen to give impartial justice. The city magistrates lived over or next to their council chamber and the Podesta lived over or next to his court, in the same way as the merchant lived over or next to his shop.

At Venice the Doge's Palace was really a town hall, accommodating an unusually complex governing body, but including handsome lodgings for the Doge. At Florence the six Priors elected by the guilds as the city executive lived and worked in the Palazzo della Signoria (today's Palazzo Vecchio) and the Podesta lived and worked in the Palazzo della Podesta (today the Bargello). The Palazzo Publico in Siena is unusually large because it combined the two functions. It had two large halls in the centre, for meetings, with the Podesta's court and lodgings to one side and the lodgings and offices of the Sienese Priors to the other.

It was this residential element which caused Italian seats of civic government to be called Palazzi Publici, rather than Town Halls or Council Houses, as in the north. But in effect they were often as much castles as palaces. Civic life in Italian towns was no sinecure, and town halls had to be at least partially fortified, against the town's own citizens rather than against outsiders; moreover, as a matter of prestige they had to have a tower which could match, and if possible outshine, the great constellations of private towers. The situation in Florence was explained by the early fourteenth-century historian Villani: the Palazzo Vecchio was begun in 1298 'by reason of the differences between the people and the magnates, for as much as the city was always in jealousy and commotion at the election of the Priors ... and the Priors, who ruled

44. The Palazzo Vecchio (1298–1314), Florence.

45. The Palazzio dei Priori (1208–57), Volterra.

the city and all the republic, did not feel themselves safe in their former habitation'.[9] The result was the culmination of a type which had found earlier expression in buildings such as the Palazzo dei Priori at Volterra (1208–57)—a highly practical answer to a specific brief, which was also a sensational expression of pride, power and splendour.

A number of town halls, both in Italy and elsewhere in medieval Europe, were built away from the market square and acquired a civic square of their own; or, alternatively, the market was removed from the market square to allow it to be used mainly or entirely for civic functions. In Paris Louis VI had moved the market from the Place de Grève to the area of Les Halles in 1136–8, and the building of the first Hôtel de Ville in the Place in 1357 established it as a square mainly used for civic or public functions; but stalls had a way of creeping in, in this and other civic squares. In Italy the best-known examples are the Piazza S. Marco in Venice and the Piazza Signoria in Florence. Both were distinct from the main market squares, although both had a market element which the Piazza S. Marco never lost. Both started much smaller and were gradually enlarged to their present size. The Piazza Signoria was created in 1298 by clearing away the ruins of the houses of the Uberti, which had been demolished in 1258 during the struggle between Guelphs and Ghibellines. It was enlarged up to its present size in four successive stages, in 1307, 1318, 1362 and 1385–6. Enlargement involved the destruction of two churches, one of which, Sta Cecilia, was rebuilt on a new site in 1385–6.

The piazza acquired public buildings in addition to the Palazzo Vecchio: the Mercanzia, the common court of the guilds, which had been founded in 1308, was given a new building on it in 1359; at some stage the Condotta, which administered military expenditure, moved into a building on it; and in 1374–81 the Loggia della Signoria (today the Loggia dei Lanzi) was built as a place in which the Priors could receive important visitors and watch tournaments and other public events on the square, as a covered alternative to the terrace in front of the Palazzo Vecchio. In between whiles, old men congregated in its shade to gossip and watch the world go by. Florentines of all ages crowded into the piazza to hear news, proclamations or new laws announced from the Palazzo and to attend public events of all sorts, from bullfights to the burning

46. The thirteenth-century granary on the Graslei, Ghent.

of heretics; on rarer occasions they were summoned by bell for a Parlementum, an open-air assembly of citizens who were called together to ratify decisions already taken rather than to take them themselves. Commercial traffic was prohibited from the square as early as 1385 with the exception of an annual cloth fair which was held on the piazza every 11 November; but this was moved to Piazza Sto Spirito in the mid-fifteenth century.[10] By then the idea of a piazza expressing civic dignity and therefore unsuitable for commercial activities had clearly crystallized.

As soon as city governments acquired the necessary powers, they began to assume responsibility for a wide variety of city services, many of them involving building; in a few cities, however, where the ruler remained the major power (notably in Paris and Rome) the responsibilities remained or were shared with him. Their activities included the cleaning, paving, draining, widening and even lighting of streets, and the creation of new ones; the formation or enlargement of squares; the building of bridges and wells; the supply of water and grain; the building of quays and the provision of cranes on them; and the building of city walls and fortifications.

Most big medieval cities had to import grain in order to feed their citizens. Maintenance of the grain supply became a major concern and was the responsibility of special committees in, for instance, Bruges and Florence. Since grain had to be imported in quantities which required large storage buildings, public grain-storage produced the first distinctive warehouses in post-Roman European cities. A public granary built at Ghent in the early thirteenth century still stands on the Grasleie, by the main river quay. In London a public granary with chapel attached was built at Leadenhall in 1444 by Simon Eyre, a rich draper and former mayor, but was destroyed in the Great Fire.[11] At Nuremberg no fewer than three large grain warehouses were built in different parts of the city between 1491 and 1502. One of them was up by the castle, and its great roof still figures prominently in the city skyline. Another, known as the Kornhaus, was down in the town, by the Kornmarkt, and later became the customs house. Carts could drive into its ground floor to load and unload, and above there were six storage floors in the roof.[12] At Gdansk the grain warehouse was built over the town mill.

47. Or San Michele (1337–1404), Florence.

The story of grain storage in Florence is a curious one. Or San Michele, one of the most splendid medieval buildings in the city and still a prominent feature on its skyline, was originally built as a grain-market-cum-warehouse. It was on the site where the city grain market had been held since at least the end of the thirteenth century. The building was started in 1336, to replace one destroyed in a fire, and was designed to contain an open arcaded market on the ground floor and storage above. The ground floor was completed early in the 1350s.

A shrine in the original market arcade had contained a picture of the Virgin which was credited with miraculous qualities, and had a religious fraternity attached to it. It survived the fire and was incorporated in a magnificent new shrine in one corner of the new market. Its fraternity became extremely rich, as a result of offerings made during the Black Death. By the end of the fourteenth century the shrine had driven out the market, and the open arcades were enclosed to form a chapel.

The openings of the stone chutes, through which grain was released from the stores above, can still be seen in the piers surrounding the chapel, and are the only survival of grain-market days. It seems uncertain how long, if at all, the warehousing above was actually in use. The space which it occupied later became the hall of the fraternity, and the building as a whole a religious centre for the guilds, who embellished it with statues by Donatello and others. The grain market was removed to a new site behind the Palazzo Vecchio, but no new covered market was built there until the early seventeenth century. The huge scale of the Or San Michele itself is evidence of the importance of grain supply to Florence at its population peak in the mid-fourteenth century. But before it was finished the Black Death had halved the population; its change of use probably reflects the fact that a grain warehouse on this scale had become redundant as well as being a tribute to the wonder-working qualities of the picture.

Town bridges were another public facility which were normally built at the expense of the city, although contributions both for building and endowing them were often made by private individuals, and a powerful ruler or local magnate sometimes contributed most or all of the cost. To build a bridge across a sizeable river was very expensive, but the possession of one was obviously of the greatest importance to both the prosperity and the convenience of a city. Early bridges were often of timber, but they were always replaced if possible by stone bridges which were fireproof and in less danger from flood; owing to the small spans of their arches they remained vulnerable, however, and many medieval stone bridges were swept away in whole or part. It was perhaps in an endeavour to get divine protection against flood that numerous medieval bridges had a chapel on them, usually with an endowed staff of priests; the chapel could also

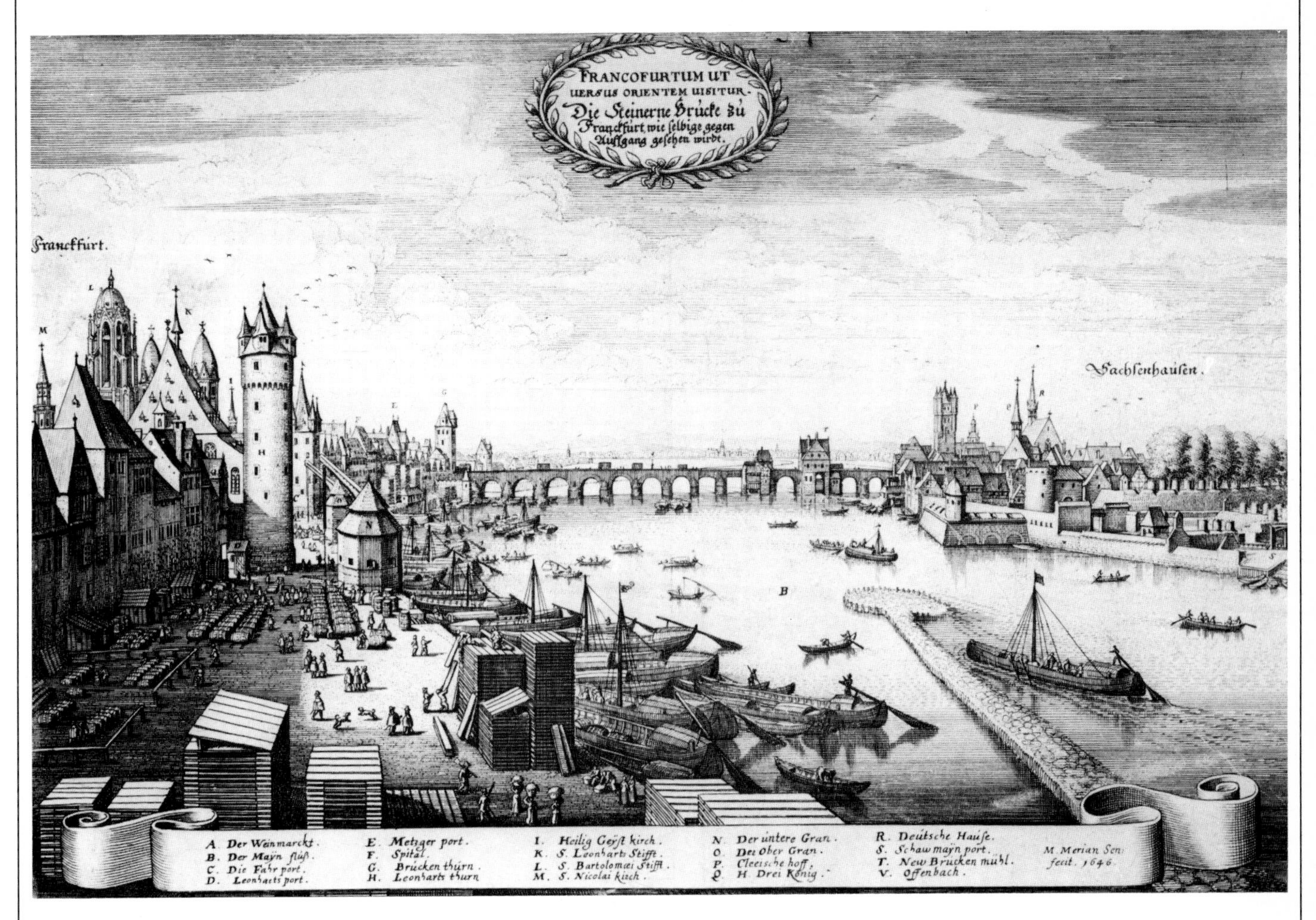

48. View from the quay at Frankfurt-on-Main. From an engraving by Mathieu Merian, 1646 (Historische Museum, Frankfurt).

be used for the collection of donations from passers-by towards the cost or maintenance of the bridge.

A popular way of recuperating part of the money spent was to build two- or three-storey shops or shops-cum-houses on the bridge, for rent. All the medieval Paris bridges ended up with buildings along them, as did two of the four Florentine ones, the original timber Rialto bridge in Venice, and London Bridge, the only bridge in or near London until Westminster Bridge was built in 1738–50. London Bridge was built in stone, replacing a timber bridge, in 1176–1209. To begin with the only building on it was a chapel, but the houses arrived in the first few years; by the sixteenth century some were as many as five storeys high. Other bridges, like the Ponte Vecchio in Florence as rebuilt in 1345, were designed to have shops from the start. The arches of the Pont au Change, the main medieval bridge in Paris, contained a number of watermills, which were rented out and provided another way of raising money.

The shops on the Pont au Change were occupied by some hundred and twenty money-changers and goldsmiths; hence the name. The Ponte Vecchio in Florence was mainly occupied by goldsmiths. A bridge in a desirable location and a crowded city could clearly command high rents, which goldsmiths and money-changers could afford to pay. The shops on the Ponte Vecchio survive, although much altered and restored. The shops on the Rialto bridge in Venice date from its re-building in stone, to a new design, in 1588. The idea of a bridge with shops was revived for the Pulteney Bridge

49. Grain merchants in Florence. From the *Specchio umano*, in which Domenico Lenzi noted the prices in the Or San Michele grain market between 1320 and 1335 (Biblioteca Laurenziana, Florence).

in Bath, which was built as late as 1769–74, probably under the inspiration (although not a copy) of a sixteenth-century bridge design by Palladio.

The provision of quays was another municipal concern. Any town heavily dependent on water-traffic was likely to have some form of quay from the earliest days, but the provision of masonry quays on a considerable scale first appears in the thirteenth and fourteenth centuries. The extensive system of quays at Bruges probably began to be created after 1270, and was certainly going full swing between 1330 and 1350. At Florence the Lungarno quay, which runs all the way along the north bank from the Ponte alla Carraia to the eastern end of the city, was constructed between about 1240 and 1300.[13] At Paris a quay was first proposed by Philippe Auguste in about 1200, but nothing seems to have been built until the 1360s.[14]

Quays had three main functions, to prevent flooding, allow for the unloading of goods and provide a roadway. At Florence, where floods from the Arno were a constant menace, the first function was the main one, and the provision of a road perhaps the second; not enough river traffic got up to Florence to make the Lungarno important as a place at which to unload it, and in any case the roadway along most of it was extremely narrow and the quay wall, for flood prevention purposes, had to be high, so that goods could only be unloaded conveniently at certain points where steps were

50. The Brauerstrasse Canal, Hamburg, in 1909. From a watercolour by E. A. Beuhne, 1909 (Museum für Hamburgische Geschichte, Hamburg).

provided. A similar situation existed in Paris, except that here the river traffic was much more important, and steps were provided at regular intervals.

At Bruges and other Flemish towns flooding was prevented and the water level controlled by dykes and sluices, so that it was possible to have low quays, along which goods could be unloaded at any point; steps were still built, however, to allow access to the water for the washing of wool or clothes, or the filling of containers.

An alternative to providing quays was to leave a beach or strand between the houses and the water, onto which boats could be pulled up. This was probably the older, and certainly the cheaper, approach, and remained common in the less prosperous or more old-fashioned places; it was the usual arrangement, for instance, in the Hanseatic cities. Sometimes the space between houses and water formed part of individual house-plots, which were developed as boat and storage yards, or on occasion finished with private wharves. By the mid or late fourteenth century yards of this kind certainly existed between Warmoesstraat and the water of Amsterdam's medieval harbour, the Damrak, and something similar seems to have existed along the Arno in Pisa.[15] There was an arrangement of the same kind in Hamburg, but here the yards were on the water-side, across the road from the houses to which they belonged, so that the water-side streets originally had houses along one side only.

Two developments tended to happen in these yards. They were often extended into the water by means of made-up ground; and in a prosperous town where pressure on open space was growing they were usually built up with houses or warehouses backing onto the older ones. Both developments can be traced in Warmoesstraat; legislation was passed in 1413 to prevent the width of the Damrak being reduced beyond acceptable limits and by the time that Cornelis Anthonisz published his bird's-eye views in 1538–44 the former yards had been solidly built up all the way along the water. A similar infill took place at Hamburg, and produced distinctive narrow waterways, with buildings sheer to the water on either side.[16]

Building on the water in this way had been a common arrangement since at least the eleventh century in Venice, where perhaps no infill was involved. As far as loading and unloading goods were concerned, buildings with water on one side and a road on the other might seem to provide an ideal system in any city where goods were transported extensively by both water and land. It meant, however, that, unless the plots were very deep, there was no room for a backyard or garden, an important consideration when goods, warehousing and residence were normally combined in the same building. It also meant that access to the water for those not living on it was inevitably reduced. It was perhaps for these reasons that extensive quay systems became the norm in the Low Countries from the sixteenth century onwards, although in other European countries they were much less prevalent.

A public crane was a distinctive feature of any medieval quay of any size which was used for unloading and loading goods. There were two main types, timber ones that could pivot on their base like a windmill, and cranes mounted on a solid masonry core which were likely to be less manoeuvrable, but perhaps could lift heavier weights. Both were worked by manpower, in the form of men working one or more treadwheels from the inside. The grandest masonry example today is at Gdansk, and is in fact a post-war reconstruction, but a very good one. The pulley for its hauling rope is sheltered from the weather under a timber shield, which projects from the stone tower like a great beak, especially impressive when seen in silhouette. One of the functions of this crane was to raise masts into position on newly built ships, and the pulley had to be high enough to make this possible.

The timber cranes were sometimes powered by two treadwheels, one to either side of the main structure, so that they looked like a combination between a crane-bird (hence the name) and a paddle-steamer. They could vary in size from relative giants like the crane on the Kraanplaats at Bruges to modest little cranes like the one at Nieuwpoort, preserved for posterity in one panel of an early sixteenth-century diptych. A good example, reconstructed on the original model in the eighteenth century, survives at Lüneburg.

The quay at Nieuwpoort, as the painting of the crane makes clear, ran outside the

51. (left) The great crane on the quay at Gdansk.

52. (above) The corn-mill and granary, Gdansk.

53. (following page) The quay at Nieuwpoort, Flanders, in the early sixteenth century. Left panel of a diptych ascribed to L. Blondeel (Stedelijke Museum, Nieuwpoort).

town walls. The Seine and the Arno were narrow enough for the river to be controllable by towers to either side, and in Pisa, Florence and Paris the circuit of walls ran both sides of the river, leaving the river banks inside the city unfortified and the city able to develop freely on both banks. If need be, the river could be closed by a chain; portions of the one used at Pisa are still hanging on the Camposanto there. In cities on a wide river or a river estuary, this kind of arrangement was impossible, and such cities, if walled at all, were invariably walled along the river as well. A quay between walls and river then became an obvious convenience. In London, however, instead of a quay being built, two small internal harbours were formed, with protected access through the river walls, at Billingsgate and Queenhythe. As a result London never had a river quay and, in spite of attempts by Wren and others to have one built in the seventeenth century, most of the City still does not have one today.

The provision of fortifications was the most prestigious, and far and away the most expensive, of the public works normally organized and paid for by the city. Walls were essential for a free city, as a safeguard of its independence, but they also offered security to any prosperous city in the unsettled days of the Middle Ages. They had other functions, however. They acted as a police and customs barrier, which enabled the city to control who came in and out, and to collect customs at the gateways; the latter function, in particular, ensured the survival of many city walls well into the eighteenth century. Perhaps as much as anything they were a status symbol, a visually overwhelming symbol of a city's power and prosperity.

Water supply was a major concern to all cities, but especially to those with a strong industrial element. The city government invariably took an interest in it. Cities with very little in the way of water had to bring it in from outside, and even cities on rivers spent time and ingenuity in canalizing and distributing their water, or supplementing it with faster-flowing streams.

A problem presented by streams, however, was that many city walls were surrounded by a moat, and an incoming stream either dispersed its water in the moat, or had somehow to be brought across it. A number of the bird's-eye views of cities which proliferated in the late sixteenth and seventeenth centuries show viaducts across the moat, bringing water into the city. At Nuremberg the little river Fischbach was brought into the city in this way from the south, and then canalized in an artificial bed lined with slabs of sandstone, and used to turn mills and to bring water to butchers, tanners, dyers, fullers and brewers.[17] At Gdansk in the second half of the fourteenth century the Teutonic Knights provided a similar canalized water supply, which split into two channels to turn no fewer than eighteen water-wheels in the gigantic town mill which was built by the Knights at the same time: it also fed an elaborate system of minor waterways, providing drinking and individual water elsewhere in the city.[18] At Antwerp, in the mid-1470s, the stream known as the Schyn, which had previously gone into the town moat, was canalized, brought across the moat, and taken through the town to the river Scheldt by way of the Place de Meir. Diverted in this way it became known as the Canal d'Herenthal and supplied water for brewers, for the common people and for horses. Antwerp had always had a system of internal canals, but their polluted water was said to be killing the horses who drank it. This was bad for trade, as the Antwerp horse fair was one of the main events of the year.[19]

There was clearly a conflict when the same water supply was used to provide industrial and drinking water. It could be dealt with to some extent by the use of wells and water-carriers, the latter bringing drinking water into the city in leather water-bags from a pure source. But at the new town of Salisbury in the fourteenth century a serious attempt was made to provide clean and dirty—or dirtiable—water in separate supplies. Clean water was taken upstream from the town off a mill leat diverted from the River Avon. The flow was controlled by two sluice gates and supplied a network of stone water channels running down the middle of most of the streets of the town. This water was for supply only. An outlet lower down the river fed what was known as the town ditch, which carried a much greater weight of water at a lower level in a zig-zag course through the lower parts of the town. Dyers, wool-washers, fullers and tanners had their premises either along the mill leat below the source of the conduits, or along the town ditch, and could dirty their water without fouling up the conduit supply.[20]

By the late seventeenth century the problems of keeping the open conduits clean and the streets round them dry was giving serious trouble and led to the system being first covered in, and finally given up in the 1850s. But it seems to have worked well enough in the first few centuries, and was certainly in advance of anything else in Europe at the time, with the possible exception of the water system at Bruges. At Paris a conduited water supply provided water to three public fountains only, at Les Halles, and in the Rues St Denis and St Martin, and the first drain was constructed in 1374.[21] It was open, as were all drains in medieval towns, where they existed.

Such rudimentary drainage and water-supply systems clearly had no chance of working if they were used for the disposal of ordure and garbage, and accordingly this was stringently forbidden by countless medieval regulations. At Paris in the fourteenth century householders were obliged by law both to clean the street in front of their house and also to carry 'boues et immondices' out of the city ('aux champs') at their own expense. Neighbourhoods associated together to hire a common cart, the rates for which

54. Life on the bridges of Paris. Details from the *Life of St Denis*, 1317 (Bibliothèque Nationale, Paris).

were fixed in 1396. In the 1370s the city had taken over responsibility for clearing certain especially dirty streets, but a comprehensive public street cleaning and clearing system was not inaugurated until 1506; a special tax was imposed to finance it.[22]

The story in Rome was a similar one. In 1452 each Roman citizen was ordered to clean the street in front of his house every Saturday from May to August. Public street cleaners were first appointed in 1525, paid for by a tax on artisans and tradespeople. An 'ufficiale delle immondizie' was created in the early sixteenth century. There were special dumping areas outside the city, where great steaming dung heaps collected. In January 1503, when the French army had been defeated by the King of Naples, several hundred robbed and stripped soldiers arrived at Rome in the night and, as reported by the Florentine diarist Landucci, 'being almost naked, they threw themselves on the dung heaps for warmth—and if the Pope had not had three or four hundred jerkins made for them, and given them money, and put them on board galleys to cross over into France, they would all have died. As it was we heard that more than 500 died of cold. They were found in the morning lying naked and dead on the dung heaps.'[23]

Landucci also described how in Florence a special group of men were employed to empty cesspits, three of whom were drowned on the job in 1511.[24] Cesspits were frequently dug for household sewage; they were often situated in the gaps between houses and had pierced seats set over them. These spaces were known as *quintane* and could become so malodorous that the phrase 'to stink like a quintana' was proverbial. One of Boccaccio's stories in the *Decameron* concerns the adventures of a horse-dealer from Perugia whose seat collapsed beneath him in a *quintana* in Naples and precipitated him into a cesspit, with unfortunate results.[25]

The streets could be kept cleaner if they were paved and had good valley-gutters laid in the paving. Paved streets in fact apeared quite early on in the main streets of the richer cities, in Paris in the twelfth century, in Florence from the mid-thirteenth century onwards, in Bruges from the mid-fourteenth. In Paris the main streets were paved at municipal expense, but the inhabitants were obliged by law, perhaps not very effectively, to pave the side streets, probably from the late thirteenth century.[26] In Rome the first post-classical regulations for street-paving, in brick and stone, date from as late as 1480, evidence of the late revival in the city owing to the long years of the Avignon papacy and the Great Schism.[27]

In a medieval city keeping a street clear of encumbrances was as much a problem as keeping it clear of dirt. A continuous struggle went on as a result of the desire of householders or shopkeepers to expand onto or over the streets, and the attempts of the city, by constantly repeated ordinances, to prevent them. The city authorities were acting on grounds of both convenience and security. Encumbrances at street level obviously impeded traffic, and balconies and projecting oriels and upper storeys were useful vantage points in street battles, of which there were all too many, especially in Italian towns. They also reduced the level of daylight in the street.

Some town authorities also went in for actual demolition of buildings, in order to widen and straighten streets, or to create or enlarge squares. Florence was a leading example, sometimes for practical reasons and sometimes for reasons which came close to being classifiable as aesthetic. The gradual creation of the Piazza Signoria has already been described. In 1294–1301 the Signoria bought up land in order to enlarge the Piazza Sto Spirito. In 1317, on a petition from the Carmelites, it paid for the creation of what became the Piazza del Carmine in front of their church, 'per il diletto dei passanti, il decoro della citta e l'utilita della chiesa'.[28] In the 1320s funds were provided for rebuilding the Via S. Gallo, north of the Baptistry, 'to increase the beauty and utility of the city of Florence and in particular to make the streets rectilinear and attractive and so that merchants transporting grain from the Mugello and Romagna can reach the market in the loggia of Or San Michele more readily'.[29] In 1339 road levels round the cathedral were lowered; previously 'the decor of that church had been much diminished and concealed'. Houses were bought in 1336–8 in order to enlarge the piazza round the Baptistry, and in 1366–90 in order to get more space at the east end of the cathedral; in the latter case new houses were built to a unified design.[30]

When the Ponte Vecchio was rebuilt in 1345 contemporary Florentines (according to Goro Dati's *Istoria*, written in about 1423) boasted of the way in which the shops were interrupted by an open space in the middle, and commercial gain given up in order to obtain a view of the river and the surrounding hills.[31] This is perhaps the first recorded expression of a river in a city being appreciated as a visual amenity as well as for practical reasons.

Florence had more and longer straight streets than any other medieval town of comparable size. Its centre was based on the grid of the Roman town. Many straight streets were laid out in the later Middle Ages, the Via Maggio as early as the 1250s. The streets, which seem such narrow tunnels today, were wide by medieval standards. Their width and straightness was probably largely conditioned by practical factors. Florence was one of the busiest industrial cities in Europe, wagons carrying corn, wool, cloth and other merchandise crowded its streets, and it had no significant amount of water transport to reduce the load on them.

In addition to new straight streets there was a certain amount of straightening and widening of existing streets in the centre, where the Roman grid had to some extent been obscured by building in the early Middle Ages. But street improvement in a densely

55. The Ponte Vecchio (1345), Florence.

56. (right) Beggars in the mid-fourteenth century. Detail from Orcagna's *Last Judgement* (Museo dell'Opera di Sta Croce, Florence).

built up central area was and is both expensive and controversial, because property there is inevitably valuable and many interests are involved. The widening of the Via Calzaioli, which is one of the main arteries of Florence and runs between the Piazza della Signoria and the Piazza del Duomo, was decreed in 1389, but until the nineteenth century only a small section of the proposed work was ever carried out.[32]

All public improvements and services had to be financed. The income of cities could derive from many sources: excise on wine, beer and spirits, customs on a wide variety of merchandise, rent of municipal lands or market stalls, the lease of offices, admission fees for new citizens, fines collected in the courts, fees for using the public scales, sale of fish from the moats—and finally direct property taxes and loans. Property taxes were a comparatively late arrival on the medieval scene; the *catasto*, the famous property tax in Florence, and one the records of which have proved an invaluable mine of information for historians, was instituted in 1427. In Nuremberg property taxes were only imposed to raise money for particular projects and were based on the good faith of individuals, who paid on the basis of their own assessment of their wealth; Machiavelli, who was used to the skilful tax-dodging of rich Florentines, cited this as evidence that in Germany 'there still prevails a good deal of the goodness of ancient times'.[33]

City loans, not surprisingly, were pioneered in Italy long before they were tried out anywhere else. The city of Paris first started borrowing money in 1522, but the Monte, the city loan in Florence, was inaugurated in early 1345, as a consolidation of all the community's outstanding obligations; the debts outstanding were mostly the result of forced loans, levied in the years 1328–43 on the basis of wealth. The Monte loan (which paid 5 percent) increased over the years, but entirely on the basis of voluntary loans; any individual's stake in it was transferable and sellable, and speculating in Monte shares became one of the precursors of playing the stock market today.

4 The Texture of Life

A large number of new towns were founded in the Middle Ages, as a result, for example, of the German expansion into eastern Europe, the English conquest of Wales, and the French conquest of Languedoc. There was nothing especially pioneering about them in terms of town-planning; they were simplified and easily laid out versions of existing towns with which everyone was familiar, and which had assumed their shapes in accord with the economic and social forces of the time. They demonstrate, in schematic form, what contemporary people expected a town to be.[1]

The town of Salisbury was founded and laid out by the bishops of Sarum between about 1213 and 1220. It must always have been planned to become what it soon developed into, a textile town bringing a comfortable addition to the bishop's revenue. The town was laid out round an off-centre market-place, perhaps designed to be easily accessible from the richer farmland to the west. The city government, such as it was, was based on the guildhall in the market square. Merchants

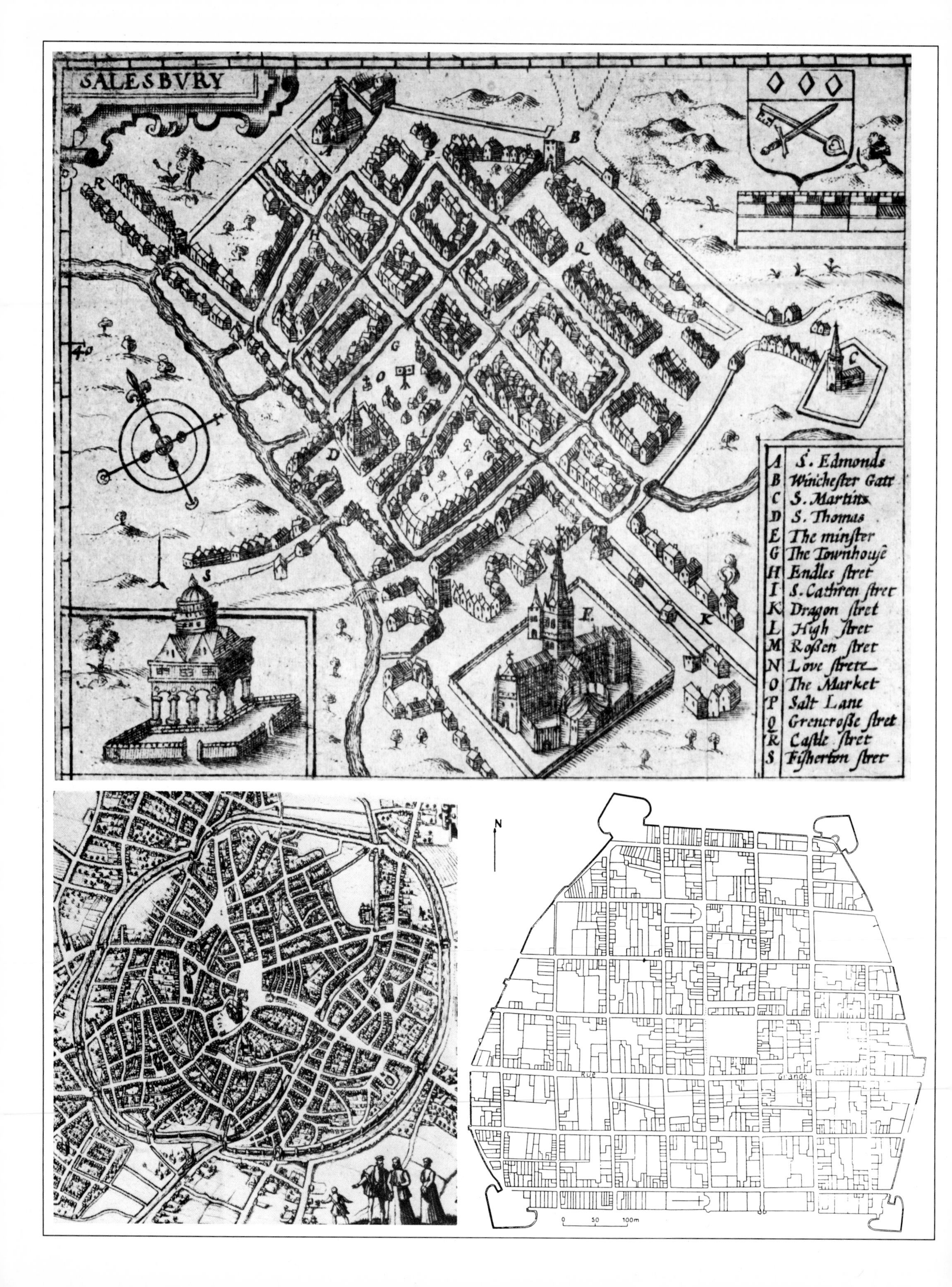
SALESBVRY
A S. Edmonds
B Winchester Gatt
C S. Martins
D S. Thomas
E The minster
G The Townhouse
H Endles stret
I S. Catiren stret
K Dragon stret
L High stret
M Rossen stret
N Love strete
O The Market
P Salt Lane
Q Grenecroße stret
R Castle stret
S Fisherton stret
N
Rue
Grande
0
50
100m

and shopkeepers moved in round the market-place and the streets immediately off it. Industry and the poor occupied the surrounding areas. Everyone lived on top of, or close to, their workplace. The main parish church was adjacent to the market, and there were two more churches away from the centre. The bishop and his canons occupied a separate enclosure to the south-west, distinct from the commercial town.[2]

For convenience of assigning plots to settlers, the town was laid out on a grid. It was not a regular or exactly rectangular grid, however, but was conditioned by various practical factors, especially by the elaborate water-supply systems, already described, the conduits of which had to have a fall and were arranged to fit the contours.

Something resembling the Salisbury scheme appeared in new towns laid out all over Europe. Convenience and practicality were their basis. A few towns (such as Cologne, near Toulouse, a town laid out in 1286) have an almost symmetrical plan, but this is more likely to have been because there were no practical factors to work against it, rather than because completely symmetrical town plans were seen as having a virtue of their own. No compunction was ever shown in skewing or breaking the grid if topography or other factors suggested it.

An obvious constraint tended to result when a new town was designed from the first (as Salisbury was not) to be fortified. Walls are expensive, and the same length of wall will include more space if built in a circle rather than in a square. But a circular walled town with streets from its gates to a central, or approximately central market square produces a web, not a grid. A web-plan is sensible from the point of view of circulation, but results in shapes between the streets which cannot be divided into standard rectangular lots. Because of this, even new towns with circular walls tended to be laid out as a grid in the Middle Ages; web plans are usually the result of gradual growth.

As was to be expected, some new towns flourished and grew, some decayed, some were never more than modest places. But medieval towns only really become interesting when they develop a degree of complexity. Most cities started off with a single open market, but if they prospered almost invariably ended up with several. Annual fairs and markets, if they started off in the centre, tended to move off to the periphery, to get rid of the inconvenience for everyone concerned of having large numbers of animals trampling through narrow and crowded streets. Covered markets and market halls appeared. The main market-place sometimes got smaller because stalls developed into shops and houses, and sometimes bigger because it was enlarged; at Nuremberg wholesale expulsion and burning of Jews in 1349 enabled the market-place to spread over the former Jewish quarter.[3] But more often the original market-place stayed the same size or became smaller, and as the town grew (and sometimes acquired new industries) it became too small for its needs and new fish markets, corn markets, yarn markets, butter markets, and so on were formed, sometimes in the open, and sometimes under cover.

The zone between the centre and the walls usually contained considerable variety too. In a textile town it was almost invariably the artisan zone, but the artisan pattern depended on the pattern of water supply and the zone was seldom if ever confined to artisan dwellings and workshops. Hospitals, almshouses and pawnbrokers tended to appear there, because that was where they were needed, and space there was cheaper. The animal market was usually held in this zone and the butchers' shambles was often pushed out there, because it was found offensive in the centre of the city. But other

57. (top left) John Speed's plan of Salisbury, *c.* 1600 (National Monuments Record).

58–9. (bottom left) Web and grid plans: Malines and (right) Carcassonne.

more prestigious uses appeared here and there, especially after the Black Death. Many cities built new and larger circuits of walls in the prosperous days of the late thirteenth and early fourteenth centuries, and as a result of the Black Death either never grew up to them, or contracted again within them; few cities got back to the level of their mid-fourteenth-century populations before the sixteenth century at the earliest. In England, for instance, it was not until the eighteenth century that Norwich grew into the four-mile circuit of walls which had been built between 1263 and 1342.

So there was usually plenty of space in the outer areas of a city within the walls, and although this could be put to artisan use, notably in the form of tenter grounds, it sometimes also served other purposes. By the end of the Middle Ages the richer citizens, starved of open space in the centre, were beginning to acquire orchards and pleasure gardens in the empty outer areas within the walls. Other increasingly frequent occupants of some part of this space were the archery companies, which began to proliferate in the fifteenth century. They were volunteer militia companies of citizens equipped with either longbows (often under the patronage of St Sebastian) or crossbows (often under the patronage of St George). To begin with they were usually formed of shopkeepers and substantial artisans, but their social prestige tended to increase over the centuries. They needed grounds on which to practise, and there was normally no difficulty in finding space for these on the outer sections of the cities within the walls. Ultimately, usually in the sixteenth century, many of them built handsome guildhouses on the edge of their grounds.[4]

Even if there was space in the outskirts it by no means followed that there was no congestion in the centre. The bird's-eye views of the sixteenth century, which usually provide the earliest reasonably reliable evidence for the plan and building-density of cities, show the centres of successful cities completely built up, often with very little in the way of private gardens. The centre was, quite simply, where everyone who could afford it wanted to be. One result of this was an almost complete absence of free-standing buildings in the centre, with the exception of prestigious public buildings and churches, and even these often acquired an adhesive fringe of shops and houses.

In the early days of cities free-standing houses were the norm. Separate buildings, each on its own little plot, have always been the usual arrangement in any new settlement. In Prato, a prosperous textile town near Florence, party walls between houses were only made lawful in the fourteenth century.[5] The use of the space between houses, the *quintana*, for latrines and garbage dumps has already been described. In Rome as late as 1565 papal legislation was ordering that such gaps should be filled in by building.[6] In the central areas of prosperous commercial and manufacturing cities (which Rome was not), they must mostly have been filled in well before that.

The building complexes of the tower societies in Italian towns were an early example of cohesive building masses sheltering many families. They seem to have grown on an *ad hoc* basis, and none of them had any kind of architectural unity. A different kind of multi-unit building was provided by terraces or rows. These are often thought of as a comparatively late phenomenon in Europe, but in fact they were built from fairly early on in the Middle Ages. There were two main reasons for building them, as almshouses or investments. They tended to be built in out-of-the-centre areas, where land was easier to come by, but this was by no means always the case. More centrally situated rows of houses were quite often built on portions of churchyards; in York, for instance, a row of eleven units (which still exists) was built in or soon after 1316 on the edge of the churchyard of Holy Trinity, in order to endow a chantry in the church.[7] In Florence in 1510 the Arte della Lana demolished a *tiratoia* which they owned in the Via dei Servi, and built twelve three-storey houses on the site, for sale.[8] Ecclesiastical bodies and guilds were frequent builders of terrace houses, since they were big owners of real estate in cities, but they were by no means the only ones. Perhaps the earliest terrace in Europe of which records survive was in Venice. It was already built by 1197; it was privately owned, and described as consisting of 'six stone houses joined together under one roof'.[9]

Terrace houses, built both as almshouses and for investment, were common in Venice from the fourteenth century, and are recorded in Florence in the late fourteenth and in Rome in the late fifteenth centuries.[10] Rows of almshouses start appearing in large numbers in Bruges and other Flemish cities from the mid-fifteenth century onwards. Almshouses are by their nature small, and none of the terraces built as investments was in the least degree prestigious; the houses were designed for artisans or the less prosperous shopkeepers, and their accommodation ranged from two to six rooms. Many had shops or workshops on the ground floor; in some examples, usually built on market-places, there were arcades before the shops. They were built as unified terraces for convenience, not effect; when a row of houses is built at one time by one builder, it is easier to build each house to the same design. The houses put up at the east end of the Duomo in Florence, as a part of the enlargement of the piazza there in 1366–90, have more pretensions, as was suited to their situation, but are not at all grand. In the Middle Ages, people of substance did not consider the possibility of living in terrace houses. Sometimes, however, sizeable houses were built in pairs, to the same design or very similar ones. There is an early pair at Tournai, and a few examples, dating from the late fifteenth century onwards, at Bruges.

Medieval houses could be divided horizontally as well as vertically, to form tenements; such subdivision to make different residential units was distinct from the very common letting off of floors or cellars for shops and workshops. Tenements probably occurred fairly early on in the Middle Ages, as a result of pressures on the central areas of successful towns, and the subdivision of properties between heirs. One would expect the earliest tenements to result from subdivisions of houses originally built for single ownership. In Venice houses were being built by the fifteenth century, and possibly earlier, with a view to being subdivided floor by floor; these subdivisions were often, but by no means invariably, intended for occupation on a family basis, by brothers or parents and children (more is said about this on p. 112).

An interesting later example of purpose-built flats is illustrated by Sebastiano Serlio's engraved design for 'una loggia per mercanti da negotiare', built in Lyons in about 1540–2.[11] It was in fact more than a loggia: it was a four-storey building, in which the merchants' loggia, eight shops, and a four-seater communal privy were on the ground floor, and on each of the three upper floors there were four self-contained apartments, two of two rooms and two of three rooms; it thus housed twelve families, even if, as Serlio admitted, in cramped conditions. The biggest room in each apartment contained a bed recess, with a mezzanine gallery for a second bed above it. The building was designed for Florentine merchants working in Lyons, which suggests that similar tenement blocks may already have existed in Florence.

In Florence, always a pioneer, both merchants and the more substantial shopkeepers

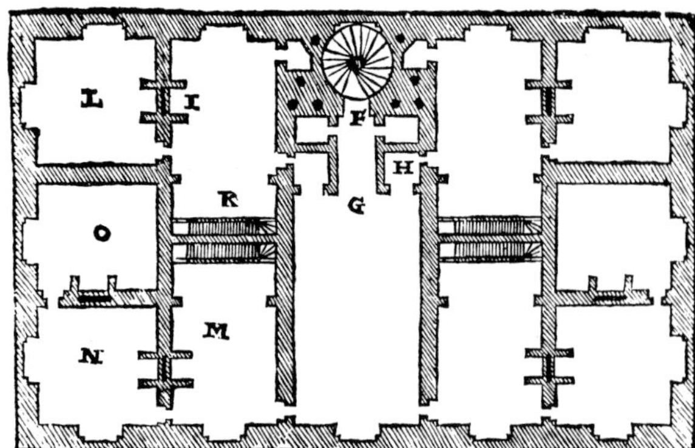

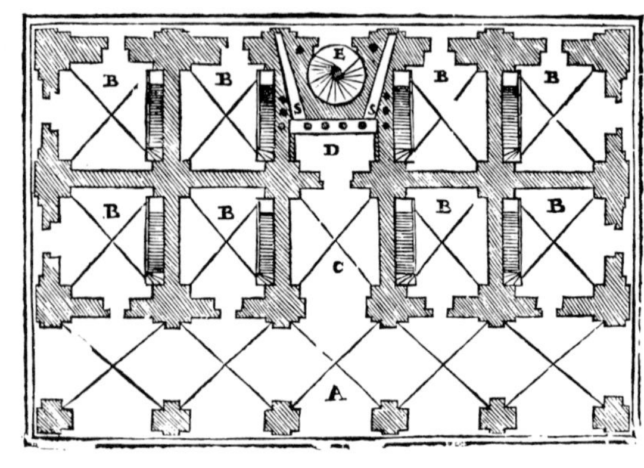

60. Lyons. Merchants' loggia, shops and apartments, *c.* 1540–2. From the Seventh Book of Serlio's *Architecture*.

seem to have begun a move to live away from their workplaces earlier than elsewhere in Europe. Francesco Datini, for instance, had at least three retail or wholesale premises in Florence in Via Porta Rossa, Via Parione and Via Por Sta Maria; but by 1399 he was living away (though not far away) from all of them, on the Piazzetta de Tornaquinci.[12] In around 1430 Andrea Banchi, who sold silk cloth both retail and wholesale in at least two premises in Via Por Sta Maria (the centre of the silk trade), was living just across the Ponte Vecchio in Via de Bardi.[13] Although Cosimo de' Medici, as the Florentine apothecary Luca Landucci put it (writing about the year 1458), 'was called the great merchant, as he had places of business in every part of the town',[14] he lived in fact in or next to none of them. In 1444 he built himself a grand palace on the northern fringe of the centre, the present Palazzo Medici-Riccardi in the Via Cavour. The palace, admittedly, accommodated the headquarters of the holding company which co-ordinated the other Medici companies throughout Europe. But this involved no more than a couple of clerks and a money chest in Cosimo's study; otherwise the palace was entirely residential, in contrast to Venetian palaces of the same date, which usually contained a large element of warehousing.

Few important medieval cities ended at their walls. Outside one or more of the gates or across the river bridge, the suburbs, the French *fauxbourgs*—false towns—formed separate little settlements. People lived in them either because they were not allowed to live inside the walls, or did not want to. In the early Middle Ages, as has appeared, textile workers were sometimes deliberately kept outside for security. By the end of the Middle Ages artisans and small masters were increasingly settling outside the walls, because they wished to be free of guild rules and restrictions. But between whatever there was in the way of suburbs around the gates, fields came right up to the walls, interspersed with the windmills which Hieronymus Bosch loved to paint. Small allotments were often cultivated, and sometimes owned, by city peasants, who lived inside the walls for security; bigger patches of property belonged to the richer citizens.

It is hard for us to get any concept of the atmosphere of a medieval town. The life-style was essentially orthodox; there was as little room for dissent as in any town under a strict communist or Islamic regime today. It was generally accepted that there were right beliefs and right ways of behaving, and that any deviation from these was punishable, often by flogging, mutilation or death. The guardians of orthodoxy were the Church and the civic government. Those who thought differently from the Church were heretics, and those who thought differently from the government were rebels.

Orthodoxy controlled the structure of the city. The city was a hierarchy, divided into ascending levels, and although movement from one level to the other was not impossible, it was not encouraged. Those on each level were expected to look and behave in a particular way—not above their stations. The city government watched over the way people behaved, and made the appropriate regulations. They were the city fathers, and the relationship between them and the inhabitants of the cities was a paternalistic one: they did their best to see that people had work and were looked after in sickness and health, but they expected them to do what they were told. The city records, especially in the late Middle Ages, abound with regulations about dress and behaviour. In Florence the cook who cooked a wedding dinner had to send the menu in advance to the city officials, so that they could check that it was not too lavish. The bride could ride to church on horseback, but had to return on foot, under pain of a fine.[15] In Siena in 1425 women were forbidden to wear silk clothes, or a train, or crepe lining which accentuated the curves of their bodies.[16] In Nuremberg, workmen were fined for parting their hair in a forbidden manner.[17]

Merchants dressed more richly than artisans, but still soberly, unless they were members of the governing body, in which case their dress was of some splendour, suited to the dignity of their position. The everyday dress of the Signoria in Florence was a toga of red damask with a silk hood bordered with fur, and velvet slippers. But even at the top levels ostentation in dress or life-style was discouraged, and often legally regulated. The merchants, as much as everyone else, and perhaps more, accepted an ethos of thrift, sobriety and hard work.

Work hours were regulated by bell from the town hall, or by city watchmen walking about the city ringing handbells.[18] They ran from sunrise to sunset, with an hour off for the midday meal. They were geared to the sun because of the inadequacy of artificial light, and as a result, of course, work-hours varied from winter to summer; in Nuremberg the shortest work day was seven hours in length, not counting mealtimes, the longest thirteen. The long winter nights may have lessened the work-load, but there was little to do in them except tell stories round the fire. All towns had a curfew, imposed at dusk, after which it was forbidden to walk about the city except on lawful business. This was an ancient custom; as early as the tenth century, night walkers in Constantinople were arrested by the city guard, whipped, and kept in fetters until brought to trial the next morning.[19] It was a necessary one owing to the inadequacy or, in most cities, total absence of street lighting. In Paris, the first attempt to light the streets was made in 1524, and announced publicly to the sound of trumpets; at nine o'clock each evening all inhabitants of the city had to put lighted candles in their windows.[20]

61. Sketches of beggars and cripples by Hieronymus Bosch (Bibliothèque Royale, Brussels).

There was a great deal of poverty in medieval cities, although of course it varied from period to period and city to city. It was likely to be greater in the textile towns, where there was a very large work force, the lower levels of which were doing poorly paid work and were immediately destitute if they were put out of a job. A town like Nuremberg, based on numerous small workshops making luxury, or at any rate expensive, goods for sale on the premises, had less poverty, but also less wealth than a town like Florence. All prosperous cities, then as now, were a magnet for the less prosperous from the surrounding countryside. In years of famine or war this meant a problem of beggars, which could assume epic proportions.

Cities were very much at the mercy of catastrophes of different kinds: from flood, famine, fire and disease. They did what they could against the first three. But dykes and river embankments could not always keep flooding rivers at bay, and stores of grain in the city granaries were not always able to outlast drought in the countries from which grain was imported, or bad harvests in the surrounding countryside. Fire was a constant hazard, especially in the northern cities, where the houses were mostly built of wood. London was frequently ravaged by fire; at the end of the twelfth century William Fitzstephen, delivering a panegyric on London, declared that 'the only plagues of London are the immoderate drinking of fools and the frequency of fires'.[21] The worst fire, before the famous fire of 1666, was in 1212, when London Bridge caught fire at either end, trapping those in the middle. Three thousand dead were said to have been pulled out of the Thames.[22] Most of Nuremberg was demolished by fire in 1340 but thereafter the city organized a fire-fighting system so efficient that outbreaks, although still frequent, were kept under control. Each district had a designated fire-fighting force, callable out at need; fire hooks, buckets, ladders and axes were mounted on specified houses; vats filled with water were kept on carts at the public baths; and the River Fischbach could be damned at intervals with fitted boards, to create a reservoir.[23]

Measures could be taken against disease too, but they were ineffective because the true causes of diseases were largely unknown. The Black Death is the most famous and worst of the plagues and epidemics that ravaged medieval cities, but by no means the only one. The record of London is nothing out of the ordinary: plague in 1258, 1348 (the Black Death, killing over half the population), 1361, 1368–9, 1407 (30,000 said to have died), 1426, 1433–4, 1450, 1452, 1454, 1474, 1499–1500 (20,000 deaths alleged), 1517, 1531 and 1535.

Death and destruction by act of God were supplemented by death or mutilation by act of man, the result of feuds within the ruling families, plots against the city

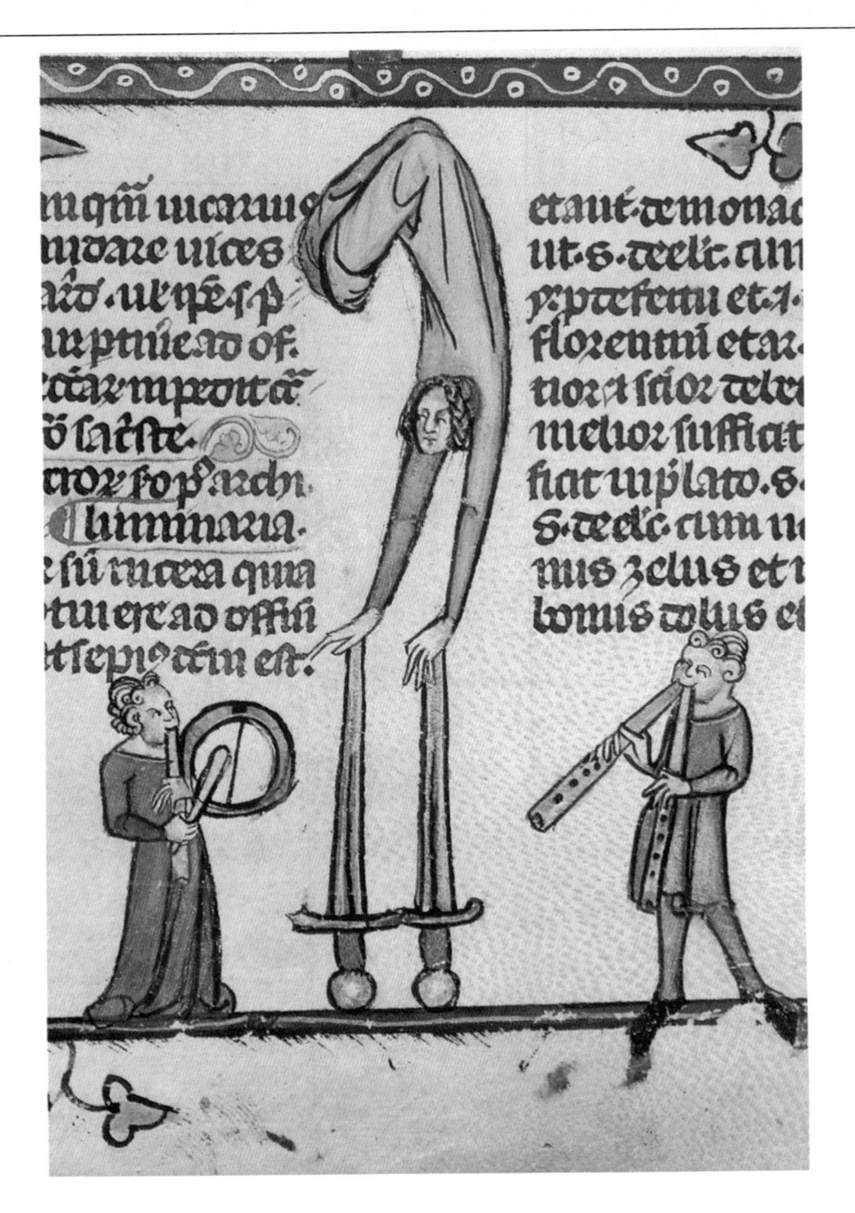

62. Fourteenth-century acrobats. From a manuscript illuminated by a monk of St Bartholomew's Priory, London, perhaps inspired by jugglers in the adjacent fair (British Library).

government, sack and pillage from outside, rivalries between different quarters of the city, struggles between artisans and merchants, massacres of Jews or burnings of heretics combined with frequent public executions for murder, theft or fraud, and public mutilations or floggings for other offences. Northern cities may have been a little less violent than Italian ones, but they were still violent.

The diary of Luca Landucci, the Florentine apothecary, between 1478 and 1500 gives some idea of the intermittently violent background to the life of a hard-working and law-abiding businessman. In 1478–9 the failure of the plot of Jacopo de' Pazzi and his associates to assassinate Lorenzo de' Medici led to riots and deaths on the piazzas, and to the façades of the Palazzi of the Signoria and Bargello being festooned with the bodies of conspirators hanging from the windows. Over a hundred were hanged within a few days; the body of Pazzi himself was disinterred from its grave by Florentine boys, dragged through the city, made to knock on its own front door, and finally thrown into the river, where crowds lined the banks and bridges to watch it floating by on its way down to Pisa.[24]

In 1478–80 a silk and wool famine caused unemployment and great distress among textile workers, the silk merchants' quarter was gutted by fire, plague raged, the Arno flooded and, as Landucci put it, 'it pleased God to chastise us'. In 1481 another plot against Lorenzo caused a smaller spate of executions. In 1484 there was a plague and a bad corn shortage. The next two years, though far from uneventful, were less cataclysmic. In 1495 a Jew was stoned to death by the crowd for disfiguring religious images. In 1494 the Arno flooded; the flood was the worst in living memory. A failed coup by Lorenzo de' Medici's son Piero led to pillage of the Medici party's houses but no deaths; another plot in 1497 caused five executions and a series of banishments. In 1496–7 there was a serious famine; 'men, women and children were falling down exhausted from hunger, and some died of it, and many died at the hospital who had grown weak from starvation'. Famine, as often happened, was followed by disease, in this case by both fever and plague. An eclipse of the sun on 29 July 1497 caused a mass flight of terrified citizens to the country.[25]

It was against this background that the Dominican friar Savonarola gained his short but extraordinary ascendency over the city. It came to an end in the spring and summer of 1498, when Savonarola was excommunicated, the Florentines turned against him, there were riots and murders, mass arrests and floggings of his supporters, and finally the hanging followed by burning of him and two other friars on the Piazza della Signoria.

But perhaps the entry in Landucci's diary for 26 February 1500 is especially revealing. It records an episode in the execution of two murderers, according to the normal Florentine method. It took place outside Landucci's shop. Landucci, it must be remembered, was a pious and kindly man.

'They were hung at the Canto delle Stinche, where they had committed the crime. They went on the executioner's cart, being tortured most cruelly with red-hot pincers all through the city; and here at Tornaquinci the brazier for heating the pincers broke. There not being much fire left, and it not sparkling properly, the Cavaliere shouted at the executioner, and made him stop the cart, and the executioner got out and went for charcoal to the charcoal-burner, and for fire to Malcinto the baker, and took a kettle for a brazier, making a great fire. The Cavaliere kept crying all the time: "Make it red-hot!", and all the people were desirous that they should be tortured without pity. The very boys were ready to assassinate the executioner if he did not do his work well, hence they (the condemned men) shrieked in the most terrible way. And all this I saw here at Tornaquinci.'[26]

The theoretical control of every aspect of life by Church or State was mitigated by the considerable inefficiency of all kinds of medieval government, where laws could be passed but there were seldom enough people available to enforce them; as a result most ordinary medieval people seem to have had a fairly cavalier attitude to the law. Against the frequent violence and suffering, and the hard lives and hard labour of most city-dwellers, must be offset the abandon with which they enjoyed themselves, when enjoyment was possible.

Holidays were the safety-valve of the medieval system. All except May Day and New Year's Day celebrated religious feasts. The number of feast days, on which work was not allowed, was on the increase through the Middle Ages, until they amounted to about fifty in most cities and, of course, all Sundays were holidays. The number was not an unmixed benefit; holidays were not holidays with pay, and could cause financial hardship to poor men who wanted to work on some holidays, and were not allowed to.

In any town there were certain holidays, usually lasting several days, which were celebrated with particular zest. They could be tied to the feast day of the town's patron saint, or to an annual fair, which itself was almost invariably attached to a feast day. They were occasions for miracle plays, football matches, horseraces, tournaments, animal baitings, fireworks, clowns, jugglers, processions and banquets. But rather than wander randomly and exhaustingly over the cities of Europe, it would perhaps be better to concentrate on one particular festival, familiar because it has survived to the present day: the Palio at Siena.[27]

The festival has had a continuous history of nearly eight hundred years, and not unnaturally it has changed a good deal over the centuries. The starting point was a procession which has been held since at least 1200 on 14 August, the eve of the feast of the Assumption. The commune and citizens, and the nobles and inhabitants of neighbouring towns and villages which had submitted to Siena, went in procession together to show their loyalty or obedience to the city (or to begin with to the bishop who then ruled the city) and their devotion to the Virgin, protectress and symbolic ruler of Siena. The procession early on became associated with a horserace, which was run through the streets. A race of this kind was a common form of popular entertainment; it may have started in Siena as an informal event, but was soon taken over by the city. The race was called a palio, because the prize was a *palio*, or banner. It became a prestigious element of the festival, and the dominant one once Siena became subject to Florence in 1555 and the Assumption Eve procession was given up.

Up till then, however, these processions were a great occasion. Like similar processions all over Europe, they proclaimed and strengthened the social format of the town: a hierarchy, but one in which everyone had a place. Its practical purpose was to present candles and banners to the cathedral. The procession was headed by a huge candle, given by the commune: it weighed a hundred pounds and was escorted by the town musicians and carried in a special cart, surrounded by children dressed up as angels. Then came the Priors of the Signoria and the public officers, each carrying twelve-pound candles; the subject nobles and village representatives, carrying candles and banners; and the people of the city, divided into their districts (or *contrade*), each accompanied by its own military company, with banners flying. The procession also included a group of prisoners, carrying candles like everyone else, and due for release to celebrate the feast. It made its way up to the cathedral, originally from the Porta Romana but later from the Palazzo Publico. At the cathedral candles and banners were dedicated, the prisoners released, and the banners hung up along the nave. The Signoria, officers, nobles and village representatives—around one hundred people—then went off to a banquet in the Palazzo Publico, and wine was distributed on the campo to everyone else.

A similar, but candle-less, procession next day took the *palio* itself up from the Palazzo Publico, and hung it from a column where the race ended, outside the cathedral. The splendour of the *palio* increased over the years at much the same rate as the festival which was named after it. By the fifteenth century it contained up to thirty yards of rose-coloured silk or crimson velvet, was lined with fur made up of up to fourteen hundred skins of the vair or miniver (a little animal like a stoat), was embroidered with the city arms in silver and gold thread, and surmounted by the lion of Siena, carved and gilt.

The race was not held on the Campo, as it is today. It was run from the Porta Romana, followed the curving main street of the town, and then took a sharpish right turn up the steep hill of the Via di Capitano to the winning post on the Piazza del Duomo. It was started by a blast on the trumpet. The horses were all Barbary horses, the thoroughbred racehorses of those days, and were entered by owners both inside and outside the city; Lorenzo de' Medici, for instance, entered a horse in the 1480s and Cesare Borgia one in 1493.[28] The jockeys had to keep their seats until the tower of S. Antonino in the Via di Città, but if a jockey fell off after that and his riderless horse ended first, it was the winner.

All sorts of other events and happenings were gradually added to the candle procession and the Palio race. Clowns, stilt-walkers (in 1464 a 'Judith on stilts with 4 servants') and visiting musicians were sent to join in the fun by Italian noblemen, by other Italian cities and even, on one occasion, by the King of Hungary, and joined in the procession. There could be up to eighty visiting musicians, including trumpeters, bagpipers, viola players, harpists and drummers, adding to the liveliness if not the musical coherence of the procession. The outfits of the bands and commune officials grew more and more splendid and multi-coloured. In the Campo there were firework displays, tournaments, baiting of bulls and other animals, races of cart-horses and buffaloes, and mock-battles—known as *giuoci della pugna*—between the different *contrade*, helmeted and fighting with wooden shields and poles. The opposing *contrada* teams adopted distinctive badges—the giraffe, the snail, the tower and so on—and from the 1480s huge artificial snails, giraffes and other devices began to take part in the processions.

In fact three palios were run every year in Siena (as two still are today), the second on the feast day of S. Ambrogio in May, the third (but only from 1487) on the feast of St Mary Magdalene in July. They were not special to Siena; palios were run all over Italy, and the kind of events which accompanied them could be found on feast days and at fairs throughout Europe. Luca Landucci's brother Gostanzo won twenty palii in at least five Tuscan towns, including Siena between 1481 and 1485, riding his own Barbary horse, Draghetto. He died in 1485; as his brother put it, 'he rushed about so much after this Barbary horse that in the end it killed him'.[29] At Rome, and in some other cities, the horses were always raced unmounted. The Rome races took place on each of the eight days of the Roman carnival, which ended on Shrove Tuesday. Its other excitements included races of children, Jews and naked old men, and the letting loose of a herd of pigs, to be stoned to death by the crowd. The carnival originally took place on the Capitoline or Palatine Hills, but in 1466 Pope Paul II moved the races down to the Via Lata which was renamed the Corso (racecourse) in consequence; the Barbary horses were stopped by a great cloth slung across the street. In Florence the main palio was run on 24 June, the feast day of St John the Baptist. The course ran straight through the town from the Porta alla Croce to the Porta al Prato; today's Via del Corso marks part of the route. As well as the palio there were perambulating shows, a candle procession, fireworks and Catherine wheels sparking off from mounts called *girandoles*, and stilt performers disguised as spirits or giants. Giants featured in many medieval feasts and processions, among them Gog and Magog in London (first mentioned in the fifteenth century) and tribes of giants all over Spain. At Pamplona, giant Moors and Normans paraded through the town and danced before the cathedral on 7 July, the feast of St Firmin, and bulls were run through the streets, as they still

63. (top right) The Palio in Florence. From a fifteenth-century cassone (Cleveland Museum of Art).

64. (bottom right). Bull-fighting in the Piazza del Campo, Siena. From the late sixteenth-century painting by Vincenzo Rustici (Monte dei Paschi, Siena).

65. Festival giants at Burgos.

are today. At Metz the dragon which paraded on feast days through the town is preserved in the cathedral sacristy.

Tournaments, held in the main square or on some other large open space, were an increasingly common feature in towns from the twelfth century. They were originally participated in by kings, princes, nobles or knights at a time when the ruler was in residence, and were often held to celebrate a royal coronation or wedding. But from the late thirteenth century they began to be organised as well by the city elites, sometimes by societies specifically formed in order to hold them. Such societies were especially common in northern Europe. The most renowned were probably the societies of the Espinette in Lille and of the Ours Blanc in Bruges, which were formed in the late thirteenth and early fourteenth centuries respectively; but by the fifteenth century they were being formed by merchants and prosperous citizens all over Flanders and Germany.[30]

Nobility by descent or knighthood by creation (or both) were the usual conditions for participation in a tournament. City tournaments may have been less discriminating, but in fact many cities, as has been described, contained an element which had inherited or acquired nobility, and many individual citizens were knighted, perhaps as a result of serving under royal or princely leadership in the mounted and armour-wearing section of the city militia; some Italian cities created their own knights. Cities were accordingly likely to include a group which took naturally to tournaments, and which enlarged itself by accepting (and often marrying into) the richer and older merchant families.

Like the palio races, tournaments were a rich man's diversion, but watched by everyone who could get a viewing-point. The *giuoci della pugna*, and similar games held all over Europe, were in a different class. They were popular contests which the establishment disapproved of, because they could get out of hand and end in deaths, or riots against the authorities. They took a number of different forms, including numerous varieties of football games, and the contests with sticks or fists held on the bridges in Pisa and Venice.

The May Day celebrations were common to all ranks, though they took different forms. May Day was a seasonal festivity which had no religious connections at all, or at least no Christian connections; it celebrated the coming of spring. Both citizens and courtiers rode or walked out into the fields, garlanded with flowers. In Italian towns young girls, often wearing chaplets of flowers, danced hand in hand in circles in the public squares. In English towns they danced similar dances, but set up poles to dance round; St Andrew's Undershaft in the City of London was so called because it stood next to a huge permanent maypole, which rose higher than the church tower.

Plays in medieval towns, on the other hand, usually had religious connections or themes, and were often held under the aegis of the Church. In the early Middle Ages they took place inside the churches; from the fourteenth century onwards they were held out of doors as well, either on wagons or on temporary stages set up in one or more of the city squares. Many were organized by the guilds or by religious confraternities. In France and Germany purely secular farces were also put on, by students, apprentices or the secular groups known as *sociétés joyeuses*, often at carnival time.

In addition to fairs and feast days, royal visits and weddings provided other occasions for processions, tournaments and other jollifications. The kings of France traditionally made a solemn entry into Paris through the Porte St Denis, after they had been crowned in the abbey of St Denis, then a few miles outside Paris, and went in procession to their palace on the Île de la Cité. The Pont au Change, which the procession crossed on the way, was decorated with a tunnel of green fronds for the occasion. A royal marriage was usually followed by a similar entry; all such processions came to be called 'joyous entries'. The marriage entry of Charles VI and his bride Isabella in 1389 was followed by four days of jousting. The extraordinarily lavish tournament which Lorenzo de' Medici gave on the Piazza Sta Croce in 1468, to celebrate the beauty of Lucretia Donati, was probably inspired by royal jousts, although given ostensibly by a private merchant whose father was effectively the ruler of Florence.

The weddings and funerals of substantial merchant or other families could also be lavishly celebrated, in defiance of sumptuary legislation, even if not on a Medici scale. In Italy one of the uses of family loggias was for wedding festivities. There is a nice description of the wedding between Bernardo Rucellai and Nannina de' Medici, which took place in Florence in 1466. A feast was held in the Rucellai loggia, and an awning was set up in the Rucellai piazza, which was adorned with garlands and coats of arms, to give shelter for dancing. Wedding gifts included a pair of calves, baskets of pomegranates, marzipan, Greek wine, quails, loaves, and an olive tree in a cart, sent in by the peasants on one of the Rucellais' country estates.[31]

Piazzas were also used for funerals. An account of a Florentine funeral on the Piazza de' Frescobaldi in 1296 describes the men sitting on the piazza on benches or mats (according to rank), while the women assisted at the funeral inside the church.[32] Funeral sermons, like other sermons, were sometimes given outdoors on the piazza.

All the events and occasions described so far have been one-off rather than regular, tied to occasional events such as weddings and coronations, or to festivals and fairs, and resulting in perhaps half a dozen big festivals in a city during a year. None of them added up to a pattern of activity sufficiently regular to call for a purpose-built building. A twice-yearly horserace down the main street, or a tournament or bullfight in one of the main squares, was tolerable and even highly enjoyable, whereas the inconvenience caused by a weekly one would have been insupportable.

None the less, these activities did have an effect on the shape of cities. The route

66. A tournament in Saxony in 1544. From a painting by Heinrich Göding the Elder (Historisches Museum, Dresden).

67. (right) Wedding or May Day dancing in Siena. Detail from *The Well-Governed City* by Ambrogio Lorenzetti, 1337–9 (Palazzo Publico, Siena).

of the Palio in Siena was periodically cleared of built-out obstructions to make sure it was clear for the race, and this must at the least have underlined its position as the main street of the city. Pope Paul II probably moved the carnival horseraces to the Via Lata so that he could watch them from his new palace, the Palazzo Venezia; and it is possible that the splendid row of palaces along the Via Albizzi in Florence were partly attracted there because they were on the route of the St John's feast day palio. More generally, the potential use of piazzas for outdoor sermons and meetings, bull-fights, tournaments and wedding dances, may have contributed to their proliferation in Italian cities.

Regular places of recreation in medieval towns were minimal, especially recreation producing permanent buildings. Most cities had at least one common, field or other open space on the edge of the built-up area, which was used by the citizens for recreation or military training: for archery, wrestling, football, skating in winter, and so on. London had Moorfields, a huge damp stretch of common land immediately north of the city walls. Florence had the Prato, or meadow, a biggish piece of open ground inside the walls on the western edge of the city by the Porta al Prato: it was here that the June palio ended. Siena had a similar meadow, known as the Piazzale del Prato, just outside the Porta; it was reserved for public use by a law of 1326.[33] Nuremberg had the river island called the Schütt, also just inside the walls. These open spaces were much valued by the citizens, and attempts to reduce or intrude on them were bitterly resented. But by their nature they produced no buildings. They were for practical use, none had anything that might be called ornamental planting, and few even had trees.

Perhaps the nearest the Middle Ages attained to regular recreational buildings was in the 'stews'—*stufe* in Italian. These were originally meant for health more than recreation: they started as public baths, using steam in some places (hence the stewing) and water in others. But since mixed bathing was usually allowed in them, they sooner or later acquired a shady reputation, and by the end of the Middle Ages were as much brothels as washing-places. They first appeared in the north. Paris had twenty-six of them by 1292. The London stews were on Bankside, south of the river and out of the city jurisdiction, on land belonging to the bishop of Winchester. They were brothels

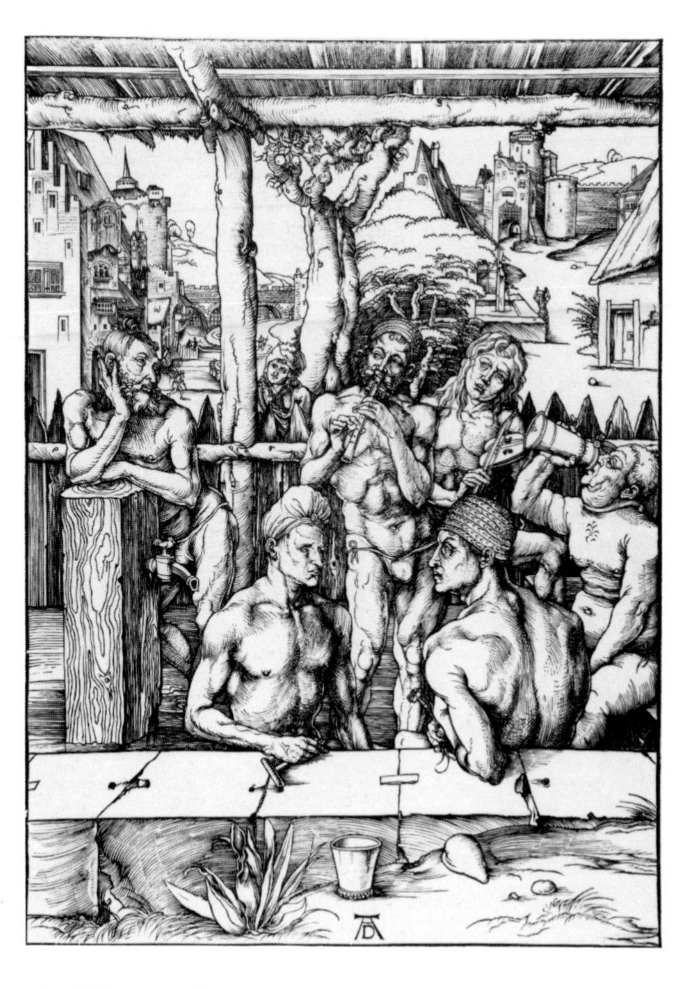

68. The baths at Nuremberg. From an engraving by Albrecht Dürer (British Museum).

69. (right) The water-house at Bruges.

by as early as 1162. The first Roman *stufa* was not opened until 1422, by a German barber, but by the end of the century many were being run by retired courtesans.[34] In Florence in 1506 a statue of Our Lady over a door opposite the Stufa di Piazza (sometimes called Stufa degli Olizzi, from the family which owned it) miraculously shut her eyes. 'It seemed as if she did not wish to see the sins that are committed there', wrote Landucci. The statue might have become a centre of pilgrimage, except that respectable women did not like being seen in the neighbourhood.

In Nuremberg the baths were closely supervised by the city. By the sixteenth century there were fourteen of them, along or near the Rivers Pegnitz and Fischbach, and a contemporary description of them ran as follows:[35]

> Come to the bath house, rich and poor
> The water is hot, you may be sure,
> With fragrant soap we wash your skin,
> Then put you in the sweating bin;
> And when you've had a beautiful sweat,
> Your hair is cut, your blood is let,
> And then, to finish, a good rub
> And a pleasant soak in a soothing tub.[36]

It all sounds very healthy and respectable; but Dürer's woodcut suggests a different story.

5

Bruges and Venice

Bruges was an essentially practical town. It existed to make and sell cloth. Its relationship to the textile industry in Flanders in the fourteenth and fifteenth centuries was much the same as the relationship of Manchester to the cotton industry in Lancashire in the nineteenth and twentieth centuries. Manchester was both a factory town and a distribution centre for the cotton textiles which were made at mill towns all over Lancashire. Bruges was a workshop town, but even more it was the distribution centre for cloth made in Ghent, Ypres and the other Flemish textile towns. Like Manchester it attracted a foreign colony, engaged in channelling its goods to outside markets. The Bruges capitalists exploited their workers just as much as the Manchester mill-owners, and the workers fought back. In the end, like Manchester, it lost its markets, as other countries started making their own cloth or undercutting Flemish prices. Then, like Manchester, it entered on a decline, for a time a catastrophic one.

SEPTEM
AOMIRATIONES CIVITATIS
BRV
OENSIS

But it was far smaller than Manchester. Its population in the Middle Ages was probably never more than 35,000, whereas Manchester had reached nearly 280,000 by 1831 and was up to over 600,000 by the end of the century. Its workers worked at home or at small workshops, not in multi-storey mills. It had no need for huge warehouses, because its turnover of merchandise was not large enough. It was much cleaner than Victorian Manchester; not only did it have no steam-engines, but it burnt no coal. Its fuel was turf, which came by river or canal from the turf-bogs in central Flanders, and made comfortable fortunes for the Bruges suppliers in doing so. Manchester's sensational skyline of factory chimneys sat beneath a huge and lurid pall of smoke. The skyline of Bruges, tower after tower rising behind the outer towers of the walls, rose sparkling clean from its setting of water and green fields.[1]

As a cloth-manufacturing town Bruges was never in the same league as Ghent, Ypres and Douai. Its merchants figured comparatively little at the great Champagne fairs. Its importance derived from its easy access to the sea. In the twelfth century English wool, on which the Flemish textile industry depended, was exported to Bruges, and the other Flemish towns came there to buy it, and to sell cloth, which Bruges exported to London. In the thirteenth century the mainland countries which bought Flemish cloth began to develop sea routes in preference to land ones, to the great benefit of Bruges. The German Hanseatic towns were firmly established there by the middle of the thirteenth century. The first Genoese galley ventured through the Straits of Gibraltar and came to Bruges in 1277; the first Venetian galleys arrived shortly after. The twice yearly arrival of the Genoese and Venetian fleets became landmarks in the commerce of Bruges and Flanders, and the Champagne fairs dwindled to insignificance.

For a time the Italians also bought English wool at Bruges. In 1313, however, England decided to confine all its European sales to one place. To begin with, the wool staple, as the monopoly was called, moved from town to town, but it was never at Bruges for more than a few years, and in 1363 settled at Calais, where it stayed for nearly two hundred years. Bruges remained the greatest cloth market in northern Europe, however; and since the merchants who came to Bruges to buy cloth also imported goods of their own to sell, it became much more than a cloth market. By the end of the fourteenth century almost anything that was available anywhere in Europe or the near east could be bought in Bruges. A Spanish nobleman, visiting in 1438, found oranges and lemons from Castille, fruits and wine from Greece, spices from Alexandria and the Levant, furs from the Black Sea, and brocades, silks and armour from Italy all on sale in its markets.[2] Merchants were coming there from all over Germany, from England, from most parts of Spain, Poland, Scotland, Ireland and Italy, especially from Genoa, Venice, Florence and Lucca; they bought and sold to each other as well as to the Flemings, although the extent to which they did this has probably been exaggerated.

The huge muddy market-place next to the castle soon became inadequate. In about 1240 the famous belfry and great halls on two floors to either side of it were built over part of the market-place to the south. To begin with, as in many other towns, the building served as both covered market and town hall. But by the end of the century trade had increased to such an extent that a large new hall had been built on the east side of the market, exclusively for selling cloth, and most of the functions of the town hall had been moved into the castle next door; here, on the castle courtyard, a grand new

70. (top) The skyline of Bruges. Details from *St Nicholas* by the Master of the Legend of St Lucy, 1490 (Groeningemuseum, Bruges).

71. (left) *The Seven Wonders of Bruges*. Attributed to P. Claessens the elder, *c.* 1550 (Beguinage, Bruges).

town hall was later built in 1377. Groceries and other luxury goods were now sold in the old halls by the belfry, cloth in the new cloth hall, corn, fruit, vegetables and pottery on the open market-place; a covered butchers' hall and markets for fish, eggs and yarn developed in other parts of the city, close to the centre, and a huge cattle and horse market took place on Fridays in the great open space on the edge of the city known as the Friday Market.

The city treasury, and the city archives, including the charters on which the powers of the city government rested, remained in the belfry, which had been rebuilt after a fire in 1280. The burgomaster publicly announced new city laws from a balcony overlooking the market-place on an upper floor of the belfry. A great axe and sword, symbol of the judicial power of the city magistrates, hung on the belfry facade, and executions took place down below, on the market square.

This split city personality, divided between the market-place and the castle square, expressed a situation of typical medieval complexity. At the back of it lay the usual power struggle between the counts of Flanders, and later their descendants the dukes of Burgundy, on the one hand, and the city government on the other.

The counts of Flanders had been enterprising and enlightened promoters of their cities from the start, and although Ghent, Ypres and Bruges, as they grew prosperous, fought for as much as they could get, and got a great deal, they never achieved the virtual independence of the great Italian cities. In Bruges the city was at its peak between 1304 and 1383, when it virtually chose its own burgomasters, aldermen and counsellors by a somewhat complicated system based on the city guilds; but from then on the counts and dukes re-established a considerable degree of control over all major appointments.

The castle belonged to the counts of Flanders; one end of it originally contained quarters for the counts, and the other lodgings for the castellan, who lived permanently at Bruges and originally ran it for the count. Once the city achieved its own government, the power of the castellan waned, and one was no longer appointed. The city took over the castellan's quarters, but kept its heart, so to speak, in the belfry.

What this meant in terms of the buildings round the castle courtyard in the fifteenth century was as follows. On the west side was the original castellan's residence, the ancient and uncomfortable Steen, which had become the city prison. In the south-west corner was the sumptuous double chapel of St Basil, a mid-eleventh-century building, the upper part of which was remodelled in 1150, to contain a phial of the blood of Christ, which Count Theodoric had brought back from Palestine. Then came the town hall, on the south side, built on the standard medieval plan with a great hall and a council room off it. Here the two burgomasters, twelve aldermen and twelve councillors of the city met, both to preside over courts and to pass legislations. On the west side, in the count's section, were the separate hall and council chamber of the Franc de Bruges, the rich area of countryside and small but prosperous towns around Bruges. It was run by the count, and had its own burgomasters and aldermen, whom he appointed. Next to this, also on the west side, was the Loove, the original residence of the counts, which had become the count's prison and the prison of the Franc.

The whole north side was filled by the great church of St Donatien, built by the counts and demolished in the French Revolution. The provost and canons of St Donatien had their own judges, bailiff and clerks and administered sixteen small separate areas of the city, given to them by the counts, in independence both of the city

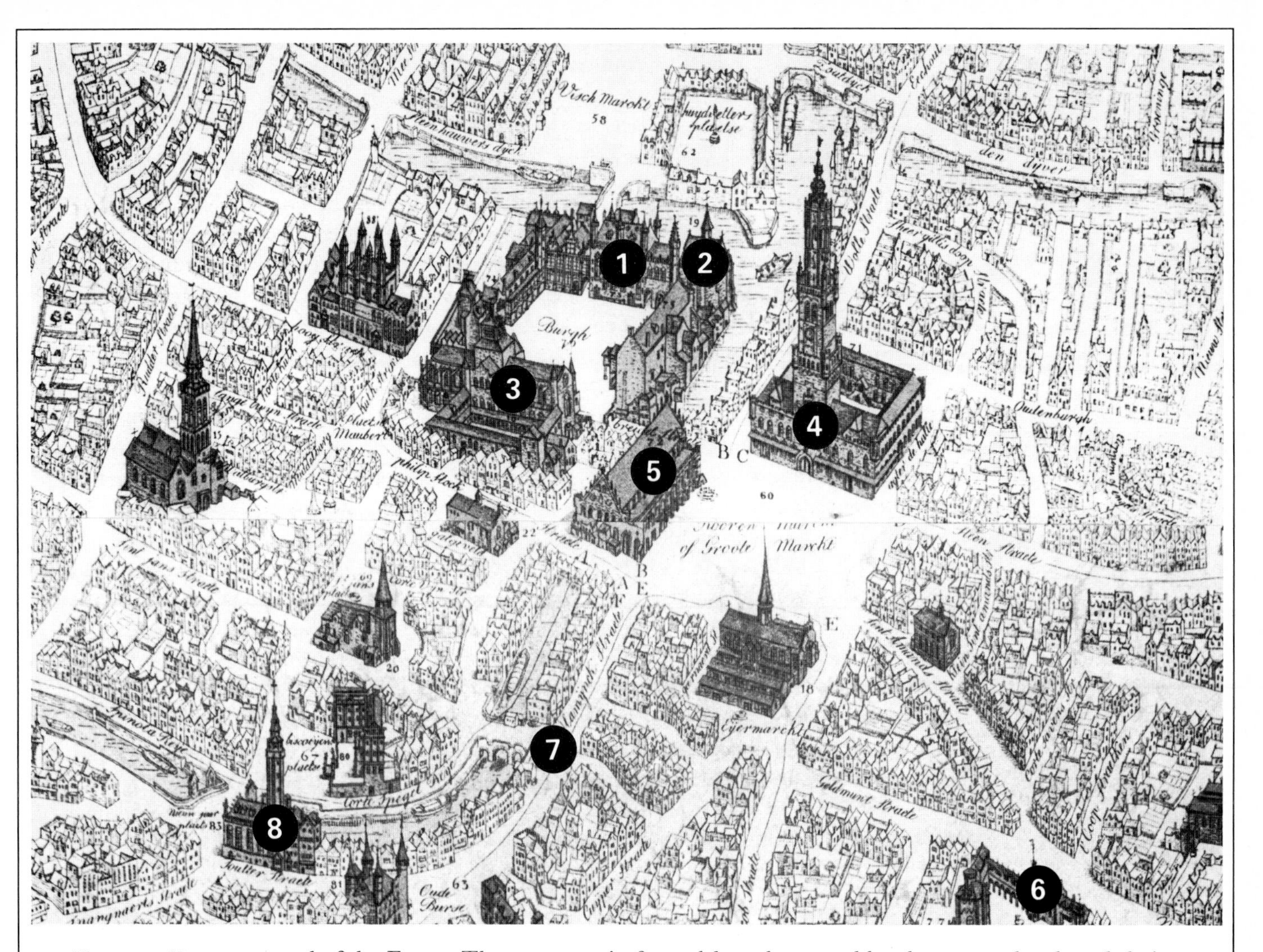

72. The centre of Bruges. Detail from the bird's-eye view by Marcus Gheeraerts, 1568.
1. Town Hall
2. St Basil
3. St Donatien
4. Belfry
5. Wool Hall
6. Cour des Princes
7. Crane
8. Poortersloge

and of the Franc. The provosts, in fact, although created by the count, developed their own power structure in a way typical of the feudal period. Berhulf, who was both provost and receiver-general of the count's lands in the early twelfth century, was head of the powerful Erembald clan, members of which also served as castellans: the clan lived in great splendour and independence in the castle court, and in 1127 assassinated Duke Charles the Good when he was worshipping in the castle chapel.[3]

Two other families, possibly both descended from members of the count's household, enjoyed rights in the town originally given to them by the count. The de la Wastines, and their successors, the Seigneurs of Ghistelles, who lived a few miles outside the city, owned the rights of collecting the main customs of Bruges; in 1477 it was they who built the little customs house which still survives as the city library. Another family had been granted the Gruut, an extremely profitable monopoly of the sale of must, the predecessor of hops in the beer-making process; they lived in the city, in the Gruuthuse, the grandest surviving medieval house in Bruges, and took their name from it.

One result of the proliferation of uses in the castle was that there was no adequate space left for the counts, or their successors the dukes of Burgundy, to live in. It was the same situation as arose with the Palace of Westminster in London, and the Palais on the Île de la Cité in Paris; the administrative and juridical functions pushed out the residential ones. Accordingly, counts and dukes built a new residence, the Cour des Princes, on the north-west side of the city; only a fragment of it remains today.

Allowing for the varying degrees of control exercised by the counts and dukes, and their grants of territories and revenues within the city, it was the burgomasters, aldermen and councillors who ran Bruges from day to day, and to do so they created a permanent civil service of some elaboration, by the standards of a medieval town. By the fifteenth century there were two treasurers, six senior clerks running the legal department, six junior clerks to do the actual clerical work, a small group of serjeants who acted as ushers and commissionaires in the town hall, up to sixteen messengers to run about the town and six mounted messengers to travel outside it, three bell-ringers for the belfry, a cook for the town hall, town criers, prison guards, a chapel sacristan, and caretakers for town hall and belfry. Outside staff included a city police force of twenty-seven, with their headquarters in a house on the market-place, a constable of the city militia, checkers of weights and measures, three town surgeons, and two keepers of the leper-house.[4] The city also licensed groups of porters all over the town, and farmed out the collecting of the taxes on beer, wine and various commodities sold in the town, and the collecting of customs not belonging to the Ghistelles family. It was from these that the city revenues mainly derived, for there were no personal taxes.

The revenues were big enough to allow the city to take on a large programme of public works, and yet not to have to raise substantial loans until the second half of the fifteenth century. Apart from building the market and town halls, and the usual massive expenditure on fortifications, they and the counts between them developed a highly sophisticated water system, which provided water for drinking, transport, power, defence and industrial use, all in operation by the mid-fourteenth century or soon after.

Bruges had—and still has, except where it has been filled in—a double circuit of waterways, strung along the little River Reie, which winds through the town and used to connect it with the sea before it silted up. The inner ring was composed of what used to be the moat round Bruges's original town walls, the outer ring of the later, double moat round the new walls, work on which started in 1297. When the inner walls were demolished, the moat, very sensibly, was not filled in. It had already been widened in 1270, and used for transporting goods; it and the river became a transport network, lined most of the way with quays, so that goods could be unloaded all over the centre of the town. The quay system, as it exists today, was largely completed by the middle of the fourteenth century. Although quays did not run along both sides of all the waterways, the system was far more comprehensive than anything else in Flanders (in Ghent, for instance) or indeed in Europe at the time. A unique sophistication was that the cloth hall was built over the River Reie. This meant that it could be built next to the market square without having to take too much ground away from it or displace existing buildings, and enabled cloth to be loaded and unloaded under cover beneath the hall in a great arcaded basement, and be carried directly up to the stalls above.

The outer circuit was not used just for defence, although it was obviously important for that. It was also a reservoir of industrial and drinking water for the town. It was fed from the inland side of Bruges, and was—and is—several feet higher than the inner water system. This enabled channels of water, controlled by sluices, to run at a reasonable speed from the outer to the inner circuit, turn water-mills in a number of places,

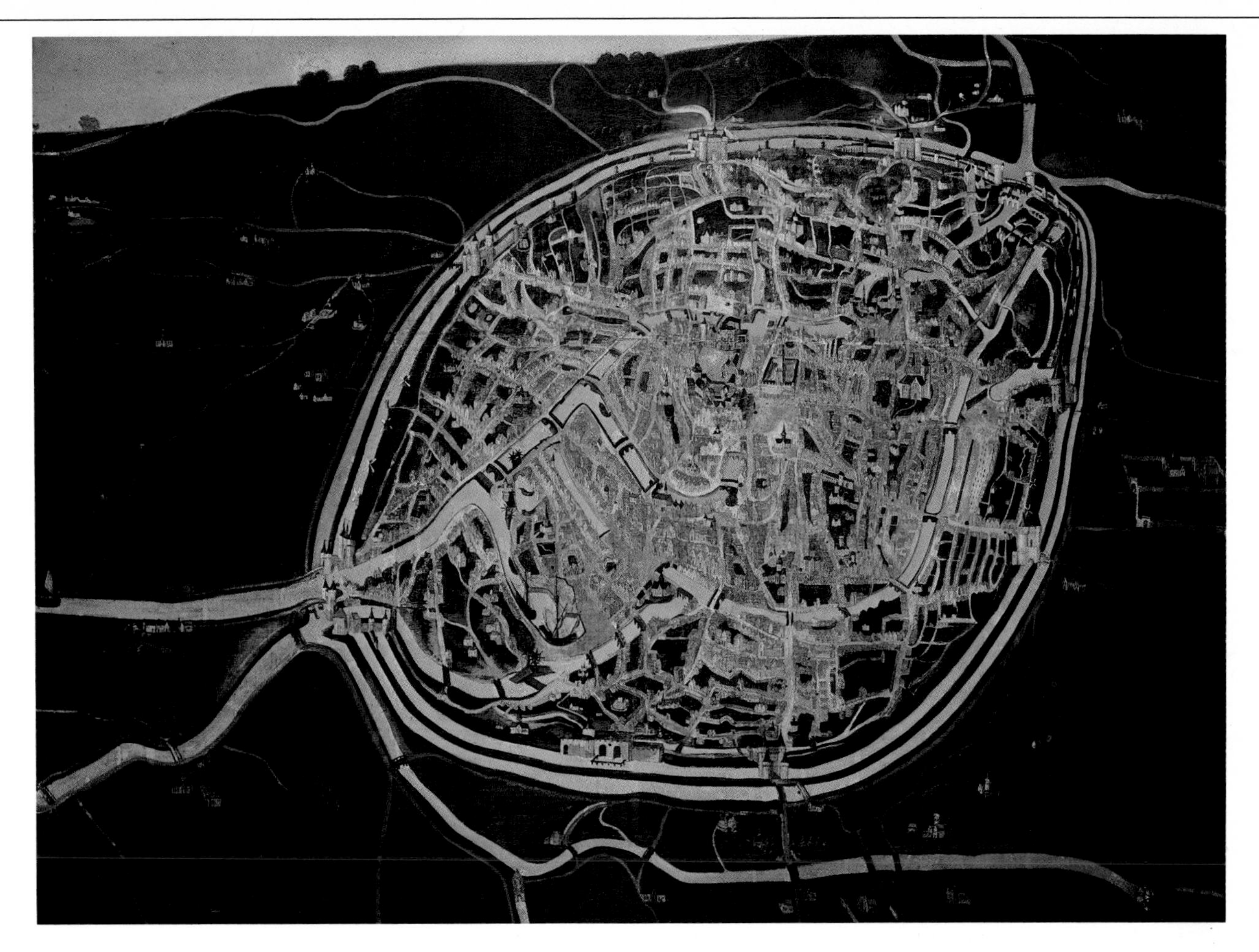

73. An aerial view of Bruges, *c.* 1500. From the painting in the Town Hall, Bruges.

and provide the flow of clean water needed by dyers and fullers for the washing, dyeing and fulling of cloth.[5]

Drinking water was pumped up from part of this circuit, by means of a chain of buckets. The chain was worked by a horse turning a horizontal wheel in a pump-house. It raised water into a tank at the top of a little water-house, from where it was fed in lead pipes to public cisterns and drinking fountains spread all over the town, or was connected, for a payment, to breweries. The system was installed towards the end of the thirteenth century; the water-house, rebuilt in 1466, still exists. The citizens of Bruges were extremely proud of it and its adjacent horse-pump; in a sixteenth-century picture called *The Seven Wonders of Bruges* they feature as one of the wonders.[6]

Much thought was also given to Bruges's water connections, both inland and to the sea. The Minnewater, that lovely limpid lake which stretches towards the centre of Bruges from the south, was probably originally formed to provide a head of water from which the lower waterways could periodically be sluiced clean; but it was enlarged in the mid-fourteenth century to be the Bruges terminus of an inland canal which in fact only came to fruition, as the Ghent Canal, in the late sixteenth century. The connection with the sea from the other end of the town was, of course, vital and also a major worry to Bruges. Ships of any size could go no further than Sluys, at the head of the sea inlet known as the Zwijn, from where boats ferried goods up and down the three miles of the canalized Reie to Bruges. The boats went up on the tide, which was held by sluice gates along the waterway as the water-level rose, so that boats could come down again at a controlled time and a good speed.[7] But a continuous losing battle had to be fought to prevent both Zwijn and waterway from silting up.

74. The establishment of the Lombard pawnbrokers on the Lange Reie, Bruges. From an engraving in Sanderus, *Flandria Illustrata*, 1641–4 (Bibliothèque Royale, Brussels).

The water system helped to establish who lived and worked where in the town. The main marketing and business area was in the centre, served by the inner ring of canals. The most profitable activities were irresistibly attracted to the northern half of this area, towards the sea. The workers, especially the cloth workers, lived and worked either in the outer areas, or on the southern and less prosperous edge of the centre. Here they had access to the water from the outer ring, rents were lower, and there were open spaces in which they could lay out their cloths to dry or be stretched, after dyeing or fulling. In the south were the distinctive settlements of the Beguines and the Bogards, communities of poor spinsters or bachelors working together at spinning or weaving under a religious rule. So the outer areas were, on the whole, the poor ones, and as a result the hospitals, almshouses and pawnshops were to be found in them. St John's, which became the biggest and best known of the hospitals, was founded in the twelfth century and its buildings still exist; its chapel is crowded with the Memlings presented to it in the fifteenth century, and opens into empty arcaded spaces once crammed with beds and people.

The main pawnshop was in the outer zone on the other side of the town, on the Lange Reie, the route to the sea. It was run by the Lombards, or the Grands Cahorsins, as they were called, who came to Bruges under licence from the count in 1281. They built themselves new premises in about 1400. The result was one of the few buildings in Bruges to show Italian influence, and its remarkable grandeur demonstrated how profitable pawnbroking could be. All classes dealt there, from the count, who had the crown jewels in pawn in 1334, to the textile workers, who pawned anything they could, from their clothes to their kitchen pots. The Cahorsins became over-ambitious, however, traded on the side, speculated in wool and probably tried to get a corner in it, but went bankrupt in 1457.[8]

75. No. 23, Kuiperstraat, Bruges. A late fifteenth-century merchant's house near the Buerseplaats, photographed in about 1900.

The Cahorsins were looked at askance by the Italian merchants who lived in the centre with the other foreigners. They did not ride or walk in the civic processions in which the rest of the foreign community had a recognized and conspicuous place. The account of the latters' part in, for instance, the procession which accompanied the entry of Duke Philip the Good to Bruges in 1440 gives some idea of their number and splendour. They were headed by 136 Hanseatic merchants on horseback, dressed in scarlet with black hoods. Then came 48 Spaniards, 40 Milanese, 40 Venetians, 12 Lucchese, 36 Genoese, 22 Florentines and smaller numbers of others.[9] The different groups were known as the 'nations', a term perhaps first used to describe the different foreign groups in the University at Paris. Each nation was headed by a consul or governor: to begin with they met in the chapels or cloisters of churches, but from the late fourteenth century they began to build their own consulates, or adapt existing houses for the purpose. They met in them to celebrate, discuss, or settle disputes, and the consul usually had an official residence in them. William Caxton, who was consul or governor of the British 'nation' in Bruges from 1462 to 1470, learnt printing in Bruges (or possibly Cologne) and printed his first book there in 1473 or 1474.

A curious feature of Bruges, and of Flanders generally, was that by the fifteenth century native merchants had largely disappeared, or at least lost all importance, except in the wine trade. They had been squeezed out by pressure on two fronts. In the twelfth and thirteenth centuries Flemish merchants, like merchants all over Europe, ran their cities with a firm hand, set up trade and craft guilds in order to keep the tradesmen and artisans under their control, and refused to let them sit on the city councils. At the same time they pursued a forward commercial policy, and travelled extensively to Germany and the Champagne fairs to sell cloth, to England to sell cloth and buy wool and to France to sell cloth and buy wine.

In the early fourteenth century the members of the trades and crafts revolted. After a series of violent outbreaks and wars, which involved both the counts (on the whole supporting the workers) and their overlords the kings of France (supporting the merchants), they managed to change the form of government in the cities to one in which the bulk of the city councils was made up of representatives of the guilds. The guilds became independent powers, rather than tools of the merchants. Meanwhile the trade opportunities for merchants were shrinking; the Hanseatic cities started to keep out Flemish merchants, the Champagne fairs disappeared and the Italians established their own representatives in Bruges. Many Flemish merchant families reacted to trouble at home and competition from abroad by retiring from business and living off rents or profitable farms or taxes, which they had acquired in their active years. Flemish overseas trade was largely carried in foreign ships and run by foreigners, based on Bruges.

The foreign merchants did not occupy their own legally defined territories, like the Hanseatics in London, Bergen, and Novgorod, or the European merchants in Alexan-

76. Interior of the Hospital of St John, Bruges, in 1778. From the painting by Johannes Beerblock (Hospital of St John, Bruges).

77. (right) The great crane of Bruges. Detail from a portrait by P. Pourbus, 1551 (Groeningemuseum, Bruges).

dria. But they all tended to congregate in the same area, the northern half of the centre, defined by the cloth hall to the south and the customs house to the north, at the end of the route to and from the sea. Here the individual merchants bought or rented houses, and the nations collectively acquired or built consulates. This was where the big money was in Bruges. The boats came crowding along the Lange Reie, between long rows of prosperous merchant houses, to unload at the quays. Wine and cloth were unloaded by the crane on the Crane Quay, the biggest and best of the medieval Flemish cranes, rearing its head like a huge ungainly heraldic bird, a short way along the water from the customs house. A special company, known as the Krajnkinders, operated the giant treadwheels to either side of the crane.

Most merchandise was liable to customs on import and export, based on the weight established by weighing machines set up by the Ghistelles family at the crane, the customs house and on the quay by the Spanish and English consulates.[10] Squads of porters in special uniforms loaded and unloaded goods and carried them between boats, weigh-beams, storerooms and market halls.[11] On the whole, goods were warehoused in cellars and vaulted ground-floor rooms in merchants' houses; but storage space was also available in some of the consulates and the inns. The earliest dateable purpose-built warehouse in Bruges was built as late as 1574.[12] In the centre of everything, on the Buerseplaats, the merchants of all the nations, but especially the Italians, congregated, picked up news, made deals, bought and sold bills of exchange, and hired boats, to ferry merchandise to and from the big ships in the Zwijn, from the ferry captains who hung around the Buerse looking for work.

One can get some idea of how the 'nations' worked from surviving statutes of the Luccan nation, dating from 1369 and 1478.[13] The Luccans came to Bruges primarily to sell silk; their numbers (excluding women and children) varied over the decades from twelve to thirty-eight. Their consulate was just off the Buerseplaats, and acted as the headquarters of what was in effect at once a trade association, a social club and a religious brotherhood. Membership was compulsory. The members annually elec-

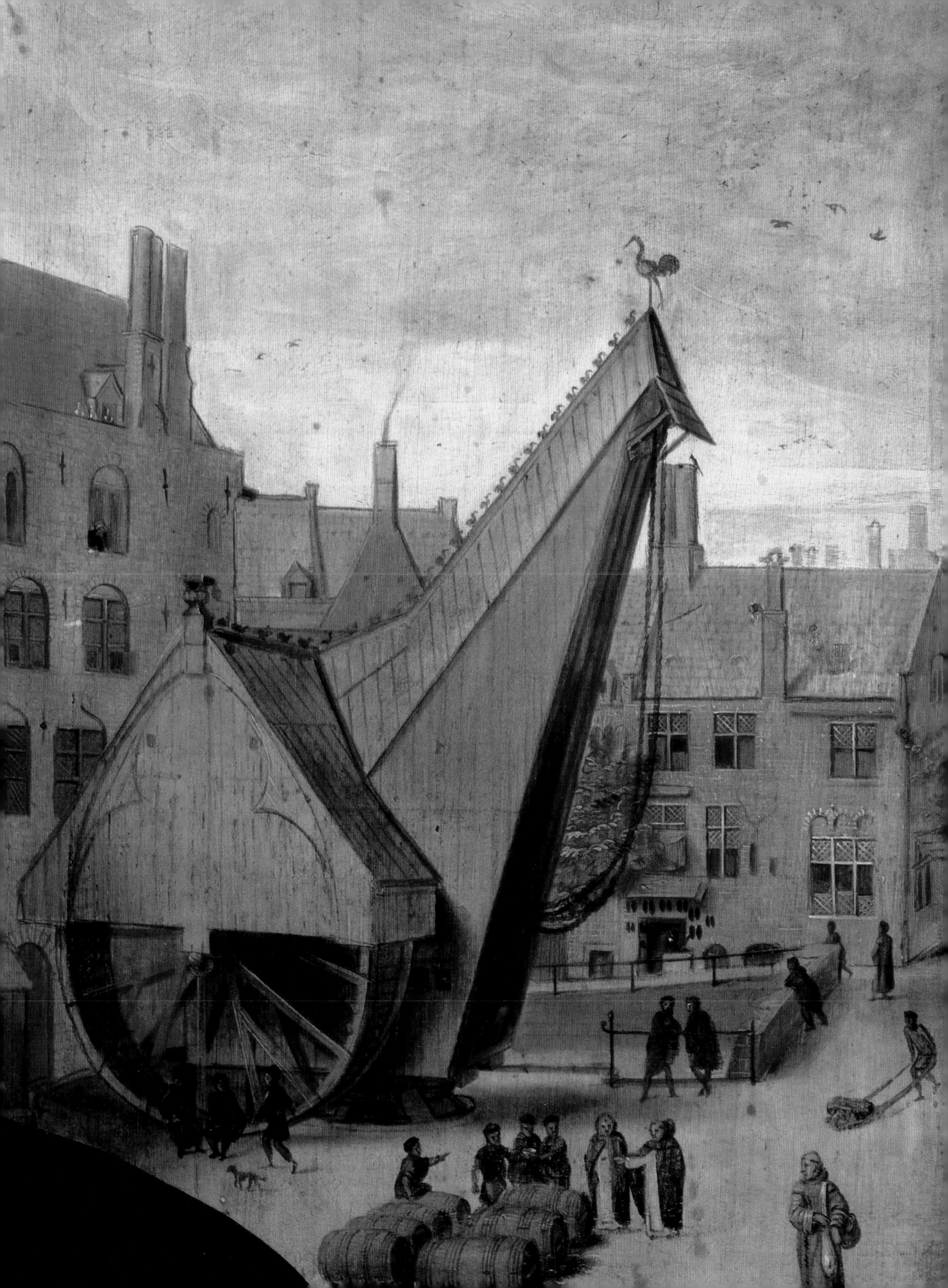

78. The Buerseplaats, Bruges, from which the term 'bourse' derives. From Sanderus, *Flandria Illustrata*, 1641–4 (Bibliothèque Royale, Brussels).

ted a consul, and two or three councillors, and there was a small permanent staff of two secretaries and two ushers. The consul adjudicated in inter-Luccan disputes, but the disputants had a right of appeal to local courts. There was a Luccan chapel in the Augustinian church (where the Genoese and Hanseatics also had chapels). High Mass was held here on the first Sunday of the month, followed by a meeting: non-attendance was fined. The feast of the Holy Cross was celebrated by a torchlight procession. Expenses were paid by a tax of 1/480, on all sales and purchases.

A few of the foreign merchants emerge out of anonymity, either because of their known activities, or because their portraits survive, or both. They tended to come into the limelight through dealing with the court, always a tempting but often dangerous activity for foreign merchants. Two of the richest Luccan merchants, Dino Rappondi and Giovanni Arnolfini, whose wedding portrait was painted in Bruges by Van Eyck, were involved with Philip the Bold and his successor John the Fearless. Rappondi, like most merchants, operated on every kind of scale; his activities ranged from supervising the building of a fort at Sluys and raising 200,000 florins for John the Fearless's ransom, to supplying the duke's wife with oranges, sugar, ginger, cinnamon and cloves.[14]

The most ambitious, and financially the most disastrous, of the Florentine merchants was Tommaso Portinari, who arrived in 1465 as the manager and local partner of the Medici company in Bruges.[15] He had put up $13\frac{1}{2}$ percent of its capital and drew 25 percent of its profits, raised to $27\frac{1}{2}$ percent in 1469; the Medici family's share of the capital varied from around 66 to 69 percent. Portinari had a staff of eight under him; an assistant manager, six factors and a *giovane*—a trainee lad related to the Medici.

He revealed his style almost straight away by buying, in 1466, one of the grandest houses in Bruges, the Hotel Bladelin, as the company headquarters and his own residence. He enlarged it by building a wing, including a vaulted cellar for the firm's merchandise. He commissioned pictures on the same generous scale. The great Portinari triptych by Hugo Van der Goes, now in the Uffizi, was commissioned by him for the hospital of Sta Maria Nuova in Florence, and he and his family feature as donors on one of the panels. He was involved in the commissioning of another superb triptych from Memling, of the Last Judgment. The ship carrying it to Italy was captured by Baltic pirates in the English Channel, and the triptych ended up in Gdansk, where it can still be seen. Portinari features both as a donor and, naked, in the central panel, being weighed by the Judgment Angel and not found wanting. It was a judgment with which his partners in Florence would not necessarily have agreed.

The Bruges company traded in pepper, almonds, sugar, cloth and silk, besides dealing in bills of exchange. One of its most profitable lines was selling silk to the ducal court. But previous partners had sensibly bound themselves not to lend money to 'lords spiritual or temporal'. Portinari reversed this policy, with disastrous results, and lent more and more money to Duke Charles the Bold. The Medicis in Florence initially allowed this because, in partnership with the pope, they were trying to corner the European market in alum and to establish a monopoly for alum from the newly discovered papal mines near Rome, which they ran. They hoped that Duke Charles would help them at the Flemish end. But even when this plan collapsed, they continued to let Portinari float loans. By 1478 the loans were so large and there seemed so little likelihood of their being repaid that Lorenzo de' Medici pulled out of the Bruges company, leaving Portinari to run it on his own. He never made a success of it, retired from business in 1488 and died in Florence in 1501, in relative poverty and in the hospital to which he had given the Van der Goes triptych in better days.

Foreign merchants in Bruges were debarred from certain activities. They were excluded from the retail trade in the city, and all their wholesale dealings had to pass through local brokers; the brokers, for instance, bought cloth in the cloth hall for the foreign merchants, and took a commission. Another important class in Bruges were the innkeepers, who were often brokers too. A third were the money-changers. They sat in a row of covered booths lining one side of the bridge across the Reie, at the north end of the cloth hall, took money on deposit as well as changing it, and made book-transfers on demand from one deposit account to another. A fourth class were the drapers, the entrepreneurs of the textile industry. All four classes were extremely prosperous. In the absence of native merchants they provided the main bulk of the Poorters, the local upper-crust of Bruges.[16]

The Poorters had their own representatives among the aldermen, and perhaps exerted more influence in the city government than appeared on the surface. Foreign merchants could join them as honorary members, without political rights. Lawyers and rich *rentiers* in Bruges were also likely to be Poorters. They formed the Bruges establishment, and their headquarters and meeting place, the elegant late-Gothic building known as the Poortersloge, was in a suitably dominant position at the head of the Lange Reie, presiding over the merchandise on which the wealth of the city was based, as it was carried in and out on the water. It was, so to speak, the Conservative Club of Bruges.

79. The white bear, crest of the jousting Order of the Ours Blanc, on the Poortersloge, Bruges.

On one corner of the Poortersloge is a small statue of a bear. This marks the fact that the building was also the headquarters of the Society of the White Bear, the Société noble et chevaleresque de l'Ours Blanc. It was a society dedicated to jousting, the most expensive and prestigious sport of the Middle Ages. The Poortersloge was, in modern terms, the Polo Club as well as the Conservative Club of Bruges.

The society had been in existence since at least 1320.[17] Its head was known as the Forestier, it held an annual feast, celebrated with banquets, dancing and jousting, and it took part in the jousts held on the market-place (or sometimes the Friday Market). The first reference to these is in 1285, and from then on they took place frequently, often lasted several days, and could be very splendid. The facades of the buildings round the market-place were decorated with tapestries and hangings, the burgomasters and aldermen (and on occasions the count or duke) watched from the windows of the Cranenburgh house, the grandest house on the square, and refreshments of bread, cheese, fruit and mead were served in the interval. The jousts were sometimes held to celebrate royal or ducal visits, and sometimes took place between the native Poorters of the White Bear and the Hanseatic merchants (as in 1305), or visiting merchant teams from outside; the Ours Blanc had a particularly lively rivalry with the Épinettes, the equivalent society in Lille.

A new dimension was introduced to Bruges in the late fourteenth century, when Flanders was inherited by the dukes of Burgundy. The dukes took a fancy to Bruges and spent considerable amounts of time there, during which Bruges became the seat of one of the most glamorous and sophisticated courts in Europe. Festivities, joyous entries, jousts and banquets succeeded each other without stint. The city paid out more than it could afford for its share, but the results must have been sensational. The celebrations following on the marriage of Duke Philip the Good to Isabella of Portugal in 1430 were especially magnificent.[18] It was when filled with enthusiasm after two days of banquets and jousting in that year that the duke proclaimed the foundation of the Order of the Golden Fleece.

As in every other medieval city, the contribution of the Church to both the life and the buildings of Bruges can scarcely be exaggerated. Its holidays were based on religious festivals; the fairs grow up round them; the guilds, the archery companies and the 'nations' all had their religious aspect, their chapels in Bruges churches, their processions, their celebrations on particular feast days. The city had managed to acquire an impressive collection of holy relics; the most famous of them, a phial of the Holy Blood, was taken in procession through the town and round the ramparts, accompanied by the aldermen, the city officials, the city militia and mounted knights, and the foreign 'nations'; the whole hierarchy of the city was on show and made public.

80. Looking up to the Poortersloge, Bruges.

The Divine Power, and the intercessing power of the Virgin Mary, the Saints and the Angels, were invoked to protect and preside over every aspect of life, and to keep the city from harm in this life and the next. Every gateway through the city walls was adorned with statues of the saints. A huge gilded figure of St Michael expelling Satan crowned the tower of the belfry, and the burgomasters made announcements to the people from its balcony flanked by statues of Sts Donatien and Élois, the town's patron saints. Even the customs officers collected customs sitting at their desks beneath a picture of the Crucifixion.[19]

The town had three ancient and prestigious collegiate-church foundations in the centre, St Donatien, Notre Dame and St Sauveur, a number of smaller parish churches, numerous convents, nine hospitals and the customary ring of religious foundations on the edge of the centre: the Dominicans, Augustinians, Franciscans, Carmelites and others. Much of the wealth of the city went into endowing and enlarging these, and in embellishing them with chapels, stained glass, vestments, plate and altarpieces.

By the end of the fifteenth century Bruges was a dazzling place. It was a manufacturing and trading town transformed. Its fleeces had become a golden fleece, its cloth cloth of gold. The foreign merchants, the ducal court, the upper clergy, the city's own rich and cultured aristocracy, living off their rents, their old-established businesses and a little gentlemanly speculation, prayed, jousted, feasted and went in processions together. In their own houses and on the altarpieces of the churches the painters who visited or lived in Bruges presented them with a world of gentle oval-faced women and calm and confident men, dressed in glowing fabrics of silk and gold embroidery and

81. The Belfry, Bruges.

exquisitely posed against a background of emerald fields and woods, or towns of miniature perfection rising from sparkling waters. Bruges itself frequently came into the paintings—sometimes in the form of details, the crane, a street corner, a courtyard, a row of gabled houses, a portion of the city walls, sometimes the whole amazing skyline.[20]

The slim towers of the Poortersloge and the Hanseatic House, and the upper stage of the belfry were new arrivals on this skyline; in some paintings the last was shown only half-built. Their appearance might seem evidence of the continuing vitality and prosperity of the town, but this was far from being the case. The Hanseatic House was built in 1478–81 on a site given by the city to the German merchants, the most important buyers in the Bruges markets, in order to dissuade them from moving to another city. The octagon, so superbly and absurdly out of scale with the rest, was added to the belfry tower in 1483–7, as a piece of desperate window-dressing. The long, losing battle against competition from English and Italian textiles was entering its last stage, and Bruges was too established, too rigid and perhaps too complacent to be able to fight it with success. There was now little to keep foreign merchants in Bruges, except the pleasantness of the life there, and even that was disturbed by furious political trouble between Bruges and the Archduke Maximilian, who had married the daughter of the last duke. For a time he was actually imprisoned in Bruges; he never forgave it, and did his best to promote Antwerp at its expense. Meanwhile, the Zwijn continued to silt up; fewer and fewer ships came to Bruges each year, and one by one the foreign 'nations' closed their houses. For a time Bruges was nicknamed 'Bruges le mort'; grass was said to be growing in its streets. It recovered, and became the modestly prosperous town which it has remained to the present day. But its great days, except as a tourist resort, were over.[21]

Superficially Bruges and Venice had much in common. Both were international trading centres, bound together by links of trade and famous throughout Europe for the wealth and variety of the goods which crammed their markets. Both were cosmopolitan and sophisticated cities. Both were threaded through with canals.

But Venice was much bigger and richer than Bruges. It was perhaps three times the size, and its merchants lived in houses of marble rather than of brick, the biggest of which could have fitted the biggest Bruges houses into a corner.[22] In the fourteenth and fifteenth centuries the people of Bruges on the whole waited for foreigners to come to them; the Venetians for centuries had gone in search of business, had travelled the world from the Atlantic coasts to China, and built up a fleet and an empire to consolidate their trade. Much of the money made in Bruges was siphoned off by the foreign merchants, especially to Germany or Italy; the Venetian profits stayed in Venice. From a merchant's point of view, Bruges was a branch-office town.

The two qualities of Venice which contemporaries wondered at were its wealth and its stability. The latter was especially a matter of amazement to the other Italian cities,

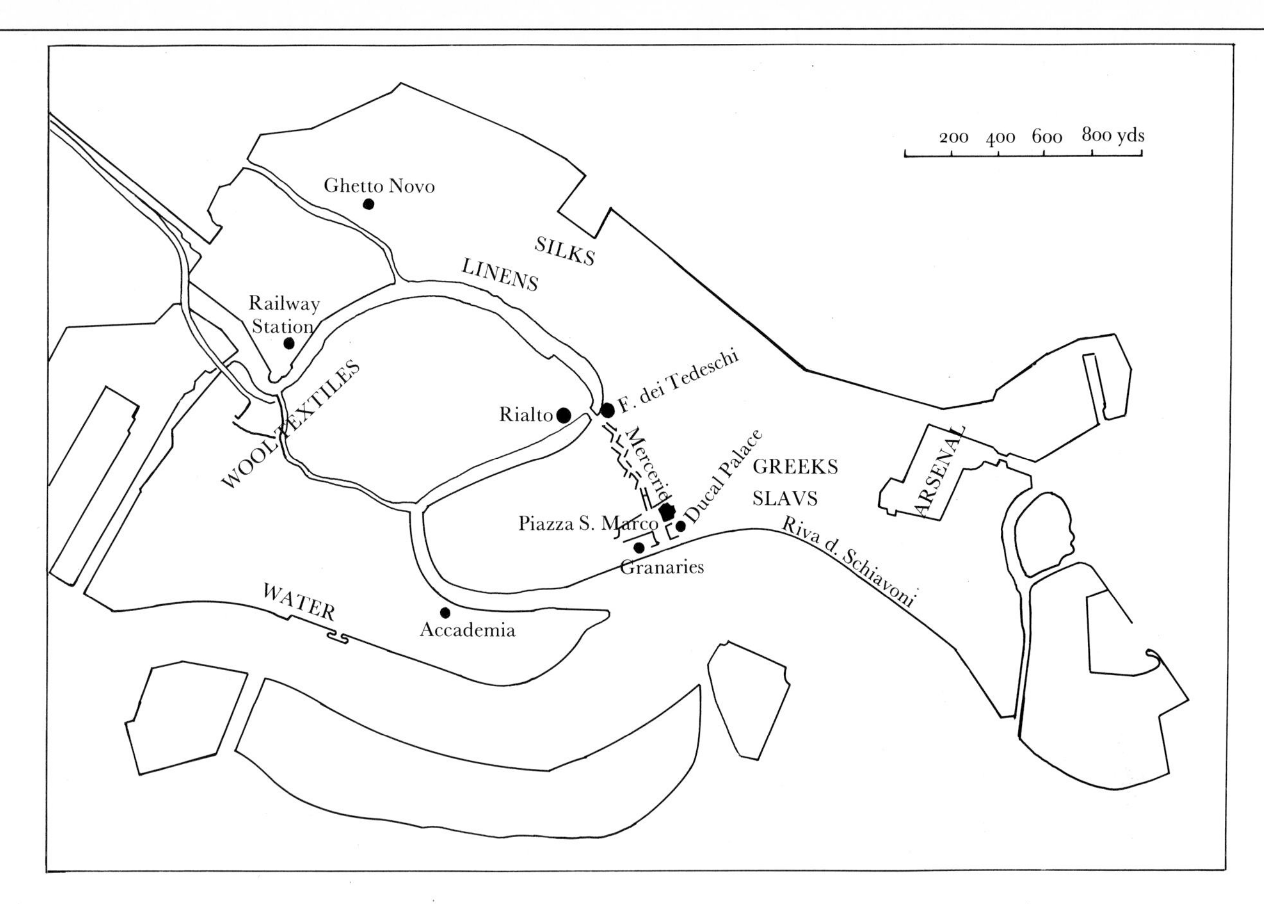

82. Plan of Venice.

as they watched their leading families busily stringing each other out of the windows of their Palazzi Publici, massacring or being massacred by their artisans, and finally succumbing to the rule of a despot. Venice preserved the same constitution with comparatively little alteration from the thirteenth century to the French conquest in 1797, and during this time, although there were conspiracies and tensions within the ruling class, there was never a major upheaval.

Like so many other cities Venice early on developed a ruling merchant class. It had become virtually independent of its distant overlord, the Byzantine emperor, by the tenth century, and completely independent by the thirteenth. In 1297 the ruling class made itself hereditary and closed its ranks. A few new families were allowed in in 1381 and a few more at the end of the seventeenth century, but on the whole the same families were running Venice in 1797 as had been running it five hundred years previously.

It is impossible to understand Venice without knowing something about the Venetian oligarchy. How did the nobles do it? A number of factors acted in their favour. Venice, securely guarded by its position and its navy, was remarkably free from outside influence. Moreover, it never had to deal with the immigrant noble families whose feuds, sense of honour and extravagant life-style caused such havoc in most Italian cities. There were certainly some landowning families among the refugees from the Lombard invasions who settled on the islands in the Venetian lagoon in the sixth and seventh centuries, but the shared trials and poverty of the early decades smoothed off any important differences in attitude, even if pride in a heroic and probably largely mythical ancestry sometimes remained. In their attitudes and life-style the Venetian ruling classes were remarkably integrated. They were also, not surprisingly, in view of the difficulties which they overcame, very able. They managed to contain two obvious threats to the supremacy of their order, from the prosperous middle classes and from the artisans. The Venetian middle classes shared in the city's commercial success; many of them were richer than all but the upper echelons of the nobility. Yet they were almost entirely excluded from the government. They could not sit on any of the councils, or serve as generals, admirals or ambassadors, let alone aspire to be procurators or Doge. Here, one would have thought, was a potential body of deeply dissatisfied people, with sufficient resources to make their discontent effective.

In fact the nobility kept them happy by giving them one prestigious and politically important office, that of grand chancellor, a useful role as members of the civil service, and a whole group of prestigious, time-consuming and completely apolitical activities as members and officials of the *scuole*.

The first *scuole* were founded about 1260. They were religious confraternities of laymen, offshoots of the flagellant movement of the thirteenth century. Through bequests they acquired increasing amounts of property, and by the fifteenth century some of them were extremely rich. Each one was affiliated to a particular church or monastic house, and to begin with had their meetings in chapels in them, but they soon built or acquired their own premises. These gradually grew more and more splendid. The typical plan consisted of a big first-floor hall, for meetings and religious services, and a hall below it (and perhaps smaller rooms off the hall) for administration.[23]

Like the great city companies in London today, the *scuole* spent the major part of their income on charity, but had a good deal left over for pageantry and feasting. They were overseen by the Council of Ten, but their internal administration was entirely their own responsibility. The nobility and clergy were admitted as members, but could not serve as officers. To be the head of one of the five (after 1552, six) *scuole* which were recognized by the Council of Ten as *grandi* became the summit of ambition for most rich non-noble citizens. For all members, belonging to a *scuola grande* ensured social contact with the nobility and a prominent place in all public pageants and processions. An energetic but less-established middle-class Venetian could go into one of the *scuole piccoli*, and campaign for its recognition as *grande*. The Scuola di San Rocco, for instance, was founded in the plague year of 1478 (both to pray for relief from the plague and to give assistance to the plague-stricken). It was upgraded in 1489, but remained one of the poorest of the *scuole grandi* until another plague in 1527 and an appallingly destructive plague in the 1570s brought donations flooding in.

Venice also escaped the labour troubles which afflicted other Italian cities. A successful industry in both silk and woollen textiles started up there in the early sixteenth century, and reached its peak around 1600 by when Venice was producing considerably more cloth than Florence.[24] But this was a late arrival. In the Middle Ages, however, Venice had the unique phenomenon of a work-force of, by 1423, 16,000 people, all working in the same place and for the same employer, instead of being minutely subdivided both as regards employers and place of work, as in the textile and other medieval industries. These were the workers in the Arsenal, a conglomeration of storehouses, workshops and shipbuilding yards which had been first constructed in 1104, had been much enlarged in the early fourteenth century, and which built and serviced the Venetian fleet.[25]

Here, one might have thought, was further potential for trouble, but in fact the Arsenal workers never presented the slightest threat to the security of the state. Once again, their quiescence was partly achieved by giving them a prominent role in state functions. They provided the Doge's bodyguard, which carried his litter in processions,

83. (top) View of the Arsenal, Venice, in the sixteenth century. By Antonio di Natale (Museo Correr, Venice).

84. (centre) The Rialto in the early eighteenth century. Detail from the painting by Gabriele Bella (Fondazione Querini Stampalia, Venice).

85. (right) Members of the Scuola di San Giovanni Evangelista processing in the Piazza S. Marco. Detail from the painting by Gentile Bellini (Accademia, Venice).

Bancho
Del Giro

kept the crowd in order with wooden clubs, and served as the crew for his great gilded barge, the Bucintoro.

But as much as anything the power of the nobility was due to their own cohesion, and to a life-style which played down individual leadership, or any cultivation of the personality, in favour of loyalty to their order and readiness for public service. Young Venetian nobles were indulgently allowed to let off a little steam, wear extravagant clothes and run around the town. But once they had sown their wild oats they were expected to be sober and hard-working.

By 1500 there were about twenty-five hundred adult male nobles. Girolamo Priuli, the Venetian diarist of the early sixteenth century, reckoned that about three-quarters of these could be classed as poor, in so far as they had few or no private resources and depended on jobs given by the government for an income.[26] This 75 percent were unlikely to get high in the hierarchy, but they were exceedingly conscious of their status and tended to be assiduous attenders of the Great Council, to which all males of noble birth belonged by right from the age of twenty-five; it was the Great Council which passed the laws and elected the magistrates, officers of state and members of the complex hierarchy of interlocking councils which ran Venice according to a carefully calculated system of checks and balances: the College, the Senate, the Signoria, the Council of Ten and a number of others. The different levels had their own distinctive dress, which they generally wore when out of doors or attending meetings in the Doge's Palace. The ordinary nobleman wore a plain black robe, sometimes described as a toga; Canon Casola, who visited Venice in 1494, thought it a dress 'which inspires confidence and is very dignified'.[27] The Senators wore purple, the College violet or blue, according to rank, the Signoria and the Ten were splendid in scarlet robes, and the Doge even more splendid in cloth of gold.

The life of the nobility, like that of Venice as a whole, rotated round two main pivots, the business centre of the Rialto and the political centre of the Piazza S. Marco. The Piazza S. Marco[28] has remained one of the most famous open spaces in the world, the significance of the Rialto has been largely forgotten, and most people think of it simply in terms of the bridge which leads to it. But in 1514 Marino Sanudo called it 'the principal place in Venice and the richest'.[29] Its site marked both the earliest settlement and the original market-place of the Venetian archipelago, on the *rivo alto*, or high bank; this was the driest site on what became the Grand Canal, and the place at which the canal was most easily bridgeable.[30] It was at the Rialto that the spices, silks, metals and other merchandise from which the wealth of Venice derived were sold in wholesale shops letting off its arcaded streets. The money-changers and jewellers also had their stalls here, and on the edge of the area were markets for meat, oil, fish, cheese, bread, fruit, vegetables and flowers. Almost the whole complex was burnt in 1514, when fire broke out in a textile merchant's shop, spread, and burnt for twenty-four hours; it was winter, the canals were frozen, and the fire service could not get water. Fra Giocondo made a scheme for rebuilding it in three square concentric zones, which was like a schematic representation of the hierarchy of commerce: a central arcaded piazza for bankers, money-changers and jewellers, four surrounding arcaded streets for textiles, and an outer perimeter of arcades for food shops.[31] In fact it was rebuilt on the same lines as before, but with Renaissance arcades instead of Gothic ones.[32]

The food markets must have been noisy places, as they still are today, but in the

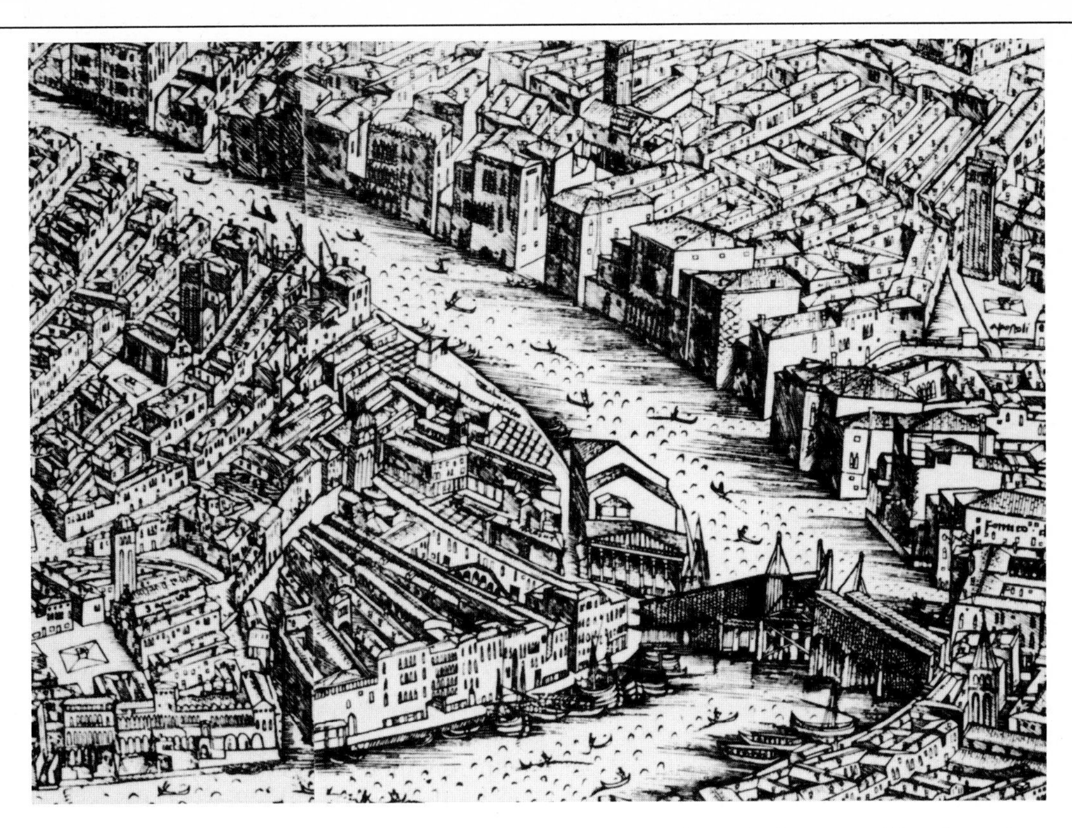

86. The Rialto area in 1500. Detail from the bird's-eye view of Venice by Jacopo de' Barbari (British Museum).

areas where the big money was being made contemporaries were impressed by the quietness with which deals were concluded.[33] The nobility frequented the Rialto as much as, if not more than, everyone else, because they were the principal merchants of Venice. They had their own particular preserve, in effect a nobleman's exchange, in the form of an arcaded loggia built in 1424 at the foot of the Rialto bridge.[34] It is clearly shown in Jacopo de' Barbari's bird's-eye view of Venice, made in 1501, and a corner of it appears in Carpaccio's painting of the *Miracle of the Holy Cross*.

Many of the nobility spent the morning at the Rialto and went to the Piazza S. Marco in the afternoon, when most of the meetings in the Doge's Palace took place. The Doge's Palace was so called because the Doge lived in one wing of it, but in fact it was just as much the Palazzo Publico of the nobility, and most of its space was given up to their meeting places. Among them was the huge hall of the Great Council, the 82-foot span of which was one of the biggest in Europe, and the smaller but sumptuous halls of the Ten and of the Senate, in the latter of which the Doge presided.

Meetings were summoned by bells from the campanile on the piazza, each of which had its name. The largest and deepest, Marangona, announced the weekly meeting of the Great Council, the next largest, Dei Pregadi, summoned the Senate, a higher pitched bell, Trottiere, rang shortly and insistently when meetings were about to start, and the smallest bell of all, Maleficio, announced the imminence of a public execution.[35]

Before and after meetings nobles chatted to each other in another loggia, at the base of the campanile, or walked up and down together in the piazzetta, by the side of the Doge's Palace, gossiping, plotting alliances, discussing elections and soliciting votes. An important nobleman could not afford to seem stand-offish to fellow nobles, with perhaps a hundredth of his income but a vote to cast in his favour; the lowness of his bow and the courtesy of his salutation were jealously watched and evaluated. A sixteenth-century poem compared this promenading stretch to a pond, in which nobles learnt to navigate the shoals of politics; its popular nickname was the Piazza del Broglio, the piazza of intrigue.

87. (left) The old Rialto bridge, Venice. Detail from the *Miracle of the Cross* by Vittore Carpaccio (Accademia, Venice).

88. (above) Venetian noblemen in the Piazzetta S. Marco, Venice, *c.* 1487. From the painting attributed to Lazzaro Bastiani (Museo Correr, Venice).

Other buildings connected with the government collected round the Doge's Palace, the piazza and the piazzetta. The prison was beyond the palace, and the mint was on the waterfront round the corner from the piazzetta. The southern side of the piazza was lined with the official houses of the nine procurators of St Mark's. The procurators were the highest-ranking officials in Venice after the Doge and the grand chancellor, their prestige was very great, but curiously enough their official job was completely non-political (although by right of their office they were members of the Senate). They had originally been appointed to look after the property of the basilica of St Mark's, but they gradually became responsible for administering many private estates and trusts as well. By the end of the fifteenth century the basilica was very rich, and the private trusts had accumulated, so their financial responsibilities were considerable. They were elected for life by the Great Council, and their houses on the piazza, along with a very small salary, came with the job.

Opposite the procurators' houses were the buildings later to be known as the Procuratie Vecchie, but only because the procurators were accommodated in them while their own houses were being rebuilt in 1582. They had in fact been built by the procurators on ground belonging to St Mark's, and were let out as apartments to employees of the government. They were rebuilt on the same lines but a storey higher in 1512. Among the eminent public servants who lived there at one time or another were the painter Gentile Bellini, and the architect Sansovino, who was appointed architect to the procurators in 1529.

Between the back of the procurators' houses and the water were the Granai, the main public granaries.[36] As Venice was almost totally dependent on imported food, the maintenance of a regular corn supply was of the first importance, so that it is not surprising that it possessed one of the largest of the numerous public granaries built in medieval Europe. The Granai in fact consisted of four separate four-storey warehouses separated by narrow lanes leading to another lane at the back of the procurators' houses; but on the waterfront the lanes were arched over so as to give the Granai one continuous facade. To judge from their architectural detail they must have been built in the fifteenth century. They occupied about the same space as St Mark's, and were a prominent feature of the waterfront until the late eighteenth century. When Napoleon turned the procurators' houses into an imperial palace in 1807 he wanted his palace to have a garden and a sea-view, and the granaries were accordingly demolished. The gardens known as the Giardinetti are on their site today.

The area round the Doge's Palace was never exclusively political and administrative. In fact the feeling that commercial activities were unsuitable for civic dignity, which had debarred them from the Piazza Signoria in Florence in 1385, seems first to have surfaced in Venice in about 1500, and operated much less effectively than in Florence. By then, apart from the activities directly or indirectly connected with government—the criminals hung in cages on the campanile, the public executions on the piazzetta, the

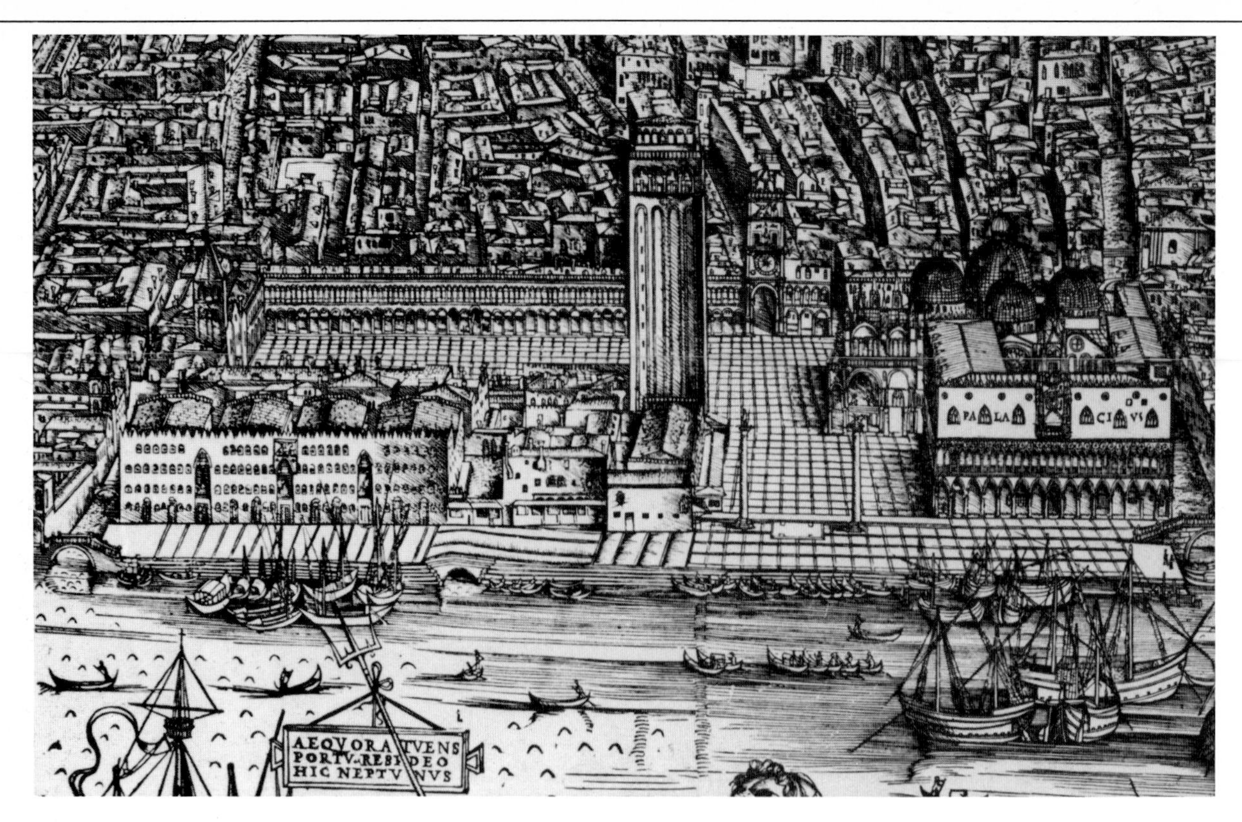

89. Piazza S. Marco and the Granai, Venice. Detail from the bird's-eye view of Venice by Jacopo de' Barbari (British Museum).

notaries working in the arcades of the Doge's Palace—there were shops all along the arcades of the piazza, a vegetable market along one side of it, money-changers' booths at the base of the campanile, butchers', bakers' and cheese-and-salami shops opposite the Doge's Palace in the piazzetta, and further meat and vegetable stalls and public latrines adhered to the bases of the piazzetta columns of St Theodore with his crocodile and St Mark's lion. Peasants hawked herbs, and sold hair for wigs displayed on poles, freaks exhibited themselves in front of the basilica, there were beggars everywhere, and once a year the whole piazza was jammed with stalls for a fair.[37]

The piazza, like main squares everywhere, was also used for a wide variety of public events, both secular and religious, from bullfights and tournaments to processions to celebrate the election of a Doge, or the great religious feasts. The butchers' guild celebrated their annual feast with a parade on the piazza, after which pigs were let loose and hunted to death, as in the carnival at Rome. At all times of crisis the people gathered in the piazza in enormous numbers, to hear the latest news announced from the Doge's Palace; victories were celebrated with bonfires on the piazza and bell-ringing from the campanile. In 1511 the alliance with the papacy, Spain and England against the French produced a five-hour parade of the Senate and clergy past St Mark's and the Doge's Palace, which were hung with tapestries and gold cloth for the occasion.[38]

The Piazza S. Marco was connected with the Rialto by two routes, the Mercerie by land and the Grand Canal by water. Both were important, in their different ways. The tortuous route of the Mercerie was always crammed with people, going to and fro between piazza and Rialto, and for this reason the best shops in Venice were on it, bursting with tapestries, brocades, hangings, carpets, silks, spices and expensive groceries. The Grand Canal was lined continuously both sides all the way to the Rialto bridge with the biggest and best houses (or, as they would later be called, palaces).

Sites on the Grand Canal were to acquire great social and aesthetic prestige, but they were originally competed for because they were the best commercial sites in Venice. They had easy access to the harbour at one end, where the big ships lay at anchor

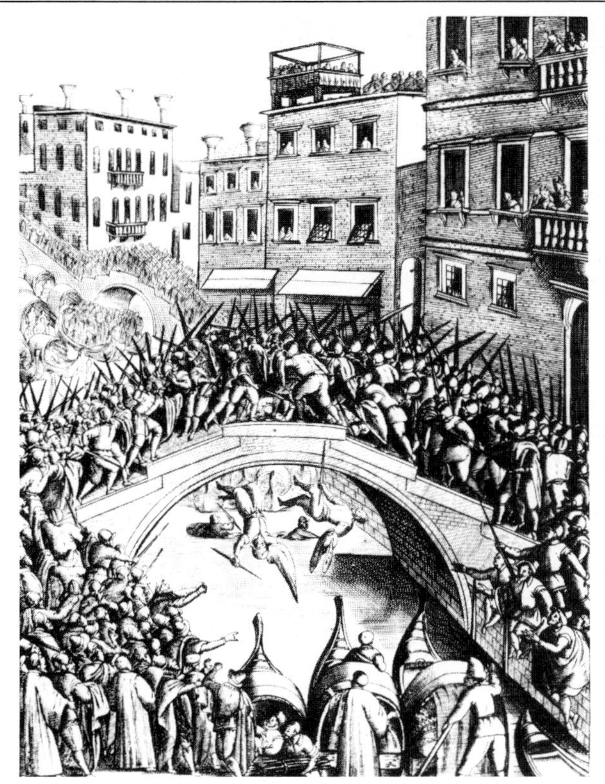

90–1. Fighting on the bridges in Venice. From Giacomo Franco, *Habiti d'houmeni e donne Venetiane*, 1610 (British Library).

or along the quays, and to the Rialto markets at the other; and the water was deep enough for small sailing craft or big barges to tie up along the palace steps. They were accordingly occupied by the most prosperous merchants in Venice, who used their lower storeys and attics for warehousing and lived on the intermediate floors in the usual medieval manner. The earlier Rialto bridges had a drawbridge in the centre; this could be pulled up to let sailing ships through, which enabled the big merchant houses to continue above the bridge. This end of the Grand Canal was also obviously convenient for merchants whose principal contacts were with the Italian mainland.

The commercial and warehousing aspect of a Venetian merchant's palace can be seen in action in the house of the Corner family on one of the best sites on the Grand Canal. The family had big plantations in Cyprus, and in August 1532 received a cargo of sugar and cotton from the island. Some of the sugar was damp, and was stored up in the roof to dry; the attics were already being used for corn storage, in the usual manner. The cotton and the remainder of the sugar were stored on the ground floor, which was already being used to store wine and timber. The hot sun dried the sugar during the day, but in order to speed up the process braziers were lit in the attics at night. The braziers set fire to the attics, the palace was destroyed and with it all the grain and sugar in the attic. The ground-floor cotton and sugar were rescued by boat, but six hundred cartloads of timber and all the wine were lost.[39]

The Arsenal, the Piazza S. Marco, the Rialto and the Grand Canal provided the pivots round which Venice rotated, but there was, of course, a great deal more to it. Almost the whole of its two main land masses, to the north and south of the Grand Canal, were closely built up by 1500. By then its population was up to about 120,000, and it reached a peak of about 183,000 in 1563 (the population of the equivalent parts of Venice today is down to 140,000).[40] The city was made up of a mass of separate districts, most of them specializing in one particular occupation, and some occupied by particular racial communities. Local feelings and rivalries were strong, and were expressed in traditional battles with fists or sticks on the bridges dividing one district

92. Venice. The Fondaco dei Tedeschi (1616) (Kupferstichkabinett, Berlin).

from the other. These were ultimately banned because they caused too much disorder.

Both the more important racial communities and the various trades and industries founded guilds or confraternities, which were known as *scuole* like the purely religious groups, and like them started by meeting in the chapel of a particular church, but sooner or later built buildings of their own. None is as grand as the buildings of the *scuole grandi*, but most of them still survive, and by plotting them one can build up something approaching a racial and occupational map of Venice.[41]

Considerable sections of Venice were given over to one aspect or other of the textile industry. Silk manufacture had been established by a large group of political exiles from Lucca who came to Venice in 1309, and it grew to be one of the most important industries in Venice. It and the much smaller linen industry were located in the northern section of Venice, north of the Grand Canal and the Rialto bridge. The wool-textile industry was a later arrival, but from 1500 it and associated crafts rapidly spread over a large area across the Grand Canal, to the west of the Rialto. All the textile industries were reasonably accessible to the Rialto, where the main wholesaling went on.

The fishing industry and the watersellers congregated along the quays of the Zattere, and had their *scuole* a little inland from it. The watersellers brought water in by boat from the mainland, and were especially important in Venice because the water from its own wells was too brackish to be drinkable, or even usable in the textile industry, and it was otherwise dependent on rainwater; this was collected underground in cisterns, and drawn out of them through well-heads, many of which still survive.

Greeks and Slavs lived to the north of the quay which is still named the Riva degli Schiavoni after the latter (it was widened in the eighteenth century, to form a general promenade or parade).[42] There were more than four thousand Greeks in Venice by the end of the fifteenth century, variously engaged. The Slavs came to Venice to serve in its army and navy: their confraternity building, the Scuola di S. Giorgio, was remodelled in 1502, when it acquired a relic of St George and commissioned the paintings by Carpaccio which it still contains. The Albanians dealt in wool and oil. The Luccan community lived and had their *scuola* in the silk district. The Milanese were mainly smiths or money-changers, and had their *scuola* near the Rialto. The Jews settled in the area still known as the Ghetto Novo in 1516.

The Germans held an especially favoured position in Venice, because metal from

93. The Procuratie Vecchie (1512) in the Piazza S. Marco, Venice.

the German mines was extremely important in its economy: it needed iron for its foundries and silver and other precious metals for export to the east, in return for spices. The German headquarters was the building known as the Fondaco dei Tedeschi, next to the Rialto bridge (today it is the post office). When it was accidentally burnt in 1505, it was rebuilt and maintained at the expense of the state. The new building, like the old one, was a communal version of a Venetian merchant's house, with warehousing down below and residences up above, in this case taking the form of seventy-two rooms of varying sizes (but all on the small side) grouped twenty-four to a floor on three floors, with access along open arcades.[43]

This kind of what amounted to a commercial hotel was only an extreme example of the shared living accommodation already common in Venice. Although free-standing houses occupied by only one family were to be found all over the city, and were especially common in the outer areas, both terrace housing and houses divided into apartments had been built there since the thirteenth century in the case of the former, and probably not much later in the case of the latter. The terrace housing which was in existence in 1197 has already been referred to, and from the fourteenth century onwards terraces became increasingly common in Venice, although no examples earlier than the later fifteenth century seem to survive.[44] Terraces could take the form of almshouses, houses built for Arsenal workers or rows of artisan houses containing shops on the ground floor; to build or buy the latter became a popular and profitable form of investment, and both the procurators and the *scuole* acquired large holdings in them.

All these terraces were made up of what the Venetians called *case di sazenti* (houses of servants) suitable for professionals, working shopkeepers, self-employed artisans or labourers; they could vary in size but were usually of two or three storeys with a front and back room on each floor, flanked by a staircase with perhaps one or two smaller rooms to front and back of it. But the procurators' houses in the Piazza S. Marco were an example of the terrace format used for *case di stazio*, houses suitable for nobles. In this they were probably unique in Venice, the result of a one-off situation in which official houses had to be provided for a group of noble officials all of equal status.[45]

The Procuratie Vecchie, opposite the procurators' houses, are an equally interesting example of what is in fact a large apartment block (incorporating shops on the ground floor) treated with considerable architectural grandeur owing to its prestigious position

94. (above) A sixteenth-century terrace on the Rio di Sta Anna, Venice.

95. (right) The Porte St Antoine, Paris, built 1585. From *L'Entrée Triomphante de . . . Louis XIV* (1662).

96. (following page) Detail of the Fontana delle Tartarughe, Piazza Mattei, Rome.

on the piazza. The present range was put up in 1512, after a fire, but replaced an earlier range of similar type. It has a curious and interesting plan.[46] The block is divided in two by a back lane, so that most of the apartments had front and back halves, joined by a bridge. This seems to be an early example both of a back street serving the same purpose as a London mews, and of a device to keep kitchen smells out of the front apartments by providing a ventilated link, in the form of the bridge.

But apartment blocks catering for all social ranks can be found in large quantities all over Venice. Many terrace blocks of tenements for modest middle-class tenants were built in the sixteenth and seventeenth centuries, some divided floor by floor, others into two-storey maisonettes.[47] Many grand Venetian houses were, or soon became, apartment blocks too. The standard plan of a big Venetian house consisted, above the ground and mezzanine floors, of a series of floors identically arranged on the plan of a central hall with smaller rooms to either side. From the fifteenth century, if not earlier, houses on this plan were often divided floor by floor between brothers or relatives. Inevitably, families started to let out floors to outsiders and then, as they acquired more than one house, to let out whole houses floor by floor. In 1529 or 1530, for instance, Aretino, the Tuscan satirist, rented a floor of a rather modest house on the Grand Canal from a noble family; then in 1551 he moved up socially and rented the best floor in a much grander house, on the Riva del Carbon.[48]

In fact, Venice led Europe by the end of the Middle Ages in the variety and sophistication of its housing stock. The logical clarity of many of the houses or individual blocks of terraces was in curious contrast to the labyrinth of canals and alleys by which they were reached. Venice, having always had the alternative of land and water communications, and never having had to adapt to the motor car, has never been under more than modest pressure to rationalize and simplify its network of communications. There, more than anywhere else in Europe, one can still get the feel of a medieval street system at its most random. There were and are no grand axial vistas, outside the Piazza S. Marco: to find the genesis of those one has to go elsewhere in Italy, especially to Florence and Rome.

Part II THE CITY TRIUMPHANT

It has had my heart since I was a child; and as with other good things, the more fine cities I saw, the more I appreciated its beauty . . . I love it tenderly, warts and all. I am only French by grace of that great city: great in its population, great in the beauty of its situation, but above all incomparably great because so many of the pleasures of life are to be found there.

Montaigne on Paris, c. 1580

6

Rome Resplendent

A late sixteenth-century painting in the Lateran Palace in Rome shows the Via Pia framed by the two groups of classical statues both believed at the time to depict Alexander and his horse Bucephalus, and running away into the distance to end where the Porta Pia pierced the walls of Rome at the end of the vista. The aesthetic qualities of a long straight street framed at its commencement and ending in a grand culminating object is clearly expressed, at the expense, in fact, of some juggling with the topography; the length of the road is shortened, for instance, in order to allow the Porta Pia to loom more large at the end of it. There is no doubt that the painter is presenting the viewer with something that he expects to be admired.

Admiration, and something more than admiration, is exactly what was expressed by the young Englishman John Evelyn, when he toured the sights of Rome in 1644. He examined the horses and enthused over their spurious contemporary reputation: 'those two rare horses, the works of the rivals, Phidias and Praxiteles, as they were sent to Nero out of Armenia'. But it was the vista that really excited him: 'Looking back, we had the entire view of the Via Pia down to the two horses before the Monte Cavallo . . . one of the most glorious sights for state and magnificence that any city can show a traveller.'[1]

Evelyn's excitement is understandable: he was having a new experience. Today we are all familiar with this kind of axial city vista, and have seen them by the dozen: up the Champs Élysées to the Arc de Triomphe, up the Mall in Washington to the dome of the Capitol, up the London Mall to Buckingham Palace and so on, almost *ad nauseam*. But when the Via Pia was created in 1561–2 there was nothing else quite like it in the world, and even when Evelyn saw it axial city vistas were rare enough. It was owing to the enthusiasm felt by him and other northern visitors that attempts to create 'state and magnificence' in a similar manner began to be made in northern Europe, and, ultimately, all over the world.

When the Via Pia was laid out the popes had been back in Rome for just over a hundred and forty years. In the previous century, while the popes were in Avignon, Rome had sunk to the position of a minor town, with a population of perhaps ten to fifteen thousand, huddled round the Tiber in the midst of the ruins of Imperial greatness. When Pope Martin V brought the papacy back to Rome in 1420, his biographer described how he found it 'so dilapidated and deserted that it had hardly any resemblance to a city'.[2]

The popes set about a policy of rehabilitation both of the papacy as an institution and of Rome as the seat of the papacy. One of its elements was the provision of splendid new buildings. 'To create solid and stable conviction in the minds of the uncultured masses', Pope Nicholas V is said to have urged on his deathbed in 1455, 'there must be something which appeals to the eye. A popular faith sustained only on doctrines will never be anything but feeble and vacillating.' Faith could be strengthened by building. 'Noble edifices combining taste and beauty with imposing proportions would immensely contribute to the exaltation of the chair of St Peter's.'[3]

New buildings took the form of new religious foundations, new hospitals and splendid new churches, above all the new St Peter's, of which the foundation stone was laid in 1506. Huge new or enlarged palaces for the pope and cardinals were used for residence, justice and administration in the traditional manner. Everything possible was done to encourage private individuals to build new houses in new quarters of the town, or to rebuild or improve in the existing town. From 1480 owners of derelict houses had to sell to anyone who wanted to rebuild on their site, and owner-occupiers wanting to rebuild and enlarge their houses were allowed to make a compulsory purchase of adjacent properties if they were not owner-occupied; from 1565 to 1571 anyone wanting to rebuild was allowed compulsory purchase from his neighbours, regardless of their status or whether he was or was not going to occupy the new building; from 1574 the privilege was limited to those intending to build splendid houses which would embellish the town.[4]

Success was shown in the rise in population. From around 20,000 in 1450 it had risen to 55,000 according to the census of 1526–7. The sack of Rome by papal troops in 1527, followed by flood and disastrous harvests in the 1530s caused the population to decline again, but it was back to the 1526 level by about 1560, and in 1592 and 1600 the census showed populations of 97,000 and over 109,000.[5]

This was the resident population. But Rome was a pilgrimage city, and one sign of its success was an increase in the number of pilgrims. They came in especially large

97. (preceding page) Looking down the Via Pia to the Porta Pia, Rome. From the fresco in the Lateran Palace, Rome.

98. Pilgrims before St Peter's, 1575. By de Cavalleris (British Museum).

numbers in the Jubilee or Holy Years, which were re-inaugurated in 1450, and took place every twenty-five years. Hard evidence for the number of pilgrims in the early Jubilee Years is lacking, but the fact that 30,800 strangers died in Rome between Christmas and the feast day of St John (24 June) in 1500 suggests the figures which were involved. In 1549 Filippo Neri founded the hospital of Sta Trinità dei Pellegrini as a hospice for visiting pilgrims, and by 1575 there were seventeen confraternities in Rome engaged in looking after them. The pilgrimage figures rose to new heights in the last decades of the sixteenth century, under the influence of the Counter Reformation. In 1575 Sta Trinità put up 174,467 pilgrims, and the total number coming to Rome was probably about 400,000. In 1600 there were probably more than 500,000 visitors, of whom about 210,000 were looked after in Sta Trinità.[6]

One result of all these pilgrims was a traffic problem. The pilgrims came both individually and in groups of around one to two hundred people, representing different confraternities. The confraternities moved in procession together, carrying banners and wearing special robes. On their arrival in Rome they were often met by Roman confraternities and processed with them through the streets; and once in Rome they processed from pilgrimage church to pilgrimage church, and over the bridge to St Peter's. About four hundred confraternities came to Rome in 1525, and six hundred in 1600. In 1575 it was described how 'the pilgrims flow almost unceasingly and one can scarcely move in the roads'.[7] In 1450 the crush of pilgrims crossing the Ponte S. Angelo on their way to St Peter's was already so great that large numbers were pushed off the bridge and were drowned.[8]

Traffic problems were increased by the entourages of the cardinals, and of the pope himself. There were around forty cardinals permanently resident in Rome in the early sixteenth century, and seventy by 1570, along with a dozen or more permanent embassies. The average size of a cardinal's household was around 150 people, and, although a few relatively poor cardinals had to make do with smaller ones, others belonging to powerful families had households of 350 to 500.[9] The ambassadors and a few important papal officials or Roman nobles had households not so far below the cardinals' average. Whenever a cardinal or ambassador rode out in the city it was beneath his dignity to travel without a large retinue of perhaps half his household. The cardinals were constantly processing to and from their residences, either to attend services at their curial churches or elsewhere, or to sit on the papal consistories which ran the Church and membership of which was their main reason for being in Rome. Ambassadors, apart from regular visits to the papal court or each other, made state entries into Rome, escorted by processions of cardinals and notables; and any movement of the pope himself was likely to be even more of an occasion.

A final complication was provided by carriages. Carriages for rich men or women to travel in, as an alternative to riding on horseback or being carried in litters, first became a prominent feature in cities in the second half of the sixteenth century, when improvements in springing made them sufficiently comfortable to be enjoyable. Rome had more of them earlier than any other city. In the 1570s or thereabouts Cardinal Charles Borromeo said that two things were necessary for success in Rome, to love God and to own a carriage.[10] By 1594 there were 888 carriages in Rome, owned by 675 people; the grander ones were pulled by six horses. Eighty of them escorted Marquis Ambrosio Spinola when he went to have an audience with the pope in 1598.[11]

Rome was never important either as a manufacturing or as a trading city. What heavy merchandise came into it mostly came by the Tiber to the two river harbours above and below the city. But even without commercial traffic, the effect of the crush of pilgrims, carriages, retinues, religious processions and everyday movement in the narrow and confused streets of the medieval city was sufficiently chaotic. It was equally difficult both to move around and to find the way from place to place, especially for pilgrims who did not know the city. From the 1470s until the end of the sixteenth century successive popes did their best to improve the circulation, by building new roads and bridges or by improving the existing ones.[12]

In the 1470s Sixtus IV set out to relieve the expected pressure of traffic on the Ponte S. Angelo in the Holy Year of 1475. He built a second bridge further upstream, the Ponte Sisto, an additional approach from the Ponte S. Angelo to St Peter's on one side of the Tiber, and a new road connecting it to what is now known as the Corso on the other. This road, today the Via dei Coronari, was called at the time the Via Recta, the straight street, evidence of how unusual such a street was in Rome at the time. For the Holy Year of 1500 Alexander VI made yet another approach road from the bridge to St Peter's, the Via Alessandrina; it too was sometimes referred to as the Via Recta. Alexander specifically stated that it was built for the convenience of pilgrims, especially in Holy Year, as well as for that of the citizens and papal court. Between 1503 and 1513 Julius II built the long Via Giulia along the bank of the Tiber; it was planned to end in another new bridge joining it to yet another grand new approach to St Peter's, but this was never built. He improved the southern approaches to the Ponte S. Angelo still further by forming what is now the Via Sto Spirito; and in the 1520s Leo X joined the bridge to what is now the Piazza del Popolo by the Via Leonina, today's Via di Ripetta.

Various other popes made or projected other road improvements; Pope Paul III (1534–50), for instance, widened and straightened the west end of the Corso up to the Piazza del Popolo, perhaps partly for the convenience of the carnival races, and formed the road now known as the Via Paolina, as a third road coming into the piazza, to serve new houses on the northern edge of the city.[13]

The popes seem from early on to have realized that new streets, apart from their value in improving the flow of traffic, could produce handsome new buildings on the sites to either side, and did their best to encourage them. But at what stage was an aesthetic quality in the straight vista of the street itself first perceived? To answer this question one needs to look at other Italian cities as well as Rome, especially at Florence. The connections between the two cities were very close in the sixteenth century. Florentine bankers ran the papal finances, almost exclusively at some periods and to a considerable extent at others. There were three Medici popes in the century. Rome relied heavily on Florence for luxury goods, especially for the silks, velvets and cloth of gold worn in religious ceremonies or at the papal court. As the century went on it acquired its own luxury industries, but these were dominated by the Florentine colony in Rome. Florentines were jewellers, sculptors, painters, dealers and booksellers. Ideas pioneered in Florence were often developed in Rome. The aesthetic possibilities of the straight street was one of them.

It is perhaps more than coincidence that the two cities in which this aesthetic first developed both had a traffic problem. Florence's need to deal with wagons carrying corn, wool, cloth and other merchandise and its lack of waterways to supplement the road system have already been described. As a result, by the fifteenth century it already had more and longer straight streets than any other city in Europe.

The improvement to the Via S. Gallo in Florence in the 1320s, was designed to increase both the 'beauty and utility' of the city of Florence, and to make the streets 'rectilinear' as well as 'attractive'[14]. This might seem to show an early perception of a straight street as visually desirable as well as convenient. But more probably it was the new building involved in the improvement that was considered beautiful and attractive, rather than the rectilinearity. Certainly a description of Florence written in the early 1420s, although it singles out wide, straight and uncluttered streets ('dirette e larghe e tutte aperte') as one of the features of Florence, does not describe them as beautiful, although the adjective is applied to many other features of the city.[15] The great paean to the beauties of Florence written by Benedetto Dei in 1472 does not mention its straight streets at all.[16]

It is tempting to connect appreciation of straight streets with the development of the science of perspective. It was in fifteenth-century Florence that this science was first developed as a means of expressing the relationship of objects to each other in space, and as a result people began to see things in a completely different way. But, if so, it was a long time before artists used their skill in perspective more than occasionally to represent long enclosed vistas, common though these were in Florence; to begin with they clearly got more enjoyment in using it to define the relationship of free-standing objects to each other.[17]

In fact it is not until the mid-sixteenth century that anything that might be called an aesthetic of straight streets became apparent. It showed itself in a number of ways: in drawings or paintings depicting long streets vanishing into the distance, or alter-

99. (right) Perspective stage-set by Vincenzo Scamozzi in the Teatro Olimpico, Vicenza.

100. (bottom) The Via Garibaldi (1558–70, former Strada Nuova), Genoa.

natively ending in a distinctive feature; in the actual building of streets which achieved, in a clearly deliberate way, the effect of the drawings; in the placing of objects to close the vista in existing streets; and in the appearance of the landscape equivalent of straight streets, long alleys or avenues in formal gardens. It was as though people had suddenly realized the aesthetic possibilities of something which had been around them for years.

Genoa was responsible for one of the most important landmarks. Its Strada Nuova was determined on in 1550, and mostly built between 1558 and 1570; it provided a 750-foot vista enclosed by grand palaces all spaced out at the same intervals and of the same height, although not of the same design.[18] It was known and admired by the Florentine Giorgio Vasari, who thought that in the whole of Italy there was no street 'more magnificent and grand'.[19] His own Uffizi followed hard on it, and was an even more powerful dramatization of a vista, owing to the buildings following the same design on both sides. In Florence, too, free-standing columns were erected on three piazzas to terminate vistas down two or more streets, in 1563, 1572 and possibly as early as 1539.[20] In the second half of the century stage designers began to make a vista down one or more streets into a feature of their stage sets. Such vistas survive in their most dramatic form in the three streets of false perspective in the theatre in Vicenza; the theatre had been designed by Palladio in 1580 but the stage set was incorporated into it in 1585 to the design of Scamozzi.

The creation of the Via Pia in 1561–2 should be seen against this background. It was designed for Pius IV,

101. Looking between the two wings of the Uffizi (G. Vasari, 1560–80) to the Palazzo Vecchio, Florence.

a Medici pope, by a Florentine artist and architect, Michelangelo. Unlike its predecessors it could not be viewed as a necessary traffic improvement; it went through land that was scarcely built on. What it undeniably achieved was to produce an effect of state and magnificence, and in doing so to exalt the reputation of Pius IV, whose name the street and gate bore.

Here again it was following an example set in Florence by Pius IV's cousin, Duke Cosimo de' Medici. It was he who had erected at least two of the columns, to celebrate his victories. The purpose of the Uffizi was to consolidate the Arti, the Mercanzia and other Florentine buildings under his control in one group of buildings; it was perhaps not accidental that the tower of the Palazzo Vecchio, which had become his own ducal palace, appeared prominently, even if off centre, at the end of the vista. In 1594 an equestrian statue of him was set up on the Piazza della Signoria; it both closed the axial vista down the Via de Cerchi and seems to have been deliberately designed to be seen, even if not axially, from as far as possible along the other streets leading into the piazza, including the central way of the Uffizi. Both he and Pius IV had realized, in fact, not only that statues, columns and gates contributed to the glory, and therefore to the power, of the regime, but that placing them at the end of a vista increased the range and impact of their message.

The works of the earlier popes in building or improving roads in Rome culminated in the road system of Sixtus V, who was pope from 1585 to 1590.[21] Sixtus was building on the ideas and achievements of others, and his roads have had a little more than their rightful share of fame. Nevertheless, they were a remarkable achievement. In 1575 a commentator had remarked that the new roads in Rome were fine as far as they went, but that they did not go far enough; they did not form a comprehensive system.[22] Moreover, they scarcely touched the old city, where visitors still continually had to ask the way through a rabbit-warren of alleys. Sixtus was a remorselessly efficient man. He set out with ruthless determination to turn his rule into a dictatorship, at the expense of the cardinals; and with similar ruthlessness he determined to cover the whole of Rome with a criss-cross network of major streets, demolishing existing buildings where necessary, and marking the intersections with obelisks. His ostensible purpose was to make it easier for pilgrims and others to find their way from church to church; the columns and obelisks were to act as signposts.

In fact, the most difficult parts of the system were never built, owing to Sixtus's death in 1590 and the expense and obstruction met with in cutting roads through heavily built-up areas. A huge Egyptian obelisk was hauled into position in front of St Peter's in 1586, but the new road that was to make it visible from the Ponte S. Angelo was not built till Mussolini's day. A road to link the obelisk in front of Sta Maria Maggiore to Trajan's Column was started but never reached the column, owing to the obstructionism of a hotel-keeper who owned property in the way.

What was achieved was almost all on the higher ground to the north-east of Rome,

DVM·RECTAS·AD·TEMPLA·VIAS·SANCTISSIMA·PANDIT
IPSE·SIBI·SIXTVS·PANDIT·AD·ASTRA·VIAM

102–3. (top left) The straight street in Florence. Street games in the Via d' Tornabuoni, looking up to and away from the column in the Piazza Sta Trinità.

104. (left) Sixtus V's street plan for Rome. From the fresco in the Sistine Library, the Vatican.

105. (above) The Piazza del Popolo, Rome, in 1604. From the painting by W. Van Nieulandt.

where the land was only thinly built on, or not built on at all. A web of roads connected the church of Trinità del Monti and the great basilicas of Sta Maria Maggiore, S. Giovanni in Laterano, Sta Croce in Gerusalemme and S. Lorenzo fuori le Mura. Sixtus's best-known achievement, on the Piazza del Popolo, in fact owed least to him. The three roads converging on the piazza were there already; the two domed churches at their junction were not built until the 1660s. His, however, was the idea of erecting an obelisk at the spot where the sight-lines of the three roads converged.

In addition to Sixtus's avowed intention of improving connections between the major churches, it is hard to believe that he was not also interested in improving the ease of movement in Rome generally. He was also well aware that new roads would help in developing the growth of a new quarter of Rome to the north-west. Special privileges were given to anyone building in the neighbourhood of the Quirinal Palace, Pius IV's Via Pia, and his own Via Felice. His predecessor Gregory XIII had started building the Quirinal in 1583; Sixtus V continued his work, and rebuilt the Lateran Palace as a summer residence. A prejudice had arisen against the low-lying Vatican as unhealthy; the malaria in that part of Rome may have been getting worse. The Quirinal, in fact, developed into the main seat of the popes in the 1590s, and remained so until 1870.

The new roads, as new roads usually do, attracted traffic, and this traffic was not always there simply in order to get from A to B. Owners of carriages were anxious to show them off and found that a pleasant way of doing so was to drive up and down the new roads. As it was enjoyable to see and be seen by as many other owners of coaches as possible while doing so, the custom arose (once again, probably initiated in Florence) of driving up and down in a particular place at a particular time—usually the cool of the evening. The custom gave a new meaning to the word 'corso': a course for parading on, rather than racing. Evelyn described how the piazza facing the Palazzo Farnese was the place where 'in summer the gentlemen of Rome take the fresco in their coaches and on foot'.[24] But the piazza was comparatively cramped; not surprisingly, the Via Pia, as the broadest and most scenic of the new roads, began to be used in the same way, as was celebrated in a seventeenth-century rhyme:[25]

A Rome à Porte Pie
L'esté, on fait le Cours.
Souvent sans qu'il ennuye
L'on y fait quinze tours.
C'est la qu'on voit paraître
Femmes, moines, et prêtres
Et c'est a qui lèvera plus haut le cu
Pour rendre le salut.*

The revival and continuous expansion of Renaissance Rome would have been impossible without an ample supply of good water.[26] To begin with this was completely lacking. By the fifteenth century the great aqueducts which had supplied classical Rome with water had fallen into ruin. The first attempt to repair them was carried out by the architect Alberti for Nicholas V in 1453. He restored the classical aqueduct which brought the water supply known as Acqua Virgo from Salone, seven miles west of Rome on the road to Tivoli. The water came to several fountains in the centre of the city, but the main outlet was the Trevi fountain. The supply was improved under Sixtus IV and Leo X but remained inadequate; the Trevi fountain dried up in summer. In 1535 most of the inhabitants of Rome were still relying on wells, or buying Tiber water from water-carriers, who filled their water-sacks with clean water upstream, and came down into the town to sell it.

Between 1566 and 1575 an extra supply-line from Salone was constructed, which brought ample water to (among others) the Trevi fountain and fountains in the Piazzas Navona, Colonna, Pantheon, del Popolo and Mattei. But these were all still in the lower town. Any extensive development of the upper ground was impossible without water, and accordingly when Gregory XIII started to build what became the Quirinal Palace in 1583 he also began to construct a new aqueduct bringing water from Pantano de Griffi, about twenty miles south-east of Rome, on the way to Palestrina. The system was completed by Sixtus V, and by 1586 the whole Quirinal area was abundantly supplied with the water called the Acqua Felice. Finally, in 1609, Pope Paul V restored an aqueduct originally built by the Emperor Augustus, and brought what was called

*At Rome, the Porta Pia / Is the place for summer parading / Often, without getting bored / Fifteen turns can be made there. / And there one can watch the sight / Of women, monks and priests / And the prize goes to whoever pays his respects / By sticking his bum up the highest.

106. The Fontanone dell'Acqua Felice (1587), Rome. From a late seventeenth-century engraving.

the Acqua Paola thirty-five miles to the Fontanone della Acqua Paola in Trastevere, across the Tiber. From there it came down to the Vatican.

Rome now had the best water supply of any of the big cities of Europe. By 1600 thirty-five new fountains had been put into service since 1575, and the city was being supplied with 20,000 m^3 of drinking water a day. Although decorative fountains had already been built in cities (the Fonte Gaia, of 1409–19, in Siena was a notable example), the first Roman fountains seem to have been completely utilitarian; certainly the Trevi fountain remained so until it was replaced in the mid-eighteenth century. It was perhaps, once again, the example of Florence which set Rome off. The much less ambitious water systems inaugurated by Duke Cosimo in Florence in the 1560s culminated in the elaborate Neptune fountain in the Piazza della Signoria, made by Giovanni da Bologna in 1565–75; a smaller but elegant market fountain centred round a statue had been erected in the Piazza S. Lorenzo in 1543.[27] In Rome it was the arrival of the second supply of Acqua Virgo in 1575 which seems to have brought the realization that city fountains could be ornamental as well as useful; soon it became apparent that, like obelisks, columns, statues and gates, they could also be used to glorify the papacy in general and the pope who set them up in particular.

A number of decorative fountains were built as suppliers of Acqua Virgo. The most elaborate was the circle of spouting dolphins in the Piazza Navona installed in 1575; the same architect's well-known fountain of 1581–8 in the Piazza Mattei was not embellished with bronze boys and tortoises until the 1650s. But all the fountains were of a modest scale, compared with what was to come. The finest of Sixtus V's fountains,

107. (above) Looking up the Via de Servi to the Piazza SS. Annunziata, Florence. From an anonymous seventeenth-century painting (Museo Firenze Com'era, Florence).

108. (top right) A papal procession on the Capitoline Square, Rome. From an anonymous seventeenth-century painting.

109. (bottom right) View of Livorno, *c.* 1600. From a fresco by B. Poccetti (Pitti Palace, Florence).

the Fontanone dell'Acqua Felice, set a new standard of grandeur and elaboration: as Evelyn described it in 1644, 'in it is a basso-relievo of white marble, representing Moses striking the rock, which is adorned with camels, men, women, and children drinking, as large as life; a work for the design and vastness truly magnificent'.[28] Paul V's Acqua Paola fountain was even more magnificent, and in a superb position, on a hill above the city where, as Evelyn described it, the morning sun lit up the waters to make 'a most glorious show'.[29] After that, pope after pope rebuilt fountains with all the effervescence of the baroque, until the Roman fountains became one of the delights and marvels of the world.

Another new feature which begins to make its first somewhat tentative appearance in Rome and Tuscany at this period is the city square designed as a unity. In the Middle Ages the idea that a large main square surrounded with handsome buildings contributed to the beauty as well as the utility of a city had been widely recognized, and carefully worded building regulations made certain, for instance, that houses built by private individuals in the Campo at Siena did not fall below a certain standard. But to build a whole square to an integrated symmetrical design was an alien concept. The Renaissance, to begin with, made no difference: a number of lovely paintings of ideal city squares survive from the fifteenth century, and they all show the squares surrounded by buildings of harmonious classical design, but without any symmetrical relationship to each other.

Courtyards of palaces, however, had been built to a symmetrical design from at least the early fifteenth century; and it was perhaps the emergence of individual rulers in Italian cities, and the concept of city spaces which were glorifications of the ruler rather than the city which led to city squares being treated with something of the unity of a palace court.

At Vigevano, a silk-manufacturing town in the duchy of Milan built under the shadow of a castle of the dukes, Duke Ludovic the Moor (who had been born in the castle) ordered the rebuilding of the market square in 1492. The new market was surrounded on three sides with arcades in the traditional manner, but they, and the facades above them, were all given the same treatment, so that, although the square is not by any means completely symmetrical, it gives a unified architectural impression.[30]

Bramante was the architect of the Vigevano piazza. In 1499 he went to Rome where,

among much else, he designed the large double court of the Belvedere, rising up the hill behind the Vatican. This was essentially a palace court, but designed to be big enough to accommodate tournaments and other entertainments; its great size may have suggested the possibilities of a similar treatment in a city context.[31]

Michelangelo's design for remodelling the Capitol in Rome was even more suggestive. Although it was more a court surrounded by the buildings of the city government than a piazza in the traditional sense, it was a brilliantly original design accessible to all in the middle of the city, and had obvious potentialities for imitation. Michelangelo's design put a new front on the Palazzo dei Senatori, the seat of the city government, remodelled the Palazzo dei Conservatori, which contained the city guilds and other city institutions, and placed a matching building opposite it, the only function of which seems to have been to complete the design. All three buildings were symmetrically grouped around the Roman statue of Marcus Aurelius on horseback, which had been set up there a few decades earlier; and in a manner reminiscent of the vista of the Via Pia, on a smaller scale, a great flight of shallow steps was carried up the hill to the open side of the square, aligned on the statue and on the steps and main entrance of the Palazzo dei Senatori beyond it.[32]

Michelangelo's design was engraved in 1568, but it took a long time in building. The Palazzo dei Conservatori was refaced in 1564–8, but the Palazzo dei Senatori was not remodelled until about 1592–1605 (although the entrance staircase had been started earlier), and the matching block opposite the Conservatori was not built until 1644–5. It was the Medici dukes, not the popes, who were responsible for the first fully symmetrical square to be built in Europe.

This was in Livorno, the port of Tuscany.[33] Livorno had been the dukes' answer to the silting up of the river at Pisa, which had previously served as the seaport for Florence. Work on a new harbour there was started in 1571, and it ultimately became the second port in Italy after Genoa. It offered the curious combination of freedom in religion and the main market for the slave trade in the western Mediterranean; the former was proclaimed in 1606 by Duke Ferdinand and brought an influx of Jews, Greeks, Moors and political and religious refugees of all kinds to swell the population. The town was planned as a working commercial one, not on an especially grand scale. It had two piazzas, a great open piazza on the harbour front, which was the site of the slave market, and the cathedral piazza in the centre of the town. This was a symmetrical square of arcaded buildings, grouped round the columned portico of the Duomo. It seems to have been designed in the 1590s, but the cathedral portico was not built until 1605.

In the early seventeenth century the dukes of Tuscany also embellished the Piazza degli Innocenti in Florence, and finished off its gradual evolution towards a kind of *ad hoc* symmetry. The loggia of the Ospedale degli Innocenti (built in about 1423) had been approximately matched across the square by the loggia of the Confraternity of the Servi di Maria in 1516; the church of the Annunziata, at the end of the square, was given a grand portico looking axially across the square and down the Via de Servi in 1601–7; a statue of Duke Ferdinand on horseback was imposed on the axis in 1608 and fountains added to either side in 1643.

Remarkable and enjoyable as the fountains, vistas, and open spaces of Rome were, they were only one facet of its character. When John Evelyn finally left Rome after a seven months' visit, he describes how 'turning about to behold this once and yet glorious city from an eminence, I did not without some regret give it my last farewell'.[34] Montaigne found that, even though he knew no one there, his visit kept him from the melancholy which plagued him.[35] Rome was unique. By the end of the sixteenth century it was less like any city that had existed before in Europe, than it was like Paris, London, Vienna, Berlin and New York as they were to develop over the succeeding centuries. It was the precursor of the great modern capital cities, at once large, cosmopolitan, complex, grand and tolerant, full of variety and extremes, regarded by some as a cess-pool of iniquity and by others as a haven of delight. But like all great cities it had its own kind of complexity.

Admittedly, much of what was to become commonplace in later cities existed in Rome only in embryo. Operas, plays and entertainments were constantly being put on, in colleges or palaces after dinner, or on carts or temporary platforms for feasts and festivals; but there were no permanent opera houses or theatres, just as bullfights and tournaments were still being put on in public squares, rather than purpose-built amphitheatres. There were no public libraries as such, but on the other hand the Vatican library, one of the greatest libraries in the world, was freely available to all, as Montaigne remarked in 1580–1: 'Anyone may visit it, and make what extracts he likes; it is open almost every morning.'[36] There were no museums; but the collections which filled the galleries and courtyards of the villas were almost all open to visitors, although access to the palaces was harder to arrange. Moreover, from 1566 the popes had been giving classical antiquities to the Palazzo dei Conservatori. This formed an increasing public collection which was originally kept in a room in the palazzo; later, when the building on the third side of Michelangelo's courtyard was finally erected, in 1645, some of the collection was moved into it and it became the world's first public museum.[37] There were no public gardens; but the gardens of villas were as open as their galleries.

In fact Rome in 1600 was not the largest city in Europe: Paris, London, Venice, Naples and Milan were certainly larger. But it had the edge on all the others because it was a genuine international capital. More than that, it was superimposed on the ruins of an earlier capital that was equally international; it was both 'once and yet' glorious. This gave it a unique double image. Those rebuilding it after the return of the popes were conscious that they were reviving ancient Rome as well as rescuing Christian Rome—or, rather, that they were both reviving the former and Christianizing it. The inscription, classical in style and lettering, on the house which Lorenzo de' Medici built for himself in Rome in 1468 referred to it as being built 'urbe Roma in pristinam formam renascente'.[38] The great Egyptian obelisk, brought to Rome in the imperial days, which Sixtus V re-erected before St Peter's, was dedicated to the True Cross, a fragment of which was placed in a container at its apex. Its inscription ran, 'Sextus V Pont. Max. cruci invictae obeliscum vaticanum ab impia superstitione expiatum iustius et felicitus consecrat'.

In 1463 Sixtus IV called Rome 'the capital of the universe'.[39] For Erasmus in 1527 it was 'the common mother of all peoples'.[40] In 1580 Montaigne found it 'the only town which is universal and common to everyone'.[41] In 1592, when Cardinal Odoardo Farnese visited the Jesuit college in the Piazza Altieri, twenty-seven languages were being spoken in the refectory.[42] In 1644 Evelyn saw, under the dome of St Peter's, 'confession-seats, for all languages, Hebrew, Greek, Latin, Spanish, Italian, French,

English, Irish, Welsh, Slavonian, Dutch, as it is written on their friezes in golden capitals'.[43] Rome was the most cosmopolitan of European cities, in terms of resident foreign colonies as well as of visiting tourists, priests and pilgrims. There were very large Spanish, and sizeable French and German colonies. Printers, butchers and innkeepers tended to be German, prostitutes and courtesans to be Spanish, solicitors to be French, and bargees to be Corsican. There were tight little groups of French, Dutch and Flemish artists and sculptors. The builders came from Lombardy, the sailors living round the river port were mostly Genoese. The bankers came from Genoa, Florence, Siena and Augsburg. The priests came from everywhere, including England.[44]

Its dual role as the capital of western Christendom and the successor of Imperial Rome made it a centre for politics, finance, education, science, art, archaeology, tourism, entertainment and pleasure, as well as for religion. A series of overlapping circles catered for the different activities; it was possible to move in one or two of them, or to savour them all; there were more options available in Rome than in any other European city.

Both as a religious capital and as capital of the biggest independent Italian state, decisions taken in Rome had political implications all over Europe, and vice versa: hence the papal legates in other capitals, and the ambassadors in Rome. The need to pass information between embassies and capitals made Rome a major communications centre; it had the best information service in Europe. The papal court and most of the embassies had their own couriers, but the messenger services run by the big merchant bankers tended to be better and more accurate. As a result the area in which the merchant bankers lived and worked—around the Vie dei Banchi Nuovi and del Banco di Sto Spirito—was the news centre for Rome. It was on the basis of news gathered from the banks that the *menanti*, the street news-sellers, sold handwritten news-sheets from at least the 1570s which were among the ancestors of modern newspapers.[45]

The main function of the merchant bankers was to raise money to service the increasing papal debts. But they also ran the papal alum mine at Tolfa—the biggest in Europe, and an important money-spinner for the papal treasury—imported, stored and speculated in the grain from the Roman marches and southern Italy which kept Rome alive, and supplied pope, cardinals and Roman nobles with silks, velvets and every variety of luxury goods.

Rome was never a manufacturing city on a large scale, although if Sixtus V had had his way he would have put the Acqua Felice to industrial use, and turned the Colosseum into a textile factory.[46] But, like all important capitals, it developed luxury industries, which gradually supplemented and to some extent replaced the goods imported from Florence, Venice and other Italian cities. The combined needs of churches and great households in Rome provided a market which attracted artists, architects, jewellers and goldsmiths from all over Italy to come and settle there. The growing reputation of their products attracted foreign buyers, especially the agents of foreign kings or princes. But these only really became important in the second half of the seventeenth century; up till then so many commissions were being given in Rome itself that it was hard for outsiders to get a foot in the market.

110. (preceding pages) The Piazza Navona, Rome, in the early seventeenth century.

But Rome could produce old works of art as well as new ones. In the course of the sixteenth century more and more people, from the pope downwards, became interested in collecting classical antiquities of all kinds, and a comfortable little industry developed, concerned with digging up, restoring, reproducing and selling them. In the late fifteenth century Florence had been a pioneer in this as in so much else; the Medici and other Florentine humanists were more assiduous collectors than the Romans. Rome took the lead in the sixteenth century, and at the same time foreigners began to show an interest in classical art and archaeology. In the 1540s, for instance, François I had around sixty plaster casts of famous classical statues made in Rome and transported to France, where bronze copies were made from them. Both the trade in antiquities, and in the making and selling of plaster casts or other forms of copy, was to increase enormously in the later seventeenth and eighteenth centuries.[47]

In the sixteenth century there was less need for copies, because it was so easy to dig up the originals. Imperial Rome had been a huge city; an apparently limitless supply of its artefacts, submerged underground by the passage of time, was only just beginning to be tapped, and much of it was easy of access. Renaissance Rome was largely contained within the walls which had been built by Marcus Aurelius in the third century. Their size and extent gave Rome a scale greater than its population, for very large areas within the walls were open land or only thinly built on. The whole area around the Forum and Colosseum came into this class, and was in striking contrast to the heavily built-up area of the medieval city next door.

One result of this was that into the eighteenth century much of Rome was given over to vineyards or grazing. Cattle browsed over the Forum and in the winter shepherds brought their sheep down from the hills to graze the city pastures around the Colosseum and elsewhere, camped in the ruins, and played their bagpipes as they watched their flocks. In the late sixteenth century the great marble basin that today forms part of the fountain between the marble horses on the Quirinal Hill was serving as a cattle trough in the Forum.[48]

Another result of the low building density in Rome was that, outside the medieval centre, there were self-sown trees and common open spaces everywhere, but especially on the hills and along the river. There was also space for many private enclosures, so that elaborate private gardens, usually built round a villa, became one of the great features of Rome. These villas were not necessarily designed for living in: they were more often places to which people who had a main residence in the centre of the city—popes, cardinals, bankers or other great people—could go for the day or a meal.[49] Some provided settings for their owner's classical statues or collections of pictures. They were used for entertainments on every scale, from intimate dinners for two or three people, to elaborate masques involving hundreds of people and costing a small fortune.

Rome was extraordinarily well provided with diversions of all varieties. The kind of events which in other cities might happen once every few months happened in Rome almost weekly. The arrival of an ambassador or a monarch, the marriage of a papal nephew, the feast days of individual nations, the carnival and religious feasts throughout the year, produced a constant succession of tournaments, bullfights, races, processions, plays and fireworks. The Piazza Navona, a classical arena which Sixtus IV had converted into the main market square of Rome in 1477, was much used for bullfights and tournaments, but in between, at all times of the year, jugglers, tightrope walkers, performing bears and other forms of entertainment were always to be found there.

The pilgrimage traffic in Rome had always had a tourist side to it, as was the case with pilgrims everywhere. Pilgrims did the rounds of the wonders of classical Rome,

which had their place in the *Mirabilia Urbis Romae*, the popular pilgrim's guide to Rome, first written in the mid-twelfth century, and copied and recopied with additions and variations for several hundred years. But in the seventeenth century more and more people were coming primarily to see, enjoy and shop in Rome, and on this type of visit religion played a minor role and sometimes no role at all.

When Montaigne came to Rome in 1580-1, he was on a tour of Italian spas in search of a cure for his gall-bladder; but he broke off from drinking the waters in order to spend several months in Rome. Like many other tourists, he complained that there were too many of his own countrymen in Rome. He toured the churches, listened to sermons for entertainment as much as for edification, inspected antiquities, gardens, vineyards and pleasure places, and visited the courtesans; according to his account, he visited them for conversation not sex, although even for the former he had to pay highly enough.[50]

One of the Aretino satires describes how foreigners would come to Rome for eight or ten days, and having seen 'le anticaglie', would want to see 'le modernaglie, cioe le signore'.[51] Courtesans were one of the features of Rome commented on by all visitors, and visited by many of them. They were a particular form of luxury goods, the direct result of the wealth, splendour and sexual imbalance of Rome. In the late sixteenth and early seventeenth centuries the ratio of men to women in Rome was around six to four; in Venice, where courtesans figured nearly as prominently as in Rome, it was about seven to six, in Florence, where they scarcely figured at all, about four to five. In Rome, the imbalance was due to the concentration of priests. The courtesans arose to cater for them in the easy-going years of the late fifteenth and early sixteenth centuries; but they were also much frequented by young nobles and rich visitors, and these kept up the demand where the Counter Reformation was reducing that from the clergy.[52]

A successful courtesan kept a carriage, lived in a fine and richly furnished house, could make elegant conversation, and had the latest books lying around, even if she did not necessarily read them. Some even had carpets on their floors, which was rare in those days. The Spanish ambassador, when visiting the famous courtesan Imperia, was afraid of dirtying the carpet by spitting on to it, and so spat on a servant instead. Imperia is said to have appreciated his consideration.[53] They were great church-goers; attending Sunday mass was an excellent way of showing themselves. They would arrive superbly dressed and accompanied by smart young admirers, and crowd the front benches. In the late fifteenth and early sixteenth centuries they frequented the church of S. Agostino, then the newest and most fashionable in Rome; several of them were buried there, under laudatory inscriptions. Many lived in the Borgo, next to St Peter's and the Vatican, for obvious reasons. In Counter Reformation times brief and unsuccessful efforts were made to expel them altogether and more successful ones to confine them to one quarter, in the Campo Marzo area around the Piazza del Popolo; in the 1599 census 438 of the 801 self-professed courtesans were living there.[54]

Whatever it was, Rome was not a conformist town. It was possible to live the life one chose there; there was room for all. In contrast to the splendid and ambitious cardinals, and the world of masques, banquets, politics and intrigue, one should remember the dedicated clergy working in the hospitals, the scholar-secretaries of great men, or an artist like Nicolas Poussin in the 1640s, living soberly and working hard, disliking

111. (top left) Two views in the garden of a Roman villa. By Christian Berentz (Galleria Corsini, Rome).

112. (bottom left) Celebration in honour of Queen Christina of Sweden in the courtyard of the Palazzo Barberini, Rome, 1656. By Filippo Lauri.

113. A Venetian courtesan painted as Venus. By Lambert Sustris, *c.* 1550 (Rijksmuseum, Amsterdam).

114. (right) Innocent X in procession by Bernini's fountain in the Piazza Navona, Rome. From an anonymous seventeenth-century painting.

excessive wealth or display, walking on the Pincian Hill for an hour or two in the early morning, painting all day, and emerging in the evening to stroll and talk on the Piazza di Spagna, where his friends among the foreigners used to gather.[55]

It could never be pretended that the right of free speech existed in Rome; but speech was freer there than anywhere else in Europe, except, perhaps, in Amsterdam. An extraordinary variety of belief, from rigid orthodoxy to extreme free-thinking was held and discussed in private, even if it was rash to make unorthodox views public. Satire flourished in Rome as nowhere else, most notoriously in the form of pasquinades; these were brief, barbed epigrams which were fixed anonymously in the night to a mutilated statue of Menalaus near the Via della Pace, and were circulated gleefully round the town the next day. The news-sheets of the *menanti* were remarkably outspoken, as Sixtus V's police complained. News-sheets from abroad, they reported, always had 'a suitably reverential and respectful tone. It is only at Rome, religious capital and haven for men of talent, that one hears of these criminal slanderers and disparagers of other people, men without fear of god or justice, who fill their papers with lies and slander', etc.[56]

Sixtus cracked down on them. But one needs to keep separate the permissive attitude of Roman society as a whole and the repressive actions of a few popes—notably Pius V and Sixtus V. Such popes were always disliked in Rome itself, and its inhabitants got their own back on them when they died. Rome at the height of the Counter Reformation must have been a little like Berlin in the 1930s: a tolerant city landed with a regime which it disliked but had to live with.

7 The Rise of the North

By the 1660s Rome was gloriously bankrupt. Its splendour had increasingly been paid for out of borrowed money. In those days, as in these, governments could run up debts with extraordinary ease, but in those days the bill had to be paid in the end.

The income of the pope was made up of two parts, 'spiritual', derived from his position as head of the Church, and 'material', derived from the Papal States.[1] In the early sixteenth century the material revenues came mainly from the Rome customs, the papal monopoly of salt and the Tolfa alum mines. The spiritual ones included *annates*, entry-taxes levied on those taking up benefices; 'compositions' paid in return for pardons or exemptions granted in the papal courts; 'tenths', special levies towards anything which could be described as a crusade; and sale of offices. The last was common in all European governments at the time; an office-holder bought his office for life, for a sum based on the profits which he reckoned could be made out of it.

The gross papal income was about 350,000 gold ducats; the combined income of the cardinals and other major benefice-holders was about twice as much again, but although this had notable effects on Roman buildings and life-style, it did not directly benefit the papacy. The income of the Venetian government in the same period was about three times as much as that of the papacy, and Venice spent much less lavishly. The policy of re-establishing their image and power by lavish building and life-style caused the popes to live well beyond their income.

Various devices were resorted to to increase it, most of them disastrous in the long run. From the late fifteenth century a number of sinecures were instituted, colleges of papal chamberlains, Knights of St Peter, and so on, and sold in return for the honour of the title and a life annuity. A public loan, the Monte, was inaugurated in 1526. In the Papal States a consumption tax was imposed from around 1530, and was followed in 1543 by the Triennial Subsidy, a heavy direct tax on property.

All this brought great wealth to the Roman bankers who raised the money and farmed the taxes. But it meant that year by year more and more of the papal income was spent on paying interest, and that the Papal States, in spite of their considerable wealth as one of the main grain-producing areas in Italy, were gradually taxed into poverty. Moreover, the spiritual income was sinking. The Reformation cut off important sources of revenue, and even the countries which remained Catholic were becoming increasingly unwilling to let church revenues go out of their countries. More generally, the Counter Reformation policy of making benefice-holders live in their benefices seriously diminished the income coming into Rome.

By the mid-seventeenth century the situation was becoming really serious, but that did not necessarily stop the popes from building. In the 1640s and 1650s Bernini's fountains on the Piazza Navona were financed by special taxes, on bread amongst others, which were bitterly resented by the Roman people. Obscene verses were circulated attacking Olimpia Pamphilia, the pope's ambitious sister-in-law, or were pinned to the rising stonework. The people wanted bread, not spires or fountains:

> Noi volemo altro che Guglie, e Fontane,
> Pane volemo, pane, pane, pane.[2]

The last extravagance was Bernini's colonnade in front of St Peter's, built against all dictates of financial good sense by Pope Alexander VII between 1656 and the mid-1660s. In 1661 the Venetian ambassador commented: 'The building of the colonnades which encircle the piazza of St Peter's will be an achievement to recall the greatness of ancient Rome . . . I am not going to discuss whether such efforts are advisable at the present moment . . . It is true that Rome is getting more and more buildings and fewer and fewer inhabitants . . . and in the Corso and the busiest streets one sees nothing but empty houses and the sign To Let.'[3]

By the 1670s Rome's great days as a city of lavish spending and consequent lavish patronage of the arts were over. Its decline was not entirely due to its own past extravagance, for Italy as a whole was in the doldrums. Italian merchants no longer ran Europe financially, dominated European commerce, and ploughed their profits into Italy. In the course of the sixteenth century the centre of European prosperity had already begun to move from the Mediterranean to the Atlantic coast; in the seventeenth century Italy finally settled down as an economic satellite of the north and west.

The main (though not the only) causes were the discovery of America and the opening up by the Portuguese of the sea route to the east. Italian, and especially Genoese, expertise had contributed to both. Christopher Columbus came from Genoa, Sebastian Cabot's family was Genoese by origin, Magellan's voyage round the world was partly financed by Genoese money; one of the first merchants settled in Goa was a Florentine. But it was the Atlantic coast which benefited; to begin with, above all, Antwerp, which for a few decades became the most prosperous city in Europe.

Antwerp had been Bruges's rival since the fourteenth century. It was the marketing centre and port for the Brabant textile industry, just as Bruges was for the Flemish one, and like Bruges it was a cloth manufacturing city as well as a cloth marketing one. To begin with the two cities were under the aegis of rival rulers, but in 1356 Antwerp was annexed by Flanders. The rivalry continued; but a ruler who favoured one city rather than the other was in a strong position to alter the balance.

In the later fifteenth century Antwerp sailed ahead of Bruges, for a number of reasons. The two cities reacted in radically different ways to the threat of their markets being undercut by cheaper English cloth. Bruges tried to keep English cloth out altogether, Antwerp started up a profitable industry importing unfinished English cloth and finishing it; the more that English cloth captured the market, the more Antwerp benefited at the expense of Bruges. Antwerp was much further from the open sea than Bruges: but at the same time as the Zwijn was silting up, the waterways leading up to Antwerp were being improved. Finally, Archduke Maximilian never forgave Bruges for its treatment of him and did everything that he could to move trade from it to Antwerp, by giving trade privileges to the latter and encouraging foreign merchants to move there. By 1500 Antwerp had effectively taken the place of Bruges, and become the main destination of the trading convoys from Venice and Genoa, and the city with which the Hanseatic traders were increasingly dealing, although they did not move their 'House' from Bruges to Antwerp until 1553. It had also developed a considerable overland trade, sending cloth to Germany and on to Italy in return for spices, as an alternative to the sea route.[4]

But what turned Antwerp from a prosperous city into a booming one was the Portuguese spice trade. This first came to Antwerp in 1501, in the form of one Lisbon-owned ship bringing a cargo of cinnamon and pepper from the east. In 1503 the Portuguese 'House' moved from Bruges to Antwerp, and Portuguese spice ships began to arrive more and more frequently. By 1509 they had driven the Venetian spice galleys out of the field by undercutting them. In 1505 Venetian pepper, imported by the old part-land, part-sea route, was selling at twenty Flemish groats a pound: Portuguese pepper, imported by sea all the way, cost between sixteen and eighteen groats, and was down to fifteen by 1510.[5]

Antwerp had a double attraction for the Portuguese. It was a conveniently central market in which they could sell spices and other eastern goods for distribution to northern and central Europe, and to France. And in Antwerp they could buy silver and copper. They needed silver to exchange for spices in India, where it was in short supply and great demand, and copper for barter in the African slave and ivory trade.

Antwerp imported its silver and copper overland from Augsburg, which had control of the silver and copper mines in central Europe. On the triple basis of English cloth, German metals and Portuguese spices Antwerp soared to prosperity. Genoa shared

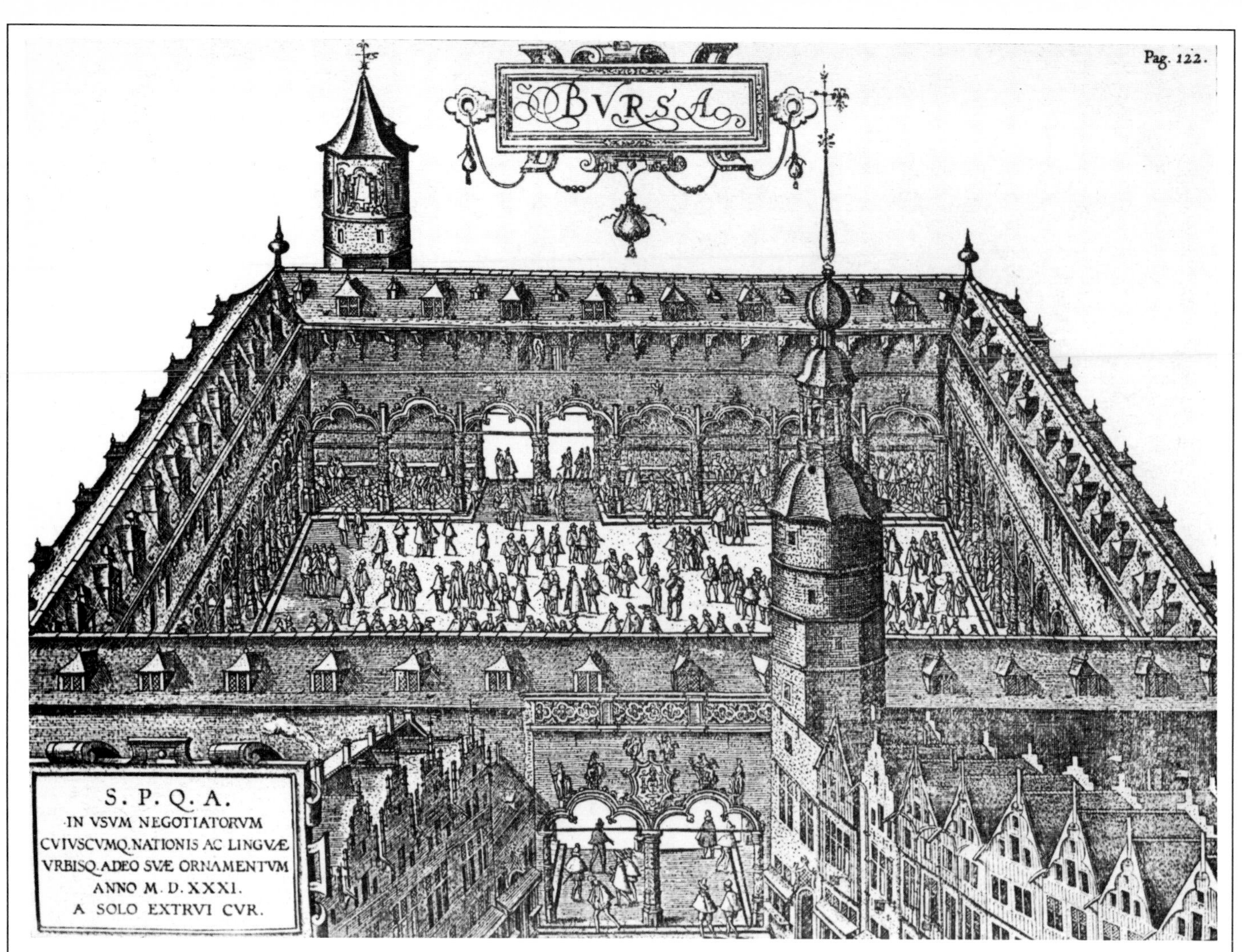

115. The Antwerp Exchange (Dominicus van Waghemaker, 1531). From an engraving in Guicciardini's *Description of Antwerp*.

in this, because Genoese bankers and entrepreneurs were well dug into the Portuguese economy. So, even more, did Augsburg, especially the Fuggers, the leading Augsburg merchants and bankers. Moreover, Antwerp diversified: in addition to finishing English cloth it moved into the newly fashionable market for lightweight textiles made with Spanish wool; its products ranged from salted herring to printed books, of which it was the main supplier to northern markets.

Big German, Portuguese, Spanish, Genoese and English colonies settled there. It attracted trade by the facilities which it provided, as well as by its convenient position. It was the most up-to-date port of the day. It had excellent quays at which sizeable ships could berth, all along the River Scheldt between the city walls and the water. The quays were well equipped with cranes, and inland canals enabled goods to be transported by water from the quays over most of the city. Carters from Hesse, in central Germany, provided overland transport from their depot in the city, which still survives. The city built the depot for them, and also provided excellent buildings for the Portuguese, English and Hanseatic merchants.[6]

Above all, in Antwerp the merchants could meet in the Bourse, or exchange, which was superior to anything previously seen in Europe. The name, but little else, came from the Buerseplaats in Bruges. Already in 1469 Antwerp had built what came to be called the old Bourse, in the form of a cloister, the first known example of this building-type adopted for use by merchants. The new Bourse, which was opened in 1531, was on the same lines, but much larger. An inscription over the entrance pro-

116. The Royal Exchange, London, in 1644. From the engraving by Wenceslaus Hollar (Guildhall Library, London).

claimed that it was for all nations (unlike the Bourse at Bruges which had been mainly frequented by Italians). It included, in addition to the walks and court, two storeys of shops selling pictures and luxury goods, the lower opening on to the walks, the upper in galleries above. It set a pattern which the larger exchanges were to follow all over Europe for the next few hundred years. London copied it in 1566–70, and Amsterdam in 1608–13.

The Bourse was described and illustrated in 1566 by Luigi Guicciardini, a Florentine merchant living in Antwerp, nephew of Francesco, the historian and politician.[7] What especially impressed him about the Bourse was its freedom from horse traffic or traffic of any other kind; there was nothing to disturb the merchants when they crowded both the open court and the walks for an hour at one o'clock and an hour in the evening, which were the recognized times for business. Merchants and merchant bankers came there to exchange information, set up deals, make bargains, negotiate loans, deal in bills of exchange, insure shipping, and buy and sell city bonds, issued both in Antwerp and in other places. In the sixteenth century charging interest on loans began to become respectable. It was officially recognized by the Emperor Charles V in 1543, and gradually condoned by the Church. In the same period marine insurance greatly increased, and the practice began to grow up of assigning, endorsing and discounting bills of exchange and the 'letters obligatory' by which merchants, when buying on credit, promised to pay a debt within a certain period. These documents, instead of being tied to particular people, began to be bought and sold as a form of

117. Bird's-eye view of Antwerp in 1635.

paper money. Goods in Antwerp were increasingly sold by sample, especially in a smaller exchange which the city built in the mid-century for the English cloth merchants. Antwerp was the pioneer in all these developments.[8] Its merchants had enthusiastically adopted double-entry bookkeeping in the Italian manner, and it was from Antwerp rather than Italy that the practice spread over the rest of Europe. The impressive buildings of the Bourse advertised the city's supremacy in business methods, as well as its prosperity.

Inevitably, the population of Antwerp increased, until by 1560 it may have been approaching a hundred thousand. The city grew, and new walls were built in 1543–53. Here again Antwerp showed how progressive it was by commissioning an Italian military engineer fgrom Bergamo to provide it with one of the earliest and most splendid examples of the new Renaissance-style of fortifications, evolved for use against cannon. These were pierced with gates, some of which took the form of triumphal arches in the classical style. The grandest was the St George's Gate, by which the Emperor Charles V, who had inherited Flanders from his grandfather Maximilian in 1516, made a 'joyous entry' to the city in 1545.[9]

The walls enclosed a large area previously unbuilt on to the north of the town. This area, known as the 'new town', was laid out with canals and quays, in the Bruges manner, but to a regular plan based on three parallel canals. The whole area was developed by Gilbert van Schoonbeke, a remarkable and able man who was one of the first Europeans to develop property on a large scale. His father, also Gilbert, had been responsible for at least one new street in the 1520s; in the 1540s and early 1550s, as Antwerp boomed and property values rose, Gilbert the younger laid out streets and built houses all over the city on what had previously been orchards and gardens. When the city got into financial difficulties over building the walls in 1548, van Schoonbeke took the contract over.[10]

Antwerp also supplied itself with a fine series of public buildings. In the beginning

118. Fireworks on the main square before the town hall, Antwerp, to celebrate the entry of Archduke Ernest in 1594 (Plantin-Moretus Museum, Antwerp).

of the century the butchers' hall was built and the medieval cathedral finished off with one of the tallest spires in Europe. Then came specialized market halls, public weigh-houses, guildhouses and above all the town hall, built in 1561–5. It made all previous town halls seem small and old-fashioned.[11]

One of the most interesting of the many pioneering activities of Antwerp lay in its provision of public walks and gardens. The idea of actually planting trees or laying out gardens in public places for the enjoyment of the public was alien to the Middle Ages. Although a number of towns had open spaces used by the citizens for games, military exercises and other forms of recreation, no attempt had been made to ornament them. But in Antwerp, by 1569 if not earlier, the former churchyard of the cathedral was cleared of tombs and planted with trees.[12] The name which it soon acquired, the Place Verte or Groenplaats, shows how unfamiliar the idea of a planted square was; one is reminded of the Via Recta in Rome. The new square became fashionable, and several of the grander foreign merchants, Welsers from Augsburg, Frescobaldi and Affaitudi from Genoa, and Diego Mendes from Portugal, had houses on it.

An even more interesting development, which was to have endless repercussions in the cities of the west, was the planting of trees on the fortifications. One of the unplanned benefits of Renaissance fortifications was that they were surmounted by a considerable width of level ground, much more spacious than the narrow walks along the tops of medieval walls. This space was often made use of for building windmills, but the combination of height and fresh air, which attracted the windmills, also attracted citizens to come and walk on them. At Antwerp the walks were made more agreeable by planting a triple row of trees along them; the order to do so was issued by the town council in December 1578.[13] The ramparts of Lucca had been planted in the same way a little earlier (they seem to have been well grown when Montaigne saw them in 1580),[14] but no other sixteenth-century city had anything similar. By 1641, when the trees on the Antwerp ramparts had reached maturity, John Evelyn commented that 'there was nothing about this city which more ravished me than those delicious shades and walks of stately trees, which render the fortified works of the town one of the sweetest places in Europe'.[15]

In the bird's-eye views of Antwerp published in the 1580s and 1590s the trees appear like little rows of newly planted cabbages. But the same views show that the new town, although laid out in the 1550s, had scarcely been built on at all: the grand building of the Hanse stands almost on its own in depressing isolation, and, although there is some building at the river end, most of the land along the canals is empty. The new town had, in fact, been a failure. Gilbert van Schoonbeke, landed with an unprofitable investment, had resourcefully taken a new tack and built a row of ten small breweries along one of the canals, supplied with water pumped up by a horse-pump from the moat of the fortifications. The pump-house is still there, much enlarged in the seventeenth century, by when it had been taken over by the city: the horse-pump remained in operation until the 1870s. The whole scheme, although initially successful, was much resented by the existing brewers at the other end of the town, and they managed to run van Schoonbeke out of Antwerp.[16]

By the mid-1550s Antwerp was, in fact, no longer an expanding market, for brewing or anything else. It had entered on a plateau of prosperity, which turned into decline in the 1560s. Although its luxury and textile industries continued to flourish, the Portuguese trade in Antwerp had decreased to such an extent that the Portuguese closed their 'House' there in 1548.

Spain had discovered silver mines of fabulous richness in South America, and Portugal was buying South American silver. It no longer needed German silver, and moved the headquarters of its spice trade to Lisbon. This obviously affected Antwerp's German trade for the worse. The situation was not improved by the religious wars in Germany. But the final decline of Antwerp was due to its own religious troubles. As in all merchant and artisan communities in the north of Europe, many of its inhabitants had been converted to Protestantism. In 1566 the Protestants broke out in an orgy of iconoclastic destruction in the churches of Antwerp. The whole of the Spanish dominions in the Netherlands revolted against Spain in 1568, but only the north succeeded in gaining independence. Antwerp, which was actively engaged in the revolt, was sacked by the Spaniards in the 'Spanish Fury' of 1576, in which seven thousand people are said to have been killed, and endured a punitive fourteen-month siege in 1584–5. By the end of the 1580s its population had halved, and many of its most enterprising citizens had moved to England or the Dutch Netherlands, the independence of which was recognized by Spain in 1609. It was the Netherlands which administered the commercial coup-de-grâce to Antwerp, by successfully blockading the Scheldt in the late sixteenth century, and finally forcing its closure to commerce to be recognized in the Treaty of Münster of 1648.

By 1600 the miracle of the Netherlands was well under way, and by the mid-seventeenth century this small new nation with almost no resources of its own and a total population of perhaps one million, had become one of the great powers of the world. The basis of its success was its shipping. Antwerp, like other Flemish towns, had never built up a merchant navy of any consequence. It waited for the ships of others to come to it. The Dutch had always lived on, in and sometimes almost under the water. From the early Middle Ages they had been intrepid sailors, and, in the

119. (top right) Widows processing in the Groenplaats by the cathedral, Antwerp. From an anonymous painting of *c.* 1600 (Museum Vleeshuis, Antwerp).

120. (bottom right) Carnival on the ice, outside the walls of Antwerp. By Denis van Alstoot (Alte Pinakothek, Munich).

absence of any significant produce of their own, were prepared to carry anything anywhere for anybody. Their range of activities gradually extended from the local coasts and waterways to the whole Atlantic seaboard, into the Baltic and Mediterranean, and finally to America, Africa and the far east.

Their successful fight for independence gave them the strength of confidence and pride, and they were helped by the difficulties of others. The troubles of Antwerp and other Flemish towns, and the Thirty Years' War in Germany, provided the Dutch with openings and also brought able and industrious refugees flooding into Holland. Their aggressive inroads into markets previously the province of other fleets and nations were backed by an increasingly formidable fighting navy. All through the sixteenth century they competed with the Hanseatic cities for the trade of the Baltic, and by the mid-seventeenth century had won the battle and acquired by far the biggest share of the market, with England a poor second.

The Baltic was the biggest supplier of timber and grain in northern Europe. Its timber was vital to the Dutch shipbuilding industry because Holland had virtually no timber of its own, and important to the English one because the Sussex forests, on which England had mainly relied for its ship timbers, had been decimated by iron smelters cutting down the trees to make charcoal. It played a major part in the growing building industry of the two countries, for the same reasons. Its grain was equally important, because neither the Dutch cities, London nor Lisbon could feed themselves from the produce of their own countries.

In the sixteenth and early seventeenth centuries Gdansk was the most prosperous, magnificent and exciting city in the Baltic. It owed its prosperity to its position at the mouth of the Vistula, up which came timber and grain from the forests and cornfields of Poland. It had been settled by German merchants, and became a semi-independent German city recognizing Polish suzerainty, but with its own government, finances, militia, currency and (until the 1640s) with its own warships. It was famed for its gaiety and wickedness. Once a year timber barges, constructed by lashing together newly felled tree-trunks, were loaded with grain and floated down the Vistula to Gdansk. There the grain was sold to the grain merchants, the barges were broken up for sale to the timber merchants, and the shippers, or the rustic Polish landowners who often accompanied their crops in order to combine business with pleasure, celebrated the sales with several days of glorious drunkenness.[17]

The grain was stored in warehouses which filled the Speicher Island, across the water from the main city. The timber was piled in stacks on another island. At the St Dominic's Fair in August, which was the main selling period, there could be five hundred ships moored in the Mottlau ready to load up with timber and grain. The grain trade reached its peak in 1618, by when the population of Gdansk was about 60,000, and the merchants were living in houses of great splendour in the centre of the city, around an equally splendid town hall. Sales declined after that, partly owing to the fact that improved drainage and farming techniques in England and Holland lessened the demand; but it remained very considerable until the end of the century. The Dutch became increasingly important in the city, until by 1650 about fifty Dutch firms had resident agents there, living in the same style as the local merchants. The English came a poor second with about twenty agents (mostly Scots, in fact), but the actual English colony was much larger.[18]

121. The town hall, Gdansk. From the engraving in R. Curicke Der Stadt Danzig Historische Beschreibung (1687).

122. Seventeenth-century houses in the Langemarkt, Gdansk.

123. (following pages) Copenhagen. Crowds attending the swearing of the oath of fealty to the new constitution, 16 October 1660 (Rosenborg Castle, Copenhagen).

The Dutch had effectively secured their timber supplies at a time when the Italians were steadily losing theirs. The final commercial decline of Italy was due less to the exploitation by other nations of the sea route to the east than to the fact that northern European shipping took over the carrying trade of the Mediterranean; and one of the reasons for this was that Italy was running out of usable timber for shipbuilding.[19] In the mid-sixteenth century Venice recovered much of its trade in spices and continued to run its own extremely prosperous cloth industry. Genoa flourished exceedingly as the city providing banking and merchandising expertise for Spain and Portugal. The splendid palaces of its Strada Nuova are evidence of the prosperity of the great Genoese merchant banking families; it was the links between Genoa, Spain and Antwerp which took both Rubens and Van Dyck to Genoa in the early seventeenth century. But Italy was increasingly unable to compete with the aggressive merchant ships which came swarming into the Mediterranean from Hanseatic, English, French and, more and more, Dutch ports. The Dutch arrived in the late sixteenth century; in 1597 the first Dutch ship berthed in Syria and took on a cargo of spices; and in the course of the seventeenth century the Dutch acquired the main share of Mediterranean commerce, followed by England and France. Italy lost all importance as a trading nation. Its ports, of which Livorno was the most up to date and Genoa the most important, were largely frequented by foreign ships.[20] In 1638 a survey of European commerce by Lewis Roberts could write off the Venetians as follows: 'The great fire of their mighty traffic being

extinguished, it will not be needful for me to rake the ashes and observe further that little coal that is yet resting unconsumed amongst them.'[21]

By then, Portugal was not doing much better. It, too, had been virtually pushed out of its markets by Dutch and English competition. By 1630 the Dutch had won control of the Indonesian spice islands and had reduced the overland spice trade to the Levant to a trickle. The Dutch managed to keep the English out of Indonesia, but the two countries shared the Indian trade, once again at the expense of Portugal.

The English today tend to think of the rivalry between them and the Dutch as one between equals. In fact it was only at the end of the seventeenth century that England began to equal Holland, and in the eighteenth century that it overtook it—as was inevitable in the long run owing to its much greater resources. In the mid-seventeenth century Holland was on top and England was trying to unseat it. Until the English navigation laws excluded Dutch ships in 1651, more Dutch ships than English ones were importing goods into England. In 1670 the tonnage of the Dutch merchant fleet was considerably larger than that of Spain, Portugal, France, England and Germany combined. In 1690, 40,000 tons of Dutch shipping traded to North America, as opposed to 28,000 of English.[22] Even in the cloth trade, no individual English town could equal Leiden. In 1660 Leiden was producing 127,000 cloths a year, more than twice the produce of Florence at its prime in the 1330s.[23] It was Dutch architecture and painting which influenced English, rather than the other way round. English gardens were laid out in the Dutch style and planted with Dutch bulbs. English houses were filled with Dutch porcelain. In 1667 Dutch ships sailed up the Thames, sent fireboats into the docks and captured the English flagship; and from 1688 England was ruled by a Dutch king.

England was still provincial, but it was not only Holland which it imitated. The influence of France was almost equally important, especially among the upper classes. A quick survey of the main cities of Europe in the 1660s would have revealed a situation somewhat as follows. In Italy, Rome, Florence, Venice, Naples, Genoa and Milan were all in different stages of decline, and their merchant families were abandoning commerce and settling down to live off the rents of the estates which they had acquired in more active days. Rome, Venice and Florence, in particular, were beginning to develop an agreeable new role as purveyors of pleasure and culture to the new rich from the north. In the Baltic, Gdansk was booming and Stockholm prosperous, but both were dominated by Dutch merchants and capital. The Danish kings were making ambitious attempts to establish Copenhagen as a political and commercial centre, much influenced by Amsterdam. In central Europe, Augsburg, Nuremberg and Prague were declining, and the rising city was Vienna, capital of a monarchy which had just won a major war against the Turks. In Spain and Portugal the great days of Seville were over, Madrid was still a relatively small place, and the commerce of Lisbon was run by foreigners. Further up the Atlantic seaboard, Antwerp had entered on a comfortable, unspectacular existence as an art-manufacturing centre and a pleasant place for foreigners to visit or stay in. Hamburg had profited from Antwerp's decline and become the main port through which English cloth was imported to the continent. London, as the principal exporter of English cloth and a capital city, was growing at extraordinary speed; by the 1660s it had a population of perhaps 400,000 and had probably overtaken Paris and become the largest city in Europe. But, though huge by contemporary standards, it was dirty, ill-built and provincial. The two most dynamic and influential cities in Europe were Paris and Amsterdam.

124. (right) New and old houses in Goudbloemstraat, in the Jordaan, Amsterdam. By Jan van den Heyden, 1682 (Amsterdam Historical Museum).

8

Amsterdam and Paris

What impressed contemporaries about Amsterdam was that it was a city entirely dedicated to making money. It could not be fitted into any of the accepted conventions for looking at and describing cities. According to these, churches, monasteries, castles, palaces, hospitals, colleges, walls, gates, bridges and squares were what visitors were expected to concentrate on, and commercial activities only received passing attention, even if they were the main reason for the existence and prosperity of the city.

But in Amsterdam this approach was unworkable. As a Protestant city the churches were relatively inconspicuous; there were no monasteries, no cathedral, no castle, no university, no college of any great importance, and the squares were as crowded with commercial activity as everywhere else. Even the civic centre of the town, the Dam Square by the town hall, also contained a fish market, a crane and a public weigh-house, and echoed to the noise of horses and sleds pulling loads of grain, sugar and wine across the clinker-brick pavement.[1] Commerce was inescapable. It seemed to visitors as though every available piece of space and all the available manpower were made to pay their way. Masts and rigging closed every vista; there were windmills on the ramparts and rope-walks on the open ground between the ramparts and the houses; the women and children in the orphanages and almshouses were set to spinning, the beggars were collected into the House of Correction, whipped, and put to rasping hazelwood to provide dye for the dyers. Even the cats were organized: in the great Admiralty warehouse there was a 'nursery room, where a woman keeps an office, to feed at certain hours of the day a great number of cats, which afterwards hunt among the stores for mice and rats'.[2]

Dedication to money-making had lifted the population of Amsterdam from about 20,000 in the mid-sixteenth century to 200,000 by the end of the seventeenth. Dutch ships had become the chief carriers of goods to Europe, and Amsterdam owned the lion's share of Dutch shipping. Its prosperity was due to a number of causes, but an essential one was its possession of a harbour with easy access to the sea on one side, and to a network of inland waterways on the other. In the great basin of the harbour as many as a hundred and fifty merchantmen and men-of-war were likely to be found lying at anchor in busy periods, as well as several hundred smaller vessels, so that anyone arriving by sea first saw the towers and spires of the city through a forest of masts, pennants and rigging stretching in a two mile curve along the water's edge. This close contact between city and harbour has been lost; in the nineteenth century the inner harbour was partly filled in to provide space for the railway station, and today trams rattle across the station square where boats used to ride at anchor, and only a token fragment is left of the Damrak, the former mouth of the river Amstel, which used to run from the harbour up to the Dam Square in the centre.

Although the harbour was deep, the deep water did not reach to the quays. The litle sea-going ships of the Middle Ages could sail right into the Damrak and unload there, but the bigger craft of the seventeenth century had to anchor in the deep water and be unloaded by lighters. A water landscape developed as a result, divided by marine fences into fields and roads, with some of the big ships grazing, as it were, in the fields, and others tethered in rows along the fences, surveying the flocks of smaller craft which crowded the inner waters: lighters, rowing-boats, coastal and inland shipping, and large low-lying barges bringing fresh water into Amsterdam. This water landscape had its own structure and buildings, built on timber platforms in the middle of the water: little shipping offices, a strange island of monstrous wooden cranes, and two timber-built inns, marooned amidst the ships and joined by long timber causeways to the mainland. They were for the use of travellers who arrived after dusk, when no strangers were allowed into the town.

Visitors who arrived in the daytime could be ferried at once to the quay by the New Bridge, which crossed the bottom of the Damrak. This was one of the busiest places in Amsterdam. Ships' captains paid their harbour dues at a little pavilion by the end of the bridge, and in an adjoining loggia placards were posted up announcing the destinations and times of departure of all the ships in the harbour. Traffic to the bridge fought its way through touts, friends, business contacts and barrow-women waiting for arrivals from the ships; the confusion was compounded by a crowd of ships' captains conferring with each other and with prospective clients, until a special platform was built for them out over the Damrak, to get them out of the way.[3]

125. Cranes in the harbour, Amsterdam.

126. (following page top) The Old Town Inn, built for travellers over the water in Amsterdam harbour. From Filips Van Zesen, *Beschreibung der Stadt Amsterdam*, 1664 (Rijksmuseum, Amsterdam).

127. (following page bottom) The harbour office by the New Bridge in Amsterdam. From Van Zesen.

128. (subsequent page top) The corn exchange, built over the Damrak, Amsterdam. From Van Zesen.

129. (subsequent page bottom) The fish market on the Dam, Amsterdam. From Van Zesen.

From the New Bridge all the way up the Damrak the quay was crammed with hoists, piles of merchandise, porters and small ships loading and unloading. Not quite halfway along, and also built out on the water, was the corn exchange. This took the form of an open square of wooden Doric colonnades; there were rows of lockers along its outer sides from which the cornfactors drew their bags of samples, and bargained with each other for the sacks of corn stored by the thousand in the great warehouses around the harbour.

The Damrak ended in the Dam. The Dam had been built across the river Amstel in the early Middle Ages, and was both the centre of Amsterdam and the origin of its name. It formed part of a dyke which ran all along the coast and prevented the sea from pouring into the low-lying polders behind it: access from the inland waterways to the sea was only by way of locks. The Dam had developed into the main city square, on or just off which were three of the principal buildings of Amsterdam, the Stadhuis or town hall, the exchange and the Nieuwe Kerk, where the city councillors worshipped. Here too was the fish market, and the long-since demolished weigh-house, where the city guard lolled in a guard room in the upper storey, and the weigh-beams hung in the big room below, operated by porters smartly uniformed in red and green. There were only three public weigh-houses in the city. Any goods sold wholesale had to be weighed in them and taxed according to their weight by both the city and the state, so there was a constant coming and going across the Dam. There were hauliers by the dozen at hand to haul goods on horse-sleds across the square, and a special stable for their horses just below the town hall—as magnificent as a king's stable, according to one account.[4]

The exchange impressed visitors as much as anything in Amsterdam. It had been built in 1608–13, out over the Amstel like the sea captains' meeting-place and the corn exchange. But it was built much more solidly, and on a larger scale, of brick and stone on a stone-arched platform. It was modelled on the Antwerp exchange, and like it had shops on the upper floors and covered walks and an open court for merchants below. Here, as a description put it in 1664, almost the whole world seemed to be assem-

DE OUDE STADS HERBERGH.

DE NIEUWE BRUGH.

KOORN-BEURS.
de Oude Kerck

DE GROOTE VIS-MARCKT.

bled to buy and sell—not only Dutch and Germans, but Poles, Hungarians, Frenchmen, Spaniards, Muscovites, Persians, Turks and even, on occasion, Indians.[5] The noise was deafening, and the variety of business transacted was extraordinarily varied. Special numbered sections of the walks were set aside for those dealing in tobacco, silk, jewels, bills of exchange, shares, property sales, groceries and cattle hides; for money-changers, Muscovy merchants, merchants trading with the West Indies or the Canaries; and for foreign merchants from France, Spain, England, Sweden, Denmark, Poland and Hamburg. In another section were the names of the shipmasters, their destination and time of departure fixed on the pillars; the destinations covered the whole known world.

The consciousness that Amsterdam's activities spread over the world, and that the world and its produce came to Amsterdam, was proudly expressed in the town hall. On its west front, Atlas lifted up his globe above a pediment in which the nations of the world offered their goods to an allegorical Amsterdam; inside, the marble floor of the huge Burgersaal was inscribed with maps of both the heavenly and terrestrial worlds. The town hall was seventeenth-century Amsterdam's one piece of flamboyance.[6] It was grander than any palace then existing in Europe (and ultimately was destined to become one), built of stone in a brick city (the stone was shipped in from Germany) and supported by 13,659 piles driven into the Amsterdam mud. Its main facades were 263 feet long, 7 feet longer than the main facades of the Antwerp town hall, a supremacy which cannot have been accidental. In fact, it contained far more space than the city had any conceivable use for and the whole upper half was almost empty.

Inside, the cool splendour of the Burgersaal and the corridors that radiated off it was in striking contrast to the noise and confusion at the Dam and the exchange. The Burgersaal, as the name expressed, was the citizens' hall, open and accessible to any citizen of Amsterdam. This was a grand gesture, but in fact walking in the Burgersaal was the only share which an ordinary citizen could hope to have in the government of the city, for Amsterdam was governed with great efficiency, but even more despotically than Venice, by a tiny self-perpetuating oligarchy of four burgomasters and seven magistrates, aided by a consultative council of thirty-six.[7]

The main floor of the lower half was occupied by burgersaal, courts, council chamber, burgomasters' rooms, treasury, and rooms for the secretariat, the trustees of the city orphanages, and the committee which adjudicated in legal cases involving insurance, and regulated the affairs of bankrupts. In the lower floor at ground level under the main rooms were the prisons, guardrooms, torture and punishment rooms, arsenal, caretaker's flat and, above all, the city bank.

The city's exchange bank or Wisselbank had been founded in 1609.[8] It was the first and for a long time the greatest public bank in northern Europe. By the end of the seventeenth century over sixteen million Dutch florins were lying on deposit in the bank vaults, and provided the town hall with a foundation as impressive in its own way as the famous 13,659 piles. The bank's reputation derived from its efficiency, convenience and total reliability. It came to be used like a Swiss bank today. Foreign governments deposited funds there, but so did foreign kings, politicians or anyone who, as Sir William Temple put it in 1672, 'thought they provided for a retreat or against a storm, and thought no place as secure as this, nor from whence they might so easily draw their money into any part of the world'.

Holland also had a comprehensive Land Registry. The ease with which money could

130. (top right) The Dam at Amsterdam, showing the town hall, weigh-house and the projected tower of the Nieuwe Kerk. Gouache by Jacob van der Ulft, 1653 (Gemeentarchief, Amsterdam).

131. (bottom right) The area round the Dam, Amsterdam, before the rebuilding of the town hall. From Flonsz van Berkenrode, Birds-Eye View of Amsterdam, 1625 (Rijksmuseum, Amsterdam).

Beurs
Nieuwe-zyds
Voor Burchwal
't Stadthuys
Wiſselbanck
Kerckhof
Nieuwe Kerck
DAM
Wage
DAMSRACK

be borrowed and transferred exceeded even the facilities offered by Italian banks, and was a matter of wonder to other Europeans. An envious Englishman described the method of raising a mortgage: 'Now I am a Dutchman and have £100 a year in the province West Friesland near Groningen, and I come to the Bank at Amsterdam and there tender a particular of my land and land tenanted . . . and desire them to lend me £4,000 and I will mortgage my land for it. The answer will be: I will send by post your particular to the register at Groningen and by return of post you shall have your answer. The register at Groningen answers—that is my land—they lend me the money. I refuse the money—I want credit and having one son at Venice, one at Nuremberg, one at Hamburg, one at Dantzic, where banks are, I desire four tickets of credit, each of them for £1,000 with letters of advice directed to each of my sons which is immediately done.'[9]

In fact, the Amsterdam bank only started to make loans to individuals in 1685, although it was lending to the city and the East India Company before then. But borrowing money from other sources was easy enough. Moreover, money was cheaper in Amsterdam than anywhere else in Europe. It could be borrowed at 3 to 4½ percent, as opposed to 6 percent or more in England. Low interest rates were one of the foundations of the city's great prosperity. Its merchants could borrow in Amsterdam and re-lend in London at a profit. They could also afford to buy at the bottom of the market, warehouse the goods bought, and wait for prices to rise.

One result of this was that the goods piled up and warehouses assumed a scale and importance they had never previously possessed. The Dutch built warehouses all over the world, but the biggest single collection of them was in Amsterdam.[10] They were a source of amazement to foreign visitors, who were used to goods being stored in much more moderate quantities in or at the back of merchants' houses. Some of these warehouses belonged to the Admiralty, or to the city; the latter owned large depositories for peat and corn, which were distributed free to the poor in the winter months. But the majority were for commercial merchandise. Amsterdam had the biggest stores of corn in Europe, but the warehouses also contained dried fish, timber, sugar, tobacco, tin, copper, wool, wine, salt, draperies, furs, books and luxury goods of all kinds, processed in Amsterdam or bought in from the Americas, the West Indies and all over Europe, as well as the eastern goods distributed from the warehouses of the East India Company. The extent of the East Indian trade was vividly demonstrated when a single Dutch vessel was salvaged in 1983 from the South China Sea, in which it had sunk in the 1640s. It contained more than twenty thousand pieces of blue-and-white porcelain, carefully packed and still in mint condition.[11]

The earliest documented reference to a warehouse in Amsterdam dates from 1548 (in which year it was already in disrepair).[12] It was at about this time that private warehouses, as opposed to public granaries, first began to appear in northern Europe as a recognizable architectural type, although it was not until the seventeenth century that they were found in really large numbers. In the early warehouses goods were raised from floor to floor internally, by hoists operated through gratings or trap doors in the floors. The technique of raising goods externally, from a pulley cantilevered out from a gable, is shown on houses depicted in an engraving of an Antwerp street dated 1567, and was probably adopted for warehouses at much the same time. The resulting small-windowed warehouses, having tiers of doors one above the other and a pulley above

132. Seventeenth-century warehouses on Realen Island, Amsterdam.

133. The Admiralty warehouse (1656, now the Naval Museum) on the Kattenburg Island, Amsterdam.

the doors were to become a distinctive feature of towns all over Europe for the next few centuries. In the earlier warehouses goods were raised by means of a rope slung over the pulley, and pulled from the ground outside the house; but during the seventeenth century the system was evolved of having one or sometimes two big horizontal wheels inside, which turned an external drum and wound up the rope accordingly.

There were warehouses scattered all over Amsterdam, but the biggest concentration was on the islands. These water-surrounded rectangular blocks of land on the harbour side of the town were formed out of marshland in the late sixteenth and early seventeenth centuries. They were (and to some extent still are) a curious little world of their own, a mixture of warehouses, shipbuilding yards, timber yards, rope-walks and sheds for drying and smoking herring round the perimeter, and housing and sometimes churches inland. The main conglomeration of granaries were on Bikkers and Realen islands; the largest warehouses were on the islands of Kattenburg, Wittenburg and Oostenburg, work on which started in 1657–8, and which were the last of the islands to be developed. Oostenburg was dominated by the sensational warehouse of the East India Company, built in 1661, with covered rope-walks adjoining on the same scale. All have since been demolished, but on the corner of Kattenburg, the smaller but far from small warehouse built in nine months in 1656 for Admiralty stores still survives as a naval museum. It contained the task force of cats already described, and also what must have been one of the first sprinkler systems: 'vast cisterns, which are kept constantly full of water, having pipes into every apartment, to let it down upon any accident of fire'.[13]

As the size of the warehouse indicates, the East India Company was one of the most important institutions in Amsterdam, and probably its biggest single money-earner. It had been set up in 1602, as an amalgamation of a number of smaller companies,

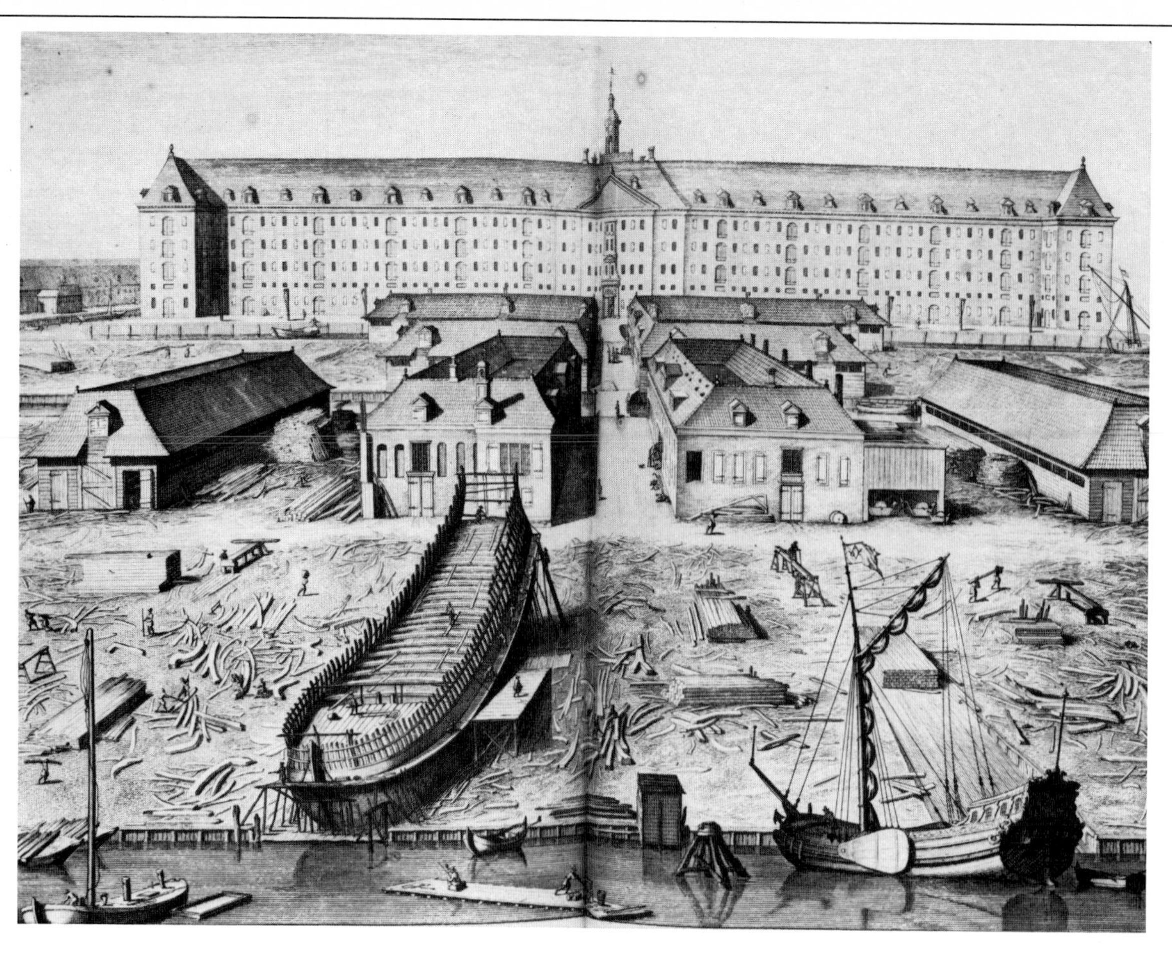

134. The East India Company warehouses (built 1661) on the Oostenburg Island, Amsterdam. By J. Muller.

the last of which had been founded in Amsterdam in 1595. Amsterdam dominated the new company and subscribed well over half its initial capital. It, the Dutch West India Company and similar companies founded at much the same time in both Holland and England were pioneers in that they were joint-stock companies, trading as units and dividing their profits among their shareholders, rather than associations of merchants trading separately but joining together for mutual support, like the Hanseatic League and the Merchant Adventurers. Shares in the Dutch companies were bought and sold on the exchange. The East India Company was extremely successful from the start, and paid dividends of 25 to 30 percent in the first six years. Its big warehouse was simply a storage depot; it had an administrative headquarters in the centre of the town, which was also a sales depot to which spices, pepper, tea, china and other goods were brought for sale as needed from the island warehouse. The West India Company had a similar arrangement, but was much less successful and had to sell its headquarters and move everything into its warehouse: the latter still stands on the Prins Hendrik Rade and is the only one of the two companies' buildings in Amsterdam to survive.

The East India Company's headquarters were on the Kloveniersburgwal, which was the fashionable place to be in the early seventeenth century. Amsterdam, rather like Bruges but on a larger scale, kept the moats of its former fortifications as it expanded and turned them into canals lined with quays and houses. It grew, as a result, in a series of circuits. The canals of the Voorburgwal and Achterburgwal mark the line of the original medieval fortifications (which consisted of ditches only, without walls), the Kloveniersburgwal and Singel the line of the next ring of fortifications, built in the 1480s. The two last were developed as a new quarter when the fortifications were

135. Map of Amsterdam by Joan Blaeu, published in 1649 (Gemeentelijke Archiefdienst, Amsterdam).

enlarged again in the late sixteenth century, and rapidly filled with the best houses and most prestigious central warehouses in Amsterdam.

A little beyond the Kloveniersburgwal were the warehousing and shipbuilding islands of Uilenburg and Valkenburg; so that when, in consequence of booming prospects and population, it was decided to enlarge the fortifications yet again and develop a big new area, this was almost inevitably on the other side of the city, beyond the Singel. Here, between about 1613 and 1615, three new canals were formed, the Heerengracht, Keizersgracht and Prinsengracht. These three canals were ultimately to work their way all round the city, and to receive great acclaim in this century as an example of farsighted and pioneering town-planning. But in fact the canals as developed in 1613–15 were hardly more ambitious than the three canals of the new town at Antwerp, laid out sixty years previously, on which they were probably modelled, and there is no evidence that it was originally planned to continue them. They were not extended until the 1660s, and the final section dates from only the eighteenth century. The first section was planned from the start to be a prestigious area, however; at a council meeting held in 1615, it was described as intended for 'beautiful houses for *rentiers* and other rich people'.[14] Industrial uses and shops were forbidden on the new canals (although shops were allowed in the radial streets that joined them), and the plots were thirty feet wide, instead of twenty, which was the customary width in Amsterdam.

In fact, with a few exceptions, it was the prosperous middle classes rather than rich *rentiers* who were attracted by the new area, and what tended to happen was that speculators bought up two thirty-foot plots and developed them as three twenty-foot ones. In the 1660s extension exactly the opposite happened: the city, having learnt from experience, divided the areas into twenty-foot plots and speculators, rightly gauging that the market had changed, bought up three twenty-foot plots and developed them as two thirty-foot ones.[15]

Warehouses were not forbidden: a sprinkling of them were built, and some of the houses probably used basements and possibly attics for storage in the traditional manner. But on the whole the area came closer to a prestigious mainly residential neighbourhood than perhaps any development yet built in northern Europe.

Industry was provided for in the area beyond the Prinsengracht, which the new fortifications were extended to include. Here a certain amount of unofficial industrial squatting had already taken place along the ditches of the polders, the fields outside the city walls. The fields were at a lower level than the city; the existing situation was accepted as a basis for development, and the area known as the Jordaan was laid out at a lower level along narrow canals running in the same direction as the polder ditches. The canals fed into the Prinsengracht, which was also formed on the lower level, so that boats could get into the Jordaan canals. Here grew up sugar refineries, potteries, printing works, glass-houses, rope-walks along the inside of the fortifications and windmills on the bastions, along with numerous modest artisan houses and the occasional large house of the more prosperous industrial entrepreneur. The iron foundries seem to have been mainly on the eastern islands, close to the shipyards. Breweries concentrated on the Brouwersgracht, which ran parallel to the harbour, and was easily accessible to barges bringing in fresh water. Water in the Amsterdam canals was kept more or less free of salt by the locks, and was much used for industrial processes, but too much went into it for it to be drinkable. Amsterdam had to rely on rain-storage and the barges for its drinking water until the mid-nineteenth century.[16]

All through the seventeenth century, row upon row of new houses rose out of the soggy soil on foundations of wooden piles, and the old barge-boarded houses built of timber were gradually replaced by the stepped or scrolled gables of new brick or brick-and-stone ones. The two grandest houses of the first half of the century were probably the 'House with the Heads' built by a rich French merchant in about 1622, but bought shortly after it was built by Louis de Geer, and the house on the Kloveniersburgwal built as a double house by Elias Trip and his brother in about 1640. Louis de Geer's family had emigrated from Liège to Holland; he became an armaments tycoon, divided his time between Amsterdam and Sweden, where he owned iron and copper mines, smelting works and foundries, helped Sweden to rise to the position of a first-rate power on the basis of its armaments, and sold his guns all over Europe. Elias Trip was also from Liège and in the same business, first as de Geer's friend and collaborator, but ultimately as his rival.[17]

The two houses are handsome enough, but, although their owners, de Geer in particular, were among the richest entrepreneurs in Europe, they nowhere near approached the grandeur of a big Florentine, Roman or Venetian palace, or one of the more important *hôtels* in Paris. The whole trend of life in Amsterdam ran against grandeur. The burgomaster walked about the streets without an attendant, 'like a shopkeeper', as an Englishman put it.[18] There was no hint of the grand manner in the layout of the three new canals, no axial vistas, columns, obelisks, grand bridges or symmetrically planned squares. In the narrow quays along the canals there was little room for horses and carriages, and a series of city regulations prohibited them or tried to limit their number by imposing heavy fines on those who owned them. The neatness and cleanliness, not

136. Houses on the Keizersgracht, Amsterdam. By Caspar Philips Jacobz. The 'House with the Heads' is on the left.

the grandeur, of Amsterdam were what impressed visitors; that and the trees along the canals, a perhaps typically Amsterdam device for getting an amenity without losing useful space. They were planted between about 1610 and 1625; in 1641 John Evelyn was delighted with the 'neat and useful' clinker brick which paved the quays, and the way in which the trees made the Keizersgracht appear 'like a city in a forest'.[19]

Entertainments were not on the grand scale either: there were no joustings, masques or grand processions. Instead there were jovial hail-fellow-well-met dinners at the club-houses of the Civic Guard, the importance of which, like that of many similar institutions in northern Europe, was as much social as military. It was a part-time guard of citizen volunteers, and being an officer in it was an almost obligatory step for younger members of the inner group of Amsterdam families, on the route to becoming a councillor, magistrate and finally burgomaster. The companies took turns at mounting guard at the city's guardhouses, and each of them held an annual dinner. The richest member often paid for a group portrait, many of which survive.[20] The Guard had developed out of the two medieval Guilds of St George and St Sebastian, which were equipped, as in other medieval towns, with crossbows and longbows respectively, and had club-houses and practice grounds on the Singel. The slightly later Kloveniers were armed with the kloven, a specially large type of bow. The Kloveniersburgwal was named after them, because their company house was originally in a tower in the city wall there, which was retained when the rest of the wall was demolished. In about 1640 the tower was handsomely rebuilt, and it was to decorate the hall of the new building that Rembrandt's *Night Watch* was painted in 1642.

The guardhouses were spread over the city: three were above the city weigh-houses, presumably because large sums of money were collected in the latter, and they were in need of security. Today the only survivor is the St Anthonis Poort, a converted gate-house of the medieval city wall, which also contained the operating theatre of the city surgeon and meeting houses for several of the city guilds. It presided over a large Monday market for ready-made and second-hand clothes, and for poultry, eggs and vegetables, through which huge anchors and cannon trundled from the neighbouring iron-foundry area, to be weighed and taxed at the weigh-house.

Allowing for changes in artistic style, one can still savour a change in atmosphere between the feasters at the St George's banquet in 1533 and 1648. The former, stiffly grouped round their bread and chicken, may have ended up as boisterously as the latter: one of them is in fact holding the words of a song about a girl. But contemporary convention clearly imposed a certain air of solemnity. Moreover, the earlier guard is

1533

far less splendidly dressed than the later one. By the mid-seventeenth century Amsterdam contained puritanical elements but on the whole was a far from puritanical city. It was religiously tolerant and sexually easy-going. The latter quality provoked indignant reactions from William Carr, who was English consul in Amsterdam in the 1680s. 'There are tolerated in the City of Amsterdam, amongst other abuses, at least 50 musick-houses, where lewd persons of both sexes meet and practise their villinies: there is also a place called the Long-Seller, a tolerated Exchange, or publick meeting house for whores and rogues to rendezvous in, and make their filthy bargains. This Exchange is open from six a clock in the evening until nine at night . . . I have heard some plead for the toleration of these wicked meetings upon pretext that when the East India fleets come home, the seamen are so mad for women, that if they had not such houses to rest in, they would force the very citizens' wives and daughters.'[21]

The licensed music-houses were scattered through the town, but the majority were close to the harbour. The prostitutes, who bore names such as Long Nell, Carmen, Blonde Venus and Joode Jet, were all legally compelled to live in the brothel quarter around the Pylsteeg, a narrow street running off the Dam opposite the town hall and a little to the south of the present red light district. This was also the area lived in by the guard of the city bailiff, who controlled the prostitutes, and benefited from their rent, and if any of them set up business elsewhere, sent his guard with drums beating and flutes playing to move them back to his own area.[22]

The pastors of the established Calvinist Church preached against licensed prostitution, just as they preached against tolerance of the Jews, and against the fact that money was spent on building the town hall rather than completing the Nieuwe Kerk: but in all cases they were blandly ignored by the city council. When Jews first appeared in Amsterdam around 1600, in retreat from the Inquisition in Portugal, they received a degree of harassment from the city authorities, but by the 1620s they had become an accepted element and by the last decade of the century, they were heavily involved in the East India trade and the sugar business, and were extremely prosperous. German Jews arrived a little later than the Portuguese ones; they came from a much poorer background, brought much less capital, and became the main barrow salesmen of the city. The grand synagogue built by the Portuguese Jews in 1670 survives on the Muiderstraat. It was in an area in which many Jews lived, but there was no specific ghetto, and the city council resisted any campaign to create one.[23]

All Protestant sects were tolerated in Amsterdam, not just the official church, as in many other Protestant states or cities. Catholics suffered certain disabilities, but these were much less than Protestants suffered in most Catholic countries. Amsterdam freely printed works banned in other parts of Europe. In all such matters the city government seems to have worked on a pragmatic basis, rather than through any ideal of tolerance. Licensed prostitution faced up to the reality of life in a teeming international port, but controlled it; religious tolerance encouraged able people to bring their talents, and often their capital, to Amsterdam; printing banned books was good business.

The Amsterdam ruling class in the seventeenth century was an able body.[24] Although totally undemocratic it was not, like the Venetian oligarchy, a closed system: it admitted any newcomer or Amsterdam-born citizen who was Protestant, rich and had acquired the right connections. When the city became officially Calvinist, large numbers of institutions formerly run by religious Orders were taken over by the city council. In

137. (top left) Feast of Company H of the Guild of St George, Amsterdam. By Cornelisz Anthonisz., 1533 (Amsterdam Historical Museum).

138. (bottom left) Banquet of the Civic Guard in their club-house on the Singel, Amsterdam. By B. van der Helst, 1648 (Rijksmuseum, Amsterdam).

addition to the Wisselbank it ran several hospitals, two orphanages, two almshouses for old people, two prisons, three schools (including a gymnasium, which was the nearest Amsterdam came to a university), two state inns for important guests, and a city lending bank, which was in effect a city pawnshop. It distributed free food and turf to those of the poor it considered deserving, and collected those it considered 'lazy beggars' into the house of correction. There were almost no beggers on the Amsterdam streets, and little serious poverty in the city. It employed all the city's porters, carriers and ferrymen. As we have seen, it initiated and supervised the expansion of the city: since this involved a comprehensive system of water management for drainage and transport, such supervision was a necessity, to prevent a chaotic situation arising.

The city government managed to create a clean and orderly environment, but not to stop the canals from smelling. It did its best. Solid sewage and garbage were collected by the city in covered wagons or canal barges and sold as field manure; the profits went to the orphanage. Three pumps, two operated by windmills and one by a horse-pump, pumped water out of the canals into the moat round the fortifications in an endeavour to keep the water in the canals circulating. At high tide a sluice gate by the St Anthonis Poort was opened in order to let sea water into the canals and scour them out.[25] None of these devices was very effective: in the summer months, as a Frenchman put it, 'cela ne remedie pas totalement l'infection qu'ils exhalent dans certains quartiers'.[26] Not surprisingly, at this period the citizens spent as much time as they could in their delightful, but never grand, summer houses along the Amstel and Vecht to the south of the city.

* * *

It would be impossible to pick out any one place as containing the essence of Paris in the mid-seventeenth century, but a visitor could have savoured a great deal of it in two: the Cours and the Palais.

The full title of the former was the Cours la Reine, but, although Paris acquired a number of Courses, it always remained *the* Cours to Parisians. It was laid out by Marie de Médicis in 1616[27] outside the city walls just to the west of the Tuileries gardens. It consisted of a triple avenue of elm trees, opening out into a circle halfway along its length; the central avenue was wider than the side ones. It ran for nearly a mile along the Seine, by where the Grand and Petit Palais now stand, between the public road by the river and the open space which was later to be planted as the Champs Élysées. Its site and name survive, but it has long since become a riverside high road, busy with traffic.

The old Cours was busy on occasions too, but with activity of a different kind. Every evening in the summer the coaches of rich Parisians paraded slowly up and down it.[28] The middle avenue had room for six coaches to drive abreast, and on average there were probably seven or eight hundred parading on it: sometimes, when the king's coach was parading, there were said to be as many as two thousand and for several hours they were jammed almost immoveably, head to tail. In 1662 the king's entourage was reported to consist of seven coaches, each pulled by eight horses; most people came in a coach and four. The coaches could be very splendid. They were covered with crimson velvet and studded with golden nails; or gilded, with gold and silver fringes;

139. The Cours la Reine, Paris. From the engraving by Aveline (Bibliothèque Nationale, Paris).

or the doors, interiors and horses were hung with hangings of white and yellow embroidered silk. The men inside them were flamboyant and exaggerated, sporting huge moustaches, plumes and hats; the women were painted and flirtatious. Sweet-sellers ran between the coaches, selling sweets and light refreshments, but also surreptitiously passing messages from coach to coach. The air, in the low evening sun, was heavy with gossip, intrigue and fantasy. The Marquis de Rouillac made a habit of carrying a box full of gloves, which he presented to the women who took his fancy. The Sieur de Molins was said to have driven the length of the Cours sticking his bottom through the window instead of his face. Around 1700 a new fashion started, of driving on the Cours at night, by music and torchlight, and getting out of the coaches to dance on the central round.[29]

Smart seventeenth-century Parisians were crazy about the Cours. They liked the view of the river, the cool air under the trees, but also the pomp, exaggeration and possibilities of showing off, conducting affairs and picking up news. They displayed their daughters there on the lookout for husbands. Madame de Montpensier, in her memoirs, said that a Parisian lady had three main pleasures in life, to wear a mask, go to the Foire St Germain, and parade on the Cours.[30] Numerous poems were written about it, in the sumptuous slow-moving verse of the time:

> J'ai vu l'alignement d'une superbe allée
> Parmi son sable d'or, des rubis éteillée,
> Couverte de rameaux dont les feuillage verts
> Conserve leur peinture, en dépit des hivers,
> Recevoir en son sein nos dieux et nos déesses,
> Dans leurs chars de triomphe, éclatants de richesses.*[31]

*I have seen the setting out of a splendid avenue / Scattered with rubies amid sands of gold, / Sheltered with branches of green foliage / Which keeps its colouring in defiance of winter, / Receiving in its embrace our gods and goddesses / In their triumphal chariots, glittering with riches. /

140–2. A President and Counsellor of the Parlement, Paris, and a Parisian gentleman. From engravings by Sebastien Le Clerc, *c.* 1664 (Bibliothèque Nationale, Paris).

According to another poem, written in 1649:

> C'est ici pour des goûts divers
> Le théatre de l'univers.[32]

The Palais was the original palace of the French kings, on the Île de la Cité. By the seventeenth century, the kings had long since ceased living there, but the courts of law, which they had presided over while in residence, remained. The most important was the Parlement de Paris, the supreme court of France rather than a parliament in the English sense. The Palais also accommodated the Chambre des Comptes, the Cour des Aides, and the Cour des Monnoies, which were the sovereign courts in all financial disputes and played a major role in French life.

The importance of the Parlement can scarcely be exaggerated.[33] Not only was it a major court of law; in the absence of an effective parliament in the English sense, it was the most effective remaining brake on the power of the king. The king was not above the law; his edicts had to be registered by the Parlement, and if it thought that they were against the spirit of the law, it could refuse to register them. In a similar manner, by issuing directives to expand or clarify existing laws and regulations, it exerted a powerful regulating influence on the life of Paris.

The Parlement consisted of three main divisions and numerous sub-divisions, made up of around two hundred counsellors and presided over by ten presidents. All its members moved through Paris with some splendour. They wore scarlet capes, decorated with different measures of fur, according to rank. The presidents wore the distinctive black velvet cap known as the *mortier*, trimmed, in some cases, with gold lace. Presidents, counsellors and their wives were attended by train-bearers; when they went to church, velvet cushions were solemnly carried before them. The presidents and members of the financial courts had similar status and wore similar dress: their financial connections often made them exceedingly rich. Membership of Parlement and the financial courts automatically conferred nobility, the *noblesse de la robe*. In the seventeenth century mem-

143. 'La Galerie du Palais'. By Abraham Bosse (Bibliothèque Nationale, Paris).

bership became hereditary and could be sold; the king appointed the senior president of the Parlement, but otherwise had no influence on its make-up. Most of the parliamentary and financial families acquired large and often superbly decorated houses in Paris, and châteaux and country estates in the Île-de-France. Most had coaches, and drove on the Cours. Many were created dukes, marquises and counts, and intermarried with the court nobility and the military *noblesse de l'épée*. They formed a formidable city aristocracy which, unlike the rest of the French nobility or the English aristocracy, was resident in the capital nine months or so of the year.

But the Palais owed its distinctive and unique character not just to the presence of the Parlement and other courts, but to the other activities which were attracted to it, as activities always tended to be attracted to major centres of power. Its enormous hall (rebuilt after a fire in 1618) and the surrounding galleries echoed to the clatter and chatter of petitioners, litigants, solicitors and lawyers, to the councillors passing to and fro in their splendour, to the bells ringing for the start of a new session, and to the trumpet blasts that preceded publication of an ordinance, or announced the arrival of the great. But they were also crowded with gossipmongers, merchants, prostitutes, fashionable strollers, and stalls selling anything from ribbons to mirrors or purses to plumes. By at least the early fifteenth century stalls had appeared in the Galerie des Merciers, which joined the great hall to the Ste Chapelle; by the end of the sixteenth they were everywhere.[34] The Palais had become the luxury shopping centre and general rendezvous of Paris, and by the eighteenth century, if not earlier, was frequently referred to as the Palais Marchand. In the 1570s a Venetian visitor described how 'in the corridors there is an immense quantity of little stalls . . . and there one invariably meets a crowd of cavaliers and their ladies, even the king and his court: the latter come for their amusement, the former have business to do . . . the Palace is like an intermediary for lovers'.[35] The atmosphere of luxury and elegance in these shopping arcades is exquisitely caught in Abraham Bosse's engraving, and gave the title for a play by Corneille.

By the early seventeenth century the Palais had acquired another function. It had become the closest approximation in Paris to an exchange. Paris, though its commercial and financial side was not unimportant, was not a great trading city like London or Amsterdam, and did not acquire a specific Bourse until 1724. But the Palais, with its concourse of people and function as the seat of the financial courts, was a natural meeting place. By 1608 the *Mercure François* was reporting that the Palais was the place where 'the bankers always have business when the court stops sitting, which is at the hour of change'.[36]

Although Amsterdam had nothing remotely similar to the Cours until the Plantage (of which more later) was laid out in the 1680s, the luxury shops and mixture of law, business and government in the Palais had obvious affinities with the area round the Dam. One big difference, however, was that the Dam area was reigned over by merchants, as was Amsterdam as a whole, the Palais by lawyers. The Parisian merchants had their main spheres of activity elsewhere, in the market area of Les Halles and in the Hôtel de Ville on the Place de Grève. But they were much less powerful than the Amsterdam merchants. The town council in the Hôtel de Ville was largely made up of merchants and rich shopkeepers, but by the seventeenth century its members were virtually appointed by the king and did what he told them to do. Socially, they were much inferior to the members of the Parlement and it was the ambition of most successful commercial families to give up commerce and move up into the Parlement or one of the financial courts. Administratively the spheres of the town council, the Parlement, and the king and his officers overlapped in a totally confusing manner, but the town council was always the inferior member.

144. 'Dame en falbala, à la promenade aux Tuileries'. From a late seventeenth-century engraving.

Not surprisingly, Paris, as a city dominated by a monarch on the one hand and rich ennobled lawyers, mostly with substantial private incomes, on the other, had a different life-style from Amsterdam. In the 1690s Martin Lister thought that 'there are no people more fond of coming together, to see or be seen'.[37] Perhaps as a result of constantly being in court or at court, rich Parisians treated life as a spectacle, in which they played a part at once dignified and important and intensely enjoyed both their own and everyone else's performance. It was not just the Cours la Reine which was 'le théatre de l'univers'. In the course of the seventeenth century Paris acquired a series of places in which to 'see and be seen', enabling Parisians to gyrate continuously between the Cours, the Palais, the Mall, the theatres, the opera, the Tuileries gardens and the boulevards, against the architectural backcloth of the Pont Neuf, the Place Dauphine and the Place Royale.

It was the kings and their officers and ministers who were the active and originating force in the period, as opposed to the municipality, which was subservient to the monarchy, and the Parlement, which was essentially conservative. Not surprisingly, the kings appreciated the role which a grand square or an impressive statue could play in boosting their image, and were much influenced by the pioneering work already done in Florence and Rome. France's two Medici queens were figures of importance in introducing Italian ideas to Paris, but not the only ones: it was the commercial links already existing between Florence and France which had produced the Medici marriages in the first place.

In 1556 Gaspar de Vega reported to Philip II of Spain that apart from the Louvre (and he did not think much even of that) Paris was interesting for nothing except its size.[38] In terms of contemporary buildings his comments were not unreasonable, and remained valid for the rest of the century.[39] François I promised big things, but in fact lived mostly at Fontainebleau or in the Loire valley, and did little in Paris except sell off royal land for building. In 1546 Henri II started to rebuilt the Louvre, but only completed one corner of the main court. In the 1560s Catherine de Médicis's grand projects for the Tuileries, on a new site just outside the city walls, got no further than a fragment. She always intended that her palace should be joined to the Louvre by a gallery along the Seine, but it was forty years or so before the link was built. The inspiration of Florence was obvious: the Tuileries was the equivalent of the Pitti, the Louvre of the Palazzo Vecchio, and the gallery a version of the series of galleries and corridors with which Cosimo I had linked his two Florentine palaces together. Italian influence was also in evidence in the Porte St Antoine, traditionally one of the two ceremonial entrances to Paris, which was rebuilt as a triumphal arch in 1585.[40] In 1578 work was started on a new bridge across the Seine; it was to cross the Seine in two parts, by way of the tip of the Île de la Cité. It ground to a halt in 1584, by when little had been achieved. The religious wars disastrously affected the pace of building, in Paris as everywhere else.

But when Henri IV was accepted as king of a united nation in 1594, he presided over a burst of new building, and pushed his schemes through with superabundant energy.[41] Paris entered on a renaissance of life and activity, not unlike the renaissance which had followed on the return of the popes to Rome. There was a difference, however. Rome was a city which had pitifully shrunk within the circuit of its walls, and which the popes were eager to see expanding to fill them again. Paris, with three to four times the population of Rome, was threatening to burst its walls, and the kings were eager to stop it from doing so. Theorists of the time declared that ancient Rome had perished because it grew too large, and that Paris was in danger of doing the same;[42] perhaps the kings, while ostensibly subscribing to this theory, were worried at the threat which the growing city would present to their own power; if so, future events were to prove them right.

A series of ordinances designed to prevent Paris from expanding beyond its walls, none of them very effective, were passed during the sixteenth and seventeenth centuries. But they made it difficult for the monarchy to promote urban improvements involving new building, except within the existing walls, where space was not easy to come by. In theory, the king had the right of compulsory acquisition of property without compensation: in fact not to compensate would have made him dangerously unpopular, and even purchase with compensation was almost invariably resisted by the property owners.[43] In effect, the great majority of royal improvements were on previously open space or replaced property which was redundant or belonged to the crown already. Quantitatively it involved only a small section of Paris, which remained a large, crowded and inconvenient city of dirty and narrow streets. But in terms of quality its effect can

145. View from the Pont Neuf, Paris. From an engraving by Aveline (Bibliothèque Nationale, Paris).

146. (top right) An entertainment in the Place Dauphine, Paris, part of the celebrations held for the entry of Louis XIV in 1662 (Bibliothèque Nationale, Paris).

147. (bottom right) The Carrousel held in the Place Royale (today the Place des Vosges) in 1615, to celebrate the marriage of Louis XIII to Anne of Austria (Musée Carnavalet, Paris).

scarcely be overestimated—largely because of the perception and drive of Henri IV. Henri's wife, Marie, was a Medici, the daughter of the Duke of Tuscany. Almost all his projects were inspired by Italian, and usually specifically by Medici, projects, but were carried a step further.

The first was the completion of the Pont Neuf. Work started up again in 1599 and the bridge was finished in 1606. It was a royal project not a city one, and was paid for by raising a special tax on wine. In one of his frequent visits of inspection Henri leapt over the considerable gap remaining between its two incomplete portions, in full view of an enthusiastic crowd. It was a typical act, and epitomized his style.

Unlike all the existing bridges, the Pont Neuf as built had no houses on it. In this it followed a design for the bridge which had been made in the 1570s, but which may or may not have been the one to which the bridge was commenced in 1578.[44] But Henri both gave the Pont Neuf a focal point and projected his own image by deciding to place a statue of himself on horseback at the point of the Île de la Cité where the bridge crossed it; in addition, he linked the statue to a new Place, the Place Dauphine, which was built on what had previously been the garden of the Palais. The statue was sited out of the traffic, on a small open square letting off the bridge; it looked across the bridge and through a narrow opening along the axis of the Place Dauphine. Henri leased the site of the Place to the then president of the Parlement, on condition that he build on it to a unified design provided by the king. It had shops on the ground floor, and was designed to provide accommodation for the bankers and merchants who congregated at the Palais for business. The idea of its unified design was probably inspired by the piazza at Livorno, but was adapted to the shape and circumstances of the site.

The bridge was twenty-eight metres wide and provided a thoroughfare not only wider than any then existing on bridges in Europe, but wider than any existing city street. It was extremely useful, and immediately became a major traffic artery. But it also provided a spacious platform from which to survey the river, and a setting for the statue far more dramatic and commanding than that achieved for the statue of any Italian ruler.

Amphitreatre de laplace Dausine
Iean Marot fecit

The land for the Place Dauphine was leased in 1606, and work started in 1609. The statue (which was made in Florence) was not ready for its site until 1614, after Henry IV's death. Meanwhile another of his major Parisian projects, the Place Royale (now the Place des Vosges), had been built.[45] Work on it had started about 1605, on vacant ground, where the Hôtel Royal des Tournelles had stood. This had been a favourite Parisian residence of Henri II, who had been accidentally killed taking part in a joust there in 1559; his widow had taken against it, and it had been demolished.

What was originally planned was rather different from what was finally built. Henri IV intended to build an arcaded square of shops, with housing above. Its inspiration was clearly the piazza at Livorno except that the north side, instead of being occupied by a church, was to be filled by one range of a great complex of workshops for the manufacture of silk textiles. In 1607 the silk-manufacturing project collapsed, the shops dropped out, and the partly built scheme was socially up-graded. What finally emerged on the site was a square with no commercial element in it at all, surrounded by houses of integrated design, lived in by the cream of Parisian society, and presided over at either end by pavilions belonging to the king and queen. It was as though the setting for a royal tournanent or pageant, with king and queen in pavilions of honour, had been turned into permanent architectural form. The square was a place for spectacle as well as habitation, and was spendidly inaugurated in 1611 by a masque and tournament held to celebrate the marriage of Louis XIII. A statue of the king on horseback followed in 1639.

As a residential square of integrated design occupied by grand people, the Place Royale was to have many successors, but it had no obvious prototype. The nearest was the Piazza S. Marco in Venice, one side of which had been rebuilt from 1584, in the form of a very grand terrace of official houses for the procurators.[46] This may have had some influence on the Place Royale, different though the circumstances were that produced it. The terrace had an arcade of shops in front, but the site was so deep that there was plenty of room for them. In the Place Royale the arcades survived without the shops, and even so cut inconveniently into the ground floor of the houses, besides preventing them from having imposing entrances. Similar vestigial arcades without shops were incorporated into London's Covent Garden, a square built under the joint influence of the Livorno piazza and the Place Royale in 1631–7.[47] Here too the arcades made the houses extremely inconvenient, although they provided a convenient walk for prostitutes when the square went down in the world in the eighteenth century.

The last of Henri IV's schemes was abortive owing to his death in 1610. It was for a series of avenues converging on a semicircular Place de France near the Temple, and was clearly influenced by the Piazza del Popolo in Rome.[48] Two more Italian-inspired developments inaugurated in this period probably owed nothing to the influence of the king. They were less obviously spectacular than the projects already described, but were to have an interesting progeny. In 1597 the municipality let part of the strip of land known as the Contrefosse, running along the outside of the city wall north of the Porte St Honoré, to a Florentine called Raphael Salvety.[49] Salvety leased the land in order to lay out a ground on which to play the Italian game of pall mall (in Italian *pallo a maglio*). This involved striking a ball with a mallet down a long fenced-in alley: it was a summer game and was normally played under an avenue of trees, for the sake of shade. Salvety's ground (where the Rue de Mail is today) was sufficiently

148. The game of Pall Mall.

successful for a second one to be laid out between the Seine and the walls of the Arsenal, at the other end of Paris. It was planted with a double avenue, one for the game and one for spectators to watch and promenade in.[50]

The pall mall at the Arsenal was extremely popular, more so, apparently, than the one by the Porte St Honoré, perhaps because of its agreeable situation by the river. A contemporary poet described its effect on a typical Parisian: 'Le Pont-Neuf et le Mail le mettent en extase.'[51] A third object for ecstasy soon arrived in the form of the Cours la Reine, which was laid out in 1616. A *cours* or *corso* was another Florentine import, but was to be taken up with even more enthusiasm in Paris than in Florence. The Cours la Reine was laid out by Marie de Médicis, on the model of the *corso* laid out by the Duke of Tuscany, in the Cascine Gardens, just outside Florence.[52] Its great success led to its being imitated at the other end of Paris by the Cours St Antoine, which took place on the Rue St Antoine, the traditional street for ceremonial entries into Paris, and spread out through the Porte St Antoine into the road to Vincennes. It was a regular event, but especially crowded on Shrove Tuesday, during the Paris carnival, when ladies came to it in masks; in 1657 three thousand carriages were said to have attended.[53]

To 'faire le cours' became a highly fashionable occupation, to play pall mall may have been fashionable to start with, but by the mid-century it had become a game for the comfortable bourgeoisie. A *Ballad of the Arsenal Mall* published in 1638 makes the players of the game say:

> Nous sommes des bourgeois, et d'habit et d'effet,
> Qui lassez du tracas de nos petite mesnages
> Venons nous promener a l'ombre des feuillages.*[54]

But mall and *cours* between them had caused a development in the long-rooted Parisian

*We are the middle classes, in dress and style./Tired out by the bustle of our little businesses/We come here to walk in the shade of the trees.

149. The *cours* on the Boulevard St Antoine, in the mid-eighteenth century. The parapet of the walls can be seen through the trees to the left (Bibliothèque Nationale, Paris).

fondness for social promenading. Promenading in coaches provided the rich with an alternative to promenading on foot; promenading at a particular time gave a new social glamour to the act; and, whether in coaches or on foot, all classes had acquired the taste for promenading in the shade of an avenue of trees.

In 1631 it was decided to built permanent stone fortifications in place of the earthworks known as the Fossés Jaunes, which had been pushed out from the main walls in 1556 in order to protect the Tuileries. The initative came from Cardinal Richelieu, and led to the first increase in the boundaries of Paris since the 1370s. The contract for the new walls specified 'derrière la muraille, un rempart de terre planté d'arbres pouvant servir du promenade'.[55] A short walk of trees of this kind had already been planted along the existing walls south of the Porte St Antoine, where they enclosed the gardens of the Arsenal. The idea clearly derived from the rampart walks planted at Lucca and Antwerp in the 1570s and earlier.

In fact no trees were planted in the 1630s, but the idea was taken up on a much grander scale by Louis XIV in the 1670s, probably at the instigation of François Blondel.[56] Between 1670 and about 1674 a new rampart, planted with trees, was constructed on the north-east side of the town, from the Porte St Antoine to the Porte St Denis. It followed the line of the old wall, of which it incorporated portions, especially the great bastion by the Porte St Antoine. This was one of the biggest in France and was known as the Boulevart St Antoine (*boulevart* being the French term for a large bastion). In the same period the Porte St Antoine was enlarged, and the medieval Portes St Martin and St Denis were rebuilt as triumphal arches, in celebration of Louis XIV's victories. The trees on the ramparts were planted in four rows, to form a central drive, sixty feet wide, for carriages, and sidewalks, twenty feet wide, for pedestrians. The arrangement was clearly inspired by the Cours la Reine, and was referred to as 'ce nouveau cours qui regne sur le boulevart'. By 1676 it had been decided to extend the rampart and *cours* all the way round the city, and its proposed line was shown on Bullet and Blondel's plan of Paris, published in that year.

By 1670 the walls of Paris were ridiculously inadequate in terms of contemporary fortification, but the proposed *enceinte* was not designed to bring them up to modern standards, and bore no relationship to the huge and hugely expensive systems which were being installed in cities on the French borders, and other cities all over Europe. Paris, as Nicolas Delamare was to boast in the early eighteenth century, was now secure enough not to need these.[57] But walls were also useful for police supervision and as customs barriers, and the new ramparts were probably intended to fulfil both functions, as well as to provide a pleasant promenade. The height of the walls and parapet which enclosed the raised *cours* was at least twelve feet, if engravings are to be relied on; an outer road, known as the Rue Basse du Rempart, ran along the bottom of the wall. In fact the ramparts never became effective as a barrier, because they took so long to build. The portion on the Right Bank was not completed until the early eighteenth century, and that on the Left Bank was still incomplete in the 1760s, by when the city had grown beyond it, and the customs limits had been extended to a new line; in many portions the wall and parapet seem never to have been constructed, and the rampart became no more than a raised drive, planted with trees. To begin with this drive was always referred to as the 'Cours', or the 'Rempart' but in the course of the eighteenth century, 'le cours qui regne sur le boulevart' became simply 'le boulevard du nord' and 'le boulevard du sud'.

A major difference between the Paris boulevards and the rampart walks at Antwerp and Lucca was that it was possible to drive along them. Commercial traffic was prohibited by an edict of 1679,[58] but the northern boulevard, in particular, became an increasingly popular drive for coaches. In the course of the eighteenth century, as the city spread beyond it, cafés and places of amusement of all kinds began to appear on it. Paris found itself with a tree-planted orbital road at least one hundred feet wide, and wider once the Boulevard and the Rue Basse du Rempart were amalgamated. The contrast with the narrow, noisy treeless streets in the centre of the city was very great, and the boulevards were to be imitated all over France and Europe, and used in Paris itself in the nineteenth century as the model for restructuring the inner city.

All this was in the future, and at the time the avenues on the boulevards were just one section of the many avenues which were being laid out all round the edge and environs of Paris. On the north-east side of the city a long triple avenue, known as the Cours Vincennes, was planted in the 1660s. It joined the royal palace and park at Vincennes to a great circuit of trees known as Le Trône, where a throne had been set up as part of the ceremonies of the entrance of Louis XIV and his newly married wife to Paris in 1660; from here the Faubourg St Antoine led to the Porte St Antoine.[59] On the other side of Paris, another long avenue, known at first as the Grand Cours, was planted in 1670 (the plans had been made in 1666) on the axis of the Tuileries. The area in between this and the Cours la Reine, was planted with a connecting avenue and a quincunx of trees, and named the Champs Élysées. The Grand Cours was carried up a rise about a mile from the Tuileries and at the top opened out into another circus, known as the Étoile, with avenues radiating from it, and views in all directions. All this was in open country. There was a carriage road along the Grand Cours, but originally it stopped at the base of the rise. It did not get up to the Étoile until 1724. The entire layout was designed by Le Nôtre as the outer extension of his 1660s remodelling of the gardens of the Tuileries, the garden facade of which was remodelled at the same time. The new gardens had a great open central walk on the axis of both the palace and the Grand Cours; a walk of trees and a raised walk along the river ran to either side. They were open to the well-dressed, but not to 'mean persons'.[60]

These walks and avenues were being laid out at the same time as the gardens at Versailles; the French had realized that the long vistas and radiating streets of Italian cities could be transferred to the countryside, and carried out there free of the complications arising from having to demolish existing houses or build new ones. The Parisian ones had a double function: they were at once a glorification of Louis XIV and an amenity for the inhabitants of the city. Paris was now supremely well equipped with shady, well-surfaced walks and roads for what was called at the time 'le plaisir de la promenade'; there was something for all classes and for all occasions, from informal driving or strolling under the trees to parading in style at fixed times. It became the practice to promenade by coach on the Cours la Reine, and then to be put down at the garden gate of the Tuileries and to walk there in evening cool.

The Parisian love of promenading was much commented on by foreigners. In 1698 Martin Lister described 'how the Parisians divert themselves; which consists chiefly in plays, gaming, walking or coaching' and thought that 'there are no people more fond of coming together, to see or be seen'. He found it all 'very diverting for people of quality'. He himself thought that the promenade of fashionable men and beautiful women in the Tuileries gardens was 'one of the noblest sights that can be seen' and selected 'the middle walk of the Tuileries in June, betwixt 8 and 9 o'clock at night', as the sight of Paris which had most pleased him.[61] But by the 1780s Mercier was complaining of the stink of urine on the terraces, where the fine people relieved themselves.

The avenues also formed part of a campaign to beautify Paris and to glorify Louis XIV, pursued with enthusiasm by Colbert, his chief minister, and to begin with backed by the king. At the centre was to be a largely rebuilt Louvre and a remodelled Tuileries, and around the circumference avenues, boulevards and triumphal arches. The way of entry to Paris by the Porte St Antoine was to be made grander still by extending the Cours Vincennes to it and by building a triumphal arch in the circus of the Trône. The front-door of Paris, so to speak, was to remain the Porte St Antoine; the Tuileries gardens and Champs Élysées, spacious and splendidly planted though they were, were the garden and recreation area at the back, leading nowhere in particular except to another recreation area, a royal hunting forest known as the Bois de Boulogne.[62]

In fact, much of this was abortive. Most of the gates were built, but the triumphal arch at the Trône got little further than the laying of foundations in 1670; the link to the Porte St Antoine was never made; only the entrance range and one other facade of the Louvre were rebuilt. As Louis XIV grew increasingly involved in Versailles, where he was in control of all he surveyed, he took against Paris, where he had to deal with a real city full of several hundred thousand real and not always complaisant human beings. The seat of executive government was moved to Versailles, and in the last twenty-two years of his life Louis XIV only visited Paris four times. A hundred years later Napoleon took over Colbert's idea and reversed it: the garden door became the front door, the triumphal arch was built on the Étoile instead of the Trône, and the avenue of the Champs Élysées ceased to be a recreational area and became a grand triumphal route leading to Napoleon's residence and seat of government in the Tuileries.

The change was a natural one then, because in the interval the western, Tuileries side had become the fashionable side of Paris. This was by no means the case in the mid-seventeenth century when the Place Royale, the adjacent great houses of the Marais and the newly developed Île St Louis had the biggest concentration of prestigious houses, conveniently placed both for the Louvre and the Palais. The centre of fashion was already beginning to move west, however, and its final shift was probably inevitable because so much was working in its favour: the fact that the Faubourg St Antoine on the east had become an industrial area, the superb framework provided by the Champs Élysées, the existence of the Cours la Reine and the Tuileries gardens, and finally the pull of Versailles, ten miles to the west of the city.

Even so, in 1685 attempts by the Crown to develop a Place Louis-le-Grand to the north of the Tuileries gardens as an up-to-date version of the Place Royale were a failure. Grand fronts were built at the expense of the king, but no one could be found prepared to build houses behind them. The fronts stood like a stage set for over ten years, surveying a huge equestrian statue of the king which had been installed with great pomp in 1692. In 1699 they were sold to the city; the city sold them on to a developer, who pulled down the 1685 fronts and built what is now the Place Vendôme in their place. The original design had had ground-floor arcades, as in the Place Royale, but these were omitted in the final version. It was a success, and with its completion in 1720 the final pre-eminence of the western districts over the eastern was made clear.[63]

In spite of all the improvements, Paris at the beginning of the eighteenth century was still basically running on a medieval plan, as can be seen by the quickest of looks at a street map of that date. Most of the streets were narrow, dirty, without sidewalks, and filled with a deafening clatter of wheels and hoofs: in the streets around the Palais, Halles and Châtelet the buildings were often six or seven storeys high, and the streets no more than fifteen or twenty feet broad. The improvements were mainly on the periphery, with one exception: the river.

Visually exploiting its river was one of the many ways in which Paris led the world in the sixteenth and seventeenth centuries. Here as elsewhere, however, it was developing an attitude which had started in Florence. In almost all medieval, or for that matter Renaissance, cities, a river was a convenience, a means of transport, an invaluable source of drinking water, a supply of power for industry, but not something to be looked at and enjoyed, at any rate to the extent that major buildings would be built with their main fronts looking on to it. The desirable site for buildings with pretension was on a square away from the river, or perhaps on a hilltop; at best, their rear facades might be on the river, for access to a convenient mode of transport.

At Florence, where the Ponte Vecchio was left open in the middle for the benefit of the river-view as early as the fourteenth century, and the Uffizi was supplied with a colonnade and upper-floor belvedere looking on to the Arno in the 1560s, some feeling for the river as an agreeable object to look at clearly existed. At Paris, which had started as a settlement on a small island in the middle of a river and spread outwards to either side, everyday life was inevitably more visually involved with the river than in most other cities. But perhaps the first building there that was deliberately planned to enjoy the river-view was the Grande Galerie of the Louvre. Catherine de Médicis's project of the 1560s was carried out by Henri IV in 1603–6 and extended five hundred yards

150. The Collège des Quatre Nations, Paris (today the Institut de France). Begun in 1662, to the designs of Louis Le Vau (Bibliothèque Nationale, Paris).

151. (right) The Café du Caveau in the Palais Royal, Paris (Musée Carnavalet, Paris).

along the riverside quay. By then the Pont Neuf had opened up a sensational river view. Parisians became actively conscious of the value of the river and the buildings along it as a spectacle. The best houses on the Île St Louis all faced outwards on to the river rather than inwards on to a central square, and were supplied with balconies from which to enjoy the view. The grandest house of all, the Hôtel de Bretonvilliers (built in 1637–43), was at the tip of the island looking upstream so that, as described a few decades later by Germain Brice, 'it seems from the windows of this house that all the boats that come continually to Paris are coming to land at its door'. Brice thought that this greatly increased 'the beauty and delight of the inside'.[64]

During the rest of the seventeenth century quays were built along almost all parts of the Seine not already supplied with them; above all the Collège des Quatre Nations, begun in 1662, was the first grand building in Europe designed to face directly on to a river. The college, which was founded on the basis of a bequest left by Cardinal Mazarin in 1661, had a somewhat different function from the buildings of the university, which it adjoined. It was intended to supply training for the manners as well as the mind. Sixty (later reduced to thirty) young noblemen or gentlemen from those parts of Italy, the Low Countries, Germany and Roussillon, which had recently been annexed to France, were educated there so that 'they may be instructed in all those exercises that are proper for persons of quality' and 'being acquainted with the French manner may have an affection for that nation from which they have received such benefits'.[65] Apart from classwork its members were taught dancing, handling arms, vaulting, and riding the great horse (or, as we would call it, haute école). It was to function under the patronage of the king, and to be linked directly to the Louvre by a new bridge across the Seine. Perhaps it was built in the way it was more to face the Louvre than to face the river: but the result was visually so impressive that other major buildings facing onto rivers were sure to follow—as indeed they did.

9 The Uses of Leisure

The crowds of fashionable people promenading in coaches on the Cours la Reine or walking in the Tuileries gardens represented a new development in the European city. They formed what was later to be called just 'society', but to begin with tended to be referred to as 'polite society', the 'beau monde' or 'people of quality'. Society had no formal existence and no legal powers, but by the eighteenth century many outsiders were desperately anxious to belong to it. It was a group of people who did things together, entertained each other, wore particular clothes, and talked, walked, behaved and decorated their houses in a particular manner. Any society had an inner ring, members of which were informally recognized as arbiters of who or what was acceptable. Whether or not someone was invited to their houses was the basic test of whether he or she belonged. Society became an extremely important element in cities, because it produced more than coaches and promenades. Theatres, opera houses, pleasure gardens, assembly rooms, racecourses, coffee-houses, shops, entire neighbourhoods and ultimately entire towns grew up to cater for it.

Medieval cities had been essentially practical. People lived in them because they had work to do, they worked hard, and their communal enjoyments were largely con-

152. Acrobats and a temple for fireworks on the Piazzetta S. Marco, Venice, during the 'Giovedi Grasso' celebrations. From an engraving by G. Antonelli, c. 1720–30 (Museo Correr, Venice).

fined to religious holidays, to regular but widely spaced events like fairs, or to special occasions, like a joyous entry or a royal marriage. All of these produced varying forms of entertainment or spectacle, some of them very elaborate ones, but none of them happened often enough to require a special building or a special setting; events were staged in churches, in the courtyards of large buildings or on the streets and squares of the cities; any structures that were put up were temporary ones. There was not enough leisure to produce a leisure industry, and the buildings to go with it.

The seeds were there, however, especially in three constituents of the medieval city. The most obvious was the court of the ruler, if there was one. Courts and courtiers needed and produced more in the way of entertainments and diversions, such as tournaments, masques, pageants and balls, than any other group in the city. In the sixteenth century these began to move out of castle halls and courtyards and to produce specialist structures and enclosures.

Another important group consisted of the landowning families who came into cities for a variety of purposes. Its members usually paid their respects at court, but did not necessarily have positions there, and were sometimes actually in opposition to it. They came to sit in council or parliament, pursue lawsuits, borrow money, and buy furniture and fittings for their houses, and coaches, clothes and jewels for themselves. They had the money and the time to amuse themselves while they were there, and usually found large numbers of their fellow landowners in the city at the same time, with an equal appetite for pleasure.

The third group was the city establishment, the group which formed city jousting societies and by the sixteenth century, if not before, was usually on social view in at least one big annual event indoors, such as a ball in the town hall. In any prosperous city it was likely to increase generation by generation in size, wealth and sophistication, in spite of an element of leakage, as some of its members transferred themselves to the country gentry and nobility.

Not every city contained all three groups, and in each city the relations between them and their relative social importance varied. But whatever the constituent parts, the resulting group combined in itself an appetite for enjoyment, a skill in devising agreeable ways of passing the time, leisure in which to enjoy them, and money with which to pay for them. This was society. The more agreeable the life which it lived,

153. Fireworks on the Elbe at Dresden, held to celebrate the visit of the King of Denmark in June 1709. From the painting by C. H. Fritzsche (Kupferstich-kabinett, Dresden).

or appeared to live, the more others wanted to join it, if they could gain acceptance. Cities acquired a new type of immigrant, immigrants with comfortable private incomes who came to them looking for a way of life rather than a job.

Society was not just concerned with having fun, however. Social position could be a tool towards acquiring political position; entertaining the right people and going to the right parties could lead to profitable jobs and rich marriages. Society's function as a discreetly disguised marriage market was an extremely important one; and to begin with there was always a close relationship between society and the ruling class. Sometimes the correlation was almost exact: in Nuremberg the Geschlechter, the families who ran the city, were legally defined in 1521 as those who received a formal invitation to the annual ball in the town hall.[1] But it seldom stayed so over the centuries; apart from anything else, running a country or a city and giving good parties called for different talents. Society became a game which was played for its own sake.

In the seventeenth and eighteenth centuries society did not necessarily shut itself apart when it amused itself. It had too much self-confidence, and it inherited a tradition of participating in popular amusements; in the Middle Ages it had been an accepted tradition for kings to disguise themselves and wander through the streets incognito. The traditional festivals continued in most European cities; carnivals grew, if anything, wilder, and all classes took part in them. Some fairs, which had become major com-

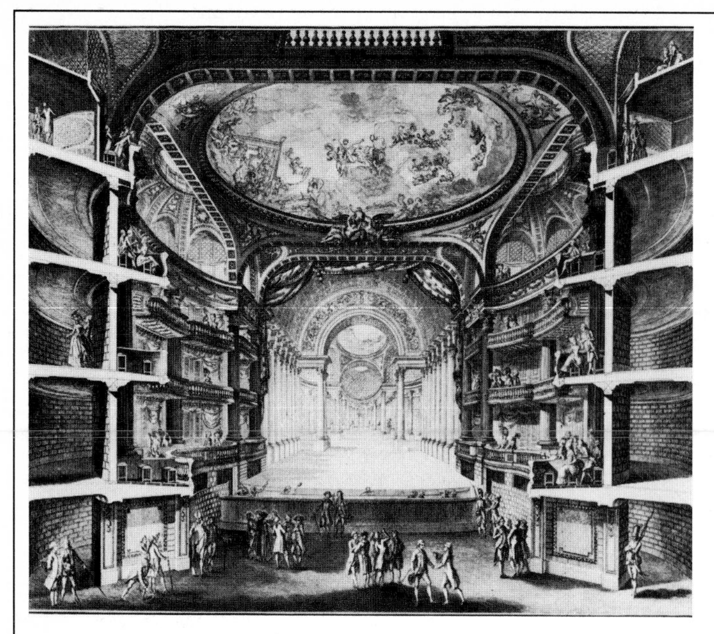

154. Interior of the Grand-Théâtre, Bordeaux, built to the design of Victor Louis in 1772–80.

155. The Assembly Rooms, York, built to the designs of the Earl of Burlington in 1731–2 (York City Art Gallery).

mercial events in the Middle Ages, became major recreational ones; among the most extravagant was St Bartholomew's Fair in London, where the cloth-selling booths gradually disappeared, and puppet-shows, plays, rope-walkers, waxworks, menageries, fire-eaters, jugglers and Punch and Judies took over. Charles II and his courtiers were frequenters, just as the Dauphin and other princes of the blood attended the Foire St Germain in Paris, in the early eighteenth century.[2] Temporary structures continued to be erected for these and similar events, and for special occasions such as peace or wedding celebrations; the latter usually produced fireworks displays, which were developed to new heights of exuberance in the seventeenth and eighteenth centuries.

From approximately the mid-sixteenth century, permanent leisure buildings began to appear in cities, at first sporadically and then in increasing numbers: first theatres, then tennis courts (which were often later converted into theatres), opera houses, cock-pits, bullrings, racecourse buildings and a variety of buildings in pleasure gardens. The development of society was a major factor in their appearance but not the only one. Increasing numbers of working people right the way down the social scale to the lower middle classes were also beginning to enjoy regular leisure activities, and buildings were being built, and walks and gardens laid out, for them. Some buildings catered for a variety of classes. Most theatres were not exclusively for the rich, and some, like the Elizabethan and Jacobean theatres in London, were built for a hard-working, mainly middle-class clientele, in face of the violent disapproval of the rich merchants who ran the city. The large number of tennis courts which appeared in Paris in the seventeenth century must have catered for a considerable social range.

The first permanent theatres were built in the sixteenth century and were of two types, deriving from two different types of medieval entertainment, those given privately in the halls, galleries or palace courtyards of rulers or great people, and those given in public, usually on wagons or temporary stages, by city guilds to celebrate particular feast days. Among early examples, the private tradition produced the theatre in Vicenza (1580–4), where the audience came by right of membership or invitation only, and the theatre at Sabbioneta (1588–90) built for a Gonzaga duke and his court; the public tradition produced the London theatres which were open to anyone who paid an admission fee. The first London theatre, known simply as The Theatre, was built in 1576 in Shoreditch, just outside the city boundaries.

Private and court theatres continued to be built right through into the nineteenth century, and so did popular public ones.[3] But the typical theatre or opera house of the seventeenth or eighteenth century was something in between the two. It was often licensed, and even subsidized by the king or relevant ruler, but entrance was through payment; it was open to any respectably dressed person, but the most prominent element was provided by the rich in boxes. There was sometimes a royal box, but it was local society rather than the local ruler which dominated this type of theatre. Sometimes, as in La Scala in Milan, its members owned their boxes, and furnished them and the anteroom behind them to their taste; arriving, circulating, recognizing the right people, cutting the wrong ones, and making conversation during the intervals and usually during the performance, were as much part of the show as the acting or singing.

The members of society enjoyed dancing and playing cards together in public places as well as in private houses, and this too produced permanent buildings, although perhaps not until the eighteenth century. Theatres were often used for dances, or the masked entertainments known as masquerades, which could take place in a separate large room incorporated in the theatre building or actually on the stage and the auditorium, perhaps with a special floor built over the latter. The great theatre at Bordeaux, the most splendid theatre of the eighteenth century, had a suite of rooms which included a café and an extremely elegant oval Salle de Concert, which could be converted as a ballroom.[4] Many town halls had a big room or rooms which could be used in the same way. A ball usually involved a room for refreshments, and a room for playing cards in, as well as a room for dancing in.

In England entertainments which just provided tea or coffee, cards and conversation were called assemblies, and were very popular in the eighteenth century, both in private houses and in public rooms. They seem to have originated in France; certainly Daniel Defoe, writing in England in 1727 when they were still a new feature, referred to them as *assemblées*.[5] Assembly rooms, which were often independent buildings of considerable size, became a great feature of English towns; they were soon used for balls as well as assemblies in the original sense, and the biggest room in them was usually a ballroom. Public assemblies were funded by subscription tickets; when they first became popular in England they got a good deal of adverse publicity, as places which involved young women in sexual intrigues and which mothers feared as encouraging 'Half-pay officers to run away with their daughters'; so Defoe put it, when declaiming against 'their pernicious tendency'.[6] Masquerades, which were basically masked assemblies, were regarded with even more suspicion by moralists, above all the extremely successful masquerades held from about 1718 until the 1730s in the Haymarket Opera House in London. To begin with they took place in a big room adjoining the auditorium, and then, when that was not big enough, they moved into the auditorium and onto the stage as well.[7]

By the mid-eighteenth century, assembly rooms and theatres had both been accepted as essential meeting places for society in any town of any pretensions. A race-meeting very commonly appeared as a third fashionable gathering place, although all classes came to watch the races. Race-meetings first became common in the seventeenth century, but it was not until the mid-eighteenth century that they produced significant buildings, in the form of stands for fashionable society, which usually incorporated a room for entertainments below the covered viewing place. The stand at York, designed by John Carr in 1754, was an early and elegant example. It was at much the same

156. Bull-fighting in the Plaza de los Toros, Seville, in the early eighteenth century.

157. (top right) Masquerade at the Haymarket Theatre, London. By Giuseppe Grisoni, 1724 (Victoria and Albert Museum).

158. (bottom right) Frederick, Prince of Wales, walking in the Mall, London. From a painting attributed to Samuel Wale.

time that permanent bullrings first began to be built in Spain and Portugal, to cater for the Iberian equivalent of race-meetings, a popular sport with a fashionable element. Previously, bullfights had been held in public squares.[8]

A promenade such as the Cours la Reine, frequented by society at a particular time of the day, usually played an important social role in any considerable town from the late seventeenth century through into the nineteenth. Promenades of this kind need to be distinguished from walks and drives in more general use, often frequented by all classes; in England the former were sometimes called parades, and the term is a useful one by which to distinguish them. From the seventeenth century onwards most towns of any importance were provided with both types.

It was typical of the development of the concept of society that the Cours la Reine was laid out as a parade for the queen and her courtiers, but developed into something much less specific: any well-dressed person in a coach and four seems to have been admitted, just as any well-dressed person was admitted to the gardens of the Tuileries. Parades had a variety of functions. From a practical point of view, in the days before the telephone, or an efficient postal service, a parade was a useful place in which those participating could meet people, pick up the latest news, and make public the fact that they were in town. It was also an obvious form of entertainment and of showing off; people came to see and be seen. Finally it was a place in which society could establish its sense of identity. Some people paraded with total confidence that they belonged, others to find out whether they belonged or not. On-the-make outsiders who were not acceptable were soon discouraged or frozen off, by the direct cut or the cold half-bow.

Parades also had a variety of sexual functions. Mothers found them a useful place in which they could show off their daughters with a view to marriage; lovers used them to make assignations. Fashionably dressed courtesans were also often to be found on them, and provided the main exception to the convention that these parades were for the socially elite. Respectable ladies of fashion presumably did not acknowledge them, but they do not seem to have objected to them either. They were there because the male half of society wanted them there.

159. Gardiner's Mall on Sackville (today O'Connell) Street, Dublin (National Gallery of Ireland).

In France, what is now the Cours Mirabeau in Aix-en-Provence is a provincial offshoot of the Cours la Reine; unlike the latter it survives as an evening promenade, though no longer a parading place for the carriages of the Provençal Parlement and local nobility, as it was when first laid out in 1651, on the site of part of the medieval walls.[9] In a number of French towns, avenues planted for pall mall, usually on or near the fortifications, became places of promenade and perhaps of parade: in 1655 Evelyn was delighted with the examples at Blois and Tours.[10] In seventeenth-century England the equivalent of the Tuileries was the Mall in St James's Park, and of the Cours la Reine the Ring in Hyde Park. Both were clearly frequented by English society in imitation of France. The Mall originated as a pall mall ground, which had been laid out and planted by Charles II in about 1660; his father had previously introduced the game to London on the site of what is now Pall Mall, which was turned into a public road when the new ground was formed.[11] Charles II's Mall was frequented by courtiers and other fashionable people, who promenaded in the avenue running alongside the ground; by the end of the century the game was no longer played, but the Mall had become the place of parade for London society, and its fame was to produce other malls all over the British Isles. According to an account written about 1720: 'Society comes to walk here on fine, warm days, from seven to ten in the evening, and in winter from one to three o'clock . . . the park is so crowded at times that you cannot help touching your neighbour. Some people came to see, some to be seen, and others to seek their fortunes; for many priestesses of Venus are abroad . . . all on the lookout for adventures.'[12]

Parading places in the British Isles in the eighteenth century could be called Malls, Walks or Parades, and were usually for walking, not driving. In Dublin there were two rival ones on either side of the river, the Beaux' Walk on St Stephen's Green, and Gardiner's Mall on what is now O'Connell Street. A mid-eighteenth-century engraving shows the latter as a kind of paddock for fashionable strollers, running down the centre of the street. Later on in the eighteenth century Gardiner's Mall went out of fashion, and the place to parade, especially on Sunday evenings, was the Rotunda Gardens just to the north of it. Here, according to a French visitor in 1796, 'Worthy mothers were thin on the ground, and seemed worried; young ladies, on the other hand, were very numerous, and seemed happily occupied; in a word, I have no doubt that this Promenade perfectly achieved its object, of helping women to find lovers.'[14]

The Unter den Linden in Berlin had an enclosure for parading reminiscent of Gardiner's Mall, although not so elaborate. The enclosure ran down the central way

160. The Unter den Linden, Berlin, in 1691. By Johann Stridbeckh (Deutsche Staatsbibliothek, Berlin).

of the avenue which gave the street its name. This was over a thousand yards long, and had been planted with two thousand nut and lime trees in 1647, to lead from Berlin through open country to the Tiergarten, a hunting park of the Electors of Brandenburg. It had become a parading place by the end of the century, by when a new quarter of the town had been laid out alongside it; and parading was to remain one of its major functions into the nineteenth century.[15]

In Hamburg the Jungfernstieg was the fashionable parade; it ran along the great medieval mill-pond known as the Alsterdamm, and promenaders could look out over the water as they walked under a double avenue of trees.[16] In Venice the Grand Canal became the setting for a glittering evening parade of the fashionable in gondolas, 'singing, playing on harpsichords, and other music and serenading their mistresses', as Evelyn described them in 1645.[17] In Antwerp the Marchioness of Newcastle, who went to live there with her husband during the Cromwellian government, described how when she 'would not bury myself quite from the sight of the world' she would drive in her coach 'about some of the streets, which we call here a tour, where all the chief of the town go to see and be seen'.[18] In St Petersburg the Nevsky Avenue became a glittering parade of carriages and strollers in the later afternoon.[19] In Spain a parade was known as a *paseo*, and a favourite form of parading was what was known as the *paseo con alamos*, a parade in the shade of the plantations of poplars known as *alamedas*; there is a reference to the custom in Seville as early as 1583.[20]

A fashionable parade tended to create, or at least help create, a fashionable quarter. The Cours la Reine played a part in drawing society to live on the west side of Paris. The Cours Mirabeau in Aix was situated between the town and the new Quartier Mazarin, which had been laid out in 1646, but plots in which were selling off very slowly; the development of the Cours as a fashionable carriage parade certainly contributed to the development of the Quartier in the late seventeenth and eighteenth centuries as the most fashionable quarter of Aix. The Unter den Linden, having started as an avenue through open fields, ended up as the most famous and fashionable street in Berlin. Property developers were conscious of the economic value of a successful parade: Gardiner's Mall in Dublin was laid out by the Gardiner family, who were developing their fields on the north side of Dublin in what proved a completely successful attempt to create a fashionable district which would rival the older one in the neighbourhood of St Stephen's Green, south of the river.

Promenades laid out or planted for more general use were equally widespread. In London the great damp common of Moorfields was drained, railed in, supplied with

161. The parade on the Jungfernstieg, Hamburg. By Christopher Suht, *c.* 1820 (Museum für Hamburgische Geschichte).

benches and laid out with avenues of elms and gravelled walks between 1606 and 1616; the city paid for the work, but collected contributions towards the cost from rich citizens.[21] In Rome the steep slopes below the church of Trinità dei Monti, where the Spanish Steps now are, had been planted with rather unimpressive walks of trees by at least the 1640s.[22] In Paris the quincunxes of trees planted in the 1670s on the Champs Élysées, became a popular resort, far less aristocratic than the neighbouring Cours la Reine, until, to the rage of Parisians, Madame de Pompadour had the trees cut down because she said that they blocked the view from her house in the Faubourg St Honoré. They were replanted to a different plan in 1764.[23]

In 1682 the city council of Amsterdam laid out a rather unusual and attractive recreational area known as the Nieuwe Plantage, on what had previously been marshy ground to the east of the city. It was divided into fifteen squares, with wide alleys between them lined with double avenues of trees; each square was subdivided into plots. These were leased out to the citizens, most of whom built single-storey houses on them, and planted out the remainder as vegetable allotments or flower gardens. The alleys became a place of resort and summer strolling for the citizens; a big inn owned by the city provided a bowling green, tennis court and open-air theatre.[24]

As Paris grew in size in the course of the eighteenth century the Parisian boulevards became more and more lively. An engraving of the 1750s after Auguste de St Aubin shows how the crowds of coaches and strollers had stimulated the appearance of cafés, street vendors, musicians and, inevitably, beggars. The engraving is titled *La Promenade des Remparts de Paris*; the expression 'boulevard' still had not gained general currency. But in 1775 it was specifically on the boulevards that Mrs Thrale spent several very entertaining evenings. By then they had become 'places of public amusement for the ordinary sort of people . . . a sort of Sadlers Wells where rope dancing, tumbling and pantomimes preside . . . saw a boy dance among rows of eggs with surprising agility'.[25]

Bordeaux was surrounded by a promenade of trees during the Intendancy of the Marquis de Tourny (1743–57); it included provision for both coaches and pedestrians, and was called a Cours to begin with, but later (by at least 1785) a Boulevard, all clearly under the influence of Paris. At Bordeaux the term 'boulevard' lost any connection with ramparts or fortifications, however, for these were preserved as a customs wall, and the boulevard ran well outside them.[26]

162. La Promenade des Remparts de Paris. From an engraving after Auguste de St Aubin (Bibliothèque Nationale, Paris).

The many improvements made at Bordeaux during Tourny's Intendancy included further planting of trees and promenades, and the laying out, from 1746, of a large public garden, the Jardin Royal: Tourny called it 'mes Tuileries', but unlike the Tuileries it seems to have been open to everyone.[27] At Nancy a 'Pepinière Royal servant de Promenade publique' was laid out in the form of a large enclosure planted with rows of trees between 1765 and 1772.[28] At Vienna the Emperor Joseph II laid out the Augarten for public use in 1775.[29] In Munich the 'English Garden' was laid out in the style of an English park at the instigation of Count Rumford, and opened in 1791. Existing royal parks on the edges of cities were also opened to the public: Hyde Park outside London on and off from the early seventeenth century, the Tiergarten outside Berlin by 1772, the Prater outside Vienna from the 1780s.[30]

Elaborate public pleasure gardens were a London innovation, and to begin with no other city had anything to compare with them. In the eighteenth century London became a rival to Paris as a pleasure city; at the beginning of the century it was imitating Paris, but by the end Paris was imitating it. This was partly the result of its growing size and wealth as both a capital and a commercial city: in the early eighteenth century it had a population of about 600,000 people and had overtaken Paris as the biggest city in Europe. But it was also due to the particular nature of London society. In the eighteenth century this was dominated less by the court than by Parliament, which had acquired a power and prestige unequalled by any equivalent institution in the rest of Europe. It was very different in its nature, function and history from the Paris Parlement; the members of the House of Lords and House of Commons normally sat for around four months a year, and, since most of them were substantial landowners and the main base of their power lay in country estates, many of them left London in the interval. These large numbers of rich people in London for only a few months had a concentrated appetite for enjoyment while they were there, of which pleasure gardens were one result.

Modest pleasure gardens in the form of areas planted with trees in formal rows, with booths for refreshments and people strolling up and down chatting to each other, strumming on musical instruments or making love, were to be found all over Europe. The Spring Gardens at Vauxhall were just such a place. They were first opened in about 1660, and were situated within easy reach of the Thames, a mile or so above London.

163. 'The Adieu to the Spring-Gardens'. Headpiece to a Vauxhall song-sheet, engraved by George Bickham after a design by H. F. Gravelot, 1737 (Lambeth Archives, London).

In 1728 an energetic new proprietor called Jonathan Tyers acquired a lease of them, and for the next thirty years was constantly elaborating them, and embellishing them with new buildings. Encouraged by the success of Vauxhall, an equally ambitious rival was opened a little further down the Thames, in the gardens of Ranelagh House, Chelsea, in 1742. By the mid-eighteenth century London had several dozen pleasure gardens of all sizes, social gradations and architectural ambitions, but Vauxhall and Ranelagh reigned supreme.

Vauxhall[31] was divided into two main parts: a grove of trees, divided by straight walks and embellished with arches and architectural conceits; and a great open space, also planted with trees, containing a bandstand and orchestra in the middle of rows of supper boxes all round. People arrived by water when it was still daylight, and wandered round the walks or listened to the music until twilight, when in a few magical moments trees, walks, bandstand, orchestra and supper boxes were suddenly illuminated with fifteen hundred oil lamps, and fifty or so lively and colourful paintings unrolled with a rattle behind each supper box. A concert of gay and pretty music or singing went on until after midnight, with intervals during which people took to the walks again, listened to the nightingales, or paraded up and down, making friends, picking up acquaintances, or admiring the occupants of the supper boxes on the pretext of looking at the paintings behind them. Those who felt like it went to the Dark Walk, which was not illuminated, or retreated into the trees on either side of it.

The charm of Vauxhall was its combination of nature, art and gaiety: the approach up the river on a fine evening, and what the *Spectator* called 'the fragrancy of the walks and bowers with the choice of birds that sang upon the trees'; the view of hayfields and evening haymakers from the outer walks; the prettiness of the buildings which grew more fantastical and elaborate through the decades; and the liveliness and good humour of the music and crowds. The people who came were a mixture of fine ladies, clergymen, apprentices, prostitutes, dukes, officers of the guards, city merchants, pickpockets and adventurers; but the variety added to the fun, and the fashionable could always retire to the semi-privacy of a supper box.

Ranelagh,[32] being later on the scene, had to establish itself with a novelty, in the form of the Rotunda. This was a circular building one hundred and fifty feet in diameter, and contained a great central fireplace, an orchestra, and a circuit of supper boxes. Outside, there were walks, a little lake, boats in which to embark on it, and a Chinese pagoda in the middle of the lake. But it was the Rotunda which was the main attraction; not surprisingly, this great amphitheatre of gaiety and music eclipsed Vauxhall for a few seasons, so Horace Walpole wrote, 'you can't set your foot without treading on a Prince, or Duke of Cumberland', and that Smollett enthused about 'this enchanted palace of a genius . . . enlightened with a thousand golden lamps that emulate the noon-day sun; crowded with the great, the rich, the gay, the happy and the fair; glittering with cloth of gold, embroidery and precious stones'.[33]

The Rotunda gave Ranelagh the edge on Vauxhall on a cool or damp evening, although Vauxhall remained unbeatable on a hot summer night. The success of the Rotunda inspired the creation of the Pantheon in Oxford Street, which opened in 1772 as a winter Ranelagh, and became the third, though shortest lived, of London's crowning trilogy of pleasure buildings. It was essentially a magnificent assembly rooms, which offered a variety of entertainment in a series of different spaces culminating in the main rotunda. This was one of the biggest and most sumptuous covered spaces in Europe, a sensational amalgam of the Pantheon in Rome and Sancta Sophia in Constantinople.

The fame of these three pleasure places is shown by the fact that from the 1760s Paris acquired numerous 'Wauxhalls', a Ranelagh and a Panthéon, having had nothing like them previously. They started to appear after the Peace of Paris in 1763, when the war between the two countries was followed by a wave of Anglomania in Paris: not all were named after English examples, but enough were to make it clear where the idea came from. None was on the scale of the London trio, and none lasted more than a few years, but they were very decorative while they lasted. There were numerous Wauxhalls, including 'le délicieux Wauxhall' next to the Foire St Germain, which lasted from about 1770 to 1784, and, much later, a 'Wauxhall d'été', with gardens and rotunda, on the Boulevard St Martin. 'Le Ranelagh' opened in 1774 in the Bois de Boulogne, for public balls and firework displays; the Panthéon was built in the centre of the city, near the Palais Royal, in 1784.[34] Most delicious of all was the Colisée, which opened in 1774 just off the Champs Élysées. The French liked Greek or Roman names; in the early nineteenth century Paris had a dance-hall called Paphos, and a Jardin de Tivoli, in the Rue de Clichy, north of the boulevard.[35] This Parisian pleasure garden was imitated by Tivoli Gardens in Berlin[36] and Copenhagen, the latter of which is perhaps the only survivor of any importance from among the many pleasure gardens which sprang up all over Europe.

Many public gardens acquired a pleasure-garden element. Both the Jardin Royal in Bordeaux and the Augarten in Vienna had a café or restaurant. By the end of the eighteenth century the Prater had acquired a whole range of diversions. The part closest to the city was covered with refreshment booths and little open-air tables; there were swings, a big open space for firework displays, a 'circus gymnasticus' for equestrian shows, a coffee-house, and a two-storey Lusthaus, where meals were served, surrounded by open galleries looking over the Danube. On holidays, and especially for the firework displays, when the whole Prater was illuminated, the gardens were crowded with coaches, and with people of all classes, from the emperor downwards. The Lusthaus,

164. The Colisée, Paris. By Gabriel de St Aubin (Wallace Collection, London).

165. (top right) The pavilion known as the Josephs-Ruhe, in the Prater, Vienna. Aquatint after Joseph Schaffer, 1787 (Museen der Stadt, Vienna).

166. (bottom right) Interior of the Rotunda at Ranelagh Gardens, Chelsea, designed by William Jones, 1742. From the painting by Antonio Canaletto (National Gallery, London).

being furthest from the city and a long walk for pedestrians, was especially frequented by society and its carriages.[37]

England invented the pleasure gardens; and it was England, too, that went several steps further and pioneered the idea of whole cities devoted to pleasure. To say 'devoted to pleasure' is admittedly an exaggeration; ostensibly, at any rate, they were devoted to health and pleasure combined.

The combination of being ill and having a good time seems an odd one, but it has a long history. To begin with, it was invariably connected with taking the waters at a mineral spring. Some way had to be found of passing the time in the long intervals between drinking or bathing in the waters. The fact that people were away from their usual environment and often in rather remote (and sometimes beautiful) places encouraged a little informality.

A guide to the baths at Plombières, on the borders of Lorraine and Germany, which was published in 1576, describes how, in the intervals of bathing in the waters, 'some sing, some play on instruments, some eat, some sleep, some dance, with the result that no one is bored and time never drags'.[38] Mary Queen of Scots relished her visits to take the waters at Buxton, in Derbyshire, as much for social as for medical reasons.[39] In 1581, when Montaigne was at the Bagni di Lucca up in the hills sixteen miles from Lucca, he gave a ball, as did several others taking the waters at the time. He invited a mixture of fellow patients, Lucca nobility and local peasants; when the dancing was over one of the local ladies presented a selection of belts, bonnets, slippers, crystal hair nets and necklaces to those of the peasant boys and girls who had danced most gracefully, and everyone went to supper.[40]

At the Bagni di Lucca there was a trellised promenade, looking over a pretty view. At Tunbridge Wells, a spa frequented by court and society twenty-five miles from London, there was a similar mixture in the mid-seventeenth century, but everything

167. The morning assembly at the Pump Room at Bath, *c.* 1737. From an etched fan attributed to G. Speren (Victoria Art Gallery, Bath).

had become a little more fashionable: the walk had become a parade, lined with smart little shops; there were rustic surroundings, bowling greens, outdoor dancing, prostitutes, adventurers and, by 1700, a card-room and a ballroom. The gentry promenading on the walk amused themselves by watching the local peasantry, who came to sell market produce at a walk down below, but did not ask them to join in the dancing.[41]

All these places were, at best, the size of large villages, as were other European watering-places, including the original Spa near Liege. Bath was the first place to develop into something more on the strength of its waters; but it developed in the spa tradition, of informal gaiety combined with rural charm. The mineral springs there had been known since pre-Roman times, and had attracted people ever since; in addition, Bath had become a modestly prosperous textile town. But its extraordinary boom came in the eighteenth century (by when its textile industry was in decline) and was mainly engineered by four men: Richard ('Beau') Nash, who became master of ceremonies in the Assembly Rooms in about 1705, Ralph Allen, who owned the main Bath-stone quarries and had houses both in and just outside the town, and two generations of architects and property speculators, John Wood the elder and younger.

Beau Nash was a 'character'. He always wore a white cocked hat, and put fashionable ladies in their places, which they seem to have enjoyed. If his contemporary biographer, Oliver Goldsmith, is to be relied on, he also had a philosophy of conduct. He believed in breaking down the barriers that still divided the different levels of upper-class and upper-middle-class society. When he became master of ceremonies, 'General society among people of rank or fashion was by no means established. The nobility still preserved a tincture of Gothic haughtiness, and refused to keep company with the gentry at any of the public entertainments of the place.'[42] Nash, using the parade and the Assembly Rooms as his tools, set out to get all classes 'from the private gentleman upwards' doing things together and talking together with no constraints except of good manners; to create a republic of gentlemen, in fact, where a duke could talk to a doctor, and a Tory to a Whig. As an admirer of his put it: 'to promote society, good manners and a coalition of party and ranks: to suppress scandal and late hours, are his views'.[43]

Nash clearly had a genius for social manipulation; he managed to put his views across by creating a way of life which people found so enjoyable that they came to Bath in greater and greater numbers to take part in it. Bath became a kind of glorified Vauxhall Gardens. It had a similar mixture of art and nature, and a similar gaiety—though a much smaller admixture of the lower classes, for the combination of getting to Bath and staying there was an expensive one.

Like Vauxhall, Bath provided both a fixed programme and informal interludes. The events in the programme consisted of visits to baths and the Pump Room in the morning, to the Parade at midday, and to the Assembly Rooms or the theatre in the evening.[44] In the intervals people wandered round the town or the surrounding countryside, met their friends, gossiped in the coffee-houses or browsed in the bookshops. There was a good deal of intrigue and gambling, but very little drinking and no late hours, for Bath was after all a health resort; so everyone, except the genuinely ill, felt very well there.

Bath evolved a combination of nature and art, or rather architecture, which fitted this way of life to perfection, but only came to maturity after the death of both Nash and the elder Wood. The first foretaste was in Wood's Grand Parade, which was built in 1740–8 and was the first promenade in England to be actually called a Parade. It took the place of his abortive plan for a Grand Parade in Queen Square, a very grand square in the style of the Place Vendôme which he had planned as a combination of enclosed space and backcloth against which visiting society would parade.[45]

The second Grand (or North) Parade was situated on low ground down by the river, and consisted of a raised paved walk bordered by a terrace of houses; the terrace was less grand than Wood had intended, because the money ran out. But the great novelty of the Parade, compared to the London Mall, his previous project in Queen Square or any existing English parade, was its view. It looked out across the river to the open countryside beyond. As the novelist Fanny Burney, who lodged in one of the houses, wrote in 1780: 'We have meadows, hills, Prior Park, the soft-flowing Avon—whatever nature has to offer, I think, always in our view.'[46]

In the mid-eighteenth century England was inaugurating the picturesque movement in landscape gardening. Formal Palladian houses were being set into informal landscapes, in which Arcadian parkland was grazed on by herds of deer and drifted down through clumps of trees to the banks of apparently natural lakes. At Bath an urban equivalent was developed. Generous slices of countryside were brought into the town, either as immediate foreground or as part of a view. The most spectacular example of this was the series of crescents which climbed up the steep hills behind the town from the 1760s onwards. Each was an exquisitely formal design, but was situated so as to look onto meadows or common land, where cows and horses grazed, and beyond them to woods and hills of the countryside across the River Avon. Vauxhall, in spite of its trees, nightingales and haymakers, had nothing to compare to this.

The first and most imposing of the Bath crescents was the Royal Crescent, which was designed and built by John Wood the younger in 1767–74. It adjoined his father's King's Circus, a splendid circle of houses, but inward-looking onto an enclosed central space. The son had opened up his father's circus by cutting it in half. In 1780 Fanny Burney was enthusiastic about 'the exquisite crescent , which to all the excellence of architecture that adorns the Circus adds all the delights of nature that beautify the Parade'.[47] In fact, it soon took over from the latter as the fashionable parade for society. It was an exquisite synthesis: the great sweep of columns suggested the unity and culture of the society which lodged in the houses and paraded in front of them, the greenery and the view kept them in touch with nature.

168. (following page top). View of Kemp Town, Brighton. By J. Bruce (Brighton Central Reference Library).

169. (following page bottom) A view on the canal at Bath.

The Bath mixture of sophisticated urban crescents and terraces looking onto natural landscapes was to be imitated all over the British Isles, at first in other spas but soon in towns of all kinds. By the end of the eighteenth century it had produced the seaside resort. In 1750 a pamphlet was published which suggested that sea water was good both for the body and for the digestion, and soon London invalids were going down to Brighton, to knock back glasses of disgusting sea water and be dipped into salt baths by formidable bathing-women.[48] Brighton, in the by now familiar fashion, became gay and fashionable as a result, and replaced Bath as the resort most frequented by London society. But the first new houses which quickly sprang up to accommodate visitors largely ignored the sea. They were grouped in a sheltered position looking onto a green called the Steyne, where the fishermen laid out their nets to dry. The Steyne became the parading place of Brighton, complete with a band playing, the Prince Regent's pavilion as a backcloth, and the fishermen and their nets to give a touch of nature.

A touch of nature was soon found insufficient, however. In the 1790s the Marine Promenade was laid out, to provide houses and a promenade looking straight out to the open sea; and by the 1840s Brighton stretched along the sea for four miles of terraces, squares and crescents, and a carriage and pedestrian promenade ran all the way in front of them.

In the mid-eighteenth century London led Europe in the quality of its shops as well as its resorts and

THE
Old
STATE
Lottery Office
for
The Sale
of
TICKETS
and
Shares
CAPEL
Street
URTON OFFICE

170. (previous page) Shops by Essex Bridge in Capel Street, Dublin. Detail from the watercolour by James Malton, *c.* 1790 (Victoria and Albert Museum).

171. The Royal Crescent, Bath (John Wood the Younger, 1767–74). From the engraving in Warner's *History of Bath*, 1801 (Bath Reference Library).

pleasure gardens. In 1775 Mrs Thrale complained that 'the shops at Paris are particularly mean'.[49] The English superiority lay mainly in having glazed shop windows. In the days of leaded lights made up of small panes of glass, a glazed window was relatively useless for the display of goods. In the Middle Ages small shop fronts were always open, and had a stall serving directly into the street: everything in the shop was visible from the street, and the shopkeeper stood behind the stall, shouting out his goods. In the larger shops, where the counter was inside, the attention of the passer-by could be attracted by hanging signs, or by a display of goods on a ledge in front. But the window behind the ledge was invariably unglazed, both so that the goods on show could be reached from inside and so that the shopkeeper could keep an eye on them.

Open shop fronts made the shop cold. The attractions of an open stall in a covered hall or gallery were obvious, especially if they were in a place frequented by people with money to spend. The shopping galleries at the Antwerp, Amsterdam and London exchanges were immediately fashionable and successful, and in the seventeenth century places such as the hall and adjacent galleries of the Palais in Paris, Westminster Hall in London and the Vladislaw Hall in Prague were lined with stalls, and remained so through the eighteenth century.[50] Booksellers, toyshops, print shops and haberdashers predominated. The Palais became the most fashionable shopping centre in Paris, so much so that by the eighteenth century it was often called the Palais Marchand.

In London the New Exchange in the Strand, which was opened in 1609, was originally intended for both merchants and shops, in the manner of other exchanges, but the merchants never used it and both its two floors of galleries became filled with fashionable shops. The Exeter Exchange, also in the Strand, was built in emulation of it in 1676, purely for shopping.

But as the technique of glass-making improved, and panes of glass could be made progressively larger, shop windows in which goods were put on show behind glass to attract the passer-by became a possibility. Paris was not well situated to exploit this, however, because of the narrowness, noisiness and dirtiness of its shopping streets, which

172. Shops in the Vlavdislav Hall of Prague Castle, in 1607. From the engraving by Aeqidius Sadeler (British Museum).

were in the centre of the city, and retained the dimensions of medieval Paris even when the buildings on them had been rebuilt. All visitors commented on these streets, which had no sidewalks, so that pedestrians were constantly in danger of being run down or spattered with mud by fast-moving traffic. 'Walking', wrote Arthur Young in 1787, 'which in London is so pleasant and so clean, that ladies do it every day, is here a toil and a fatigue to a man, and an impossibility to a well-dressed woman.'[51] 'The renowned Tournefort', according to the Russian traveller Karamzin writing in 1790, 'who had travelled almost the entire world, was crushed to death by a fiacre on his return to Paris because on his travels he had forgotten to leap in the streets, like a chamois.'[52] In this ambience, browsing in shop windows was not likely to flourish.

Almost all London streets had sidewalks, and Pall Mall and the Strand, the two main eighteenth-century shopping streets, were wider than any equivalent in Paris. In the course of the eighteenth century shops in galleries went out of fashion, and the shopping streets gradually filled with shops with glazed shop fronts. The panes grew larger as the century progressed; behind the panes goods were carefully arranged to make a show. A key moment in the development of the London shop was the demolition of the New Exchange in 1734. It was replaced by a terrace of unified design which had glazed external shop fronts all the way along, and living accommodation for the shopkeepers above the shops.[53]

Living above the shop remained the norm. Shops were family businesses, and seldom occupied more than the ground floor of one house, unless there were workshops attached, as in the case of a furniture shop: Chippendale's business in St Martin's Lane occupied four houses, and a big yard at the back.[54] Just how handsome and profitable one of these small shops dealing in luxury goods could be can still be seen in Artillery Lane, Spitalfields, where Francis Rybot, a seller of silks (probably both wholesale and retail), had a shop front of the greatest elegance installed about 1757, and lived above it in richly decorated rooms which would not have disgraced a lord.[55]

113
OMBRES CHINOISES DE SERA- PHIN
MAGASIN
CHANGE DE TOUTES SORTES DE MONNAIES
CABI- NET DE CON SULTA- TION AL'EN TRESOL
CAFE AMERICAIN

174. General view of the courtyard of the Palais Royal, Paris, built to the designs of Victor Louis in 1780–4 (Bibliothèque Nationale, Paris).

173. (left) 'La sortie du Numero 113', Palais Royal, Paris. From the watercolour by Opiz, 1815 (Musée Carnavalet, Paris).

Shops in the London manner quickly spread over the British Isles, but Paris had nothing to equal them until the 1780s. In that decade the commercial development of the garden of the Palais Royal made it the shopping centre of Europe, and produced one of the most memorable and enjoyable places ever to have been created in a European city.

The developer was the Duc de Chartres, of the Orleans branch of the Bourbons. His family had been living in the Palais Royal since 1661, and in the absence of the king at Versailles its members had become the leaders of Paris society. The duke was an Anglophile, as extravagant as he was rich, and always short of money. When he decided to develop the big garden at the back of the palace in 1780, there was an outcry, because the garden was a very pleasant one and was open to the public. The result of the re-development was so delightful, however, that criticism rapidly died down once the buildings were opened in 1784. They were an extravagant success, and immediately replaced the Palais Marchand as the most fashionable rendezvous in Paris.

They took the form of a covered arcade running round three sides of a very large court or garden. There were shops all along the arcades, glazed in the English manner, and three storeys of accommodation above them. The court was planted with trees and embellished with fountains. In the centre (added a little after the rest) was a sunken top-lit 'circus'—in fact a long colonnaded hall, intended for concerts, balls and shows of all kinds.

Mrs Thrale described the Palais Royal as 'a sort of Vauxhall with tents, fountains and a colonnade of shops and coffee-houses surrounding it on every side'.[56] Arthur Young called it 'in the style of our Pantheon', and Thiery's 1787 guide to Paris, 'a kind of perpetual fair'.[57] It was as though the Piazza S. Marco in Venice had been amalgamated with Vauxhall, Ranelagh and the best shops in London. Shopping at its most luxurious and entertainment at its most enjoyable were concentrated into one highly decorative ensemble right in the centre of Paris.

The variety which it contained on its two main floors was prodigious.[58] It included an exquisite theatre, a puppet-show, a silhouette-show, a waxworks, and a theatre in which child actors performed. There were auction rooms, concert rooms, a salon for chessplayers, gambling clubs, purely social clubs, a Turkish bath, apartments to rent, several small hotels, numerous cafés, and eating places run by *restaurateurs*—a chic new phrase invented for the Palais Royal. The upper floors contained very agreeable rooms which were rented out to bachelors, prostitutes and artists. In the main building of the Palais visits to one of the best private picture collections in Europe could be arranged by members of the public without too much difficulty. The shops varied in size: some occupied only one bay of the arcade, some as many as nine, most were on one floor only, but some were on two. There were tailors, print-shops, picture-shops, jewellers, glass-shops and shops selling every kind of luxury goods. The Magasin des Effets Précieux, which ran through nine bays of the first floor, sold pictures, marbles, bronzes, porcelain, jewellery, watches, furniture, lustres and materials. It and other shops in the Palais Royal were the first in Paris to do away with bargaining, and to sell for a fixed price. But the prices were extremely high.

'Everything', wrote Karamzin, 'that can be found in Paris (and what cannot be found in Paris) is in the Palais Royal . . . Should an American savage come to the Palais Royal, in half an hour he would be most beautifully attired and would have a richly furnished house, a carriage, many servants, twenty courses on the table, and, if he wished, a blooming Lais who each moment would die for love of him. Here are assembled all the remedies for boredom and all the sweet banes for spiritual and physical health, every method of swindling those with money and tormenting those without it, all means of enjoying and killing time. One could spend an entire life, even the longest, in the Palais Royal, and as in an enchanting dream, dying, say "I have seen and known all".'[59]

Gambling and prostitution formed an increasingly important part of the attractions of the Palais Royal, crowded it with foreign soldiers after the Battle of Waterloo, and were finally repressed by Louis Philippe (the Duc de Chartres's son) in 1837, a step which effectively finished its prosperity and central role in the social life of Paris. The prostitutes had rooms on the upper floors, were relatively inconspicuous in the daytime, but came out in force at night. Karamzin was as charmed by them as by everything else. 'We left the galleries', he wrote, 'and sat down to rest in a chestnut-lined walk . . . Here silence and a half-light reigned. Although the arcades shed their light upon the green boughs, it was lost among the shadows. From another walk floated soft, sweet sounds of tender music. A slight breeze stirred the tiny leaves of the trees. "Nymphs of joy" approached us one after another, threw flowers at us, sighed, laughed, invited us into their grottoes, with promises of untold delight, and vanished, like phantoms of a moonlit night.'[60]

On 12 July 1789, one year before Karamzin wrote his rhapsodies, a young lawyer called Camille Desmoulins had emerged from one of the Palais Royal cafés and made an impassioned speech to the excited crowds assembled in its gardens. He ended by inciting the citizens of Paris to take arms against the royal troops, who were camped just outside the city. Others joined him and from the centre of the Palais Royal riots spread all over Paris. On 14 July the Bastille was stormed and taken. The Palais Royal and its cafés remained the centre for news, speeches and debate all through the Revolution. Continuous political excitement was combined with increasing extravagance of dress and behaviour in those who frequented it. The music grew wilder, the prostitutes more fantastic. Papillon, Sophie Beau Corps, la Sultane, l'Orange, la Bacchante, la Venus, paraded up and down in the arcades and gardens among the revolutionaries.[61] The fact that leisure and pleasure could help to generate ideas leading to action was demonstrated in the most bizarre possible manner.

Cities produced ideas as well as goods. Their role as places for the collection and dissemination of knowledge, and for the generation of ideas on the basis of that knowledge, had become increasingly important from the sixteenth century onwards. The increase of leisure in cities, of which the social activities of polite society were one aspect, played an important part in this, but much of it was due to the original basic activities

175. A view in the Palais Royal gardens (Bibliothèque Nationale, Paris).

of cities. Information was collected for the purposes of trade or government, schools were founded to train the future members of the governing class. Above all, cities were places in which all kinds of people mixed together. 'Lutetia', said the Emperor Charles V, using the Latin name for Paris, 'non urbs est, sed orbis.'[62] 'Ceste ville est un autre monde, dedans sa monde florissante' was inscribed on Mathieu Mérian's plan of Paris, published in 1615. The idea that a city was a world in miniature was to become a very common one. All the peoples of the great world, or so it seemed, were drawn together into a big city, and all kinds of different activities were to be found there. Moreover, all successful cities attracted men of ability, intelligence and ambition, and the increasing amount of leisure enabled people to sit back from the grind of merely keeping alive, to meet one another, to talk and let their intelligences wander.

From the point of view of the government, big cities were worrying places, potentially useful but also potentially dangerous. The ideas and inventions which they turned up might lead to the prosperity of the nation and the glory of its ruler, but they might be subversive. They were worried with reason, for the concepts that people had the right to think, write and print what they wanted and that kings had no innate God-given right to rule both originated in cities. So rulers did their best to control and canalize their intellectual and creative energies.

In the fifteenth century groups in cities all over Italy, or in villas just outside them, began to meet together.[63] They met under the influence of the new interest in classical literature and art, and they called themselves academies, after the park and district in Athens in which Plato talked with his pupils and taught them his philosophy. The Italian academies met to do many different things: to compose, write and read their own poetry, to read and discuss the classical authors, to read addresses on ethics or other subjects, to act plays or to perform music. To begin with, they had no organization and no purpose-built buildings of their own. In the course of the sixteenth century they began to specialize and to organize themselves. They acquired members, rules and ultimately buildings. They gave courses of lectures, and accepted pupils; in some cases (in Florence, for instance) they developed into full-scale universities. Specialized academies appeared, of sculptors and painters, or of people interested in law, language, archaeology, natural history, chemistry or even fencing, riding, dancing, playing cards and shooting.

Rulers began to take an interest in academies and to give them their patronage. The pioneer was Duke Cosimo I of Tuscany, who in 1540 made himself the protector of a small philological academy which had been founded a year or two previously, and turned it into the Accademia Fiorentina, a more formally constituted academy for the study of the Italian language. In about 1563 he went on (at the suggestion of Giorgio Vasari) to found the Accademia del Disegna, for artists and sculptors. Much later, in 1657, his descendant set up the Accademia del Cimento, to discuss, lecture and make experiments concerning physics and astronomy. Meanwhile, in 1593 the Accademia di S. Luca for artists had been founded by Cardinal Federigo Borromeo in Rome, under papal protection; and official academies had spread to northern Europe (as, to some extent, informal or unofficial ones had already done). Academies or societies for the cultivation and rational development of the German or French languages were set up by the Prince of Anhalt in Weimar in 1617, and by Richelieu (in the form of the Académie Française) in Paris in 1635. Louis XIV became a great founder of academies: the Académie de Danse in 1661, the Académie de Musique, which was in effect a royal opera company, in 1666, the Académie Royale des Inscriptions et Belles Lettres in 1663, the Académie Royale de Peinture, on the basis of an earlier group, in 1667, the Académie Royale des Sciences in 1666, the Académie de l'Architecture in 1671. The Académie des Sciences gave royal recognition to a group (including Descartes and Pascal) which had already been meeting since the 1640s; in the same way the slightly earlier Royal Society ('for improving Natural Knowledge'), which was founded in London in 1660 and given a charter by Charles II in 1662, grew out of an informal group which had started to meet in London in 1645. An informal scientific Accademia dei Lincei had been founded in Rome in 1603, and was joined in 1611 by Galileo; it collapsed, however, as a result of Galileo's prosecution by the Inquisition in 1632. A few years later John Milton, freshly returned from Rome, reported to Parliament that the learned men there 'did nothing but bemoan the servile condition into which learning among them was taught; that this it was had damped the glory of Italian wits; that nothing had been there written now these many years but flattery and fustian'.[64]

It was not surprising that three great cities, Rome, Paris and London, should have become major centres of scientific research and discovery. Books could be bought in them, instruments bought or made there, like-minded people were more likely to be found there, and so were the comfortably-off well-disposed amateurs who could help to subsidize scientific research, even if they did no more than dabble in it themselves. The importance of the Royal Society can be exaggerated, but it is hard to exaggerate its effects when combined with the independent activities of London-based scientists, not all of whom belonged to it.

Its membership consisted of a hard core of serious scientists, an outer fringe of well-off people who attended meetings as a pleasant way of passing the time, and a good many in between the two. There were comparatively few merchants in the Society: the average membership in the years 1660 to 1685 were made up of 31 percent of doctors and professional scholars, 30 percent of aristocrats and landed gentlemen, 21 percent of courtiers, politicians and government officials and office-holders, 7 percent of clergymen, and 6 percent of merchants and tradesmen.[65] The serious scientists came from a variety of backgrounds, but most of them had either private incomes or jobs which provided them with a good deal of leisure. It was not only the leisure and luxury industries which benefited from the annual movement of the well-off into London and out of it again. But scientific research out of London was also stimulated by the contacts with the centre provided by scientists or intelligent amateurs with country estates. These provincial activities were further encouraged by correspondence between provincial scientists or societies and the Royal Society officials, and by its annual publication of transactions. Its function as a clearing-house for information and ideas was arguably more important than its meetings and the discussions and experiments which took place at them, which were often of a fairly superficial nature. Discussion and experiment took place in other venues in London too, possibly more fruitfully: in private houses and in coffee-houses.

Coffee-houses played an important part in the development of science, as they did in that of an extraordinary variety of activities. The story of their rise and their continued influence is one of the more curious episodes in the history of the western city.[66] Coffee was being drunk in Persia and Arabia in the fifteenth century and spread all over the Turkish empire in the sixteenth, but it was not until the mid-seventeenth century that it was introduced to western Europe, usually, to begin with, by people with some kind of Levantine connection. The first known coffee-houses in England opened in Oxford in 1650 and moved to London in 1652. There were eighty-two of them in London by 1663, and about five hundred by the early eighteenth century. A coffee-house or 'maison de café', was opened in Paris by a Levantine in 1643, but was a failure. The arrival and considerable social success of Soliman Aga Mustapha Raca as ambassador from the Sultan to Louis XIV brought coffee (which he offered to his guests) into fashion in Paris, and a number of cafés started up. But it was not until a Sicilian, Francesco Procopio, opened a 'maison de café' on the Rue de Tournon in 1675, and then in the Rue des Fosses St Germain in 1686, and supplied them with marble tables, crystal chandeliers, Italian sorbets and ices, and a counter selling confectionery, that 'maisons de café' became really fashionable in Paris. By 1700 their name had been abbreviated to caffés or cafés. There were about three hundred of them by 1716, eighteen hundred by 1788 and four thousand by 1807.

Cafés and coffee-houses soon started to sell tea and chocolate as well as coffee, and by the beginning of the eighteenth century, if not earlier, most of them were providing meals and alcoholic drinks as well, and some had beds for the night. In London, and soon elsewhere in cities all over the British Isles, one reason for their quick and phenomenal success was that they started up when the newsbooks, newsletters and 'diurnals' which were the forerunners of newspapers were beginning to become important, and from the very beginning had them available for the use of customers. Printed news was supplemented by word of mouth and by advertisement. Soon coffee-houses became places for the dissemination and discussion of news all over Europe. In cities where newspapers were largely restricted to official publications, semi-professional tellers of news appeared; in Paris they were called *nouvellistes*. In London in 1663 coffee was attacked as:

A loathsome potion not yet understood,
Syrup of soot, or essence of old shoes,
Dashed with diurnals or the book of news.[67]

In 1701 a guidebook to Amsterdam describes the arrival of the English post in the Caffé François, in the Kalverstraat, the clientele crowding to read the London newsletter, and the lively discussions and political arguments that followed: it calls the café a 'Political Academy'.[68]

Government looked on cafés, or at least some cafés, with suspicion. In 1685 an official of the Paris police wrote to his subordinate: 'The King has been informed that in several places in Paris, where coffee is on sale for drinking, there are assemblies of all kinds of people, especially strangers. For which reason His Majesty orders me to direct you to prepare a list of all such places, and ask you if you think that it would be expedient to close them in future.'[69] They were not closed, because the government found it more profitable to infiltrate police spies into them in order to pick up information, report on any subversive conversations, and make arrests or take other suitable action in consequence. In England in the 1660s the government was using coffee-houses more creatively, for propaganda purposes: in 1665, for instance, during the Dutch War, it introduced stories of Dutch maltreatment of British sailors by way of the coffee-houses, in the hopes that from there they would 'spread like leprosy'.[70]

In spite of police spies, coffee-houses and cafés remained places in which people discussed what they liked and said what they thought. Soon, like Italian academies in the sixteenth century, they began to specialize. In London particular coffee-houses were scientific, literary, political, artistic, commercial or for gambling. Some houses became the provinces of particular individuals. In the late seventeenth century Robert Hooke, curator of experiments and for a time secretary to the Royal Society, kept court in Garraway's Coffee House, across the road from the Society's premises in Gresham's College. In the early eighteenth century Joseph Addison presided over Button's Coffee House in Covent Garden, where he sat surrounded by friends and admirers, writing articles for his periodical *The Guardian*; outside contributors could deliver articles and letters through the mouth of a gilt lion's head and paws, which he installed as a letter-box.[71]

The coffee-houses round the Royal Exchange in the City had their own distinctive clientele and development. As business on the Royal Exchange grew, and it became uncomfortably crowded, different groups of merchants started to meet and transact business in adjacent coffee-houses, which had already specialized in newspapers relevant to their particular interests. Three of the most important organizations of the City grew out of these coffee-houses: the Baltic Exchange out of the Baltic Coffee House in Threadneedle Street, Lloyd's out of Lloyd's Coffee House in Lombard Street, and the Stock Exchange out of Jonathan's, in Change Alley. The gaming coffee-houses were in yet another world. They were all close to the fashionable residential streets of the West End. Playing cards for money was allowed in London coffee-houses (whereas playing cards at all was forbidden in Parisian cafés in the eighteenth century), but those who wanted to play for high stakes tended to form clubs which met within the coffee-houses, perhaps so that they could be confident of playing with people who could pay up if they lost. The best known was White's Club, which originally met in White's Chocolate

176. The lion's head on box originally in Button's Coffee House, London, and today at Woburn Abbey.

House in St James's Street; in 1755 the Chocolate House element disappeared and it became a fashionable gambling club pure and simple, occupying its own 'great house in St James's Street'.

In Paris cafés acquired special characteristics, in much the same way as London coffee-houses; but a big difference between them was that women went to Paris cafés. The Café Procope was carried on by Procopio's son, and became the most brilliant of the cafés frequented by artists and writers. Officers frequented the Café Militaire, actors and actresses the Café des Baucheries, financiers the Café du Prophète Élie, writers and chessplayers the Café de la Régence. The prostitutes of the Palais Royal were to be found in the Café des Aveugles, in the basement of one of the Palais Royal arcades; it was so called because it had an orchestra composed of blind musicians.[72]

Up till the early nineteenth century cafés and coffee-houses did not generate their own buildings, although the rooms which they occupied could be handsomely decorated. Even academies and societies produced comparatively little in the way of new buildings in the period. Louis XIV put most of his academies into different parts of the Louvre; the Royal Society occupied part of the existing buildings of Gresham's College in the City. It was not until 1780 that it and the recently founded Royal Academy moved into quarters specially built for them as part of the new government complex at Somerset House. The commercial and gaming coffee-houses, in which large sums of money were expended, generated buildings, but ceased to be coffee-houses in doing so. The first purpose-built coffee-houses arrived in the early nineteenth century, and even then were usually combined with some other use. Many, like the Exchange Coffee House in Boston, Massachusetts (1805–9), were also hotels; the wonderful Café Pedrocchi in Padua (1816–31) was also what amounted to an assembly room.[73]

But their importance as meeting places and generators of ideas was very great. A 'Rules and Orders of the Coffee-House', published in London in the late seventeenth century, proclaimed that

177. Interior of the Café Pedrocchi, Padua, designed by G. Jappelli in 1826. From a lithograph by A. Tosini (Museo Civico, Padua).

178. (right) Copenhagen. The castle and royal dockyard (begun 1598) from a view of the city after J. Van Wijk, 1611 (National Museum, Copenhagen).

> Gentry, Tradesmen, all are welcome hither,
> And may without Affront sit down Together.[74]

The couplet gave a somewhat exaggerated picture of their democratic nature, for few tradesmen or artisans had the leisure or the money to spend much time in them. None the less, they were places in which people from different social backgrounds could meet and talk together. In Old Slaughter's Coffee House in St Martin's Lane in London in the mid-eighteenth century, artists, writers and sculptors, who lived in and around Covent Garden, met with the printsellers and owners of furniture shops, who had their premises in St Martin's Lane; contacts made there helped to introduce the rococo style to England.[75] The ideas of the Enlightenment circulated and were discussed in cafés all over Paris by the lively and intelligent professional classes who were increasingly frustrated by the ossification of the French political and social system, and by those of the nobility who sympathized with them. Apostles of Enlightenment such as Voltaire, Rousseau, Diderot, d'Alembert and Condillac frequented the Café Procope and the Café de la Régence.[76] The presence of these five people in Paris, and their meeting together there, epitomizes the way in which a city could bring people together: Voltaire, the son of a Parisian notary, d'Alembert, a Paris foundling, Condillac, a Lyons nobleman, Rousseau, a plebeian from Geneva, Diderot, a Langres bourgeois. They met in Paris and they circulated round Europe; in every city coffee-houses, clubs, salons, societies and academies contributed to provide an international network of contacts. By the 1780s the Paris cafés had become intensely political. It was the society which met in them, and their equivalents from provincial cities who came up to Versailles for the meeting of the Estates-General in 1789, who launched the Revolution.

But the Revolution was launched with the help of the sansculottes, trousered artisans, masters of small workshops, and shopkeepers; they lived in a different part of Paris and were disaffected for different reasons. But they crowded into the Palais Royal gardens or the debating clubs to listen to the speech-making or to take part in it, and café intellectuals such as Danton or Desmoulins made contact with them.[77] The French Revolution revealed for the first time the explosive potentialities of one particular combination in cities as they grew in size: the combination of a disaffected intelligentsia with a disaffected working class.

10 A New Scale

Fashionable society, and its growing desire to amuse itself, introduced an extremely important new element into the cities of the seventeenth and eighteenth centuries, but of course they were changing in other ways as well. The great increase in trade resulting from the opening up of America and of the sea route to the east, the steady growth of European population, the decay of the city-state and growing power of the nation-state combined to produce bigger cities and bigger buildings. The age of the grand town hall had passed for the time being with the completion of the Amsterdam Stadhuis; there was to be nothing on that scale again until the mid-nineteenth century. But government departments of all types were moving from rooms in the palace of the ruler or from nondescript or unassuming buildings of their own into impressive new ones. Palaces were rebuilt or remodelled on a larger scale, and acquired specialist new buildings, to contain libraries or works of art. Newly prosperous commercial cities required new exchanges, old ones were rebuilt, and smaller specialist exchanges broke off from them. There were to be no hospitals larger than the Ospedale Maggiore in Milan until the very end of the eighteenth century, but there were more and more on a similar scale. As standing navies and armies grew in size, a new range of buildings appeared to service or accommodate them. The first commercial docks, and an increase in the scale and number of warehouses, produced a new townscape of the docklands.

It was the national capitals which benefited most; the

179. The rampart walk at Vienna in 1824. By P. D. Raulino (Museen der Stadt, Vienna).

increase in population and prosperity of their nations inevitably brought them an increase in legal, political and financial business, and this, together with their social prestige, their own commercial trade, if any, and their growing service industries swelled their own populations. London, at once a major port and commercial and financial centre, and a legal, political and social capital, increased in size from about 200,000 to just under a million between 1600 and 1800. Paris, very much less important commercially, but the capital of a much larger nation, rose from about 250,000 to 550,000 in the same time. The rivalry between the two capitals led to a rivalry in their provision of public buildings. Other capitals joined in, with increasing impact from the mid-eighteenth century onwards: Berlin, as the capital of the pushing new kingdom of Prussia, St Petersburg as the new capital of an ancient nation increasingly ambitious to make its mark, Vienna as an old city, which had grown rapidly after the Turkish danger had been dealt with in the 1680s and 1690s.

Many of the new buildings were very large, and many were on the outskirts of cities, for reasons of health, security, convenience, or because it was too expensive to find space for them in the centre. Huge blocks of many-windowed hospitals, barracks, prisons, colleges or warehouses, often rising out of gardens or green fields, became a distinctive feature of the approach to all cities of any size.

Many cities on the continent were still fortified; indeed city fortifications reached new heights of expense and elaboration in the seventeenth century. Apart from the large quantities of land occupied by the ramparts of the city itself, there was often a separate citadel either free-standing or attached to the main *enceinte*, and for reasons of security and field of fire an area round the ramparts had to be left open for what

180. The Koniglichen Invalidenhaus, Berlin (Landbildstelle, Berlin).

were known as the glacis and the esplanade: the banks sloping down from the ramparts, and the levelled area beyond them.

So much space next to a busy city was inevitably made use of in time of peace, and as military presence grew less it tended to be infiltrated on more and more, until, when and if the fortifications were finally declared redundant, a huge area became available for redevelopment. At Bordeaux a tree-planted promenade known as the Allées de Tourny was laid out on the glacis of the citadel in 1745; the theatre was built on it in 1772–80; and finally, in the 1780s, the citadel was demolished and, after a hiatus due to the Revolution, was laid out as a new quarter of the city.[1] At Vienna the esplanade was kept more or less open and the city leap-frogged over it to form a ring of suburbs; the esplanade and ramparts became a promenade and a green-belt scattered with trees and cafés; finally, in the 1860s, both were redeveloped as the Ring.

Citadels were often built as much to overawe the city as to protect it; the citadels of Florence (Fortezza da Bassa, started 1534) and Antwerp (1567–72) are examples. Both had some accommodation for troops. But the normal arrangement was for troops to be billeted out in the houses of civilians; it was not until the eighteenth century that barracks began to become a conspicuous city feature. It was superannuated soldiers and sailors, not active ones, who generated the most conspicuous naval and military buildings of the seventeenth century. The hospitals and hôtels built for them in that century were hospitals in the all-embracing medieval sense, providing food, shelter and medical care for the thousands of maimed or retired servicemen left behind by the wars. The Hôtel des Invalides was built just outside Paris in 1670–7; then came the Royal Hospital, Kilmainham, on the edge of Dublin (begun 1680) and the Royal Hospital, Chelsea (1682–91), on the edge of London. Later examples included the Invalidenhaus in Berlin (1747–8) and the Allgemeines Krankenhaus in Vienna; the latter catered for the poor as well as for soldiers.

All these were built on the scale of palaces (or of colleges, which provided the models for Chelsea and Kilmainham), but apart from their size their buildings were unassuming. Those of the Invalides were always the most elaborate, and the addition of a splendid domed chapel in 1680–91, and the planting of avenues all round it, made it the most conspicuous building in the environs of Paris. England responded with the two domes and grand stone façades of the Royal Hospital, Greenwich, which was built for retired sailors and commenced in 1691.

Dockyards grew larger and more elaborate, and at the end of the eighteenth century acquired a new function. They had originally developed as enclosed basins in which ships could be repaired, refitted, or find shelter during winter, and the hulks of newly built ships could be fitted out; they were not places in which to load or unload cargoes. The actual basins were combined with workshops, warehouses for stores, rope-walks, timber yards and slips or strands on which ships could be built or repaired. Large dockyards already existed in medieval times, at Genoa and the Arsenal in Venice; in 1598 Christian IV began a smaller arsenal next to the castle in Copenhagen.[2] The Venice Arsenal grew more elaborate century by century, and some of its sixteenth-century buildings, such as its covered rope-walk (1579–83) and covered wet dock (1573), were superbly robust examples of functional design. It did not, however, have lock-gates to keep the water-level constant, because these were not necessary in the Mediterranean; and it did not have dry docks.

Dry docks began to appear as ships grew bigger, and hauling them out of the water to repair their hulls became more of a business. A dry dock was constructed at Plymouth in 1495, and a number of others followed, but neither their gates nor their timber-lined sides coped effectively with soil-and-water-pressure. It was not until the late seventeenth century, at Plymouth and Portsmouth, that Edward Dummer constructed stone-lined docks with outward-angled gates, which could deal with both problems. The first English wet dock or basin was constructed in the same period, at Portsmouth; unlike the Mediterranean basins it and subsequent basins had lock-gates. Previously, English warships had laid at anchor in natural harbours or inland waterways, and they continued to do so at many English naval bases. But in the course of the eighteenth century the great naval dockyards at Plymouth, Portsmouth and Chatham became more elaborate even than the Arsenal at Venice.[3]

All these dockyards were naval rather than commercial. The sixteenth- and seventeenth-century islands at Amsterdam, on the other hand, were mainly commercial, and with their associated warehouses, timber yards, shipyards and rope-walks were essentially docks, although their waterways were not enclosed. At London the Howland Great Wet Dock at Rotherhithe, in use by 1703, was commercial, and so was the first wet dock in Liverpool, constructed in 1724–6; the former provided winter moorings for one hundred and twenty ships, and had dry docks attached.[4]

But none of these docks was concerned with handling passengers or merchandise. The huge East India Company warehouse on Oostenburg Island in Amsterdam admittedly warehoused merchandise as well as ships' stores and accessories, but the waterways adjacent to it were too shallow to take the big East India Company ships, which anchored in the haven outside. The first basins or wet docks constructed for loading and unloading were on canals and narrow inland waterways, where mooring space was limited. The first dock of this nature for sea-going vessels was probably the one at Hull, built in 1775–8.[5] But the most impressive conglomeration was at London. As the trade of the Port of London grew the congestion in the Thames became insufferable, and to deal with it a series of docks were built in quick succession: the West India Docks (1800–2), the Commercial Docks (1802–7), the London Docks (opened 1805), the East India Docks (opened 1806), and the St Katherine's Docks (opened 1828). They were all built (as was the Hull dock) by private companies, which issued shares to raise the necessary capital.[6] The broad stone quays, high walls and long lines of huge warehouses of the new docks became one of the sights of London. They were built on the edge of the city or even, in the case of the West and East India Docks, out in open country, but they soon generated a whole new area of houses for dock

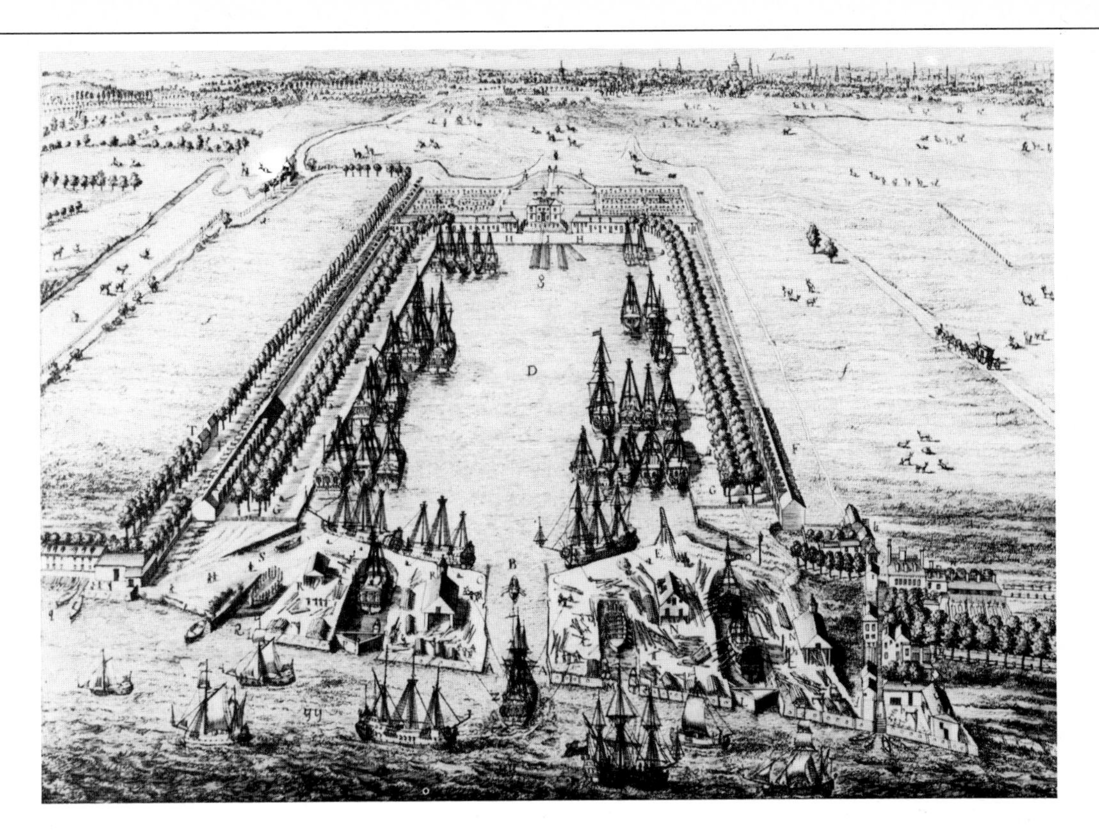

181. The Howland Great Wet Dock (*c.* 1700), near Deptford (Guildhall Library, London).

workers and dock officials, and inns, doss-houses, brothels and places of entertainment for the ships' crews.

It was not until later in the nineteenth century that European cities had anything to compare with England's great naval and commercial dockyards. England was a pioneer, too, in the provision of barracks on any scale. Perhaps the earliest were the huge range of barracks built mainly for English soldiers just outside Dublin in 1706;[7] barracks at Berwick-on-Tweed followed in 1717. Berlin, in spite of its military ambition and large military population (33,386 out of a population of 145,021 in 1786), quartered most of its garrison in the town; in parts of Berlin every household was compelled by law to accommodate one soldier.[8] The first barracks, such as the one built on the Jakobsville in about 1750, were very unassuming. The most conspicuous military building in eighteenth-century Berlin was the Zeughaus, which was built in 1695–1706 on one of the best sites in the centre of the city. It has all the trappings of a baroque palace, but in fact was an arsenal for the storage and display of firearms and cannon.

Paris owed its barracks to the Maréchal de Biron, and to his appointment as colonel of the regiment of Gardes-Françoises in 1745. He inaugurated a programme which by 1787 had produced no fewer than fourteen barracks for twenty companies of the guards, scattered all over the city, as well as a separate depot containing a military school and the headquarters of their band.[9] They were unpretentious buildings, like most barracks, but very elegant; they had none of the grandeur of the huge École Royale Militaire, which was designed by Jacques-Ange Gabriel in the 1750s as a prestige building, as prominently sited as the Invalides.

Then, as now, the needs of war could generate inventions which were useful in peace. Just as wet and dry docks were first constructed for naval dockyards, but spread to commercial ones, the type of hospital which was to have most influence in the nineteenth century was pioneered in the eighteenth at the Royal Naval Hospital at Stonehouse, near Plymouth. Instead of being built as one building, like virtually all earlier hospitals, this was built in the form of fifteen separate pavilions, to reduce the risk of infection.

182. The barracks at Dublin, the main buildings of which were built in 1701–6. From the aquatint in James Malton's *Dublin*, 1799 (National Library of Ireland, Dublin).

183. (top right) The Allgemeines Krankenhaus, Vienna, with the Narrenthurm in the centre. Aquatint after Joseph Schaffer, 1787 (Museen der Stadt, Vienna).

184. (bottom right) The Royal Naval Hospital (1756–64) at Stonehouse, near Plymouth.

It was built in 1764–5, and may have owed something to an unexecuted pavilion plan by Wren for the Royal Naval Hospital at Greenwich. Its fame was such that in 1787 it was visited by a French Royal Commission, which had been appointed to make recommendations for the rebuilding of the by then notoriously insanitary Hôtel-Dieu in Paris.[10]

Their report, which recommended adoption of the pavilion plan, was abortive owing to the revolution of 1789, and the type did not come into general use until the mid-nineteenth century (although it was adopted by Thomas Jefferson for the very different functions of the University of Virginia in 1825). Most hospitals continued to be built on traditional cross, courtyard or block plans, although there was a tendency for wards to get smaller. Very large hospital buildings, usually surrounded by fields, became a distinctive feature of the outskirts of sizeable cities. Paris had already acquired the Hôpital de St Louis in 1607–12, the Hôpital des Incurables in 1635–9, and the Hôpital de la Salpêtrière in 1660. All these were built at the inspiration and partly at the expense of the king.

In London the large new building of Bethlehem Hospital was built by the City of London Corporation in 1676, but the money was mostly raised by subscription. It was a lunatic asylum (the word 'bedlam' comes from the local pronunciation of 'Bethlehem') and was built in Moorfields, the great recreational area on the edge of the City: far from being thought to detract from the pleasantness of its walks, a visit to the hospital to gape at the lunatics became a favourite recreation for London citizens.

English hospitals in the eighteenth century were almost invariably built as the result of subscriptions or private benefactions, supplemented by their own endowments if the rebuilding of an older hospital was involved. The Rotunda Hospital in Dublin was partly supported by subscriptions to the Rotunda, the main Dublin Assembly Rooms,

which adjoined the hospital and was built at the same time for that purpose. Most of these hospitals were of comparatively modest size. It was the powerful centralized monarchies on the mainland of Europe which built huge hospitals. Apart from the Paris examples, they include the Frederiks Hospital in Copenhagen (1758), the Albergo dei Poveri at Naples (1751), the Julius Hospital in Würzburg (1798, a rebuilding of an almost equally large hospital of 1576–85) and the Allgemeines Krankenhaus in Vienna. The last was converted from its original seventeenth-century purpose to a general medical hospital on a very large scale by the Emperor Joseph II; he added new buildings for maternity cases and lunatics.

The building for lunatics consisted of a hollow round tower, the Narrenturm, six storeys high, with twenty-eight cells to a floor. Hospitals for lunatics in the seventeenth and eighteenth centuries were increasingly divided into cells rather than wards, and could be nearer to prisons in type than to hospitals of other kinds. New prisons on

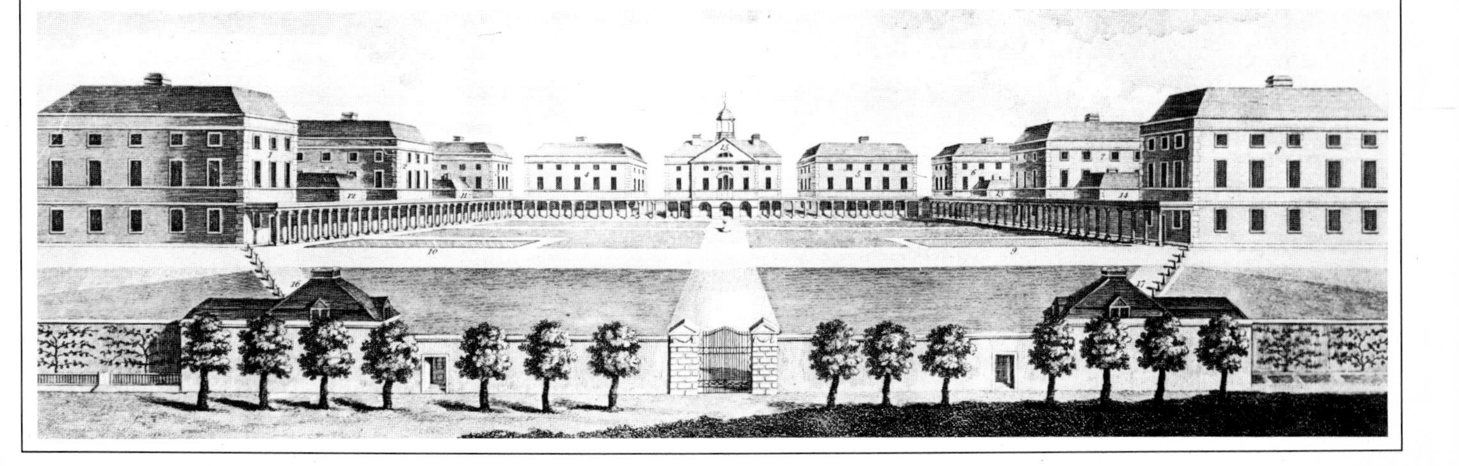

185. Section of the Hôtel de la Marine et des Affaires Étrangères, Versailles, in the mid-eighteenth century (Bibliothèque Municipale, Versailles).

a large scale were another feature of the eighteenth century: they gradually replaced prisons in portions of town halls, as at Amsterdam, or in old buildings, often medieval towers or castles adapted for the purpose, such as the Bastille in Paris. The most impressive aesthetically was Newgate in London, rebuilt in 1770–85 on a site where there had been a prison since the Middle Ages, and therefore in the centre of the Georgian city. But the most influential was the Maison de Force outside Ghent.[12] This was erected in 1772–5 on a radial plan which was to have much influence in the nineteenth century.

New parliament buildings, government offices or law courts were in a different situation; for the most part, they had to be central, as did commercial or financial buildings such as banks or exchanges. But on the other hand, they did not necessarily have to be large. The administrative staff which ran eighteenth-century states was tiny compared to the numbers involved today. Any size which government buildings possessed was usually due to the fact that they were more than just office buildings, and contained a number of other functions. They often included residential accommodation for their chief officer or officers. The section of the Hôtel de la Marine et des Affaires Étrangères (*c.* 1770) at Versailles shows, in addition, printing works, model-rooms and a very large library; only ten of the forty-two rooms shown appear to be occupied as offices.

But buildings of this type, being central, tended to be designed for show; moreover, there was a growing feeling that the dignity of government should be expressed in government, legislative or judicial buildings of all kinds, not just in the residence of the king or the seat of the town council. An element of international competition developed, often expressed on the river frontages of capital cities, which were increasingly seen as public or processional ways lined with splendid buildings, instead of, or as well as, commercial highways. In Paris a new building to house the mint was built in 1768–75 on the banks of the Seine, next to the Collège des Quatre Nations. According to a contemporary biography of its architect, the grandeur of the river front was intended to 'proclaim the idea of the depot being the symbol representing national opulence'.[13] The front was grand beyond its practical functions: the great central feature contained a sumptuous council chamber far in excess of the needs of the members of the council. It was soon followed by the new Somerset House (1776–8) on the Thames in London, which replaced a royal palace which had become redundant, and consolidated accommodation for a variety of different academies and government offices into the largest of eighteenth-century government buildings; by the new Academy of Art (1764–88), Academy of Science (1783–9) and later the new Exchange (1805–10) on the banks of the Neva in St Petersburg; and by the new Customs House (1781–91) and Four Courts (1786–1803) on the banks of the Liffey, in Dublin, both with grand fronts and prominent, functionally quite unnecessary, domes. The former, as James Malton's *Picturesque and Descriptive View of the City of Dublin* (1799) proudly and correctly proclaimed, was 'the most sumptuous edifice appropriate to such a use in Europe' and 'aids to convey very exalted ideas of Dublin, in the approach from the Bay'.

Dublin had also rebuilt its Parliament House in 1729–39, and built an imposing Royal Exchange in 1769–79. By the end of the eighteenth century it had the grandest public buildings of any capital in Europe. It was an extraordinary achievement for a city with a population of only 140,000 and only a modest degree of independence from the central government in London. Two factors contributed to it: the considerable commercial prosperity of Ireland in this period, and the pride of its Protestant upper classes in having forced the English government to hand over legislative independence in internal affairs to the Parliament in Dublin.[14]

Customs houses were important in the British Isles because there, as elsewhere in the seventeenth and eighteenth centuries, there was virtually no direct taxation of income, and very little of capital; the main source of national revenue was taxes on consumption, especially customs and excise. But different countries had different systems. In Holland an important contribution was made by taxes on wholesale sales; all such sales had to pay tax on weight at the public scales at the weigh-houses. Hence the prominence of weigh-houses at all Dutch towns, the frequent provision of a guard-room above them, to secure the considerable sums of money collected in them, and the convenience for merchants of having premises not too far away from them.

In many European countries customs were payable on entering cities within the country, as well as when entering the country itself. The income from these city dues could be very large and it was important to make sure that they were not evaded. At Bordeaux, for instance, the medieval walls were retained as a customs wall up till the Revolution, and any gaps were filled with iron grills; for that reason even the river frontage of the Place Royale was closed in by a great ironwork screen.[15]

Sometimes new customs walls were constructed. When a city was growing in size it was clearly in the interest of those collecting the dues to enlarge the customs boundary. This happened at Berlin in 1734–6. The boundaries of Friedrichstadt, one of the five separate towns of which Berlin was made up, were much enlarged and a new customs wall was built to define them. It was pierced by monumental gates at the points where roads were allowed through. The Brandenburg Gate was built as a customs barrier as well as a grand entry to the city, and continued to act as one when it was rebuilt in its present form in 1788–91.

At Paris the customs situation had become highly unsatisfactory by the 1780s. Louis XIV's ramparts had probably never been effective, and the customs boundary had anyway been extended beyond them. Barriers were set up on all roads and streets where they crossed the boundary, among them a great ironwork screen across the Champs Élysées known as the Grille de Chaillot; but there was no intervening wall.[16] The loss to the revenue was very considerable. In 1780 the Ferme-Générale, the group of financiers which leased the collecting of these and other revenues from the king, was reorganized. The new tax farmers determined to enlarge the customs boundary yet again, and to mark it by a proper wall, punctuated by properly manned barriers and customs posts. The result was a series of over fifty individual *barrières* (of which only a handful survive) round what was then the perimeter of the built-up area of Paris. They varied in size, but were all examples of the originality and fertility of design of their architect, Claude-Nicolas Ledoux, who also designed the Hôtel des Fermes as a new headquarters for the Ferme-Générale.

From the sixteenth century onwards the opportunities for designing a new town of any size in Europe were few and far between. Such towns as were founded were seldom intended to have populations of more than a few thousand. Even Livorno, which grew to be such a success, was planned on relatively modest lines. There was no need, in towns of this scale, for anything complex: a central square, with a church on or adjacent to it, a surrounding grid or web of streets, and fortifications round the whole if so desired, were all that was called for. Livorno in Italy in the sixteenth century, Richelieu in France in the seventeenth, were planned on these lines. The Renaissance taste for symmetry and centralized plans gave such towns a pattern-book regularity, but as mechanisms they differed very little from the towns of the Middle Ages.

But when the greater part of the City of London was destroyed by fire in 1666, an unrivalled opportunity arose for planning a city on the grand scale (by the standard of those days), to contain over one hundred thousand people. At least six plans were produced. In the end none of them was used; the City was rebuilt on the lines of the old streets, with a few modifications. But the plans are interesting as showing the concepts of what a large city might be which existed at the time; and at least two of them were to be imitated in plans for other cities, which were actually carried out.

The plans were of two sorts, plain and fancy. Two of the three fancy ones were drawn up by John Evelyn, and one by Christopher Wren.[17] They might be described as court plans, and show the influence of the papal network in Rome, and the gardens of Vaux-le-Vicomte and Versailles. They are so close to each other that they must be the result of shared discussions, but in the final stages the two men seem to have worked independently. Wren's, not surprisingly, is the most stylish. In the year before the fire, proposals had been made to increase the effect of the three radial streets leading off the Piazza del Popolo in Rome by building two churches at their junction; the proposals were engraved, and clearly influenced the way in which Wren planned to site St Paul's. But the elaborate star-shaped intersections at either end of both his and Evelyn's plans suggest the radiating avenues of Le Nôtre.

Neither Wren nor Evelyn was seduced by the remorseless elegance with which Le Nôtre's avenues work towards one culminating château or palace. They use the papal system to create a multi-focal city. The main focal points are St Paul's, the Exchange, the Customs House and London Bridge, all of which were to be rebuilt on the site

186. (top right) The Customs House, Dublin, built to the designs of James Gandon in 1781–91. From an aquatint in James Malton's *Dublin*, 1799 (National Library of Ireland, Dublin).

187. (bottom right) Looking across the Neva to the Exchange and Academy of Sciences at St Petersburg (British Library).

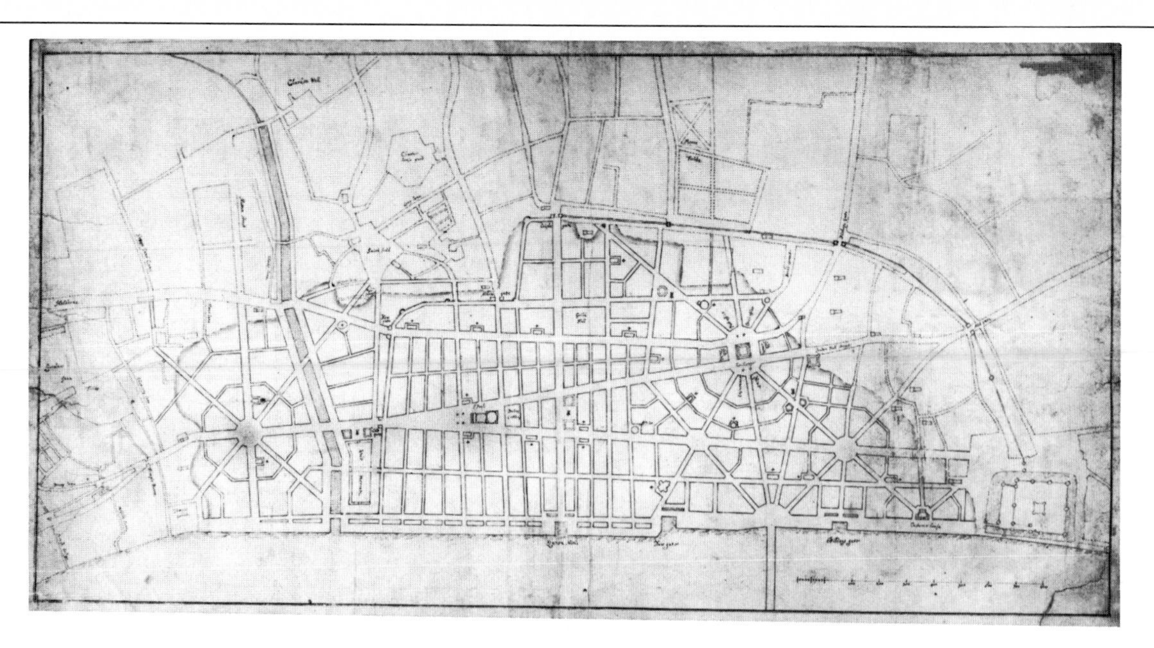

of their predecessors; minor focal points are provided by the city gates and the ancient harbour basins of Queenhithe and Billingsgate. The Guildhall, the seat of city government, is given no prominence, whereas the Royal Exchange is made the converging point of a huge web of streets; the plans suggest a City such as Charles II must have longed for, extremely prosperous and entirely subservient to the king.

The other three plans are based on the grid, the grid, and nothing but the grid.[18] The only break in their remorseless chequerboard is the provision of a number of squares; buildings sited to end a vista play no role of any importance. One of the three, by Valentine Knight, survives only in his description of it, in which he makes clear the reason for his grid; it could easily be sub-divided into rectangular plots of identical size. It and all grid plans were a land surveyor's and real-estate dealer's dream: easy to lay out, and easy to sell.

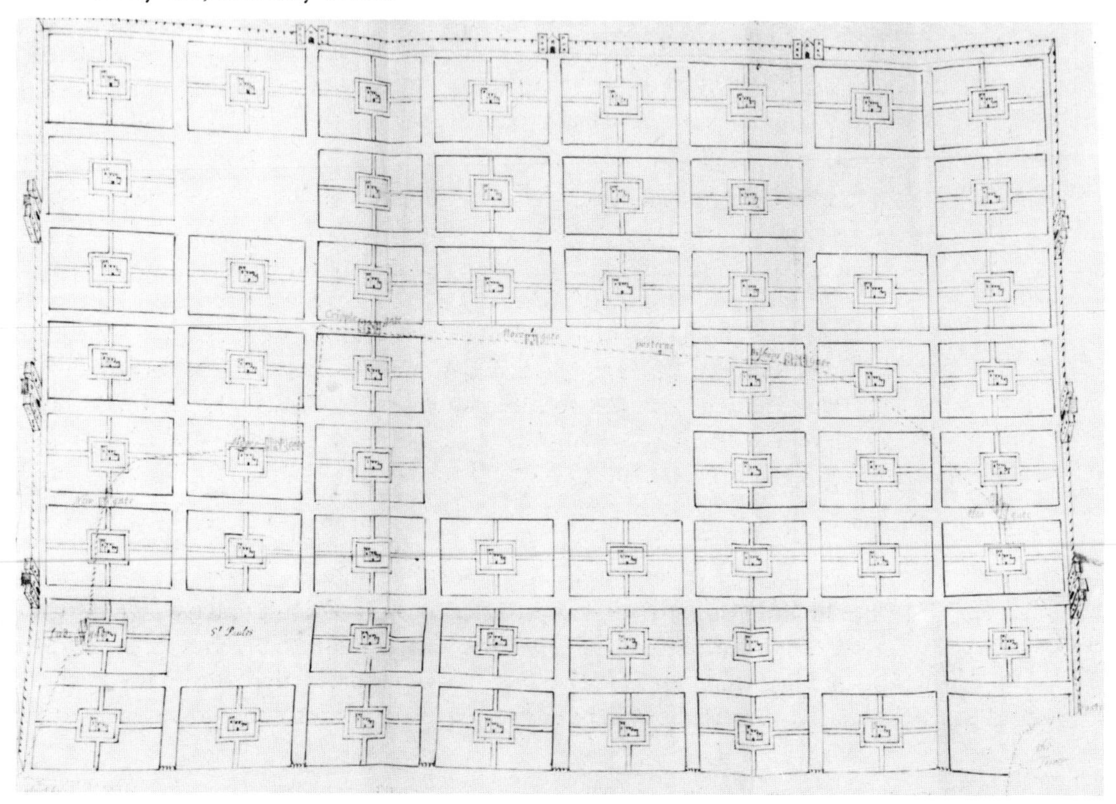

Plain and fancy plans were to remain the staple ones for all new town developments of the next hundred and fifty years. There was to be only one other equivalent opportunity to that of rebuilding London after the fire, and it also was missed. Peter the Great's new capital city of St Petersburg was to be given a degree of cohesion and even splendour, as a result of alterations made from the mid-eighteenth century onwards, but the original plan was *ad hoc* and unimaginative.

Turin, which grew very rapidly in the seventeenth and early eighteenth centuries, expanded in a series of grids, relieved by squares. The streets which formed the grids were mostly about eighty feet wide, with the exception of the Contrada di Po, laid out in 1673, which was a hundred feet wide, and cut through the grid on a diagonal, from the main gate to the castle. This was part-converted into a baroque palace and set in the middle of a large new square. The street layout was controlled by the dukes of Savoy; the new buildings had repetitive façades, and each new grid aligned with the previous ones, although the intervals between the streets were often different.[19]

Berlin was another rapidly growing city, and, like Turin, its growth was closely controlled by its rulers. It, too, developed mainly on a series of grids, although at its southern point at the end of the Friedrichstrasse, Friedrich Wilhelm I essayed a rather provincial layout in the manner of the Piazza del Popolo. But it is more usual in seventeenth- and eighteenth-century cities to find smaller independent grids, not necessarily aligned with each other, the result of independent property speculators laying out separate areas. In Paris the Île St Louis, the streets round the Rue de Richelieu and the Pré-aux-Clercs area are all examples. None of them included squares, nor did later lay-outs, such as the extensive development of the area known as the Chaussée d'Antin, north of the boulevard, in the 1770s and 1780s. The residential square never caught on in Paris, or on the continent in general, to the extent which it did in England.

Two main reasons can be suggested for this. One was the difference in plan between the better houses in Paris and the better houses in London. In Paris, as Lister put it in 1698: 'All the houses of persons of distinction are built with port-cocheres and courts within.'[20] He reckoned that there were about seven hundred of these houses in Paris. All that was seen of them from the street was normally a wall with an archway in it, and sometimes the windows of subsidiary buildings. In London, on the other hand, even the rich were accustomed, from at least the early seventeenth century, to living in houses the main doors of which opened onto a public thoroughfare.

The Parisian type was clearly unsuitable for squares; the point of a square was destroyed if the façades of the houses were hidden from the outside world. But no one wanted houses of the English type. A compromise solution was tried in the houses of the Place Royale and in a number of other places. Each house was entered by a porte-cochère, which went through the house into a courtyard at the back: a staircase went straight up from the porte-cochère to the main rooms on the first floor of the house above it. Carriages drove in at the porte-cochère, put their passengers down at the foot of the stairs, and went on into the courtyard. It was an ingenious arrangement, but it could never be as dignified as the traditional one and it had the disadvantage that having the courtyard at the back made it difficult to have a garden.

Another reason was that in Paris and London there were different attitudes to the open space of a square. In 1687 it was reported that the space at the centre of the Place Royale 'is about to be converted into a garden and is to be enclosed with a palisade

188–9. (left) Designs by Christopher Wren and (below) Richard Newcourt for rebuilding the City of London after the fire of 1666 (All Souls College, Oxford; Guildhall Library, London).

190. King (now Soho) Square, London, built and laid out in 1680–1. From an engraving of 1754 (Guildhall Library, London).

of iron, into which none may enter but those belonging to the houses about the place, who only are to have keys'.[21] The grill was erected, at the expense of the occupants, and the gardens laid out, but the occupants were not allowed to keep them private. As Brice put it in 1725, 'their outlay was completely superfluous, because a square should never be obstructed or circumscribed, on the contrary access to it should be free and easy'.[22] In French tradition a square was a public place, and the tradition was too strong to be broken. Being a public place, it was in danger of filling up with noisy activities. The Place Vendôme, for instance, was crowded out once a year with the Foire St Ovide, when booths and stalls were erected round the statue of Louis XIV, and the Parisians crowded in to enjoy themselves.

In England, squares had often contained markets, but the idea that a square was necessarily a place for public assembly was very much less strong. There was never any difficulty about enclosing the centre of squares, once the idea had caught on. The first residential squares in London, Covent Garden, St James's Square and Bloomsbury Square had open centres on the continental model. The first square to contain an enclosed garden for the residents was King Square (today Soho Square) which was laid out in 1680–1;[23] its example may have inspired the abortive attempt to enclose the centre of the Place Royale. By the mid-eighteenth century there were eleven residential squares in central London, and eight of them had enclosed gardens. Covent Garden, where the open centre had become a market, rapidly went out of fashion. A private central garden became the essential requisite of success for a residential square, of which there were sixteen west of the City by the 1790s.

There were a number of grand detached houses with their own forecourts and sizeable gardens in London, but never perhaps more than two dozen of them, as opposed to the seven hundred porte-cochère-cum-courtyard houses of Paris. Most upper-class residents of the West End of London were satisfied with a house in a row, preferably facing onto a square, and often with only a very small garden of its own. The reason for this was probably that London society spent less time in London than Paris society did in Paris. For a peer or country gentleman who came up to London for three or four months a year, a free-standing house with a large garden was not worth the expense. But they were ready to pay a little more for the convenience and improved outlook

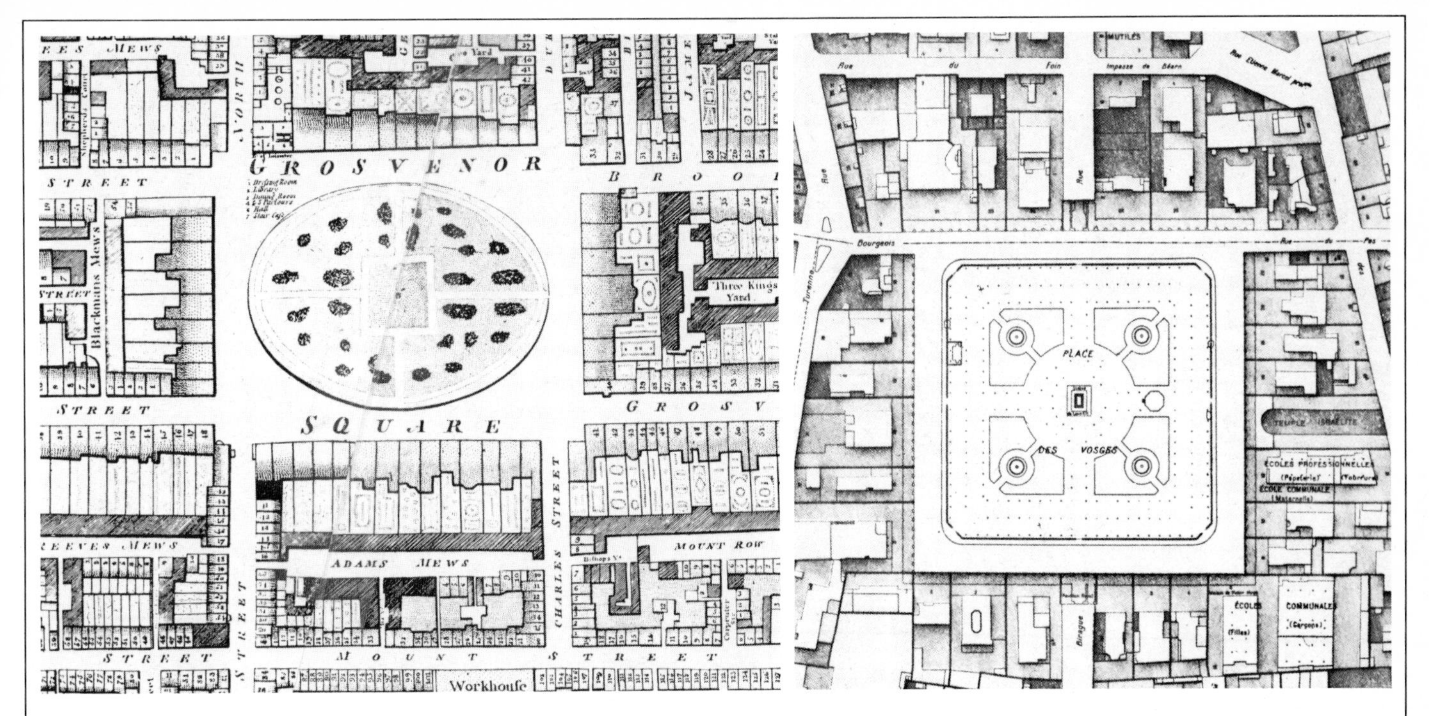

191. Grosvenor Square and surrounding streets in 1799. Detail from R. Horwood's plan of London.

192. The Place des Vosges, Paris. From a plan of *c.* 1940.

of a house on a square rather than in a street. Between Covent Garden in 1631 and Bedford Square in 1775, none of the London squares had any architectural pretensions; they were built of brick, several were not even of integrated architectural design, and in those that were no effort seems to have been made to prevent lessees of individual houses rebuilding or remodelling them. Stone was scarcely used, except for the handsome doorcases framed by wrought-iron standards or stone obelisks supporting lamps, which was all most houses had in the way of external ornament.

The impressive size of the area of London which was developed with mainly upper-class houses between 1680 and 1750 is less evidence of the growing prosperity of London, than of the growing inclination of English landowners to spend a season there—of the growth of society, in fact. Development was almost all promoted by ground landlords, mostly on land which they had inherited rather than on land which they had bought to develop. Individual estates were normally laid out on a grid and around a square, but little effort was made to relate one ground landlord's grid to the next one. Apart from a square all the larger developments provided a church and a market, the latter always placed inconspicuously away from the square. Shops were sometimes allowed on the less important streets, but never on the squares nor, to begin with at any rate, on the streets leading into them.

All the more important squares were built for carriage-owners. Parisian carriage-owners could keep their carriages and horses in the courtyards of their houses; the larger houses often had a stable court off the main one. London carriage-owners without court-yards had to find somewhere to put them. The answer was already present in embryo in Covent Garden, where the grander houses along the north side had coach-houses at the end of their gardens; access to them was by a narrow back street, running parallel to the houses. St James's Square had a similar arrangement serving one side of the square. But it was not until the Grosvenor estate was laid out around Grosvenor Square from the 1720s onward that what became the standard London plan was devised, in which parallel rows of houses were served by a common back street, known as a mews, lined all the way along with stables. The planning of the mewses on the Grosvenor estate is of a somewhat *ad hoc* nature, and problems arose in servicing the houses when the grid of streets was interrupted by a square. By the end of the eighteenth century,

193. Clearing away the night-soil. From an eighteenth-century bill-head (St Bartholomew's Hospital, London).

however, the alternation of mewses, squares and streets was being worked out with pattern-book regularity.[24]

Mewses had one other advantage besides providing access to stables. The new eighteenth-century estates in London were all provided with covered drains normally running under the middle of the streets. But these were to take away surface water. Sewage was removed in the traditional manner, in covered carts, which in London normally operated at night. The mewses provided a back way in which sewage (including horse dung) and rubbish of all kinds, could be loaded up and carried away inconspicuously. They were the urban equivalent of the back stairs, which had appeared in English houses of any size a little earlier. Just as an elegant lady no longer had to pass a bucket of ordure coming down the stairs as she went up them, she no longer had to meet a night-cart being loaded up at her own front door, as she returned from a ball.

The streets in these London estates were comfortably wide, and all had broad sidewalks. The wider streets in both Covent Garden and Mayfair were sixty feet wide; as the Mayfair houses, like all later ones in central London, were set back from the sidewalk edge, in order to provide sunken 'areas' to bring light to the basement, the distance between street frontages was about ten feet more. In the later estates they were a little wider: around Berkeley and Cavendish Squares they were about sixty-five (plus ten) feet. These were all quiet residential streets, and worth comparing with the thirty feet of the widest medieval streets in Paris, the sixty feet frontage to frontage of the Corso and other main streets in sixteenth-century Rome, and the mere twenty-five feet of the Via Nuova, the grandest late Renaissance street in Genoa. In Dublin, where a Wide Streets Commission was set up in 1756, to encourage new wide streets and widen existing ones, residential streets were wider still, and varied between seventy-five and one hundred feet.[25]

The advent of carriages in large numbers to prosperous towns in the seventeenth century had certainly encouraged the laying out of wider streets, but these London and Dublin streets, none of which was busy, could cater for more than any foreseeable weight of traffic. Their width was no doubt largely for visual reasons, but reasons of health probably also played a part. The 'miasma' theory, that illness could be caused by stagnant air, and that a grid of spacious streets helped to ventilate a district and therefore kept it healthy, had already appeared in the late seventeenth century, and was especially strong in the eighteenth.[26]

In London, and in England generally, as in Amsterdam and Holland, the ideal for which everyone aimed was the single family house, however small. Tenements existed: in both London and Amsterdam in the seventeenth and eighteenth centuries a great many houses apparently designed for single family occupancy were let off floor by floor, or even room by room, to different individuals or families. But this was a matter of economic constraint: few people lived that way out of choice. In Paris, on the other hand, although those at the top of the social pyramid lived in houses with porte-cochères, a great many comfortably-off families lived with reasonable content in one-floor apartments. Purpose-built apartment blocks were common in seventeenth- and eighteenth-century Paris, just as they were in Venice and Vienna, whereas they were virtually non-existent in London and Amsterdam.

Brice, writing in the late seventeenth century, commented how in Paris 'there are continually several distinct families in one house, which is rarely to be seen in other towns, where every one desires to dwell apart'.[27] He put the phenomenon down to the laws against the expansion of Paris, which produced a high density and forced families to live together. But another factor which needs to be borne in mind is the development in Protestant countries of the nuclear family, confined to parents and children, and the survival in Catholic countries of the extended family. Even the grandest houses in Paris were likely to contain separate apartments in which different generations and different siblings lived; the grand houses in Mayfair were seldom if ever divided up in this way (and therefore could, on the average, be smaller than their Parisian counterparts). Division into apartments for families could develop easily enough into apartments for letting out. In Paris in the eighteenth century, apart from buildings specifically built as apartment blocks, even the owners of houses in the Place Vendôme often occupied only the main floor and let out the rest. Lady Mary Wortley Montagu, visiting

Vienna on her way from London to Istanbul in 1716, found narrow streets 'and what is an inconveniency much more intolerable, in my opinion, there is no house that has so few as five or six families in it. The apartments of the greatest ladies, and even the ministers of state, are divided but by a partition from that of a tailor or a shoemaker.'[28]

Handsome although squares of conventional shape can be, it is always a pleasure to turn to the squares which are not square. These started to appear at much the same time as that at which architects realized that rooms need not be square either; squares in towns are, after all, essentially external rooms. The Piazza S. Ignazio in Rome was laid out in 1727; it served a traditional Italian function as a piazza in front of the main entrance of a church, but was laid out on an ingenious and delightful plan of rococo curves. The Amalienborg Place in Copenhagen was a residential square obviously inspired by the Place Vendôme in Paris; it was laid out in 1749 by Frederik V of Denmark whose statue on horseback stands in the centre of the square, and like the Place Vendôme it is octagonal in plan. But, whereas the diagonal sides of the Place Vendôme are very short, in the Amalienborg Place all the sides are the same length so that the octagonal effect is much stronger. The statue of Frederik V looks down one of the streets leading out of the square to the façade of the Marble Church: the combination of humane scale, geometrical variety and symmetrical relationships makes it one of the most delightful of eighteenth-century squares.

At Berlin in the 1730s Friedrich Wilhelm I laid out square, octagonal and circular squares just inside the gates of his new customs wall round Friedrichstadt to mark the point of entry to the city. At much the same time squares of varying shape were laid out round the perimeter of Bordeaux; the grandest was the Place Royale, which was open on one side to the river, and had cut-away corners, like the Place Vendôme. Some of the Bordeaux squares were used as markets; and squares on the edges of cities could also serve a useful function as places in which to welcome important visitors. Eighteenth-century pictures of the Piazza del Popolo in Rome showing it crammed with the carriages and spectators who came to watch the interminable procession which escorted a new ambassador to the Quirinal give some idea of the numbers which could be involved on these occasions.

At Nancy the series of contrasting spaces formed by the Place Royale, the Place de la Carrière and the oval forecourt of what used to be the Intendancy are an example of a patron and architect using the constraint of an existing situation to create something which looks as though it had been carefully contrived for aesthetic reasons on an unencumbered site.[29]

The town of Nancy, for long the capital of the independent Duchy of Lorraine, had been occupied by France during the wars of the late seventeenth century, but was returned to the dukes by the Treaty of Rysuick in 1697. The town in fact consisted

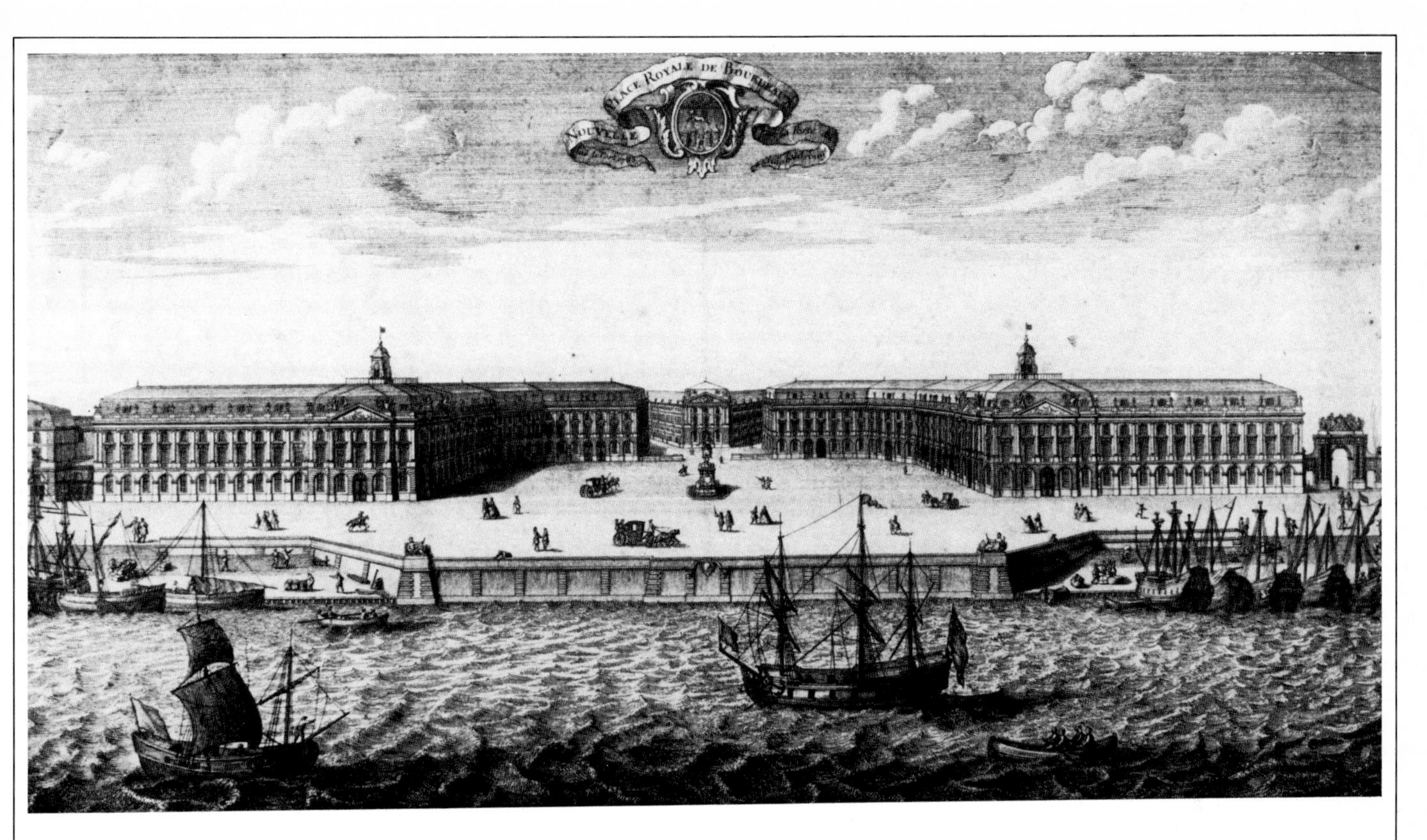

195. The Place Royale, Bordeaux (Archives Municipales, Bordeaux).

194. (left) Bird's-eye view of the Hallesche Tor, Berlin, *c.* 1735. From an anonymous painting destroyed in the 1939–45 war (Markisches Museum, Berlin).

of two towns, the old town, and the rather larger new town laid out next door to it on a grid plan designed by an Italian, Jerôme Citoni, in 1588. Both had their own city governments and their own fortifications. By the Treaty of Ryswick the fortifications of the old town were allowed to remain, but those of the new town had to be demolished; in their place a customs wall was built round it in 1701. In 1737 Lorraine was again ceded to France, and Louis XV installed his father-in-law, the exiled King Stanislas of Poland, as Duke of Lorraine.

In 1744 the city of Paris celebrated Louis XV's recovery from a near-fatal illness by determining to dedicate a new square and statue to him; the result was what is now the Place de la Concorde. A number of provincial cities followed its example, including Bordeaux and Nancy. In 1750–5 Nancy built a Place Royale on what had been largely open space, forming part of the glacis of the fortifications of the old town. These were still maintained, although tree-lined walks had been planted along the ramparts. A new town hall was built on the new Place, and a statue of Louis XV installed in its centre.

The project was inspired and closely controlled by Stanislas and his architect, Louis Heré: the latter designed all the new buildings. They made it part of a much larger scheme of improvement. The new Place had been deliberately sited on the axis of the square known as the Carrière on the old town. This was a long narrow open space which had been formed on previously open ground when the town walls were extended in 1552, and been used for tournaments. In 1717–22 Duke Leopold of Lorraine had started to build a grand new palace looking down the Carrière, but in 1722 he followed Louis XIV's example and abandoned Nancy for a new palace at Luneville, fifteen miles away. Stanislas also lived mainly at Luneville, and gave the shell of Leopold's palace to the city, which demolished it.

Heré rebuilt or refronted the buildings on the Carrière, and joined it to the Place Royale by forming a new, grand gateway in the ramparts and making a bridge enclosed by buildings across the moat. He planted trees in the Carrière and refaced or rebuilt

196. Aerial view of the Place Royale and Place de la Carrière, Nancy.

the buildings on it. The city was persuaded to build a residence for the Intendant, Louis XIV's financial representative in Nancy, on the site of the abortive palace, in 1751–3.

At the end of the day Nancy had acquired a series of contrasted spaces which also provided it with a new administrative, social, commercial and residential centre, and had turned the constraints of the site to brilliant advantage; apart from the bridge and gate negotiating the fortifications of the old town, the grills behind the Place Royale fountains marked the customs wall of the new one.

The functions of the new town hall were as much social as administrative; it was in frequent use for balls and concerts. The Place also accommodated two large private houses, the customs office and the Academy of Music. The L-shaped buildings which enclosed the way across the moat contained shops, a billiard room and the first cafés to be opened in Nancy. The Carrière became a parade for Nancy society, and was lined by the houses of the city notables, including an especially elegant one for Heré himself. At the end nearest to the Place Royale were new law courts and a new bourse.

The great open space facing the Winter Palace in St Petersburg was formed in 1819–29 on a truly imperial scale. Its southern side was filled with a crescent of buildings occupied by the general staff, and acted as a foil to the palace and a kind of amphitheatre from which to survey the military parades which took place on the square. It may show the influence of English crescents. But these, as has already been discussed, expressed a different conception from that behind geometric squares on the continent. They were designed to enable the buildings on them to look out onto a view, not to look inwards into an enclosed space. All the early crescents were open to a view, whether of the surrounding countryside, as at Bath, or the sea, as at Brighton. In later lay-outs,

197. Looking past the General Staff Building and Winter Palace to the Admiralty and Isaac's Cathedral, St Petersburg. From the painting by Theodore Yakovlevitch Aleksyeev, d. 1825 (Private collection).

however, crescents were sometimes included merely as a variant on terraces or squares, in order to give a new development a suitably fashionable air; for a similar reason ordinary nineteenth-century terraces are sometimes called parades, although they were never used for parading in the full eighteenth-century sense.

Crescents built to look at a view, elegantly shaped enclosed squares, and a plan which brought the country into the town and enabled the town to look at the country, all reached their apogee in the New Town at Edinburgh. Its growth is a textbook example of the growing importance of society. Edinburgh was a capital city, but a capital which had lost its main function. Its parliament had gone as a result of the Act of Union of 1707, and there was little in the way of government offices. Commercially the city had never had much importance. What remained were lawyers, barristers, doctors, architects, artists, bankers and shopkeepers, to cater for the needs of the Scottish upper and middle classes, along with a small but famous university and an excellent high school. In the course of the eighteenth century Scottish peers and landed gentry increasingly began to come to Edinburgh for the pleasure of a season in the city, as well as to consult their lawyer or their doctor. They acquired apartments or houses, and other people with private incomes but no large landholdings settled there permanently. They were encouraged to do so by the enterprise of the lord provost and town council, who laid out the original New Town in 1767, to the design of James Craig, and by the various ground landlords who added to it.

Craig's New Town consisted of two squares linked by a central street, with a grid of streets to either side. In the original plan there were churches in both squares, closing the vistas of the central street. The 'town' was really no more than a residential area for the upper and upper-middle classes. Everyday shopping was catered for in the back-

198. Edinburgh. Bird's-eye view of Randolph Crescent and Ainslie and Moray Places.

199. (right) In the Park Street Cemetery, Calcutta.

streets, but there was no major shopping street, and no major public buildings other than churches and assembly rooms.

This conventional grid plan had an out-of-the-ordinary situation, along the levelled spine of a hill, looking across a marshy valley to the Old Town on one side, and down to the Firth of Forth on the other. The site may have been chosen mainly for reasons of health and ventilation; certainly north or east winds still ventilate its streets all too effectively in the winter. But the houses on the outside of the grid had superb views, to open country on one side and the Old Town on the other.

The New Town was extensively added to, especially in the years after the Napoleonic Wars, by when the influence of Bath and of Regent's Park in London was apparent. The Post Office Directory of 1829 shows thirteen crescents and four circuses, interspersed with block after block of regularly planned terraces. Spatially the most exciting development was on the estate of the Earl of Moray, where a crescent led into an oval and the oval into the dodecagon of Moray Place. Everywhere, art and nature were boldly mixed together. A great swathe of landscaped gardens divided Craig's New Town from the development to the north, all the main squares, crescents and circuses looked onto areas of informally planted grass and trees, and there were, and are, views everywhere, out to the surrounding hills and down to the Firth of Forth. At the back of the Moray estate the ground drops sharply down into the tree-lined valley of the stream known as the Water of Leith, and a path along the stream leads past a little classical temple built over a mineral spring; walking there, one could be in a gentleman's park rather than in the middle of a great city.[30]

11 The City as Export

The spread of European activities to America and the far east led to the founding of settlements in both areas, some of which grew into great cities. The first ones were established by the Portuguese and the Spaniards. To begin with these seem to have been planned in a fairly haphazard manner, but in the second half of the sixteenth century they were systematized into what became virtually a mass-produced article. Grid-planning prevailed, because it was so convenient.

The standards were laid down in Royal Ordinances concerning the laying out of new towns, often referred to as the Laws of the Indies.[1] They were issued by Philip II of Spain in 1573; although Spain and Portugal were united under the same kings between 1580 and 1640, they seem never to have been observed in Portuguese colonies. They took the kind of town with which Spaniards were familiar at home, and systematized it, on the basis of a grid. Everything was to centre on the main square which was to be used for tournaments, festivities and celebrations, as well as a market-place. Its length was to be at least one and a half times its

width, 'as this proportion is the best for festivals in which horses are used or any other celebrations which have to be held'. It was to be not smaller than two hundred by three hundred feet, and not larger than three hundred by eight hundred; four hundred by six hundred was recommended as a good average size. The lots around it were to be reserved for the main church, the town hall, shops, dwellings for merchants, and a building for the royal council. Twelve streets were to converge on the square, four main ones in the middle of each side, and subsidiary pairs at each corner. The streets were to provide the basis of the town grid, which was to be set at 45 degrees to the compass points, so that the streets did not face the principal winds. The main square and streets were to have arcades, 'for these are a great convenience for those who resort thither for trade'. 'In cold climates the streets shall be wide; in hot climates narrow, however, for purpose of defence and where horses are kept, the streets had better be wide.' Churches and monasteries were to be spaced out over the town, with smaller squares in front of them, 'so that the teaching of religious doctrine may be evenly distributed'. Waste-producing activities, such as slaughterhouses, fisheries and tanneries, were to be situated where the waste could easily be got rid of, for instance on the river or the sea, below the town. There was to be a common for pasturing cattle and for recreation, and it was to be big enough to allow for the needs of the town, even if it should grow greatly.

These regulations were adhered to, with variations, all over Spanish America. They were sensible and practical. The grid could be expanded as and when desired. The one difficult decision was the size of the central square: the likely ultimate size of the town had to be estimated, and if it was overestimated a small town could be left with a huge and desolate square.

The regulations were not designed to produce visually impressive towns. The governor was expected to live over the poultry, vegetables and eggs of the market. A consistent grid plan does not allow vistas to be closed by important buildings. In some towns the grid was adjusted to enable this, but it did not happen very often.

The differences between the grid plans of Spanish America and those of English America were not very great. There is no reason to suppose that one influenced the other; they derived from a common original. But the end result was very different, for reasons which had little to do with the plan. It was the arcades in the main square and streets, the enormous numbers of churches and monasteries, the distinctive nature of the houses, and the much greater extremes between wealth and poverty, which differentiated the Spanish colonial cities. Before the nineteenth century no inhabitant of a city in British America could approach the wealth of the mine-owners in Spanish America; no British governor had rule over territories as large, or command of a life-style as lavish, as a Spanish viceroy. Even in India only a handful of individuals became as rich, and only in Calcutta at the end of the eighteenth century did the governor-general begin to live in comparable splendour. Spanish-American towns, moreover, had a start of a hundred years or so. By the mid-seventeenth century the capitals of various provinces had established a society with several generations of wealth behind it, and a way of life which attracted the great landowners to come and spend substantial amounts of time there, as in Europe.

200. Mexico City from the distance. Detail from a picture by Thomas Egerton (Government Art Collection).

The houses in these cities almost invariably followed the Spanish tradition. They were built round courtyards which varied in size according to the importance of the house; and in any successful settlement these courtyard houses soon cohered together and filled up each block with a solid mass of housing, pitted with courtyards. Two traditional forms of recreation, also imported from Spain, added to their distinctive character. Any town of any size had an *alameda*, on the edge of the town, for the evening parade; and once bullfights had been moved out of the main square, in the late eighteenth or early nineteenth century, every town of any size had a bullring.

The main towns in Spanish America were Lima, Quito, Havana and Mexico City. Mexico City was the largest and most glamorous, because of its wealth, setting and history. Behind it hovered the vision and the ghost of the Aztec city of Tenochtitlan, itself less than two hundred years old when Cortez and his companions first looked down and saw the gold-plated pyramids of the city rising from the centre of an inland sea in the middle of a girdle of mountains.

When the Spaniards obtained possession of the city in 1519–21 they destroyed the main temple in order to build their cathedral on part of its site, and turned the temple courtyard into the main square. All the buildings of the Aztec city were destroyed. What was left were the lakes around the city, the mountain setting, the canals that came into the city from the lakes, the water supply which the Aztecs had brought in from springs in the hills by means of two aqueducts (which the Spaniards rebuilt), and the Indians themselves. They were allowed to keep most of their land; the Spaniards created a separate Indian nobility, inferior to the Spanish one but not without prestige. The Indian peasants continued to farm the countryside, to build shanty villages round the city, and to come floating in by boat on the canals every morning, bringing flowers and vegetables to sell in the markets.

The lakes gradually disappeared, but there was still a great deal of water left in them into the nineteenth century. The city was approached by causeways across the lakes. There were no fortifications, but customs barriers of rather decorative architecture, called *garitas*. The main square was enormous, approximately nine hundred feet square, the biggest in Spanish America. On it were the cathedral, the viceroy's palace, merchants' houses, and arcades as laid down in the Laws of the Indies. 'These are filled with gay shops, peddlers, caffés, old clothes, toys, flower-venders, sweetmeats, book-stalls, cutlers, curiosity-hunters, antiquities (veritable and doubtful) and the usual crowd of loungers and quid nuncs.'[2] The description was made in 1844, but the scene would probably not have been all that different a hundred years earlier. One-third of the square was filled with a very large market. It was not until the early nineteenth century that a market in front of the viceroy's palace was thought to be inapposite, or at any rate that anything was done to move it; in the early 1800s it was removed to a covered market hall adjoining the square, which was cleared for a central statue of Charles IV on horseback, in a balustraded enclosure. The statue did not last in this position, for it was removed when Mexico broke away from Spain in 1823. All that was left was the pedestal, which survived in lonely isolation and earned the square the name of the Plaza del Zocalo, square of the pedestal. The name has remained to this day, and has spread, so that now every main square in Mexico is called a *zocalo*.[3]

The palaces of the Spanish nobility and ennobled Spanish mine-owners in Mexico City were built, with increasing splendour, in the streets within a short distance of the main square, alternating with churches, colleges and monasteries. From their colonnaded courts, filled with plants and caged birds, their owners emerged every evening in their coaches, to congregate on the Alameda. All the society of the city was to be found there, from the viceroy downwards; everything was done after the European pattern, but with the element of exaggeration and fantasy with which European models tend, and still tend, to be transformed in Mexico. Thomas Gage, an Englishman who was there in the 1640s, was fascinated by it. 'The coaches', he wrote, 'do exceed in cost the best of the court of Madrid and other parts of Christendom; for there they spare nor silver, nor gold, nor precious stones, nor cloth of gold, nor the best silks from China to enrich them. And to the gallantry of their horses the pride of some doth add the cost of bridles and shoes of silver.' He reckoned that about two thousand coaches assembled there every evening, 'full of gallants, ladies and citizens, to see and be seen, to court and be courted, the gentlemen having their train of blackamoor slaves some a dozen some half a dozen waiting on them, in brave and gallant liveries, heavy with gold and silver lace, with silk stockings on their black legs, and roses on their feet, and swords by their sides'. Some of the men came on horseback, rather than in coaches.[4]

As on the Cours la Reine in Paris refreshments were carried from coach to coach, intrigues simmered, rows developed; 'at this meeting are carried about many sorts of sweetmeats and papers of comfits to be sold, for to relish a cup of cool water, which is cried about in curious glasses, to cool the blood of those love-hot gallants'. Courtesans were much in evidence as on most seventeenth-century parades; a church and hospital for reformed prostitutes was suitably located along one side of the Alameda.

Once Philip V was recognized as the first Bourbon king of Spain by the Treaty of Utrecht in 1712, Spain became especially open to French influences. One result of this was that promenading by coach up and down a *cours* (in Spain called a *paseo*) became fashionable as an alternative to parading round and round an *alameda*. In Mexico a number of viceroys planted trees along existing roads or laid out new ones on the outskirts of the city as *paseos*. The most elaborate was the Paseo Nuevo or Paseo de Bucareli, laid out by a viceroy of that name in the 1770s. It followed the model of the Cours la Reine, and was enlarged half way along to a circle (called a *gloriette* in Mexico) on which carriages could line up to watch the parade. It became fashionable to move on from the Alameda to the Paseo Nuevo, especially on feast days, when it was crammed with coaches.[5]

The Paseo was raised a few feet above the surrounding meadowland and those parading on it had a pleasant view, over to the city on one side and on the other past Chapultepec Castle, the hilltop summer residence of the viceroys, to the surrounding mountains. The men pirouetted on their horses down the middle of the road, showing off before the ladies; the coaches drove up and down or parked in the Gloriette 'where the ladies amuse themselves for hours, examining the equipages that roll by, and nodding, smiling and shaking their fans at their acquaintances as they pass . . . The gay throng disperses, as the moon rises behind the mountains, pouring a flood of clear light, bright as the day in other lands, over the tranquil landscape.'[6]

Another *paseo* which was fashionable at certain times of the year was the Paseo de las Vigas. The went alongside one of the canals, and the diversion of promenading there was to watch the Indians, who came out on the water in the evening in crowds of little boats, singing and playing instruments. On certain nights of the full moon fashionable society took to the water too, and it became a Venetian scene of carnival gaiety, with the vicereine in a gilded boat covered with flowers and strung with Chinese lanterns, and all Mexican society singing and serenading in boats around her.[7] The last *paseo* to be laid out in Mexico City developed into the main thoroughfare of the modern city. From the 1870s onwards the avenue of trees which the emperor Maximilian had planted on the road to Chapultepec was remodelled as a *paseo* with *gloriettes*, on the model of the Paseo de Bucareli. It was named the Paseo della Reforma and by the end of the century was punctuated by no fewer than six *gloriettes*, most of them embellished with fountains or statues.[8]

Western cities were exported to the east as well as to the west. Goa had been the first great western city in the east; but by the end of the eighteenth century Goa was in decay, the French had lost all but a foothold in India, and none of the Dutch settlements could compare in size or prosperity with Calcutta.[9]

Calcutta had prospered both as a centre of trade and as a seat of government. Trade had created it in the first place. There was no other reason for settling in a place which for seven months of the year has one of the world's most awful climates. But Calcutta was on the Hooghly, the Hooghly connected with the Ganges, the Ganges and its tributaries gave access to Bengal, and Bengal was the richest province in India. In return for English guns, clocks, machinery of all kinds and textiles, Calcutta collected raw silk, silk goods, cotton, cotton fabrics, rice, sugar, saltpetre, indigo and opium, and exported them to ever-increasing markets in the west and the east.

All these goods piled up in the East India Company's warehouses, inside Fort William at the centre of the European settlement. Calcutta was entirely a company creation. The company's ships had the monopoly of trade to Europe, and the goods which the company bought and sold made up the bulk of their cargoes. Company employees, along with a small group of licensed independent merchants, were allowed a quota in the company ships, and could trade privately inside India and to the east. In 1765 the company took over the collecting of the Mogul emperor's revenues in Bengal; in effect this meant ruling Bengal, at first nominally for the emperor, but in the end for the company, with an increasing element of control by the English government. Calcutta became a seat of government, revenue collection and law courts, and from 1772 a governor-general and council in Calcutta were in charge of all the East India Company's Indian possessions, not just of Bengal.

Government began to loom larger than commerce in the company's activities. All its employees, except those in a separate and less prestigious commercial section, were banned from private trading inside India in 1772, and from private trading of all kinds in 1793. Its monopoly of shipping goods to Europe was eroded and finally abolished in 1813; from the same year independent merchants no longer had to be licensed by the company. Until 1833 it still traded, and it kept its profitable monopoly of opium production in Bengal. But in Calcutta trade was increasingly taken over by the private companies, or agency houses, as they came to be called.[10] Most of the officials of the East India Company deposited their savings with them, and on this basis they built ships, founded banks, invested in newspapers and real estate, revived the indigo trade, and exported opium to Hong Kong, besides acting as agents in a wide variety of different concerns and looking after the company officials and their families from the cradle to the grave and beyond. The merchants of the agency houses were respected and often very rich, but European society in Calcutta was now dominated by a pyramid of government officials, judges and lawyers, with the governor-general at its peak. This society

201. (top right) The Zocalo, Mexico City. From an anonymous picture, *c.* 1700 (Corsham Court).

202. (bottom right) Aerial view of Mexico City. From a lithograph of Casimir Castro.

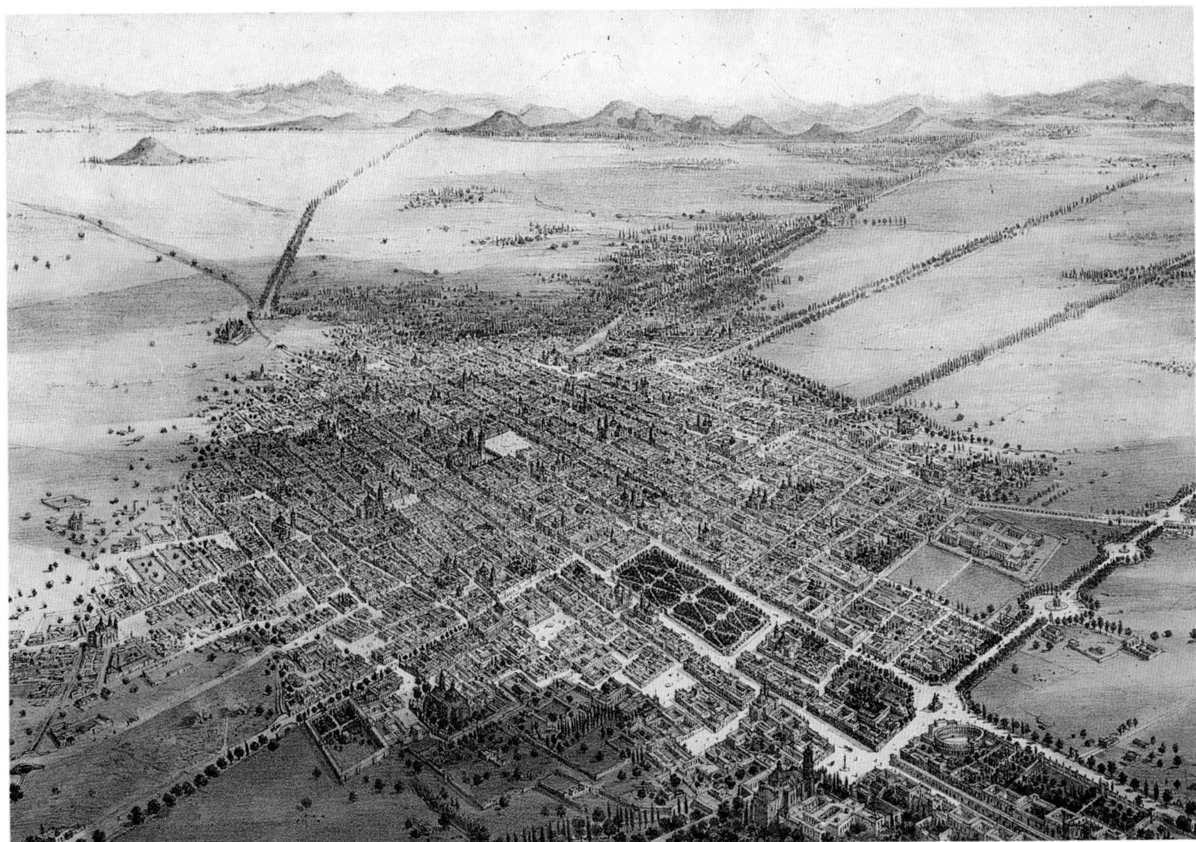

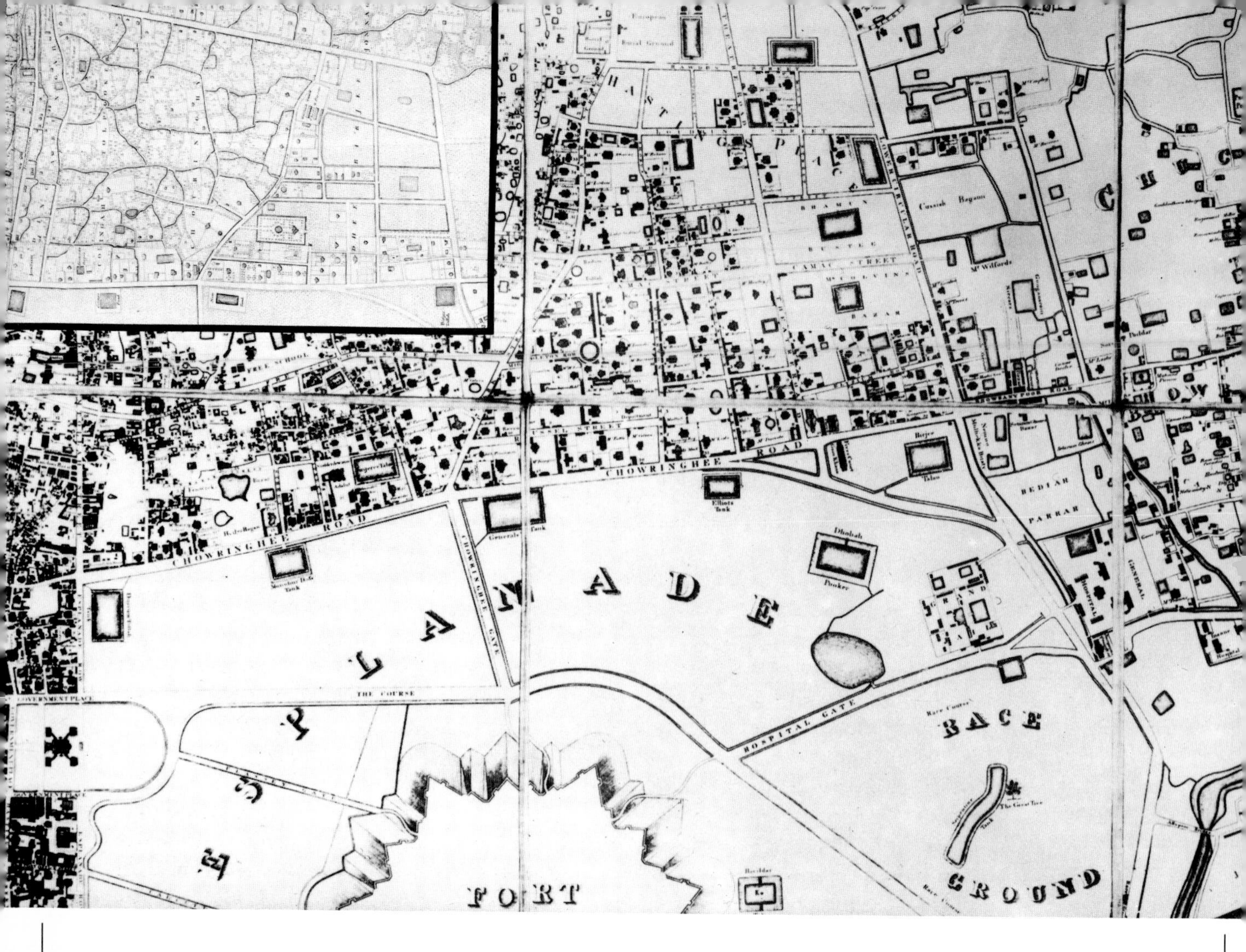

203. The Esplanade (Maidan) and Chowringhee areas of Calcutta. Detail from the plan by J. A. Schalch, 1824, with inset of Chowringhee from the plan by A. Upjohn, 1794 (India Office and Libraries).

numbered only a few thousand people. To the north of the European quarter a densely packed and far more populous Indian town had its own elite of rich merchants (or merchants turned landowners) who traded throughout India and the east, and built up fortunes at least as large as those made in the agency houses. Here, hidden and surprising in a warren of bazaars, tenements and chaotic alleys, were temples of mixed Hindu and Palladian architecture, and grand houses in which white Ionic or Corinthian verandahs led to courtyards in the Indian style, and shrines to Hindu household gods.[11] The Marble Palace, built by the Mullick family in the 1830s, is the best known of these houses, but a comparatively late one and by no means the only surviving example.

There was much else in Calcutta to intrigue visitors.[12] There was the approach up the huge and dirty Hooghly, the nine-mile parade of colonnaded houses glimpsed through the greenery of Garden Reach, the first distant vista of the city, white and sparkling through the masts across the water, the Europeans in their pleasure-barges being lulled with music and cooled with claret as they lay back under huge embroidered sunshades, the little boys in white muslin and coloured sashes who held the sunshades over them, the smoke rising from the pyres in the burning-ghats along the river banks, or the dead bodies of those whose relatives could not afford a pyre, floating down the river covered with crows. There was St John's Church on a Sunday morning after a ship from England had come in, when the English girls emerged from their palanquins, the shoals of purple-faced company officials leered and peered as they helped them into church, and the girls smirked back, in the hopes of a quick marriage and a rich widowhood. There were the houses themselves, the high first-floor rooms opening onto pillared verandahs, the adjutant cranes standing frozen on one leg along the parapets, the swarms of servants with strange names: the mace-bearing chobdar, who organized the household, the jemadars, who acted as a bodyguard, the palkee-bearers, who carried the palanquins, the mussalchees who held the torches, the khansamahs, who waited at table, the hookabardar, who looked after the hookah, the abdar, who kept wine cool with saltpetre. Not least, there were the Park Street cemeteries, where most Europeans were likely to end up in a few years' time, with pyramids and temples to cover their bones and inscriptions to record the grief of those who lost them too soon.[13]

The heart of British Calcutta was the Esplanade, not yet called the Maidan. This very large open space was yet another example of the side-benefits which European cities derived from their fortifications. In 1756 Calcutta was captured, sacked and looted by the local nawab. Once the city had been re-taken it was decided that a larger, stronger and better-sited fort must be built. The new fort was on the river, like the old one, but outside the town instead of in the middle of it, and surrounded by an open space about five hundred yards in radius, instead of being hemmed in by buildings. In accordance with the military terminology of the time, the open space was known as the Esplanade.

Besides immediately becoming the recreation and exercising area for all the Europeans in Calcutta, the Esplanade was rapidly lined on two sides with grand new buildings: the council house, accountant-general's office, court house and government house to the north on the edge of the original settlement, and a long row of splendid private houses stretching down the east side along Chowringhee Road. Against this architectural backcloth processed rajahs on elephants, on their way to government house, camels and camel-riders, Indian women in closed-in bullock carts resembling little huts on wheels, soldiers, pedestrians of all kinds, and Europeans being conveyed in palanquins or coaches, or dashingly driving themselves in phaetons. The racecourse at the southern end of the Esplanade became a favourite resort for duels in the dawn light, and on the western edge lawyers strolled under the trees of Respondentia Walk, which ran along the river by the court house. On moonlit nights 'elegant walking-parties' wandered over the enormous empty spaces, or palanquins on their way back from dinners or balls passed at the double, while the mussalchees ran in front, waving their flaming torches and shouting 'Tok, Tok' to clear the way.[14]

Social life on the Esplanade came to a climax every evening on the broad quarter-mile drive known as the Course. Here, when the appalling heat had slightly abated, and the low sun shining through the dust turned the white Chowringhee houses gold or pink, British Calcutta drove or rode up and down, and dashing Calcutta ladies showed off their charms, proudly conscious of their status in a society in which the men greatly outnumbered the women. 'The manners of Calcutta', according to a novel of Calcutta life written in 1789, 'are somewhat contradictory—now all softness and femininity and now all courage and resolution . . . They take a particular pleasure, on the one hand, in obliging and informing strangers—melt into tears at every tale of sorrow—and sweetly sympathize with those whose spirits are depressed; on the other hand, you behold them so little attentive to female decorum, and so fearless of danger, that a scarlet riding dress, which gives them most the appearance of the other sex, enraptures

204. (above) A European lady in a palanquin before Writer's Buildings, Calcutta. Detail from a plate in T. & W. Daniell's *Views of Calcutta*, 1788 (India Office Library, London).

205. (right) Houses of rich Indian merchants in the Black Town, Calcutta, seen from the Hooghly. Detail from a plate in *Views of Calcutta*, 1788 (India Office Library, London).

them—and to drive a phaeton and pair with a vivacity, *à dégagement*, or whatever else may be the proper epithet, to mark their skill and unconcern, in the midst of numberless spectators is their delight; . . . the ladies of gaiety and *ton* always make a point, on these occasions, of having a gentleman-companion, who lolls at his ease; the office of managing the rein, &c., being wholly assumed by the lady . . . A servant . . . runs on each side the horses, with long-handled flappers in their hands, sometimes held by their manes and sometimes at a little distance; and the effect is both striking and pleasing.'[15]

The Course at Calcutta had obvious affinities with the French *cours*, the Italian *corsi* and the Spanish *alameda* and *paseo*.[16] But it seems unlikely that any Spanish lady would have taken the reins herself on a public promenade, and although there were certain similarities, in extravagance of turn-out and perhaps provinciality of outlook, between Calcutta and Mexico City, the differences were equally striking, not least the different form of the houses. Instead of the densely built-up city blocks, thick walls, small external windows and colonnaded courtyards favoured by the Spaniards when building in hot climates (both dry and humid), the English preferred free-standing houses, large windows, no courtyards, and external colonnades in the form of verandahs.

They built in this way for coolness and for health. Both were thought to be promoted by detached houses, as a result of their having through-ventilation, and being open to any available breeze. In the 1780s William Hickey recommended 'a good habitation in an open airy part of the town' as one of the essentials for health in Calcutta.[17] There was very little terraced housing in the European quarter; even in the original nucleus around Tank (now Dalhousie) Square, the houses were detached, although much more closely spaced than in Chowringhee. Quite a few people lived out of the town altogether in what were known as garden houses, and commuted up or down the river to work.

Houses along or off the Esplanade provided what soon became the fashionable mean between houses in the centre and garden houses. Those living in them were conveniently close to the public buildings and could frequent the evening promenade on the Course, but could also use the Esplanade in the cool of the morning for riding (another of Hickey's essentials for health) and still enjoy big gardens and plenty of space. Chowringhee developed into what was perhaps the first example of the kind of prosperous residential suburb of detached houses that was to become a distinctive feature of dozens of western cities in the nineteenth century.

Building along Chowringhee Road started in the late 1770s. As soon as the prime lots along the Esplanade had been bought up, the development moved into the land to the east. By 1784 an L-shaped area between Chowringhee Road, and what are now Free School Street, Park Street, London Street and Theatre Road had been laid out on an irregular grid and was filling up with large detached houses on big plots.[18] Property development became a popular form of speculation, indulged in, not always success-

206–7. Late eighteenth-century houses in Park Street and (right) Short Street, Calcutta (India Office Library, London).

fully, by a variety of different people. Some of the houses were built and rented out by Indian, English or Armenian merchants; in 1787 J. Z. Kiemander, a Dutch missionary, and his son went bankrupt as a result of speculative house-building; Camac Street and Wood Street were developed around 1780, and then sold off, by two Engineer officers, Lieutenant William Camac and Colonel Wood.[19]

The first English houses to be built in Calcutta did not have verandahs; they looked much the same as houses built at the time in England. Verandahs seem first to have appeared in the 1760s; the name and possibly the idea were taken from Portuguese houses, but the friendly vernacular of Portuguese verandahs, such as can still be seen in Goa, was translated into a classical language of arcades or Doric and Ionic colonnades inspired by Palladian prototypes. In some of the earlier houses the verandah took the form of a two-storey portico attached or recessed on the middle of one façade of the house, but it soon became usual to cover the whole of one side (usually the southern) with two- or three-storey verandahs. Verandahs were clearly still not universal by 1777, when William Hickey rented a house without one, and had one added by an Indian builder. Verandah columns were normally built of brick, but the lintels were of timber; houses and verandahs were covered over with the local white stucco called chunam, which possessed 'the delicacy and lustre of marble', according to the Daniell brothers.[20]

The verandahs were invariably hung with green mats or Venetian blinds, which provided a gay contrast to the white stucco, and could be rolled up and down as needed; they became agreeable outdoor living rooms, set out with chairs and card-tables. The interiors of Calcutta houses were almost always very simply decorated, however large, but the verandahs could make the outsides look extremely grand; as William Hodges

208. Houses in Chowringhee from the Esplanade. From a lithograph by William Wood (British Library).

put it in the 1780s, they had 'the appearance of Grecian temples; and indeed every house may be considered as a temple dedicated to hospitality'.[21]

Children were not much in evidence in these hospitable houses. In the late eighteenth century European wives were increasingly taking the place of Indian mistresses, but the Calcutta custom was to keep children out of the town, in country cottages which also provided an agreeable retreat from the social whirl. According to the anonymous author of *Hartly House* (1789), 'these retreats . . . are at Calcutta called Bungilos, and possess all the charms and beauties of rural existence. Hartly Bungilo consists of a suite of apartments on a ground floor, with a thatched roof and verandahs, and stands in the centre of a garden.' Here the heroine admired Mrs Hartly's closet, which was decorated 'with a pink paper from China', chatted with 'the gouvernante . . . the widow of a clergyman', and played the harp by moonlight.[22] Bungalows were an adaptation for European use of a distinctive type of Bengali peasant hut; the name derives from the Hindu or Mahratti *Bangla*, which simply means 'of or belonging to Bengal'. They were to have a world-wide progeny in the nineteenth and twentieth centuries. The first identified references to them as adapted for Europeans occur in the 1780s, but it has not been established who first adapted them, when and why, or whether they spread from Calcutta to the out-stations or vice versa.[23]

In the decades around 1800 Calcutta was an interesting place. It had lost much of the crudity of the 1770s, when flash young men 'covered with lace, spangles and foil' indulged in 'the barbarous custom of pelleting each other with little balls of bread, made like pills, across the table', and the ladies joined in the fun.[24] The growing splendour of its public buildings culminated in the new government house, built on the Esplanade in 1798–1803. The city was a pioneer in a number of different ways. It was the first place where Europeans seriously studied Sanskrit and Indian antiquities; the Asiatic Society, founded by Sir William Jones in 1784, had established a library and a journal which was exploring all aspects of Hindu life. The multiple interests of the agency houses were later to inspire the founding of the first American trusts.[25] The big Calcutta shops were pioneering the kind of general sales which were to form the

209. Silk and cloth merchants visiting a European house. From the lithograph after a drawing by Mrs Belnos (India Office Library, London).

basis of the department stores in Paris and New York. As early as 1784 Messrs Baxter and Ord, who kept what was called a 'Europe shop', were advertising that they had bought up the cargo of 'Captain Johnson of the *Berrington*', and could accordingly offer for sale millinery, pianofortes, mahogany furniture, wines, ale, cheese, pickles, herrings, feathered hats, boots, shoes, fancy cloths, doeskin breeches, gloves, vinegar, oil, mustard, guns, telescopes, books, perambulators, spectacles and speaking-trumpets.[26] In 1789 it was affirmed that British women visiting the Europe shops were capable of 'spending 30 or 40,000 rupees in one morning, for the decoration of their persons; on which account many husbands are observed to turn pale as ashes, on the bare mention of their wives being seen to enter them'.[27]

The best known of these Europe shops was Dring's Long Rooms, in the Lall Bazaar. The rooms stretched for two hundred feet, divided by a screen of columns in the centre, and their variegated contents were celebrated in 1828 by Sir Charles D'Oyly in his poem *Tom Raw the Griffin*.

> Here rich gilt, bronze, and di'mond cut epergnes,
> And alabaster vases, meet Tom's view,
> With plated dinner sets, and silver urns,
> And strings of pearls, and shawls of splendid hue,
> And diamond necklaces, or false or true,
> Boots, shoes, and cotton stockings, silks and laces,
> Toys, walking sticks, and vermicelli too,
> Milroy's neat hunting saddles—cues, and maces,
> Preserves, pale ale, and hams, and jockey caps for races.[28]

The fondness of Calcutta people for gambling was put to constructive use by a system of public lotteries. Public lotteries had taken place since the Middle Ages, and the proceeds were often put to some charitable purpose;[29] but in Calcutta the system was carried much further. In 1784 St John's Church had been built on the proceeds of a lottery, organized by a lottery commission of nine gentlemen. More lotteries for a variety of purposes followed in the 1790s. In 1803 they began to be organized for the particular purpose of public amenity, first under a Town Improvement Committee, set up by Lord Wellesley in 1803, and then under Lottery Commissioners, set up in 1817. Lotteries paid for the town hall (1813), numerous tanks, improved sewage, roads, paths, balustrades and Respondentia Walk on the Maidan, the Kidderpore Bridge, and a variety of new roads, including Strand Road (1828) along the river front, and the long sequence of Wellesley, Wellington, College and Cornwallis Streets, running north–south along the inside edge of both the English and the Indian towns. The achievement was considerable, although in Calcutta as in almost all western cities since the Middle Ages, the problems of acquiring property in heavily built-up areas prevented any attempts at piercing new roads through the confusion of the Indian town, where they were most needed.[30]

210. View from the verandah balcony of a house in Macao.

The lottery prizes were drawn in the town hall, once it was completed, by two little charity boys from the orphanage; 'every nation, colour, trade, and caste were there', and the boys were 'provided for by the lucky possessor of the capital prize'.[31]

But interesting and innovative though the shops and lottery-financed improvements of Calcutta were, its main importance in the history of the western city was that here for the first time were to be found a splendid town built round what was, in effect, a great public park, and residential neighbourhoods of prestigious free-standing houses, set in their own gardens.

Buildings two or more storeys of which were protected on one side by verandahs supported on classical columns became a common feature of tropical cities developed or influenced by the British. In some cases the idea undoubtedly derived from British buildings in India, especially in Calcutta. The type appeared early in the nineteenth century in Canton, and a little later in Hong Kong, both of which had close trade connections with Calcutta, and in Macao, where the Canton merchants and their mistresses retired in the summer. In America, the verandahed houses of Charleston, South Carolina (where the verandahs are called piazzas), are often so similar stylistically to Calcutta ones that it is tempting to surmise whether there was any direct influence.[32]

But the planning of American towns and cities bore little relation to that of English settlements in India. From early on, if they were laid out on any plan at all, it was based on the universal and practical grid, and usually contained an open central square. New Haven, Connecticut, for instance, which was first settled in 1638, was laid out on a grid of nine squares, each of 825 feet, the central one of which was left open as what is now called the Green.[33]

Philadelphia, which was laid out between 1681 and 1683 as the main city of William Penn's new settlement of Pennsylvania, was unusual, not because it was on a grid but because the grid was such a large one. Since Roman days no new western city had been planned on such a large scale, or anything approaching it. The original plan involved a grid a little under two miles long and one mile wide, running between the Schuylkill and Delaware Rivers. This is not large by twentieth-century standards, but

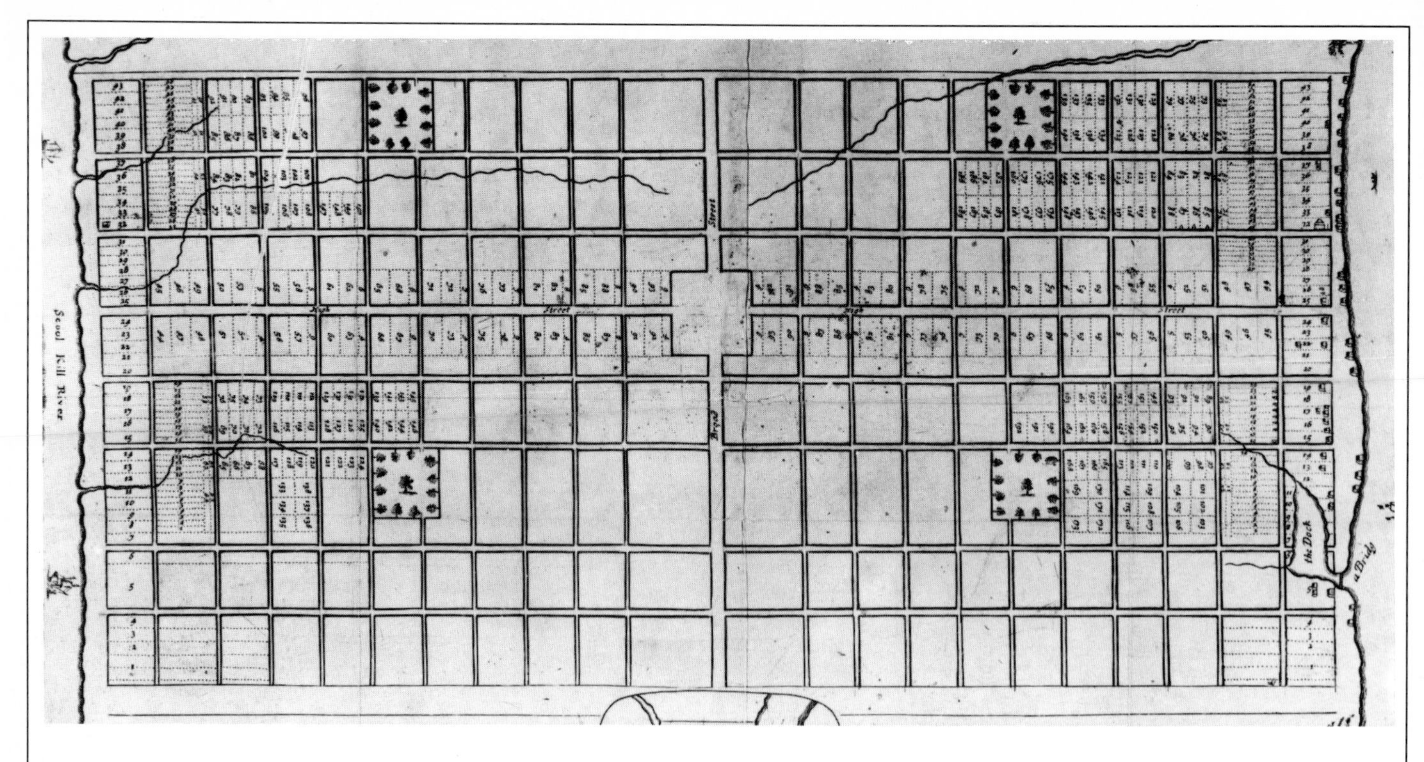

211–12. The original plan for Philadelphia, 1682 (north to the top), and (right) Philadelphia in 1762, from the plan by Nicholas Scull (west to the top) (Cornell University; Library of Congress, Washington, D.C.).

it was as large as London or Paris, and larger than any other western city of its day. It was almost certainly modelled on the plans for rebuilding London after the Great Fire of 1666, but the plain plans not the fancy ones, as was suitable for a Quaker city. But, unlike the London plans, it was carried out—even if it took a hundred and fifty years to fill the grid.[34]

This grid, like those of its London models, contained a number of open squares, regularly disposed: in its case one central main square and four subsidiary ones. The two main streets were one hundred feet wide, the width recommended by Evelyn in his plan for London, and the other streets were fifty feet wide. On the main square, which contained ten acres, it was planned to build 'a Meeting-House, Assembly or State House, Market-House, School-House, and several other buildings for public concerns'. All this was in the European tradition, close enough, indeed, to the Spanish grids in America.

There were important differences, however. The four subsidiary squares were not designed to contain markets or churches, as in the London or Spanish plans. They were 'to be for the like uses as the Moor-fields in London', that is, laid out with walks and planted with trees, for the exercise and recreation of the townspeople. Moreover, Penn recommended that each individual house be free-standing, 'that so there may be ground on each side for gardens or orchards, or fields that it may be a green country town, which will never be burnt, and always be wholesome'.[35]

Behind all this lay both practical necessity and possibly an attitude to life. The first settlers in British-American towns could not expect to live off the native population, for there was no native agriculture to speak of. Land plots in towns were always big enough for each settler to have a sizeable garden which often amounted to a smallholding, although it could be supplemented by a bigger allotment on the edge of the town. The very large green at New Haven was perhaps originally intended as common pasture. The smaller settlements were mainly settlements of farmers, who went out into the surrounding fields in the daytime. Even in the bigger settlements the artisans and shopkeepers in the towns were expected to feed themselves at least partly off their own homegrown produce. In 1685 Penn claimed that the first Philadelphian settlers could

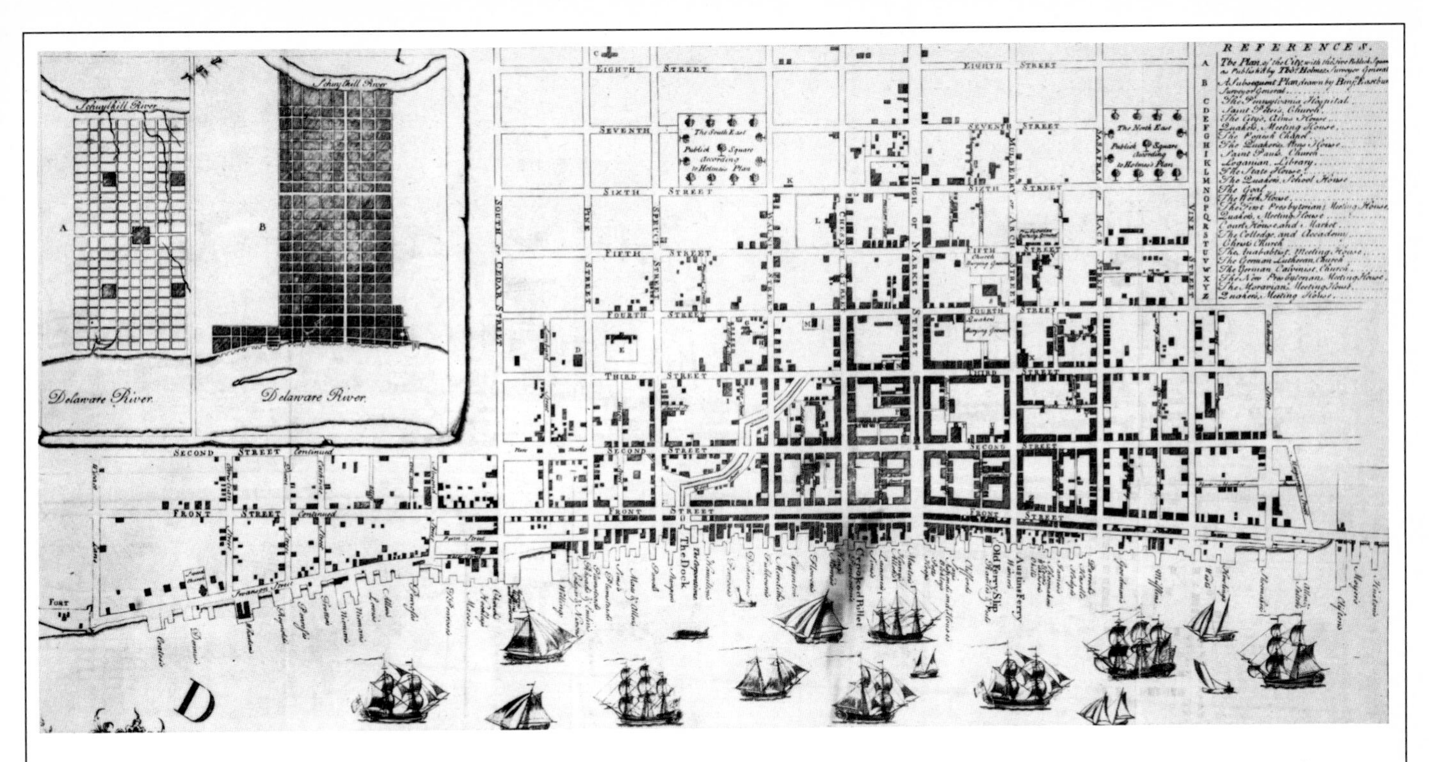

already live 'comfortably', what with 'their Garden Plots (the least half-an-acre), the fish of the river, and their labour, to the countryman who begins to pay with the provisions of his own growth'.[36]

Fire prevention was another reason for free-standing houses; Penn had probably actually seen the rapidity with which the close-packed houses of London had burst into flames in the Great Fire of 1666. The 'wholesomeness' of plenty of fresh air circulating between houses was another argument in favour of detachment. Perhaps it is not reading too much into it to see as well a conscious rejection of the big European city in favour of the 'green country town', however much magnified over English examples, as a better place in which to live. Most English-American settlements were founded by independent groups, getting away from something in the home country which they disliked, rather than by government action, as in Spanish America. In Philadelphia the actual names of the state—Penn's wooded land—and the choice of street names suggest some such attitude. As Penn put it in 1685: 'The names of those streets are mostly taken from the things that spontaneously grow in the country, as Vine Street, Mulberry Street, Chestnut Street, Wallnut Street, Strawberry Street, Cranberry Street, Plumb Street, Hickory Street, Pine Street, Oake Street, Beach Street, Ash Street, Poplar Street, Sassafrax Street and the like.'[37]

References to other settlements in America in the early eighteenth century stress their airiness, the fact that the houses are free-standing in large gardens, and their safety from fire. When the Swiss nobleman Baron Christopher von Graffenried laid out New Bern in North Carolina in 1710 he described his approach as follows: 'Since in America they do not like to live crowded in order to enjoy a purer air, I accordingly ordered the streets to be very broad and the houses well separated one from the other. I marked three acres of land for each family, for house, barn, garden, orchard, hemp-field, poultry-yard and other purposes.'[38]

New Bern was destroyed by Indians in the year after its settlement, but Savannah, Georgia, which was laid out in 1733, adopted a similar but rather differently organized system. Each settler was granted fifty acres, made up of a farm of just over forty-five acres, a five-acre allotment on the edge of the town, and a house plot sixty feet by

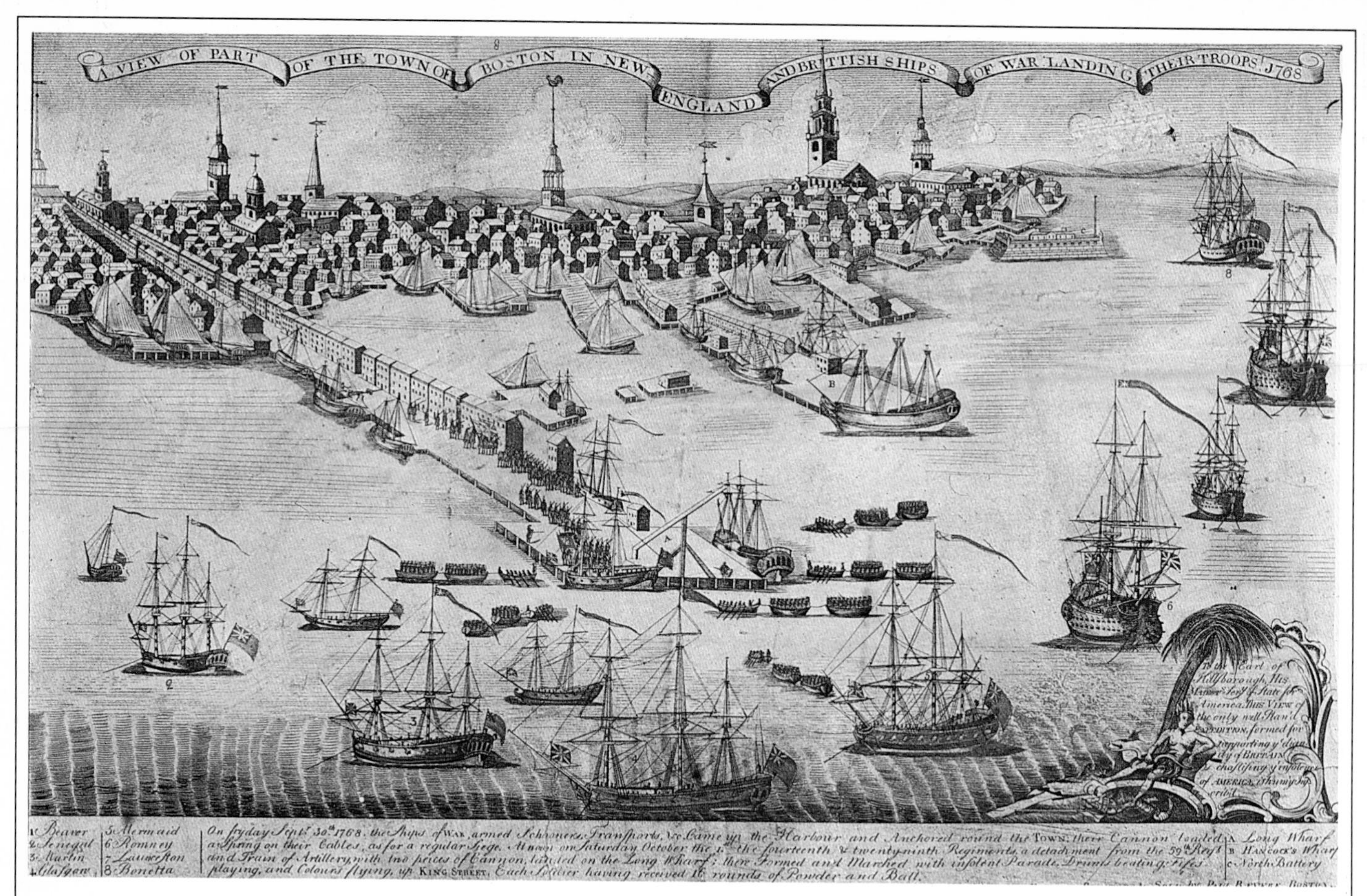

213. Boston, Massachusetts. View of the harbour in 1768, by Paul Revere (New York Public Library).

ninety; the plots were laid out on a grid plan around four squares. The basic city plot was accordingly smaller than in Philadelphia or New Bern; but even so, as the *London Magazine* put it in 1745: 'the houses are built some distance from each other, to allow more air and garden room and prevent the communication, in case of any accident, by fire'. Immediately round the town was common land, left open 'for convenience of air', according to the original land grants.[39]

In fact in any town which was commercially successful, economic pressure, combined, perhaps, with the example of towns in England, quickly got rid of the detached houses, at any rate in the more prosperous areas. By 1800 Savannah had become a delightful town, but a town of terraces in the English manner. Philadelphia, instead of spreading evenly and thinly over its half-acre plots, coagulated in terraces in the neighbourhood of the Delaware and the main street; the richer merchants obtained the best sites immediately along the river, and made passages under the road to the wharves.

Philadelphia never acquired a quay running along the river in the European manner. Instead, timber wharves were built out into the river at right-angles to the shore. In 1685 there was only one such wharf, but by 1762 there were sixty-six of them giving the plan of the town a distinctive comb-shaped profile along the water.[40]

The arrangement became a standard one in American ports, most of which were on inland waterways, wide enough to take such wharves without the river passage being obstructed, and having little or no tide to complicate berthing alongside them. At Boston a row of houses was built along the biggest of the wharves, and in the end the space between the wharves began to be filled up with made-up ground, and the town spread out over what had been water. Much of Boston grew up in this way; it was no different from what had happened in, for instance, Amsterdam in the Middle Ages, but was carried out on a much larger scale.[41]

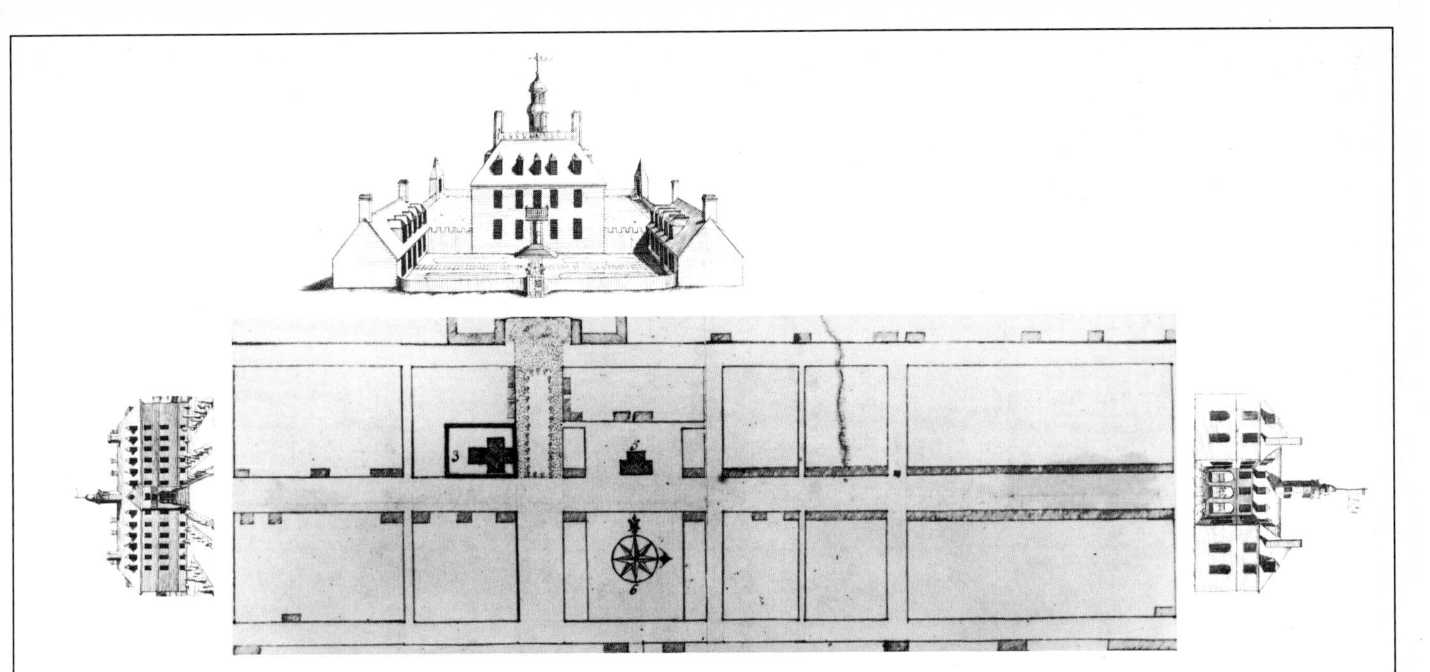

214. Williamsburg, Virginia, in 1781, with insets (left to right) of the College, Governor's Palace and Capitol. From an engraving of *c.* 1737.

All the early towns in British America owed their prosperity to trade, and, although some of them became seats of government for individual colonies, it was their wharves, shipping and merchants' houses which impressed contemporary visitors, not their government buildings. But Williamsburg was founded in 1698 specifically as the seat of the state government of Virginia, and from the start there was little likelihood of it ever becoming a trading centre, because it was not on a river.

Towns, in fact, had notably failed to take root in Virginia. The colony owed its prosperity to tobacco, grown on plantations strung along its many waterways. These were deep enough for English ships to come straight to the plantations and take on cargoes of tobacco in return for assorted goods brought out from England. The function of the towns as intermediate distribution centres was by-passed; the plantation-owners lived on their plantations like barons in their castles, visited each other, and showed no inclination for urban life; what towns there were were miserable places, and none more miserable than Jamestown, the original capital.

Yet by 1724, only twenty-six years after it had been founded, Williamsburg was described as a 'delightful, beautiful ... and thriving city' where the people 'live in the same neat manner, dress after the same modes, and behave themselves exactly as the gentry in London; most families of any note having a coach, chariot, berlin, or chaise ... and at the Governor's House upon birth-nights, and at balls and assemblies, I have seen as fine an appearance, as good diversion, and as splendid entertainments in Governor Spotswood's time as I have seen anywhere else'.[42]

What had been created, in fact, was a city in miniature for polite society, not for commerce. It proved immediately attractive to the plantation-owners of Virginia, who not only crowded the town out whenever the Virginian Assembly or Courts were sitting, but brought their wives and daughters with them. By 1718 Williamsburg had acquired a theatre, the first in British America; dances were given in an assembly room in the main inn, as well as in the governor's house, and the Virginian gentry could buy coaches, silver, lace, furniture, and jewellery there as well as more utilitarian goods.

Williamsburg owed its success partly to its three handsome public buildings, the college, the governor's house and the state house (the first state house in America to be called a Capitol), but also to the beauty of its plan. The broad main street of the town, the Duke of Gloucester Street, was closed at one end by William and Mary College

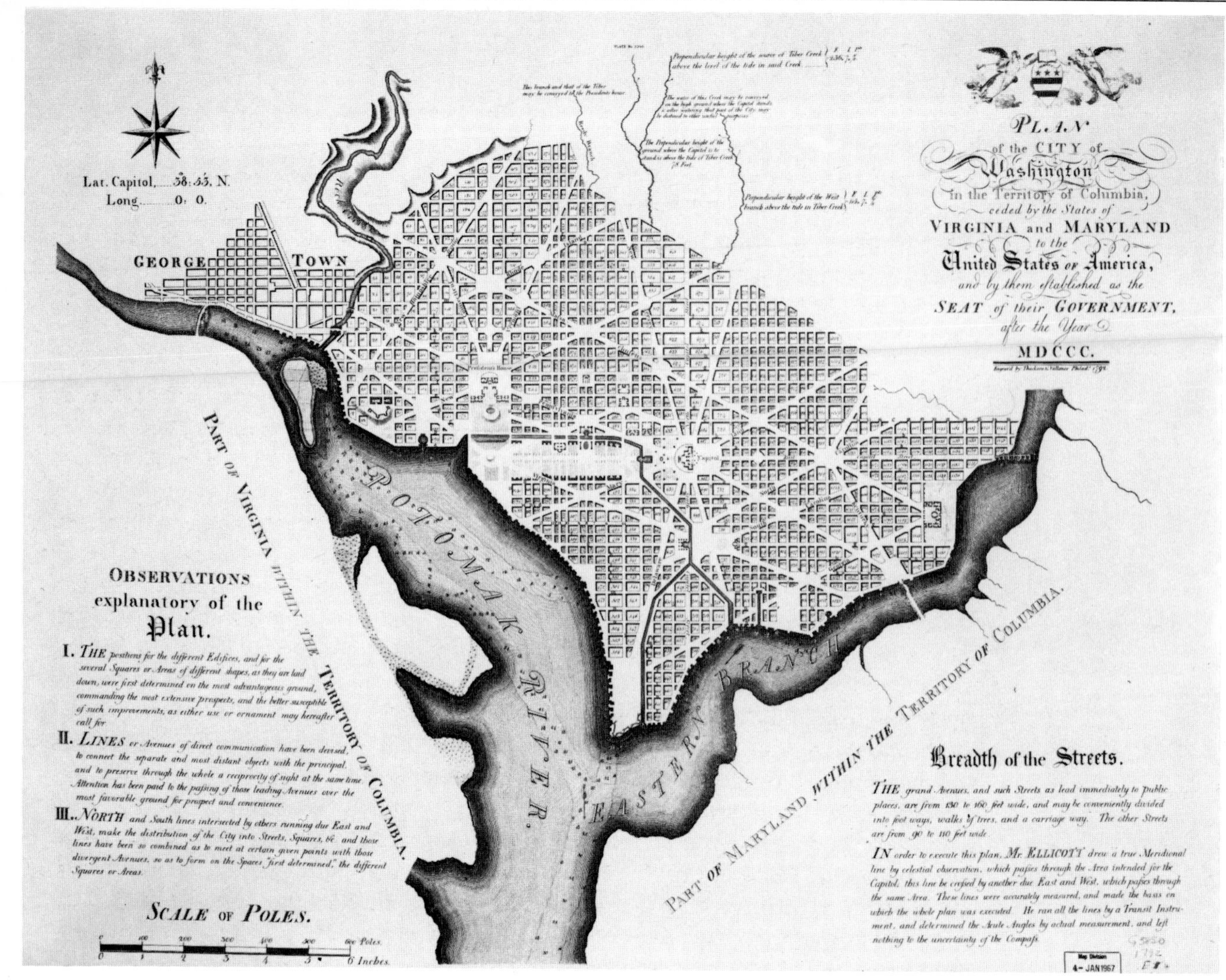

215. L'Enfant's plan for Washington (Library of Congress, Washington, D.C.).

and at the other by the Capitol; not quite half-way along it an even broader street led up to the governor's house or palace. The Duke of Gloucester Street was 99 feet broad, Palace Street was 210 feet. An entirely satisfying sense of civilized order was suggested by this arrangement of the three focal points: government, Crown and college. Perhaps the symmetry would have been even more appropriately finished off if the church had faced the palace on the other side of the main street; but the church was on its present site before the town was laid out. The final touch was provided when Palace Street and the Duke of Gloucester Street were planted with avenues of catalpas between 1730 and 1749.[43]

Williamsburg was a small provincial place; the roads were never paved, and coaches drove up to the axles in dust in the summer; even the grandest of the buildings were not very grand, and off the main streets scattered houses quickly melted into the surrounding countryside. But its plan was as original as anything then existing in Europe and America, and had no obvious prototypes: even the very simple device of a long wide street with prominent buildings at either end had no equivalent in the western world in 1699.

In 1790 the capital of the new independent states of America, which had been temporarily situated in New York and Philadelphia, finally settled permanently on the banks of the Potomac at Washington. The job of laying out the new town was given to a Frenchman, Major Pierre L'Enfant. L'Enfant borrowed plans of Frankfurt,

Karlsruhe, Amsterdam, Strasbourg, Paris, Orléans, Bordeaux, Lyons, Montpellier, Marseilles, Turin and Milan from Jefferson.[44] 'Notwithstanding I would *reprobate the idea of imitating*', he wrote to him, 'yet the contemplation of what exists of well improved situation, even the parallel of these with defective ones, may serve to suggest a variety of new ideas.'[45] In fact the only one of the city plans which clearly influenced Washington is that of Paris. The plan is a synthesis of the Champs Élysées and other elements from Paris with Williamsburg and Wren's plan for rebuilding London, combined with inspired use of the topography of the site. Although there is no evidence that L'Enfant visited Williamsburg, it was well known to both Jefferson and George Washington; and the resemblances between Washington's plan and Wren's plan for London are so striking that it seems inconceivable that L'Enfant did not know of it.

The plan that L'Enfant presented in sketch form in 1791, and which was engraved and made public in the following year, is arguably the most brilliant town plan ever conceived. Like Wren's plan it was based on a grid, for convenience of laying out lots for sale, and a web of diagonals, for convenience of quick and clear movement through the city and in order to provide visual relief from the monotony of the grid. The two main monuments, the president's house and the Capitol, were directly connected by one of the diagonal avenues, but were also linked indirectly in a way clearly suggested by the relationship of Capitol and governor's house in Williamsburg. The Capitol was at the end of a tree-lined 'Grand Avenue', off and at right-angles to which another green space led up to the president's house.

But the Washington arrangement differed from the Williamsburg one in two major particulars. At Williamsburg the three focal points had been Capitol, governor's house and college; at Washington the place of the college was taken by the Potomac. The Capitol, built on top of the highest eminence on the site, was to look down the grand avenue and across the river, and the president's house to have a clear view along the river reach, towards the neighbouring town of Alexandria, by way of a promontory of land on which L'Enfant suggested erecting a 'Majestic Colum or a grand Perysemid,' which would 'completely finish the landscape'. What L'Enfant was aiming for, as he told George Washington, was 'a sense of the real grand and truly beautiful only to be met with where nature contributes with art and diversify the objects'.[46] Analogies with Bath are immediately obvious, although there is no evidence that L'Enfant had knowledge of it, let alone visited that city.

Furthermore, the grand avenue was not planned as a public road, like Duke of Gloucester Street in Williamsburg, but as a 'public walk'; by about 1796 it had been named 'The Mall'.[47] On either side of it was to be a mixture of public buildings and private gardens stretching up to grand houses, suitable for ambassadorial residences. L'Enfant described it as a 'place of general resort . . . all along side of which may be placed play houses, room of assembly, accademies and all such sort of places as may be attractive to the learned and afford diversion to the idle'.[48] L'Enfant clearly envisaged his Mall as crowded with people, a mixture of the completely pedestrian Mall in London and of the partly pedestrian Champs Élysées in Paris, with its pleasure-resorts like the Colosée, and the big gardens coming down to it from the houses on the Faubourg St Honoré. It would, he wrote in his broken English, give Washington 'a superiority of agreements [*agréments*, amenities] over most of the city of the world'.[49]

If the network of diagonal roads derives from Wren, the way in which they were

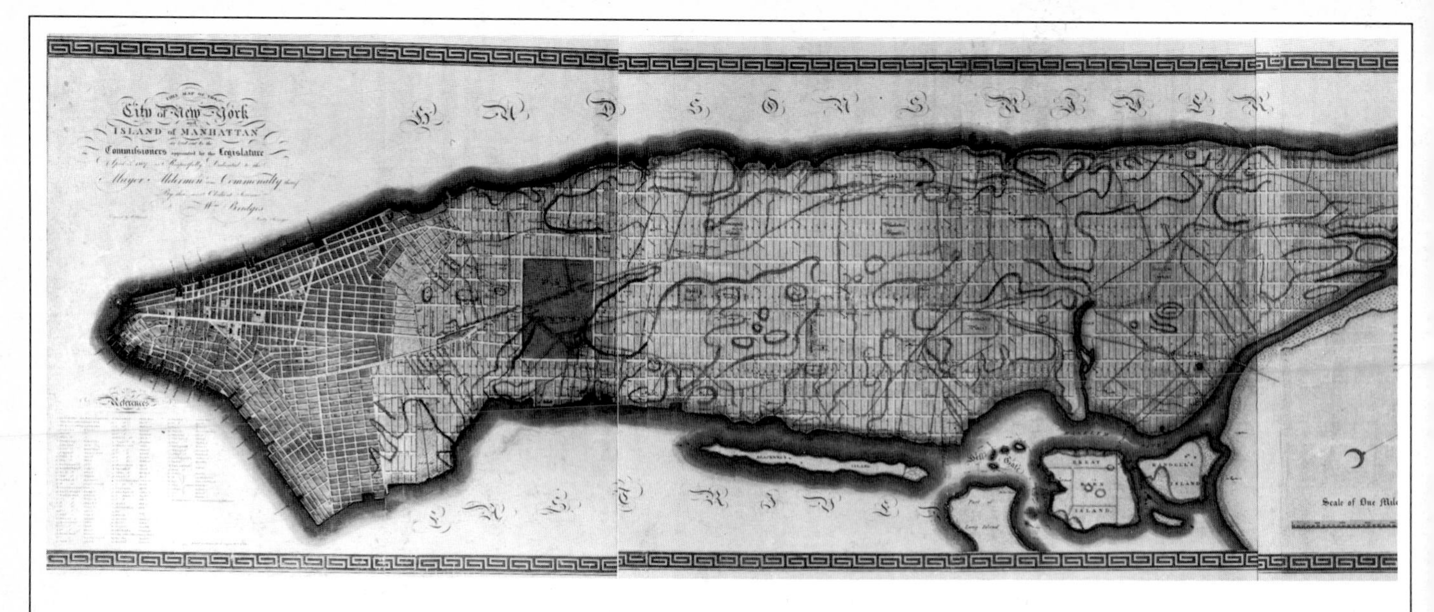

216. New York. The Commissioners' Map, 1811 (Museum of the City of New York).

217. (right) Traffic at Dearborn and Randolph Streets, Chicago, in 1909 (Chicago Historical Society).

218. (following page) India House, Manchester. By Adolphe Valette, 1912 (Manchester City Art Gallery).

219. (subsequent page) Back-yards in Manchester (Manchester Public Libraries).

to be planted with a double line of trees giving shade to walks to either side of the carriageway derived from the Paris boulevards; but they were to be wider, 160 feet at their widest. Like the boulevards, they were intended to provide 'a variety of pleasant rides' and to encourage the growth of the city along them.

Washington was envisaged by L'Enfant as becoming a great commercial centre as well as a national capital. The south-eastern quarter of the city, along the deeper waters of the eastern branch of the Potomac was to be the commercial and naval quarter. Little of this materialized, since by the time that Washington had developed into a city of any size, water transport was rapidly being overtaken in importance by rail transport, promoted by East Coast money which ignored Washington. The Mall was not planted until the 1840s, and then as an early Victorian park of winding walks; it never became the busy parade between grand private houses, theatres and assembly rooms envisaged by L'Enfant. The park in turn was cleared away for the beaux-arts improvements of the early 1900s.

If Washington marked the epitome of the fancy plan, while it was slowly taking shape the epitome of the plain plan developed much more quickly in New York. In 1811 three commissioners were asked to produce a plan for the future development of New York City, then a flourishing port with a population of about 70,000. Like L'Enfant, they thought in terms of a world city, but in every other respect their approach differed from his, and disapproval of Washington emanates from every paragraph of their report. 'One of the first objects which claimed their attention', it ran, 'was . . . whether they should confine themselves to rectilinear and rectangular streets, or whether they should adopt some of those supposed improvements, by circles, ovals, and stars, which certainly embellish a plan, whatever may be their effects to convenience and utility. In considering that subject, they could not but bear in mind that a city is to be composed principally of the inhabitations of men, and that strait-sided and right-angled houses are the most cheap to build and the most convenient to live in. The effect of this plain and simple reflection was decisive.' Furthermore, open spaces 'for the benefit of fresh air, and consequent preservation of health', could be kept to a minimum, as Manhattan was an island amply ventilated by two 'large arms of the sea' instead of standing 'on the side of a small stream such as the Seine or the Thames'. For the same reason land was expensive, and the more that was built on the better economic sense it made.[51] Accordingly they took their rulers and divided Manhattan up into a grid of streets, relieved only by a few small squares and a parade ground.

Part III THE EXPLODING CITY

"The other part of me wanted to get out and stay out, but this was the part I never listened to. Because if I ever had I would have stayed in the town where I was born . . . I might even have got rich—small-town rich, an eight-room house, two cars in the garage, chicken every Sunday and the Reader's Digest on the living-room table, the wife with a cast-iron permanent and me with a brain like a sack of Portland cement. You take it, friend. I'll take the big, sordid, dirty, crooked city."

Raymond Chandler

12 Manchester and the Industrial City

'Manchester: a sky turned coppery red by the setting sun; a cloud, strangely shaped resting upon the plain; and under this motionless cover a bristling of chimneys by hundreds, as tall as obelisks. Then a mass, a heap, blackish, enormous, endless rows of buildings; and you are there, at the heart of a Babel built of brick . . .

'Earth and air seem impregnated with fog and soot. The factories extend their flanks of fouler brick one after another, bare, with shutterless windows, like economical and colossal prisons . . . and inside, lit by gas-jets and deafened by the uproar of their own labour, toil thousands of workmen, penned in, regimented, hands active, feet motionless, all day and every day, mechanically serving their machines . . .

'What dreary streets! Through half-open windows we could see wretched rooms at ground level, or often below the damp earth's surface. Masses of livid children, dirty and flabby of flesh, crowd each threshold and breathe the vile air of the street, less vile than that within . . . Even to walk in the rich quarter of the town is depressing . . . But they [the rich] are powerful: there is the compensation. The life of the head of an industrial or commercial house can be compared to that of a princeling. They have the capital sums, the large aims, the responsibilities and dangers, the importance and, from what I hear, the pride of a potentate . . . they are the generals and rulers of human toil. Quarter of a million sterling, half a million sterling, such are the figures they deal in . . . The warehouses of finished cotton goods and other fabrics are Babylonian monuments. One of them is two hundred yards long and the bales of cloth are handled by steam-driven machinery. A cotton mill may contain as many as three hundred thousand spindles . . .

'Always the same impression: enormousness. But are work and power all that is required to make a man happy?'[1]

So wrote Hippolyte Taine, recalling a visit to Manchester, probably made in 1859. Manchester had been having that kind of effect on people since the 1820s, especially on those who were seeing a new industrial town for the first time. In the 1820s and 1830s, when there were few such places, it was, as Asa Briggs has called it, 'the shock city of the age'.[2] People were fascinated, amazed and appalled by it. For a newcomer the first distant view of Manchester and its smoking chimneys must have been as extraordinary as a first view of Constantinople in the tenth century, or of New York in the early twentieth century. And it was as extraordinary from close-up as from a distance. All the usual conventions had been turned upside down in it. Even in great commercial centres like Amsterdam or London, the skyline was still presided over by the towers and domes of churches and public buildings; the warehouses, impressive though they were, did not dominate the city. In Manchester factory chimneys far outnumbered church towers, eight-storey mills towered over squalid little houses, opulent warehouses, some of them as large as the mills, were grander and bigger than the town hall. From 1830, when the first passenger railway line in the world joined Manchester to Liverpool, viaducts carried steaming and smoking trains above the roofs of the smaller houses, and added another large, bizarre and unfamiliar element to the townscape. 'Here man is an insect', Taine wrote of the mills. But it was 'for the insect man' that the machines laboured; 'it is he who commands their toil'.

In his novel *Coningsby* Benjamin Disraeli called Manchester 'the most wonderful city of modern times' and wrote of 'illumined factories with more windows than Italian palaces, and smoking chimneys taller than Italian obelisks'.[3] To the Berlin architect Karl Friedrich Schinkel, 'the machine and the buildings for it called factories' were 'the miracles of the new age', but he was also horrified by them: they were 'monstrous masses of red brick, built by a mere foreman without any trace of architecture, and for the sole purpose of crude necessity'.[4] For Thomas Carlyle, Manchester was 'every whit as wonderful, as fearful, as unimaginable, as the oldest salem or prophetic city'.[5]

Yet, although in many ways Manchester was a pioneer and a prototype, in other ways it was a throw-back. To find a city as teeming, raw and rough as Manchester was in the 1830s one has to go back to Florence or Ghent in the 1330s. The Manchester cotton lords were as thrusting, ambitious, powerful and successful as the Italian or Flemish merchants and entrepreneurs who dominated the medieval textile towns. Their labour relations were as bad: even so, the Peterloo Massacre of 1819, in which a meeting of protesting handloom weavers in Manchester was dispersed by soldiers and yeomanry, and eleven people were killed, was nothing compared to the mass slaughters in Italy or Flanders in the fourteenth century. Manchester was full of poverty, squalor and disease, but so were the medieval textile towns, even if they lack the abundant documentation which exists on the problems of Manchester. Pigs roamed the back streets in Manchester, as they had roamed the back (and sometimes the main) streets of the medieval towns.[6] Like them, Manchester attracted immigrants by the thousand in spite of all its problems, and added to its problems in doing so. But as a Manchester 'middle-class gentleman' said to Frederick Engels after listening to a diatribe against the horrors of the town: 'And yet there is a great deal of money made here. Good morning, sir.'[7]

Manchester was both a manufacturing and a marketing town, as Bruges had been and for similar reasons. It had plenty of water for the production process, and excellent connections to a major port and to other manufacturing towns, at first by water and later by rail. An aerial view of Manchester is as riddled with water as an aerial view of Bruges. Its natural water sources were the Rivers Medlock, Irwell and Irk, at the junction of which it is situated; but in the late eighteenth century its winding and not very efficient connections by river were improved by a network of canals. By a piece of good fortune for Manchester, it was a few miles away from rich coal-mines at Worsley; these belonged to an enterprising aristocrat, the Duke of Bridgwater, who risked all his fortune in promoting canals in order to sell his coal.

Even so, in 1800 Manchester was only one of several hundred textile towns scattered over Europe. In the Middle Ages the Flemish textile towns has prospered so extraordinarily because they were the first in the field; by 1800 the field was well worked and only special circumstances could suddenly push one town, or group of towns, into a pre-eminent position. For Manchester these were to be the arrival of steam-powered spinning machinery and looms combined with the development of North America as a major cotton-growing area.

For some time Manchester, like many textile towns in the Middle Ages and afterwards, had been engaged in processing a raw material which was imported from abroad. It and its Lancashire neighbours were further from the best wool-growing areas in England than the Yorkshire, East Anglian and West Country textile towns, and had difficulty in competing with them; accordingly, by the eighteenth century they had mostly moved over to working up imported cotton. They originally got their cotton from the Levant by way of Turkish merchants in London, who had a monopoly through their membership of the Levant Company. Cotton was not native to America; it was first introduced there in 1770 but only grown in large quantities from 1792 when a mechanical gin was invented which separated the raw cotton. Once it became a major American crop, Liverpool was a much more convenient port by which to enter England than London. Liverpool had very little fresh water and could not develop as a manufacturing town itself. But it could import cotton to Manchester, which was ideally situated both to process cotton and to distribute it. Five bags of American cotton were imported into Liverpool in 1785, 6 in 1786, 108 in 1787, 196,467 in 1807, 458,693 in 1820, and 1,033,773 in 1837.[8]

In the 1760s Hargreave's spinning jenney and other inventions had revolutionized the wool- and cotton-textile industry, by means of the machine-powered factory; spinning in factories was supplemented by weaving in factories when the power-loom which

had been invented in the 1780s first became practical and economic in the 1820s. To begin with, factories depended on water power, and were dispersed according to its availability. The steam-engine, which was first effectively adapted for factory use in the 1780s, enabled a much greater concentration of power in individual factories, and of factories in particular districts. Lancashire had the coal and could get the cotton. Factory methods enabled cotton to be both spun and woven much more cheaply. Cotton yarn was selling in Manchester for 38 shillings per pound in 1786, and for *2s. 11d.* in 1833. A piece of cotton calico sold for *24s. 7d.* in 1814, and *6s. 0¼d.* in 1833.[9] Not surprisingly, there was an economic explosion, of which Manchester and Liverpool were the main beneficiaries. Not only did all the countries of the world want cotton, but in each country more people could afford to buy it. The economic explosion produced explosions of population and building. The population of Manchester increased from 41,032 in 1774 to 270,901 in 1831, and was over 600,000 by 1900. For a few decades mills, warehouses and houses could not be built fast enough to keep up with the demand, even though the introduction of gas to Manchester in 1817 enabled mills to work night and day in two shifts, their multitudinous windows blazing in the dark.

The transport system of Manchester was as quick to benefit from the steam-engine as the factories. Manchester did not make the mistake of relying on its canals and neglecting railways in consequence. It and Liverpool between them were pioneers, and Manchester had more railways sooner than any other town in Europe. It had its first railway in 1830, six years before London.[10] By 1840 it was served by six railway lines, and was connected to Liverpool, London, Birmingham, Leeds and Sheffield; it was a bigger railway centre than London, although London was rapidly overtaking it.

In many ways the structure of the textile industry in Manchester resembled that which had been traditional in Europe since the Middle Ages. The manufacturing process was organized by entrepreneurs, who collected the goods in shops or warehouses, from which they sold their products to merchants for distribution: some entrepreneurs, as in the Middle Ages, tried to by-pass the merchants and sell direct to the retailers. But the factory system and expanding markets had combined to change the scale, almost out of recognition. The artificers who had previously worked either at home or in small workshops were now concentrated into mills, producing more in a week than a Florentine business could produce in a year. Both entrepreneurs' warehouses, the equivalent of the Florentine woolshops, and merchants' warehouses grew in size accordingly.

The prime locations had not changed all that much since the Middle Ages. Mills and dye-houses were still normally next to water. The first mills in Manchester, being powered by water, had to be by the Irwell, Irk or Medlock; the steam-powered mills drew the water for their boilers, and the dye-houses for their vats, from rivers or canals. Canals and rivers were also useful in case of fire. Manchester first acquired a piped-water system in about 1810, but it seems to have been some time before mills and dye-houses started to use waterworks water, which had to be paid for, instead of free water from rivers and canals. As the latter got increasingly polluted, however, waterworks water came more into demand: clean water was essential for dye-works and it corroded boilers much less quickly than polluted water. But wherever they got their water supply from, mills, dye-works, tanneries and gasworks deposited their waste to join the sewage in the rivers. By 1845 the Irk was described by Engels as 'a narrow, coal-black, foul-smelling stream . . . in dry weather, a long string of the most disgusting, blackish-green,

220. (preceding pages) Manchester. By William Wylde, 1851.

221. (right) A canal view in Manchester.

222. Warehouses in Portland Street, Manchester, in 1858.

slime pools are left standing . . . from the depths of which bubbles of miasmatic gas constantly arise and give forth a stench unendurable even on the bridge forty or fifty feet above the surface of the stream. But besides this, the stream itself is checked every few paces by high weirs, behind which slime and refuse accumulate and rot in thick masses.'[11]

Manchester was not entirely given over to spinning, weaving and selling cotton. A number of associated or similar industries flourished or sold their products there: silk-throwing and weaving, dyeing, bleaching, cloth-printing, the manufacture of tapes, ribbons and everything that came under the general heading of small-ware, and the rubberizing of cotton cloth by the process made popular by Charles Macintosh. Dry-salters provided dyes and fixatives for the dye-works. Factories making steam-engines and mill machinery were a natural by-product of the cotton-mills, as were factories making locomotive engines and locomotives for the railway lines. Workers in these heavy industries were amongst the best paid in Manchester.

Manchester's trade and industry, the cotton industry in particular, worked in three concentric zones: the exchange at the centre, a middle zone of warehouses and an outer zone of mills. The first exchange had been built in a room over the market hall, and opened in 1729 in the middle of the market-place; it fell out of use because those doing business there disliked fighting their way through butchers' stalls and market crowds to get to it. A location near the market was desirable, however, because manufacturers who lived outside Manchester but bought or sold on the exchange liked to combine this with visits to the market; Tuesday was market day, and was still the busiest day on the exchange in 1839. By then a grand new exchange had been built, and was enlarged in 1836 and 1845–9. It was then said to be the largest covered space used for exchange purposes in the world; but it was enlarged again, to two and a half times its former size, when the exchange was rebuilt in 1869–74.[12]

There were two kinds of warehouses in Manchester: transit warehouses belonging to the canal and railway companies, which were built by the canal basins and goods stations and were often very large but seldom ornamental; and the commercial warehouses belonging to individual manufacturers and merchants. The best location for the latter type was near the inns and hotels, where the outside buyers stayed, and the exchange, where their owners went to buy and sell. As the exchange was on Market Street, and most of the inns and hotels in or near Market Street and its western extension, Piccadilly, the warehouses of this type congregated most thickly to the north and south of the Market Street axis.[13]

The outside buyers and country drapers staying in the main inns and hotels were besieged with offers from 'hookers-in'—touts who got a one percent commission on any business they brought to the warehouses—and from warehouse clerks, all extolling the goods of the business or businesses which employed them.[14] A high proportion of warehouse goods were sold directly from the warehouses. The alternative system, of sending representatives round the country to sell goods by sample, had already existed

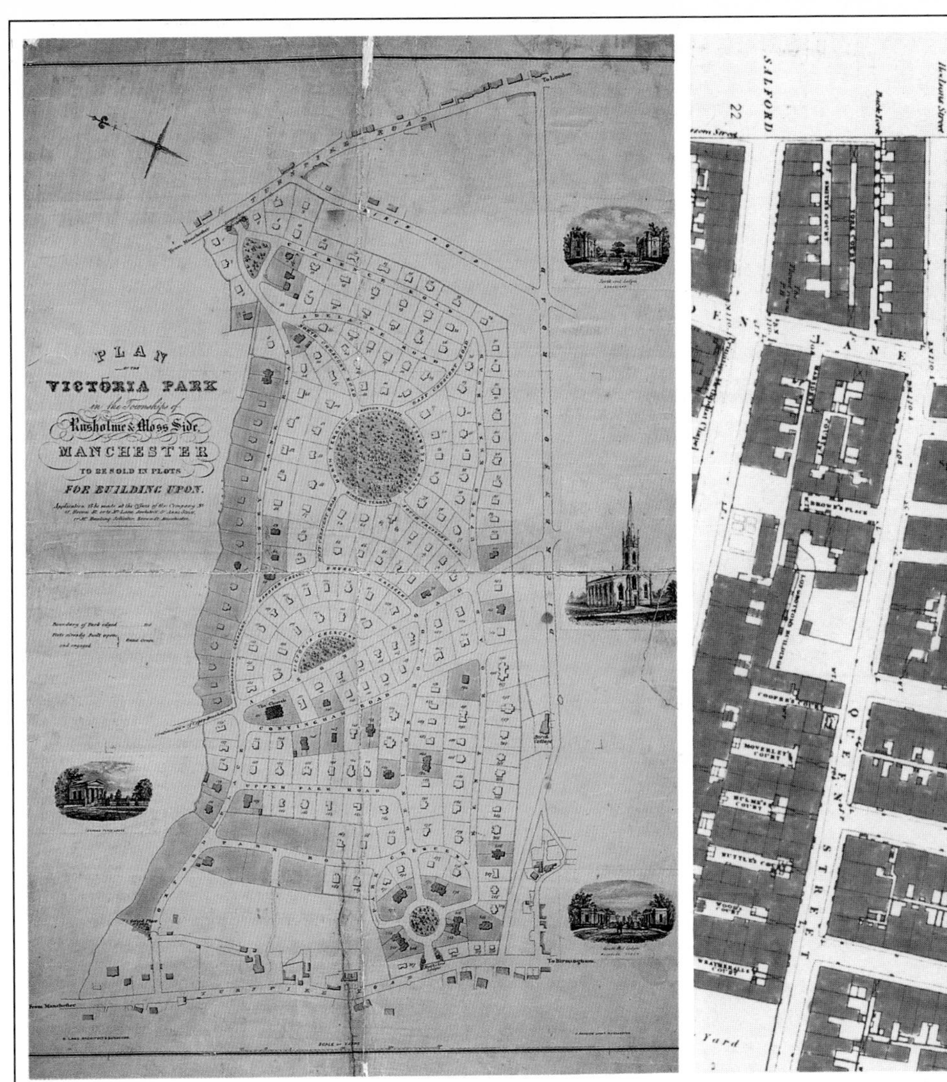

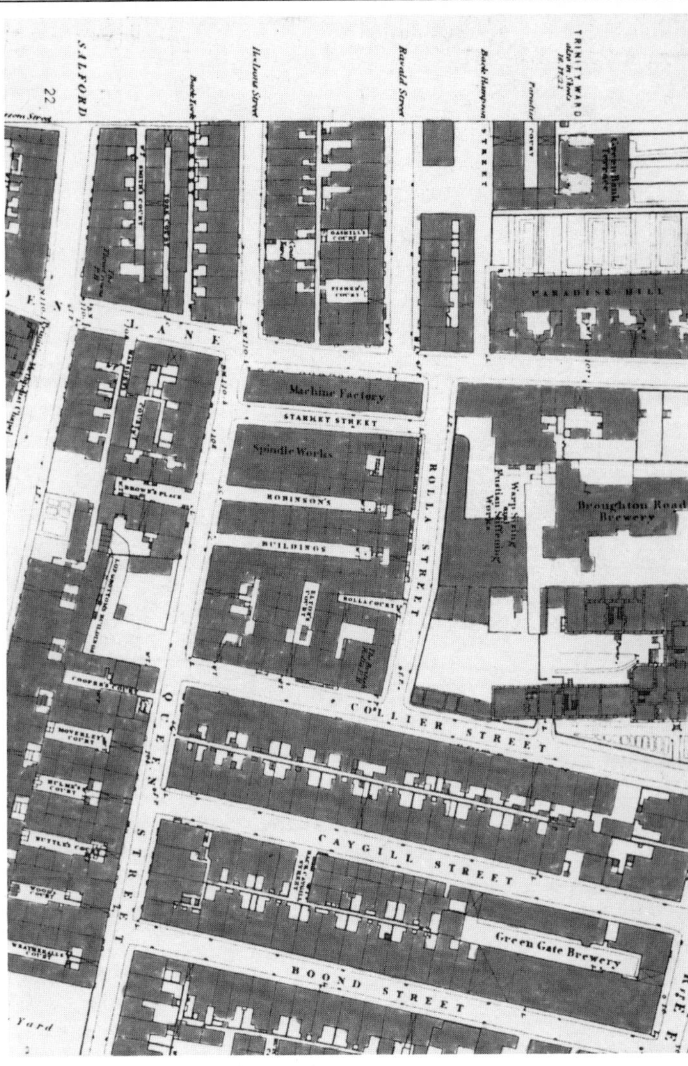

223–4. Richard Lane's layout for Victoria Park, Manchester, 1837, and (right) detail from the 1848 Ordnance Survey, showing working-class housing in Salford (Manchester Public Libraries).

by the mid-eighteenth century, when the representatives were called 'bagmen'. By 1800 the system was growing in importance and the bagmen in consciousness of their status; they became 'travellers', and later 'commercial travellers'. Some of the pre-rail travellers became legendary and heroic figures, who travelled superhuman distances against all odds to establish records or steal a march on their competitors.[15]

The more that sales made through travellers or catalogues predominated over sales made on the premises, the less important a central site was to become for a warehouse; ultimately, in western cities, warehouses were removed to cheaper peripheral sites, if possible convenient for railway or other transport, and only an administrative and decision-taking office was left in the centre. But in nineteenth-century Manchester warehouses still dominated the centre. They were intended to be seen and visited, and became increasingly impressive. Drapers and shopkeepers flocked to them from all over the country, and engravings of them on the firm's bill-heads became a guarantee of success and reliability for overseas buyers. In 1839 Edward Walters, a Manchester architect, built the first of a series of warehouses in the style of an Italian palace. Victorian merchants and manufacturers were always intrigued and flattered by comparisons between themselves and the merchants of the Renaissance. The palazzo style caught on, and became popular all over the country.

The earlier Manchester merchants had lived close to or above their warehouses, in the traditional way. One of the best addresses was Mosley Street, which was a new street laid out on what was then the edge of the town in the 1780s and 1790s. By the end of the eighteenth century it was lined with handsome brick houses, some with warehousing at the rear in Back Mosley Street.[16] There were more warehouses, or dwelling-houses with warehouses attached, or houses converted to warehouses, in Church Street, High Street and Cannon Street. Some belonged to merchants, others to manufacturers. Many of the mills belonging to the latter were outside Manchester, often in a different town or several different towns, but they found a warehouse in Manchester valuable as a sales outlet. Robert Peel, for instance, started a calico-printing works in Bury in 1774 in partnership with two others. In 1780 the three men opened a warehouse in Cannon Street, Manchester. The firm prospered almost unbelievably, and expanded into importing and exporting, yarn-spinning, cloth-weaving and cloth-bleaching, as well as cloth-printing. In the end it had works at Bury, Radcliffe, Heywood, Bolton, Warrington, Blackburn, Burnley, Padiham, Walton, Stockport, Bradford, Lichfield and Tamworth.[17] Robert Peel died in 1830, a baronet, former member of Parliament, and owner of large estates and a country house in Staffordshire. He left two million pounds, and a son who was to become prime minister.

Manufacturers who owned Manchester warehouses, and were prosperous but not on the Peel scale, had to decide whether to live by the mill or by the warehouse; often one partner lived at one, and another partner at the other. Then in the 1830s a significant change began to take place. As Love and Barton's *Manchester as It Is* put in 1839: 'Within the last few years Mosley-Street contained only private dwelling-houses: it is now converted almost entirely into warehouses; and the increasing business of the town is rapidly converting all the principal dwelling-houses which exist in that neighbourhood into mercantile establishments, and is driving most of the respectable inhabitants into the suburbs. So great, about the year 1836, was the demand for such conversions, that some of the land in Mosley-Street, intended for warehouse erections, sold for a rental of 14*s.* per square yard per annum. On land purchased at so high a rate new buildings have generally been erected; and, to make the most of it, a more than usual number of warehouses are raised on a limited space, the towering height of which makes up for their contracted width.'[18]

The respectable inhabitants did not need much driving to get them into the suburbs. Apart from being able to sell or redevelop their original homes for a handsome profit, developments in the south of England were making suburban life fashionable, and developments in Manchester were making city life increasingly noisy, dirty and smelly. The first migrants moved to terraces on the edge of the town, like St George's Street in Hulme, or the Crescent in Salford, built in the early nineteenth century on a hill above the River Irwell. But by the 1830s villas had become the thing. In 1835 a 'company of gentlemen' acquired one hundred and forty acres two miles to the south-east of Manchester, and began to develop it with detached or semi-detached villas 'free from any possible nuisances that may arise from the vicinity of smoke and manufactures; and to combine, with the advantage of a close proximity to the town, the privacy and advantage of a country residence'. They called the development Victoria Park.[19]

In fact Victoria Park was a little too far out; it only really got under way in the 1850s. But villas further in proliferated, far enough to be away from 'smoke and manufactures', close enough to put their owners within an easy drive or ride of the centre.

There they lived, as Engels described it, 'in free, wholesome country air, in fine, comfortable houses, passed once every half or quarter hour by omnibuses going into the city'.[20] It was a little tedious, however, to drive or take an omnibus out to the suburbs for dinner in the middle of the day (Manchester merchants dined at one). Although previously merchants and manufacturers had taken it for granted that they ate at home, clubs began to appear in the centre, on the London model, starting with the Union Club, which opened in Mosley Street in 1825. 'Many gentlemen', wrote Love and Barton, 'who have been compelled, by the encroachment of commercial buildings, to take up their abode in the Country, doubtless appreciate the comforts of an establishment in town, conducted with all the regularity, and enjoying all the exclusiveness, of a private dwelling.'[21]

The 'respectable inhabitants' moved to the suburbs; the less respectable continued to live near the centre. Mill-workers lived as near their mills as they could: apart from having to get to the mill and back without the advantage of carriages, they normally went home for their meals. Children worked in the mills for the same hours as their fathers, until the hours were reduced by Act of Parliament in 1833 and again in 1847. The system was explained to Robert Southey by a Manchester gentleman in 1808: 'He took us to one of the great cotton manufactories, showed us a number of children who were at work there, and dwelt with delight on the infinite good which resulted from employing them at so early an age . . . "You see these children, sir," said he, "they get their bread almost as soon as they can walk about, and by the time they are seven or eight years old bring in money. There is no idleness amongst us; they come at five in the morning, we allow them half an hour for breakfast, and an hour for dinner; they leave work at six, and another set relieves them for the night; the wheels never stand still."'[22]

The mill-workers were the aristocracy of labour in Manchester; by the standards of the time they got good wages, three times the rate of agricultural wages in many southern counties. They only suffered hardship when there was a recession. This happened with appalling regularity, however, for Manchester's periods of great prosperity were interrupted every ten years or so by vicious recessions, the result of over-production and over-confidence in the boom years. Mill-workers lived, for the most part, in rows of little houses newly built by speculative builders (or, more rarely, by mill-owners) in the neighbourhood of the mills.[23] They were often badly built, and much too closely spaced together, back-to-back or round small internal courts; in the early decades of the nineteenth century they suffered from an almost total lack of any services, and only the invaluable pigs helped to mitigate the squalor. Their worst feature was that, in some cases, they had basements which were unfit for habitation, but inhabited. These were the notorious cellars of Manchester which, along with accommodation in old, rotting, half-timbered houses in the oldest parts of the town (where the worst cellars also were), provided Manchester with some of the most appalling accommodation in England. It was lived in by casual labourers, out-of-work vagrants who had come to Manchester in the hope of work and failed to find it, and hand-loom weavers who were desperately trying to compete with power-looms at starvation wages. A high proportion of all three groups were Irish.

Bad housing and bad drainage combined to produce the death rate recorded in 1842, when it was compared with that in Rutland.[24]

Average age of death

	Manchester	Rutland
Professional persons and gentry and their families	38	52
Tradesmen, farmers and graziers and their families	20	41
Mechanics, labourers and their families	17	38

If there was a great deal of death in Manchester, there was also a great deal of life. Love and Barton's *Manchester as It is* decribes the centre in 1839: 'the bustle and activity, the loading and unloading of waggons, the carriers' carts waiting to receive packages, and the dyers' and bleachers' vans waiting to deliver pieces, the waggon-loads of cotton, the immense iron-hooped bales for exportation, drawn along the streets'.[25] In her novel *North and South* Elizabeth Gaskell characterized Manchester people of those days: 'their energy, their power, their indomitable courage in struggling and fighting, their lurid vividness of existence', while all round 'the chimneys smoked, the ceaseless roar and mighty beat and dazzling whirl of machinery struggled and strove perpetually'.[26] In many ways Manchester in the 1830s was an exciting place; but no attempt to explain away or mitigate can disguise the fact that it was also a very terrible one.

By the 1870s it was possibly less exciting, and certainly a great deal less terrible. Many of its problems had been due to the fact that it had had to cope with mass immigration and dramatically rapid expansion, equipped with little more than the administrative powers of a village. In 1832 it acquired two members of Parliament; in 1839 it acquired its own council: in 1853 it became a full-blown city, complete with aldermen and lord mayor. The Manchester Statistical Society, which had been founded in 1833, carefully collected the statistical evidence on which reforms could be based. The Borough Police Act of 1844 and the Sanitary Improvement Act of 1845 set up a sanitary code which was strengthened over the decades, and on the basis of which housing conditions slowly began to improve. Three public parks were opened in 1846. The water supply was much extended from 1847. Facilities in individual houses were still often very bad, but from 1854 the Manchester Baths and Laundry Company provided handsome buildings in which working men and women could wash themselves and their clothes; the motives of its promoters were of the best, but they were gratified to find that the baths also payed a dividend.[27] The great complexes of the Chorlton, Prestwich and Crumpsall hospital-workhouses were built in 1864–7 on the pavilion plan: Florence Nightingale thought that the plan of Chorlton 'will be of the best, if not the best, in the country'. In 1870 a joint-stock company was set up for the erection of 'decent, well-arranged habitations let at small rentals'. The company followed the advice of its architect, who urged the 'erection in situation of such value of blocks and dwellings in flats, though I was well aware of prejudice in the mind of the Lancashire working man against such buildings'. Then as now do-gooders were confident that they knew what was good for people.

At the back of all these schemes was a growing group of philanthropic bankers, doctors, architects, clergymen, businessmen and mill-owners. But the mills were leaving Manchester as property values rose, and moving to the outer suburbs or the surrounding towns. Meanwhile public libraries, an art gallery, a college which was to develop into a university, grand assize and police courts, the great Free Trade Hall in which the Hallé Orchestra gave its concerts, theatres, hotels, music-halls, churches, chapels, public houses and more and more warehouses in the grand palazzo manner diversified the city. They could be sumptuous, learned, flamboyant, flashy or eccentric: all were solidly built and all quickly turned black with Manchester soot. But it was still over no ignoble city that the tower of the new town hall rose between 1868 and 1877, on the edge of a great new square. It was also over a beautiful, or at least a romantic city; but it needed a Frenchman, Adolphe Valette, to reveal its beauty to Mancunians.[28]

225. The Town Hall (Alfred Waterhouse, 1808–77), Manchester.

The pattern which had been pioneered in Manchester was to be repeated, with variations, all over the world. Cities (or interested parties within cities) promoted a communication network of railways and/or steamer-lines, of which their city became the nexus. Improved communications increased existing trades and manufactures and usually stimulated new ones, such as shipyards and boiler or locomotive works. An industrial and manufacturing zone grew up on the edge of the city, with a large immigrant population of workers to go with it. In the centre, trade and services also boomed, land values rose and the residents were often pushed out into other neighbourhoods. In general, population invariably increased, and if it increased very rapidly, as it frequently did, congestion resulted, existing services, such as they were, collapsed, labour troubles and epidemics broke out, often on a disastrous scale, and the ensuing reactions led to the provision of drainage systems, improved water supply, hospitals, public parks, public schools and sometimes public housing, along with a central administration enlarged to cope with its new responsibilities. In the middle of the city the scale of everything steadily increased. Grand new buildings appeared: town halls, law courts, public libraries, museums, colleges, art galleries, hotels, department stores, covered markets, railway stations, theatres, exchanges, banks and insurance offices. Existing streets were widened and new ones opened (although usually not on a sufficient scale in either case). If the city in question was a national capital, a whole hierarchy of new national government buildings was superimposed on the local ones.

Of course there were variations, depending on local factors. All cities acquired residential suburbs, but in those where there was a long tradition of the upper classes living in the centre, they usually continued to do so, even if not always in exactly the same place; in other cities, such as Manchester, the rich and the middle classes deserted the centre entirely. The factory and workshop zone varied from city to city; in some it became a continuous, or practically continuous, belt interposed between the suburbs and the centre, in others it adjoined one portion of the centre only.

All this was the result of technological breakthroughs which not only allowed both production and population to grow, but also enabled people, goods and information to be conveyed faster, more easily, more cheaply and in greater quantities. The textile industry, for long the major industry of the western world, was revolutionized by a series of inventions which made possible the factory production of woollen, cotton, silk and linen textiles. Steamships and steam-engines distributed the resulting goods rapidly (by previous standards) and in very large quantities round the world. From the mid-nineteenth century hydraulic machinery provided a new means of raising and lowering people and goods. Metal cables and trusses, and the engineering skills which knew how to use them, allowed far greater spans to be bridged, and the result was sheds on a heroic scale to shelter trains or markets, and bridges which improved communications in all parts of the world. A series of inventions in the iron and steel industries enabled them to keep pace with the demand for mill machinery, engines, rails, trusses, cables, and plates for ships and engines. Improved drainage and sewage systems, better hospitals and improvements in medicine increased population, and demand increased with them. As a result of the development of steam ploughs and of mechanical reapers, binders and threshing machines, more food was produced to feed more people. The rising need for raw materials generated great new, or newly great, cities: Sydney for the wool trade, Buenos Aires and Chicago for meat and corn, New Orleans for cotton. Cable and wireless communication round the world enabled orders to be transmitted and the state of markets to be known with far more speed and accuracy than before, and greatly reduced the element of risk in exporting goods for sale. Mass-advertising encouraged more and more people to buy more and more goods. A general increase in wealth not only kept markets expanding, but also increased the size of the leisure classes and the leisure of the working classes, brought people crowding in to settle or visit in the great cities, and sent more and more people travelling for pleasure.

These developments needed capital. Inventions only become effective if there is capital to promote them. One reason why English production outstripped that of all other nations in the late eighteenth and first half of the nineteenth century was that it was easier to borrow money there.

The City of London, in particular, became adept at different ways of collecting money for investment, and provincial cities copied its methods. The system of selling transferable shares to fund joint-stock companies, which had launched the East India and other great trading companies in the seventeenth and eighteenth centuries, was used to finance most of the canals and virtually all the railways. The London banks developed a close relationship with banks in the country, and large amounts of surplus capital from rich agricultural districts found its way to London, from where it was lent out in turn to borrowers in London or in industrial areas. Insurance companies of all kinds enjoyed a great boom from the 1820s onwards, and attracted yet more capital.[29] Many insurance companies were also joint-stock companies, but until 1825 the Bank of England was the only joint-stock bank allowed by law in England, although in Scotland they had long been legal. A financial panic in 1825 caused the failure of so many private banks with inadequate reserves that the ban was lifted; from then on joint-stock banks became increasingly important all over the country.

All this investment capital was used to finance development in the British Isles and abroad. In America, the Louisiana Purchase of 1803, was financed by two private London banks, Hope's and Baring's. Railways, harbours, and services of all kinds in cities round the world were financed from London, and designed by British engineers using plant and equipment made in Britain. The Galleria, the great shopping arcade of Milan, was a London project.[30] But inevitably City capital was also used to help finance the growth and rebuilding of London itself.

226. (right) Jones, Loyd and Co.'s Bank (P. C. Hardwick, 1843), Lothbury, City of London.

13 London and the Growth of the Suburb

Money from the City was the fertilizer which helped to produce the gay shop-fronts, stucco colonnades and variegated vistas of Regent Street—the first Regent Street, that is, as built in 1813–27, not as rebuilt in the 1920s. Its development marked a breakthrough in the history of the western city, less because of its architectural quality, although that was by no means to be despised, than because, after centuries of still-born projects, it was the first example in Europe of a major street being successfully driven through a congested city centre.[1]

The idea of such a street was not new; something like it had already been suggested by John Gwynn in his *London and Westminster Improved*, published in 1766. It became more than ever relevant once it was decided to develop what became Regent's Park as an area of upper-class housing, which would need easy access to the fashionable West End if it was to succeed. There were four major requisites for the new street: an individual who had the energy to push the scheme through, a good route, an Act of Parliament and about a million pounds.

The individual appeared in the person of John Nash, the Prince Regent's friend and favourite, a very gifted

227. The Regent Street Quadrant. From the drawing by T. H. Shepherd, engraved for *Metropolitan Improvements*, 1829.

if rather flashy architect with a taste for property speculation. He chose a route with great skill, along the eastern edge of fashionable London, close to all the right places but passing through areas where property was relatively cheap and there were few people who could make an effective fuss about being uprooted. The Act of Parliament was passed without too much difficulty. Most of the initial capital was lent by the Royal Exchange Insurance Company and the Bank of England.[2]

Nash even managed to make aesthetic capital out of his difficulties. The various twists and turns which the street had to take, in order to keep down costs and avoid the property of occasional powerful and intransigent owners, were used to give diversity and variety to the route. One of the most prominent sites along it was taken in 1819 by another insurance company, the County Fire Office, and at the southern end, two palatial clubhouses, the Athenaeum and the United Services Club, looked across Waterloo Place at each other.

Clubs and insurance offices were to become prominent features of nineteenth-century London. The columned and arcaded front of the County Fire Office introduced a new standard of grandeur for business premises. For the next thirty years insurance companies produced a far greater number of grand buildings than banks did.[3] They needed to attract the custom of as many people as possible, whereas banks still concentrated their attentions on people of substance who came to them, very often, through personal contacts. Traditionally banks either looked like very superior shops, or like private houses in part of which banking happened to take place; one of the partners almost invariably lived over the bank. It was the new joint-stock banks which first began to go in for commercial grandeur, and the private banks were forced to imitate them in self-protection.[4]

The club-houses were built in much the same style and on the same scale as the

228. The staircase at the demolished Army and Navy Club (C. O. Parnell and A. Smith, 1848–51), Pall Mall, London.

insurance offices. They had a different character from eighteenth-century clubs, which were essentially for gambling. For a modest annual subscription they offered their members all the amenities of the mansion of a plutocrat; foreign visitors were amazed by their luxury and silently efficient service. By the mid-century their success in London was so great that they had killed the coffee-houses and made public houses places to which no one above the lower middle classes would think of going.[5]

Although nineteenth-century London acquired increasing numbers of buildings built on an impressive scale, as a whole it was far from impressive. A capital city in the administration of which the national government had virtually no say, and which was divided up into a patchwork of jealously independent territories run by the Cities of London and Westminster and about sixty parish councils, was never going to acquire any kind of comprehensive civic grandeur. It was not until 1855 that a Metropolitan Board of Works was set up as a central authority and even then its powers were very limited. What London had to offer for cities round the world to imitate was not in the centre but the suburbs. Here, along the leafy groves of St John's Wood and Camberwell, up and down the hills and valleys of Kentish Town and Clapham, detached and semi-detached villas were spreading year by year.

The established custom of merchants and shopkeepers living above or close to their work, which was being abandoned in Florence as early as the fifteenth century, first began to show signs of breaking in London in the seventeenth. When Lincoln's Inn Fields was surrounded with grand new houses in the mid-seventeenth century Sir John Banks, 'one of the greatest merchants of the day', was one of a number of merchants who left their houses in the City to come and live there—in his case, in 1672.[6] From then on the residents in the new streets and squares in the West End of London always included a proportion of the richer City families. By 1766 John Gwynn, in his *London and Westminster Improved*, was complaining that wealthy merchants, who ought to live in the City, 'are thrust out of the way of their business and obliged to live in a part of the town entirely unsuitable to their interests in every respect . . . mixing among persons of quality'.[7] Gwynn attributed this to the lack of suitable houses in the city, but it seems more likely that the merchants who moved actually wanted to mix among persons of quality.

These were not moves out of the city, however, but moves from one city to another, from the commercial City of London to the polite City of Westminster. To retreat from the city into the country was a different kind of operation altogether, and one for which there was a long tradition, both for City merchants and for Westminster gentlemen. In the eighteenth century Twickenham and other villages along the Thames were studded with detached houses in big grounds, summer retreats of politicians, placemen or poets, among which Horace Walpole's Strawberry Hill or Lady Suffolk's Marble Hill

229. Villas on the Thames at Twickenham. From an engraving after S. H. Muntz, 1756 (Guildhall Library, London).

are perhaps the best-known examples. Merchants also acquired, within easy reach of the City, similar houses to which they could go at weekends, or to which they sent their families in the summer. But such houses were not at first considered as houses from which to travel into London to work; they were holiday houses for people with houses in London, or sometimes permanent retreats for Londoners who had retired.

Houses of this kind were increasingly referred to as villas. The word 'villa' had had a complex and fluid history in England since the seventeenth century, but by the late eighteenth century it was normally used to mean a small to medium-sized gentleman's house in a rural setting, not necessarily near a town. Used in this sense it could be stretched to cover both a sizeable country house in the middle of a park and estate, and a small house having no more ground to it than a comfortably sized garden, but distinguishable as a gentleman's house by the elegance of its design and a careful separation between rooms for gentry and servants. From at least the mid-eighteenth century a very small gentleman's house was sometimes called a cottage rather than a villa: the idea of a gentleman living in a cottage was perfectly acceptable, and by the 1790s the influence of the romantic movement had even made it fashionable. In that decade the gentleman's *cottage ornée* appeared, equipped with thatched roof, rustic wood verandah and a great deal of honeysuckle, with servants discreetly at hand to ensure that the simple life was not too simple.

Many villas and cottages within easy reach of London were built by merchants and businessmen. Sometimes they were satirized for building above their station, especially if the villa was considered in bad taste: a poem of 1757 made fun of the 'cit's country villa',[8] and William Cowper was scathing about them in 1780:

> Suburban villas, highway-side retreats,
> That dread the encroachment of our growing streets,

230. Villas on Herne Hill, Camberwell, London, in about 1830. From the drawing by J. Thomson (Guildhall Library, London).

Tight boxes neatly sash'd, and in a blaze
With all a July sun's collected rays,
Delight the citizen, who, gasping there,
Breaths clouds of dust, and calls it country air.[9]

But a pretty villa or cottage was clearly suited to the needs and life-style of this class, members of which usually wanted to be considered gentlemen, and on the whole were accepted as such, as long as they had enough money, and dressed and behaved in a gentlemanly manner.

Architectural pattern-books of designs for cottages and villas, executed and unexecuted, began to appear in the 1790s, and increased steadily in numbers in the early nineteenth century. Richard Elsam's *Essay on Rural Architecture* (1803), for instance, contained designs for both villas and 'small, comfortable, genteel cottages . . . for the gentleman of fortune'. These cottages were seen as country retreats to which to retire 'as a relaxation from business'. 'Beyond doubt', he wrote, 'there is a considerable satisfaction in a convenient comfortable retreat, near a town, where a gentleman has an opportunity of participating in the sports of the field, in agriculture, or in gardening; and at other intervals, when the mind is so disposed, to intermix in the company, and gay amusements, of his neighbourhood.'[10] The villas in these books were in a variety of styles; the cottages sometimes had rustic elements, but were often just small, neat, classical houses, one or two storeys high. A pretty garden was considered an essential adjunct.

A further development came when City gentlemen gave up town residences altogether, and started to commute into the City from their country villas, or villas in villages on the outskirts of London. The development becomes noticeable in the mid-eighteenth century, or even earlier, when Clapham, which was pleasantly situated on a hill above London and had had a daily coach to Gracechurch Street in the City

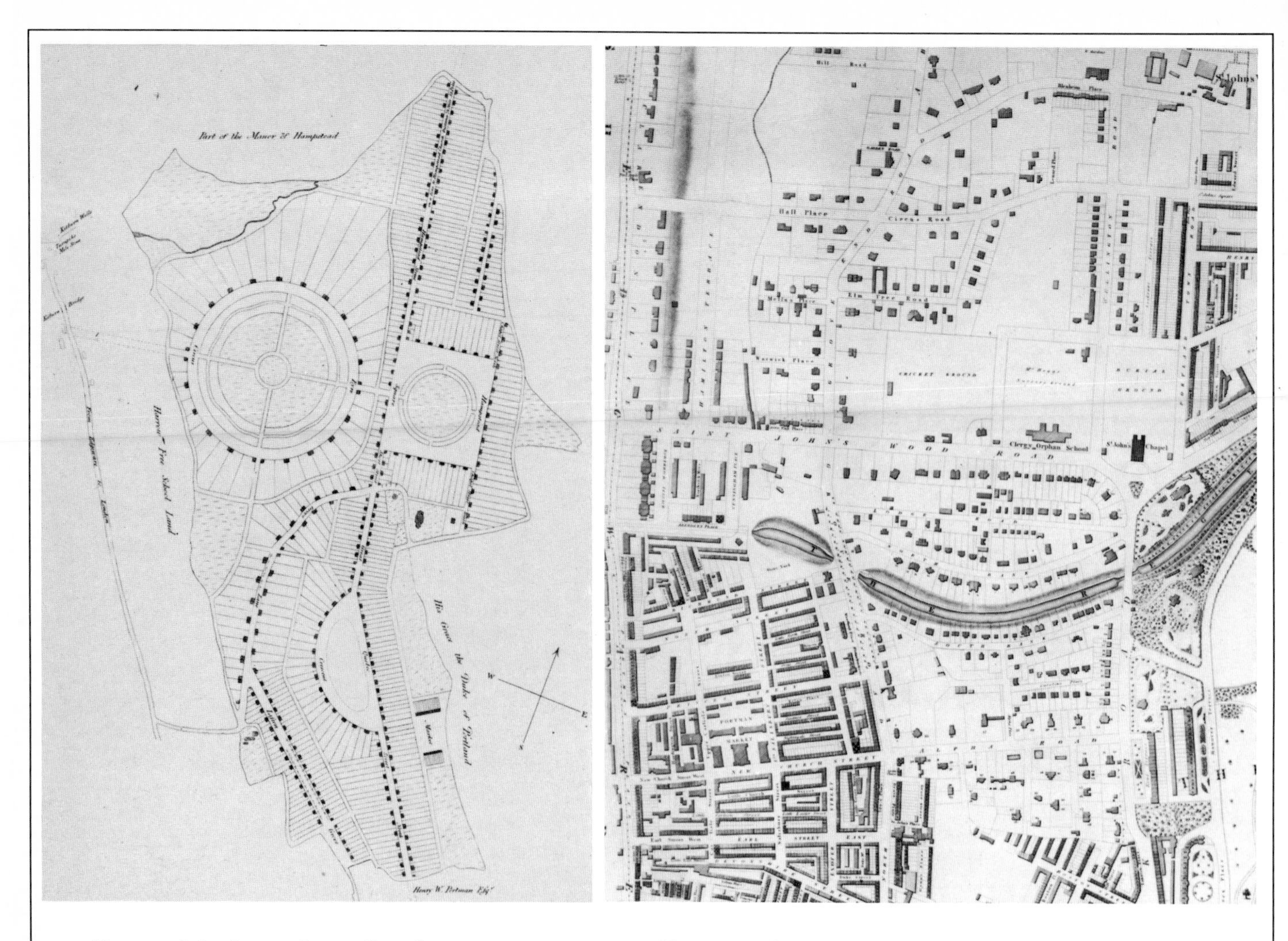

231. Unexecuted plan for the development of the Eyre estate in St John's Wood, 1794 (British Library).

232. St John's Wood in 1819. Detail from the plan by Horwood.

since 1690, began to attract a small group of prosperous City merchants. They built or acquired substantial houses on or near Clapham Common, and caught the coach down to London in the morning.[11]

Until the end of the eighteenth century, villas and cottages, whether designed as holiday retreats or as homes for commuters, were purpose-built for their owners. Speculative builders built houses in terraces, often just a single terrace built out in the fields, waiting for London to catch up with it. But the possibility of building speculative estates of villas or cottages clearly had not occurred to property developers, or, if it had, had been dismissed.

Then in 1794 Spurrier and Phipps, auctioneers, of Copthall Court in the City, published a plan for the 'improvement' of the estate of the Eyre family, in the area known as St John's Wood, at that time open fields in the northern half of the parish of St Marylebone. The plan showed a lay-out of a circus, crescent, square, and connecting streets, but instead of being arranged in conventional terraces it was entirely given up to semi-detached houses.

The semi-detached house was not a new feature in England, but previously it had been used entirely for labourers' cottages, usually in estate villages built by improving landlords. Its advantage was that it was cheaper to build than a detached cottage, but could have a bigger garden than a terraced one. The earliest examples are at Chippenham in Cambridgeshire, built by Lord Orford around 1702–10. Here the cottages are pseudo-semi-detached, each pair being in fact joined by lower outbuildings. Completely semi-detached cottages were built in Sir Robert Walpole's model village at

Houghton in Norfolk from 1729 onwards. Thereafter they were built in considerable quantities all over the country, and designs for them were published by Nathaniel Kent and John Wood in 1775 and 1781, in two books specifically devoted to labourers' cottages.[12] The type was introduced to London in 1781 by John Soane, in the form of two rows of semi-detached artisans' cottages in Southwark: they were called Adam's Place after the developer. In 1784 Soane designed a small crescent of semi-detached cottages for Hammels Park in Hertfordshire, but they were never built.[13]

There is no evidence as to whether it was the unknown architect, the ground landlord or the auctioneers who thought up the idea of up-grading the semi-detached cottage as the basis for a speculative lay-out of houses for gentlefolk in St John's Wood. In any case, nothing happened. Probably the French wars put an end to the scheme, as they did to so much other speculative building all over England. In 1803 the scheme was still live enough for a new version of the circus to be designed by John Shaw. It was shown on a map of London published in 1807 as the 'proposed British Circus'; it now consisted of a circular road lined on both sides with detached or semi-detached houses, the houses in the inner ring having access through their own gardens to a communal circular 'pleasure ground'.[14] This scheme never got built either, but meanwhile, the southern end of the estate was being more modestly and successfully developed with a lay-out of detached and semi-detached houses called Alpha Cottages. These are shown in the 1807 edition of Horwood's map of north-west London, and first appear in the rate-books in 1808.

Alpha Cottages were sufficiently successful for a large northward extension of the development to be planned in 1811. Its completion was delayed because in 1812 the newly formed Regent's Canal and Dock Company got permission by private Act of Parliament to build a canal through the middle of the Eyre Estate, in order to join up the existing canal basin at Paddington to the Thames at Limehouse. The work was not finished until 1820. The extension was delayed, and its lay-out had to be altered—and Thomas Lord was forced to move his cricket ground a few hundred yards to the north. In the end the canal proved a benefit to the estate, however, for rows of cottages or villas, known as North Bank and South Bank, were built along either side of it and were amongst the area's most agreeable features.

By 1821 St John's Wood contained several hundred cottages or villas, detached and semi-detached, thickly sown towards the south, and gradually thinning out towards the north.[15] The area had its own chapel, built in 1813–14, its own inn, assembly rooms, and pleasure garden at the Eyre Arms, and its own cricket ground. It was more than a cluster of houses; it had developed into a full-blown suburban neighbourhood, the first in England. It became popular with people who wanted to live cheaply, quietly, or conveniently for visits into or out of central London—which meant artists, architects, writers, retired East India Company officials and rich men's mistresses. Around 1820 one could have met William Blake being entertained by the architect C. H. Tatham in Alpha Cottages, and Keats and Wordsworth being entertained by Benjamin Robert Haydon in Upper Lisson Grove, just south of the villas.[16] Ugo Foscolo, the Italian poet and revolutionary, lived in Digamma Cottage, which he had built for himself on the canal in 1822.[17] Edwin Landseer, who had been taught by Haydon, settled in a house in St John's Wood Road in 1825. The East India Company officials, whose memorials figure prominently in the St John's Wood Chapel, may have been attracted

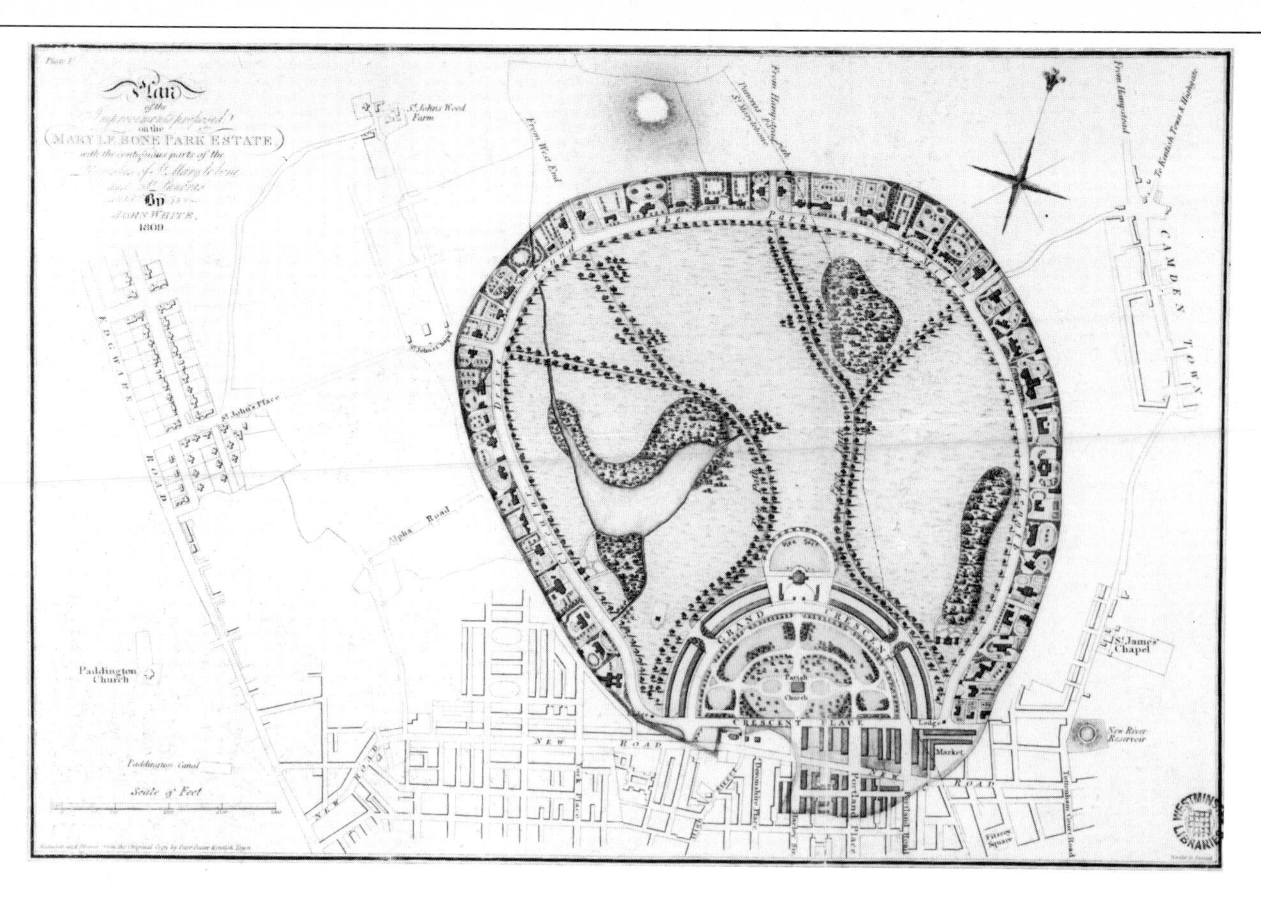

233. Proposed development of Marylebone Park, by John White, 1809 (Westminster City Archives).

to retire there by the neighbourhood's resemblance to the garden quarters of Calcutta and other Anglo-Indian quarters; it is possible that the developers were aware of this. The number of kept women in the area has probably been exaggerated, but they were certainly present, enabling later Victorians to let off steam about 'dark demoralizing scenes' and 'dissipated men of affluence'.[18]

While St John's Wood was getting under way something much more ambitious was germinating next door, and gradually developing into Regent's Park.[19] Marylebone Park, a hunting park enclosed by Henry VIII, had long been cut up into farms, and had been held by the Duke of Portland on a long lease which was due to expire in 1811, when it would revert to the Crown Lands. As it was just to the north of fashionable London, it clearly had great potentiality. In 1809 the Duke of Portland's surveyor, John White, unofficially presented three suggestions as to how it might be 'improved'.[20] Much the most interesting of these showed it developed as a landscaped park complete with lake, having terraces and a crescent to the south, and very grand villas facing onto a circular drive all round the perimeter of the rest. The scheme was much more ambitious than St John's Wood with its modest cottages. The idea of houses looking onto a park was reminiscent of the terraces built round Sydney Gardens in Bath in the 1790s,[21] but the grand sweep of villas was suggestive of the great houses round the Esplanade in Calcutta.

However, the job of laying out the park was given in 1811 to John Nash, as architect to the Department of Woods and Forests. His first scheme envisaged covering the whole area with circuses, crescents and terraces, interspersed with pleasure-grounds dotted with large villas. By the time the scheme was published in 1812 the houses had been thinned out, and what was planned was a very large landscaped park, complete with lake, with terraces all round, a circus in the middle of the park, and villas scattered over the park. The circus was clearly modelled on Shaw's British Circus, but had terraces

234. Looking towards Cornwall and Clarence Terraces across the lake at Regent's Park. Engraved from the drawing by T. H. Shepherd, 1829.

instead of villas. In the end the circus was never built, and only eight of the proposed forty to fifty villas materialized—or, to be exact, seven villas and one cottage. The canal, which Nash had originally envisaged as coming through the middle of the development, was pushed to the northern edge, and from 1823 two rows of cottages on the St John's Wood model, but rather more fanciful, were built on either side of the canal where it emerged from the park: they were called Park Village West and East. Park Village West, unlike South Bank and North Bank, still survives.

Although the Regent's Park development drew most of its ideas from Bath, it was important because it showed that the mixture of city and country, which people had become used to in a holiday or health-resort context in Bath or elsewhere, could be introduced into a major city. Moreover, Regent's Park improved on Bath in one respect, even if against Nash's original intention. In Sydney Gardens the terraces looked onto a comparatively modest pleasure garden, at Regent's Park they surround a full-scale park, an urban version of a gentleman's park in the country and just as large, complete with winding island-dotted lake and long vistas through groves of trees. 'Look at the beautiful expanse of the Lake before us', wrote James Elmes in his *Metropolitan Improvements* of 1829. 'See the exquisite diversity of scene, occasioned by the islets or holmes that lie upon its tranquil bosom, in all the variety of nature, when at the same time they are the effects of art . . . A house, situated like one of these, possesses the double advantage of town and country. By its contiguity to the fashionable and business part of the metropolis, it forms a complete town residence; and by the romantic beauty of the decorated landscape by which it is surrounded, it is equal to any part of the country for health and domestic retirement for men of business.'[22]

From about 1820 one can watch the villa lay-out and the city park spreading, with variations, all over the country. Many of the earlier examples were designed by London-based architects, and others were clearly inspired by London examples. The influence

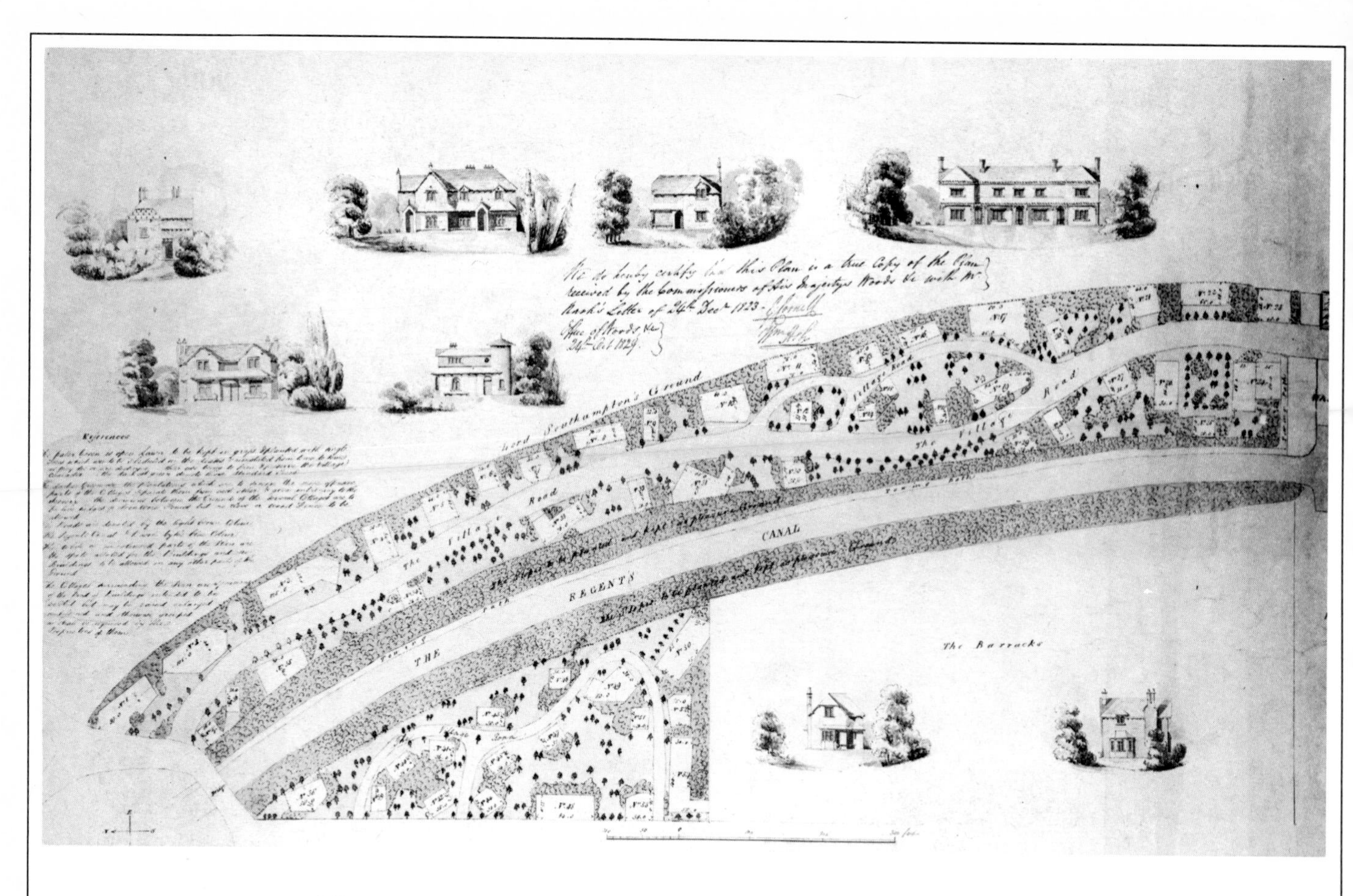

235. John Nash's original plan for Park Village, Regent's Park, 1823 (Public Record Office).

236. (top right) Plan of the Park Estate, Cheltenham, 1833 (Gloucester County Library).

237. (bottom right) No. 14, Lansdowne Road, North Kensington. From a watercolour of *c.*1860.

of Regent's Park was great, but can be exaggerated, the influence of St John's Wood was probably just as important, and so was that of White's proposals for Marylebone Park.[23]

A park, to begin with, was thought of as an adjunct and amenity for the houses round it, rather than for the city or town as a whole, and a park development was always connected with a housing development: access into the park was often confined to the families in the surrounding houses. Regent's Park was not opened to the public until the 1840s. The houses round a park could be mainly or entirely villas, as in John White's plan, or a mixture of terraces and villas, as in Regent's Park; but villas actually inside the park, as in Regent's Park, are almost never to be found, probably because they cut up the park and caused problems of access and security. Any park of any pretentions had to have a lake. The earliest and one of the best examples of a villa park is Calverley Park in Tunbridge Wells, laid out in 1828 by Decimus Burton, who had designed several of the Regent's Park villas, and whose father had been deeply involved in contracting both for Regent Street and the Regent's Park terraces.[24] The Park in Cheltenham (a town much favoured by retired East India Company officials) was laid out in 1833 with villas only round a small park; its lay-out was clearly inspired by John White's.[25] Early examples of mixed villas and terraces are to be found in Prince's Park, Liverpool, laid out by James Pennethorne and Joseph Paxton from 1842, and Birkenhead Park, across the Mersey from Liverpool, laid out according to Paxton's designs from 1843.[26] Birkenhead Park was of particular interest because it was open to the general public, as, clearly enough, was the People's Park in Halifax, also laid out by Paxton in 1856.

The concept of a park acquired so much prestige that 'Park' began to occur in place-names even if there was no park. The two Park Crescents built in Brighton and Worthing

PLAN
PARK ESTATE
THE
PARK

238. A view of Park Crescent (A. H. Wilds, *c.* 1830), Worthing (Worthing Municipal Library).

to the designs of Amos Wilds, in 1829 and about 1830, both had no more than a large pleasure-ground. Kensington Park in west London was laid out on a large scale from the 1840s. It had a series of pleasure-grounds enclosed by villas or terraces, the small private gardens of which led directly into the pleasure-ground, on the model of Shaw's Grand Circus in St John's Wood; this very agreeable arrangement had in fact already been used in Park Crescent, Brighton, and Moray Place in Edinburgh.[27] But there was no park. At Victoria Park in Manchester and the Castle Park in Nottingham there was not even a pleasure-ground; Castle Park was at least built on what had been the deer park of Nottingham Castle, even if it entirely obliterated it. By the 1860s parkless parks or parkless neighbourhoods with 'Park' in their name abounded all over the country. 'Grove' and 'Gardens' also became popular ways of suggesting that a street had 'the double advantage of town and country'. Another way of giving a neighbourhood a rural air was to abandon both grid and geometric road systems and lay out an estate with winding roads, on the model of the winding paths in the parks.

Nash had introduced winding roads into the Park Villages in 1823, and they became a great feature of the seaside villa districts of Torquay, which were laid out from the 1840s onwards. There they were suggested by the need for the roads to climb up and down very steep slopes; they were also adopted with enthusiasm at Bournemouth, where they were rather less necessary, and made a pretty showing in the St John's College estate in north Oxford, where the ground is virtually flat. The social geography of some Victorian towns and suburbs can be accurately measured by seeing where the winding roads stop and the straight roads begin.

Hippolyte Taine walked through the suburbs of Manchester and Liverpool in the 1860s and found them strange and depressing places, in spite of the 'sweetness and calm' of the 'natural beauties'. They were too calm for him. 'The townsman', he wrote, 'does everything in his power to cease being a townsman, and tries to fit a country-house and a bit of country into a corner of the town.'[28]

The villas in Regent's Park were, as was remarked at the time, 'planted out from the view of each other, so that the inhabitant of each seems, in his own prospect, to be the sole lord of the surrounding scenery'.[29] Such had always been Nash's intention.

239. View of the Norham Manor Estate, North Oxford, 1860 (Bodleian Library, Oxford).

Contemporary depictions of the villas show them, not unreasonably, without a hint, or with only the tiniest hint, that they were not in the depths of the country. The same convention was used, rather less reasonably, to depict the even grander villas of the 1840s in Kensington Palace Gardens, which in fact were built on a row of comparatively small plots, very much in view of their neighbours.[30] The convention appears again, with delightful absurdity, in a watercolour of about 1860 depicting Mrs Louisa Macdowall's modest villa in Lansdowne Road, Kensington Park. The villa appears as a free-standing house in its own spacious gardens, without another building in view. In fact it was semi-detached, in a row of other semi-detached villas, and what is shown as garden in front of it was actually the public road.[31]

When John Hughes (father of the author of *Tom Brown's Schooldays*) moved to a rather similar semi-detached villa in The Boltons in Fulham in about 1853, he referred to the neighbourhood as 'this wild back-settlement, two miles beyond Hyde Park Corner . . . I consider myself, for all social purposes, as living in the country, out of the pale of the Red Book.'[32] The Red Book was the street directory of socially acceptable London, and in London there was no great social prestige attached to living in a villa neighbourhood. 'Society' continued to live in terrace houses in the centre, or, in a few very grand instances, in detached houses surrounded by terrace houses, as it had been doing since the early eighteenth century. The fact that no more than eight Regent's Park villas ever got built suggests that there was a limited demand for them. People in society did not need 'the double advantage of town and country'; when they felt like the advantages of the country, they went to their country houses. That, at least, was the fiction, and those who did not own country houses lived in the fashionable areas of London according to the same conventions as those who did. The grand villas in Kensington Palace Gardens were inhabited, of necessity, by rich people, but they were not fashionable rich people: they included three building contractors, a lace merchant, a tea merchant, a timber merchant, a Spanish merchant banker and a steel manufacturer. The Spanish de Murieta family did have social ambitions, and managed to establish itself on the edge of the Prince of Wales's set; but then they immediately moved off to the socially much grander ambience of Carlton House Terrace, looking over St James's Park.[33]

240. A road in Sydenham, South London, in 1871. From the painting by Camille Pissarro.

241. (right) Detail of the auditorium, the Opéra (1861–75), Paris. From C. Garnier, *Nouvel Opéra de Paris* (British Library).

A very different situation reigned in the new industrial towns. Here the cream of local society all moved into villa neighbourhoods, and by the later nineteenth century no one with any social pretentions lived in a terrace or in the centre of the town. In Manchester, Victoria Park was soon overtaken by even bigger villas further out, at Didsbury, Altrincham and Bowdon; in Birmingham, Edgbaston became the best address;[34] in Nottingham, it was Castle Park, soon to become *the* Park;[35] in Liverpool the select areas were Prince's and Sefton Parks, and the parkless Grove and Fulwood Parks.

The growth of suburbs was facilitated and partly caused by better public transport, first the horse omnibuses which spread over London in increasing numbers from the 1820s, then local railway lines, horse trams and finally electric trams. To begin with, the cost of transport inevitably made them impractical for the working classes, and as big nineteenth-century cities generated large numbers of middle-class people prepared to move out to them, they developed as very extensive one-class areas. The first suburbanites were not necessarily smug, conventional or respectable. St John's Wood, the first English suburb, had a slightly raffish and dashing aura, and the function of a suburb as a place in which to keep a mistress lasted well into the century. Nor did living in suburbs imply a rejection of the city; it was a way of getting, or trying to get, the best of both worlds.

14

Paris and the Boulevards

'The first lights are being lighted, and the great banquet begins.' In these words Eduardo de Amicis opens his description of an evening on the Paris boulevards in 1878.[1] The whole nineteenth-century world flocked to Paris to enjoy the banquet; it was Paris not London which was looked to as the epitome of all the modern city had to offer. Its remodelling under Napoleon III and Baron Haussmann gave it a spaciousness and scale which no other city possessed, but which city after city did its best to emulate. It had its own unmistakeable flavour, to be found in the gilt and glitter of the opera house, in the lush cast iron of lamp-standards, kiosks and urinals along the boulevards, and in the bedded-out flowers that filled its parks and gardens: fuchsias, cannas, petunias, pelargoniums and begonias, including the hirsute and almost oriental opulence of the emperor's own flower, the Begonia Rex Imperator.[2]

In the 1840s Paris was still a city of contrasts, as it had been for the last hundred years and more. The hub or centre of the city was largely composed of a warren of narrow and filthy streets, and impossible traffic jams, from which the visitor, having hopelessly lost his way, would emerge suddenly and surprisingly onto the luminous open spaces of the quays and the Seine, or the gaiety and trees of the boulevards. The Directorate and, still more, the Empire had, it is true, introduced some major new features. The most obvious for the visitor were the long, elegant arcades of the Rue de Rivoli, the Arc de Triomphe gradually rising at the end of the Champs Élysées, the triumphal column which had replaced the statue of Louis XIV on what had now become the Place Vendôme, and the grand portico of the Chamber of Deputies, surveying the portico of the Madeleine across the Seine and the renamed Place de la Concorde.

Equally or even more important, but off the main tourist route, were the great new markets and abattoirs, some of them on confiscated religious property, the new public cemeteries on the edge of the city, and the waterways and waterworks of the Canal d'Ourcq, which had brought a major new source of both water supply and water transport to Paris.[3] But nearly all the improvements had used existing vistas and been made, in the traditional manner, on open or largely open ground or by rebuilding buildings in public or imperial ownership. The Rue de Rivoli, for instance, occupied for the most part what had previously been the gardens of houses and religious establishments along the south side of the Rue St Honoré; its creation involved much fewer difficulties than that of its near contemporary, Regent Street in London.[4]

By 1870 the transformation of Paris had become the wonder of the world. Napoleon III, sitting at his desk at the Tuileries with a map of the remodelled Paris covering the wall before him, Persigny, his minister of finance, and Baron Haussmann, his Prefect of the Seine, had achieved what all previous governments and monarchs throughout Europe had failed to achieve, and driven a network of straight and broad roads through a crowded and ancient city, remorselessly demolishing everything which stood in their way. London's Regent Street, considerable achievement though it was, paled into insignificance compared with what was done in Paris.

But Paris remodelled was not just the expression of the ambition and power of an absolute ruler (which Napoleon III actually never was). It was made possible by the particular situation of Paris in these years.[5] From about the 1830s France experienced what amounted to its own industrial and financial revolution. Cities like Lille, Rouen and Rheims went over to the factory system. Paris became the centre of a railway network: the first railway arrived in the 1840s and by the 1870s Paris was the terminus of ten lines. An effervescence of manufacturing activity resulted. By 1848 Paris had become the world's greatest manufacturing city, with more than four hundred thousand workers employed in industry. Admittedly, many of these were working in small old-fashioned workshops, especially along the little River Bièvre, which had been an industrial river since the Middle Ages. But there were big textile works, and heavy industry factories and chemical works as well. Paris had had important iron works since the 1820s. Gouin and Company (later to be known as the Société de Batignolles, from the location of its factory on the north-west outskirts of Paris) started as a locomotive factory in 1847 and later expanded to construct factory machinery, and to contract for bridge building and engineering works of all kinds all over the world. By 1855 it was employing two thousand workers. Other big engineering works in Paris included

Désouches, which made railway coaches, and Cavé, which made iron-clad boats. In the 1860s Gustave Eiffel set up what were to become his famous works just outside Paris at Levallois-Perret.

All this activity, and similar activities all over France, needed financing. Paris developed into a great money market. One expression of this was the Bourse, architecturally the grandest exchange in Europe. It was built on the site of a suppressed convent; its foundations were laid in 1808, but it was not opened until 1826. But what was really more important in the financial history of Paris was the development from the 1850s onwards of a new kind of bank to supplement the old private banks. The Crédit Mobilier (1852), the Crédit Industriel and Commerciel (1859), the Crédit Foncier (1861), the Société de Dépôts et de Comptes Courants (1863), the Crédit Lyonnais (1863) and the Société Générale (1864) were the French counterparts of the joint-stock banks of England, but they were active much sooner than the English banks in establishing a network of local branches and local agencies, and in attracting the savings of small people. The cumulative result of this gave them very large reserves. They had made the discovery that a million deposits of five hundred francs are as good as five hundred deposits of a million francs. The Crédit Mobilier and the Crédit Foncier were both the creations of Émile Pereire, a brilliant but over-adventurous financier, who crashed, taking his companies with him, in 1867. He was a pioneer and took too many risks, but during the years of his prosperity he and his companies were of the first importance in the development of Paris.

The creative basic assumption made by Napoleon and his ministers was that, in a city as rich and on the up as Paris, work on the enormous scale which they envisaged would pay for itself in the end. The expenditure was an investment, recoverable from rising tax revenues and increased property values. Accordingly, it was decided to borrow on a scale on which no city had ever borrowed before. The decision was so disliked by Haussmann's predecessor as prefect, Jean Jacques Berger, that he was dismissed. In the end the cost of public works between 1853 and 1869 was 2,554 million francs, or about £102 million. Of this about 500 million francs, or £20 million, was raised by city loans—as compared to the £400,000 borrowed for the public works involved in Regent Street. About a quarter of the loan was taken up by the Crédit Mobilier, but a high proportion was sold direct to small investors, in 500 franc bonds. These costs are exclusive of the very large, but unknown, sums spent by the contractors to develop the sites along the new roads. Pereire's Crédit Foncier was set up specifically to lend money to them, and lent out £16 million repayable in an eight-year period on the completion of the works. Pereire also formed a property development company, as an off-shoot of the Crédit Immobilier, which built two very large hotels, and a substantial portion of the buildings on the new streets.

The task of redeveloping Paris was made easier because it was a single administrative unit with an ancient tradition of strong local government dominated by the state, in complete contrast to the multitude of separate authorities in London. Although, at the Revolution, the ownership of property had been recognized as one of the essential human rights, a law of 1841 had legalized compulsory purchase with compensation if Parliament declared the work a public utility. The 1852 law was modified to allow compulsory purchase to be initiated by the executive. This put the Parisian executive in an extremely strong position, even though further legislative measures, which were

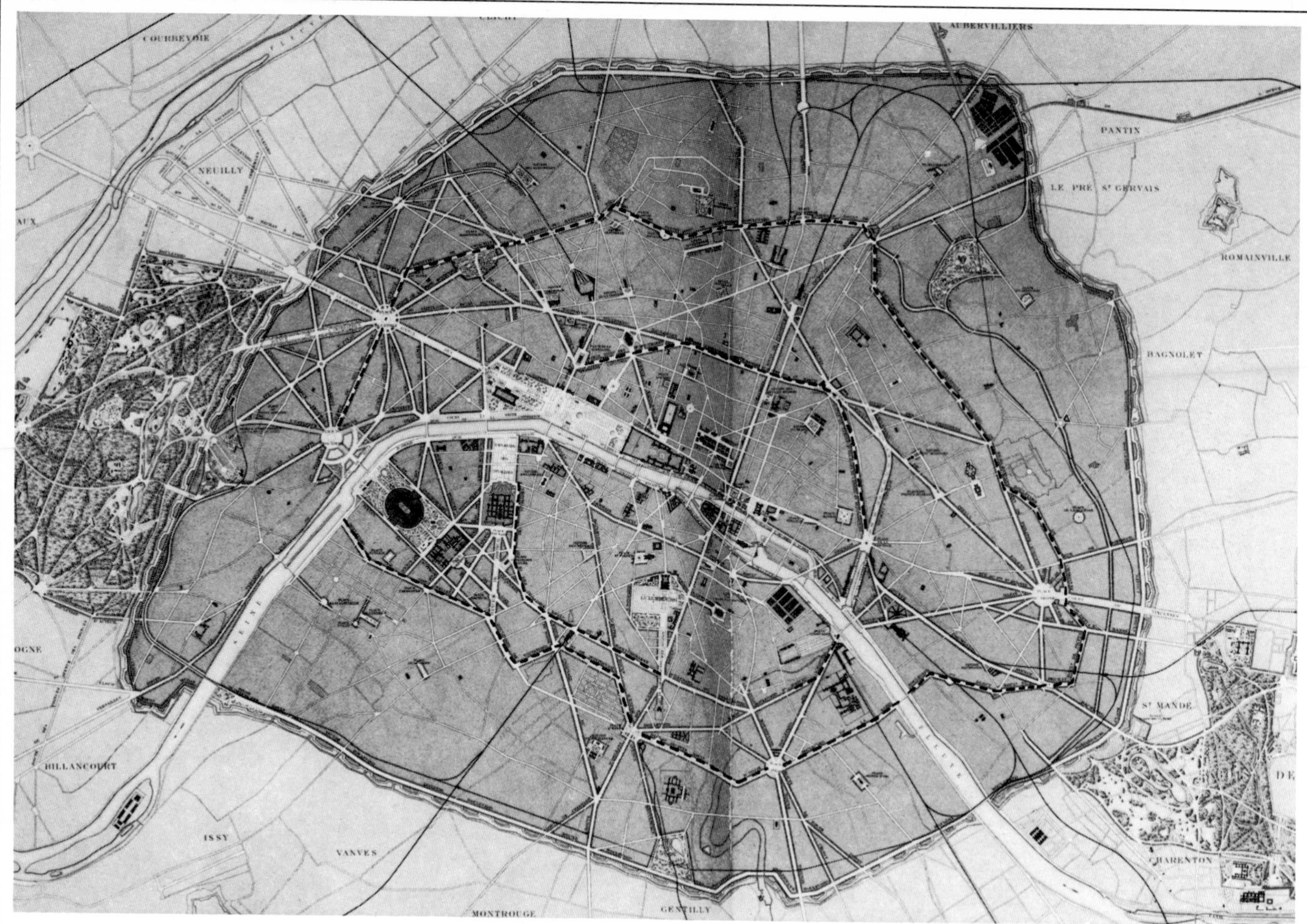

242. Napoleon III's Paris. From A. Alphand, *Les Promenades de Paris*. The dotted lines show the original inner boulevards (1670–*c.* 1760) and the *boulevards exterieures* formed on the line of the customs wall of 1787.

243. (top right) The lake, temple and rocks in the Parc des Buttes-Chaumont, Paris.

244. (bottom right) The Boulevard des Italiens, Paris, by the Café Tortoni. By Eugène Guerard, 1856 (Musée Carnavalet, Paris).

passed as the result of lobbying by property owners and leaseholders along the lines of the proposed new roads, greatly increased the cost of purchase.

Having the money and the power to push the redevelopment schemes through would not necessarily have been enough if the schemes had produced sufficiently strong disaffection among the population of Paris. In fact enough people did well out of them to prevent this. As usual in the nineteenth century, it was the poor who suffered. The non-leaseholding occupants of demolished property were evicted with little if any compensation and no right to re-housing, as was the standard procedure for compulsory purchases in Europe for most of the nineteenth century. The amount of concern that this caused was minimal; the well off, on the whole, simply welcomed the fact that a lot of undesirable slum property had disappeared. The evicted poor, though considerable in numbers, were not sufficiently unified to form an effective protest lobby.[6]

The proprietors and leaseholders, on the other hand, got very good compensation. Moreover, all those who bought city bonds had acquired a financial stake in the new work. As usually happens, there was a difficult period when work had been going on for a few years, and before the ultimate benefits had become clear; the new issue of city bonds floated in 1860 took two years to sell (and then, finally, at a discount), whereas the issues of 1855 and 1865 were sold in a day. As the work approached completion it became a matter of civic and national pride.

The best-known products of Haussmann's remodelling of Paris were the new boulevards, but these were only part of a comprehensive scheme of urban renewal. A number of old roads were widened or straightened and new roads other than boulevards created, including an eastern extension of the Rue de Rivoli, the roads

around the Étoile, and the Avenue de l'Opéra (although the last was not actually achieved until after the Third Empire). Several new public squares were formed. The Bois de Boulogne and the Bois de Vincennes were turned into public parks, and two new parks created, the Parc des Buttes Chaumont and the Parc Monceaux, the latter based on a smaller private park. New hospitals, schools, colleges, barracks, prisons and a new opera house were formed. Huge new iron market halls were built at Les Halles. The water and gas supplies were improved, and a new public drainage system installed.

Napoleon III, living in London from 1838 to 1840, had walked or driven up and down Regent Street or through the parks (and kept a mistress in St John's Wood). English influence was much in evidence in his work in Paris. The initial idea of a self-financing scheme was probably inspired by Regent Street. The Parisian drainage system owed a good deal to the one which was installed from 1844 by the Metropolitan Board of Works in London. Above all, the public parks and public squares were obviously modelled on Regent's and St James's Parks and the London squares—but with significant differences.

245. A concert in the Champs Élysées in 1856 (Bibliothèque Nationale, Paris).

The boulevards and avenues were an extension in network form of the orbital Parisian *grands boulevards* of the seventeenth and eighteenth centuries. Like the earlier boulevards, they were planted with avenues of trees, and most were approximately the same width. Some were much wider however; the Boulevard Richard le Noir and the Avenue de la Grande Armée were seventy metres wide, the Avenue de l'Imperatrice a hundred and twenty.[7] The original boulevards, moreover, had been intended for pleasure and exercise, not to solve traffic problems, and up to the mid-nineteenth century had kept this use, even though they were also beginning to be used to some extent as a ring road. The new boulevards in the middle of the city were rapidly crowded with traffic, which inevitably moved into the old boulevards as well, so that they lost most of their former leisurely character. But the entertainment element, and the crowds of people walking up and down for pleasure as much as business, remained a feature of most of the boulevards, new and old. Their treatment varied, in fact, a good deal according to their location. Some had a planted strip down the centre or along each side, and in others the whole centre was given over to traffic.[8]

Refreshments and entertainment figured prominently in much that was done under Haussmann. The revamping of the east end of the Champs Élysées, for instance, was designed to enhance its traditional character as an open-air recreation area for Parisians of all classes. In addition to the Palais de l'Industrie, in which the 1857 Exhibition was housed, it was embellished with a circus, a building for displaying panoramas (the embryo prototype of the cinema show), two restaurants, three *cafés concerts* (outdoor cafés at which music and singing was put on), two ice-cream stalls, a cake stall, an open-air refreshment buffet and a bandstand, in addition to fountains, flower-beds and numerous cast-iron urinals. The whole area was lit up at night when, in the words of Adolphe Alphand, the engineer and garden designer who laid it all out, 'la foule que se present dans les bosquets, la musique, la voix des chanteurs, le murmure des eaux, donne a cette charmante promenadé un air féerique'.[9]

One of the main distinctions between the Parisian and London parks was that restaurants, cafés and even (in the Bois de Boulogne) a racecourse figured prominently in the former, and were almost completely lacking in the latter. There was a pleasure-garden element in the Parisian parks, part of a tradition dating back to the eighteenth century which had owed much to English pleasure gardens; but in England in the mid-nineteenth century the non-conformist or evangelical lobbies were strong enough to bring about the gradual closure of all the pleasure-gardens and to exclude anything to do with drink or betting from all the new parks.

The new squares formed under Haussmann were English-inspired in so far as they were thickly planted oases of greenery surrounded by terraces of buildings, but in contrast to the quiet seclusion of English squares they were designed to be gay and public places. The whole of Third Empire Paris was in fact designed for enjoyable motion. Private carriages, hackney cabs and the Compagnie Générale des Omnibus (later to be supplemented or replaced by horse and electric trams) conveyed large numbers of people relatively effortlessly all over the town through the new roads and boulevards, which were brilliantly lit at night. Crowds milled under the trees on the wide sidewalks, sat out in the cafés to watch the crowds, or looked at the window displays in the great plate-glass windows of the new shops. Alternatively, they could walk through the new department stores, and up and down their splendid curving staircases, or savour the novel excitement of the passenger lifts, which gave changing vistas of the different galleries as they rose magically up and down. The rich had their own particular carriage promenade in the Champs Élysées, and the new opera house gave them one of the most splendid staircases in the world on which to show themselves.

The opera house, however magnificent, was an example of a long-familiar type; the two new hotels, the Grand Hôtel de Louvre and the Grand Hôtel by the Opéra, were new to Europe, but inspired by American examples; but the great new stores were both a new and specifically French development.[10]

It is arguable that Paris became the shoppers' Mecca because of its appalling pre-Third Empire street system. As described in an earlier chapter, Parisian shops were under no great pressure to go in for window displays and fine shop windows, because walking in its narrow streets without sidewalks was a pedestrian's nightmare. Accordingly, the best shops tended to be off the streets. The Palais Royal had been sensationally successful, but its arcades were open; the fashionable new development from about 1800 onwards was the *passages*, shops in covered top-lit arcades, in fact a reversion to the now deserted galleries of the Palais Marchand. At least seventeen of them were opened in Paris between 1800 and 1830, and imitations of them spread all over Europe and America.[11]

The next stage was that of the bazaars. These were another form of off-street shopping. The term had first been borrowed from the east for European shopping in 1816, when three houses in Soho Square in London were adapted as the Soho Bazaar.[12] This was a charitable venture; the houses were filled with stalls, which were let out to the relatives of those who had been killed in the recent wars. The idea was taken up on

DEHODENQ RESTAURATEUR
CAFÉ GLACES
DÉJEUNERS
A LA FOURCHETTE

a more ambitious scale in Paris. Le Grand Bazar was opened on the Rue St Honoré in 1825, for similar charitable purposes but on a larger scale. But it was the Bazar de l'Industrie (1827–9), in what is now the Boulevard Montmartre, which introduced the building form which became associated with bazaars. It was constructed of cast iron, and consisted of two storeys of galleries for stalls, grouped round an open nave. The Bazar de Boufflers, which opened on the Boulevard des Italiens in 1829, had two narrow parallel naves surrounded by galleries, all of ornamental cast iron of remarkable elegance. It was sometimes known as the Galerie de Fer; 'Galerie' became an alternative to 'Bazar' as a name for these structures. The Bazar Montesquieu or Bazar de Fer followed in 1830, and the three-storey Galeries du Commerce et de l'Industrie in 1837. In the latter the galleries were joined to each other across two naves by bridges.

All these later bazaars were purely commercial. Their ambitious use of iron developed naturally out of the fact that Paris was already a centre for iron foundries, and that its iron industry was expanding. They were brilliantly lit by gas (which was introduced into Paris in 1829); this contributed to their success, but also to their destruction, for their contents were highly inflammable, even if their iron structure was not. None has survived, but the type still exists in GUM, the great Moscow store, which was built as a bazaar of independent stalls, as it still is today. It is a late example of the type (built in 1888–93), but a very splendid one.

246. (left) The Passage des Panoramas, Paris, *c.* 1810. From the anonymous painting in the Musée Carnavelet, Paris.

247. (below) The interior of GUM (A. N. Pomerantzev, 1888–93), Moscow.

Long before GUM was built the architectural format of the bazaar had been adapted for big stores under single ownership. Such stores had in fact been developing in Paris since the 1830s, in the form of what were called *magasins des nouveautés*. They sold silks, woollens, cloths, shawls, lingerie, hosiery, gloves, ready-to-wear and occasionally furs, umbrellas and sewing goods; this selection, circumscribed though it may seem, was a novel one in Paris, where most shopping had been organized by guilds up to 1789, and shops traditionally kept to very narrow ranges. They advertised, and sold at a fixed and marked price, which was also still something of a rarity in Paris, although the practice had been pioneered in the shops of the Palais Royal in the 1780s. But the *magasins des nouveautés*, unlike the extremely expensive and relatively small Palais Royal shops, pioneered a technique based on bulk-buying, big stocks, low prices and quick turnover.

Several of the *magasins des nouveautés* grew to a considerable size in the 1850s, but they grew on an *ad hoc* basis, by absorbing and knocking together adjacent shops or houses. It was not until the 1860s that grand buildings started to be erected for them. The bazaar plan adapted perfectly for the purpose: if the nave was enlarged into a central hall, the height and numbers of galleries increased and lifts and a grand staircase built to connect them, something well lit, easy to get around in and visually sensational resulted; and by the 1860s the proprietors of big stores were very much alive to the advertisement-value of visual effect. The best known,

VOYAGE
VOYAGE
CONFECTION

but not quite the earliest, of these stores was the Bon Marché in the Rue de Sèvres on the Left Bank, which was built in 1869–72.[13] Its architect was Louis-Charles Boileau, and its ironwork was made for Aristide Boucicaut, the proprietor, by Gustave Eiffel, who had recently set up his foundry just outside Paris.

The growing wealth and population of Paris and France provided the clientele, iron and glass produced a new aesthetic, and the result was one of the most enjoyable and exciting groups of buildings ever erected. Great new stores were constantly being built in Paris up till the early 1930s; concrete and marble contributed to a new look from about 1910, but the basic plan remained very much the same. The stores gradually stocked more and more goods until they developed into full-scale department stores. They pioneered sales, mail-order, catalogues and advertising of every kind, and provided a complete world for their customers, in which sales areas were supplemented by restaurants, cafés, bars, picture galleries and reading-rooms. They were visually at their most exciting in the 1890s and early 1900s when Art Nouveau ironwork twisted and flickered over staircases, domes and balustrades and burst out through the stonework of their exteriors. In his novel *Au Bonheur des Dames* (1882), Zola, at once fascinated, exhilarated and appalled, described the excitement caused by these great shops 'burning like a beacon', their catastrophic effect on the small shops in the neighbourhood, the throb and fever of the crowds in a big sale, the women going on mad sprees of buying, the displays in which 'material was streaming down like a bubbling sheet of water falling from above and broadening out on the floor . . . women pale with desire were leaning over as if to see their reflections'; and beyond the hubbub of business the 'sensation of the vastness of Paris—a city so vast that it would always be able to supply customers'.[14]

It was not only Paris which supplied the customers for the shops, however. They came to Paris from all over France and from all over the world. They came at all times, but the major occasions of their coming were the great exhibitions of 1855, 1867, 1878, 1889 and 1900. In the nineteenth century Paris was much more successful than any other city in putting on exhibitions.[15] London's two exhibitions, of 1851 and 1862, both had around six million visitors. The failure of the 1862 exhibition to improve on the attendance figures of the 1851 one discouraged any further exhibitions in London until the White City exhibition in 1908, and that had only eight million visitors. Meanwhile the number of visitors to Paris exhibitions climbed up from five million in 1855 to eleven million in 1867, sixteen million in 1878, thirty-two million in 1889 and nearly fifty-one million in 1900.[16]

The 1855 exhibition in Paris had been centred on a rather uninteresting temporary building in the Champs Élysées. The 1867 exhibition, on the Champ de Mars, had an extremely interesting main exhibition hall, divided up into concentric circles of glass galleries. But the feature of the exhibition which radically altered the character of all exhibitions in the future was that it was not confined to one building. The surroundings of the main building were laid out as a garden of winding paths, scattered all over which were several dozen little pavilions, of all types and styles. Several of these served as or contained bars, buffets, restaurants or entertainments: among them the belly-dancers from Morocco were as popular as they were erotic. The de Goncourts described how, 'at the English buffets in the Exhibition, there is a fantastic quality about the women, with their splendid beauty, their crude pallor, their flaming hair; they are like whores of the Apocalypse, something terrifying, frightening, inhuman. Their eyes

248. (left) The main hall in the Galeries Lafayette (Ferdinand Chanut, 1910), Paris.

gaze unseeingly into the distance. A cross between clowns and cattle, they are magnificent, alarming animals.'[17]

From the beginning, the great nineteenth-century exhibitions had attracted people who came to be entertained as well as instructed. But in the Paris exhibitions the entertainment element grew much stronger, and it was not just the exhibitions but all Paris which put itself on show for the visitors who flocked there. Apart from coming to see the exhibition, they came there to shop, to go to the shows and the opera, drink in the cafés, savour the crowds and the bright lights on the boulevards, revel in the city's scale and opulence, and in many cases gratify or titillate their sexual appetites. There were at least as many prostitutes in London as in Paris; in the 1860s Hippolyte Taine was appalled by their number and squalor.[18] But the image of Paris as the city where sex was glamorous and open, where prostitutes had their own recognized aristocracy, where the cancan was danced in the cabarets and where novels openly featured aspects of life which no English novelist would dare mention had a perpetual fascination, especially for Protestant nations.

The most glittering description of Paris as seen by a foreigner is that written by an Italian, Eduardo de Amicis, who came in 1878. For him Paris seemed a 'vast gilded net', a 'Tower of Babel', 'a great opulent and sensual city, living only for pleasure and glory'. 'The Boulevards are blazing', he writes of Paris at night. 'Half closing the eyes it seems as if one saw on the right and left two rows of flaming furnaces. The shops cast floods of brilliant light half across the street, and encircle the crowd in a golden dust. The kiosks, which extend in two interminable rows, lighted from within, with their many coloured panes, resembling enormous Chinese lanterns placed on the ground, or the little transparent theatres of the marionettes, give to the street the fantastic and childlike aspect of an Oriental fete. The numberless reflections of the glasses, the thousand luminous points shining through the branches of the trees, the inscriptions in gas gleaming on the theatre fronts, the rapid motion of the innumerable carriage lights, that seem like myriads of fireflies set in motion by the wind, the purple lamps of the omnibuses, the great flaming halls opening into the street, the shops which resemble caves of incandescent gold and silver, the hundred thousand illuminated windows, the trees that seem to be lighted, all these theatrical splendours, half-concealed by the verdure, which now and then allows one to see the distant illuminations, and presents the spectacle in successive scenes—all this broken light, refracted, variegated, and mobile, falling in showers, gathered in torrents, and scattered in stars and diamonds, produces the first time an impression of which no idea can possibly be given.'

Looking back from all this he 'thinks with amazement of those solitary, silent little cities from which we started, called Turin, Milan and Florence, where every one stands at the shop door, and all seem to live like one great family. Yesterday we were rowing on a small lake, today we are sailing on the ocean.'[19]

The Paris which de Amicis and other visitors saw was, of course, only a section of Paris. All round it other aspects of a great and complex city were to be found. There was government Paris, learned Paris, business Paris, religious Paris; and in a huge swathe all round the city were the industrial areas of Paris to which no visitors ever went, and in which about half of its population of 1,851,792 were living in 1876.[20]

This area included the traditional workshop districts in the Faubourg St Antoine to the east, and around Gobelins and the Bièvre to the south. But it was mostly made

249. The Moulin de la Galette, Paris. From the painting by Renoir, 1876 (Musée de Jeu de Paume, Paris).

up of the new arrondissements which had been included in the city by Napoleon III, between the customs wall of the 1780s, which he demolished in order to form an outer ring of *boulevards exterieures*, and Louis Philippe's fortifications. Rather more than half this industrial population were employed in small workshops, but the factories stretched beyond the city boundaries, especially to the north towards St Denis. All this great slice of city was filled with foundries, chemical works, railway-carriage workshops, railway yards, steam laundries, cloth mills, canal docks and warehouses, and the huge Third Empire abattoir up in the north-east, with its porters as massive as the beef which they slaughtered.

Here and there the area contained unbuilt-on land which was invaded by squatters who built shanty towns of mud, stones, tarred paper and driftwood. The quarry-galleries off the railway tunnel which ran through the former quarry and pleasure-garden area of Belleville (where Haussmann formed the most scenic of the Third Empire parks) filled up with beggars and thieves.[21] Some of this down-and-out population came from the central slums which had been destoyed to make way for new boulevards; others were immigrants who had failed to find work. An influx from the provinces helped to raise the population of Paris from a million to nearly two million between 1841 and 1870. The new population settled mainly in the outer zone, for the most part in bleak courtyard tenements, such as Zola described in *L'Assommoir*.[22] The old porte-cochère

Les Abattoirs de la Villette
Cour d'abattage
Hélio

250. (top left) The Abattoirs de la Villette, Paris (Bibliothèque Nationale, Paris).

251. (bottom left) Leather worker on the Bièvre, Paris (Musée Carnavalet, Paris).

252. (above) Sugar warehouses in La Villette, Paris (Bibliothèque Nationale, Paris).

plan, which had been evolved for the houses of the rich in the sixteenth and seventeenth centuries, had been adapted to produce the apartment blocks, built round a courtyard approached through a porte-cochère, in which most middle-class Parisians lived in the nineteenth century. Suitably stripped of amenities, it proved equally adaptable for working-class tenements; many still survive today, lived in by African and Arab workers rather than French ones.

Only one of these working-class areas gradually impinged on the consciousness of the centre. It had an odd history.[23] The hill of Montmartre was originally occupied by windmills, little pleasure gardens, and a few substantial houses built by those who came there for quiet and the view. It was submerged beneath the great industrial and working-class invasion of outer Paris, but it was too precipitous for the factories and goods yards which were built to its east and west, in La Chapelle and Batignolles. It became an area of small workshops, small tenements and little houses; the pleasure gardens continued, among them one around a disused windmill, the Moulin de la Galette. The Boulevard de Clichy and Boulevard de Rochechouart at the bottom of the hill became a mainly working-class entertainment area, of circuses, cabarets and brothels.

South of these *boulevards exterieurs* was the more prosperous area around Notre Dame-de-Lorette. Being immediately to the north of the part of Paris in which the financiers lived and worked, it attracted the two classes who hoped to get business from them, artists and the high-class prostitutes who came to be called Lorettes. In the 1880s some

253. The Moulin Rouge, Paris.

254. (right) Looking from Central Park to the San Remo Apartments on the West Side, New York.

of the artists began to move up into Montmartre, partly because it was cheap, partly because they found subjects to paint in the circuses, pleasure gardens and laundries around the *boulevards exterieurs*, partly, perhaps, because a cult of the working classes was developing. In his novel *Bel-Ami* (1885) de Maupassant makes Madame de Marelles claim to have 'common tastes' ('des gouts canailles'); she indulges in fantasies about wearing working-class clothes and gets a thrill from going to cheap cafés and dancehalls. When Zola's novel about working-class Paris, *L'Assommoir*, was dramatized, a ball was given on its opening night at which everyone who attended wore working-class fancy dress.[24]

The artists went to the existing places of amusement in the area, but they also began to start up cabarets of their own. People who were getting bored of the conventional amusements on the *grands boulevards* began coming up to the *boulevards exterieurs*. For a few decades Montmartre became a mixture of studios, tenements, workshops, dance-halls, cabarets and circuses, frequented by artists, gangsters, prostitutes and people of all classes and countries who came there to be amused. The Moulin de la Galette ceased to be the modest pleasure garden which Renoir had painted, frequented by clerks or factory-workers and their girls, and became a huge and hectic dance hall. The Moulin Rouge opened, an had an artificial windmill instead of a genuine one, to draw the public. Ultimately the amusements and the tourists drove out the artists and most of the working classes. But in the interval the artists who had come to the area to escape from middle-class conventions and set up their own way of life had given birth to the concept of the avant-garde.[25]

15 America and the Birth of the Skyscraper

It was in the first half of the nineteenth century that the United States of America first began to make a cultural impact on Europe. In the early 1800s what was called, rather mysteriously, an 'American cottage' appeared in an English pattern-book.[1] A fashion for American gardens came shortly afterwards, to be followed by a more enduring fashion for American prisons. Top-lit prison galleries, with many storeys of cells opening onto balconies at either side—similar to the arrangement soon to be adopted for Parisian bazaars—first appeared in 1820, in the prison at Auburn, in New York State. In the Eastern Penitentiary at Philadelphia, designed in 1825, John Haviland arranged galleries of this kind like the spokes of a wheel around a central observation hall, from which the entrances to all the cells could be supervised. The principle of supervision from the centre had been worked out in 1791 by Jeremy Bentham for a projected semicircular 'Panopticon'; the spoke plan derived from the Maison de Force at Ghent; Haviland amalgamated the two. He went on to design prisons all over the United States, which were copied all round the

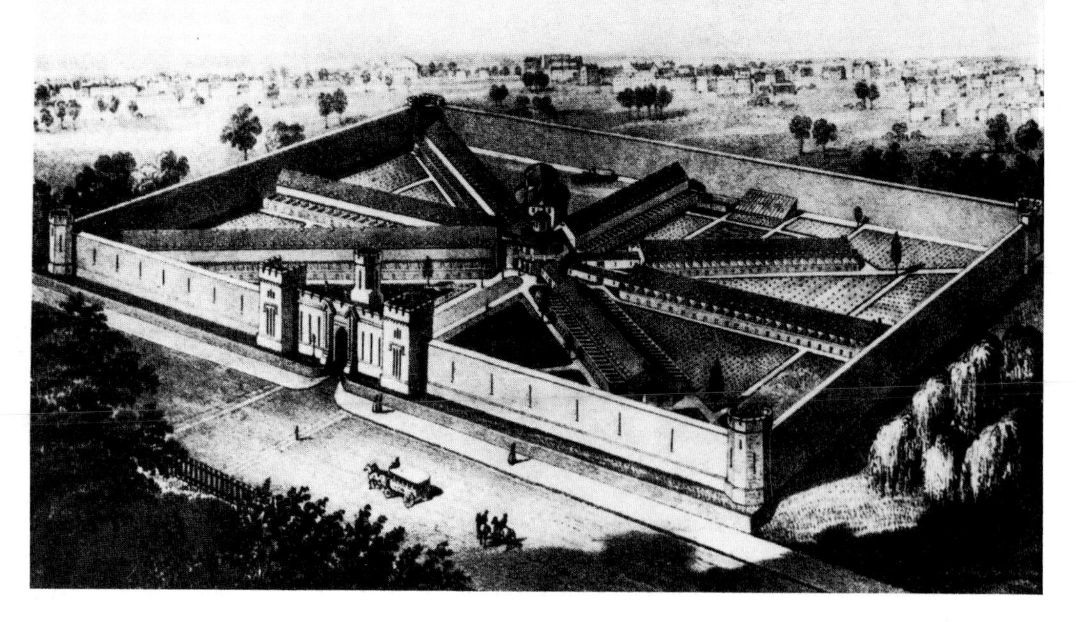

255. The Eastern Penitentiary (John Haviland, 1825), Philadelphia.

world. Observation teams were sent from Paris to examine American prisons in 1833 and 1837.[2]

American hotels began to lead the world at about the same time, certainly in size and probably in standards of accommodation.[3] One curious reason for their size was that from early on large numbers of people, including entire families, lived all the year round in them. Barnam's City Hotel in Baltimore (1825–6) had more than two hundred bedrooms, Astor House in New York (1832–6) three hundred and nine (and seventeen bathrooms), the St Charles in New Orleans (1837) six hundred. The Continental in Philadelphia (1858–60) could accommodate eight to nine hundred people in a mixture of suites and single rooms. These numbers are worth comparing with the Queen's Hotel, Cheltenham, in England (1836–8), puffed at the time as 'the grandest hotel in Europe', which had about one hundred and ten bedrooms. 'The American Hotel is to an English hotel what an elephant is to a periwinkle', wrote George Augustus Sala (an Englishman) in 1866.[4] The English had to console themselves by commenting, with some truth, that most American hotels looked like barracks.[5]

Inside, however, the scale and splendour of their public rooms were often in keeping with the number of their bedrooms. The Exchange Coffee House at Boston (1806–9), in which a merchants' exchange occupied the ground floor, inaugurated a feature which was to become common in American hotels, and has been revived in post-war decades. The centre was occupied by a circular domed rotunda, surrounded by several storeys of balconies, the upper ones of which gave access to the bedrooms. A similar arrangement existed in the circular hall of the St Louis Hotel in New Orleans (1839) and the rectangular hall of the Palace Hotel in San Francisco (1874–6). The latter measured 144 feet by 84, and carriages could drive into it to deposit guests, watched by other guests sitting out around the court. 'Balconies extend entirely around each storey, upon the rails of which are ranged, in harmonious blending, choice tropical plants and shrubs intermingled with evergreens.'[6] The balconies gave access to the hotel's 850 bedrooms and 437 bathrooms. The arrangement was another variant of the bazaar and prison-gallery theme (the prison-gallery type was in fact to be closely copied in the Taj Hotel, Bombay, in 1903).

The first hotel in Europe to have the scale and lavishness of an American hotel was the Grand Hôtel du Louvre in Paris (1855), which had about seven hundred bedrooms.

256. The Grand Court, Palace Hotel (John Gaynor, opened 1874), San Francisco.

The fact that it was inspired by American examples was recognized at the time.[7] In 1860 Théophile Gautier remarked that Paris was getting like Philadelphia, and in 1870 Édmond de Goncourt complained that it was being 'Americanized' and that 'the Parisian of the past felt lost here'.[8] They were thinking, perhaps, of big hotels and wide straight streets, although there is no reason to believe that there was any American influence behind the new boulevards; indeed the influence here was working in the other direction.

The Capitol in Washington was another building which had European repercussions, apart from spawning numerous domed capitols all over the States. Its dome began to be built in 1855, and the image of a great domed building on a hilltop must have inspired the Palais de Justice in Brussels, which was started in 1868. Domes began to appear over parliament houses too: the English architect Gilbert Scott put one on his unsuccessful competition design for the Reichstag in Berlin in 1872, and one was actually built over the parliament house in Budapest in 1882.

America, in short, was now rich enough to support large prisons, large hotels and large capitols, and, since much of its wealth came from trading with Europe, Europe was becoming conscious of what was going on there. Even so, most of the cultural influence was still going the other way. The many German immigrants brought beer halls and concert halls to American cities, but curiously little else. The influences were preponderantly English and French. The reasons for the English influence were obvious. France had links of trade with America, but more important were the links of sentiment between the world's two great republics. One result of this was that many American architects went to be trained in Paris.

The English villa and the English suburb were quickly adopted in America, partly, perhaps, because they could be grafted onto the American tradition of the free-standing house on its smallholding. But most of the grand, and many of the less grand, buildings built in America from the 1850s onwards showed strong French influence. Many rich Americans, accustomed to living in hotels, transferred very happily to French-style apartments. The English park spread all over America, but it tended to have more going on in it, in the French manner, and to be combined with French-style boulevards. All these developments can be watched in New York and Chicago, cities which also pioneered what was to be the most sensational American export to Europe and the world, the skyscraper.

In 1830 there were still pigs rooting on Broadway, within sniffing distance of the skirts of the fashionable ladies who were promenading up and down looking in the shop windows. The pigs did not last much longer on Broadway, but they were not legally debarred from roaming the New York streets until 1867. By 1930 skyscrapers twenty to thirty storeys high were surveying their rooting areas, and the population of New York had risen from a little over 200,000 to nearly seven million. The growth of Chicago in these hundred years was proportionately even more sensational. In 1830 there were probably more pigs than houses in Chicago; its population was about 50.

257. By the City Hall on Broadway, New York, in 1818. Engraved from the watercolour by A. L. Klinckŏwstrom (British Library).

By 1870 it was nearly 300,000, by 1890 over 1,200,000, by 1930 3,376,000. The two cities were closely bound up with each other; New York (with help from Boston) created Chicago, but Chicago helped to create New York.

Any town with New York's situation, on an island with deep storm-free anchorages along both sides, comparatively small tides and quick access to the sea, was bound to become a prosperous place. For the first hundred and fifty years of its life, however, its growth was slowed down by the fact that there was little for it to export, for its hinterland consisted of poor farmland and contained no known mineral resources. Like Amsterdam, its merchants found an opening as carriers of the goods of other people; moreover, unlike Amsterdam, all the timber which it needed for shipbuilding was easily accessible up the broad waters of the Hudson. New York clippers entered the market with such vigour that by the early nineteenth century they were carrying more cotton from Charleston to Europe than was being carried in ships built in Charleston.[10]

The economy of New York was transformed by the opening of the Erie Canal in 1825. The canal ran from Albany on the Hudson to Buffalo on Lake Erie. New York now had easy water access, by way of the Hudson and the canal, to the Great Lakes and through them to the corn and beef of the Midwest (and the furs of the North), at a time when the growing population of Europe was less and less able to feed itself. As more of the Midwest was opened up, New York prospered in proportion. In the 1840s it overtook its East Coast rivals, Boston and Philadelphia, both as a commercial and as a financial centre. Its position was officially recognized in 1846 when the Treasury in Washington opened a sub-Treasury in New York, as the office by means of which the Washington government kept in touch with the money market and from which the bulk of government pensions and interest on government bonds was paid out. The New York Stock Exchange, which had been founded by a group of brokers meeting under a cottonwood tree in Wall Street in 1792, began its rapid growth into one of the great financial institutions of the world. Its prosperity was offset, however, by periodic financial panics, of which that on 13 October 1857 was one of the worst.

By then Chicago was literally jacking itself out of the mud. It had been built on a flat plain barely above the level of Lake Michigan, and the filth and muddiness of its streets were indescribable. In 1856–7 the Chicago town council decided that the general level of the city was to be raised over four feet above the previous one. Roads and sidewalks were rebuilt accordingly, and the buildings were jacked up to align with them. As Chicago was still mostly built of timber, this was a feasible operation, although a lengthy one. Some were of masonry, however, including the Briggs Hotel, which was five storeys high and weighed 22,000 tons. It was raised four and a half feet while its normal operations as a hotel continued.[11]

Chicago owed its prosperity to its position and to its facilities as a harbour. Storms blow up quickly in the Great Lakes, and harbours are very necessary; the Chicago River, on and around the two branches of which Chicago is built, provided a port which, if nothing very marvellous, was serviceable. Even more important, Chicago was at one end of the shortest route from the Lakes to the Mississippi by way of the Illinois River, the route that linked the two biggest inland water systems of North America to each other. It was partly a land link, however. Clearly, Chicago would profit by turning it into a complete water link, and accordingly the Illinois and Michigan Canal was commenced in 1836 and opened in 1848.

At the time of the completion of the canal, St Louis was the leading city of the Mississippi–Missouri basin, and was growing fast. It dominated a network of over fifteen thousand miles of waterway. It was flourishing so much as a result of the opening up of the Midwest that both citizens and visitors had visions of its replacing Washington as the national capital.[12] The canal must have seemed just as likely to turn Chicago into a satellite of St Louis as to draw trade from the Mississippi into the Great Lakes. It certainly had no apparent effect on the prosperity of St Louis, the population of which rose from 16,469 in 1840 to 77,860 in 1850 and 160,773 in 1860. The population of Chicago was rising even faster, but in 1860 it was still only 109,260.

St Louis had not bargained for the combined influence of East Coast finance and the railways. New York, and to a lesser extent Boston, were determined to divert in their direction as much as possible of the traffic which went down the Mississippi. Railways supplied the necessary tool, and money from the East Coast was poured into building them. Chicago was connected to New York by rail in 1852. By 1856 it was at the centre of a network of ten trunk-lines, stretching all over the Midwest. St Louis suffered from the Civil War, and from too much confidence in the power of its great river. It acquired its own railway network too late. By 1870 Chicago had overtaken it in both population and trade, and by 1880 was the fourth biggest city in America.

As an importer, processer, packager and exporter of goods, Chicago rapidly became one of the wonders of the world.[13] Its wealth was based on grain, timber, livestock, and the shipping and railways which brought them in and out. The Chicago River hemmed in the original town to north and west with a belt of shipping, wharves, factories, warehouses, grain elevators and working-class housing; railway yards between the river and the lake shut it in to the south. The river, which was by no means large, was choked with shipping and filthy with industrial waste; the ten bridges which crossed it had to be raised every few minutes to let ships through, to the despair of waiting land traffic. The lake front had no moorings for shipping and was therefore free of industry; but in the 1850s the Illinois Central railway line succeeded in getting a franchise to build its tracks along it. When the industrial belt round the city could absorb no more, the Calumet River and Lake south of the city were developed as a second industrial area.

The grain trade was concentrated at the mouth of the river, where enormous grain elevators, between the river and the rail tracks, were dealing with 60 million bushels of grain a year by 1870. Lumberyards, selling 1,500 million feet of timber a year, lined the south branch of the river and slips off it. In 1865 the stockyards were consolidated

258. Bird's-eye view of central Chicago in 1893 (Chicago Historical Society).

259. (right) Section of Montgomery Ward and Co.'s mail-order establishment, c. 1900, Chicago (Chicago Historical Society).

in one yard covering nearly one square mile, four miles south of the town. As early as 1863 it was claimed that the hogs processed in Chicago in a year would reach, head to tail, all the way to New York. By 1905 seventeen million animals a year were passing through the yards.

These primary industries produced a whole range of secondary ones. By the 1870s the odds were that the corn sold in Chicago came from crops which had been cut by McCormick reapers; by then these were being despatched all over America from the works which Cyrus Hall McCormick had opened in 1847 on the Chicago River, opposite the main clutch of grain elevators. By 1865 Chicago was rolling its own rails, and by the early 1880s it was producing its own railroad cars, at the factory built by George Pullman by the Calumet Lake, complete with a model town for the workers adjoining. Out of the lumber trade grew an industry for mass-producing timber buildings and one of the biggest furniture industries in the world.

Chicago also became a major shopping centre, distributing goods by mail-order all over the Midwest, and displaying them in its department stores along State Street for the Midwest to come and buy. To begin with the stores normally combined wholesale and retail in one building, but as they grew the wholesaling was often hived off to a separate building; a similar process took place in New York. By the 1890s Marshall Field's store was running special buses to the North-Western Station 'always crowded with ladies on a shopping trip from the suburban towns'.[14] Its huge wholesale warehouse was as grand and grim as any Florentine palace, and when the retail store was rebuilt in 1902–7 it became one of the three largest department stores in the world.

Mail-order started in America in the 1850s, but first became big business in the 1870s, when Montgomery Ward of Chicago developed the first major mail-order firm. By 1876 he was advertising 3,899 items in his catalogue, and selling pretty well anything from swaddling clothes to tombstones. The firm never had a shop; but the mail-order idea was taken up by the big department stores, and by 1900 Sears, Roebuck had overtaken Montgomery Ward.[15]

The growth of Chicago and the Midwest brought very great wealth to New York

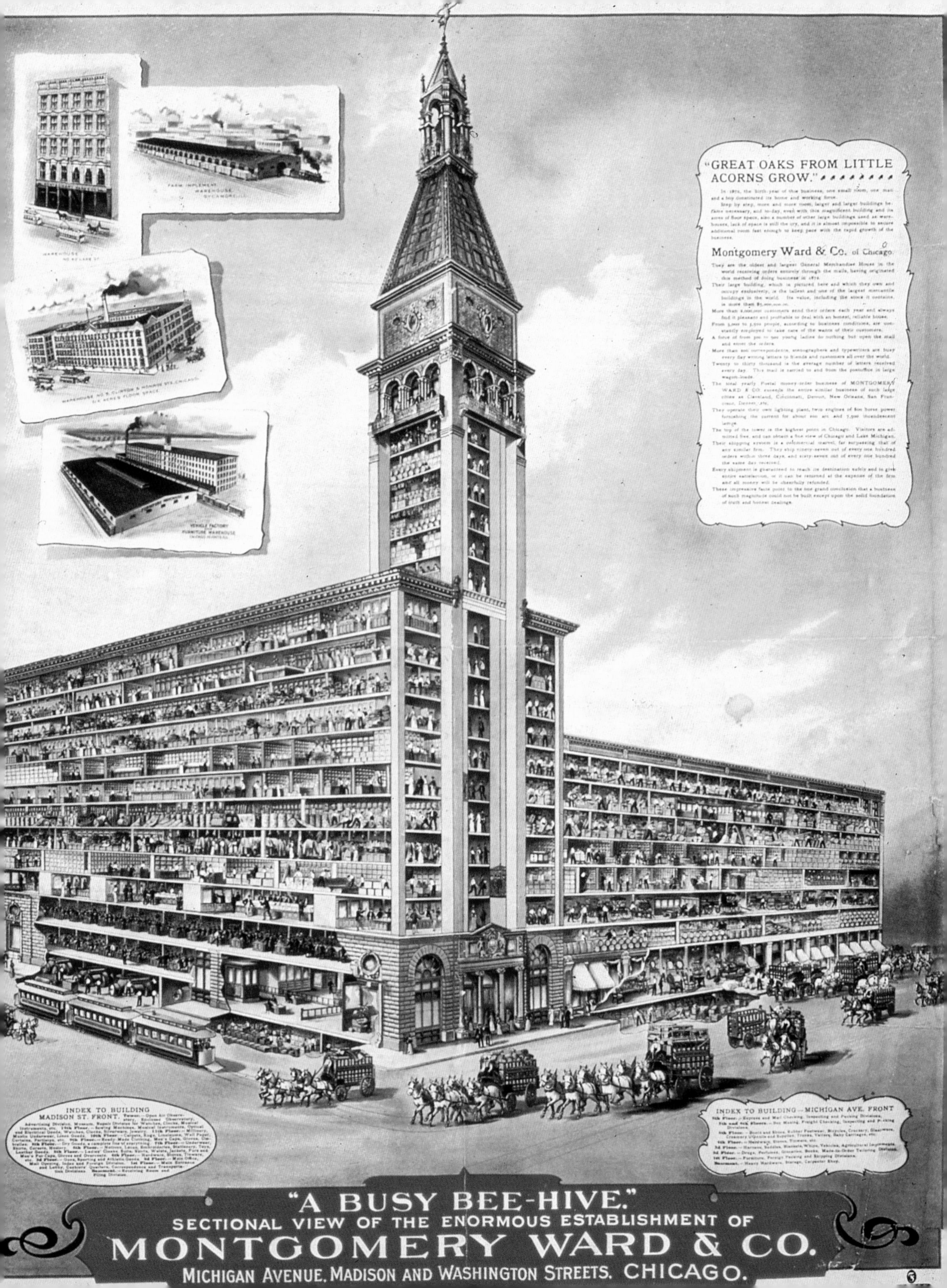
"GREAT OAKS FROM LITTLE ACORNS GROW."
Montgomery Ward & Co. of Chicago.
INDEX TO BUILDING
MADISON ST. FRONT.
INDEX TO BUILDING—MICHIGAN AVE. FRONT
"A BUSY BEE-HIVE."
SECTIONAL VIEW OF THE ENORMOUS ESTABLISHMENT OF
MONTGOMERY WARD & CO.
MICHIGAN AVENUE, MADISON AND WASHINGTON STREETS. CHICAGO.

260. Grain elevators by the Chicago River (Chicago Historical Society).

and considerable wealth to Boston, partly because of the trade which they did with the area, partly as a return on the capital which they continued to invest in it. But New York was by no means limited to being the link between Europe and the Midwest. By the end of the nineteenth century it was far and away the most important link between Europe and the whole of America, between North America and South America, and between different parts of North America, especially between New England and the southern states. Its harbour could take more and bigger ships than Boston, Philadelphia and Baltimore, and as ships grew in size it benefited accordingly. It was the terminus of railways spreading all over the United States. By 1891 it was exporting 39.2 percent and importing 63.6 percent of all United States exports and imports. Thirty transatlantic steamship lines ferried passengers and mail between it and Europe. As King's *Handbook of New York* put it, in the kind of language which was increasingly to be used about New York: 'the commerce and finance cannot be adequately measured in words or figures. The aggregate transactions every day reach an amount so stupendous that the figures are beyond comprehension.'[16]

Moreover, like Paris, Chicago and other cities at the centre of big distribution networks, New York had become a major manufacturing and industrial city. But, as the population grew, there was very limited space for this function of New York on Manhattan Island. Besides, although Manhattan was easily approachable by water, it was correspondingly hard to get at by land. One of the ironies of its history is that the city which by and large created the railway system of America had the greatest difficulty in connecting itself to the system. Railways had problems in getting there, and once they got there they had problems in penetrating the tightly built-up city. Before 1910 only two routes came into Manhattan. One came down the middle of what was then Fourth Avenue. Technically it had acquired a franchise to go downtown; but since by a local ordinance all steam-engines had to stop at 42nd Street, leaving the carriages to be pulled by horse the rest of the way, the terminus, not surprisingly, ended up at 42nd Street. The building of Grand Central Station here was to be of the greatest importance in the future development of New York. But no goods traffic came in by this line, because there was no suitable or adequate space for goods yards. The only railway line for goods traffic ran down the western side of Manhattan, along the Hudson. It had neither enough tracks nor a big enough downtown goods yard to provide adequate service for the wharves and warehouses in the southern half of Manhattan. Moreover, it was a surface line, and the rail traffic was continually interrupted by the cross traffic going from the wharves into the city.[17]

These two lines linked New York to the north and west. All trains from the south and south-west, including trains from Philadelphia and Washington, had to stop on the other side of the Hudson from New York, in Jersey City; by the end of the century nine lines had terminuses there. Various schemes to tunnel under the Hudson came to nothing, and it was not until 1910 that a railway tunnel was finally completed. It went under the Hudson, across Manhattan by way of Penn Station, and under the East River to Long Island. But this line still only carried passenger traffic.

Lack of space and transport facilities on Manhattan, combined with high land values there, meant that nearly all of New York's heavy industry and a good deal of its warehousing settled across the water, in the Bronx, Brooklyn, Queen's, Staten Island and Jersey City, where, apart from other conveniences land was cheap. All these areas were originally outside New York City; the city boundaries were extended to include Queen's, the Bronx, Brooklyn and Staten Island in 1898, but Jersey City, being in another state, was never absorbed. Commercially and financially, however, these districts across the water had long been dominated by Manhattan. By the end of the nineteenth century their waterfronts were lined with wharves, warehouses and factories, and most of the bigger, noisier and dirtier industries had settled there.

Sugar refineries and oil refineries packed into Brooklyn, shipbuilding yards into Staten Island; oil-refineries and other industries in Jersey City fouled its creeks and destroyed its profitable oyster-beds; the Bronx acquired railway repair-yards and also the Otis Works, which supplied lifts and lift-machinery to the world. Inland from the waterfront were the closely packed tenements of the industrial workers, and as tunnels and bridges gradually connected the outer boroughs with Manhattan more and more people who either could not afford or did not want to live there came to live in them, or spilled out from Manhattan to relax on the Long Island beaches and enjoy the roller-coasters and giant elephant of Coney Island. But for outsiders this was and is unknown and unvisited New York, in which 78 percent of its inhabitants were living in 1938.

So Manhattan, unlike Chicago, was left with all the dirtier and more unsightly activities of a great city safely across the water, and with one of the cleanest, clearest and freshest atmospheres of any of the great urban complexes of the world. There was still enough water traffic coming to it to line both sides of the island with wharves for at least half its length. Big steamships, including all the great passenger ships, used the more spacious Hudson River and wharved on the west side; grain barges from the west, and sailing ships, the numbers of which remained considerable well into the 1890s, crowded up the East River, especially to the wharves on South Street. The ferrying of goods and passengers to and fro from Manhattan to the outer boroughs added to the variety and amount of shipping which made the great open spaces of the harbour a romantic and extraordinary sight—and in the 1920s and 1930s the skyscrapers of Lower Manhattan rose out of the middle of it all. By then, however, the sailing ships had all but disappeared. King's *Handbook* described the scene in 1893: 'Almost every variety of vessel is found in these waters: the brilliant excursion-steamboats, melodious

261. Shipping on South Street by Wall Street ferry, New York, in 1865.

with band-music, and waving with flags and streamers; ark-like canal boats from the Great Lakes, distended with wheat and corn; the swift Norfolk schooners, redolent of fine tobacco and of early vegetables; oyster-boats from the Connecticut coast, small and pert in outlines and motion; huge full-rigged ships from Calcutta laden with indigo; sooty steam-barges from the Pennsylvania coal-regions; Nova Scotia brigs, laden with fine apples and potatoes; heavy old whalers, making port after long Arctic voyages; schooners from the West Indies and Honduras, crammed with tropical fruits; fishermen from the Grand Banks, heroes of the saltest northern seas; Mediterranean merchantmen, with rich cargoes from the Levant; and hundreds of other types . . .' including tugs, ferryboats, yachts belonging to New York millionaires, early oil tankers, curious tower-like structures serving as floating granaries, which supplemented the granaries on the mainland, and great passenger steamships from Europe.[18]

From the bowels of the last the immigrants poured out. For New York, in addition to importing and exporting anything from pianos to bananas, also imported cheap labour in quantities unequalled anywhere else at any time in the history of the world, and packed its human imports into tenements almost as tightly as it packed imported goods into warehouses. The supply came from those parts of Europe which were unable to produce enough food or afford enough American corn to feed their expanding populations. The Irish came first, followed by the Germans, Poles, Slavs, Italians, Greeks and Jews, the last mainly from Russia and victims of religious persecution rather than economic pressure. The immigrants worked on building sites, on the wharves, in the warehouses, in clothing factories, or in the heavy-industry factories across the rivers; or alternatively they were re-exported, especially to the stockyards, warehouses, factories and workshops of Chicago.

262. Warehouses of the 1870s in Broome Street, New York.

Behind the Manhattan wharves were steamship offices, bars, doss-houses, ship's outfitters and warehouses, especially the warehouses which stored goods sold by sample in the downtown exchanges, and which did not need to be near their markets. The warehouses closely connected with the shops, or where buyers wished personally to inspect the goods, were further inland. Much the biggest congregation of these were the dry-goods warehouses. Iron-fronted warehouses of the 1860s and 1870s lined, and still line, the streets of what is now SoHo, in order to be close to the shops and hotels on Broadway, and not too far from the wharves (or were actually on Broadway, where they often combined wholesale and retailing business); taller brick-fronted warehouses were built to the north in the 1880s and 1890s, following the fashionable shops as they moved uptown. The warehouses dealt in both American and European textiles, and were occupied by a mixture of commission or agency businesses, or by the New York show-houses of individual American mills. As they were visited by buyers, they were designed to inspire confidence and look handsome, like the warehouses of Manchester. The earlier ones arrayed their fronts with cast-iron Corinthian columns, arches and entablatures, bought ready-made from New York manufactories; but some of the later brick warehouses were just as splendid, and often rather more inventive in their architecture.[19]

Buying and selling textiles, making up textiles into clothing, and buying and selling clothing were collectively much the biggest source of employment in New York, and the textile workshops were the biggest single industry there. Whole buildings or the upper storeys of warehouses in the dry-goods area were occupied by workshops; but garment manufacture moved north like the shops, and ended up between 25th and 30th and 39th and 41st Streets, where it still is today. For a long time a great deal of the work was done in small workshops on the ground floors of tenements, or by families working at home in tenement flats. This small-scale manufacture of clothing, much of it for sale in small retail shops, was largely a Jewish affair, and was the main industry of the very large Jewish tenement area to the east of Broadway.[20]

There was not much space for the poor to live in Manhattan. Their tenements filled two long strips, a narrow one on the west and a much wider one on the east, between the buildings on the waterfront and the warehouses, shops, offices, entertainment areas and better housing in the centre. By the end of the century New York housing was certainly the most congested, and arguably the worst, in any large city in the world. The first immigrants who came in large numbers moved into what had been respectable eighteenth-century houses at the lower end of Manhattan, the occupants of which had moved to newer houses further north. The old houses suffered the habitual fate of houses which have gone down in the world, and became decayed and overcrowded slums. In New York the word 'tenement', which was to get such an ill name, legally meant

263. Tenements in the lower East Side, New York, with inner rooms lit by small light shafts.

any housing unit that was occupied by more than three families, rich or poor. In common speech, however, it was always used in the later nineteenth century to signify working-class flats. The first purpose-built tenements were put up around 1850, apparently with the best intentions. They were welcomed as being designed 'for the express purpose of rescuing the poor people from the dreadful rookeries they were then living in'. They were the so-called 'railroad tenements', which ran back as much as 240 feet from the main street frontage, and were chopped up into tiny two-room apartments, lit by narrow alleys to front and back. Many had no form of plumbing, and they soon became as bad slums as the buildings which they were designed to replace. The 'front-and-back' tenements which were evolved a little later were, if anything, worse, because their bedrooms often had no windows or ventilation of their own, and were no more than recesses at the back of the living rooms. A tenement-house law passed in 1879 made this illegal and limited the percentage of a lot which a tenement could occupy. A competition sponsored by the *Sanitary Engineer* for a plan to meet the new regulations produced the dumb-bell plan, which dominated the tenement world for the next forty years or more. Tenements built to this plan were rolled out by the thousand. A series of laws concerning maximum heights, or the need for fireproof construction over certain heights, kept them to a maximum of seven or eight storeys before 1901, and six storeys after it. No tenements had lifts.[21]

A Tenement House Commission was set up in 1900 and a Tenement House Act passed in 1901, administered by a new Tenement House Department. Among other requirements, it increased the minimum size of the courtyards. The pre-1901 tenements were grim to live in, especially in the hot New York summer and if the air shafts were used as refuse dumps, as they often were. As a report of the Department put it in 1903, 'Often at night, when the small rooms opening upon the air shaft are so close and ill-ventilated that sleep is impossible, mattresses are dragged upon the floor of the parlor and there the family sleep altogether in one room. In summer the small bedrooms are so hot and stifling that a large part of the tenement house population sleep on the roofs, the sidewalk and the fire escapes.'[22]

The description is reminiscent of Calcutta today, and it is interesting to compare densities. The density of Manhattan as a whole in 1894 was 143.2 people per acre, or 91,648 a square mile. The density of Paris at this period was 126.9 per acre, of Berlin 100.8. The density of Calcutta in 1961–3 was 101,010 people per square mile. The density of the Tenth Ward in New York in 1898 was 747 people per acre, or 478,080 a square mile; it was 'possibly the most crowded district in the world'.[23] Tenements in New York, of course, had many more storeys than Calcutta housing, which is seldom more than three or four storeys, and often lower. By 1900 there were 42,700 tenements in Manhattan, housing 1,585,000 out of its total population of around two million.

264. View in Mulberry Street, on the lower East Side, New York, in 1900.

Most purpose-built tenements were not slums, or at least they were one or two levels above the rotting private houses which had been turned into tenements, like the houses at the notorious Five Points in the Bowery. Much depended on the extent to which they were overcrowded. It may come as a surprise to those who have read about New York tenements actually to see them for the first time. As far as the street fronts are concerned, they are often handsome buildings. They are solidly built of brick, almost always have generous and richly detailed cornices, and often handsome window surrounds as well. The fire-escapes, which were made obligatory for multiple-family dwellings by the law of 1867, are often decorative objects, and their cumulative rhythm has its own extraordinary quality. Many visitors to New York remember the fire-escapes as much as the skyscrapers. They were much used for sitting out, hanging washing, talking to neighbours, and sleeping in hot weather. Since there was little inducement to stay inside a tenement flat, the neighbourhood streets were extremely lively.

As far as the members of polite New York society were concerned, the waterfront only existed when they took a steamer to Europe or a ferry to catch the train to Washington or Philadelphia, and the tenements did not exist at all. They lived an inland life, in a strip running down the centre of Manhattan. Their businesses, their houses and the shops, theatres and restaurants which they frequented were all in this.

In fact, offices and commerce, being able to pay higher prices for property than houses, exerted a constant pressure on the housing in the strip and pushed it, like toothpaste out of a tube, further and further north up the central strip. An alternative explanation is that the rich, as newer and more fashionable houses were built to the north, moved into them, and commerce and offices moved in to fill the gap. Probably both explanations have an element of truth. The most fashionable housing moved north

265. Fashionable 'turn-outs' in Central Park, New York. 'Sketched from the life' by T. Worth (Museum of the City of New York).

along Fifth Avenue, perhaps because Fifth Avenue started from Washington Square, which was the most fashionable residential square in New York in the 1840s. The speed at which it moved was remarkable, and can be accurately charted by following the peregrinations of the Astor family: from Lower Broadway between 1800 and the 1830s to Lafayette Place in the 1840s, Fifth Avenue around 34th Street in the 1880s and up Fifth Avenue to 84th Street (looking over Central Park) in the 1890s. The shops moved up Broadway, and then up Fifth and Sixth Avenues, following the fashionable people.

Central Park, once it had been laid out and had begun to mature and look attractive, was a magnet to help pull housing to the north. The great plan for the development of New York laid down in 1811 made minimum provision for public open space; and the largest space which it had provided, the 'Parade Ground' between 23rd and 34th Streets had long since been built over. But when large public parks began to be considered desirable, following on their provision in London and Paris, New York set aside a very large area in what was still unbuilt-on land for that purpose. The park was laid out by the landscape architect F. L. Olmsted and his partner Calvert Vaux from 1858. Olmsted wanted all classes in New York to enjoy Central Park, and created a skilfully varied mixture of attractions: winding footpaths tunneling under winding carriageways, secluded boulder-strewn woods, lakes for boating, fishing and skating, restaurants and look-out platforms, and a great public Mall for promenading under four rows of trees. But inevitably, owing to its position, Central Park in its earlier years was more used by the better off. The daily carriage promenade along its Fifth Avenue side became the equivalent of the Ring in Hyde Park in London. Inevitably, too, it was on this side of the park that the rich started to build their houses, as the culmination of their move up Fifth Avenue.

By the time that they reached Central Park, the rich of New York were quite amazingly rich. Moreover, as Moses King put it, 'Many enormously wealthy Americans have come here to live and enjoy the fortunes accumulated elsewhere.' To have a box in the New York opera, a carriage in which to drive up and down on Central Park, a house on Fifth Avenue, and a holiday cottage in the Louis-Quinze style in Newport became the summit of ambition for silver kings (and queens) from Nevada, steel kings from Pittsburg, corn kings from Chicago, rail kings from San Francisco and oil kings from Cleveland. All these rich people, native and immigrant, produced shops, hotels, restaurants and theatres. But so, too, did the very much larger numbers of merely prosperous New Yorkers, and the great numbers of people who came in on business, but wanted to see a show or two and have a good time while they were there. New York became America's biggest shopping and amusement centre.

While the multi-millionaires acquired their plots and built their brassy mansions on the Fifth Avenue side of the park, property speculators were busily promoting the West Side. This had obvious potentialities; not only Central Park to the east, but the Hudson River to the west, at a point where the wharves ended and the ground rose, so that any houses built there had a superb view across the river.

Two roads were laid out to attract buyers to the area, both of which broke the 1811 grid: a winding road along and above the river, known as Riverside Drive, and a nine mile avenue following the line of the old Bloomingdale Road, which was a continuation of Broadway, but was renamed the Boulevard (later to be called Broadway Boulevard, and today just numbered in with Broadway). The latter was laid out in about 1867, in imitation of the Paris boulevards, with 'two capital roadways, separated by a central strip of lawns, trees, and flowers. When finished, it will be one of the most beautiful driveways in the world . . . much of the way over high ground, commanding beautiful views.'[24] Commonwealth Avenue, in Boston's reclaimed Back Bay area, had already been laid out on the same French model in 1856.[25] But the Boulevard seems to have been the first road so named in America. It was to have an abundant progeny.

Some huge and opulent free-standing houses were built along Riverside Drive, and the rest of the area, after a slow start, was quickly and profitably developed in the 1880s with a mixture of terrace houses and apartment blocks. It was in this part of New York that the apartment block became domesticated in America. The first New York example had been built, to the designs of Richard M. Hunt, on 18th Street, between Third Avenue and Irving Place, and a few more were built in the 1870s, none of them very large. The early ones were called 'French flats', perhaps a name put in circulation by real estate agents, in order to free the buildings of any associations with tenements.[26] Owing to the high price of land and lack of space in Manhattan, and the American practice of living in hotels, it was inevitable that they would catch on in the end; some of them, in fact, started as residential hotels rather than apartment blocks. On the West Side the grandest examples were built overlooking the Park, where the Dakota (1881–4) was the first of a series which got bigger and more opulent decade by decade. 'Apartment-life', wrote Moses King, still slightly patronizingly, in 1893, 'is popular and to a certain extent fashionable. Even society countenances it, and a brownstone front is no longer indispensable to at least moderate social standing. And

266–7. Non-establishment and establishment millionaires on Fifth Avenue at Central Park, New York. The house of Senator Clark, a silver king from Nevada, at the end of its twenty-three year life, and (right) one of a pair of Vanderbilt houses.

as for wealthy folk who are not in society, they are taking more and more to apartments.'[27] 'Wealthy folk who are not in society' neatly categorizes the upper West Side; even the multi-millionaires along Riverside Drive were multi-millionaires who had not quite acquired the social confidence with which to launch themselves on Fifth Avenue.

There was very much less economic pressure to build apartment houses in Chicago, but none the less they began to be built in the 1870s, and in the end Chicago was to have examples as splendid as any in New York. They were undoubtedly built under New York influence, and possibly with New York capital. Chicago was always torn between a desire to imitate New York, and the desire to be different from it.

The most obvious single difference between the two cities was that the row house flourished in New York to the exclusion of the detached house, while in Chicago exactly the opposite was the case. Like any American new town from the seventeenth century onwards, Chicago started off as a collection of separate houses, each on its own plot. In the eighteenth century the force of fashion, combined with economics, had tended to replace such houses with terraces, but Chicago developed at a time when the detached suburban house was the new mecca of the middle classes, and as a result comparatively few terrace houses were built. There was none of New York's pressure from lack of space either. To north, west and south flat open space stretched as far as the eye could see. In fact, three rival communities of wealthier Chicagoans developed, on the north side, the west side and the south side, each thinking themselves better than the others. The south side had the advantage, however, that to get to it it was not necessary to cross the river and its industrial surroundings, or to face the delays of waiting for the bridges to open. Even before the great fire of 1870, Michigan and Prairie Avenues on the south side had established themselves as the streets where the richest people

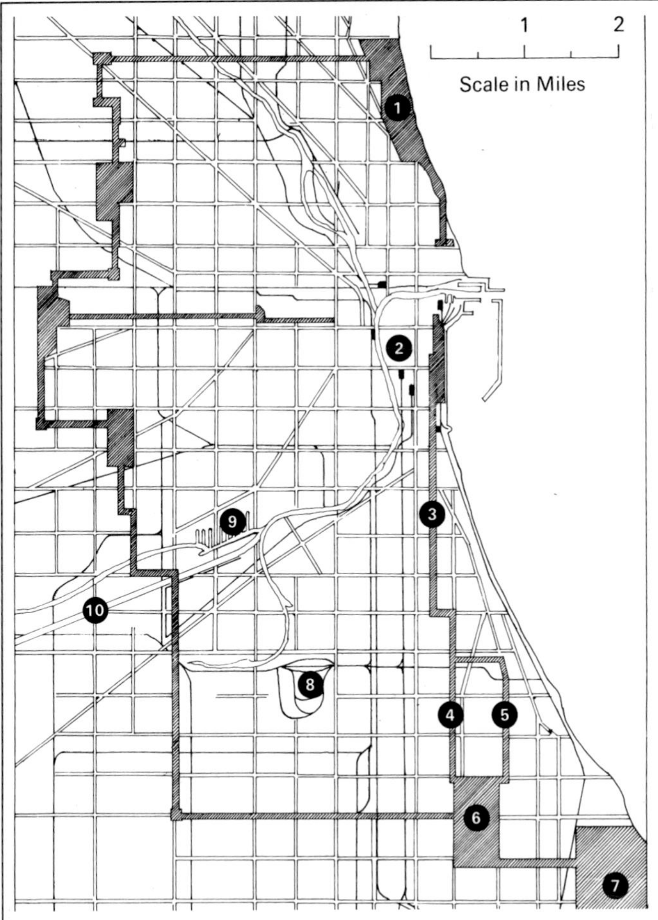

268. Chicago in about 1890, showing the park and boulevard system.
1. Lincoln Park
2. City Centre
3. Michigan Avenue
4. Grand Boulevard
5. Drexel Boulevard
6. Washington Park
7. Jackson Park (site of World's Fair)
8. Stock Yards
9. Timber Wharfs
10. Illinois Canal

lived. As Chicago boomed, something of a property developers' war developed, as the various real estate interests tried to attract the right sort of people to different previously undeveloped areas. As in New York, developers were very conscious of the part which a park and a nicely laid out and planted carriage promenade played in making an area fashionable.

At much the same time as Broadway Boulevard was laid out in New York, Chicago acquired a linked park-and-boulevard system of a remarkably ambitious nature. It was made possible by an unlikely coalition of idealists and real estate men. As early as 1849 a Chicago enthusiast, John S. Wright, had suggested that Chicago would soon need parks, and had written: 'of these parks I have a vision. They are all improved and connected with a wide avenue, extending to and along the lake shore on the north and south, and so surround the city with a magnificent chain of parks and parkways that have not their equal in the world.'[28]

Wright's idea came to fruition in 1869, when the Illinois General Assembly created independent South, West and North Park Commissions. Their members were appointed by the governor, given powers to buy land, collect taxes and borrow money, and required to lay out parks and linking 'boulevards' (specifically so called). By 1873 Sarah Lippincott enthusiastically described the 'complete circumvallation of the city which at no distant day will furnish one of the grandest drives in the world'.[29] But the boulevards had a cash value too; when Washington Street was declared one, land values along it doubled. By 1874 it was reported that 'the south and west parks have been for five years a stimulus to land speculation and investment and a key to the situation in the real estate market. With the backing of Chicago speculators, the success of the parks was assured.'[30]

The boulevards varied from 200 to 400 feet in width. Commercial traffic was not allowed on them, and most of them had a middle drive for carriages, and rides for horses to either side, or alternatively a middle strip of parkland. When the system was laid out it was in completely open country. Some portions were more successful than others. Grand and Drexel Boulevards immediately became fashionable, linking as they did the already fashionable Michigan Avenue on the north to Washington Park, where the racecourse was, on the south. This was where the Chicagoans who imitated smart New York promenaded. 'There the richly attired ladies and stylish looking gentlemen reigned supreme, and the common people did not block their way.'[31] On one Sunday afternoon in 1881 it was reported that 4,700 carriages moved south on Grand Boulevard.[32] In winter-time the promenaders changed over to sledges.

The North Siders had the advantage, however, of being able to promenade along the lake, which was blocked by the railway on the south side. Lake Shore Drive, which joined Lincoln Park to the centre, was laid out as a boulevard in the 1870s, and in the 1880s and 1890s was extended through the park and up to Evanston. The big houses built in the 1880s and 1890s on southern Lake Shore Drive, and on Astor Street behind it, were as splendid as any in Chicago: the area soon became known as the Gold Coast. The hefty granite houses in these smart sections of Chicago were built detached, semi-detached or in terraces; cumulatively they were the nearest Chicago came to the closely built-up streets where the rich lived in New York.

In contrast to those of the well-off who lived as close to the centre as they respectably could were those who lived as far away as the available transport could conveniently take them. They took the train in the evening and went off to what they liked to think of as villages, usually with rural-sounding names; Lake Forest, Lake Bluff, Riverside, River Forest, Highland Park, Deerfield, Oak Park and so on. Many of these areas started as places to which people removed in the summer, and developed into places where people lived all the year round. Lake Forest, one of the earliest of the settlements, was also one of the furthest out. It was twenty-five miles from the centre, and was laid out on a pattern of winding roads in 1857. Riverside, laid out by F. W. Olmsted in 1869, also had winding roads, and open greens running between the lines of houses. But variations on a grid were more common, with wide streets planted with avenues of trees, and houses a little further apart, to give a country feel.[33] Settlements away from the lake were plugged for 'immunity from the effects of the raw and chilling lake winds', settlements on it were 'kissed on one cheek by Michigan's waves, fanned from behind by prairie breezes, jeweled with happy homesteads set in waving green, and wreathed about with prairie wild flowers'. This was Evanston, as described in 1891.[34] However, Chicago inexorably advanced up to the boulevards, beyond them and finally up to and beyond the commuting villages. The advance was made possible by steadily improving transport: horse buses from 1850, horse trams from 1858, cable-cars from 1882, electric cars from the late 1880s and an elevated railway from 1890. Developments consisted mostly of detached houses, some of brick but more of timber, with a mixture of small brick apartment blocks, usually three storeys high.

Chicago tenements bore no relation to New York ones. Even the very poor lived superficially like the better off, in detached timber houses. The differences were that houses meant to be lived in by one family were crammed to bursting with five or six; that further rows of timber houses had often been built in their back yards; and that few of the houses had proper sanitation and neither the houses nor the roads were maintained. The areas to the west of the river and around the stockyards were jammed with these houses, interspersed with saloon bars, cheap shops and restaurants, and pawnbrokers. The stockyards, the lumberyards and the garment industry were the main employers of their inhabitants. Successive waves of immigrants moved into them, and moved on as soon as they acquired enough money to do so, leaving the houses in even worse condition for the next wave. On the near west side after 1870 'the Americans largely gave place to the Irish and the Germans, who in turn receded before the advancing host of Russian Jews and Italians, who still later gave way before the Greeks and Bulgarians, who are now in turn being superseded by Mexicans and Negroes'.[35] In the neighbourhood of the stockyards the Irish gave way to Germans, and the Germans to Slovaks, Poles and Lithuanians. Many of the houses and tenements belonged to the more successful members of the nationalities who lived there, or to those who had arrived with a little capital; some proved appallingly bad landlords. As the various nationalities went up in the world, they moved to the west, north-west or south-west, into newer,

269. Tenements on upper West Side, Chicago.

better maintained and less crowded houses and apartment blocks. Out of the whole great belt of low housing that resulted, huge churches rose every few hundred yards, for even the Catholics worshipped by nationalities, in Polish, Italian, Irish and Slovak churches. The result had (and still has) a curiously medieval effect.

Up to the 1880s the skyline of the central areas in both Chicago and New York consisted of church spires or domes interspersed with the domes, cupolas or towers of public buildings and, in Chicago, of rival railway stations. In 1891 Maitland's American Standard Dictionary was the first known dictionary to include the word 'skyscraper': 'a very tall building such as now are being built in Chicago'. A few years later 'and New York' could have been added to the definition. By 1920 the churches and public buildings had been submerged by the rising tide of skyscrapers in both cities: the downtown silhouette which was ultimately to be exported all over the world had arrived.[36]

The skyscraper is widely believed to have resulted from two main forces: a technological breakthrough combined with a land shortage. About the former there is no doubt. When Elisha Graves Otis stood on top of his suspended lift at the American Institute Fair at New York in 1854 and cut its cable, he was demonstrating more than a safety device: he was also making dramatically clear that one of the main obstacles to buildings growing high had been removed. The invention of the telephone in 1876 got rid of

270. Lower Manhattan seen across Brooklyn Bridge, New York.

another obstacle. In 1884 William Le Baron Jenney, a Chicago architect who had had an engineering training in Paris, worked out the steel-frame construction that was to make very high buildings structurally possible and high buildings of all kinds much cheaper, along with the foundation system that enabled them to be built in the boggy ground of Chicago.

The land-shortage theory is superficially attractive. In New York, Wall Street was at the tip of an island; the centre of Chicago was hemmed into a small area by the river and the railway yards. But it does not, in fact, bear looking into.

Offices are in a very strong position to acquire premises because, above the ground floor (where successful shops can pay more), they can afford to pay much higher rents than any other form of accommodation. A businessman in one room a few square feet in area can earn as much money as a factory full of heavy machinery or a warehouse full of merchandise, and afford to pay rents which would be unthinkable for all but a multi-millionaire to pay for an apartment or a house. For the same reason, the business district of a city needs, proportionately to the money which it earns, very much less space than the commercial or residential district.

In fact, both the New York and Chicago business districts would have had no great difficulty in expanding. One can stand on Brooklyn Bridge today and look over to where the cliffs of Wall Street drop suddenly into a belt of four- or five-storey buildings along Pearl Street, Water Street, Front Street and South Street. By 1900 the collapse of business from sailing ships along the South Street wharves had already made this a run-down area ripe for redevelopment. But it was not redeveloped. Similarly, the Chicago business area could easily have expanded to the south, where an area of cheap bars and brothels was equally vulnerable to redevelopment.

Chicago buildings started to go high simply because, once it was technically feasible,

271. Downtown from the Chicago railway yards in 1941.

the financial situation in downtown Chicago was extremely propitious for building them. Their appearance was not a sign that Chicago was more adventurous than the East Coast cities, for in fact the capital to build them came mainly from Boston and New York. Astute businessmen in those cities realized what was in it for them. Office rents in Chicago were high (though not as high as in New York) because business was booming on the Chicago Stock Exchange and in the Board of Trade (which in spite of its confusing name was effectively the corn exchange); as was always the case in business areas, the businessmen wanted to be within a few minutes walk of the relevant exchange. In addition, central area property could be picked up unusually cheaply. The large-scale rebuilding after the 1870 fire had been followed by a slump in 1873, resulting in large numbers of foreclosures on mortgaged properties. Around 1879 the mortgage companies, having completed the necessary legal procedures, started to sell off the properties at bargain prices. Investors, as a result, had the opportunity of building ten storeys and upwards on land which had sold, not just for six-storey prices, but for cheap six-storey prices.[37] It was not surprising that in 1880 Peter Brooks, the Boston financier, wrote to his Chicago agent that 'Tall buildings will pay well in Chicago hereafter, and sooner or later a way will be made to erect them'.[38] The Brooks family built the ten-storey Montauk Building in 1882, and the sixteen-storey Monadmock Building in 1891. Both had outer walls of conventional masonry construction; the Monadmock was the highest such building ever to be built, and its extension built in 1893 went over to steel-cage construction. Meanwhile, the pioneer steel-cage Home Insurance Building had been built in 1884–5 ten-storeys high as the Chicago branch of a New York insurance company. From the late 1880s up till 1893 buildings of from twelve to sixteen storeys went up all over central Chicago in considerable numbers. Most of the money to build them came from the East Coast, in the form of loans, direct promotions, or investment by East Coast banks and insurance companies in building bonds issued for individual buildings.

High buildings in New York kept step with the Chicago ones as far as height was concerned, but were ten years behind in going over to the complete skeleton frame. High masonry buildings had in fact preceded Chicago: the ten-storey Equitable Life Assurance Building in 1868–70, the ten-storey Western Union Telegraph Building in 1873–5, the eleven-storey Tribune Building in 1873–5. The sixteen-storey World Building, of mixed load-bearing masonry and steel-frame construction, was the highest office building in the world when it was built in 1889–90. The Manhattan Life Insurance Building, built in 1893–4, was twenty storeys high, including the tower, and from then on New York skyscrapers soared away from Chicago ones in height.

It has become the convention to compare the stripped elegance of the Chicago skyscrapers with the columns, domes and spires of the New York ones, to the detriment of the latter. The difference in style in fact reflects the different situations in the two cities. New York was a head-office city and Chicago a branch-office one. The East Coast investors who financed the Chicago skyscrapers wanted the maximum return on their investment, and no frills. As H. B. Fuller makes his architect complain in his novel on a Chicago skyscraper, *The Cliff Dwellers*, published in 1893: 'over the whole thing hovers incessantly the demon of Nine-per-cent'.[39] Nine percent was a wonderfully good return in a society where money could be borrowed at five or five and a half percent; but to get it it was necessary for the building to be no more than an iron cage with the necessary services running through it, cheaply clad in tile, brick or terra-cotta. When the client wished to make more of a splash, the 'Chicago style' was often thrown out of the window: to advertise the virtues of temperance the firm which had designed some of the simplest and most elegant of the early skyscrapers provided the Women's Christian Temperance Union with one ebulliently tricked out with turrets, machicolations, steep roofs and dormer windows.[40]

All the early New York high buildings were designed to make a splash rather than to give the maximum commercial return. They were the headquarters of insurance companies, of newspapers, and of cable or telegraph companies which were often in competition with each other, and knew the value of height, splendour and a memorable silhouette in establishing their image or increasing their sales. Advertising skyscrapers continued to figure prominently in New York. The whole world could instantaneously recognize the silhouette of the Singer Building (1902), the Woolworth Building (1911) and the Chrysler Building (1930). The Singer Building is said to have paid for its construction by one year's extra sale of sewing machines in Asia alone. The contractor who built the Woolworth Building was deeply upset on his client's behalf because he knew that as an investment it could never make a proper return. 'Then Mr Woolworth let me into his secret—that there would be an enormous hidden profit outweighing any loss. He confessed that the Woolworth Building was going to be like a giant signboard to advertise around the world his spreading chain of five-and-ten-cent stores.'[41]

Not all New York skyscrapers were built as headquarter buildings; many were constructed as straightforward investments. But it was the brand-image buildings which set the style; so that whereas in Chicago some, at any rate, of the advertising skyscrapers were merely more elaborate versions of the investment ones, in New York it tended to be the other way round.

272–4. Three early skyscrapers: (left to right) Tacoma Building, Chicago (Holabird and Roche, 1887–9); Metropolitan Life Tower, New York (N. Lebrun and Son, 1906–9); Singer Building, New York (Ernest Flagg, 1908).

The first skyscraper boom in Chicago lasted only two years. In 1893 buildings over ten storeys high were prohibited there by law. The law seems to have passed easily enough, for several pressure groups were in favour of it. Owners of property in the immediate neighbourhood of the business area wanted to stop it expanding vertically in order to encourage it to expand laterally. Owners of undeveloped sites in the business area objected to being assessed for taxes on the basis of their sixteen-storey potentiality. Owners of existing skyscrapers wanted to keep a monopoly. In fact, office space had been over-supplied, and rents were falling as a result. The height limit was raised to 260 feet in 1902, and reduced to 200 feet in 1911, as a result of over-supply following another building boom.

This stop–go system reflected the fact that Chicago was only rich enough to support a limited number of skyscrapers. New York, being far bigger and richer than Chicago, could support many more and much bigger ones. It was also easier to raise money there. There was an enormous amount of capital of all kinds available in New York, and property developers became adept at finding new ways of tapping it. The main lenders were the savings banks and the insurance companies. Insurance had become a very big business in America. By 1910 the biggest company dealing in it, and the biggest insurance lender in the New York property market, was the Metropolitan Life Insurance Company. In 1910 the insurance which it had in force amounted to $2,216 million, nearly ten times the amount held by any one life insurance company in 1870, and three times as large as the largest in 1870 (its insurance out was to climb to over $20,000 million by 1935). In 1909–10 it moved into a temple in the sky on the upper storeys of its new 700-foot office block which for a short time was the world's tallest building. It proudly symbolized both the prosperity of Metropolitan Life and the part it was playing in the creation of New York.[42]

The height of buildings related directly to site value (but the desire to advertise or compete could push buildings up beyond their economic height). The site value related to the rents available in the area. In 1903 the difference in rents between Chicago and New York resulted in office land being four times as expensive in the latter, so that its office buildings were inevitably higher.[43] Land with low buildings on it in expensive areas sold for prices which forced the purchaser to rebuild, if he wanted an economic

275. Looking from Brooklyn Bridge across South Street to the towers of Wall Street, New York.

276. (right) The grid and the hills collide, at San Francisco.

return on his money. Owners of low buildings were equally under pressure to sell or redevelop, because buildings were taxed on the basis of the potential value of the site. Real estate manuals published tables giving the recommended height for buildings, depending on the land value. Values altered dramatically from area to area. The Department of Taxes issued land value maps for the purposes of assessment. In 1910 the highest value shown in Wall Street was $24,750 a foot frontage, whereas in and around South Street, a few blocks away, they varied between $800 and $1,200; closeness to the stock exchange was the controlling factor.[44]

In 1916 a new Building Zone Regulation laid down that 'no building shall be erected in excess of twice the width of the street, but for each one foot that the building or a portion of it sets back from the street line, four feet shall be added to the height limit'. Previously there had been no height limit on office buildings; now their developers could still effectively build them any height they liked as long as they worked out the set-backs. The distinctive skyscraper silhouette of the 1920s and 1930s was the result. From 1897 apartment blocks were allowed to be built up to 150 feet high in streets over 79 feet wide, and 100 feet high in streets under 80 feet wide, providing that they had lifts and full fireproofing, which in effect meant providing they were apartments for the well-off, not working-class tenements. Apartment blocks looking over open ground, such as Central Park, had no height limit.[45]

Apart from apartment blocks, there was effectively no height limit on New York buildings, so that an aerial view of Manhattan was (and to a large extent still is) a three-dimensional diagram of property values and rent levels. By 1910 manufacturing lofts were being built up to fifteen storeys high, and by the 1920s up to twenty-four storeys. By 1930 the economic height limit for apartment blocks free of zoning restrictions was about twenty storeys. The most sensational new phenomenon of the 1920s and 1930s was the development of the area round Grand Central Station as an alternative business district for headquarters of corporations, real estate offices and other firms which did not need to be close to the downtown exchanges.

In 1930 it was calculated that the optimum height for an office building with ground-floor shops opposite Grand Central Station was sixty-three storeys.[46] The Chrysler Building was built seventy-seven storeys high a block away in 1929–30, but in its case the advertising element pushed it well above the economic optimum. The Grand Central Station area and Wall Street developed as two islands of very tall buildings, surrounded by much larger areas of lower, though in some areas far from low, buildings. Of course the most prestigious gambit was to build a low building on a very expensive site, to show how rich one was.

16 Cities Round the World

All over the world cities were exploding in size, for the same kind of reasons as those which had caused London, Paris and New York to explode. They had to find ways of dealing with their new size and their huge new populations, and they all drew on the three great cities for ideas. City after city equipped itself with London-style clubs, parks and suburbs, Paris-style boulevards, cafés, apartment blocks and department stores, and New York-style hotels, prisons, office blocks and gridded street plans, the last sometimes applied with cheerful disregard of the rise and fall of the land. More adventurous places acquired a few New York-style skyscrapers or a Paris-style avant-garde, and all of them acquired grand new public buildings. They grew into great, teeming smoky cities, where trains rumbled into cavernous railway stations, trams clanked and clanged through streets of high buildings, crowds jammed the cafés, bars and theatres, gas-light flared through shop windows or onto wet pavements, and the proud towers of town halls or parliament buildings rose over all. All the cities had similar problems, which they seldom entirely solved but to which they never succumbed. They experienced fires, epidemics and hunger, but no huge holocausts of death by starvation or the plague, and only one fire which destroyed almost an entire city. They produced stone-carvings by the acre, and statues by the gross, but also hospitals, drains, police and fire services, sewage-systems and waterworks.

The flow of influences was neither regular nor always direct. On the whole, public parks came from England by way of Paris, and tended to have a strong Third Empire strain in them; and once Cesar Ritz had given his Parisian imprint to the hotel it was imitated round the world, even in America, from where the great hotel had originated. America had its own tradition of big stores, which derived from the wholesale-cum-retail warehouse of many separate floors, rather than the galleried halls of the bazaar. When Alexander Stewart's great Marble Dry Goods Store opened on Broadway in New York in 1848 it was grander than any store then existing in Paris: none the less Parisian influence was soon visible in the fashion shows (the first in America) which were given there in a 'Ladies' Parlor' lined with full-length mirrors imported from Paris.[1] Ultimately and inevitably Paris-style galleried halls and grand staircases arrived in America, but they were confined to a minority of stores, some of which, like the City of Paris in San Francisco, acknowledged their sources. In England the big department store was a comparatively late arrival, and scarcely existed as a building-type before 1900. Fire regulations tended to keep out grand stairs and galleried halls. There was reason behind them, for Paris-style stores were a serious fire hazard.

The English suburb caught on much more in some countries than in others. In America it was an immediate and lasting success. It arrived later in Germany, but by the end of the nineteenth century Charlottenburg, to the west of the Tiergarten, was developing a villa suburb which was rapidly becoming the most fashionable residential area of Berlin (although in fact a separate borough until 1920), and all German cities of any size had their villa areas. Both Vienna and Paris had villa suburbs, and there were some wild and wonderful houses in them, but in neither city did they compete in size or fashion with the mixture of apartments and grand private palaces in the centre. Villas proliferated in Mediterranean seaside resorts, but both the old and new rich of the older Italian towns continued to live in the centre, even in Milan, which was the city most in key with developments in northern Europe. When Pirelli made his fortune as a rubber manufacturer he moved into the centre from his house by the works in the outskirts, exactly the opposite of what his equivalents had been doing in Manchester.[2]

Continental cities had their own tradition of apartment blocks, although in most cities they increasingly showed signs of French influence. In America, apartment blocks were a French import, and they were called 'apartments' accordingly. In England the first big blocks of flats for middle- or upper-class occupation began to appear in the mid-nineteenth century, under French influence, and from the 1880s onward they were built in considerable numbers, especially in London. But it was only in the 1920s and 1930s that they caught on to anything like the extent which they had in America, and then the fashion came from America rather than France.

The tree-planted boulevard had existed in Paris since the seventeenth century, and its influence had been felt long before Haussmann's transformation of the city. But the

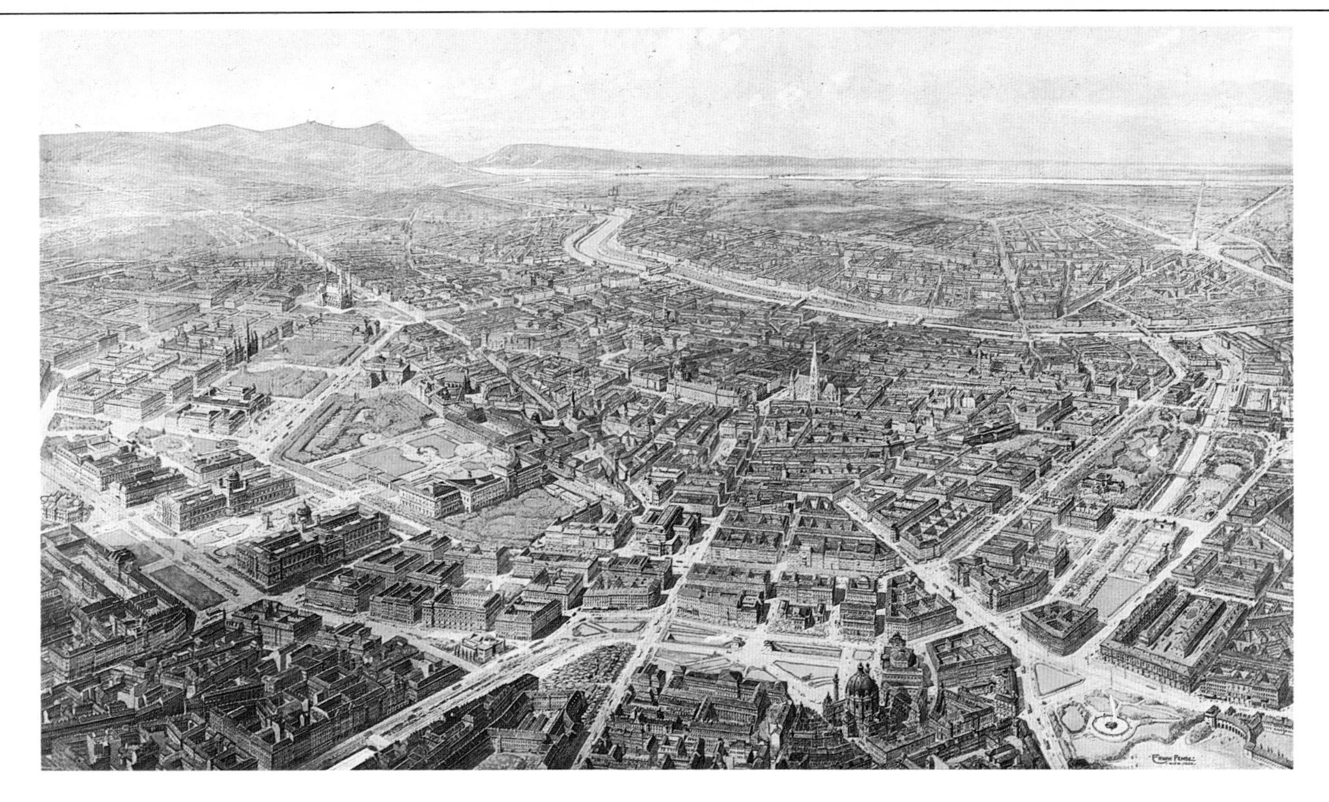

277. A bird's-eye view of the Vienna Ring. By Franz Pendl (Museen der Stadt Wien).

fame and prestige of Paris as he left it gave a great boost to the provision of broad tree-lined streets, often with bridle-paths and strips of parkland or planting incorporated in the Haussmann manner; the roads, like his, often provided routes for tram-lines, which sometimes pushed out the bridle-paths. These new roads could be called either 'boulevards' or 'avenues', as indeed Haussmann's had been. In 1859, for instance, the fortifications of Antwerp were demolished, not because the city was no longer considered to need fortifications but because a ring of much more elaborate ones was constructed farther out. The old tree-lined walks along the original rampart disappeared, and in their place a ring of Haussmann-style avenues appeared. Similar improvements were carried out in cities all over Europe: in Brussels, for instance, the boulevards already formed in the old Paris style around 1820 were Haussmannized later on in the century; in Liège a broad boulevard and a small park were formed by filling in a former branch and dock of the River Meuse.[3]

Most European boulevards, or boulevard-style avenues, were laid out through areas which were already built up. In America, although the idea, the configuration and the name came from France, boulevards were put to a different use, and laid out on unbuilt-on land, in order to attract houses, if possible the houses of the rich. All these roads had the common feature of a strip of planting down the centre of the roadway, or alternatively two strips, one to either side; the planted area often incorporated a ride for horses. They were sometimes called boulevards, but just as often avenues. Most American cities acquired at least one where the best people had their homes—like Summit Avenue in St Paul, Minnesota, where the rich Protestants lived and snubbed the Catholic Scott Fitzgerald and his family.[4]

Much the grandest new boulevard layout in Europe after Haussmann's was the Ring in Vienna.[5] The demolition of the city's seventeenth-century fortifications and the laying-out of the ground which they and their esplanade had occupied was decreed by the Emperor Franz Josef on 20 December 1857. A plan was finally settled on in 1859: the Ringstrasse was opened in 1865, but building went on into the 1880s. It is hard not to regret the great green belt around the walls, and the walks along the top of them, which were lost in consequence. But by redeveloping them Vienna immediately put herself on a par with Paris as a great modern city, and overtook London or any other of the capital cities of the world. The space involved was very large and could without difficulty accommodate a series of grand new public buildings, large residential areas for the well-off, and parks, squares and open spaces. Moreover, developing it had none of the financial problems of redeveloping Paris; the ground was vacant, and a large part of the cost could be raised by selling off building sites.

The Parisian Victor Tissot, visiting Vienna around 1880, complacently announced that everything there imitated Paris: he found French plays, French dances, French fashions, and 'all the German hairdressers call themselves Hippolyte'. 'Whatever people say, and whatever they do', he concluded, 'the influence of Paris reigns supreme, because it is the city of good taste, wealth and the arts.'[6] But, although Parisian influence was obviously at work, the Ring was by no means a copy. It was a clever piece of planning even if too little of the gaiety of the Viennese cafés found a way into its architecture.

The new development was based on two circular roads, the inner and grander Ringstrasse and the outer Lastenstrasse. Instead of all the public buildings being grouped together, the characteristics of the different parts of the old, inner city were projected into the Ring, so that different portions of it assumed different characteristics, each with its relevant public buildings and accommodation for the relevant people to live in as well as to work. The Ringstrasse started, for instance, with textile warehouses and offices on the Danube Canal; then came the commercial and financial section, centred round the new exchange; then the university; then a civic and national government section, around the new town hall and parliament house; then a museums section, with the great buildings of the Kunsthistorisches and Naturalhistorisches Museums looking at each other across a square. From the university to the museums was the most concentrated line of public buildings, since this was the portion nearest to the Hofburg, the royal palace. After that the Ring was running along the part of the city where most of the baroque palaces of the wealthy still were, and it changed character accordingly: here, well spaced out, were the opera house, the Kursalon, which was Vienna's equivalent of an assembly rooms, the park, and the Flower Hall, venue for the flower shows and an annual ball which was one of the landmarks of the Vienna season. In between were the big hotels, the grandest apartment blocks, and the stretch of the Ringstrasse known as the Corso (next to the Schwarzenbergplatz) which became the pedestrian promenade area for Vienna society.

In the gaps between public buildings all round the Ringstrasse, in the new streets off it, and on the outer circuit, serried ranks of new apartments were built, sometimes over ground-floor shops or offices, sometimes occupying whole buildings. There were a very few grand single houses, inevitably in the fashionable section and occupied by a couple of archdukes and a prince or two. Also, inevitably, in this section were the so-called 'Zinspalaste', or tenement palaces, where the main floor was occupied by a high-ceilinged and sumptuously decorated apartment with a grand staircase leading up to it, and the rest was let off in less pretentious apartments. The social status of the residents in the rest of the Ring varied according to the character of each section; when residents of the financial quarter grew rich enough, they usually moved over to the fashionable side. Most of the old nobility continued to live in their town palaces

278. The Ring, by the Parliament House and Town Hall, Vienna (Museen der Stadt Wien).

within the Ring or their garden palaces outside it, but enough moved into the right section of the Ring to give it the required social cachet.

Outside New York and Chicago the skyscraper spread slowly and in small numbers; outside North America it scarcely existed before the 1950s. Two forces worked against it, economics and the law. There were not many cities which had sufficiently large office zones and sufficient prosperity as a financial centre to raise rents to the level at which skyscrapers became an economic investment. In America, where the skyscraper was regarded with pride as a national product, most big cities acquired a handful of them between 1900 and 1940, but they were often built for prestige or advertisement rather than economic return, and outside New York and Chicago no American city had more than a handful of buildings over twenty storeys tall before 1940.

In Europe the three main financial centres, London, Paris and Berlin, which could have afforded skyscrapers, were all capital cities, and a sense of hierarchy led to high buildings being prohibited by law: it was for long unthinkable that cathedrals, palaces or public buildings should be overshadowed by commercial structures. In Berlin height limit was related to street width, but the maximum height was 72 feet.[7] In Paris there was a similar relationship; the maximum height to the cornice line was fixed at 20 metres from 1859 to 1967, although the permissible height above the cornice was periodically raised, allowing a total height of up to 25 metres in 1859 which had risen in stages to 30 metres by 1902.[8] The modest increase allowed in 1902 was bitterly criticized at the time as permitting 'great buildings *à l'américaine*, these skyscrapers which insolently stretch up to dominate a place which is not made for them'. In 1913 it was forecast that soon 'we shall see the humiliated, miserable appearance that will be offered by the Louvre, the Arc de Triomphe, the Hôtel de Ville, the Luxembourg Palace, Notre Dame . . .'.[9] The permitted total height in the centre was raised by a mere metre in 1967, although 37 metres was allowed in the outlying arrondissements.[10]

In London there were no height regulations before 1895, and one skyscraper—or what seemed a skyscraper to English eyes—was erected in 1875–89, in the form of an unlovely tower of flats known as Queen Anne's Mansions, at the end of Queen Anne's

279–80. The elephant house in the zoo, *c.* 1850, and (right) the main hall of the Antwerp railway station, *c.* 1900.

Gate in Westminster. It was fourteen storeys and 171 feet high. Queen Victoria was furious, because it looked down on Buckingham Palace. It was partly as a result of her representations that when a new London Building Act was passed in 1894, building heights were limited to a total of 80 feet up to the cornice line, and 20 feet above it.[11]

It was, of course, quite acceptable for public buildings of sufficient importance to raise their spires or domes above this level. By the end of the nineteenth century there was an accepted inventory of public buildings which all cities of any pretensions had to have and which they endeavoured to build as grandly as possible: a town hall, law courts, exchange, opera house or big theatre, at least one museum or art gallery, at least one grand railway station, a customs house, if the city was a port, and, in the case of a national capital, a royal residence or residence of head of state, parliament house and one or more big ministries. All of them had at least one public park, as large and as central as possible, and most of them had a zoological garden.

Most of these building types had a history going back into the eighteenth century and beyond. Museums and art galleries had assumed a new function and importance, however. They had started as buildings—or, more often, portions of buildings—in which rulers kept their collections; they developed into buildings which rulers regularly opened to the respectable segment of the public; they finally emerged as buildings belonging to the city or the nation, often on the basis of a royal collection presented to the nation, or commandeered by it. The ideal behind the last stage was expressed in a memorandum written by Aloys Hirt for Friedrich Wilhelm of Prussia in 1798. Works of art are 'a heritage for the whole of mankind . . . Only by making them public and uniting them in display can they become the object of true study, and every result obtained from this is a new gain for the common good of mankind.'[12]

By 1798 two great public collections already existed. In 1753 nearly £100,000 had been raised in England by public lottery with which to buy and house the large but miscellaneous collection left on option to the nation by Sir Hans Sloane. The collection

281. Franz Krüger. *Parade, Berlin, 1837* (Staatliche Museen zu Berlin (DDR) National-Galerie).

was installed in the late seventeenth-century Montagu House in Bloomsbury. It was supported by grants from Parliament and added to from time to time; but it was badly arranged and until 1805 access was only by written application and guided tour. The national museum in the Louvre, founded by decree of the National Assembly in 1793, was a more recognizable ancestor of the great public museums of the nineteenth and twentieth centuries. The booty of foreign wars poured into it, and it rapidly became very large, filled with contents of superb quality, regularly open free to the public and attended in large numbers (as opposed to the one hundred and twenty a day coming to the British Museum at peak periods in 1810). Its Grande Galerie, 1332 feet long, was approached by an almost equally grand staircase. In 1815 many of the contents were removed, but by then an international pattern had been set.[13]

Grandiose designs for museums, along with equally grand designs for public libraries, academies, exchanges and hospitals, had featured prominently in the designs put in for the Grand Prix of the Academy of Architecture in Paris in the 1770s and 1780s. The concept of great buildings erected at public expense for the good of humanity was a product of the French Enlightenment. During the wars that followed on the French Revolution, the good of humanity became overlaid with concepts of national glory and honour. It was during the wars that statues of national heroes and monuments to national glory first began to join or replace the statues of monarchs or monuments erected to them which for long had been the only commemorative features of cities. There had always been an element of rivalry between cities, but it grew stronger. A city's public buildings were symbols of the might of the law, the dignity of government, the prosperity of commerce and the greatness of the human spirit; they were often a necessary result of growing populations and growing administrative functions taken on by government; but they were also a sign that the city was keeping up with, or doing better than, other cities and other capitals. Grand processional ways fulfilled a similar function; existing roads were adapted, or new ones built, in order to provide them.

282. The Parliament House (Imre Steindle, 1882–1902), Budapest.

Vienna could make use of the space from its demolished fortifications to provide itself with all the space for public buildings which it needed. In Bombay part of the esplanade of the fort was used to provide sites for new Gothic law courts, secretariat and university of Venetian magnificence. But other cities had problems in finding suitable sites and adequate space for buildings which traditionally were sited in the centre. The river was sometimes exploited: the French Foreign Office on the Quai D'Orsay joined the great public buildings already on the Seine, the Italian Palazzo di Giustizia was built on a new quay, the Lungotevere, which was built along the Tiber in the 1870s and 1880s, and the Hungarian Parliament House rose between 1882 and 1902 on the banks of the Danube. The Victoria Embankment, constructed in 1864–70, gave London its first riverside quay of any length, and there were projects for building new law courts and a new opera house on it, to join Somerset House and the Houses of Parliament and form an enfilade of grand public buildings along the Thames.[14] The projects came to nothing; but by the early 1900s the new building of the London County Council on the opposite bank could satisfy the most insatiable demands of civic pride.

In all big cities a grand opera house formed the apex of a pyramid of buildings designed for entertainment or social gatherings. These included theatres, music-halls, cabarets, circuses and hippodromes on the one hand, and cafés, restaurants, bars, casinos and clubs on the other. The nineteenth century proved particularly good at producing buildings of this kind. The high populations and high densities of cities, the numbers of people still living in the centre, the increasing quality and quantity of public transport, helped to generate them in very large numbers; and the cheapness of machine-cast or machine-made ornaments enabled even places catering for customers of modest income to go to town in their possession of tiles, mirrors and ironwork, with gay and glittering results.

New-style western cities were not confined to Europe and North America. Buenos Aires was the most notable example in South America.[15] On the strength of Argentine corn and beef, of a network of railways of which it was the terminus, and of the harbour works constructed in the 1880s, it became the Chicago of South America; its slaughter-house area was actually called Nuevo Chicago. Its nomination as the capital of the Argentine in 1880 accelerated its growth; its population rose from 40,000 in 1800 to 180,000 in 1870 and 1,300,000 in 1910. The immigrants who provided its workforce came mostly from Italy and Spain, the capital to develop it from England, but the architecture from France. The great Plaza de Mayo around which city life revolved was, admittedly, a Spanish-style feature, enlarged in 1884 to become South America's equivalent of the Zocalo in Mexico City; but the tree- and shop-lined Avenida de Mayo which led off it became Buenos Aires' equivalent of a Paris boulevard, the opulent houses which the very rich built to the north of the Plaza de Mayo could almost all have been taken straight out of the 8th Arrondissement in Paris, and most of the new buildings were designed by architects trained in the Paris École des Beaux-Arts.

The fact that Paris had full-time schools of architecture and engineering and London did not (the schools run by the Royal Academy and Architectural Association offered only evening classes until well into the twentieth century), gave Paris a long lead as a supplier of ideas and urban forms to cities, reinforced as it was by Paris's dominant image as the world's gayest, most sophisticated and most civilized city. Architects came to be trained there from all over the world, but especially from both North and South America. Although France and England were both involved in the internal affairs of Egypt (until England finally took virtual control in 1882), the new quarters of Cairo and Alexandria were laid out in the second half of the nineteenth century in the French rather than the English manner, with broad tree-lined streets, big opera houses and, in Cairo, a central square or small park in which serpentining paths led to a restaurant, a theatre and a little lake, like a miniature amalgamation of the Champs Élysées and the Bois de Boulogne.[16]

Cairo and Alexandria were cities which, though nominally in an independent country, were virtually run by European nations. Tokyo was the new capital of a country which remained independent, but took with enthusiasm and increasing success to western technology and some western ways.[17] The capital was moved to it from Kyoto, and its name changed from Edo to Tokyo, in 1868. The city was already a very large one, with well over a million inhabitants, but it was entirely oriental, a congregation of temples, gardens, tea-houses, markets and single-storey wooden houses based on a chaotic street plan and spread out round the moat and walls of the great palace or castle of the shoguns, which now became the Imperial Palace. Although very much bigger, it was closer in character to a European city of the Middle Ages than anything surviving in Europe.

Over the next fifty years, during the reign of the Meiji emperor, it acquired much of the equipment of a big western city: it became the centre of a railway network, it acquired a modern port, tramways, railway stations, a belt of factories, parks, statues, monuments, department stores, western-style mansions for the rich industrialists, and one broad tree-lined street running through the new brick-built area known as Ginza Town. It even acquired a skyscraper, known as the Asakusa Twelve Storeys. This was an octagonal brick tower, built with the help of an English consultant, William Barton, and opened in 1890. It had the first elevator in Japan, imported from the United States. After eight floors of shops, there was a floor for exhibitions, a floor of rotating arc lights, and a top floor equipped with a balcony and telescopes.

One of the most curious products of the Meiji period in Tokyo was the Rokumeikan. This was a combined assembly rooms and hostel for important guests, erected by the State in 1881–3. It was a classical building of some charm and dignity. It was designed by Josiah Conder, an English-born architect, who designed most of the important buildings in Tokyo in the late nineteenth century. Its function was to educate the Japanese upper classes in the ways of western high society, and to show visitors from the west how well the Japanese could behave as European-style ladies and gentlemen. Classes were given there to teach waltzes and quadrilles. It was the venue for garden parties,

283 (top left) The Café Griensteidl, Vienna. By R. Völke (Museen der Stadt Wien).

284. (bottom left) The Börsig ironworks, Berlin, c. 1845 (Berlin Museum).

285. (above) Horse-drawn buses in Ginza Bricktown, Tokyo. From a print by Hiroshie III (Tokyo Central Library).

charity bazaars, receptions and balls, in which Japanese couples in bustles and white ties danced round to a European orchestra.[18]

The Japanese took with innocent enthusiasm to all new western fashions, and moved apparently without emotional disturbance from western to traditional Japanese ways of behaviour and back again. They still do so today but, usually at any rate, the western element has grown much stronger. In Meiji Tokyo nine-tenths of the city remained little touched by western influences, and many of the new buildings were in a curious but attractive mixture of western and Japanese styles. The mixture was especially strong in the architecture of the new department stores, a western import which the Japanese adopted with particular zest, and of which they have remained addicts ever since. It was to be found inside the stores as well as out; in the Mitsukoshi store in its early days customers took their shoes off when they entered and replaced them with slippers specially supplied at the door; but while they shopped they were entertained with western airs played by a boy band dressed in red and green kilts.[19]

Tokyo also acquired its factory areas, on the eastern side of the city or around the harbour. From the early nineteenth century industrialization spread apace in Europe and America, and by the late nineteenth century it was spreading round the rest of the world. England quickly lost its monopoly of new factories, and the docks and railway yards which they helped to generate. Many of the old Flemish textile cities, Ghent foremost among them, went over to the factory system and had a new period of prosperity; Antwerp once more became a major port and financial centre for the textile and other industries, with industries of its own as well. An Englishman, William Wood, had started up a cotton-mill in 1824, other industries followed, and between the 1850s and the early 1900s a great complex of docks was constructed.[20] In 1850 the Port of Antwerp was dealing with less than a twentieth of the tonnage of shipping going through the Port of London, but was up to 75 percent by 1912. By then the Port of Rotterdam was much the same size as Antwerp, and that of Hamburg was a little larger.[21] Lvov (Lemberg) in Poland, and Brno (Brunn) in Czechoslovakia, developed as the Manchesters of the Russian and Austrian empires; Brno had started to industrialize on the basis of imported English machinery but was beginning to produce its own as early as 1818. In North America textile towns sprang up all over New England. In France the long-established silk industry in Lyons went over to factory production, and Rheims and

Rouen became the centres of the cotton industry. The visual results at Rouen were described by de Maupassant in his novel *Bel-Ami* (1885): 'Then the city appeared on the right bank, dimmed by the morning mist, with gleams of sunlight on her roofs and her array of steeples, some pointed and some squat, pierced and wrought like giant jewels, her towers, square or round, topped with heraldic crowns, her belfries and bell turrets, the entire Gothic population of church roofs dominated by the slender spire of the cathedral, that astonishing pinnacle of bronze, ugly, odd, immense, the tallest in the world. But opposite, on the other side of the river, stood up, round and curving outwards at the top, the slim factory chimneys of the vast suburb of Saint-Sever. More numerous than their brethren the steeples, they lifted their tall brick columns far out into the countryside, and blew their black, coal-laden breath up into the clear sky. And the tallest of them all, as tall as the pyramid of Cheops, almost equal of her haughty opposite number at the cathedral, the great fire-vent of the Foudre towered up like a queen of the toiling, smoking population of the factories, just as her neighbour was the queen of the throng of sacred monuments . . . One could see the barges moving up and down stream, drawn by tugs like bloated flies, belching forth their clouds of thick smoke. Islets, afloat on the water, lay end to end, or with long gaps between them, like beads of unequal sizes on a great gleaming rosary.'[22]

Industry on a large scale was not confined to provincial towns. Paris, Berlin, St Petersburg and Vienna, besides being capital cities, were also the biggest industrial centres in their countries. This was the consequence of their becoming the centres of national transport networks, which in turn was due to their being both political capitals and major centres of finance; their convenience from the point of view of transport and finance offset the fact that none of them was close to major sources of raw materials. In 1846 Berlin was the terminus of a web of five railway lines, the only railway lines in Germany. By 1882 (when Berlin had been the capital of the newly united German empire since 1871) a mesh of railways had spread all over the country, but Berlin, now served by ten lines, was still overpoweringly their focus. A circular line was constructed on the edge of the city in the 1870s, and became the main location for industry. This had previously started up in the form of iron foundries and machine-building works, of which the great Borsig works (where the first German locomotive was built in 1837–41) was one of the first and the most important; from the 1840s, when firms such as Siemens, AEG and Bergmann were founded, Berlin became a world centre of the electrical industry.[23]

In addition to its docks, London acquired shipyards in the lower reaches of the Thames, a factory area in Lambeth, and a considerable amount of light industry, but it never became industrialized to the same extent as the big continental capitals. By the time it had developed as a transport centre alternative centres serving a rapidly growing industrial area had already developed in the north. One result of this was that the central government was never vulnerable to industrial action in the same way as in Paris and St Petersburg, where a rampant working class in collusion with city intellectuals were able to close in on the inner city and take it over in 1870 and 1917.[24]

Large areas of working-class housing inevitably developed to serve both industry and transport and the everyday needs of cities. Most old cities of any size already had such areas in or near their centres. They could be once-fashionable districts which had gone down in the world or areas which had originally been developed as working-class

286. Berlin. Workshop courtyards of 1906, at No. 11, Rütterstrasse, Kreuzberg.

housing on the edge of the city, and had become central as the city grew in size. Being made up of old houses, they were often in bad repair, and, being central, they were almost invariably overcrowded. They were tempting subjects for redevelopment, whether for new buildings or new roads; they were cheaper to buy up than other areas, and developing them could produce a grand new road or building and get rid of an undesirable area at the same time. The London Law Courts, for instance, after the Embankment project had foundered, were built on what had previously been a rookery of slum houses to the north of Fleet Street. The idea that the occupants (as opposed to the owners or leaseholders) of such areas had any rights to compensation for rehousing only developed gradually, and in some countries.

While such districts in the centres of cities were tending to contract, great belts of new cheap housing appeared on their outskirts, many built as adjuncts to new industries. Almost every big city evolved its own form of overcrowding its working classes. Much depended on the standard block size in different cities, and the standard size of plots within the blocks. In most English-speaking countries working-class families resisted to their utmost efforts to persuade them into multi-storey tenements, but terraces were built back-to-back in innumerable British industrial towns, and detached houses were built with cracks of only two or three feet between each house in Melbourne and Chicago. In Europe, tenements proliferated, with many variations. In Berlin, for instance, the ground over which the city rapidly expanded between the 1850s and the 1914–18 war was laid out in very large blocks, up to 400 metres square, following the plan worked out in 1858–62 by James Hobrecht for the Police President, who ran Berlin.[25] It was intended that these blocks should be subdivided by minor roads, but in fact they were developed in a series of courtyards running back from the street frontage; one complex usually consisted of three or even four courtyards leading into each other, a greater or lesser proportion of which was often occupied by workshops or even by small factories. As a result, a curious contrast developed: on the frontages endless vistas of six-storey tenements, all exactly seventy-two feet high, vanishing into the distance to either side of wide streets; behind them a warren of high, enclosed courtyards, humming with people and machinery. The street frontages were often rather elaborately decorated with stucco ornaments, Italianate in the mid-century, but gradually dissolving into oriel windows, balconies and gables towards 1900. In the courtyards a successful business sometimes installed a show façade of coloured tiles, but on the whole there were no frills. The whole courtyard system had obvious and serious drawbacks, but it also had a powerful character of its own, and the innumerable small workshops that resulted from it were conveniently close to where people lived and provided a back-up to the big factories that gave the Berlin industrial economy great resilience and flexibility.

Most cities built their tenements on some variant of a courtyard plan, unless the standard plot was too narrow for more than a light well, as in New York. In Buenos Aires the standard tenements were called *conventillos*. The type developed out of the low single-storey or two-storey houses which well-off families built to the south of what became the Plaza de Mayo in the eighteenth and early nineteenth centuries. These were built round a series of patios, running back from the street front, usually on a standard plot of 28.4 feet width, and from three to six times as deep as they were wide. In the customary fashion, the original owners moved out of these charming houses into newer and grander houses to the north of the Plaza de Mayo. Spanish and Italian immigrants came crowding in, and, by gross overcrowding and subdivision of what was there already and by reducing the size of the patios by new building, landlords were sometimes able to accommodate 350 people in a space formerly occupied by 25. The type was copied for new buildings: by 1907 there were twenty-five hundred *conventillos*, new and old, large and small, occupied by 150,000 people.[26]

* * *

In 1842 New York celebrated the opening of the new water supply which had been brought to it from Croton, in the hills on the mainland to the north of Manhattan; it replaced the supplies from entirely inadequate reservoirs, wells and rainwater on which the city had previously relied. The festivities included a procession eight miles long, bigger even than that which had celebrated the opening of the Erie Canal in 1825.[27] At a prefixed time the supply was connected, water gushed from the fountains in the city square, and the massed choir of the Sacred Music Society launched into a hymn which had been written for the occasion:

> Water leaps as if delighted
> While her conquered foes retire.
> Pale Contagion flies affrighted
> With the baffled demon, Fire . . .[28]

The residents of nineteenth-century cities were vividly aware of what new services could do to make city life tolerable, and celebrated their arrival accordingly. The astounding growth of their cities was frequently accompanied to begin with by a breakdown of existing services and a complete lack of new ones in new areas, especially the poor ones. But the cities fought back. The history of city services in this period was often one of confusion, overlap and lack of central planning, the motives behind their provision were mixed, but the cumulative results were formidable. The tramways and cable-cars have mostly gone, many of the railway lines have been closed, gas has been replaced by electricity, but in many cities much of the public transport, the public services and virtually all the underground services are, for better or worse, still substantially based on nineteenth-century systems and buildings.

The gas lighting which spread round the cities of the world at extraordinary speed once it had been pioneered in London in 1812 reduced crime, added to the number and gaiety of city amusement areas and all after-dark activities, and provided Victorian intellectuals with a new hobby of walking through empty city streets at night. But the arrival of a new water supply called for special celebration because, as the New York Sacred Music Society pointed out, it was so obviously life preserving. Bad onslaughts of fire or disease were often the direct causes of the installation of a proper water supply. Hamburg established an excellent public system from 1848, in reaction to the fire which destroyed a large section of the town in that year.[29] In the year before, Manchester had bought up the city's private waterworks company and set about improving the supply as an immediate reaction to the cholera epidemic in 1847–8. Cholera had reached Europe in 1833, and was immediately and appallingly lethal; in the 1840s it began to be realized that it spread by way of contaminated water. The hard core of those committed to the improvement of working-class conditions quickly received the support which they needed once the wealthy began to be alarmed that they might be infected by the poor. Between 1840 and 1880 most big cities acquired new water supplies, or greatly improved their existing ones.

The steam-pump provided the driving force of the new systems. The raising of water to a higher level by artificial means had been practised since medieval times. The water-house at Bruges, in which water was raised by a horse-wheel working a bucket chain, was first installed in the late thirteenth century, as described in Chapter Five. In the sixteenth century water began to be pumped up by pumps powered by water-wheels, often set in the arches of bridges, where the current ran faster. Two such systems, at Constance and Augsburg, were visited by Montaigne in 1580.[30] An English engineer, Peter Morice, installed another under London Bridge in 1581.[31] In Paris there were water-wheel pumps on the Pont Notre Dame, installed in the mid-seventeenth century, and on the Pont Neuf, installed about 1600 and remodelled in 1712. The Pont Neuf water-house was called La Samaritaine, because it carried a bas-relief showing the Good Samaritan giving water to the traveller.[32]

The York Water Company in London was using steam power to pump Thames water up to the West End squares by the early eighteenth century, and other companies followed. In Paris the brothers Perrier installed steam-pumps at Chaillot, on the Right Bank in the city suburbs, in the 1770s, and another pumping-station was built across the river at Gros Caillou in about 1830 (with a covered-in swimming pool attached).[33] At New Orleans a system worked by steam-pump was installed in about 1810.[34] At Perth in Scotland the elegant little classical engine-house which Adam Anderson designed in 1832 still survives; it has a boiler-house chimney disguised as a Doric column.

287. Tourists in the Paris sewers. From *Illustrated London News*, 29 January 1870.

Most of these early water systems supplied water to parts of the cities only, usually the richer parts. The water was often pumped up directly from the river, and the quality was bad and got worse as cities grew and rivers were increasingly polluted. Most were installed by private individuals or companies. Water supply was so important that its provision was increasingly taken over by the cities themselves, but many city water supplies were run by independent companies well into the twentieth century, as were gas and electricity supplies and all forms of city transport. The quality of service and water usually improved in the course of the nineteenth century, however, as filtering systems were gradually introduced and the water supply was taken from rivers above the cities rather than in their centres. The stand-pipe, into which water was pumped to provide pressure for the system and to take water into upper floors, first became common in the mid-century, and lofty stand-pipe towers, variously embellished, joined towers containing water reservoirs to form a new feature of city skylines.

Getting rid of sewage was the other side of the coin to bringing in fresh water. London was a pioneer in doing so. In 1844 its drainage system was put under the control of a public body, and between 1845 and 1875 it was supplied with a comprehensive drainage system designed and installed by Joseph Bazalgette.[35] One of the functions of the new embankments along the Thames was to take the lower of three levels of main sewers, which discharged below the city, aided by pumps placed at strategic points. The pumping stations were treated with some architectural splendour, as cathedrals of hygiene: they had something to celebrate, for the Bazalgette system effectively got rid of cholera in London. Most other cities were much less advanced. There were public tours of the main sewers of Paris, and none of those of London, for the excellent reason

288. The main Dresden railway station (1892–8) in 1927.

that the Paris sewers took only surface water: sewage was still removed in carts, as in preceding centuries. Many cities remained in this situation into the twentieth century; until the 1950s large areas of Tokyo were still dependent on cess-pits, emptied by carts or lorries.[36]

The standpipe-tower which still rises out of the north-eastern quarter of Berlin is part of the water system installed for a British company by the engineering firm of Fox and Crampton in 1856 and taken over by the city in 1873. Services of all kinds were installed in cities all over the world by London-based and London-financed companies. They installed and ran, for instance, the gas works of Buenos Aires (1875 and 1878); Bombay, Amiens, Boulogne and Rouen (1835); Hong Kong, Singapore and Smyrna (1862); and Montevideo (1872). Apart from Berlin, the water systems which they installed included those in Amsterdam (1852), Odessa (1872), St Petersburg (1874–7), Beirut (1873–5), Alexandria (1879), Antwerp (1880) and Shanghai (1880). They ran tramway or omnibus companies in Barcelona (1872), Gothenburg (1879), Seville (1886), Hawaii (1888) and numerous different companies in Buenos Aires.[37]

The current did not only run in one direction, however. Other cities, Paris and New York in particular, also became active round-the-world promoters of services. The London omnibus system was run by a company based on Paris, where the horse omnibus had been introduced in the 1820s;[38] the London underground was mostly installed by Charles Yerkes, the American financier who had provided much of the Chicago transport system in the 1880s and moved into New York subways in the 1890s; his life was the basis of three of Theodore Dreiser's best novels.[39] In between horse omnibuses and electrically powered underground trains came horse trams, cable-cars,

289. Berlin. Stand-pipe of the waterworks installed by Fox and Crampton, 1856 (Berlin Museum).

290. (right) *A River Side Street*. From the illustration by Gustave Doré in Blanchard Jerrold, *London, A Pilgrimage*, 1872.

elevated railways and electric trams; the cable-car was invented in San Francisco in the 1870s to deal with the apalling gradients caused by applying a grid street system to a hilly city, and was adopted by a number of cities built on flat or relatively flat ground, such as Chicago (from 1882) and Melbourne (from 1885), before being progressively pushed out by the electric tram in the 1890s and early 1900s.

Inter-city trains had increased city populations and caused great problems of congestion, which transport systems within the city helped to diffuse. But to begin with they catered for those of the middle classes who could not afford, or did not want, to run a carriage. They were too expensive for ordinary working men, unless special cheap fares were imposed by law on certain services at certain times. This happened on London railway and tram lines in the 1870s, and on Melbourne railways from 1883 and trams from 1885, and made working-class suburbs possible in those cities.[40] In Buenos Aires, working-class fares on some services were imposed by law, but the transport companies ran them with such deliberate inefficiency that they were of little use.[41] From about 1900, however, the cheaper running costs of electrified systems combined with competition between different lines began to bring ordinary fares down in most big cities, which expanded accordingly.

At the heart of every transport system the great railway stations were as distinctive as any new type of building produced in the nineteenth century. Behind gigantic triumphal arches of masonry or spired and turreted hotels, their huge ribbed carcases of glass and iron were filled with the hiss of steam and the tramp of feet, translucent with light shining mysteriously into dim distances of smoke or darkness, and vibrant with the sense of far-off places. That mixture of the practical and the romantic which made Victorian cities exciting was nowhere to be found in a more concentrated form.

17

Babylon or Jerusalem

Two hundred years ago or so it was possible to see the whole of any city in the world, without having to go several thousand feet up in an aeroplane to do so. One could see London from Highgate, Rome from Monte Mario, or Paris from Montmartre. 'Ecco Roma' the travellers would cry—or whatever else was appropriate—as they reined in their horses. And there in front of them would be the whole bag of tricks—a forest of roofs, with towers, domes or spires breaking out of it, but a forest with edges, an island with water or green fields visibly flowing up to its shores. This was what people expected a city to be, and it was not so very different from the medieval city with its spires and towers rising from behind a circuit of walls. The walls had gone for the most part, the cities had grown, but the human eye could still encompass them.

Then, in the nineteenth century, things began to change. The population of London hit a million in about 1811, Paris in the 1840s, Berlin in the 1880s. By the end of the century there were at least a dozen cities of over a million inhabitants, and ones of over half-a-million proliferated. One could climb a hill, but one no longer saw the whole city, one saw a forest that had no

291. *Belshazzar's Feast.* Engraving from the painting by John Martin, 1820 (British Museum).

edges, no obvious shape, no clarity, often, because of the smoke that billowed out of it, or the fog or haze that engulfed it.

It was a new situation, and it produced a new metaphor, or at least the new use of an old metaphor. These new monster cities were called Babels or Babylons. Until archaeologists got to work in the mid-nineteenth century, the real Babylon was a place about which nobody knew very much, except that Herodotus had described it as very large, and the Bible as very wicked. It had been the scene of Belshazzar's feast, at which mysterious writing had appeared on the wall, to interrupt the king's orgy, followed by the destruction of the city. The Tower of Babel had come to a bad end too, and Babel was normally identified with Babylon. In the Book of Revelations Babylon was given short shrift. It was 'Babylon the great, the mother of harlots and abominations of the earth ... Babylon the great is fallen ... that great city that was clothed in fine linen and purple and scarlet and decked with gold and precious stones and pearls ... is utterly burned with fire.'[1]

In the Middle Ages Babylon was freely used as a metaphor for a wicked city or a luxurious one—than, as now, one was presumed to go with the other—rather than for a huge city, perhaps because there were no huge medieval cities, and the concept of one was beyond the medieval imagination. As London swelled, the metaphor came into specialized use to describe its vastness. But the idea of wickedness or luxury was always at the back of the drawer, ready to be pulled out by those who wanted it. Cowper compared London to Babylon in his poem *The Task*, which came out in 1785. A few decades later Byron called London 'mighty Babylon' and described Don Juan's descent to it through 'a whirl / of wheels, and war of voices and confusion'.[2] By then the metaphor was coming into general use. Its popularity was partly the result of two pictures exhibited in London in 1819 and 1820.

In 1819 John Martin put his picture *The Fall of Babylon* on show at the Royal Institution. It was a new kind of picture, for him or anyone else, and it made his reputation. It shows a vast city, half-classical, half-Egyptian, stretching its quays, colonnades and

292. Warehouse, New Quay, Liverpool, *c.* 1835.

bridges as far as the eye can see; rising up in the background is an enormous mysterious Tower of Babel. The Fall is going on in the foreground, where hundreds of diminutive human beings are being busily but rather inconspicuously raped or massacred. It was the huge city, not the fate of its inhabitants, which captured the imagination of the public who crowded round the picture.

Next year Martin followed up *The Fall of Babylon* with *Belshazzar's Feast* and turned his success into a triumph. He had determined, he announced, that 'the picture shall make more noise than any picture ever did before',[3] and indeed it immediately became famous all over Europe. It showed the feast in the setting of a similar gigantic Babylon, but by night instead of day. The result was sensational. The city was lit by a lurid red glow, lightning flashed out of the clouds, torches flared, huge colonnaded tunnels vanished into blackness, and the terror of the milling crowd, fleeing from the writing on the wall, came across with extraordinary vividness.

Martin was believed at the time, not only to have been in part inspired by the new monster cities of his own day, but also to be a prophet of the cities of the future—and the lurid gas-lit immensity of the Victorian city bore out this opinion. The French writer Michelet came to England in 1834, and was fascinated by its new architecture, outside London as well as in it. He claimed that Englishmen were describing this architecture as Babylonian and saw it reflected in the paintings of Martin. 'The buildings without end of huge towns such as London and Edinburgh', he wrote, 'immense streets, endless colonnades . . . warehouses on the docks of London and Liverpool . . . all these are fused together, systemized and idealized by Martin. He is, in my view, an architectural prophet.'[4]

Babylon was in the air. 'The modern Babylon' became a familiar nickname or journalistic cliché for London,[5] and, inevitably, as Paris grew, it too began to be called Babylon. Victor Hugo described it as such in 1831. Balzac followed him in the 1840s. By 1860 de Goncourt was complaining that the new boulevards were destroying the Paris he loved and turning it into 'London or some Babylon of the future'. In 1871 Gautier visited Gustave Doré's studio and was greatly struck by a painting of Paris seen from Montmartre. 'The enormous city', he wrote, 'is bathed in smoke, pricked with points of light. It seems like one of those Ninevehs or Babylons which the prophet glimpses in a dream.'[6] In 1864 the novelists Chevalier and Labourdieu started (but never completed) a trilogy called *Les Trois Babylones: Paris, Londres, New York.* In the 1890s G. W. Steevens apostrophized Chicago as 'Queen and guttersnipe of cities, cynosure and cesspool of the world . . . the first and only veritable Babel of the age'.[7]

In 1870 Victor Hugo had agreed with de Goncourt that Paris was going the way of London, but remarked, 'It has two things, thank heavens, to distinguish it from England: the comparative beauty of its climate and the absence of coal.'[8] London was indeed filthy dirty by then. Tennyson had already referred to it as a 'great black

Babylon'.[9] At the end of the century Henry James called Paris a 'vast bright Babylon'.[10] London as the black Babylon and Paris as the bright Babylon did in fact represent two types of nineteenth-century city. The black Babylon was an essentially English invention, the city of mills, warehouses, docks, counting-houses and railway viaducts, the city where vast numbers of people toiled like ants in the smoke and fog—for, odd as it may seem today, it was the passionate intensity with which the English worked and their apparent inability to enjoy themselves which struck foreign visitors of those days. London was the biggest of these black Babylons, but the term was also applied to other industrial cities, especially to Manchester. In the 1860s, as we have seen, Hippolyte Taine called Manchester 'a Babel built of brick'. He described its warehouses as 'Babylonian monuments'; de Quincey called them 'huge Babylonian centres of commerce'.[11] In the 1880s Melbourne, Australia's only industrial city, was described as the 'modern Babylon' or 'modern Babel', the towers of which 'satanically gleam'.[12]

In contrast, the bright Babylon of Paris was a city of luxury and pleasure. In his novel *Cousine Bette*, for instance, Balzac describes Olympe Bijou, a sixteen-year-old Parisian street girl with a mouth like a half-burst pomegranate, a passionate breast and dreamy dark eyes. She is 'one of those living masterpieces that only Paris in the whole world can create; for only in Paris exists the endless concubinage of luxury and want, of vice and sober virtue, or repressed desire and ever-renewed temptation, which makes this city the heir of Nineveh, Babylon, and Imperial Rome'.[13]

Balzac is clearly using Babylon here to express a somewhat different reaction from that, for instance, expressed by the journalist W. H. Stead in his famous and furious article 'The Maiden Tribute of our Modern Babylon', which blew the lid off the London trade in twelve-year-old girls.[14] As a metaphor, Babylon was able to concentrate in one word all the qualities and connotations which made the new huge cities of the nineteenth century unlike anything which anyone had experienced before. But it could be used with different inflections. These different uses are a useful way of pin-pointing three different types of nineteenth-century reaction to the new cities—hate, love and love–hate.

The love–hate reaction is clearly present in Balzac's description of Paris and Olympe Bijou. But it is especially to be found in French reactions to London and other black Babylons in England. One can feel a delicious frisson running through Hippolyte Taine, as, in the early hours of the morning, he rides in a hansom cab through the deserted gas-lit squares of Belgravia: 'A sepulchral light shone over the great empty Babylon, casting the whiteness of a shroud upon its colossal artefacts.'[15] It was fascination, and the ensuing violent aesthetic response, which makes Gustave Doré's vision of London so compelling. It is to be found in his illustrations to *London—a Pilgrimage*, written by Blanchard Jerrold, and published in 1872. Doré's reaction to what Jerrold calls 'our wonder-working Babylon' was a London dramatic, baleful and beautiful, a London of docks, of gaslight, of fog, of looming figures and pullulating life, of wealth and poverty equally wrapped in haze and darkness.

The most curious example of this fascinated French response to London is to be found in Huysmans's novel *A Rebours*. Huysmans may never have been to London, but he must have seen Doré's engravings of it, and been inspired by them to depict the reactions of his hero Des Esseintes, when the latter decides to go to London.

'His mind', Huysmans wrote, 'conjured up a picture of London as an immense, sprawling, rain-drenched metropolis, stinking of soot and hot iron, and wrapped in a perpetual mantle of smoke and fog. He could see in imagination a line of dockyards stretching away into the distance, full of cranes, capstans, and bales of merchandise, and swarming with men . . . All this activity was going on in warehouses and on wharves washed by the dark, slimy waters of an imaginary Thames, in the midst of a forest of masts, a tangle of beams and girders piercing the pale, lowering clouds. Up above, trains raced by at full speed; and down in the underground sewers, others rumbled along, occasionally emitting ghastly screams or vomiting floods of smoke. And meanwhile, along every street, big or small, in an eternal twilight relieved only by the glaring infamies of modern advertising, there flowed an endless stream of traffic between two columns of earnest, silent Londoners, marching along with eyes fixed ahead and elbows glued to their sides.

'Des Esseintes shuddered with delight at feeling himself lost in this terrifying world of commerce, immersed in this isolating fog, involved in this incessant activity, and caught up in this ruthless machine.'[16]

This kind of reaction tended to be that of visitors from outside, who saw the cities as immense impersonal machines or awesome stage-sets, and had no knowledge of, or deliberately ignored, the complexities of personal relationships and overlapping groups which lay behind them. In contrast, from the very beginning there were those who instinctively delighted in great cities and if they called them Babylons did so in a sympathetic spirit.

At the time when London was first being described as Babylon, Dr Johnson was at hand to express the unqualified enthusiasm of a born city-lover for what he called its 'wonderful immensity'. Just because it was so immense it 'comprehended the whole of human life', and he accordingly made his famous dictum that 'the man who is tired of London is tired of life'.[17] His absurd little friend Boswell found that London gave him the same kind of electric charge that still thrills visitors to that great transatlantic Babylon and collection of Towers of Babel, New York. 'I can talk twice as much in London as any where else', he wrote.[18] Similarly, George Borrow described how he first came to London as a young man, wondered at the 'forests of masts', 'chimneys taller than Cleopatra's needle', 'huge wreaths of black smoke which formed a canopy—occasionally a gorgeous one—of the more than Babel City', and felt that 'I had never walked with the same ease and facility on the flagstones of a country town as on those of London'.[19] The early nineteenth-century painter Benjamin Robert Haydon felt much the same on Highgate Hill. 'So far from the smoke of London being offensive to me, it has always been to my imagination the sublime canopy that shrouds the City of the World. Drifted by the wind or hanging in gloomy grandeur over the vastness of our Babylon, the sight of it always filled my mind with feelings of energy such as no other city could inspire . . . Often have I studied its peculiarities from the hills near London where, in the midst of the drifted clouds you catch a glimpse of the great dome of St Paul's announcing at once civilization and power.'[20]

Henry James had the same kind of reaction to what he called 'the murky modern Babylon'. 'For the real London-lover', he wrote, 'the mere immensity of the place is a large part of its merit.' He revelled in 'the rumble of the tremendous human mill', in 'the thick dim distances, which in my opinion are the most romantic town vistas in the world', in 'the atmosphere, with its magnificent mystifications, which flatters and superfuses, makes everything brown, rich, dim, vague'. For him London was 'an epitome of the round world', the 'particular spot in the world which communicates the greatest sense of life'.[21]

He felt just as strongly about Paris. In his novel *The Ambassadors* he describes his hero contemplating Paris on a sparkling sunny morning, and seeing it as a city of endless variety—but in a quite different way from London. 'It hung before him this morning, the vast bright Babylon, like some huge iridescent object, a jewel brilliant and hard, in which parts were not to be discriminated nor differences comfortably marked. It twinkled and trembled and melted together, and what seemed surface one moment seemed all depth the next.'[22]

At exactly the time at which Henry James was writing, the Impressionists were at work painting Paris in all its aspects, lights and moods, and the result was the most wonderful cumulative portrait of a great city which has ever been created. This was the city that was to attract artists and writers from all over the world, the 'Babylon revisited' of Scott Fitzgerald, the 'lovely Babylonian capital' of his friend Morley Callaghan.[23] In these and similar uses the term 'Babylon' had travelled a long way from its traditional role. It was being used as a celebration by people who had accepted the complexity of the big city, who accepted the fact that it was too big to comprehend as an asset not a liability, who found it, in fact, enormously exciting.

By no means everyone reacted to great cities in this way. There were those who were horrified by them—horrified by their size, by the noise, dirt, poverty and disease which they generated, and by what was seen as their artificiality, as opposed to the 'natural countryside'; they would have agreed with Cowper's endlessly quoted if scarcely accurate phrase 'God made the country and man made the town.'[24] The degree of reaction varied, however, between those who accepted great cities as agents of civilization, but tried to transform them by liberal injections of 'the advantages of the countryside', and those who rejected them altogether. The latter class inevitably produced alternatives, in theory or action; they both designed other types of settlement and tried to build them.

The counterpart of Babylon was Jerusalem. Ideal cities were called by many names. They could be 'the City of the Sun', or 'Thelema', or 'Hygeia', or 'the City on a Hill'; but lurking at the back of all of them was the concept of the millennium, and of the New Jerusalem. The fount of millennialism was St John's account of his vision, as related in the Book of Revelations: the seven seals opened by seven angels to release seven plagues on the world; the consumption by fire of 'Babylon the great, the mother of harlots and abomination of the earth'; the casting into the bottomless pit of the dragon, 'that old serpent which is the devil'; the coming of Christ on earth to reign among the chosen for a thousand years; the loosing of the devil out of his prison for 'a little season'; the second coming of Christ, the Last Judgment, and the final dispensation as related by John: 'And I saw a new heaven and a new earth ... And I John saw the holy city, new Jerusalem, coming down from God out of heaven ... And God shall wipe away all tears from their eyes; and there shall be no more death, neither sorrow, nor crying, neither shall there be any more pain.'[25]

The meaning of Revelations, and the extent to which it was to be taken as a metaphor or a true forecast of the future, was to be a subject of endless speculation both by Bible commentators and by ordinary people who read their Bible. The concept of a life on earth freed from death, pain and sorrow was sufficiently compelling even if it were coming at some unknown point in the future, but it became much more exciting if it was thought to be imminent, as it was by various sects through the centuries. Others believed that the millennium did not have to be waited for, but could be brought about by men, once they had the necessary change of heart. Different individuals had different views about what it might involve. 'Why may we not have our Heaven here (that is, a comfortable livelihood on the earth) and heaven hereafter too?' wrote Gerrard Winstanley in 1649.[26] A similar attitude was expounded by Robert Owen in 1816: 'What idea individuals may attach to the term Millennium I know not; but I know that society may be formed so as to exist without crime, without poverty, with health greatly improved, with little, if any, misery, and with intelligence and happiness increased an hundredfold; and no obstacle whatsoever intervenes at this moment, except ignorance, to prevent such a state of society becoming universal.'[27]

Owen was a deist, who took the concept of millennialism out of its religious background and adopted it with an enthusiasm which in his case became obsessive. But it remained powerful in religious sects of all kinds. In the eighteenth century Emanuel Swedenborg and his disciples believed 'the blessed millennium' to be 'on its way to a speedy revival in the church'.[28] Swedenborg's writings, such as his *The New Jerusalem and its Heavenly Doctrine*, had great influence on William Blake. In his *Jerusalem* and other works, Blake presented the picture of the children of Albion who had been 'cast forth to the Potter to build Babylon because they had forsaken Jerusalem'.[29] Jerusalem was personified as in prison in Babylon. But it was recoverable; so Blake declared, in what was to become his best-known poem

And did the Countenance Divine
Shine forth upon our clouded hills?
And was Jerusalem builded here
Among these dark Satanic Mills?

I will not cease from Mental Fight
Nor shall my Sword sleep in my hand
Till we have built Jerusalem
In England's green and pleasant land.

In the Book of Revelations the New Jerusalem in fact comes down out of heaven after the Second Coming, not the first, and does not form part of the millennium. Many thought that it, like related concepts such as the Heavenly City and the City of God, was a metaphor for something which was to be built in the hearts and souls of men. But to those who believed that the millennium was achievable in the present, the idea of founding actual cities or settlements as one way of bringing it about was immediately attractive. There was a long history of such settlements, but they increased greatly in number in the nineteenth century, both as projects and as actual schemes, in direct reaction to the increasing size and problems of the contemporary city.

Older religious literature had produced some striking images of heavenly or transcendent cities, but little detail. In Bunyan's *Pilgrim's Progress* the pilgrim travels to a heavenly Jerusalem (also called Mount Sion, or the Cœlestial City) which is described as standing 'upon a mighty hill'.[30] Bunyan probably derived its situation from

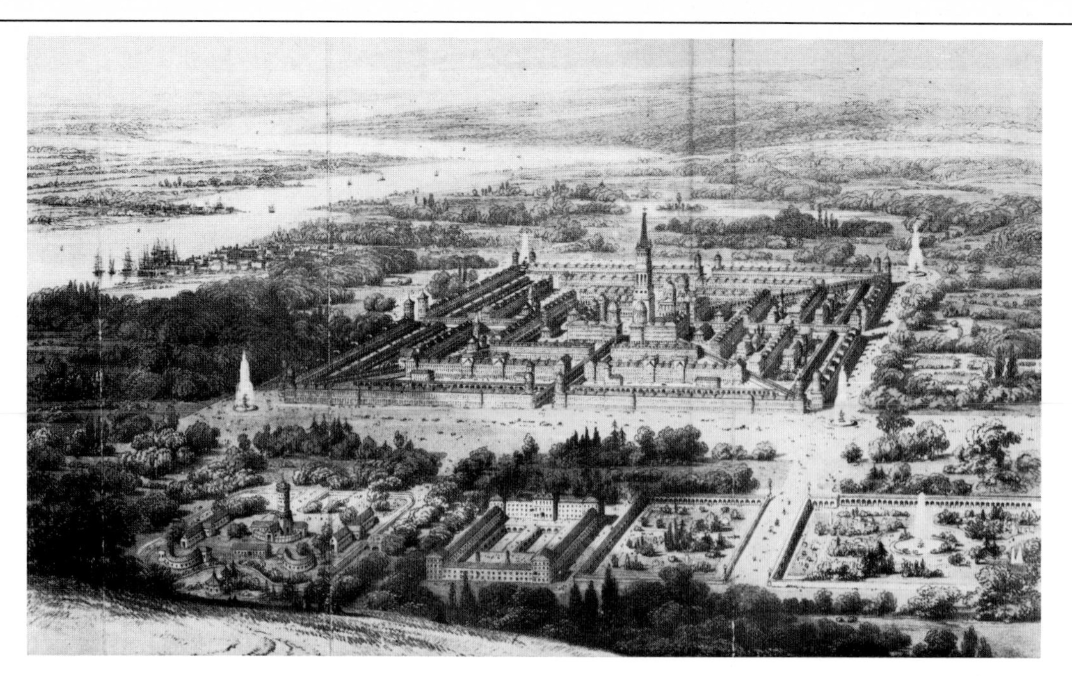

293. Proposed model town of Victoria. From James Silk Buckingham, *National Evils and Practical Remedies*, 1849.

a hint in Revelations and from Christ's saying as recorded in St Matthew's Gospel: 'Ye are the light of the world. A city that is set on a hill cannot be hid.' The phrase was to be in constant use in the nineteenth and twentieth centuries, but more as a metaphor than as a programme for building; few ideal settlements were actually built on hilltops. Bunyan's city was made of pure gold, so that mortals could not look at it when the sun shone on it. In Revelations the New Jerusalem was also built of gold (but its gold was 'like unto clear glass') on foundations of precious stones; its light was 'clear as crystal' and it had no need of sun or moon, 'for the glory of God did lighten it'.[31] It was square and had twelve gates; otherwise no information is given as to its plans. But in the early seventeenth century Thomas Campanella had described his own version of a New Jerusalem in some detail, and his description was to be much read in the nineteenth century, and to exert considerable influence. He called it Civitas Solis, the City of the Sun. It was laid out in seven concentric circles, the middle ones of which were 'built upon a high hill'; on top of the hill was 'a rather spacious plain, and in the midst of this there rises a temple, built with wondrous art'.[32]

There was much variation in the projects, realized and unrealized, for ideal cities and settlements in the nineteenth century, but they all had certain qualities in common. They were designed in conscious reaction against large contemporary cities. Instead of fog, smoke, congestion, soot-blackened buildings, poverty and huge populations, they offered clear air, sun, openness, greenery, moderate prosperity for all, and populations of at most 60,000, and usually less. Light and greenery were advocated for practical reasons but given a more than practical value; they became symbols of regeneration.

Robert Owen himself never built a new city; at both New Lanark in Scotland and New Harmony in Indiana he took over existing buildings. But at least two published designs showed his influence, and probably also that of Campanella. James Silk-Buckingham's city of Victoria, which he published in his *National Evils and Practical Remedies* in 1849, was designed as a series of concentric zones of building, although on a square plan, not Campanella's round one. In between the zones were broad, tree-lined streets. The city was to be run by a company in which all its residents had shares, and was to be pacifist, teetotal and religiously tolerant, and to have communal laundries and restaurants. The inner circuit took the form of a covered gallery one hundred feet wide, decorated with pictures and statues. A band was to play in it every evening, and it was to open as 'a Public Promenade for all classes'. The model city of Queen Victoria Town, shown in Robert Pemberton's *The Happy Colony*, was somewhat similar in concept, but even closer to Campanella's, for it was based on a circular plan. It was to be the model for a group of agricultural settlements in a notional colony of 200,000 acres in New Zealand. 'To establish labour societies in primitive lands', wrote Pemberton, 'founded on *universal* labour, knowledge, science, harmony and love will infallibly lay the foundations of the millennium.'[33]

Large numbers of millennialistic settlements were founded in the nineteenth century, but they were nearly all on a pathetically small scale compared to the Silk-Buckingham and Pemberton schemes, and even so foundered, usually as a result of a combination of impracticality, incompetence and lack of money. The one major exception took the form of settlements built by idealistic owners of industrial works for their workers. Saltaire in the 1850s, Bournville and Port Sunlight in the 1890s, all showed the influence of Owen and his followers. Bournville and Port Sunlight showed other influences too. They were at once more suburban and village-like than Victoria or Queen Victoria Town; they included a proportion of detached and semi-detached houses, and the brick gables and half-timbered architecture of their little houses were in a different vein to the long terraces of the earlier schemes.

The rediscovery of the English vernacular, the attacks by Ruskin and William Morris on contemporary capitalism, Morris's idealization of the Middle Ages and the rural village or country town, his celebration of London as it used to be:

> Small and white and clean,
> The clear Thames bordered by its garden green[34]

Ruskin's advocacy of small cities, any part of which was within a few minutes walk of 'a belt of beautiful garden and orchard',[35] all helped to form a climate of opinion. By the end of the century Ebenezer Howard's *Tomorrow: A Peaceful Path to Reform* (1898), soon to be retitled *Garden Cities of Tomorrow*, found an immediate, an enthusiastic, and in many cases a moneyed readership.

Howard published a schematic design for his proposed city which clearly showed the influence of Silk-Buckingham and Pemberton. It was divided into concentric circular zones, one of which consisted of a glazed ring-shaped 'crystal palace'; its recommended population was 58,000 and a ring of satellite cities were to have populations of 32,000. All the cities were to be full of gardens and greenery. He supported his case with a mixture of practical argument and rhapsodic exaltation. 'Yes', he wrote, 'the key to the problem how to restore the people to the land—that beautiful land of ours, with its canopy of sky, the air that blows upon it, the sun that warms it, the rain and dew that moisten it—the very embodiment of Divine love for man—is indeed a *Master-Key*, for it is the key to a portal through which, even when scarce ajar, will be seen to pour a flood of light on the problems of intemperance, of excessive toil, of restless anxiety, of grinding poverty—the true limits of Governmental interference, aye, and even the relation of man to the Supreme Power.'[36]

Above all, he used the phrase 'garden city'. It caught people's imagination. In 1902 a Garden City Association was founded in England, and a Deutsche Gartenstadt-Gesellschaft in Germany. In 1902–3 the former set about building the first garden city at Letchworth in Hertfordshire; in striking contrast to the way in which nineteenth-century settlements had failed to raise a few thousand pounds, the necessary £156,000 to buy the land and get the project under way was raised without difficulty. In 1905 A. R. Sennett published *Garden Cities in Theory and Practice* in which he plotted the spread of garden cities or related projects round Europe and America. 'A Garden City!' he wrote, 'To the summer toilers in our smoke-beshrouded towns, half-suffocated in their narrow stagnant streets ... how refreshing the name! ... As we desert the lanes of Nature for the cities of artificiality, we desert quietude, happiness and integrity for bustle, unrest, and insincerity.'[37] He wrote a great deal more in the same vein.

Hampstead Garden Suburb, which was initiated in 1906 and laid out on the edge of London in 1908, represented a halfway stage to a full-blown garden city which was to become increasingly common in the following decades. It was not a self-contained and self-supporting town as Letchworth was, but it was similarly controlled by a company in which all the residents had shares, and it set out to create a community of like-minded people and to provide them with shared social facilities. It actually was, if not a city, a community on a hill, and its hilltop was occupied by something very like 'the rather spacious plain' and 'temple built with wondrous art' of Campanella's City of the Sun. The circumstances of the time produced, in fact, two churches, one Anglican and one Non-Conformist, both free-standing in the middle of a square, on one side of which was an Institute for the residents: the lay-out and many of the houses were designed by Raymond Unwin, the buildings on the square by Edwin Lutyens.

294. A plan of Welwyn Garden City by Louis de Soissons, *c.* 1921.

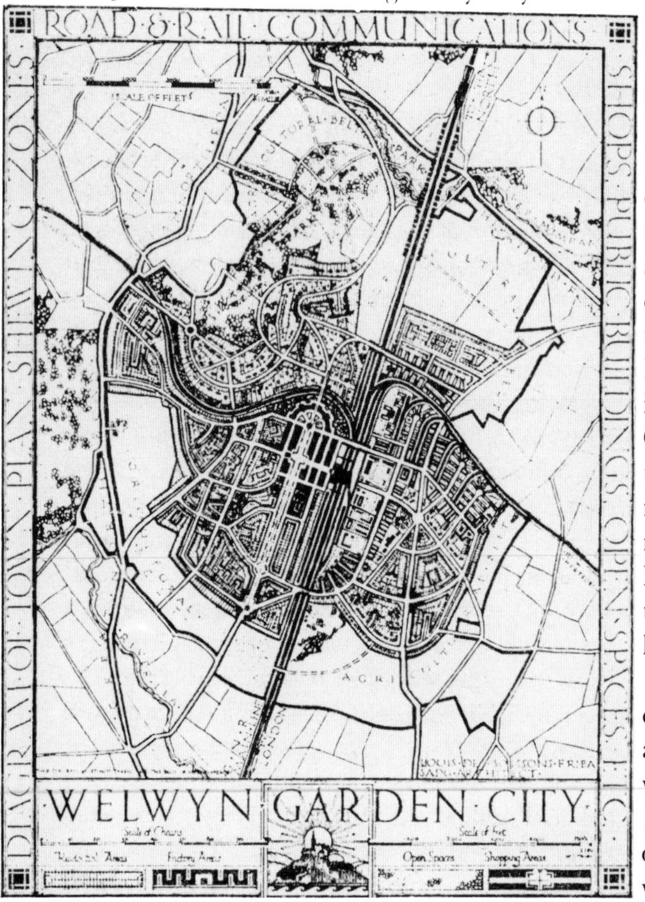

Early designs for Welwyn Garden City, which was launched in 1920, showed it above a symbolic rendering of a city on a hill, even though it was not on one. C. R. Ashbee's abortive plans for Ruislip Garden City (*c.* 1910), just outside London, actually would have been on a hill (although a modest one) and were clearly influenced by Campanella, of whom Ashbee was an admirer; the City of the Sun was a phrase which he constantly used. He had founded his own ideal community, the Guild of Handicraft, in the East End of London in 1888. In 1902, as an alternative to building its own settlement, the Guild had moved *en masse* to Chipping Campden in Gloucestershire, the epitome of those modest country towns which the garden-city movement had adopted as the ideal antithesis to the monster city. 'I am glad', he wrote in his journal in December 1901, 'that the men themselves have decided that on the whole it is better to leave Babylon and go home to the land.'[38]

The growing reputation of garden cities was made clear in 1912, when two garden capitals were initiated at Canberra and New Delhi.[39] The plan of Canberra was the result of a competition which was won in May 1912 by Walter Burley Griffin, of Chicago. The plan of New Delhi was made public in 1913, and was the work of a planning commission the dominant member

295. The World's Fair, Chicago, 1893. Looking past the Columbia Fountain to the Electricity and Manufacturers Pavilions (Avery Library, Columbia University, New York).

of which was Edwin Lutyens. The New Delhi plan shows the influence of that of Canberra, and those of both Wren's London and L'Enfant's Washington. But their long vistas, diagonal avenues and star-shaped constellations of roads were accompanied by very low densities and so much open space that almost all resemblance to a conventional great city was lost. The influence of the garden cities was clear, but so was that of what was known as the City Beautiful movement in America.

The City Beautiful was born in Chicago. In 1893 the World's Columbian Exposition was held there to celebrate the four hundredth anniversary of the discovery of America; it was popularly known as the World's Fair. It followed the model which had been worked out in the Paris exhibitions, and consisted of a great many kiosks and pavilions of all sizes congregated together to form what amounted to a separate exhibition city. It was the biggest exhibition yet to be held in the nineteenth century; it did not attract quite as many visitors as the Paris 1889 Exhibition (around 27 million as opposed to 32 million), possibly because a major financial depression hit America in 1893. But even so, it was successful enough to pay a ten percent dividend to those who had put up the money for it.

One reason for its success was that it had much the most inventive and enjoyable plan of all the exhibitions held up to its time. The plan was really more interesting than its grand classical architecture, which had all the limelight. It was a water city, like Venice. The water was grouped in two linked areas, a formal T-shaped combination of basin and canals, and a winding lagoon with a wooded island in the middle. The buildings were arranged in sympathy with the water, shading from the great formal axis, where the domed Administration Building looked down the water of the basin, to winding walks scattered with pavilions, at the far end of the lagoons.

The Exposition was designed to be enjoyable and easy to use.[40] There was a main railway terminus by the great basin, and an elevated railway running round the periphery. Foot-sore visitors could also be ferried from place to place by gondolas or silent electric launches on the waterways, or recover their energies in an abundance of restaurants, cafés, tea-houses, lunch-counters and refreshment stands, at ground level and on roof-terraces on the pavilions. A novel and outstandingly successful feature of the exhibition was the separate amusement area which was attached to it. A long pedestrian way known as the Midway Plaisance led up to the main entrance of the

296. Chicago as the City Beautiful. A drawing by Jules Guérin, from D. H. Burnham and E. H. Bennett, *The Plan of Chicago*, 1909.

main exhibition and passed through a crammed conglomeration of attractions that ranged from 'A Street in Old Cairo' to a giant Ferris Wheel; the latter was the inspiration of the surviving great wheel erected in the Prater in Vienna in 1900.

F. L. Olmsted was the landscape architect for the Exposition, and the brilliance of the plan and conception of the exhibition owed much to him. Inevitably it suggested the possibility of an alternative to the high densities, grid plans and crowded conglomerations of tall buildings of the central areas of Chicago and New York. In 1895 Daniel Burnham, the Chicago architect who had been the chief architect to the Exposition, started work on a plan for the improvement of Chicago which could turn it into what he called the City Beautiful.[41] The phrase was a variant on the House Beautiful, a term which contemporary house architects had taken from Bunyan's *Pilgrim's Progress* and made much use of. Burnham suggested a Chicago opened up with broad tree-planted boulevards and wide streets, and enriched with grand classical buildings on the model of those which had been built at the Exposition, especially around the great basin. In 1901–2 he was the leading spirit on a commission which presented a new plan for Washington; the plan cleared away the nineteenth-century naturalistic park which had taken over L'Enfant's Mall and re-created it as a broad formal vista lined with grand public buildings. In 1903 he designed a similar Mall on a smaller (but far from small) scale as a central space for a new civic centre at Cleveland. In 1904 he produced a grand plan for San Francisco on the same lines; it was never carried out, but its influence led to the building of the civic centre there, in which a domed city hall and other public buildings in the grand manner surrounded a great open square. His Chicago plan was officially adopted by Chicago in 1907; much of it was never carried out, but it did lead to a good deal of street widening and the formation of a great area of public parks, laid out on formal lines between the city and the lake. Lutyens's gigantic open spaces at New Delhi are in the same tradition; the King's Avenue leads from the War Memorial Arch up through the two blocks of the Secretariats to the Viceroy's Palace, and space not all that much smaller than the entire City of London is allotted to about fifteen buildings. At Canberra another great central vista runs from the Capitol across the lake to the war memorial.

Schemes for more open cities could have a variety of points of view behind them. It is worth contrasting the attitudes of Olmsted and A. R. Sennett, author of *Garden*

Cities in Theory and Practice. Sennett's comparison of the country girl, 'the modest, unaffected, truth-loving maiden, replete and content, in the charms of Nature's adorning', to the 'woman about town, a creature of guile, artifice and insincerity',[42] can be set against Olmsted's dry remark that anyone who has been to 'what stands for festivity' in the remoter farms of New England 'will hardly think that the ardent desire of the young woman to escape to the town is wholly unreasonable'.[43] Olmsted believed in great cities as centres of enlightenment, civilization and enjoyable living, but believed equally strongly in the necessity for public parks and a reduction of density in residential areas. Sennett thought that 'Concentration of population in any one spot is unnatural ... If these agglomerations of populace be a necessity, and are at the same time repugnant to the natural law, the remedy must be a compromise ... the towns must be made more like the country.'[44] Olmsted, in fact, thought that cities were wonderful places which could be improved, Sennett that they were terrible places which had to be made bearable. Sennett's point of view was the predominant one in the garden-city movement. The Garden City Association became the Garden City and Town Planning Association in 1908 and the Town and Country Planning Association in 1932; the mainstream of modern town-planning stems from it, and resulted in people who disliked great cities being put in charge of them all over the world.

Advocates of the City Beautiful were not as extreme as advocates of the Garden City. They believed in great cities, but great cities rescued from squalor and confusion and made noble and spacious. Even so, Olmsted and Burnham should not be bracketed together. Both the Garden City and the City Beautiful tended to use space less so that something could happen in it than for its own sake, either as a symbolic representation of national or civic dignity and power, or as a symbolic rejection of the congestion of 'unnatural' cities. Olmsted's schemes were all conceived in terms of people. The 1893 Exposition was brilliantly worked out to provide an enjoyable and working ambiance for huge crowds. The City Beautiful schemes provided bigger spaces for use by fewer people; the emphasis was on dignity, not enjoyment. Burnham admired great cities, but his point of view was basically that of a successful professional man who lived in a prosperous suburb (Evanston in his case) and was driven by his chauffeur to his downtown office five days a week. The schemes bore only a comparatively superficial resemblance to their historical exemplars. The Parisian boulevards went through crowded residential areas, the populations of which came flocking into them for exercise and amusement. The Champs Élysées was primarily an area for public amusement and social promenading, and only occasionally a triumphal way into Paris. L'Enfant's Mall was designed as a broad walk between an avenue of trees, and he envisaged it as thronged with people walking up and down; Burnham made it an empty space, the only function of which was to provide a vista from the Capitol to the Washington Monument, and the Monument to the Capitol.

A great City Beautiful avenue, such as the Mall in London as it was remodelled in 1903–4, could provide a suitably spacious setting for processions, parades and the reception of foreign statesmen or domestic heroes. It is arguable that the most successful product of City Beautiful thinking was its railway stations; their huge classical portals added drama to the act of entrance or departure from the city, and their great vaulted halls echoed to the hurry and stir of the crowd which by the nature of their use frequented them.[45]

297–8. Early London County Council estates: Cookham House, Boundary Street Estate, Tower Hamlets, 1893–1900, and (right) Du Cane Road, Old Oak Estate, Hammersmith, 1905–13.

The early garden cities and garden suburbs were all built either by the co-operative efforts of individuals, or by companies for their workers. It was not until the end of the nineteenth century that public housing provided by the state or the city made its first significant appearance. Up till that time it never seems even to have occurred as an option to governments or city councils. The one exception was when they as employers provided housing in the form of barracks or the terrace housing built for the workers in the Arsenal in Venice.

In England a Royal Commission on the Housing of the Working Classes sat in 1884–5. The commission was one of the products of that mixture of fear, bad conscience and goodwill which had made the conditions of the working classes, especially in big cities, a major subject of concern in the mid-Victorian years. It reported, among much else, that the private sector, philanthropic bodies and building trusts were unable to provide new working-class housing in the amounts and to the quality that was needed. The Housing of the Working Classes Act, passed by Parliament in 1890, enlarged the previously limited powers of local authorities to build housing. It became law three years after the London County Council had been set up as a central body with limited control (which was gradually increased) over the Cities of London and Westminster and the patchwork of parish vestries which had previously run the London conurbation. The council was elected on a wide franchise, and the first elections were won by the Progressives, a mixture of Liberals and Fabian Socialists. As a reforming organization it set up a Housing of the Working Classes Branch of its Architects Department in 1893, and recruited a group of gifted, dedicated and idealistic young architects to staff it. The first two important projects to be designed by the branch were both the result of slum clearance and road-widening schemes. They were the Boundary Street Estate in Bethnal Green (1893–1900) and the Millbank Estate behind the Tate Gallery in Westminster (1897–1902). Between them they housed nearly ten thousand people.

These ten thousand had to be fitted in on relatively small sites, and of necessity the housing took the form of flats in five-storey (or occasionally six-storey) buildings. Five storeys was usually considered the limit for flats without lifts. Lifts could not be included on the London County Council estates because of the expense, since they had to be built for an economic return, without any subsidy from the rates; even as it was, the flats had to be let at rents higher than most of the families which they had displaced could afford.

The architecture of the two estates was the result of a very successful attempt to use good materials with the minimum of ornament in such a way as to avoid the grim image of almost all the working-class housing produced by companies, trusts and charities in the previous decades. But it was not what its architects would have built, if free of constraints; by temperament they were garden-city men. The 1890 Act had authorized local authorities to buy unbuilt-on land for housing, but only within the municipal boundaries; this limited the options in London, and made anything resembling a garden city virtually impossible. A second Act, passed in 1900, allowed the purchase of land outside municipal boundaries. The London County Council bought thirty-nine acres at Tooting in January 1900, and three more out-country estates in the next few years. On them they built what became known as cottage estates, of pleasant two-storey houses, a few of them semi-detached but most built in short terraces, interspersed with occasional tree-lined avenues, public gardens or little squares, and all having reasonably sized private gardens. Owing to the financial constraints, the density was around 25–30 dwellings to the acre, considerably higher than in middle-class garden cities and suburbs or company villages, but low compared to that of the Boundary and Millbank Estates. These cottage estates provided an alternative to flats that was to be imitated by councils all over the British Isles in ensuing decades.[46]

On the continent, public housing became important later than in England. Holland followed on fairly closely, and the fact that it was not involved in the 1914–18 war enabled large areas of housing to be built in the war years, especially in Amsterdam. In Austria and Germany, on the other hand, public housing became a major public issue as a result of the disastrous end of the war, the collapse of the previous regimes, the departure of the two emperors, and the emergence of Social Democrat and Socialist administrations. Both Vienna and Berlin, which had previously had some of the most congested working-class housing in Europe, built on such a scale and with such panache that by the 1930s the tide of influence had altered, and it was English authorities which were beginning to imitate continental ones.

In both Berlin and Vienna a situation not unlike that resulting from the creation of the London County Council came into existence, but in a more dramatic and comprehensive way; both cities had much bigger industrial populations than London. Vienna had elections based on a new and wider franchise, and elected a Socialist government, as it was to continue to do in all free elections up to the present day. In Berlin a new and larger authority was created in 1920, as in London in 1890, but with considerably greater powers; it united the old centre of Berlin and all the surrounding and previously independent boroughs under one authority. Responsibility for zoning and building

299. The Karl-Marx Hof, Vienna.

regulations was transferred to this from the state-appointed police-president, who had previously run Berlin, somewhat in the same way as the Préfet de la Seine continued to run Paris. Most of the working-class housing which was built subsequent to the reorganization was not in fact technically public housing, but it was essentially a creation of the city government. It was built by a number of public construction companies or building societies, the majority of the shares in which belonged to the local authorities or the trade unions. One of the biggest of the building societies was run by Martin Wagner, who was also in charge of the municipal department of urban planning.[47]

All continental public housing included an element of terraced or even occasionally semi-detached or detached houses, probably built under English garden-city influence. But in all of them flats predominated. They were an accepted and customary form of living on the continent, and there was none of the working-class prejudice against them that existed in England; moreover, under the influence of Communism and the Modern Movement in architecture they began to acquire the same kind of mystique, as symbols of liberated and communal life, which cottages with gardens had acquired for garden-city enthusiasts in England.

In Vienna, post-war poverty and inflation, an acute housing problem, a Socialist city government and a flamboyant mayor in the person of Karl Seitz produced an equally flamboyant housing programme.[48] The city was able to buy up land in large quantities at low prices, and by 1933 it had completed nearly 60,000 dwellings, most of which took the form of flats. Some of the estates were very large. The flats on them were small and poorly finished, but externally the buildings were palaces for the people: their architecture was heroic, and they were to be generators of a heroic mythology, for they became the bastions of the Communist party and scenes of sieges and machine-gun battles in the days following the *Anschluss*.

A sensational enfilade of semicircular arches surmounted by lean and splendid statues pierces the great cliff of the Karl Marx Hof, the grandest of the Vienna estates. But its architecture is not so megalomaniac as photographs suggest. It is built around three sides of a very pleasant garden, its materials are an agreeable mixture of red brick and grey rough-cast, and its scale, although grand, is not oppressive. Moreover, through the great arches is a railway station, fifteen minutes by train from the city centre.

This Vienna housing was disapproved of by the Modern Movement architects who designed the working-class housing in Berlin, Frankfurt and other German cities. Their own buildings were in a much lower key, and carefully avoided grand gestures, ornaments, pattern-making or any overt form of historicism. Again, photographs can be misleading, especially those taken shortly after the buildings were completed, which

300–1. Berlin. Two views in the Hufeisensiedlung, Britz, designed by Bruno Taut in 1928.

usually make them seem much starker than they became once planting matured. One of the best known of the estates, the Hufeisensiedlung (Horseshoe Estate), built to the designs of Bruno Taut in 1928, is a remarkably pleasant place. The horseshoe of flats round which the estate centres and from which it takes its name, looks into an oval bowl of greenery, which drops down to a pond and a cluster of trees; a path goes round the green, and between it and the buildings are private gardens belonging to the flats; the flats have deep inset balconies big enough to serve as outdoor rooms. The feeling that this is a place designed so that the poor could emerge from the dark courts of the Berlin tenements and enjoy the same kind of amenities as the well-off comes across with pleasing strength.

The plan of the Hufeisensiedlung horseshoe is the same as that of the housing of the 1840s and 1850s in the Ladbroke Grove area in London: a circuit of terraces looking onto private gardens, which in turn let into a central communal garden. The resemblance may be a coincidence; but certainly there was no tradition of terrace architecture in Germany or Austria, whereas England was full of prototypes for terrace layouts and for the kind of interpenetration of housing by natural landscape which is found in many of the German schemes. By and large, neither they nor the Austrian housing are more than marginally revolutionary in terms of architecture or planning. They are arranged in terraces, circles or squares in much the same manner and to much the same scale

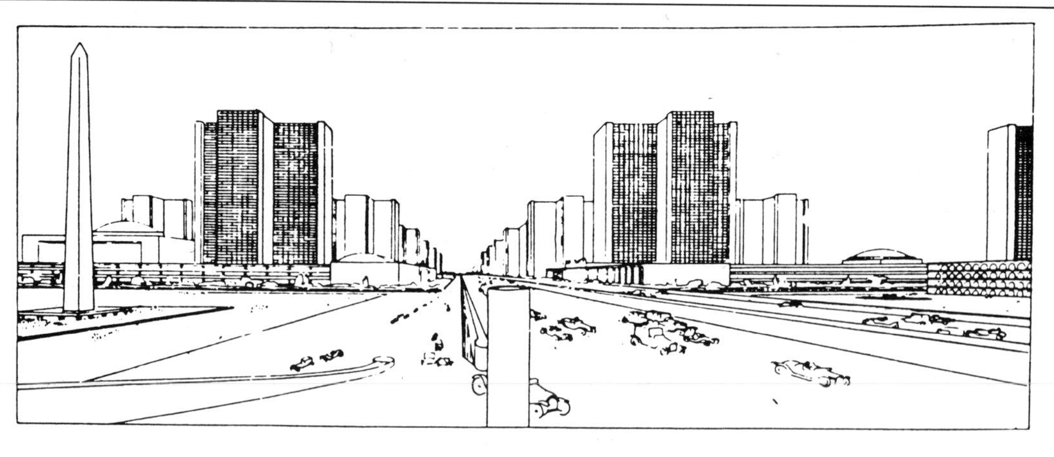

302. *Ville Contemporaine* From Le Corbusier, *Urbanisme*, 1925).

as the eighteenth- and nineteenth-century terraces of Bath or Kensington; their height is limited, as the heights of those were, by the fact that none had lifts, and they are built of conventional materials. They are none the worse for that.

More obviously sensational visions of the city of the future were produced in these years, of which far and away the most influential were the various drawings published by Le Corbusier to show a *ville contemporaine* in his *Urbanisme* (1925) and other publications. They projected a new image, of cities which developed vertically rather than horizontally, allowing green space to flow into them and around the great glass towers in which the citizens lived, enjoying fresh air, sunshine and access under cover to restaurants, nurseries, shops and laundries.

In fact Le Corbusier's schemes had their roots in what had gone before, just like any other schemes, as he himself made clear by calling them 'vertical garden cities'. What he had done was to mate the skyscraper with the garden city, decommercializing the skyscraper and modernizing the garden city in the process. Even the glass buildings by which he and other architects of the Modern Movement were fascinated as symbols of enlightenment had a long lineage behind them, going right back to the light, 'clear as crystal', and the walls 'of pure gold, like unto clear glass' of the New Jerusalem in Revelations.[49]

Le Corbusier built nothing resembling his *ville contemporaine* before 1939. It had one child in the pre-war period: the Cité de la Muette at Drancy, built by the Department of the Seine as one of a group of satellite *cités jardins* near Paris. The estate was begun in the early 1930s and was to consist of a mixture of three-storey ranges and sixteen-storey blocks, built of prefabricated units. It was left unfinished, served for a time as a police barracks and a prison, and has never been used for the purpose for which it was built.[50] In the 1930s, if one had put the gleaming glass skyscraper by the side of a little wooden bungalow as contrasting housing types, it would have been supposed that one was contrasting the former as the type of the future with the latter as a type on the way out. But in fact it was the bungalow which was to win, for its recognizable descendants are still being built by the hundreds of thousands today, whereas residential tower blocks have fallen into disgrace, and are as likely to be blown up as put up.

The detached house with its own garden, of which the bungalow proved to be one of the most popular forms, owed its power to the fact that three different types of symbolic value could accrue to it: it could be seen as a miniature country house in a park, a homestead on a smallholding, or a domestic sanctuary in a Garden of Eden. The snob-value of a suburban villa as a country house in miniature established its popularity in England, and early nineteenth-century concepts of domesticity reinforced it; on the other hand, the fact that the upper classes, when in London, continued to live in terraces, and the formidably large terraced areas of London which resulted, offered an alternative

303. Cottage residence at Hawthorn, Melbourne. From *The Australasian Builder*, 1890 (Latrobe Library, University of Melbourne).

image, which probably helps to explain the long survival of terrace houses at all social levels in all parts of the British Isles. For different reasons, builders of garden cities, garden suburbs and working-class cottage estates were consciously trying to create communities, and favoured terraces because they suggested, however misleadingly, a communal spirit.

In both cases the semi-detached house provided a compromise that was to be remarkably popular in the British Isles, but almost nowhere else. When the Northern Line was opened from Charing Cross to Golders Green in 1907 it was clearly a semi-detached house which was advertised on the tube line's poster, however coyly disguised. Tube lines, motor buses and local railways, combined with cheap working-men's fares, opened up new stretches of territory to those who were still working in city centres; rising wages and the growth of the building societies supplied the necessary finance; and in the 1920s, when cheap Morrises and Fords came on the market, a whole new dimension was added to the lives of ordinary people. Car ownership, which had been 109,000 in England in 1919, had risen to around two million by 1939. In the 1920s private developers gave up building terrace housing almost completely in favour of semi-detached or detached houses; terraces survived only on public housing estates or in central London, where they maintained their social prestige. One reason for favouring semi-detached houses as opposed to terraces was that the gap between each group of two left the occupants space in which it was possible to build a garage; up till 1939 garages were seldom provided by the developer except as optional extras, for the percentage of car owners was still not high enough.[51]

In English-speaking countries other than England the semi-detached house found few takers. In America the tradition of the detached house had never been entirely lost, and in America, Australia, New Zealand and South Africa a detached house in its own bit of ground, whether in the country or the town, was probably the ideal for which most immigrants were hoping. Terrace houses were also built in considerable numbers to begin with and under English influence in Australian towns, just as they had been from the eighteenth century in East Coast American towns, but outside New

304. Melbourne. Design by C. D. Figgis for suburban villas, Malvern, *c.* 1890 (Latrobe Library, University of Melbourne).

305. (right) Golders Green, London Transport Poster.

York and, rather surprisingly, San Francisco the terrace house had gone out of fashion in both countries by 1900, if not before. Meanwhile, the detached house could be found right the way down the social scale.

In Melbourne, working-class families had lived mainly in detached houses from the very beginning, and they continued to do so when equivalent families in most big American cities were living in tenements. As R. E. N. Twopenny, in his *Town Life in Australia*, put it in 1883: 'Terraces and detached houses are universally disliked, and almost every class of suburban house is detached and stands in its own garden.'[52] To begin with, the working-class housing was in the centre, or in inner suburbs (which, as was usually the case in Australia, became separate municipalities). It was made up of single-storey cottages containing one to three rooms, almost invariably built of wood, and closely packed together near the docks, sawmills, breweries, brickfields, tanneries or soap factories where their occupants worked. The houses were usually on low, flat and often damp ground. Building societies were active in Melbourne from at least the 1860s, and many houses were acquired through building societies, and even built by them. The end result was not unlike the rows of detached wooden houses in inner Chicago: but the single-storey Melbourne cottages were much smaller than the Chicago ones, and so were not subdivided into tenements. But as their condition deteriorated over the years, they became slums.[53]

Melbourne enjoyed great prosperity in the 1880s; between 1881 and 1891 its population expanded from 268,000 to 473,000. Its original suburbs grew larger, and new suburbs appeared. The development was stimulated by feverish activity on the part of real estate agents and building societies, and nearly all took the form of detached houses in gardens. The poorest stayed in the deteriorating wooden suburbs in the centre, but loans, low rail fares and good wages enabled clerks, artisans and the better-paid labourers to move into little three- or four-roomed brick cottages. Inevitably, the better-off got the better land, however, and their bigger houses in bigger gardens spread over the hilltops. Melbourne became a huge conurbation of low-density houses.

In America the low-density residential suburb spread down the social scale after 1900 rather than before. Suburban development reached a peak in the 1920s, when cheap cars, cheap building techniques, easy loans and mass-advertising spread suburbs in ever increasing circles round all the East Coast and Midwest cities. But these were still suburbs built round conventional high density centres. Meanwhile a new vision of a vast city of houses, gardens, low buildings and low densities, in which the conventional city centre shrank to unimportance, was emerging in the west at Los Angeles, partly by accident and partly by design.

The first question about Los Angeles is why it is there at all. In *This Country of Yours* (1932), Morris Markey describes how he wandered round Los Angeles trying to answer it. 'The Chamber of Commerce people told me about the concentration of fruit, the shipping, the Western branch-factories put up by concerns in the East. But none of these things seemed the cause of a city. They seemed rather the effect, rising from an inexplicable accumulation of people.' In the end he was forced to conclude that 'alone of all the cities in America, there is no plausible answer to the question'.[55]

UNDERGROUND

SANCTUARY.

"'Tis pleasant, through the loopholes of retreat,
To peep at such a world; to see the stir
Of the great Babel, and not feel the crowd;
To hear the roar she sends through all her gates
At a safe distance, where the dying sound
Falls a soft murmur on th' uninjured ear."

William Cowper.

J. R. & Co. Ltd.

THE SOONEST REACHED AT ANY TIME

GOLDERS GREEN

(HENDON AND FINCHLEY)

A PLACE OF DELIGHTFUL PROSPECTS

If the Chamber of Commerce had handed him a history of its organization written as early as 1899, it would have answered him: Los Angeles, it claimed, was 'the best advertised city in the globe, Chicago alone excepted'.[56] Ralph Hancock put it more exuberantly in 1949: 'Here is one dusty little Mexican pueblo starting out deliberately to make itself great by intelligent, consistent, scientific advertising, and now, after sixty years, there lies the result, sparkling like an overgrown movie set, mile on mile of the most beautiful residences in America, street on street of the last word in efficient commercial buildings, stack on stack of statistics so amazing that they challenge every doubt. Advertising, ballyhoo, publicity, the most ancient of California's professions and still the greatest outlet for its citizens' over abundant exuberance, did it.'[57]

A mid-nineteenth-century geographer looking at a map of California would have noticed that it had two great natural harbours, one in the north at San Francisco, and one in the south at San Diego. He might reasonably have concluded that San Francisco and San Diego would become the main cities of northern and southern California respectively. That is what the people of San Diego thought. As the natural corollary, they worked for a south transcontinental railway to end at San Diego, just as the transcontinental line to the north ended at San Francisco. Los Angeles, by better lobbying and better publicity, arranged for the line to come to it, and by successful lobbying of Congress in Washington, persuaded the central government to subsidize an enormously expensive artificial harbour, to connect with the railway.[58] This was not the limit of its achievements. Advertising cities was not a new idea in the 1890s. In *Martin Chuzzlewit* Dickens had made cruel fun of the way in which new midwestern cities puffed themselves.[59] The Statue of Liberty advertised New York City as much as, and more than, it advertised Liberty, as New York businessmen were well aware.[60] But Los Angeles—and, in particular, the Los Angeles Chamber of Commerce—developed the puffing of cities into an art form.

It is a tenet of faith among advertisers that advertisements only work for something which is worth advertising. The success of Los Angeles rested on the climate of southern California. Several million people, freezing in the midwest winters and grilling in the midwest summers, needed to be told that if they cashed their savings and booked to southern California, they would find the best climate in the world waiting for them, in their own country. Los Angeles set out to tell them this, and to make sure that when they bought their ticket it was to Los Angeles that they booked.

California had been ceded by Spain to America in 1846. San Francisco quickly grew to prosperity, on the basis of its harbour and the Gold Rush. In 1869 the completion of the Central Pacific Railway gave it its transcontinental link. But it was not till the 1870s that the dim little Spanish pueblo at Los Angeles, and the settlements in its neighbourhood, began to attract any attention.

Americans came to southern California for four reasons, to grow oranges, to have a holiday, to get well and to die. Given water, its soil is wonderfully fertile; its beaches stretch for ever; its climate is dry, and never too hot or too cold; and invalids, especially consumptives, do better there than anywhere in Europe, or at least that is what Charles Nordhoff asserted in his best-selling *California: For Health, Pleasure and Residence* (1872). In 1883 Major Ben Truman weighed in, in his *Tourist Illustrated Guide to California*, with the kind of language that seemed to flow automatically from the pens of those writing about Los Angeles: 'Almost everything grown on earth can be raised in Los Angeles

306. The California Pavilion at the World's Fair, Chicago, 1893 (Chicago Historical Society).

County. The pomegranate flourishes side by side with the potato, the banana with the tomato, the orange, lime and apricot with the peach, pear and apple. The guava and the plum, the olive and the squash, are found in Los Angeles County, in the most loving companionship side by side . . . But the winters of Los Angeles—ah! While all is rude, and cold, and leafless, and flowerless, and changeable in all the States east of the Sierra, in Los Angeles wind and weather are almost perfection . . . everywhere there are roses—such roses as rival those of Paestum, or of the Bosphorus—white, cream, blood-red and plush—freighting the very atmosphere with their incomparable odors and aromatic sweets. You may drive out to the delicious orange groves . . . or you may dash down to a beach where the foaming billows of the Pacific roll distantly away to a tropical southern sea.'[61]

By the mid-1880s all was set up for the big splurge. Los Angeles City was the centre of a prosperous farming and fruit growing area, and growing fast. Down on the coast, Santa Monica was getting a reputation as a resort. Up in the hills, the city of Pasadena was founded in 1886 by a group of well-off citizens from Indiana, and consumptives began coming to spend the winters there. Visitors came by sea or by rail. In 1873 Los Angeles had paid through the nose to the Southern Pacific Railroad for the privilege of becoming the terminus of its line. In 1884 it connected with the Santa Fé, a second southern transcontinental line. It was now joined to the East by two lines. In 1886 a price war resulted; at one stage tickets from Kansas City to Los Angeles were being sold for a dollar. Midwesterners poured in by the thousand. Admittedly, most of them trickled back again, but the inrush had given businessmen in Los Angeles plenty of food for thought. The Los Angeles Chamber of Commerce was set up in 1888. In 1890

307. The walnut elephant in the Chamber of Commerce permanent exhibition, Los Angeles (California Historical Society).

Frank Wiggins, a Quaker from Richmond, Indiana, was appointed head of its publicity, and became one of the city's forgotten founders.

The Los Angeles myth was largely created in the next ten years, by Frank Wiggins and others.[62] In 1891 a journalist had remarked that 'if you dangle a golden orange before the eyes of a Northern man you can lead him anywhere'.[63] Wiggins became a genius at dangling oranges. In 1891 he was in charge of an exhibition of citrus fruit which was sent to Chicago; it was originally billed to be called the Citrus Fair, but it was probably he who had the name changed at the last minute to the Orange Carnival. It had over 100,000 visitors. But this, of course, was nothing to the 1893 World's Fair in Chicago. The Californian pavilion there was the only state pavilion of any size apart from the Illinois one, and it was much the more entertaining of the two. It was almost the first building to be designed in the so-called California Mission Style, and in contrast to the grand classical fronts of the other pavilions it vividly suggested a land where one could enjoy oneself in the sun. The pavilion itself was designed in San Francisco, but the displays were dominated by southern California, which also managed to get hold of the entire courtyard of the great Horticultural Pavilion.[64] Frank Wiggins

308. Los Angeles display at the Toronto Fair of 1930 (California Historical Society).

ran the Southern California World's Fair Association, which organized the displays. On opening day 'cartload after cartload of fruit was thrown out into the vast throng gathered in front of the building. It took a hundred Columbian guards to maintain order and keep a passageway into the street.'[65] In the Horticultural Building southern California showed an Orange Tower in the form of a triumphal column, an Orange Bell and an Orange Globe; they were made up of 25,000 regularly changed oranges, and consumed 375,000 oranges in the course of the fair. The courtyard was planted with an orchard of real lemon and orange trees, covered in fruit: 'this surprising display awakened lively interest in myriads of visitors; especially those who, living all their lives under sterner skies, had never before had the privilege of enjoying such a sight'. In the main California Pavilion a live palm tree, 128 years old, was planted beneath the dome; there was a Cleopatra's Needle made up of olive-oil bottles, a giant pyramid of raisins, a life-size knight on horseback covered with prunes ('probably no single feature of the California Building attracted more general notice'), and fruit and oranges everywhere which were lavishly handed out free to any visitors who wanted them.[66] A special booklet, *The Land of Sunshine: Southern California*, was published for the exhibition. Los Angeles figured prominently in it. Two illustrations were captioned 'From snow to roses in thirty-eight minutes: Los Angeles County'. A photograph of a house almost invisible under a cascade of climbing roses was captioned: 'One hundred thousand gold-of-ophir roses, Los Angeles County: this view taken in February'.

Both the midwestern press and the midwestern public loved the Californian displays. It was claimed that ten million people saw them. 'People of all nations, classes and colors rushed for the California Building', reported the Salt Lake City *Tribune*. 'Always fresh, and green, and cool', said the Wisconsin *Eagle*. The Chicago *Times* went over the top: 'California enshrined the purple and gold of her sun-kissed fruit with the nation's colours, and scattered in the lap of the world the treasures of her vineyards ... There is an air of prosperity and abundance about it all that is seen in no other State building.' 'Why can't I go and live there permanently?' wrote a visitor from Wisconsin in the comments book. He probably did.[67]

Through the 1890s Wiggins and the Los Angeles Chamber of Commerce sent displays to exhibitions all over America. For two years they kept a travelling exhibition, 'California on Wheels', moving round the Midwest. A permanent exhibition was maintained in Los Angeles, the most prominent object in which was an enormous elephant, entirely made out of walnuts.[68] The Chamber maintained a steady flow of publications, and even scattered ten thousand leaflets about Los Angeles across the Alaskan snows of the Klondyke.[69] In 1894 a group of Los Angeles businessmen started up a magazine, *The Land of Sunshine*; a gifted editor, Harry Lummis, ran it and got it a paid circulation bigger than that of any other magazine west of Chicago. Los Angeles started up a 'Fiesta de Los Angeles' and Pasadena an annual Rose Carnival. When San Francisco was shattered by earthquake in 1906 the Los Angeles Chamber of Commerce hastily weighed in with the announcement, 'Geologists say that the rock formation underlying the city of Los Angeles is of such a nature that it is as safe from the danger of earthquake as any locality in the United States'. Year by year the publicity machine grew, the epithets and slogans rolled out, the orange architecture at the exhibitions piled up in more and more fantastic structures.

And the Midwest responded. 'Retired farmers, grocers, Ford agents, hardware merchants, and shoe merchants from the Middle West and other parts of these United States, thousands and tens of thousands of them ... Toil-broken and bleached out they flock to Los Angeles, fugitives from the simple, inexorable justice of life, from hard labor and drudgery, from cold winters and blistering summers of the prairies.'[70] The population of Los Angeles was 11,000 in 1880, 50,000 by 1890. By 1926 there were huge electric signs all over the city '2,000,000 population by 1930'. By 1930 the population was in fact 2,300,000. By 1970 it was 8,351,266.

This was the population of the urbanized area, not of Los Angeles City. The great conurbation of Los Angeles developed because several dozen smaller cities, of which the city of Los Angeles was the biggest, grew until they merged together. New cities or would-be cities were starting up all the time. Some prospered and some failed. Some ultimately went in with Los Angeles City, usually because they wanted to share in its water supply. Some—Long Beach, Santa Monica, Pasadena, Beverly Hills, Santa Ana—are still independent.

By the early 1900s the beach of Los Angeles County was lined with a series of separate resorts: Santa Monica, Ocean Park, Venice, Playa del Rey, El Segundo, Manhattan

309. The Dragon Gorge Amusement Ride, Ocean Park, *c.* 1910 (Henry E. Huntington Library, San Marino, California).

Beach, Hermosa Beach, Redondo, Long Beach, Naples, Huntington Beach, Newport Beach. Most of them had piers. Ocean Park had an oriental plunge-bath complete with minarets, and a dragon gorge scenic railway. Venice had a grand canal, a lagoon, a St Mark's Hotel, an enormous auditorium and the world's largest roller-coaster. Some beach resorts considered that they had more class than others. All of them soon acquired permanent residents. In the years around 1900 the older, iller, staider or richer visitors went to the great hotels up in the hills around Pasadena, and many of them settled there permanently. Santa Ana and San Fernando were trading centres for the orange groves. San Pedro and Wilmington were where the inadequate natural harbour had always been, and from 1899 the great breakwaters of the new harbour were gradually constructed there. Los Angeles City was the business and transport centre for the whole area, and the seat of county administration. In the mid-1890s oil was first discovered on the coast, and every year more and more long-necked oil pumps moved their heads up and down, driving some of the beach resorts into decline in the process. In 1910 the first movie was made in Hollywood, and Los Angeles acquired yet another dimension.

By then the whole area had acquired what amounted to an official religion. It was loudly proclaimed by the publicity men, who may or may not have believed in it, but it certainly meant a great deal to many of the people who came to live there. It was a religion based on the garden-city gospel, but with a difference. It taught that the conventional big city was corrupt, diseased, cruel and artificial, and that the city of oranges and the sun was kindly, helpful, natural and innocent. But it was also going to be very large: it would be a Garden of Eden, but an Eden for a million Adams and Eves, living in little homes in a million little paradises.

In 1894 an article in the *Land of Sunshine* proclaimed the theme of the little home. Los Angeles was a good place for the invalid, the artist and the poet, but it was best of all for the modest man who had escaped from the 'chilling winds of the East' and taken up a smallholding. 'Its growing orange groves he sees and beholds resplendent in the sunlight he came so far to seek. His home, however small and humble, stands embowered in roses . . . the children of the homemaker no longer spend half their time behind sealed windows and doors, but like healthy young animals as they should be, live in the sunshine, become strong in body and limb, and grow into goodly men and women without a trace of sallow bleach upon their rugged sun-burned faces.'[71] In 1907 Dana Bartlett was proclaiming in his book *The Better City* that Los Angeles 'shall be a city of homes, and therefore a city without slums. Instead of the pent-up millions in other cities, that from necessity or choice know only a contracted indoor existence, here will be found only healthy, happy families, scattered over a vast area.'[72] The image of the smallholder living off his orange groves was fading, however; instead, Bartlett explained how, given cheap fares and rapid transit, 'the working man can be induced to locate with his family far from the noisy city'.

A similar picture was painted by W. E. Smythe in 1910. 'The sunshine and the rain are as kind to the poor as the rich, and the rose blooms as sweetly for the bungalow as for the palace . . . A true Southern Californian city would be a garden filled with homes. Many of these homes would be very humble, costing but a few hundred dollars, yet they would represent a very high average of beauty and comfort, thanks to the marvellous climate. In order to accommodate a great population, such cities will naturally spread over a vast area—the vaster the better.'[73] The themes of the wicked Eastern city and the new way of life in the West were constantly repeated. In 1914 the Los Angeles *Examiner* thought that 'it is our departure from "village ideals", the simple comely life of our fathers, that has nurtured the blight of demoralizing metropolitanism'.[74] In the 1920s Clarence A. Dykstra urged that the city should spread 'until it meets the country, and until beautiful forms of urban life blend almost imperceptibly with beautiful forms of rural life'.[75] G. Gordon Whitnall called for 'not another New York, but a New Los Angeles. Not a great homogeneous mass with a pyramiding of populations and squalor in a single center, but a federation of communities co-ordinated into a metropolis of sunlight and air.'[76]

By and large, this is what Los Angeles became. Admittedly, Los Angeles City had a conventional downtown, but a law passed in 1906 had forbidden buildings over thirteen storeys high in it, and by the end of the 1930s a large chunk of it was being demolished for a civic centre as huge and blank as any City Beautiful could hope for. And all around it there was indeed a federation of communities, made up of hundreds of thousands of individual homes, most of them modest homes for modest people. In 1907 Dana Bartlett had pointed out the possibilities of 'cheap bungalows or California houses'.[77] The bungalow was not the only kind of house to be built in Los Angeles, but it was built in very great numbers and it epitomized the Los Angeles spirit.

310. (right) A view in Los Angeles.

EST PARKING ONLY

311. Bowen Bungalow Court, No. 549, East Villa (Alfred Heinemann, Assoc., 1912), Pasadena (Greene and Greene Library, Gamble House, Pasadena).

Bungalows on the Anglo-Indian model were built all over the hotter zones of the British Empire from the early nineteenth century up to the 1930s, but the bungalow came to California by way of England, and changed in the process.[78] The first English bungalows were built on the Kent coast in the 1860s and 1870s, and were what thirty years previously would have been called 'cottages' under a new name. The name was probably chosen for the sake of novelty, in order to sell them, for visually the little houses bore no resemblance at all to Indian bungalows. The name caught on, however, and as more English bungalows were built they started to live up to their name, and look like bungalows, to the extent that they became cottages with a bit of verandah attached, and with a big roof which (unlike those in Indian bungalows) often contained one or two attic rooms. They became popular as seaside or country retreats for people who thought of themselves as artistic or progressive. It was in this form that they reached the East Coast of America in the 1880s and from there they moved on to California by way of the Midwest. A typical California bungalow was constructed of wood, and had a roof of very shallow pitch with extremely deep eaves, but not necessarily a verandah. To begin with they were built in modest quantities by artistic people in comfortable circumstances.

By the 1920s making, building, selling and promoting bungalows had become a major industry. It was not confined to California; more than a hundred thousand bungalows were built in and around Chicago between 1920 and 1930.[79] The bungalow boom owed something to the energy and money that was put into its promotion, but basically bungalows succeeded because they were cheap, practical, and proved capable of inspiring great affection in the people who lived in them. Bungalows could be chosen by catalogue from a big mail-order firm, or a firm specializing in bungalows, and would arrive in numbered sections ready for erection. A flood of bungalow catalogues and bungalow magazines was published, and there were even bungalow songs:

312. Opening festivities at Grauman's Chinese Theater, 18 May 1927.

For I oft get bungalonely
In the mingled human drove
And I long for bungaloafing
In some bungalotus grove,
In a cooling bungalocation
Where no troubling trails intrude,
'Neath some bungalowly rooftree
In east bungalongitude.[80]

A special development of the Californian bungalow was the bungalow court, which first appeared in Los Angeles in 1909. It consisted of around ten to twenty bungalows, grouped round a pedestrian court; the bungalows were usually built for rent and were very popular with summer visitors.

The wide dispersal of Los Angeles would have been impossible without transport. Many people believe that Los Angeles was created by the motor car, but in fact it was there in essence before cars became of any importance. It developed as it did because an area in which literally dozens of separate independent cities, big and small, were scattered over a wide area, received an influx of immigrants, and acquired a system of electric-cars and local railways which connected what was there already and made

RCH BRIDAL & TUXEDO
2ND FLOOR

it easy to fill the gaps in between. By the early 1900s most of the system was owned by Henry E. Huntington, whose uncle had been one of the promoters of the Central Pacific Railroad. New lines seemed to appear almost daily: 'it would never do', he explained in 1904, 'for an electric line to wait until the demand for it comes. It must anticipate the growth of communities and be there when the home builders arrive.'[81] When the home builders did come, they usually found that the land was owned by the Huntington Land and Improvement Company.[81] By 1913 Huntington had joined the select group of American multi-millionaires to whom the great dealer Joseph Duveen was prepared to sell pictures, and was installing them in his great white palace at San Marino, next door to Pasadena. He was not a bungalow man.

Once mass-production of motor cars started up in the 1920s, Los Angeles took to them happily and painlessly. Inevitably, they helped to fill the remaining gaps of open land, and to encourage the richer citizens to build hilltop houses from which they could survey the poor ones in the plains below. The bungalow court developed effortlessly into the motel.[82] Downtown Los Angeles began to crumble as shops moved out of the centre along Wilshire Boulevard, where there was space for two great strips of car parking behind the towers and glitter of the great new stores. In the late 1930s the first freeway was built, from Los Angeles City to Pasadena.

The real estate interests christened the stores along Wilshire Boulevard 'Miracle Mile'. Los Angeles ballyhoo was working full-time. 'Salesmanship became a fine art. College professors lectured on overcoming sales resistance. Preachers promoted.'[83] In 1919 building permits for $28 million of work were issued, and by 1923 they were up to $200 million. Clean air and perpetual sunshine had made Los Angeles the world capital of the film industry, the stars lived out their unreal lives on Beverly Hills, huge shrines in the Chinese, Egyptian and Roman styles were erected for the celebration of the new religion, and crowd scenes gave employment to those who had failed to make a living out of oranges. Down by the harbour more and more long-necked oil pumps nodded their heads up and down, infiltrated the beach resorts, and created a new group of Los Angeles millionaires. What was happening to the city of healthy, happy families, and the cult of sun and oranges? Louis Adamic weighed in in 1926: 'Actually, and in spite of all the healthful sunshine and ocean breezes, it is a bad-place—full of old, dying people, and young people who were born old of tired pioneer parents, victims of America—full of curious wild and poisonous growths, decadent religions and cults of fake science, and wild-cat business enterprises, which, with their aim at quick profits, were doomed to collapse and drag down multitudes of people'.[84]

In fact, in spite of all the hopes of Dana Bartlett and his school, Los Angeles was becoming neither a Better City nor a City Beautiful nor an Earthly Paradise but a World City, just as complex and cosmopolitan as any conventional city of the past, a city in which almost anything could be found by those who knew where to look for it, pouring filth into the air as freely as Manchester had poured it into its rivers, a city of wild and wonderful and banal buildings, a city of bungalow-slums in junk-strewn gardens, a Mexican city, negro city, Japanese city, a city of oil-wells and art galleries, surfboards and sunsets, palm trees and Pepsi-Cola, the city of Philip Marlowe and Charlie Chaplin, of Mickey Mouse and Frank Lloyd Wright, of weirdoes, professors, gangsters, gurus, millionaires and nice ordinary people, a failed Jerusalem, a low-density Babylon.

313. (left) Painted street façade in Broadway, Los Angeles.

314. (following page) Case Study House (Pierre Koenig, 1958), Hollywood Hills, Los Angeles.

EPILOGUE

When travelling on the circle line in Tokyo a year or so ago, I was intrigued by the frenzy of advertising on display in the compartments. In addition to the usual row above the windows, as in the London Tube, there were advertisements projecting on banners from the walls, advertisements pasted on the doors, ceiling, windows and dividing screens by the doors, and advertisements wrapped round each individual strap hanger. It was all part of the chaotic tangle of signs and advertising to be found everywhere in Tokyo; J. M. Richards once surmised that the Japanese, having totally tamed their countryside, deliberately kept their jungle in the cities.

Advertising of this degree of wildness seems a specifically Japanese characteristic; even in Hong Kong it is not quite so frenetic. But a few months after visiting Tokyo, I was amused to read Eduardo de Amicis's account of his visit to Paris in 1885. When sitting in a café on the boulevards he had been struck by the omnipresent inescapable advertising. The facades opposite him were smothered with advertisements; advertisements were printed on the table tops; his drink arrived in an advertising glass; when he looked down to the ground, advertisements were printed in the asphalt at his feet. It was all, he felt, so different from the quiet surfaces even of Milan or Turin in his native Italy.

Cities pass through phases, and come out of them again, and in many ways Tokyo today is where Paris was a hundred years ago, which is perhaps one cause of the charm of that superficially hideous city. Tokyo, like Paris in the 1880s, has its big organizations and its big factories, but these rest on the foundation of thousands and thousands of small family businesses, shops and workshops. Little shops, bars and restaurants, open at all hours, crowd the streets, fill upper floors and line arcades both above ground and below it. Amazingly large areas of Tokyo are given over to amusement: if one wants to get any feel of what Montmartre was like in the 1890s, one is more likely to do so in Asakusa or Yoshiwara than in the sleazy streets of Montmartre today. Into the bars, clubs, cabarets and strip shows in these areas Japanese businessmen crowd at the end of their long day, to be chatted up by pretty little girls and to put off as long as possible their return to the minute flats in which they live in as cramped conditions as most nineteenth-century Parisians. And, as in nineteenth-century Paris, the great Tokyo department stores still provide a self-contained world far livelier and more enjoyable than anything to be found in the declining department stores of the west: up to fifteen storeys of restaurants, art galleries and shopping of every kind, crammed to bursting with shoppers and laughing shop girls, and surmounted by roof-top gardens and amusement parks, in which one can ride a roundabout high above the city or fish for live fish while Bach blares from the loud speakers.

But as a building in Tokyo more than thirty years old is a rarity, its nineteenth-century life-style is expressed in the universal language of the Modern Movement. Tokyo has good modern architects and good modern (and even post-modern) buildings, but, like most great cities today, what makes an impressive showing when collected into a book on the contemporary architecture of Tokyo is swamped on the ground by a basic townscape of dirty concrete and material resembling cardboard, already turning tatty after a life of ten or twenty years. It is only at night that the entertainment districts lose their daytime junkiness and become a wonderland of neon lighting, for the old Japanese genius for fireworks has transposed naturally into modern electronics.

A great many cities are experiencing vicissitudes which are nothing new in the history of cities, except in their scale, although they are often treated as if they were. Individual cities are in trouble, as some cities always have been, because they have lost the main purpose for which they came into existence, and have not found adequate new ones. Textile towns in New England and the north of England have lost their trade to Japan and Korea, just as Flemish ones lost trade to Italy or England in the later Middle Ages. Ports like Liverpool and Calcutta are in trouble, because they depended on an industry which no longer exists, or because they cannot take new and bigger ships, just as Venice was in trouble in the seventeenth century, or Bristol in the early twentieth.

Other cities have troubles as the result of too much prosperity, not too little, just as they have always had them. Any large or relatively rich city is bound to attract poor immigrants, who flood in filled with hopes of prosperity, which are often disastrously disappointed. The cities accept them either because they cannot stop them, or because they find them useful, since they are prepared to work all hours and to do the dirty work which the city's established population no longer wants to take on. There are shanty towns on the edge of Bombay or Brazilia, just as there were shanty towns on the edge of Jacobean London or Third Empire Paris. As an alternative to squatting on the outskirts, the very poor continue to move into houses or apartment blocks from which the well-off have removed to newer and more fashionable areas. There are slums in seventeenth-century palaces in Mexico City, or columned classical mansions in Charleston, or once-prosperous middle-class apartment blocks in Harlem, just as there were slums in the half-timbered houses of merchants in Manchester at the beginning of the nineteenth century, or once-elegant *conventillos* in Buenos Aires at the end of it. What is new is the scale. Descriptions written by eighteenth-century travellers of the poor *leperos* in their blankets who formed the main mass of the population of Mexico City, and of the glaring contrasts between wealth and prosperity to be found there, are remarkably reminiscent of descriptions of Mexico City today; but the *leperos* were numbered in thousands, and the poor of modern Mexico City in millions.

Travelling round the cities of the world today one is constantly meeting life-styles which relate to cities of the past; in some Indian cities bullock-carts, bicycles, camels and Rolls Royces happily mingle in one street together. But there is a type of western and specifically American city towards which other cities seem to be developing, so that it is likely that in the long run in Tokyo and many similar cities small family businesses will gradually disappear, residences become larger, and home life based on television, videos and computer games replace the life of the street.

But even the modern model is not all that modern. Almost all the elements which have become so common in post-war cities existed before 1939, and some before 1900, even if only in a handful of examples: skyscrapers, low-density suburbs, covered and underground shopping arcades, multi-storey car parks, freeways, airports, civic centres, art centres, low-density suburbs, and housing estates of tower blocks. The suburban shopping malls which are the great new feature of American life and are spreading from there to Europe, have roots going right back to the twelfth century, to the covered selds of Cheapside, or the great halls of Flanders, but their immediate ancestor is a shopping centre in Kansas City built in 1923. This was a baby, however, compared to the great malls of Chicago or Houston. Here again it is the scale which is different. Skyscrapers have grown to twice their pre-war height. Freeways have proliferated and created a new landscape of their own. Suburbs stretch for hundreds instead of tens of miles. The urban populations of one or two million, which so amazed the nineteenth century, have been replaced by complexes of ten or twenty million.

The whole monstrous growth rests on a real basis of economic prosperity, but behind it lie two myths: the myth of the city as a fabulous Eldorado, which tempts immigrants from rural poverty and brings them flooding into city centres, and the myth of the country as a Garden of Eden, which a few generations later sends them flooding out again to the suburbs.

Both myths are powerful, but the second is the dominant one, because the people who believe in it are on the whole richer and better established, and in many cases control the destinies of cities, or did so until recently. The belief that the country is basically good and the city basically wicked can be traced deep back into the past, but its particular modern form stems from the reaction against the many and undeniable horrors of big nineteenth-century cities. Out of this arose the Garden City Movement, the City Beautiful Movement and the Modern Movement. The three ideologies conflicted on many points, but all were united in their condemnation of high-density, closely knit cities, and in a belief that little which had been built in the nineteenth and early twentieth centuries was of any architectural value.

Between them, they gained control of a planning system which developed from the modest embryos of the early twentieth century into mammoth post-war organizations endowed with powers and financial resources on a scale that made even Haussmann seem modest. These were faced with problems of decay, war-time destruction and overcrowding the gravity of which one tends to forget today, but the orgy of destruction which they initiated went far beyond practical necessity. Economic factors played their part, and property developers and anyone else who had a financial stake in redevelopment joined in enthusiastically when given a chance, but the basic impetus was an ideological one. Modern Babylons were to be opened up to the light, and their surplus population decanted into new Jerusalems. In the 1950s and 1960s the consequent blowing-up of cities by redevelopment caused at least as much destruction as the blowing-up of cities by bombing in the preceding wars. I can remember visiting Belfast in the early 1970s and being appalled at the damage which the troubles there had apparently caused. Further investigation showed that bombed or burnt-out buildings were comparatively few and far between, and that most of the acres of devastation were due to the city's planning department.

The corresponding gains were of arguable value. To begin with, the quality of most of what was built was, and still is, appalling. In the 1950s the Modern Movement captured the fields of public and commercial building round the world, except for a few pockets of resistance here and there. Some wonderful and exciting buildings were built as a result. But the Modern Movement is an élitist style, not one for run-of-the-mill builders or architects. Only a very good designer can cope with a system that excommunicates all ornament and all except the most undercover forms of historicism. Travelling round the cities of the world today, one can trace with appalling consistency the moment when the traditional styles were put to death and the Modern Movement moved in, usually in its shoddiest and most banal form.

Moreover, although a certain amount of rebuilding of cities is inevitable and desirable, far more was destroyed than was necessary. Many areas were demolished against the wishes of their inhabitants. Complex relationships which had been built up over the years were destroyed for ever, and it proved correspondingly difficult, as it always has done, to create instant new neighbourhoods, and even more to create instant new towns or cities. In certain economic conditions a new town, if planted in the right place, can grow at amazing speed, as exemplified by Chicago. But a city founded for theoretical reasons starts with the dice loaded against it. New capitals may be necessary for political purposes, and the functions of government today are complex enough to give them an immediate basic population as well as a reason for existing; even so, experience shows that it is many decades before they can hope to become more than the ghost of a city. In other new cities, like Milton Keynes in England, no amount of enthusiasm, intelligence or promotion can get rid of the basic fact, that there is no particular reason for the city to be there in the first place.

Two dominant types of modern city seem to be emerging. In one a single high-density downtown, culminating in a burst of skyscrapers, is surrounded by a girdle of motorways, beyond which low-density suburbs stretch to the horizon. This is the Houston, Calgary or Toronto model, which poorer cities like Brisbane or Birmingham do their best to copy. It may seem to have fulfilled Olmsted's plea, made in 1870, for cities with high-density centres surrounded by residential areas full of greenery and open space. As a model it presents serious problems of getting people in and out of the centre, problems with which no system of motorways, however lavish, seems able to cope. The resulting island clusters of skyscrapers can be visually sensational, especially as they light up in the low evening or morning sun, like New Jerusalems of the twentieth century. But out of working hours they become cities of the dead, and the size of their buildings makes them curiously unreal even when they are in use. The economics of modern skyscrapers tend to be concealed by their builders, but many are clearly built as the result of wars of prestige between rival property or business empires, rather than to get the maximum return. Skyscrapers are becoming a bit of a bore.

The other model is the Los Angeles one, the low-density multi-centre city. Los Angeles has shown that a city of this type can produce much of the complexity and variety of a conventional high-density city. It is a more sensible model, particularly as improving technology makes the diffusion of work increasingly practicable, and other cities are beginning to develop towards it. At Houston (a city which has no zoning laws), office skyscrapers are beginning to wander away from the centre across the surrounding suburbs, each followed by a lower block of car parking, like a dog on a lead. In cities of all kinds shopping centres scattered round the out-of-centre areas have long ago taken most of the profit and point out of central shopping districts. The model has serious disadvantages, however. It is extraordinarily wasteful of space, and therefore of energy; it is largely dependent on the motor-car, and correspondingly hard on young, old or poor people. But if the dominant ambition of the majority of people is going to remain that of living in their own house on their own plot of ground, Los Angeles is the city of the future.

If so, it is arguable that the next step after Los Angeles is the complete dissolution of the city, as was already advocated in Los Angeles in 1910: nations where 'beautiful forms of urban life blend almost imperceptibly with beautiful forms of rural life'. There seems no reason why modern industry and manufacture, which is mostly clean and quiet, should not be diffused over very wide areas; there is nothing particularly new

315. Downtown Houston

about this, however, for industry has always tended to move out from cities. But no form of technology is ever going to get rid of the value of face-to-face contacts in government, education or business, or of the tendency of people of a certain kind to congregate where the options are richest; and as long as this is the case cities of some form will continue.

In fact all types of city, from the most diffused to the most concentrated, have their own sets of advantages and disadvantages. The decision how and where to live is obviously conditioned by economic constraints, but is as much an aesthetic as a practical one. I have been shown with pride by local residents many a desirable suburb, where the sprinklers sprinkle on green lawns, and handsome period houses look at each other around the golf course. I know instinctively that such areas are for them but not for me. I have to confess to the intense enjoyment with which I explored collapsed eighteenth-century houses converted to tenements amid the teeming streets of Calcutta, or walked through the huge desolate stage sets of what is left of pre-war East Berlin, where towering tenement façades are still pockmarked with shellfire, and half the balconies have dropped off the houses, like over-ripe fruit; and to my corresponding lowering of spirits when I entered neat new estates built round carefully landscaped courtyards, on both sides of the Berlin Wall.

What any city lover misses in such areas is the sense of drama in its widest sense: the sense that many varieties of human life are concentrated on one stage. Fallen glory or heroic ruin provides one kind of drama, even if adapted for self-indulgent spectators rather than ill-housed inhabitants. But the drama of big cities is endless in its variety. There are dramas of architecture, like the old London vistas, few and far between now, where Board Schools, churches and public houses lifted their heads and proclaimed their different gospels above the long rows of little houses; or dramas of geography, like the crazy grid of San Francisco, or the Bristol terraces gazing down into the Clifton Gorge. There is the constant gentle drama of life going on. From my own second-floor living room in Notting Hill I can look several hundred yards in four different directions down four different sets of streets. I can watch fifty different neighbourhood cats, rubbing against the legs of passers-by, stalking birds, and nosing hopefully among the garbage cans. I can watch the first wave of school children hurrying past, with or without their mothers, alternating with smart young girls off to television studios or estate agents' offices, and the second wave of senior citizens, out for their laboured morning constitutionals. I can see, at various times, lovers, roller skaters, policemen, the local busybody, the local lavatory attendant, who exercises neighbourhood dogs for a moderate fee, and the local cripple, processing slowly past in his electric chair, waving to people on the pavement. Twice a year a religious procession goes past, once a year the steel bands and dancers of the Notting Hill carnival. I am within two to ten minutes walk of a street market, at least six churches and chapels, four cinemas, four good restaurants and many bad ones, and at least twenty pubs. I am twenty-five minutes from Piccadilly Circus. The area has its disadvantages, but it does me well enough.

NOTES TO THE TEXT

NOTES TO CHAPTER 1

1. The standard work on the topography of Constantinople is R. Janin *Constantinople Byzantine* (Paris 1964). See also R. Guilland *Études sur la topographie de Constantinople Byzantine* (Berlin and Amsterdam 1964) and R. Krautheimer *Three Christian Capitals: Topography and Politics* (Berkeley 1983).
2. *Works of Liudprand of Cremona* (tr. F. A. Wright, London 1930) pp. 207–8.
3. 'Travels of Rabbi Benjamin' in Thomas Wright *Early Travels in Palestine* (London 1848) pp. 74–5.
4. Liudprand *Works* p. 209.
5. Odon de Deuil's account of the Crusade of Louis VII, from Guizot *Collection des Mémoires* (1825) XXIV p. 322.
6. 'Travels of Rabbi Benjamin' pp. 75–6.
7. Liudprand *Works* p. 267.
8. Geoffrey de Villehardouin *Chronicles of the Crusades* (tr. F. Marzials, London 1908) p. 65.
9. See R. Krautheimer *Early Christian and Byzantine Architecture* (Pelican History of Art, London 1965) p. 367. The point is of some interest, because the plan became one of the basic types of European renaissance architecture.
10. See Iris Origo 'The Domestic Enemy: Eastern Slaves in Tuscany in the Fourteenth and Fifteenth Centuries' *Speculum* XXXIX (July 1955) 321–66.
11. 'Travels of Rabbi Benjamin' p. 123.
12. Francesco Balducci Pegolotti *La Practica della Mercatura* (ed. A. Evans, Cambridge, Mass. 1936).
13. Information, Alison Cooper, who is writing a Ph.D. thesis at Manchester University on Manchester warehouses.

NOTES TO CHAPTER 2

1. *Cambridge Economic History of Europe* II *Trade and Industry in the Middle Ages* (ed. M. Postan and E. E. Rich, Cambridge 1952) pp. 336–7.
2. For the Celys, see *The Cely Papers* (ed. H. E. Malden, Royal Historical Society Camden 3rd Series, 1900), and for the Brownes and their buildings, Royal Commission on Historical Monuments (hereafter R.C.H.M.), England *The Town of Stamford* (London 1977) especially pp. 37–42.
3. For Sassetti, see R. de Roover *The Medici Bank* (New York 1948) and F. E. de Roover 'Francesco Sassetti and the Downfall of the Medici Banking House' *Bulletin of the Business Historical Society* XVII (1943) 65–80. There is some uncertainty about the attribution, since the inscription on the picture is a later addition: see F. Zeri and E. E. Gardner *Italian Paintings in the Collection of the Metropolitan Museum of Art: Florentine School* (New York 1971) pp. 133–5.
4. The Medici palace in Milan as described in Filarete's *Treatise on Architecture* (ed. J. R. Spencer, New Haven 1965, I pp. 325–7).
5. The classic authority on the bill of exchange remains R. de Roover. See especially his *L'Évolution de la lettre de change XIVe-XVIIIe siècles* (École Pratique des Hautes Études. VIe section. Centre de Recherches Historique. Affaires et Gens d'Affaires 4, Paris 1953) p. 62.
6. R.C.H.M. England *Salisbury* (London 1980) pp. xl–xli, 60.
7. Rörig 'Der Markt von Lübeck' *Wirtschaftskräfte im Mittelalter* (Cologne 1959) pp. 36–133.
8. A. Vandenpeerebom *Ypresia* (Bruges 1878) I.
9. The hall is now the Museum of Archaeology and Applied Art.
10. See Derek Keene 'A New Study of London before the Great Fire' *Urban History Yearbook 1984* (University of Leicester Press) p. 14.
11. See the Basinghall Ward section of John Stow *Survey of London* (1st ed. 1598, Everyman ed. pp. 256–9).
12. R. de Roover *The Rise and Decline of the Medici Bank 1397–1494* (Harvard Studies in Business History 21, Cambridge, Mass. 1963) p. 108. There is a useful general account of the Florentine banking system in the same author's *The Medici Bank* (New York and London 1948) pp. 1–4.
13. For Italian pawnbrokers, see R. de Roover *Money, Banking and Credit in Medieval Bruges* (Cambridge, Mass. 1948) pt. II.
14. A. Weitnauer *Venezianischer Handel der Fugger* (Munich and Leipzig 1931) p. 134, quoting Matthäus Schwarz, bookkeeper to Jakob Fugger, writing in 1516.
15. See, for instance, the examples quoted in Hidetoshi Hoshino *L'industria laniera fiorentina dal basso medioevo all'eta moderna* (Rome 1978) pp. 309–10.
16. Contract given in L. F. Salzman *Building in England down to 1540* (Oxford 1952) pp. 478–82.
17. H. Gordon Selfridge *The Romance of Commerce* (London 1918) p. 216.
18. M. de Cervantes Saavedra *Don Quixote of La Mancha* (1st ed. 1605–15) pt. I, ch. XX.
19. *Cambridge Economic History* II p. 393, quoting Giovanni Villani, the contemporary historian.
20. Giovanni Fanelli *Firenze* (Le città nella storia d'Italia, 1980) p. 70.
21. For a useful short account of the organization of the Florentine wool-trade, see R. de Roover 'Labour Conditions in Florence' in N. Rubinstein (ed.) *Florentine Studies* (London 1968) pp. 277–313.
22. G. A. Brucker 'Ciompi Revolution' in *Florentine Studies* p. 319. There had been many more before the Black Death: see Hoshino *L'industria laniera* p. 207.
23. Serlio's unpublished Sixth Book of Architecture (written *c.* 1541–7) included four designs for single-storey houses for poor artisans. See *Sebastiano Serlio on Domestic Architecture* (ed. M. N. Rosenfeld, New York and Cambridge, Mass. 1978) pl. XLVIII.
24. Jean Schneider *La Ville de Metz au XIIIme et XIVme siècles* (Nancy 1950) pp. 128, 138 ff.
25. Fanelli *Firenze* p. 29.
26. R. Brentano *Rome before Avignon* (London 1974) p. 13.
27. Adornes *Itineraire* f.5(a), quoted Jacques Heers *Family Clans in the Middle Ages* (Amsterdam and Oxford 1977) p. 160.
28. For the Genoese *alberghi*, see Heers *Family Clans* pp. 78 ff. and D. O. Hughes 'Kinsmen and Neighbours in Medieval Genoa' *The Medieval City* (ed. Miskimin, et al., New Haven 1977) pp. 95-112.

NOTES TO CHAPTER 3

1. There is a short but valuable account of hospitals, with a bibliography, in N. Pevsner *History of Building Types* (London 1976) pp. 139–45. The most recent full-length monograph is J. D. Thompson and G. Goldin *The Hospital: A Social and Architectural History* (New Haven and London 1975).
2. Thompson and Goldin *Hospital* p. 22.
3. Ibid. p. 31.
4. Ibid. pp. 51-3 and fig. 55.
5. The best and most recent account of early university architecture is Michael Kiene 'Die Grundlage der europäischen Universitätsbaukunst' *Zeitschrift für Kunstgeschichte* 46 (1983) 63–114.
6. From a description of Nuremberg by Christopher Scheurl, 1516, quoted by Gerald Strauss *Nuremberg in the Sixteenth Century* (Bloomington, Indiana 1976) p. 61.
7. Paris is now splendidly served by the multi-volume *Nouvelle Histoire de Paris*, in which see especially Pierre Lavedan *Histoire de l'Urbanisme à Paris* (Paris 1975), with a valuable bibliography.
8. D. M. Nicholas *Town and Countryside: Social, Economic and Political Tensions in Fourteenth Century Flanders* (Bruges 1971) pp. 254–8.
9. G. Villani *Cronica ecclesiastica* (Florence 1844–5) I, viii, 26.
10. Fanelli *Firenze* p. 61.

11. Stow *Survey of London* 'Lime Street Ward' (Everyman ed. p. 139).
12. Strauss *Nuremberg* p. 18. See also J. C. Smith *Nuremberg: A Renaissance City* (Huntington Art Gallery, University of Texas 1983) pp. 6–14.
13. Fanelli *Firenze* pp. 34, 65.
14. Lavedan *Urbanisme* p. 111.
15. H. H. van Regteren Altena and H. J. Zantkuyl 'A Medieval House Site in Amsterdam' *Berichten van de Rijkdienst voor het, Oudheidkundig Bodemonderzoek* 19 (1969) pp. 233–66; David Herlihy *Pisa in the Early Renaissance* (New Haven 1958) pp. 92–3.
16. J. Bracker, C. Prange, et al. *Alster, Elbe and the Sea* (Hamburg 1981) pp. 70, 90, pls. 11, 24.
17. Strauss *Nuremberg* p. 20.
18. I. N. R. Davies *God's Playground: A History of Poland* (Oxford 1981) I p. 303. Information, Professor Edmund Cieslak.
19. P. Génard *Anvers à traver's les ages* (2 vols. Brussels 1887–92) I p. 51.
20. R.C.H.M. *Salisbury* I pp. xxxii–xxxvi.
21. Lavedan *Urbanisme* pp. 116–17.
22. Ibid. pp. 115–16, 169.
23. Delumeau, *Vie économique et sociale de Rome dans le 2me moitie du XVme siècle* (Paris 1957) I pp. 243–5; Luca Landucci *A Florentine Diary* (London and New York 1927) 10 January 1503.
24. Landucci *Diary* 4 August 1511.
25. *Decameron*, 2nd day, 5th tale.
26. Lavedan *Urbanisme* p. 115.
27. Delumeau *Vie économique* I p. 240.
28. Fanelli *Firenze* pp. 41–2.
29. G. A. Brucker *Renaissance Florence* (New York 1969) p. 28.
30. Fanelli *Firenze* p. 46.
31. Ibid. p. 66.
32. Ibid. p. 42.
33. Strauss *Nuremberg* pp. 71–2.

NOTES TO CHAPTER 4

1. Plans of many basti des are given in P. Lavedan and J. Hugueney *L'Urbanisme au moyen âge* (Geneva 1974).
2. See R.C.H.M. *Salisbury*.
3. Strauss *Nuremberg* pp. 23, 119.
4. A fine example is the Schiesshalle of the Guild of St George at Gdansk (1487–94, altered 1591).
5. I. Origo *Merchant of Prato* (London 1957) p. 365.
6. Delumeau *Vie économique* I p. 243.
7. R.C.H.M. England *York* (London 1981) V pp. 143–5.
8. Landucci *Diary* 15 June 1510.
9. Juergen Schulz 'The Houses of Titian, Aretino, and Sansovino' *Titian, his World and his Legacy* (New York 1982) p. 106 n. 10.
10. Fanelli *Firenze* p. 46; Delumeau *Vie économique* I pp. 280–8; P. Tomei 'Le case in serie nell'edilizia Romana dal 400 al 700' *Palladio* II (1938) 83; R. A. Goldthwaite *The Building of Renaissance Florence* (Baltimore and London 1980) p. 18.
11. Rosenfeld *Serlio* (see ch. 2 n. 23) p. 25, fig. 15 and fn.
12. Origo *Merchant of Prato* pp. 86–7, 240, 318, and for this aspect of Florence generally, see Goldthwait *Renaissance Florence* pp. 102–3.
13. F. E. de Roover 'Andrea Banchi, Florentine Silk Manufacturer and Merchant in the Fifteenth Century' *Studies in Medieval and Modern History* (University of Nebraska, Lincoln) III (1966) 221–86.
14. Landucci *Diary* p. 2.
15. J. Lucas-Dubreton *Daily Life in Florence in the Time of the Medicis* (trl. A. L. Sells, London 1960) pp. 101–3; John Gage *Life in Italy in the Time of the Medicis* (London 1968) pp. 193–6.
16. Giovanni Cecchini and Dario Neri *The Palio of Siena* (Siena 1958) p. 51.
17. Strauss *Nuremberg* p. 113.
18. The first docks began to come into use at the end of the Middle Ages.
19. Liudprand *Works* (see ch. 1 n.2) p. 38.
20. Lavedan *Urbanisme* I p. 169.
21. William Fitzstephen *Libellum de situ et nobilitate Londini*, printed in Stow's *Survey of London* (Everyman ed. p. 506).
22. Stow *Survey of London* 'Bridges' (Everyman ed. p. 24).
23. Strauss *Nuremberg* pp. 189–90.
24. Landucci *Diary* pp. 15–19 ff.
25. Ibid. p. 117.
26. Tornaquinci was the corner where the Via Vigna Nuova and the Via Spada join the Via Tornabuoni.
27. My account derives mainly from Cecchini and Neri's *Palio of Siena*.
28. Landucci *Diary* July 1485; Cecchini and Neri *Palio of Siena* p. 68.
29. Landucci *Diary* 12 September 1485.
30. Maurice Keen *Chivalry* (New Haven and London 1984) pp. 90, 209; Juliet Vale *Edward III and Chivalry* (Woodbridge, Suffolk 1983) ch. 2.
31. Eve Borsook *Companion Guide to Florence* (London 1973) p. 210.
32. F. Schevill *History of Florence* (1937) p. 165.
33. Lando Bartolotti *Siena* (La città nella storia d'Italia series, 1983) p. 121.
34. Lavedan *Urbanisme* p. 126 (Paris); Stow *Survey of London* 'Bridge Ward Without' (Everyman ed. pp. 360–1); Delumeau *Vie économique* I p. 417 (Rome).
35. Landucci *Diary* 13 November 1506. The Florentine stews are the subject of a comedy by the mid-sixteenth-century dramatist G. M. Cecchi, *Lo Stufavolo*.
36. Strauss *Nuremberg* p. 194.

NOTES TO CHAPTER 5

1. For general works on Bruges, see especially J. A. Van Houtte *Des Geschiedenis van Brugge* (1982) and *Bruges: Essai d'histoire urbaine* (Brussels 1969); the still invaluable A. Duclos *Bruges: Histoire et souvenirs* (Bruges 1910, without index, reprinted with index 1976); V. Vermeersch *Bruges: mille ans d'art* (Antwerp 1981, with a useful bibliography).
2. Pero Tafur, quoted Malcolm Letts *Bruges and its Past* (London 1924) p. 133.
3. J. B. Ross 'Rise and Fall of a Twelfth Century Clan' *Speculum* XXXIV (1959) 367.
4. Duclos *Bruges* pp. 171–4.
5. For the water system at Bruges, see especially L. Gilliodts Van Severen *Inventaire des Archives* Intro. pp. 394, 440, 468, 472; Duclos *Bruges* pp. 42–3, 82, 84, 86–7, 541–2; articles by Marc Ryckaert in *Bruges and the Sea* (ed. V. Vermeersch, Antwerp 1982) pp. 13–23, 27–44.
6. For the water-engine, see Duclos *Bruges* pp. 231–2. A description of 1511 is printed in Van Severen *Inventaire* Intro. pp. 432–9.
7. Pero Tafur's description of the system in 1438 is printed in Letts *Bruges* p. 132.
8. De Roover *Money, Banking and Credit* (see ch. 2 n. 13) pt. II.
9. R. Vaughan *Philip the Good: The Apogee of the Burgundian State* (London 1970) p. 245.
10. Duclos *Bruges* p. 40.
11. Ibid. pp. 174–8.
12. Luc Devliegher *Les Maisons à Bruges* (Lannoo, Tielt and Amsterdam 1975) p. 301 and fig. 445. It was at Potterierei 5, and was demolished in 1859.
13. De Roover *Money, Banking and Credit* pp. 17–19.
14. Ibid. pp. 86, 89–90.
15. Ibid. pp. 34–40, 86–8. For the Hôtel Bladelin, see Devliegher *Maisons à Bruges* pp. 237–42.
16. For the brokers, see J. A. Van Houtte 'Les Courtiers au moyen-âge' *Revue historique de droit français et étranger* 4th series XV (1936) 105–41, and for the money-changers, de Roover *Money, Banking and Credit* pt. III.
17. Van Severen *Archives* IV pp. 471 ff, and for jousts at Bruges in general, II pp. 433 ff.
18. Letts *Bruges* pp. 37–43.

19. It is listed in an inventory of 1481. Van Severen *Cartulaire de l'ancien Grand Tonlieu de Bruges* (1908) no. 2719.
20. The so-called Master of the Legend of St Ursula was especially fond of the skyline of Bruges, which appears in the background of paintings by him in the Groeningemuseum and St James, Bruges, and the museums of Minneapolis and Detroit.
21. The commerce and manufacture in Bruges was in fact overtaken by that of Antwerp, rather than killed by it; Bruges recovered a degree of prosperity, especially after the opening of the canal to Ostend in the 1620s and its enlargment in the 1660s; its real collapse as a manufacturing town came in the early nineteenth century, when it failed to go over to the factory system.
22. There is a useful account of the Venetian nobility in R. G. Finlay *Politics in Renaissance Venice* (London 1980).
23. For *scuole* of all kinds at Venice, see S. Gramigna and A. Perissa *Scuole di Arti Mestieri e Devozione a Venezia* (Venice 1981) and Deborah Howard *The Architectural History of Venice* (London 1980) pp. 97–101.
24. See D. Sella *The Wool Industry in Venice in the Sixteenth and Seventeenth Centuries* (1983) and his 'The Rise and Fall of the Venetian Woollen Industry' *Crisis and Change in the Venetian Economy* (ed. B. Pullan, London 1980) pp. 106–26.
25. F. C. Lane *Venetian Ships and Shipbuilders of the Renaissance* (Baltimore 1934).
26. Finlay *Renaissance Venice* p. 75.
27. M. M. Newett (ed.) *Canon Pietro Casola's Pilgrimage to Jerusalem in the Year 1494* (Manchester 1907) p. 143.
28. For the piazza, see Giuseppe Samona, et al. *Piazza San Marco: l'architettura, la storia, le funzioni* (Padua 1970).
29. Sanudo, quoted by Deborah Howard *Jacopo Sansovino* (New Haven and London 1975) p. 48.
30. For the Rialto, see R. Cessi and A. Alberti *Rialto: l'isola, il ponte, il mercato* (Bologna, 1934).
31. G. Vasari *Le vite de' piu excellenti architetti, pittori, e scultori italianis* (ed. G Milanesi, Milan 1878–85) V pp. 269 ff.
32. Howard *Sansovino* pp. 50–7.
33. Ibid. p. 50, quoting M. A. Sabellico, published in 1502.
34. Cessi *Rialto* p. 61.
35. Finlay *Renaissance Venice* p. 20.
36. Samona *Piazza San Marco* pp. 50, 53; Maurice Aymard, *Venise, Raguse et le commerce du ble* (Paris 1966).
37. Finlay *Renaissance Venice* pp. 19–20.
38. M. Sanudo *I. Diarii* (ed. R. Fulin, et al., Venice 1879–1903) XIIII pp. 132–41.
39. Ibid. LVI p. 751.
40. Today's quoted population figures for Venice include Mestre.
41. For the *scuole*, see Gramigna and Perissa, *Scuole.*
42. Ibid. p. 65.
43. Howard *Sansovino* p. 50.
44. See G. Gianighian and Pavanini *Dietro i palazzi: tre secoli di architettura minore a Venezia 1492–1803* (Venice 1984) and Schulz 'Houses of Titian' (see ch. 4 n. 9).
45. Their plan is reproduced in Samona *Piazza San Marco* between pp. 68–9.
46. Plan reproduced and discussed in Schulz.
48. Schulz 'Houses of Titian' pp. 83–9.

NOTES TO CHAPTER 6

1. Evelyn *Diary* 10 and 12 November 1644.
2. Georgina Masson *Courtesans of the Italian Renaissance* (London 1975) p. 11.
3. P. D. Partner *Renaissance Rome 1500–1559* (Berkeley 1976) p. 16.
4. Delumeau *Vie économique* I pp. 230 ff.
5. Ibid. I pp. 280–1, 422–3; Partner *Renaissance Rome* p. 48.
6. Delumeau *Vie économique* I pp. 169 ff.
7. Ibid. I p. 171.
8. Ibid. I p. 169.
9. Partner *Renaissance Rome* pp. 83, 117, 135 ff.
10. Delumeau *Vie économique* I p. 443.
11. Ibid. I p. 445.
12. Ibid. I pp. 297–306, 324.
13. Ibid. I pp. 306–8.
14. See ch. 3 n. 29.
15. Goro Dati, quoted by Fanelli *Firenze* (see ch. 2 n. 20) p. 54.
16. Quoted by Fanelli Firenze pp. 82, 85.
17. The latest historical study of perspective is Lawrence Wright *Perspective in Perspective* (London 1984).
18 See E. Poleggi *Strada Nuova: una lottizzaziane del Cinquecento a Genova* (Genoa 1968).
19. Vasari *Le vite* (see ch. 5 n. 31) VII p. 553.
20. Column in Piazza Sta Trinita erected 1563, surmounted by statue of Justice, 1581; in Piazza S. Felice erected 1572; in Piazza S. Marco erected 1539, to celebrate marriage of Cosimo.
21. Delumeau *Vie économique* I pp. 313 ff.
22. Ibid. p. 295.
23. Ibid. pp. 317–18.
24. Evelyn *Diary* 6 November 1644.
25. Quoted by M. Poete *Le Promenade à Paris au XVIIme siècle* (Paris 1913) p. 106, giving no date or source.
26. For the Rome fountains, see Delumeau *Vie économique* I pp. 328 ff. and Cesare D'Onofrio *Acque e fontane di Roma* (Rome 1977).
27. Eve Borsook *Companion Guide to Florence* (London 1973) p. 235. For the extensive series of early fountains in Naples, see D'Onofrio *Acque e fontane* pp. 213–19.
28. Evelyn *Diary* 12 November 1644.
29. Ibid. 25 January 1645.
30. Illustrated and discussed in Arnaldo Bruschi *Bramante* (London 1977) pp. 64–6.
31. Ibid. pp. 87–113.
32. See James S. Ackerman *Michelangelo* (London 1961) pp. 54–74.
33. For Livorno, see Giacinto Nudi *Storia urbanistica di Livorno* (Venice 1959) and Evelyn *Diary* 21 October 1644.
34. Evelyn *Diary* 18 May 1645.
35. *Diary of Montaigne's Journey to Italy* (ed. E. J. Trachmann, London 1975) p. 161.
36. Ibid. p. 144.
37. F. Haskell and N. Penny *Taste and the Antique* (New Haven and London 1981) pp. 8, 15, 63–4.
38. Partner *Renaissance Rome* p. 18.
39. Evelyn *Diary* 19 November 1644.
40. Quoted by Delumeau *Vie économique* I p. 248; Partner *Renaissance Rome* p. 32.
41. Delumeau *Vie économique* I pp. 217–18.
42. Ibid.
43. Evelyn *Diary* 19 November 1644.
44. Delumeau *Vie économique* I pp. 199–204; Partner *Renaissance Rome* pp. 77–80.
45. Delumeau *Vie économique* I pp. 25–36.
46. Ibid. I p. 320.
47. Haskell and Penny *Taste and the Antique* pp. 2–6, ch. III, etc.
48. Ibid. pp. 136, 258.
49. For the villas, see D. R. Coffin *The Villa in the Life of Renaissance Rome* (Princeton 1979).
50. Montaigne *Journey* p. 161.
51. Partner *Renaissance Rome* pp. 55–6.
52. See Masson *Courtesans* and Delumeau *Vie économique* I pp. 416–32.
53. Delumeau *Vie économique* I p. 419.
54. Ibid. I p. 428.
55. Anthony Blunt *Nicolas Poussin* (London and New York 1967) pp. 171–2, quoting G. P. Bellori (1672).
56. Delumeau *Vie économique* I pp. 230–6.

NOTES TO CHAPTER 7

1. Partner *Renaissance Rome* pp. 58 ff.
2. Francis Haskell *Patrons and Painters* (rev. ed. New Haven and London 1980) p. 150.

3. Ibid. p. 152.
4. For the economy of Antwerp in this period, see especially H. van de Wee *The Growth of the Antwerp Market and the European Economy* (3 vols., The Hague 1963).
5. Ibid. II p. 126.
6. Génard *Anvers* (see ch. 3 n. 19) I p. 78.
7. Luigi Guicciardini *La Description de la cité d'Anvers* (tr. F. de Belleforest, Antwerp 1920) p. 41.
8. Van de Wee *Antwerp Market* II p. 330.
9. Guicciardini *Anvers* pp. 33–5.
10. For van Schoonbeke, see Génard *Anvers* II pp. 63 ff.; E. Sabbe *Anvers, metropole de l'Occident* (1951) pp. 23–7, 53–4.
11. The town hall and its accommodation is described in Pevsner *Building Types* (see ch. 3 n. 1) p. 32, using an inventory of 1570 given in F. Prims *Het Stadhuis van Antwerpen* (Antwerp 1930).
12. It is shown planted in the bird's-eye view of Antwerp by Virgilius, 1569, but not in the view in Guicciardini, 1564.
13. City Archives PK 917, fol. 163, 18 December 1578.
14. Montaigne *Journey* (see ch. 6 n. 35) p. 198.
15. Evelyn *Diary* 5 October 1641.
16. For van Schoonbeke's breweries, see Génard *Anvers* II, and F. Smekens *The Brewer's House: A Concise Guide* (Antwerp Archaeological Museums), with a bibliography listing further publications by Génard and others.
17. I. N. R. Davies *God's Playground: A History of Poland* (2 vols., Oxford 1981) I, ch. 8.
18. Ibid. I, ch. 8.
19. See F. C. Lane 'Venetian Shipping during the Commercial Revolution' in *Crisis and Change in the Venetian Economy in the Sixteenth and Seventeenth Centuries* (ed. B. Pullan, London 1968) esp. pp. 40–1.
20. See F. Braudel and R. Romano, *Navires et marchandises à l'entrée du port de Livorne 1547–1611* (Paris 1951).
21. Lewis Roberts *The Merchant's Mappe of Commerce* (London 1638) p. 75.
22. *Cambridge Economic History* (see ch. 2 n. 1) II p. 210.
23. See the table in K. G. Ponting 'Sculptures and Paintings of Textile Processes at Leiden' *Textile History* 5 (1974) 135, based on publications by N. W. Posthumus.

NOTES TO CHAPTER 8

1. Amsterdam is wonderfully well provided with detailed early illustrated guidebooks and in fact pioneered this type of publication. I have mainly used Filips Van Zesen *Beschreibung der Stadt Amsterdam* (Amsterdam 1664), because the text is in German, rather than M. Fokkens *Beschrijvinge der wijdt-vermaarde Koopstadt Amstelvedam* (Amsterdam 1662) and O. Dapper *Beschrijving van Amsterdam* (1663). Other enjoyable accounts are the much reprinted *Le Guide d'Amsterdam* (I have used the 1701 edition) and the relevant section of William Carr *A Description of Holland* (London 1701).
2. Carr *Description* p. 30.
3. Van Zesen *Beschreibung* pp. 172–6.
4. Dapper *Beschrijving* p. 450. For the weigh-houses, see Van Zesen *Beschreibung* pp. 233–4 ff.; Carr *Description* (1697 ed.) p. 47.
5. Van Zesen *Beschreibung* p. 232–3: *Guide* pp. 91–3.
6. For the town hall, see K. Freemantle *The Baroque Town Hall of Amsterdam* (Utrecht 1959).
7. For a useful account of the Amsterdam city government, see Freemantle *Town Hall* p. 15.
8. For the Wisselbank, and finance in Amsterdam generally, see Violet Barbour *Capitalism in Amsterdam* (Ann Arbor, Michigan 1963) pp. 43–6 ff.
9. Quoted by H. I. Bloom *The Economic Activities of the Jews of Amsterdam in the Seventeenth and Eighteenth Centuries* (Port Washington, N.Y. 1969) p. 174.
10. For Amsterdam warehouses, see M. Revesz-Alexander *Die Alten Lagerhäuser Amsterdams* (The Hague 1928). There is a good description of the islands in *Guide* (1734 ed.) pp. 23–33.
11. They were sold by Christie's Amsterdam on 12/13 June 1984.
12. The warehouse later became part of the City Lending Bank on Lombardsteeg, and was restored in recent years by Henk Zantkuyl.
13. Carr *Description*, p. 30.
14. Information, Henk Zantkuyl.
15. Information, Henk Zantkuyl.
16. For a mid-seventeenth-century drawing of a brewer's water-barge, see Amsterdam Historisch Museum *Amsterdam in z'n Element* (exhibition catalogue 1966–7) fig. 12 in the section 'Watervoorziening, riolering en waterverversing'.
17. Barbour *Capitalism in Amsterdam* p. 36.
18. Peter Burke *Venice and Amsterdam* (1974) p. 66, quoting Henry Sidney, *c.* 1680.
19. Evelyn *Diary* 20 August 1641.
20. See the catalogue *Group portraits in the Amsterdam Historical Museum: Pt. 1, Civic Guard Portraits*, with a short bibliography. There is a description of the guard and its duties in *Guide* (1734 ed.) pp. 40–3.
21. Carr *Description* p. 70.
22. *Guide* p. 55. There is a list of music and gaming houses and of prostitutes names in J. F. Van Slotte *Bijdraage . . . Prostitutie te Amsterdam.* (Amsterdam 1937) pp. 34–5.
24. For an analysis, and a comparison with Venetian ruling classes in the seventeenth century, see Burke *Venice and Amsterdam.*
25. Dapper *Beschrijving* p. 425; *Guide* pp. 35–7.
26. *Guide* p. 35.
27. The standard late seventeenth- and early eighteenth-century guide to Paris, published in many editions, is Germain de Brice *Description de la Ville de Paris*, translated into English by James Wright as *A New Description of Paris* (1688). I have used the 1688 English translation and the French edition of 1725. For a shorter but lively account, see Martin Lister *A Journey to Paris in 1698* (London 1699).
28. Most guides (Sauval, 1724; Brice, 1725; Galignani, 1829) date it 1616, others (Thiery, 1787) date it 1628.
29. There is an excellent chapter on the Cours la Reine in Marcel Poete *La Promenade à Paris au XVIIe siècle* (Paris 1913). See also *New Description* II p. 154; Lister *Journey* pp. 178–9. Poete dates the Cours to 1628.
30. Poete *Promenades à Paris* p. 107.
31. Ibid. p. 109.
32. Ibid. p. 120.
33. For the Parlement, see J. H. Shennan *The Parlement of Paris* (London 1968).
34. Ibid. pp. 101–2; O. A. Ranum *Paris in the Age of Absolutism* (New York 1968) pp. 12, 146–7.
35. Poete *Promenade à Paris* p. 29.
36. Ibid. p. 43.
37. Lister *Journey* p. 14.
38. Quoted by Lavedan *Urbanisme* (see ch. 3 n. 7) p. 173.
39. Even so, a good deal was built, especially in the way of private hotels. See David Thomson *Renaissance Paris: Architecture and Growth 1475–1600* (London 1984).
40. Thomson *Renaissance Paris* p. 202 n. 23. It was enlarged under Louis XIV.
41. For Henri IV's activities in Paris, see A. Blunt *Art and Architecture in France 1500–1700* (1953) pp. 91–103 and Ranum *Paris in the Age of Absolutism.*
42. Lavedan *Urbanisme* p. 189, quoting Colbert.
43. Ibid. pp. 183–4.
44. Ibid.
45. See Lucien Lambean *La Place Royale* (Paris 1906).
46. See ch. 5 pp. 117, 121.
47. See *Survey of London* (ed. F. H. W. Sheppard) XXXVI *The Parish of St. Paul Covent Garden* (London 1970) pp. 64–76.
48. Blunt *Art and Architecture* p. 96, pl. 72.
49. Poete *Promenade à Paris* p. 136.
50. Ibid. pp. 137–8.
51. Ibid. p. 142.
52. Lavedan *Urbanisme* p. 299.
53. Poete *Promenade à Paris* pp. 99 ff. First mentioned in 1622–3, and therefore the precursor of the Cours la Reine if the later date for the latter is correct.
54. Ibid. p. 139.

55. Lavedan *Urbanisme* p. 186.
56. *New Description* p. 77.
57. Nicolas Delamare *Traite de la Police* (2nd ed. Paris 1722–38) I p. 103.
58. For this and various other edicts concerning the boulevards, see *Lettres, instructions et memoires de Colbert* (ed. P. Clement, 1868) V pp. 555–7.
59. A contemporary plan of the Cours de Vincennes is illustrated by Lavedan *Urbanisme* Pl. 49. Le Trône is now the Place de la Nation.
60. Samuel Johnson *Works* (Everyman ed. London 1906) I p. 577.
61. Lister *Journey* p. 180.
62. See Lavedan *Urbanisme* pp. 178 ff.
63. Ibid. pp. 221–7.
64. *New Description* I p. 147.
65. Blunt *Art and Architecture* p. 188; *New Description* II p. 151. For other academies for training gentlemen in the Faubourg St Germain, see *New Description* II p. 113.

NOTES TO CHAPTER 9

1. Strauss *Nuremberg* (see ch. 3 n. 6) p. 79.
2. Lister *Journey* p. 175.
3. For a useful account of theatres, see Oscar G. Brocket *History of the Theatre* (Boston and London 1977); also Pevsner *Building Types* (see ch. 3 n. 1) pp. 63–90, with a short bibliography.
4. M. Louis *Salle de Spectacle de Bordeaux, par M. Louis* (Paris 1782) p. 9.
5. D. Defoe *Tour through the Whole Island of Great Britain* (reprint of 1st (1724–7) ed., London 1927) I p. 52 (Bury St Edmunds).
6. Ibid. I p. 217 (Lyme Regis).
7. See Hugh Phillips *Mid-Georgian London* (London 1964) pp. 88–91, 276–7.
8. I have found no adequate architectural or social study of bull-rings.
9. J.-J. Gloton, *Renaissance et baroque à Aix-en-Provence* (Rome 1979) II pp. 244–5.
10. Evelyn *Diary* 28 April and 2 May 1644.
11. Phillips *Mid-Georgian London* pp. 42-6.
12. *A foreign view of England in the reign of George I and George II* (ed. M. van Muyden, 1902) pp. 47–8.
13. For Stephen's Green, see Constantia Maxwell *Dublin under the Georges* (London 1936) p. 116 and *Autobiography and Correspondence of Mrs. Delany* (London 1861–2) 1st series I p. 300.
14. De la Tocnaye *Promenade d'un Français dans l'Irlande* (2nd ed. 1801) p. 26.
15. See e.g. F Nicolai *Beschreibung der . . . Berlin* (3rd ed. Berlin 1786) I pp. 171–2; French ed. 1813, pp. 60–1.
16. *The Picture of Hamburg* (London and Hamburg *c.* 1810) pp. 162–3.
17. Evelyn *Diary* June 1645.
18. *Lives of William Cavendish Duke of Newcastle and of his Wife* (ed. M. A. Lower, London 1872) pp. 300–1.
19. *A Picture of St. Petersburg . . . at the Twelve Different Months of the Year* (London 1815) p. 21.
20. *Diccionario historico de la lengua Espanola* (Madrid 1933) II, 'paseo con alamos', quoting B. de Escalante *Dialogos del arte militar* (1595).
21. See the Moorfields section of F. Lambert 'Some Recent Excavations in London' *Archaeologia* 71 (1921), especially pp. 80–93.
22. They are shown in an anonymous late seventeenth-century painting, reproduced by S. and G. Cartocci *Yesterday's Rome* (Rome 1978) p. 82.
23. Galignani *New Paris Guide* (1829 ed.) p. 678.
24. See *Amsterdamse Monumenten* I (1983) 'Wonen in de Planage (1); *Guide d'Amsterdam* (Amsterdam 1734) pp. 48, 261.
25. Hester Thrale *The French Journals of Mrs. Thrale and Dr. Johnson* (ed. M. Tyson and H. Guppy, Manchester 1932) 29 September and 17 October 1775.
26. See F. G. Pariset (ed.) *Bordeaux au 18me siècle* (Bordeaux 1968) pp. 554–80 and plan rep pl. XXX; *Description Historique de Bordeaux* (1785) pp. 36–7.
27. Pariset *Bordeaux* pp. 556–8, 574 ff.
28. Christian Pfister *Histoire de Nancy* (Paris and Nancy 1902a) III pp. 684 ff.
29. *Nouveau Guide par Vienne* (Vienna 1792) p. 191.
30. Ibid. p. 194.
31. There are useful recent accounts of Vauxhall in two exhibition catalogues: David Cole *The Muse's Bower: Vauxhall Gardens 1728–1786* (Gainsborough's House, Sudbury, Suffolk 1978), with a short bibliography, and 'Vauxhall Gardens' in *Rococo* (Victoria and Albert Museum, London 1984) pp. 74–98, with footnotes.
32. For Ranelagh, see M. B. M. Sands *Invitation to Ranelagh 1742–1805* (London 1946).
33. Quoted in *The London Encyclopaedia* (ed. B. Weinreb and C. Hibbert) p. 637.
34. A. Braham *The Architecture of the French Enlightenment* (London 1980) p. 111; Thiery *Guide* (see ch. 8 n. 28) I p. 17 (Ranelagh), p. 224 (Panthéon and Wauxhall); Thrale *Journals* p. 905 (Colisée).
35. 'Public Gardens' in Galignani *New Paris Guide* (1829 ed.) pp. 660–3; Paphos illustrated in M. Poete *Une vie de Cité: Paris de sa naissance à nos jours* (2 vols. and album, Paris 1925) album pl. 374.
36. The Berlin Tivoli had an early switchback, shown in a coloured woodcut of *c.* 1820 in the Museum of the History of Berlin. There were similar switchbacks (called *montagnes*) in Paris from 1817 (Galignani New Paris Guide p. 660).
37. *Nouveau Guide par Vienne*; watercolours of *c.* 1815–20 by B. Wigand, T. D. Raulino and others in Vienna Historical Museum.
38. Montaigne *Journey* (see ch. 6 n. 35) pp. 12–14.
39. Antonia Fraser *Mary Queen of Scots* (London 1969) pp. 437–9.
40. Montaigne *Journey* pp. 216–18.
41. A. Savidge *Royal Tunbridge Wells* (Tunbridge Wells 1975).
42. Oliver Goldsmith *Life of Richard Nash of Bath* (London 1762).
43. M. Williams *Lady Luxborough Goes to Bath* (Oxford 1946) p. 5.
44. The schedule is described in John Wood *Essay Towards a Description of Bath* (2nd ed.) ch. XVI.
45. Ibid. pp. 346, 350.
46. *Diaries and Letters of Mme d'Arblay* (ed. C. Barrett, London 1904–5) I p. 327.
47. Ibid. I p. 329. For the Circus's use as a parade, see P. Egan *Walks through Bath* (Bath 1819) p. 162.
48. Clifford Musgrave *Royal Pavilion* (London 1959) pp. 1–13.
49. Thrale *Journals* p. 100.
50. For Westminster Hall, see Phillips *Mid-Georgian London* p. 20 and fig. 10. Law cases were heard in corners of the hall, between the shops, until 1820.
51. A. Young *Travels in France* (ed. M. Betham-Edwards, London 1890) pp. 92, 103.
52. N. M. Karamzin *Letters of a Russian Traveller* (New York and Oxford 1957) p. 185.
53. Phillips *Mid-Georgian London* p. 135, fig. 173.
54. Ibid. p. 117.
55. *Survey of London* (ed. F. H. W. Sheppard) XXVII *Spitalfields and Mile End New Town* (London 1957) pp. 227–36.
56. Thrale *Journals* p. 198.
57. Young *Travels* p. 302, referring to the Circus; Thiery *Guide* I p. 271.
58. The fullest contemporary account is in *Tableau du Nouveau Palais-Royal* (London 1788).
59. Karamzin *Letters* p. 215.
60. Ibid. p. 182.
61. François Fosca *Histoire des Cafés de Paris* (Paris 1934) p. 73; *Nouveau Palais-Royal* p. 82.
62. Karamzin *Letters* p. 187.
63. For academies, see N. Pevsner *Academies of Art, Past and Present* (Cambridge 1940).
64. J. Milton *Areopagitica* (1644; *Milton's Prose*, ed. M. W. Wallace, Oxford 1925, p. 305).
65. Michael Hunter *Science and Society in Restoration England* (Cambridge 1981) p. 71.
66. See Fosca *Cafés de Paris*; Bryant Lillywhite *London Coffee Houses* (London 1963), with detailed alphabetical gazeteer; A. Ellis *The Penny Universities* (1956).

67. H. R. F. Bourne *English Newspapers 1621–1887* (London 1887) II p. 48.
68. *Guide d'Amsterdam* p. 65.
69. Fosca *Cafés de Paris* p. 29.
70. *Diary of Samuel Pepys* (London 1983) X (Companion) p. 71, quoting Cal. State Papers Domestic 1664–5, p. 365.
71. *The Diary of Robert Hooke* (ed. H. W. Robinson and W. Adams, 1935) passim; Lillywhite *London Coffee Houses* under 'Button's'.
72. Fosca *Cafés de Paris* p. 32.
73. Pevsner *Building Types* p. 174. The London Coffee House Hotel and Tavern, Ludgate Hill, had about 85 bedrooms in 1812 (Plans in City of London Record Office, R.5).
74. Hunter *Science and Society* p. 77.
75. M. Girouard 'English Art and the Rococo, I—'Coffee at Slaughter's' *Country Life* (13 January 1966) 58–61.
76. Fosca *Cafés de Paris* pp. 52–69.

NOTES TO CHAPTER 10

1. Pariset *Bordeaux* pp. 633–4.
2. J. A. Skovgaard *A King's Architecture Christian IV and his Buildings* (London 1973) pp. 39–40. The complex consisted of an arsenal, covered dock for shipbuilding or repair, and warehouse, all round an enclosed dock.
3. See Jonathan Coad *Historic Architecture of the Royal Navy* (London 1983).
4. *London Encyclopaedia* (see ch. 9 n. 33) p. 398; C. N. Parkinson *Rise of the Port of Liverpool* (Liverpool 1952).
5. Victoria County History: *East Riding of Yorkshire* (London 1969) I pp. 185 ff.
6. Weale *Pictorial Handbook of London* (1854) pp. 339–44; Port of London Authority *London, the Port of the Empire* (London 1914).
7. James Malton *A Picturesque View of the City of Dublin* (Dublin 1799, facs. 1978) pl. 30 and text; Maurice Craig *Dublin* (Dublin 1969) p. 94. Now called Collins Barracks.
8. H. G. Pundt *Schinkel's Berlin* (Cambridge, Mass. 1972) pp. 14–18.
9. Thiery *Guide* (1787) I pp. 78, 81, 147, 187, 468, 472, 611; II pp. 208–9, 214, 229, 260, 554, 564.
10. Thompson and Goldin *Hospital* (see ch. 3 n. 1) pp. 142–6.
11. Ibid. pp. 67–9.
12. Pevsner *Building Types* pp. 161–2, fig. 10.4.
13. Allan Braham *The Architecture of the French Enlightenment* (London 1980) p. 120.
14. For Dublin prosperity at this period, see L. M. Cullen *An Economic History of Ireland since 1660* (London 1972).
15. Pariset *Bordeaux* pp. 554 etc. The grill across the Place Royale is shown on the plan of *c.* 1790, reproduced Pariset, pl. XXIX. The gates were shut at 11 p.m.
16. The pre-customs-wall barriers are still shown on M. Pichon *Nouveau Plan routier de la Ville et Faubourgs de Paris*, 1787. For the customs-wall, see E. Fremy 'L'Enceinte de Paris construite par les fermiers generaux' *Bulletin de la Société de l'Histoire de Paris* 39e annee (1912) pp. 115–48.
17. S. E. Rasmussen *London, the Unique City* (Harmondsworth 1960) ch. 6 'Town Planning Schemes in 1666'. For the Evelyn plan, and his explanation of it, see article by S. Perks *Journal of the R.I.B.A.* 3rd s. XXVII pp. 467–70.
18. For Newcourts plan, see 'The Rebuilding of London after the Great Fire: A Rediscovered Plan' *Town Planning Review* XVIII (1939) pp. 155–61.
19. For Turin, see Pierre Lavedan *Histoire de l'urbanisme: renaissance et temps moderne* (Paris 1959) pp. 513–14.
20. Lister *Journey* (see ch. 8 n. 27) p. 8.
21. *New Description* (see ibid.) I p. 93.
22. Brice *Description* (see ibid.) II p. 203.
23. Philips *Mid-Georgian London* pp. 230–1.
24. The Bryanston and Montagu Square areas, on the Portman estate in Marylebone, laid out *c.* 1810, are a good example.
25. See E. McParland 'The Wide Street Commissioners' *Irish Georgian Society Bulletin* XV (1972) 1–32.
26. See F. H. Garrison *Introduction to the History of Medicine* (4th ed. Philadelphia and London 1929) pp. 270–1, 367.
27. *New Description* I p. 6.
28. *Letters of Lady Mary Wortley Montagu* (ed. Wharncliffe, London 1893) I p. 235.
29. Pfister *Nancy* (see ch. 9 n. 28) II pp. 50–4, 219–32, III pp. 479 ff.
30. For Edinburgh, see A. J. Youngson *The Making of Classical Edinburgh* (Edinburgh 1966) and Colin McWilliam *Edinburgh* (1984) in the Buildings of Scotland series.

NOTES TO CHAPTER 11

1. Zelia Nuttall 'Royal Ordinances concerning the Laying Out of New Towns' *Hispanic American Historical Review* V (1922) 249–54, with full translated text of the Ordinances.
2. Brantz Mayer *Mexico as It Was and as It Is* (New York 1844) pp. 39 ff.
3. For the history and changing appearance of the Zocalo, see M. M. del R. de Redo *El Zocalo* (Mexico City 1974).
4. T. Gage *New Survey of the West Indies* (1648, 1928 ed.) p. 91.
5. Described in J. R. Poinsett *Notes on Mexico* (Philadelphia 1824), quoted by J. Conder *Modern Traveller* (1830) XXV p. 296.
6. Mayer *Mexico* pp. 39 ff.
7. See T. C. Yturbide and M. M. del R. de Redo *Biombas Mexicanos* (Mexico City 1970) p. 99, quoting J. de Viera *Compendiosa Narracion de la Ciudad de Mexico* (1777, new ed. 1952).
8. Many plans in Mexico City archives. Maximilian's avenue is shown in a lithograph by Casimiro Castro, reproduced in F. Benitez *Historia de la Ciudad de Mexico* (Mexico City 1982) II p. 284. It bore no relationship to the present Paseo or the Champs Élysées, and there seems no foundation for the often repeated story that he planted it in imitation of the latter.
9. For life in Calcutta in the late eighteenth and early nineteenth centuries, I have drawn especially on *Memoirs of William Hickey* (ed. A. Spencer, 4 vols. 1913–25); Anon. *Hartly House, Calcutta* (3 vols. London 1789, a novel); E. Fay *Original Letters from India* (1819, new ed. 1925); K. Blechynden *Calcutta Past and Present* (London 1906) p. 210. T. and W. Daniell's illustrations of Calcutta are reproduced in Mildred Archer *Early Views of India* (London 1980) with selections from the accompanying text. *Calcutta 200 Years: A Tollygunge Club Perspective* (Tollygunge Club, Calcutta 1981) contains much information and reproduces many contemporary illustrations.
10. See S. B. Singh *European Agency Houses in Bengal* (Calcutta 1966).
11. There is an especially good collection of such houses in and around Maharaja Nabakrishna Street, by the Sogha bazaar.
12. Fay *Letters from India* pp. 171–2, 208; *Hartly House* I pp. 15, 38; Blechynden *Calcutta* pp. 127, 195.
13. Harold Holloway *The South Park Cemetery, Calcutta* (Calcutta 1978), with photographs by Elizabeth McKay, is a short but useful guidebook.
14. *Hartly House* I p. 19.
15. Ibid. I p. 119. For the Course, see also Sir Charles D'Oyly *Tom Raw the Griffin* (London 1828) Canto III, Stanzas XX ff.; Hickey *Diaries* III p. 292; Fay *Letters from India* p. 189.
16. It is not clear whether the term 'Course' derived from *cours*, or from the fact that the evening parade originally took place on the race-course.
17. Hickey *Memoirs* III p. 354.
18. A photocopy of William Hickey's notes (1789) on the Daniell views of Calcutta is in the India Office Library, and is full of information and gossip about the contemporary occupants of the Chowringhee houses.
19. Blechynden *Calcutta* p. 210.
20. Hickey *Memoirs* IV pp. 117–18 and illustration; *Hartly House* I p. 21; T. and W. Daniell *Picturesque Voyage to India by way of China* (London 1810).
21. W. Hodges *Travels in India during the Years 1780–3* (London 1793) p. 15.

22. *Hartly House* I pp. 109–11.
23. A. D. King *The Bungalow: The Product of a Global Culture* (London 1984) pp. 14–41.
24. Hickey *Memoirs* II p. 137.
25. Lanier *A Century of Banking in New York 1822–1922* (New York 1922) p. 189.
26. Quoted Blechynden *Calcutta* p. 124.
27. *Hartly House* I pp. 87–8.
28. D'Oyly *Tom Raw* Canto IV, Stanza XXXVI.
29. There is a useful article on lotteries in the 11th (1910) edition of the *Encylopaedia Britannica*.
30. Blechynden *Calcutta* pp. 193–4; H. E. A. Cotton *Calcutta Old and New* (Calcutta 1907) pp. 165 ff.
31. D'Oyly *Tom Raw* Canto V, Stanza LIII ff., with illustrations.
32. 'Piazzas' are also found in New York State from *c.* 1770. See J. Poesch *Country Life* 163 (1978) 1170–1.
33. J. W. Reps *The Making of Urban America: A History of City Planning in the United States* (Princeton 1965) pp. 128–30.
34. Ibid. pp. 157–65.
35. Penn's instructions to his Commissioners, 1681, printed in S. Hazard *Annals of Pennsylvania* (Philadelphia 1850) pp. 527–30.
36. W. Penn 'A Further Account of the Province of Pennsylvania, 1685', printed in A. C. Myers *Narrative of Early Pennsylvania, West New Jersey and Delaware 1630–1707* (New York 1912) p. 262.
37. Ibid. p. 260.
38. Reps *Urban America* p. 177.
39. Ibid. p. 192.
40. For early wharves, see Myers *Narrative* pp. 261, 331.
41. For Amsterdam, see p. 60 of this book; for Boston, see Reps *Urban America* pp. 140 ff.; W. M. Whitehill *Boston: A Topographical History* (Cambridge, Mass. 1959).
42. J. W. Reps *Tidewater Towns: City Planning in Colonial Virginia and Maryland* (Williamsburg 1972) p. 184.
43. Information, Graham Hood.
44. E. S. Kite 'L'Enfant and Washington' in Institut Français de Washington *Historical Documents* Cahier III (1929) pp. 48–9.
45. Ibid. p. 42.
46. 'L'Enfant's Reports to President Washington' in *Records of the Columbia Historical Society* 2 (1899) 30, 32. This gives L'Enfant's original and often broken English, which Kite corrected.
47. It was called the Mall by at least 1796. See Junior League of Washington (ed. T. Froncek) *An Illustrated History of the City of Washington* (New York 1979) p. 71
48. 'L'Enfant's Reports' p. 36.
49. Ibid. p. 43.

NOTES TO CHAPTER 12

1. Hippolyte Taine *Notes on England* (tr. E. Hyams, London 1957) pp. 219–22.
2. A. Briggs *Victorian Cities* (London 1963) p. 92.
3. Disraeli *Coningsby* (1844).
4. Quoted by Pundt *Schinkel's Berlin* pp. 166–8.
5. Quoted by Briggs *Victorian Cities* p. 90.
6. Frederick Engels *The Condition of the Working Class in England* (London 1969) p. 86. First published in 1845.
7. Briggs *Victorian Cities* p. 102.
8. Love and Barton *Manchester as It Is* (Manchester 1839, facs. Manchester 1971) p. 15. The figures from 1807 onwards probably contain a small proportion of West Indian cotton.
9. Ibid. p. 18.
10. See R. S. Fitzgerald *Liverpool Road Station, Manchester* (Manchester 1980).
11. Engels *Working Class* p. 83.
12. T. Swindells *Manchester Streets and Manchester Men* (3rd series, Manchester 1907) pp. 149–59. There is a good account of the operations of the Exchange in *Encyclopaedia Britannica* (11th ed. 1910) under 'Cotton', p. 280.
13. Swindells *Manchester Streets*, passim; Love and Barton *Manchester* pp. 200–2.
14. Swindells *Manchester Streets* pp. 103–4.
15. E.g. Samuel Smiles *George Moore: Merchant and Philanthropist* (London 1878) pp. 65–96.
16. Nathan Rothschild started his English career as a cloth merchant living in Mosley Street, with a warehouse behind. Swindells *Manchester Streets* (1st series, 1906) p. 199.
17. Ibid. pp. 96–9.
18. Love and Barton *Manchester* pp. 200–1.
19. Ibid p. 181.
20. Engels *Working Class* p. 79.
21. Love and Barton *Manchester* p. 136.
22. Reference mislaid.
23. There is no adequate modern study of working-class housing of that period in Manchester, but the 1.056 Ordnance Survey maps of 1850 provide invaluable documentation.
24. Briggs *Victorian Cities* p. 98, quoting *Report on the Sanitary Condition of the Labouring Population of Great Britain* (1842).
25. Love and Barton *Manchester* p. 200.
26. E. Gaskell *North and South* (1855) chs. 49 and 50.
27. Anthony Pass 'Thomas Worthington: Practical Idealist' *Architectural Review* (May 1974) 268–76, from which the information and quotes in the rest of the paragraph also derive.
28. See Manchester City Art Gallery *Adolphe Valette* (exhibition catalogue October–November 1976).
29. J. O. Stalson *Marketing Life Insurance* (1942) pp. xxxvii ff.
30. Information, Peter Ferriday.

NOTES TO CHAPTER 13

1. For Regent Street, see H. Hobhouse *A History of Regent Street* (London 1975); J. Summerson *The Life and Work of John Nash* (London 1980) pp. 75–89, 130–46; James Elmes *Metropolitan Improvements: or London in the 19th Century* (London 1829; facs. New York 1978) pp. 88–116.
2. Summerson *Nash* pp. 81, 84, 87.
3. John Weale *Pictorial Handbook of London* (London 1854) p. 110.
4. For the London and Westminster Bank, City of London, 1837, an early and elaborate joint-stock bank by Cockerell and Tite, see David Watkin *The Life and Work of C. R. Cockerell* (London 1974) pp. p. 221–5.
5. M. Girouard *Victorian Pubs* (New Haven and London 1984) pp. 4–7.
6. Pepys *Companion* (see ch. 9 n. 70) p. 18.
7. J. Gwynn *London and Westminster Improved* (London 1766) p. 15.
8. R. Loyd *The City's Country Box*, quoting E. F. Carritt *A Calendar of British Taste 1600 to 1800* (London 1949) pp. 282–3.
9. Cowper 'Retirement' (first published 1780).
10. R. Elsam *Essay on Rural Architecture* (London 1803)pp. 6–8.
11. See the Clapham entry in the *Encyclopaedia* (see ch. 9 n. 33).
12. Gillian Darley *Villages of Vision* (London 1975) pp. 2–8.
13. P. de la R. du Prey *John Soane: The Making of an Architect* (Chicago 1982) pp. 219–32, 261–4.
14. John Summerson 'The Beginnings of Regent's Park' *Architectural History* 20 (1977) 58, pl. 19.
15. The villas of St John's Wood have been grievously depleted, and there is no adequate modern study of the estate to replace A. M. Eyre's gossipy *St. John's Wood* (London 1913).
16. *The Richmond Papers* (ed. A. M. W. Stirling, London 1926) p. 24; *The Autobiography and Journals of Benjamin Robert Haydon* (ed. M. Elwin, London 1950) pp. 316–19.
17. J. Harris 'C. R. Cockerell's Iconographica Domestica' *Architectural History* 14 (1971) 19.
18. D. J. Olsen *The Growth of Victorian London* (London 1976) p. 217, quoting A. Cox *The Landlord and Tenant's Guide* (1853).
19. For Regent's Park, see Summerson 'The Beginnings', and Elmes *Metropolitan Improvements* pp. 8–87.
20. John White *Explanation of a Plan for the Improvement of Marylebone Park* (London 1813).
21. W. Ison *The Georgian Buildings of Bath* (London 1948) pp. 95–8,

166. The Bath and Avon Canal is made a decorative feature of Sydney Gardens, as Nash intended the Regent's Canal to have been in Regent's Park.
22. Elmes *Metropolitan Improvements* p. 47.
23. See John Archer '*Rus in Urbe*: Classical ideals of Country and City, in British Town Planning' *Studies in Eighteenth Century Culture* (ed. H. C. Payne, University of Wisconsin, Madison) 12 (1983) 159–86.
24. Christopher Hussey 'Tunbridge Wells: Calverley Park' *Country Life* 145 (1969.2) 1080–3, 1166–9.
25. Archer '*Rus in Urbe*' p. 173.
26. G. F. Chadwick *The Works of Sir Joseph Paxton* (London 1961) pp. 46–53.
27. For Kensington Park, see *Survey of London* (ed. F. H. W. Sheppard) XXXVII, Northern Kensington (London 1973) pp. 194–257.
28. Taine *Notes on England* (see ch. 12 n. 1) p. 220.
29. Elmes *Metropolitan Improvements* p. 86, quoting Charles Ollier, 1823.
30. *Survey of London* XXXVII, Northern Kensington, pp. 151–93.
31. Ibid. p. 249.
32. Ibid. XLI, Southern Kensington: Brompton, p. 206.
33. M. Girouard *The Victorian Country House* (London and New Haven, 1979) p. 422; Post Office Directory, London.
34. For Edgbaston, see David N. Cannadine *Lords and Ladies: The Aristocracy and the Towns 1774–1967* (Leicester 1980).
35. Kenneth Brand *The Park, Nottingham* (Nottingham Civic Society 1984).

NOTES TO CHAPTER 14

1. E. de Amicis *Studies of Paris* (New York 1882).
2. The flowers are illustrated in Vol. II (*planches*) A. Alphand *Les Promenades de Paris* (2 vols. Paris 1867–73).
3. Lavedan *Urbanisme* (see ch. 3 n. 7) pp. 348–54.
4. Ibid pp. 338–9, pls. 168–70.
5. See Rondo E. Cameron *France and the Economic Development of Europe 1800–1914* (Princeton 1961); Louis Chevalier *La Formation de la population Parisienne au XIXe siècle* (Paris 1950).
6. For the development of Paris in this period, see *Mémoires du Baron Haussmann: Grand Travaux de Paris* (2 vols. Paris 1979; partial reprint of Haussmann's *Mémoires*, 3rd ed. 1893) and David H. Pinkney *Napoleon III and the Rebuilding of Paris* (Princeton 1958).
7. Sections are given in Alphand *Promenades* II.
8. Ibid.
9. Ibid. I p. lix.
10. See Bernard Marrey *Les Grands Magasins: des origines à 1939* (Paris 1979).
11. See J. F. Geist *Arcades: The History of a Building Type* (Cambridge, Mass. 1983).
12. John Timbs *The Curiosities of London* (new ed. 1867) pp. 40–2.
13. Marrey *Grands Magasins* pp. 68–83; Michael B. Miller *The Bon Marché* (Princeton and London 1981).
14. *Au Bonheur des Dames*, ch. IV.
15. For exhibitions, see C. Beutler *Weltausstellungen im 19 Jahrhundert* (exhibition catalogues Neue Sammlung, Staatliches Museum für Angewandte Kunst, Munich 1973); Pevsner *Building Types* pp. 236–56.
16. Pevsner *Building Types* p. 323, quoting Beutler.
17. *Pages from the Goncourt Journal* (ed. R. Baldick, Oxford 1962) p. 130.
18. Taine *Notes on England* (see ch. 12 n. 1) pp. 29, 31.
19. De Amicis *Studies* pp. 29–30.
20. Chevalier *Formation de la population.*
21. Paul Feval, et al. *Paris-Guide* (Paris 1867) p. 1452.
22. Coupeau's tenement was in the Rue de la Goutte d'Or (Paris XVIIIme).
23. See especially Louis Chevalier *Montmartre du plaisir et du crime* (Paris 1980).
24. See the plates in Philip Jullian *Montmartre* (Oxford 1977) pp. 55–7.

NOTES TO CHAPTER 15

1. J. Plaw *Ferme Ornée or Rural Improvements* (London 1795) includes designs for a pair of cottages 'in the American style'; these had been erected at Belmont in Kent before 1787 (H. Colvin *Biographical Dictionary of British Architects* p. 642).
2. For American prisons, see Norman B. Johnston *The Human Cage* (New York 1973); Pevsner *Building Types* pp. 166–8.
3. For hotels, see Pevsner *Building Types* pp. 169–92, with bibliography. There is no adequate modern monograph on them.
4. *Temple Bar Magazine* II (1866), quoted by J. Williamson *The American Hotel* (New York 1930) p. 49.
5. Pevsner *Building Types* p. 179, quoting Robert Kerr.
6. B. E. Lloyd *Lights and Shades of San Francisco* (1876) pp. 50–3.
7. *Revue générale de l'architecture* XIII (1855) 135–6.
8. *Goncourt Journal* pp. 53, 179.
9. Baron Axell Klinckowstöm, quoted by H. W. Lanier *A Century of Banking in New York* (New York 1922) p. 12; Jacob Riis *How the Other Half Lives* (1957 ed.) p. 8.
10. Carl Condit *The Port of New York* (1980).
11. H. M. Mayer and R. C. Wade *Chicago: Growth of a Metropolis* (Chicago 1969) pp. 94–6.
12. Lawrence Lowic *The Architectectural Heritage of St. Louis* (exhibition catalogue, Washington University Gallery of Art, St Louis 1982) pp. 70, 107.
13. Mayer and Wade *Chicago* is the standard contemporary history of Chicago, with innumerable illustrations; David Lowe *Lost Chicago* (Boston 1975) has interesting insights.
14. *Chicago and its Environs* (Chicago 1893) p. 100.
15. Robert Hendrickson *The Grand Emporiums: The Illustrated History of America's Great Department Stores* (New York 1980) pp. 220–34.
16. Moses King *King's Handbook of New York City* (Boston 1893, facs. New York 1972) p. 58. *King's Handbook* is an invaluable source for the 1890s, as is the Federal Writer's Project *New York City* (ed. Lou Gody, New York and London 1939) for the 1930s.
17. Condit *Port of New York* I pp. 25, 110–12 ff.
18. *King's Handbook* p. 71.
19. Ibid. pp. 871–912.
20. Federal Writers' Project *New York City* pp. 108–24.
21. For tenements, see especially *The Tenement House Problem* (ed. R. W. de Forest and Lawrence Veiller, New York 1903) and New York Tenement House Department *1st Report* (1903).
22. *Tenement Report* (1903) I pp. 132–6.
23. C. N. Glaab and A. T. Brown *History of Urban America* (1967) p. 159.
24. *King's Handbook* p. 148. It is called 'Bloomingdale Road or Boulevard' in Trow's *New York City Directory* (1868).
25. W. M. Whitehill *Boston: A Topographical History* pp. 150 ff.
26. *Real Estate Record and Builder's Guide* (anniversary number, 1868–94) pp. 32 ff.; Andrew Alpem *Apartments for the Affluent* (New York 1975).
27. *King's Handbook* pp. 242–3.
28. Glen E. Holt 'Private Plans for Public Spaces: The Origins of Chicago's Park System 1850–75' *Chicago History* 8 (1979) 173.
29. For the parks and boulevards (so called in the original legislation), see also S. J. Lippincott *New Life in New Lands* (New York 1873) p. 12.
30. Theodore Turak 'William le Baron Jenney: Pioneer of Chicago's West Parks' *Inland Architect* (Chicago, March 1981) 39.
31. Andreas Simon *Chicago, The Garden City* (Chicago 1893) p. 48.
32. Homer Hoyt *One Hundred Years of Land Values in Chicago* (Chicago 1933) pp. 133–4, quoting *Real Estate and Building Journal* (12 May 1883).
33. E.g. Evanston: Meyer and Wade *Chicago* pp. 74–83; Oak Park: ibid. p. 178–82. For Riverside, see ibid. pp. 183–5.
34. Meyer and Wade *Chicago* p. 78.
35. Edith Abbott *The Tenements of Chicago 1908–1935* (Chicago 1936) p. 93. For tenements generally, see Edith Abbott and Jane Addams *Twenty Years at Hull House* (New York 1910).
36. The most recent work on skyscrapers is Paul Goldberger *The*

Skyscraper (New York 1981, London 1982).
37. Hoyt *Land Values* pp. 130–1.
38. Meyer and Wade *Chicago* p. 128.
39. H. B. Fuller *The Cliff-Dwellers* (1893, reprint 1968) pp. 95–6. *Real Estate and Building Journal* (28 January 1893) 107, quotes a 10 per-cent return in Chicago as feasible, as against 6 percent in New York.
40. For contemporary comments and illustrations of Chicago skyscrapers, see *Industrial Chicago* (6 vols. Chicago 1891–6), and Kirkland *Chicago*, especially II pp. 347 ff. The standard more recent monographs are C. W. Condit *The Rise of the Skyscraper* (Chicago 1952) and *The Chicago School of Architecture* (Chicago 1964).
41. L. J. Horowitz and B. Sparkes *The Towers of New York: The Memoirs of a Master-builder* (New York 1937) pp. 2, 118.
42. Hoyt *Land Values* p. 153.
43. *Real Estate Record* (29 January 1910) 212; J. O. Stalson *Marketing Life Insurance* (1942) pp. 798–801.
44. Table given in R. M. Hurd *Principles of City Land Values* (New York 1903).
45. *Real Estate Record* (3 December 1910) 941, where a selection of the maps are reproduced. Further maps in Hurd *City Land Values* p. 158.
46. W. C. Clark and J. L. Kingston *The Skyscraper: A Study in the Economic Height of Modern Office Buildings* (New York 1930).

NOTES TO CHAPTER 16

1. Hendrickson *Grand Emporiums* (see ch. 15 n. 15) p. 35.
2. Adrian Lyttelton 'Milan 1880–1922: The City of Industrial Capitalism', from *People and Communities in the Western World* (ed. G. Brucker, Homewood, Illinois 1979).
3. K. Baedeker *Belgium and Holland* (1910 ed.) p. 250.
4. See Ernest R. Sandeen *St Paul's Historic Summit Avenue* St Paul, Minnesota 1978).
5. The Ring is exhaustively covered by the multi-volume *Die Wiener Ringstrasse: Bild Einer Epoche* (ed. R. Wagner-Rieger, Wiestaden 1970–9).
6. V. Tissot *Vienne et la vie Viennoise* (2nd ed. Paris 1881) p. 197.
7. Arthur Shadwell *Industrial Efficiency* (2nd ed. London 1909) p. 130.
8. For Paris building regulations, see Norma Evenson *Paris: A Century of Change 1878–1978* (New Haven and London 1979) pp. 147–59.
9. Paul Leon 'La Beaute de Paris' *Revue de Paris* (15 November 1909) 104.
10. Evenson *Paris* pp. 177–8. 37m was allowed in the outlying arrondissements.
11. Priscilla Metcalf *James Knowles, Victorian Editor and Architect* (Oxford 1980) pp. 304–8. The fuss was caused by the extension to the mansions added 1888–9.
12. The letter is translated in N. Pevsner *Academies of Art* (London 1940) pp. 194–7.
13. Pevsner *Building Types* pp. 120–1.
14. David B. Brownlee *The Law Courts* (New York and Cambridge, Mass. 1984) pp. 181–90.
15. See John R. Scobie *Buenos Aires: Plaza to Suburb 1870–1910* (New York 1974).
16. 'Cairo' entries in Larousse *Grand Dictionnaire Universel* (1867 ed.); *Encyclopaedia Britannica* (1910–11 ed.).
17. See Edward Seidensticker *Low City, High City: Tokyo from Edo to the Earthquake* (New York and London 1983).
18. Ibid. pp. 68–70, 98–100.
19. Ibid. pp. 109, 113.
20. Roger Binnemans and George van Cauwenbergh *Ons Antwerpen* (Antwerp 1976) pp. 76–9; *Antwerpen 1830–1980* (exhibition catalogue, Stadsfeestzaal Meir, Antwerp 1980) pp. 36 ff.
21. Table in Port of London Authority *London: The Port of the Empire* (London 1914).
22. G. de Maupassant *Bel Ami* pt. II ch. I.
23. See Gunter Kuhn and Manfred Hamm *Berlin: Denkmäler einer Industrielandschaft* (Berlin 1978), with many photographs of industrial Berlin; Horst Matzerath 'Berlin 1890–1940' in *Metropolis 1890–1940* (ed. A. Sutcliffe, London 1984) pp. 289–318.
24. For the industrial aspects of St Petersburg, see James H Bater *St Petersburg: Industrialization and Change* (London 1976).
25. Sutcliffe *Metropolis* pp. 21, 294–7.
26 Scobie *Buenons Aires* pp. 51–3, 147–55.
27. Martha J. Lamb *History of the City of New York* (1877–80) II pp. 730–1.
28. Ibid.
29. *Illustrated Guide to Hamburg and its Environs* (compiled J. Thompson, Hamburg 1866) p. 36; Illustrations of waterworks in Museum für Hamburgische Geschichte.
30. Montaigne *Journey* (See ch. 6 n. 35) I pp. 60, 135.
31. Illustrated 'London Bridge Waterworks' *London Encyclopaedia* (see ch. 9 n. 33).
32. Lavedan *Urbanisme* (see ch. 3 n. 7) p. 168; *New Description* p. 182; John Evelyn *Diary* 24 December 1643, 21 June 1650.
33. Thiery *Guide* (1787) I pp. 47–51; Bacler d'Albe *Promenades pittoresque et lithographiques dans Paris et ses environs* (Paris 1822) p. 20, pl. 25.
34. The Pump-House is illustrated on the margin of Tanesse's plan 1813, reproduced Reps *Urban America* fig. 50.
35. For Bazalgette, see *London Encyclopaedia* p. 238 (drains and sewers).
36. R. P. Dore *City Life in Japan* (London 1958) p. 64.
37. Extracted from *Stock Exchange Gazette* (1889).

NOTES TO CHAPTER 17

1. Revelations XVIII:8.
2. *Don Juan* Canton XI.
3. William Feaver *The Art of John Martin* (Oxford 1975) p. 49.
4. See Jean Seznec *John Martin en France* (London 1963) p. 29.
5. *The Modern Babylon* was the title of a book of sketches of London life published in the 1830s.
6. V. Hugo 'Hymne' *Chants du Crepuscule* (1831); *Pages from the Goncourt Journal* (ed. R. Baldick, Oxford 1978) p. 53 (Gauthier).
7. G. W. Steevens *The Land of the Dollar* (Edinburgh and London 1897) pp. 144–5.
8. *Goncourt Journal* p. 179.
9. *The Letters of Alfred, Lord Tennyson* (ed. C. Y. Lang and E. F. Shannon, Cambridge, Mass. 1981) I p. 157.
10. Henry James *The Ambassadors*.
11. De Quincy *Confessions of an Opium Eater* (*Works*, 1863 ed. I p. 131).
12. Graeme Davison *The Rise and Fall of Marvellous Melbourne* (Melbourne 1978) pp. 72, 248, 256.
13. Balzac *Cousine Bette* (1846) ch. 31.
14. Published in the *Pall Mall Gazette* (July 1885).
15. Taine *Notes on England* (see ch. 12 n. 1) p. 37.
16. J. K. Huysmans *A Rebours* ch. XI (tr. R. Baldick, Penguin Classics, London 1959, pp. 133–4).
17. J. Boswell *The Life of Samuel Johnson* (Everyman ed., London 1906) II p. 131.
18. Ibid. II p. 178.
19. George Borrow *Lavengro* ch. XXXI.
20. Haydon *Autobiography and Journals* (see ch. 13 n. 16) p. 47.
21. Henry James *Essays on London and Elsewhere* (London 1893) pp. 1, 9.
22. James *The Ambassadors* (1903) Bk II, ch. 2.
23. Morley Callaghan *That Summer in Paris* (New York 1963) p. 116.
24. W. Cowper *The Task* I p. 749.
25. Revelations XXI: 1–4.
26. W. H. G. Armytage *Heavens Below* (1961) p. 19.
27. Ibid. p. 77.
28. Ibid. p. 59.
29. W. Blake *Jerusalem* I.24.

30. J. Bunyan *Pilgrim's Progress*.
31. Revelations XXI: 10–12, 16–23.
32. T. Campanella 'Civitas Solis' in *Ideal Commonwealth* (ed. Henry Morley, 1885) pp. 216–18.
33. R. Pemberton *The Happy Colony* (London 1854) pp. 112–13.
34. W. Morris *The Earthly Paradise* (1868) Prologue.
35. J. Ruskin *Sesame and Lilies* (1865) sec. 138.
36. E. Howard *Garden Cities of Tomorrow* (London 1902) p. 13.
37. A. R. Sennett *Garden Cities in Theory and Practice* (1905) I pp. 1–2.
38. Fiona MacCarthy *The Simple Life: C. R. Ashbee in the Cotswolds* (London 1981) p. 36. Ashbee's bird's-eye view of his proposed Ruislip Garden City is illustrated as fig. 55 of his *Where the Great City Stands* (London 1917).
39. For New Delhi, see R. G. Irving *Indian Summer: Lutyens, Baker and Imperial Delhi* (New Haven and London 1981).
40. See Stanley Appelbaum *The Chicago World's Fair of 1893: A Photographic Record* (New York 1980), with a full bibliography.
41. See Thomas S. Hines *Burnham of Chicago: Architect and Planner* (New York 1974), especially chs. 7–10, 14.
42. Sennett *Garden Cities* II p. 3.
43. Olmsted 'Public Parks and the Enlargement of Towns' (1870), reprinted in *Public Parks* (Brookline, Mass. 1902) p. 12.
44. Sennett *Garden Cities* II p. 4.
45. There is a fine in-depth study of Pennsylvania Station, New York, in Carl Condit *The Port of New York* (Chicago 1980) I pp. 239–311.
46. For early L.C.C. housing, see Susan Beattie *A Revolution in London Housing* (London 1980).
47. Sutcliffe *Metropolis* (see ch. 16 n. 21) pp. 210–13, 306–8.
48. M. Tafuri and F. Dal Co *Modern Architecture* (New York 1979) p. 193.
49. Revelations XXII: 18.
50. Martin Pawley *Architecture versus Housing* (London 1971) p. 37, pl. 28.
51. For a study of the semi-detached house, see P. Oliver, I. Davis and I. Bentley *Dunroamin: The Suburban Semi and its Enemies* (London 1981).
52. R. E. N. Twopenny *Town Life in Australia* (London 1883) p. 37.
53. See Bernard Barrett *The Inner Suburbs: The Evolution of an Industrial Area* for a study of a working-class suburb in Melbourne.
54. See Davison *Melbourne*, especially chs. 7–8.
55. M. Markey *This Country of Yours* (Boston 1932).
56. C. D. Willard *The Chamber of Commerce of Los Angeles* (Los Angeles 1899) p. 144.
57. Ralph Hancock *Fabulous Boulevard* p. 307.
58. R. M. Fogelson *Fragmented Metropolis* (Cambridge, Mass. 1968) pp. 43–62, 108–119.
59. Dickens *Martin Chuzzlewit* chs. 21–3, etc.
60. See M.Trachtenberg *The Statue of Liberty* (London 1976).
61. B. Truman *Tourist Illustrated Guide to . . . California* (San Francisco 1883).
62. For Wiggins, see Willard *Chamber of Commerce* pp. 262–3 and Boyle Workman *The City that Grew* (Los Angeles 1935) pp. 355–6.
63. Hancock *Fabulous Boulevard* p. 115, quoting Charles D. Warner.
64. 'A Famous Festival' *Land of Sunshine* (Los Angeles, March 1895) 73.
65. For a detailed description of the Californian exhibits and pavilion, see *Final Report of the California World's Fair Commission* (Sacramento 1894).
66. Ibid. p. 102.
67. Ibid. p. 113.
68. Willard *Chamber of Commerce* pp. 120, 151–5 ff.
69. Ibid. pp. 145–51.
70. Louis Adamic *Laughing in the Jungle* (1932).
71. *Land of Sunshine* (November 1894) p. 117.
72. Dana Bartlett *The Better City* (Los Angeles 1907) p. 71.
73. W. E. Smythe 'Significance of Southern California' *Out West* 32 (April 1910) 297.
74. *Examiner* (28 February 1913); quoted by Fogelson *Fragmented Metropolis* p. 191.
75. C. A. Dykston 'Congestion de Luxe—Do we want it?' *Pacific Outlook* 40 (June 1927) 226 ff.
76. Fogelson *Fragmented Metropolis* p. 163.
77. Bartlett *Better City* p. 74.
78. Anthony D. King *The Bungalow* (London 1984) pp. 65–155.
79. Information from exhibition *Apartments and Bungalows in Chicago 1890–1940* (Chicago Historical Society, Spring 1984).
80. The full poem is quoted in Robert Winter *The Californian Bungalow* (Los Angeles 1980) p. 42, along with a number of others.
81. Fogelson *Fragmented Metropolis* pp. 89, 104.
82. Winter *Californian Bungalow* p. 66–7.
83. W. W. Robinson, Vice President, Title Guaranty & Trust Co., quoted by Hancock *Fabulous Boulevard* p. 127.
84. Adamic *Laughing in the Jungle* p. 220.

PHOTOGRAPHIC ACKNOWLEDGEMENTS

Bulloz: Front endpaper; Roger Mann: vi; Foto Mas: 6, 13, 37; Scala: 7, 8, 18, 19, 31, 56, 64, 67, 83, 85, 87, 107, 109; Alinari: 12, 22, 44, 45, 47; ACL Bruxelles: 14; Edward Piper: 15, 38, 46, 69, 79, 80, 81, 221, 225, 279, 280; Bibliothèque Nationale, Paris: 16, 95; H. Maertens, Bruges: 17, 70, 73, 77; Mansell-Alinari: 21, 96, 101; Mark Girouard: 23, 24, 51, 52, 93, 94, 122, 132, 133, 199, 206, 207, 254, 263, 275, 276, 299, 300, 301, 310; Giancarlo Costa, Milan: 26; Artothek, Munich: 34; Giraudon: 40, 147, 151, 244, 246, 249; Helga Schmidt-Glassner, Stuttgart: 43; B. T. Batsford: 65; Van Haelewyn, Bruges: 71; Stedelijk Fotodienst, Antwerp: 75; OCMW, Bruges: 76; Biblioteca Herziana: 100; Italfoto-Gieffe, Florence: 102, 103; British Architectural Library/RIBA: 106, 196, 226, 255, 312; Paolo Folchetto, Rome: 111; By gracious permission of Her Majesty the Queen: 158, 220; By kind permission of the Marquess of Tavistock and the Trustees of the Bedford Estates: 176; Aerofilms: 198; By permission of Lord Methuen: 201; Christie's Colour Library: 210, 240; Colonial Williamsburg: 214; Debuisson, Paris: 243; Popperfoto: 247, 282; Chevojon, Paris: 248; Lightfoot Collection: 261; Museum of the City of New York: 267; Bettman Archive/BBC Hulton Picture Library: 270; Andreas Feininger/Colorific: 271; Manfred Hamm: 286; GLC Photographic Library: 298; John Malmin, Los Angeles: 312; Julius Shulman, Los Angeles: 314.

INDEX

(Back endpaper) London from a balloon in 1851

THE RIVER